Managing the Testing Process:

Practical Tools and Techniques for Managing Hardware and Software Testing

D1372301

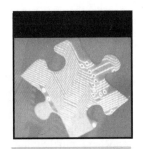

Managing the Testing Process:

Practical Tools and Techniques for Managing Hardware and Software Testing

Rex Black

Wiley Publishing, Inc.

Publisher: Robert Ipsen
Editor: Ben Ryan
Developmental Editor: Kathryn A. Malm
Managing Editor: Angela Smith
New Media Editor: Brian Snapp
Text Design & Composition: Benchmark Productions, Inc.

Designations used by companies to distinguish their products are often claimed as trademarks. In all instances where Wiley Publishing, Inc., is aware of a claim, the product names appear in initial capital or all capital letters. Readers, however, should contact the appropriate companies for more complete information regarding trademarks and registration.

This book is printed on acid-free paper. ∞

Published by Wiley Publishing, Inc.

Published simultaneously in Canada.

This publication is designed to provide accurate and authoritative information in regard to the subject matter covered. It is sold with the understanding that the publisher is not engaged in professional services. If professional advice or other expert assistance is required, the services of a competent professional person should be sought.

Library of Congress Cataloging-in-Publication Data:

ISBN 0-471-22398-0 (paper : alk. paper)

Wiley also publishes its books in a variety of electronic formats. Some content that appears in print may not be available in electronic versions.

For more information about Wiley products, visit our Web site at www.wiley.com.

Printed in the United States of America.

10 9 8 7 6 5 4 3 2 1

Contents

About the Author

Rex Black (Rex_Black@RexBlackConsulting.com) is the president and principal consultant of Rex Black Consulting Services, Inc. (www.RexBlackConsulting.com), an international software and hardware testing and quality assurance consultancy. A hands-on practitioner for two decades, he and his teams of expert test engineers, test toolsmiths, and test technicians help clients such as Bank One, Cisco, Compaq, Dell, General Electric, Hitachi, Household Finance, Motorola, Netpliance, Schlumberger, Sun, Williams Communications, and others with implementation, consulting, training, and staffing for testing, test automation, and quality assurance projects. He has worked with these clients on projects throughout the United States and in Canada, France, Germany, Holland, Italy, Japan, Singapore, Spain, Switzerland, Taiwan, and the U.K.

His popular first book, *Managing the Testing Process,* is now in its second edition, and joined by his new book, *Critical Testing Processes.* Rex also wrote the entry on test management for Wiley's *Encyclopedia of Software Engineering* along with numerous articles and papers. Rex is an internationally recognized speaker and trainer on the topic of testing, offering courses for practitioners ranging from beginners and seasoned pros alike. When he is not working at a client's site, presenting a training seminar, or in his office writing, Rex relaxes at home or outdoors with his wife and business partner, Laurel Becker, his daughter Emma Grace Black, and his faithful canine friends Max and Cosmo.

Acknowledgments

This book is a Second Edition, and that only happens when the First Edition is a success. So, first off, I'd like to thank those of you who bought the First Edition. I hope it's proven a useful reference for you. A special thanks goes to those who wrote reviews and sent me e-mails! I have addressed your suggestions for improvement in this Second Edition.

A book only gets into people's hands through a lot of behind-the-scenes hard work by a publisher's team. A special thanks to the fine people at Wiley, especially Kathryn Malm, Angela Smith, and Frank Scalise, but most especially Ben Ryan, who has been shepherding *Managing the Testing Process* along from the very beginning in 1998. I'd also like to thank my friends at Microsoft Press who helped me with the First Edition: Erin O'Connor, John Pierce, Mary Renaud, Ben Ryan (again), and Wendy Zucker.

In the course of learning how to manage test projects, I have worked with many talented professionals. At the risk of omitting somebody and in random order, I'd especially like to thank the following people for their help over the years:

Dr. Shahram Zaman, Dr. Art Gooding, Dr. Richard Baker, Kyle Marple, Tom Bohner, Amos Hare, Jim Magdich, Troy Sukert, Bill Schoneman, Bob Petersen, Jeff Fields, Dave Desormeau, Joe Mata, Jerry MacMillan, Armand Aghabegian, Bob Hosale, Neal Pollack, Chris Baker, Greg Cummings, Shawn Panchacharam, Summer Chien, Dr. Bertrand Chen, Barton Layne, Kefetew Selassie, Craig Rittenhouse, Terry Newgard, Gary Hochron, Greg Scala, Rob Gowans, Dr. Alonzo Cardenas, Dr. Shoichi Minagawa, Albert Saenz, Torsten Baumann, Wayne Blackard, and Judy McKay.

This material appears in one-day, two-day, and three-day courses called "Managing the Testing Process" that I have presented literally all around the world. I thank all the attendees of those seminars for their help making this material better in the Second Edition.

Some excellent professionals reviewed this manuscript and gave me the benefit of their time and insight: Dr. Boris Beizer, Rick Craig, Jakob Jensen, Reynolds MacNary, Dr. Patricia McQuaid, Jay Nelson, Eric Patel, and Dr. Deepti Suri.

Of course, my appreciation goes out to all my past and current colleagues, subcontractors, employees, clients, and employers. I especially want to thank the clients who graciously agreed to the anonymous use of data and documentation from their projects to illustrate many of the tools and techniques I discuss.

In the realm of "without whom," of course, I thank my parents, Rex, Sr., and Carolynn, for their love and support over the years. My greatest appreciation goes to my wife and business partner, Laurel Becker. *Managing the Testing Process* twice taken me away from a lot of things in my life, but I especially appreciate my wife's support in terms of her own time given up with me. Laurel also contributed by reviewing and formatting these materials, which was a tremendous help.

I've changed a few of my ideas since I wrote the First Edition, but the biggest change in my life has involved the arrival of my daughter. I guess all parents have dreams for their children's success, and I have to admit that "Senator Emma Grace Black" has a nice ring to my ears. However, in the course of writing this book, Emma managed to find some mechanical bugs in the construction of my laptop merely by touching it, so she may well follow me into the field of hardware and software testing. And I'd like that, too. Whatever she chooses to become, this book is dedicated to her.

Please attribute all errors, omissions, mistakes, opinions, and bad jokes in this book solely to me.

Introduction

So, you are responsible for managing a computer hardware or software test project? Congratulations! Maybe you've just moved up from test engineering or moved over from another part of the development team, or maybe you've been doing test projects for a while. Whether you are a test manager, a development manager, a technical or project leader, or an individual contributor with some level of responsibility for your company's test and quality assurance program, you're probably looking for some ideas on how to manage the unique beast that is a test project.

This book can help you. The first edition, published in 1999, sold over 10,000 copies in its first two years on the shelf. I've received dozens of emails from readers, some wanting to ask me a question or two, some thanking me for writing the book, and some pointing out errors. As I started work on this second edition in 2001, I received an email from a reader in China who had read the book in its Mandarin-language translation. People have written reviews—mostly positive, but with suggestions for improvement, too—in various publications and Web sites. I am pleased with the reception this book has received, and thank all of you who read the first edition, especially those who have given me ideas on how to make this second edition better.

This book contains what I wish I had known when I moved from programming and system administration to test management. It shows you how to develop some essential tools and apply them to your test project, and offers techniques that can help you get and use the resources you need to succeed. If you master the basic tools, apply the techniques to manage your resources, and give each area just the right amount of attention, you can survive managing a test project. You'll probably even do a good job, which might make you a test project manager for life, like me.

The Focus of This Book

I've written *Managing the Testing Process* for several reasons. First, in what some have termed the "software crisis," many projects suffer from a gap between expectations and reality when it comes to delivery dates, budgets, and quality, especially between the individual contributors creating and testing the software, the senior project managers, and the users and the customers. Similarly, computer hardware development projects often miss key schedule and quality milestones. Effective testing and clear communication of results as an integrated part of a project risk-management strategy can help.

Second, I perceived a gap in the literature on software and hardware testing. I have read books targeting the low-level issues of how to design and implement test cases, as well as books telling sophisticated project managers how to move their products to an advanced level of quality using concepts and tools such as the Capability Maturity Model, ISO 9000, Total Quality Management, software quality metrics, and so forth. However, I believe that test managers like us need a book that addresses the basic tools and techniques, the bricks and mortar, of test project management.

The tips and tools offered in this book will help you plan, build, and execute a structured test operation. As opposed to the all-too-common ad hoc and reactive test project, a structured test operation is planned, repeatable, and documented, but preserves creativity and flexibility in all the right places. What you learn here will allow you to develop models for understanding the meaning of the myriad data points generated by testing so that you can effectively manage what is often a confusing, chaotic, and change-ridden area of a software or hardware development project. This book also shows you how to build an effective and efficient test organization.

To that end, I've chosen to focus on topics unique to test management in the development and maintenance environments. Because they're well covered in other books, I do not address two related topics:

Basic project management tools such as work-breakdown-structures, Gantt charts, status reporting, and people management skills. As you move into management, these tools will need to be part of your repertoire, so I encourage you to search out project management books—such as the ones listed in the bibliography in Appendix B—to help you learn them. A number of excellent training courses and curricula currently exist for project management as well.

Computer hardware *production* testing. If your purview includes this type of testing, I recommend books by W. Edwards Deming, Kaoru Ishikawa, and J. M. Juran as excellent resources on statistical quality control, as well as Patrick O'Connor's book on reliability engineering; see the bibliography in Appendix B for details on these and other books referenced here.

Software production, in the sense of copying unchanging "golden code" to distribution media, requires no testing. However, both hardware and software production often include minor revisions and maintenance releases. You can use the techniques described in this book to manage the smaller test projects involved in such releases.

The differences between testing software and hardware are well documented, which might make it appear, at first glance, that this book is headed in two directions. I have found, however, that the differences between these two areas of testing are less important from the perspective of *test project management* than they are from the perspective of *test techniques*. This makes sense: hardware tests software, and software tests hardware. Thus, you can use similar techniques to manage test efforts for both hardware and software development projects.

Canon or Cookbook?

When I first started working as a test engineer and test project manager, I was a testing ignoramus. While ignorance is resolvable through education, some of that education is in the school of hard knocks. Ignorance can lead to unawareness that the light you see at the end of the tunnel is actually an oncoming train. "How hard could it be?" I thought. "Testing is just a matter of figuring out what could go wrong, and trying it."

As I soon discovered, however, the flaws in that line of reasoning lie in three key points:

- The tasks involved in "figuring out what could go wrong, and trying it"—that is, in designing good test cases—are quite hard indeed. Good books have been written on the art of test case engineering, many in the last decade. Unfortunately, my professors didn't teach about testing, even though Boris Beizer, Bill Hetzel, Cem Kaner, and Glenford Myers had all published on the topic prior to or during my college career. As the second half-century of software engineering begins, that is finally beginning to change. However, the level of exposure to testing that most software-engineers-in-the-making receive remains too low.

- Testing does not go on in a vacuum. Rather, it is part of an overall project—and thus testing must respond to real project needs, not to the whims of hackers playing around to see what they can break. In short, test projects require test project management.

- The prevalence of the "how hard can testing be" mindset only serves to amplify the difficulties that testing professionals face. Once we've learned through painful experience exactly how hard testing can be, it sometimes feels as if we are doomed—like a cross between Sisyphus and Dilbert—to explain, over and over, on project after project, why this testing stuff takes so long and costs so much money.

Implicit in these points are several complicating factors. One of the most important is that the level of maturity of an organization's test processes can vary considerably: testing can be part of a repeatable, measured process, or an ad hoc afterthought to a chaotic project. In addition, the motivating factors—the reasons why management bothers to test—can differ in both focus and intensity. Managers motivated by fear of repeating a recent failed project see testing differently than managers who want to produce the best possible product, and both motivations differ from those of people who organize test efforts out of obligation but assign them little importance. Finally, testing is tightly connected to the rest of the project, so the test manager is often subject to a variety of outside influences. These influences are not always benign when scope and schedule changes ripple through the project.

These factors make it difficult to develop a "how to" guide for planning and executing a test project. As academics might say, test project management does not lend itself to the easy development of a canon. "Understand the following ideas and you can understand this field" is not a statement that can be applied to the field of testing. And the development of a testing canon is certainly not an undertaking I'll tackle in this book.

Do you need a canon to manage test projects properly? I think not. Instead, consider this analogy: I am a competent and versatile cook, an amateur chef. I will never appear in the ranks of world-renowned chefs, but I regularly serve passable dinners to my family. I have successfully prepared a number of multicourse Thanksgiving dinners, some in motel kitchenettes. I mastered producing an edible meal for a reasonable cost as a necessity while working my way through college. In doing so, I learned how to read recipes out of a cookbook, apply them to my immediate needs, juggle a few ingredients here and there, handle the timing issues that separate dinner from a sequence of snacks, and play it by ear.

An edible meal at a reasonable cost is a good analogy for what your management wants from your testing organization. This book, then, can serve as a test project manager's "cookbook," describing the basic tools you need and helping you assemble and blend the proper ingredients.

The Tools You Need

Five basic tools underlie my approach to test management:

A thorough test plan. A detailed test plan is a crystal ball, allowing you to foresee and prevent potential crises. Such a plan addresses the issues of scope, quality risk management, test strategy, staffing, resources, hardware logistics, configuration management, scheduling, phases, major milestones and phase transitions, and budgeting.

A well-engineered system. Good test systems ferret out, with wicked effectiveness, the bugs that can hurt the product in the market or reduce its acceptance by in-house users. It also possesses internal and external consistency, is easy to learn and use, and builds on a set of well-behaved and compatible tools. I use the phrase "good test system architecture" to characterize such a system. The word *architecture* fosters a global, structured outlook on test development within the test team. It also conveys to management that creating a good test system involves developing an artifact of elegant construction, with a certain degree of permanence.

A state-based bug tracking database. In the course of testing, you and your intrepid test team will find lots of bugs, a.k.a. issues, defects, errors, problems, faults, and other less printable descriptions. Trying to keep all these bugs in your head or in a single document courts immediate disaster because you won't be able to communicate effectively within the test team, with programmers, with other development team peers, or with the project management team—and thus won't be able to contribute to increased product quality. You need a way to track each bug through a series of states on its way to closure. I'll show you how to set up and use an effective and simple database that accomplishes this purpose. This database can also summarize the bugs in informative charts that tell management about projected test completion, product stability, system turnaround times, troublesome subsystems, and root causes.

A **comprehensive test tracking spreadsheet.** In addition to keeping track of bugs, you need to follow the status of each test case. Does the operating system crash when you use a particular piece of hardware? Does saving a file in a certain format take too long? Which release of the software or hardware failed an important test? A simple set of worksheets in a single spreadsheet can track the results of every single test case, giving you the detail you need to answer these kinds of questions. The detailed worksheets also roll up into summary worksheets that show you the big picture. What percentage of the test cases passed? How many test cases are blocked? How long do the test suites *really* take to run?

A **simple change management database.** How many times have you wondered, "How did our schedule get so far out of whack?" Little discrepancies such as slips in hardware or software delivery dates, missing features that block test cases, unavailable test resources, and other seemingly minor changes can hurt. When testing runs late, the whole project slips. You can't prevent test-delaying incidents, but you can keep track of them, which will allow you to bring delays to the attention of your management early and explain the problems effectively. This book presents a simple, efficient database that keeps the crisis of the moment from becoming your next nightmare.

This book shows you how to develop and apply these five basic tools to your test project, and how to get and use the resources you need to succeed. I've implemented them in the ubiquitous PC-based Microsoft Office suite: Excel, Word, Access, and Project. You can easily use other office-automation applications, as I haven't used any advanced features.

The Resources You Need

In keeping with our culinary analogy, you also need certain ingredients, or resources, to successfully produce a dish. In this testing cookbook, I show you how I assemble the resources I need to execute a testing project. These resources include some or all of the following:

A **practical test lab.** A good test lab provides people—and computers—with a comfortable and safe place to work. This lab, far from being Quasimodo's hideout, needs many ways to communicate with the development team, the management, and the rest of the world. You must ensure that it's stocked with sufficient software and hardware to keep testers working efficiently, and you'll have to keep that software and hardware updated to the right release levels. Remembering that it is a *test* lab, you'll need to make it easy for engineers to keep track of key information about system configurations.

Test engineers and technicians. You will need a team of hardworking, qualified people, arranged by projects, by skills, or by a little of both. Finding good test engineers can be harder than finding good development engineers. How do you distinguish the budding test genius from that one special person who will make your life as a manager a living nightmare of conflict, crises, and lost productivity? Sometimes the line between the two is finer than you might expect. And once you have built the team, your work really begins. How do you motivate the team to do a good job? How do you defuse the land mines that can destroy motivation?

Contractors and consultants. As a test manager, you will probably use "outsiders," hired guns who work by the hour and then disappear when your project ends. I will help you classify the garden-variety high-tech temporary workers, understand what makes them tick, and resolve the emotional issues that surround them. When do you need a contractor? What do contractors care about? Should you try to keep the good ones? How do you recognize those times when you need a consultant?

External test labs and vendors. In certain cases, it makes sense to do some of the testing outside the walls of your own test lab—for instance, when you are forced to handle spikes or surprises in test workloads. You might also save time and money by leveraging the skills, infrastructure, and equipment offered by external resources. What can these labs and vendors really do for you? How can you use them to reduce the size of your test project without creating dangerous coverage gaps? How do you map their processes and results onto yours?

Of course, before you can work with any of these resources, you have to assemble them. As you might have learned already, management is never exactly thrilled at the prospect of spending lots of money on equipment to test stuff that "ought to work anyway." With that in mind, I've also included some advice about how to get the green light for the resources you really need.

On Context

I've used these tools and techniques to manage projects large and small. The concepts scale up and down easily, although on larger projects it might pay to implement some of the tools in a more automated fashion. In that case, the tools I've described here can be prototypes or serve as a source of requirements for the automated tools you buy or build.

The concepts also scale across distributed projects. I've used the tools to manage multiple projects simultaneously from a laptop computer in hotel rooms and airport lounges around the world. I've used these tools to test market-driven end-user systems and in-house information technology projects. While context does matter, I've found that adaptations of the concepts in this book apply across a broad range of settings.

Simple and effective, the tools comply with industry standards and bring you in line with the best test management practices and tools at leading software and hardware vendors. I use these tools to organize my thinking about my projects, to develop effective test plans and test suites, to execute the plans in dynamic high-technology development environments, and to track, analyze, and present the results to project managers. Likewise, my suggestions on test resource management come from successes and failures at various employers and clients.

Because context matters, I've added a new chapter at the end of this edition that discusses the importance of fitting the testing process into the overall development or maintenance process. This involves addressing issues such as organizational context, the economic aspects of and justifications for testing, lifecycles and methodologies for system development, and process maturity models.

Using This Book

Nothing in this book is based on Scientific Truth, double-blind studies, academic research, or even flashes of brilliance. It is merely about what has worked—and continues to work—for me on the dozens of test projects I have managed. You might choose to apply these approaches "as is," or you might choose to modify them. You might find all or only some of my approaches useful.

Along similar lines, this is not a book on the state of the art in test techniques, test theory, or the development process. This is a book on test management, both hardware and software, as I have practiced it. In terms of development processes—best practices or your company's practices—the only assumption I make is that you as the test manager became involved in the development project with sufficient lead time to do the necessary test development. The last chapter addresses different development processes I have seen and worked within. I cover how the choice of a development lifecycle affects testing.

Of course, I can't talk about test management without talking about test techniques, to some extent. Because hardware and software test techniques differ, you might find some of the terms I use unclear or contradictory to your usage of them. I have included a glossary to help you decipher the hardware examples if you're a software tester, and vice versa. Finally, the test manager is usually both a technical leader and a manager, so make sure you understand and use best practices, especially in the way of test techniques, for your particular type of testing. Appendix B includes a listing of books that can help you brush up on these topics if needed.

This book is drawn from my experiences, good and bad. The bad experiences— which I use sparingly—are meant to help you avoid some of my mistakes. I try to keep the discussion light and anecdotal; the theory behind what I've written, where any exists, is available in books listed in the bibliography in Appendix B.

I find that I learn best from examples, so I have included lots of them. Because the tools I describe work for both hardware and software testing, I base many examples on one of these two hypothetical projects:

- Most software examples involve the development of a Java-based word processing package named SpeedyWriter, being written by Software Cafeteria, Inc. SpeedyWriter has all the usual capabilities of a full-featured word processor, plus network file locking, Web integration, and public-key encryption. Speedy-Writer includes various JavaBeans from other vendors.

- Most hardware examples refer to the development of a server named DataRocket, under development by Winged Bytes, LLP. DataRocket provides powerful, high-capacity file and application services as well as Web hosting to LAN clients. It runs multiple operating systems. Along with third-party software, Winged Bytes plans to integrate a U.S.-made LAN card and a Taiwanese SCSI controller.

As for the tools discussed in this book, you can find examples of these at www.rexblackconsulting.com. I have spent a lot of time improving these templates for this second edition. I also have added some case studies from real projects. In those chapters that describe the use of these tools, I include a short section guiding you in the use and study of these templates and case studies should you want to do so. That way, you can use these resources to bootstrap your own implementation of the tools. These tools are partially shown in figures in the chapters in which I describe them, and I have improved the readability of these figures for this edition. However, screen shots of worksheets and forms can only tell you so much. Therefore, as you read the various chapters, you might want to open and check out the corresponding case studies and templates from the Web site to gain a deeper understanding of how the tools work.

Please note that the tools supplied with the book are usable, but contain only small amounts of "dummy data." This data should not be used to derive any rules of thumb about bug counts, defect density, predominant quality risks, or any other metric to be applied to other projects. I developed the tools primarily to illustrate ideas, so some of the sophisticated automation that you would expect in a commercial product won't be there. If you intend to use these tools in your project, allocate sufficient time and effort to adapt and enhance them for your context.

For those wanting to practice with the tools before putting them into use on a real project, I have included exercises at the end of each chapter. These additions, new to this edition, also make this book suitable as the test management textbook for a course on testing, software engineering, or software project management. (Solutions to these exercises are found on the Web at www.rexblackconsulting.com.) Given that testing is increasingly seen by enlightened project managers as a key part of the project's risk management strategy, including material such as this as part of a college or certification curriculum makes good sense.

Finally—in case you haven't discovered this yet—testing is not a fiefdom in which one's cup overfloweth with resources and time. I have found that it's critical to focus on testing what project managers really value. Too often in the past I've ended up wrong-footed by events, spending time handling trivialities or minutiae while important matters escaped my attention. Those experiences taught me to recognize and attend to the significant few and ignore the trivial many. The tools and techniques presented here can help you do the same. A sizeable number of computer test organizations are disbanded in their first couple years; this book will help keep you out of that unfortunate club.

Although it's clearly more than simply hanging onto a job, success in test management means different things to different people. In my day-to-day work, I measure the benefits of success by the peace of mind, the reduction in stress, and the enhanced professional image that come from actually managing the testing areas in my purview rather than reacting to the endless sequence of crises that ensue in ad hoc environments. I hope that these tools and ideas will contribute to your success as a testing professional.

What's New and Changed in the Second Edition?

For those of you who read the first edition and are wondering whether to buy this second edition, I've included the following synopsis of changes and additions:

- I've added a new final chapter that discusses the importance of fitting the testing process into the overall development or maintenance process. I address organizational context, the economic aspects of and justifications for testing, lifecycles and methodologies for system development, and process maturity models.

- I have added case studies for many of the tools and techniques discussed in the book. These case studies came from real projects, which, happily, are not encumbered by nondisclosure agreements. I have included some background information to help you understand these case study documents.

- I have increased the number of templates and examples, and improved the format of some tools. I also added some new metrics. The templates include the tools to generate those metrics. Some of the templates originally published with the book, while usable, contained minor errors. (Readers of the first edition—being test professionals—caught and pointed out these errors to me.) I have corrected those mistakes.

- Some of the figures in the first edition were crowded into small spaces and had tiny fonts. I've revised and expanded the figures for better readability. I've also corrected some figures that became misplaced during the final edit.

- In addition to case studies, I have also added some exercises, some originally used in my three-day "Managing the Testing Process" class, and some created specifically for this second edition. These exercises can be used for self-study, book club, or classroom education. (Professor Patricia McQuaid selected the first edition as the textbook for a software testing course at California Polytechnic State University.) I have worked with some respected members of the software engineering academic community to ensure the usefulness of these exercises.

- The templates, case studies, exercise support files, and other tools, rather than being supplied on a breakable, hard-to-update CD-ROM, are now posted on the Web at www.rexblackconsulting.com. I will update and correct those templates as time goes on, so this book will, in a sense, be continuously improving.

- Finally, little has changed in terms of the challenges facing those who manage test projects since I wrote the first edition. Every time I teach my two- and three-day "Managing the Testing Process" classes, which are drawn directly from this book, at least one attendee tells me, "It's amazing how every issue we've talked about here in class is something that has come up for me on my projects." However, I have learned some new tricks and broadened my mind. For example, I criticized exploratory testing in the first edition, but I have learned through talking with successful practitioners as well as trying it out myself that, carefully managed, exploratory testing is a useful technique.

If you read the first edition, enjoyed it, and found it useful, I think these changes and additions will make this second edition even more useful to you.

Defining What's on Your Plate: The Foundation of a Test Project

Testing requires a tight focus. It's easy to try to do too much. There is a virtually infinite number of tests that you *could* run against any nontrivial piece of software or hardware. Even if you try to focus on what you think might be "good enough" quality, you can find that such testing is too expensive or that you have trouble figuring out what "good enough" means for your customers and users.[1] Before I start to develop the test system—the testware, the test environment, and the test process—and before I hire the test team, I figure out what I *might* test, then what I *should* test, and finally what I *can* test. Determining the answers to these questions helps me plan and focus my test efforts.

What I might test are all those untested areas that fall within the purview of my test organization. On every project in which I've been involved, some amount of the test effort fell to organizations outside my area of responsibility. Testing an area that is already covered by another group adds little value, wastes time and money, and can create political problems for you.

What I should test are those untested areas that directly affect the customers' and user's experience of quality. People often use buggy software and computers and remain satisfied nevertheless; either they never encounter the bugs or the bugs don't significantly hinder their work. Our test efforts should focus on finding the critical defects that will limit people's ability to get work done with our products.

---

[1] To my knowledge, James Bach first applied the phrase "good enough" to software quality. You can find his thoughts on the subject at www.satisfice.com.

What I can test are those untested, critical areas on which my limited resources are best spent. Can I test everything I should? Not likely, given the schedule and budget I usually have available.[2] On most projects, I must make tough choices, using limited information, on a tight schedule. I also need to sell the test project to my managers to get the resources and the time I need.

What You *Might* Test: The Extended Test Effort

On my favorite development projects, testing was pervasive. By this, I mean that a lot of testing went on outside the independent test team. In addition, testing started early. This arrangement not only made sense technically, but also kept my team's workload manageable. This section uses two lenses to examine how groups outside the formal test organization contribute to testing: the first lens is the level of focus—the *granularity*—of a test; the second is the type of testing performed within various test phases. Perhaps other organizations within your company could be (or are) helping you test.

From Microscope to Telescope: Test Granularity

Test *granularity* refers to the fineness or coarseness of a test's focus. A fine-grained test case allows the tester to check low-level details, often internal to the system; a coarse-grained test case provides the tester with information about general system behavior. Test granularity can be thought of as running along a spectrum ranging from structural (white-box) to behavioral (black-box and live) tests, as shown in Figure 1.1.

Structural (White-Box) Tests

Structural tests (also known as "white-box tests" and "glass-box tests") find bugs in low-level operations such as those that occur down at the levels of lines of code, database schemas, chips, subassemblies, and interfaces. These structural tests are based on *how* a system operates. For example, a structural test might reveal that the database that stores user preferences has space to store an 80-character username, but that the field only allows 40 characters to be entered.

Structural testing involves a detailed knowledge of the system. For software, testers develop most structural tests by looking at the code and the data structures themselves; hardware structural tests compare chip specifications to readings on oscilloscopes or voltage meters. Structural tests thus fit well in the development area. For test staff—at least those separated from low-level details and without programming or engineering skills—structural testing can be difficult.

---

[2] See Boris Beizer's, *Software Testing Techniques*, Cem Kaner, et al.'s *Testing Computer Software*, or Glenford Myers' *The Art of Software Testing*, for discussions on the difficulty of achieving "complete" testing, however one defines "complete."

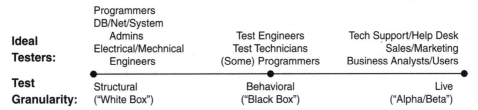

Figure 1.1   The test granularity spectrum and owners.

Structural tests also involve knowledge of structural testing techniques. Not all programmers learn these techniques as part of their initial education and on-going skills growth. In such cases, having a member of the test team work with the programmers as subject matter experts can promote good structural testing. This person can help train the programmers in the techniques needed to find bugs at a structural level.

Behavioral (Black-Box) Tests

Behavioral tests (also known as "black-box" tests) are often used to find bugs in high-level operations, at the levels of features, operational profiles, and customer scenarios. They are functional tests based on *what* a system should do. If DataRocket can achieve an effective throughput of only 10 Mbps across two 1-gigabit Ethernet connections acting as a bridge, a black-box network performance test can find this bug.

Behavioral testing involves a detailed understanding of the application domain, the business problem being solved, and the mission the system serves. Behavioral testing is best done by testers who understand the design of the system, at least at a high level, so that they can effectively find bugs common to that type of design. For example, programs implemented in Java can—depending on the Java Virtual Machine that runs them—suffer from serious performance limitations.

In addition to the application domain and some of the technological issues surrounding the system under test, behavioral testers must understand the special behavioral test techniques that are most effective at finding such bugs. While some behavioral tests do look at typical user scenarios, many are designed to exercise extremes, interfaces, boundaries, and error conditions. These are places where bugs thrive, and behavioral testing is primarily a search for defects, just as structural testing is. Good behavioral testers use scripts, requirements, documentation, and testing skills to guide them to these bugs. Simply playing around with the system or demonstrating that the system works under average conditions are not effective techniques for behavioral testing, although many test teams make the mistake of adopting these as the sole test techniques. Good behavioral tests, like good structural tests, are structured, methodical, and often repeatable sequences of tester-created conditions that probe suspected system weaknesses and strive to find bugs, but through the system under test's external interfaces. Behavioral testing is the primary test technique for most independent test organizations.

Live Tests

Live tests involve putting customers, content experts, early adopters, and other end users in front of the system. In some cases, we encourage the testers to try to break the system. Beta testing is a well-known form of bug-driven live testing. For example, if the SpeedyWriter product has certain configuration-specific bugs, live testing might be the best way to catch those bugs specific to unusual or obscure configurations. In other cases, the testers are trying to demonstrate conformance to requirements, as in acceptance testing, another common form of live testing.

Live tests can follow general scripts or checklists, but live tests are often ad hoc or exploratory. They don't focus on system weaknesses except for the "error guessing" that comes from experience. Live testing is a perfect fit for technical support, marketing, and sales organizations whose members don't know test techniques but do know the application domain and the product intimately. This understanding, along with recollections of the nasty bugs that have bitten them before, allows them to find bugs that developers and testers miss.

The Complementary and Continuous Nature of Test Granularity

The crew of a fishing boat uses a tight mesh net to catch 18-inch salmon and a loose mesh net to catch six-foot tuna. They might be able to catch a tuna in a salmon net or vice versa, but it would probably make them less efficient. Likewise, each test technique is most effective at finding certain types of bugs. Many great test efforts include a mix of all three types.

While my test teams focus on behavioral testing typically, I don't feel bound to declare my test group "the black-box bunch." I've frequently used structural test tools and cases effectively as part of my system test efforts. I've also used live production data in system testing. Both required advanced planning, but paid off handsomely in terms of efficiency (saved time and effort) and effectiveness (bugs found that might've been missed). The concept of test granularity implies a spectrum, not a set of "either/or" categories. Mixing these elements can be useful in creating test conditions or assessing results. I also mix planned test scenarios with exploratory live testing. I use whatever works.

A Stampede or a March? Test Phases

The period of test execution activity during development or maintenance is sometimes an undifferentiated blob. Testing begins, testers run some (vaguely defined) tests and identify some bugs, and then, at some point, project management declares testing complete. As development and maintenance processes mature, however, companies tend to adopt an approach of partitioning testing into a sequence of phases (sometimes called *levels*). Ownership of those various phases can differ; it's not always the test team. There are various commonly encountered test phases, although these often go under different names.

IS THE "WHITE-BOX/BLACK-BOX" MODEL WRONG?

The "white-box/black-box" model is widespread. Glenford Myers contrasts "white-box" and "black-box" approaches in *The Art of Software Testing*, a pioneering book. Cem Kaner, Jack Falk, and Hung Nguyen refer to test cases as following a "glass-box" or "black-box" paradigm in *Testing Computer Software*, as does Jeffrey Voas and Steve McGraw in *Software Fault Injection*.

The model is also handy. With my clients, I have found that the use of the "white-box" and "black-box" models to explain the type of testing used in particular projects or phases helps make communication easier. The concepts are quite intuitive.

However, the model is not ubiquitous. Bill Hetzel, in *The Complete Guide to Software Testing*, describes six types of test cases: requirements-based, design-based, code-based, randomized (especially in terms of the underlying data), extracted (from live data), and abnormal (or extreme). Of these, he does point out that requirement-based tests are "black box," design- and code-based tests are "white box," and extracted tests are "live." However, the index contains neither the phrase "black-box" nor "white-box."

Some argue that the model is an oversimplification, and a dangerous one at that. Boris Beizer, who wrote a book called *Black Box Testing*, has had second thoughts about the phrase, which he describes in his essay, "The Black Box Vampire." He argues that the better model is to think in terms of the "structural" and "behavioral" spectrum, with a fault model (i.e., how the bugs were created) providing an orthogonal testing dimension as well. He argues that the "white-box/black-box" model makes testing look simpler than it is, encourages a possibly negative division of test work between programmers and testers, feeds into the mindset that testers are lower skilled than programmers, and fosters a false belief that "black-box" testing is about demonstrating compliance to requirements.

Who's right? To me, the issue is the usefulness of the abstraction or simplification of the rich set of techniques available. I find the abstractions intuitive and clarifying, although I don't get too hung up on the matter. I prefer to think in terms of quality risks, and then let the choice of critical quality risks drive the selection of test techniques.

Unit Testing

Unit testing involves the testing of a piece of code, the size of which is somewhat ambiguous in practice, although it is often a function or a subroutine. It is also not usually a test phase in a project-wide sense of the term, but rather the last step of writing a piece of code. The test cases might be structural or behavioral in design, depending on the developer or the organizational standard. Either way, it is "white-box" testing in the sense that the programmer knows the internal structure of the unit under test and is concerned with how the testing affects the internal operations. As such, programmers almost always do the unit testing, sometimes testing their own code, sometimes testing other programmer's code.

Component or Subsystem Testing

During the component or subsystem testing, testers focus on bugs in constituent pieces of the system. Component test execution usually starts when the first component of the product becomes functional, along with whatever scaffolding, stubs, or drivers needed to operate this component without the rest of the system.[3] In our SpeedyWriter product, for example, file manipulation is a component. For DataRocket, the component test phase would focus on elements such as the SCSI subsystem: the controller, the hard disk drives, the CD-ROM drive, and the tape backup unit.

Component testing tends to emphasize structural or white-box techniques. In addition, components often require hand-built, individualized support structures. Component testing is a good fit for programmers and hardware engineers in these cases. If a component is standalone, however, black-box techniques can work. For example, I once worked on a Unix operating system development project in which the test organization used shell scripts to drive each Unix command through its paces using the command-line interface—a typical black-box technique. We later reused these component test scripts in system testing. In this instance, component testing was a better fit for the test organization.

Integration or Product Testing

Integration or product testing involves testers looking for bugs in the relationships and interfaces between pairs of components and groups of components in the system under test, often in a staged fashion. Integration testing must happen in coordination with the project-level activity of *integrating* the entire system—putting all the constituent components together, a few components at a time. The staging of integration and integration testing must follow the same plan—sometimes called the *build plan*—so that the right set of components come together in the right way and at the right time for the earliest possible discovery of the most dangerous integration bugs. For SpeedyWriter, integration testing might start when the developers integrate the file-manipulation component with the graphical user interface (GUI) and continue as developers integrate more components one, two, or three at a time, until the product is feature complete. For DataRocket, integration testing might begin when the motherboard is attached to the power supply, continuing until all components are in the case.[4]

Not every project needs a formal integration test phase. If your product is a set of standalone utilities that don't share data or invoke one another, you can probably skip this. However, if the product uses application programming interfaces (APIs) or a hardware bus to coordinate activities, share data, and pass control, you have a tightly integrated set of components that can work fine alone yet fail badly together.

---

[3] See Boris Beizer's, *Software Test Techniques* or Glenford Myers', *The Art of Software Testing*, for good discussions on support structures for component testing.
[4] See Rick Craig and Stefan Jaskiel's book, *Systematic Software Testing*, for an overview of the integration process and how to design an integration test suite. Alternatively, if you can find a copy, check out Boris Beizer's, *Software System Testing and Quality Assurance*, which is very complete and well-explained. Alternatively, wait for Ross Collard's upcoming series of books on software testing for an updated discussion of integration.

The ownership of integration testing depends on a number of factors. One is skill. Often, the techniques needed to perform integration testing are structural; some test teams do not have sufficient internal system expertise. Another is resources. Project plans sometimes neglect or undersize this important task, and neither the development manager nor the test manager will have the resources (human or machine) to do this. Finally, unit and component testing tends to happen at the individual-programmer level when owned by the development team—each programmer tests her own component or swaps testing tasks with her programmer peer—but this model won't work for integration testing. In these circumstances, unfortunately, I have seen the development manager assign this critical responsibility to the most junior member of the programming team. In such cases, it would be far better for the test team to add the necessary resources—including appropriately skilled people—to handle the integration testing. When the product I'm testing needs integration testing, I plan to spend some time with my development counterparts working out who should do it.

String Testing

String testing zeroes in on problems in typical usage scripts and customer operational "strings." This phase is a rare bird; I have seen it used only once, when it involved a strictly black-box variation on integration testing. In the case of SpeedyWriter, string testing might involve cases such as encrypting and decrypting a document, or creating, printing, and saving a document.

System Testing

During this phase, testers look for various types of bugs in the entire system, fully integrated. Sometimes, as in installation and usability testing, these tests look at the system from a customer or end user point of view. Other times, these tests are designed to stress particular aspects of the system that might be unnoticed by the user, but critical to proper system behavior. For SpeedyWriter, system testing would address such concerns as installation, performance, and printer compatibility. For DataRocket, system testing would cover issues such as performance and network compatibility.

System testing tends toward the behavioral area of the testing spectrum. I apply structural techniques to force certain stressful conditions that I would be hard-pressed to create through the user interface—especially load and error conditions—but I usually find my testers measuring the pass/fail criteria at an external interface. Where independent test organizations exist, they often run the system tests.

Acceptance or User Acceptance Testing

Thus far, the description of each test phase has revolved around looking for problems. Acceptance testing, in contrast, often tries to demonstrate that the system meets requirements. This phase of testing is common in contractual situations, when successful completion of acceptance tests obligates a buyer to accept a system. For in-house IT or MIS development efforts, completion of the acceptance tests brings the green light for deployment of the software in a production environment. In commercial software and hardware development, acceptance tests are sometimes called "alpha tests" (by in-house users) and "beta tests" (by current and potential customers). Alpha and beta tests, when performed, might be about demonstrating a product's readiness for market, although many organizations also use these tests to find bugs that can't be (or weren't) detected in the system testing process.

Acceptance testing involves live or "near live" data, environments, and user scenarios. The focus is usually on typical product usage scenarios, not extreme conditions. There-fore, marketing, sales, technical support, beta customers, and even company executives are perfect candidates to run acceptance tests. (Two of my clients—one a small software startup and the other a large PC manufacturer—use their CEOs in acceptance testing; the product only ships if the CEO likes it.) Test organizations often provide test tools, suites, and data that have been developed during system testing, support for the acceptance test-ing, and, with user "witnessing," sometimes also perform the acceptance test.

Pilot Testing

Hardware development often involves pilot testing, either following or in parallel with acceptance tests. Pilot testing checks the ability of the assembly line to mass-produce the finished system. I have also seen this phase included in in-house and custom software development, where it demonstrates that the system will perform all the necessary operations in a live environment with a limited set of real customers. Unless your test organization is involved in production or operations, you probably won't be responsi-ble for pilot testing.

Why Do I Prefer a Phased Test Approach?

As you've seen, a phased test approach marches methodically across the test focus granularity spectrum, from structural tests to behavioral black-box tests to live tests. Such an approach can provide the following benefits:

- Structural testing can build product stability. Some bugs are simple for develop-ers to fix but difficult for the test organization to live with. You can't do perfor-mance testing if SpeedyWriter corrupts the hard disk and crashes the system after 10 minutes of use.

- Structural testing using scaffolding or stubs can start early. For example, you might receive an engineering version of DataRocket that is merely a motherboard, a SCSI subsystem, and a power supply on a foam pad. By plugging in a cheap video card, an old monitor, and a floppy drive, you can start testing basic I/O operations.

- You can detect bugs earlier and more efficiently, as mentioned previously.

- You can gather better metrics and use best-practice techniques in your testing effort. For example, both Stephan Kan and Pankoj Jalote have described defect removal models that provide for quantitative quality assessments as part of declaring each phase complete.[5]

---

[5] See Jalote's, *CMM in Practice* and Kan's *Metrics and Models in Software Quality*.

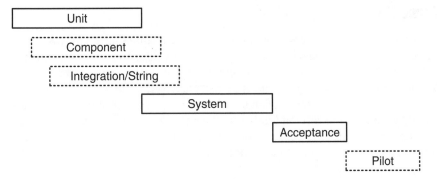

Figure 1.2 The test execution period for various test phases in a development project.

- Phases provide real and psychological milestones against which you can gauge the "doneness" of testing and thus the project.

The last two benefits are explained in more detail in Chapter 4, "An Exciting Career in Entomology Awaits You: A Bug Tracking Database," which discusses defect metrics, and in Chapter 9, "The Triumph of Politics: Organizational Challenges for Test Managers," which explores the politics of test projects.

Test Phase Sequencing

Figure 1.2 shows a common sequence of the execution activities for various test phases. On your projects, the execution activities in these phases might be of different relative lengths. The degree of overlap between execution activities in different phases varies considerably depending on entry and exit criteria for each phase, which I'll discuss in Chapter 2, "Plotting and Presenting Your Course: The Test Plan." Quite a few companies omit the test phases that are shown with dotted lines in the figure. There's no need to divide your test effort exactly into the six test phases diagrammed in Figure 1.2; it's better to start with the approach that best fits your needs and let your process mature organically.

When I plan test sequencing, I try to start each test phase as early as possible. Software industry studies have shown that the cost of fixing a bug found just one test phase earlier can be lower by an order of magnitude or more, and my experience leads me to believe that the same argument applies to hardware development.[6] In addition, finding more bugs earlier in testing increases the total number of bugs one will find. And since the nasty, hard-to-fix problems often first rear their ugly heads in behavioral testing, moving into integration or system testing early buys the project more time to fix them. Finally, on unique, leading-edge projects, I need to test basic design assumptions. The closer to "real world" I make this testing, the more risk mitigation I achieve.

---

[6] For just two examples, see Kan's, *Metrics and Models in Software Quality* and Campenella's, *Principles of Quality Costs.*

The First Cut

At this point, you have some ideas about how other organizations attack the division of the test roles. Now you can look at the testing that already goes on in your organization and locate gaps. If you are establishing a new test organization, you might find that folks who tested certain areas on previous projects believe that they needn't continue testing now that *you're* here. (I touch on this topic more in Chapter 9 when I discuss how development groups can become "addicted" to the test team.) After identifying past test contributions, I make sure to close the loop and get commitments from individual contributors (and their managers) that they will continue to test in the future.

What You *Should* Test: Considering Quality

Once I've identified the areas of testing that might be appropriate for my test organization, my next step is to figure out what I should test. To do this, I must understand what quality means for the system and the risks to system quality that exist. While quality is sometimes seen as a complex and contentious topic, I have found a pragmatic approach.

Three Blind Men and an Elephant: Can You Define Quality?

There's a management parable about three blind men who come across an elephant. One touched the tail and declared it a snake. Another touched a leg and insisted that it was a tree. The third touched the elephant's side and claimed that it was a wall.

Defining quality can be a similar process. Everyone "knows" what they mean, but disagreements abound. Have you debated with developers over whether a particular test case failure was really a bug? If so, weren't these debates in fact about whether the observed behavior was a quality issue? What, really, is quality? What factors determine its presence or absence? Whose opinions matter most?

J. M. Juran, a respected figure in the field of quality management, defines quality as "features [that] are decisive as to product performance and as to 'product satisfaction'…. The word 'quality' also refers to freedom from deficiencies… [that] result in complaints, claims, returns, rework and other damage. Those collectively are forms of 'product *dis*satisfaction.'"[7] Testing focuses on the latter half of this definition. I often call possible bugs *quality risks,* while referring to the observed symptom of bugs as *failure modes.* At the most general level, the process of testing allows the test organization to assess the quality risks and to understand the failure modes that exist in the system under test.

After a product is released, customers or users who encounter bugs might experience product dissatisfaction and then make complaints, return merchandise, or call technical support. This makes the users and customers the arbiters of quality. Who are these people,

---

[7] J. M. Juran, *Juran on Planning for Quality",* pp. 4–5. In *Quality Is Free,* Phillip Crosby argues that quality is conformance to requirements—nothing more and nothing less. But when was the last time you worked on a project with complete, unambiguous requirements?

and what do they intend to do with the product? For our purposes, let's assume that customers are people who have paid or will pay money to use your product and that they expect your product to do what a similar product, in the same class and of the same type, should reasonably do. The users might also be customers, or they might be people who did not pay for the product or its development, but use it or its output to get work done.

Testing looks for situations in which a product fails to meet customers' or users' reasonable expectations in specific areas. For example, IBM evaluates customer satisfaction in terms of capability (functions), usability, performance, reliability, installability, maintainability, documentation/information, service, and overall fitness for use. Hewlett-Packard uses the categories of functionality, usability, reliability, performance, and serviceability.

The Perils of Divergent Experiences of Quality

As people use a product—a car, an espresso machine, a bar of soap—they form opinions about how well that product fulfills their expectations. These impressions, good or bad, become their *experience of quality* for that product. Test teams try to assess quality during test execution. In other words, you and your test team use the test system—the testware, the test environment, and the test process as discussed in Chapter 3, "Test System Architecture, Cases, and Coverage"—to gauge, in advance, customers' experiences of quality. I refer to the extent to which the test system allows testers to do this as the *fidelity* of the test system.

Figures 1.3 and 1.4 provide visual representations of two test systems. In Figure 1.3, test system A allows the tester to cover a majority of the product's quality risks and also to cover those areas that affect customer A's experience of quality. Test system B, shown in Figure 1.4, fails in both respects: it covers a smaller portion of the product's features, and, worse yet, the portion tested does not cover customer B's experience of quality.

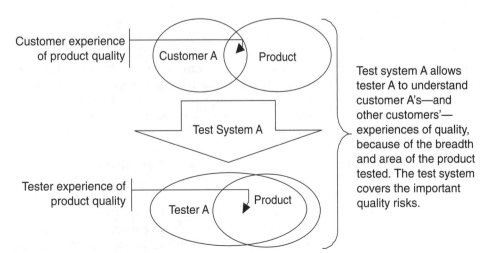

Figure 1.3 A high-fidelity test system.

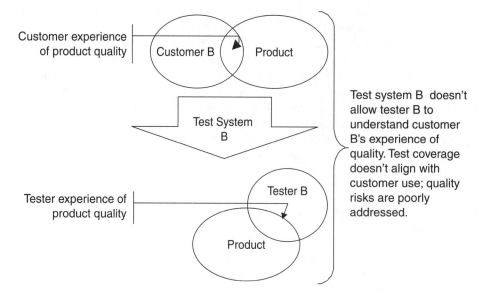

Test system B doesn't allow tester B to understand customer B's experience of quality. Test coverage doesn't align with customer use; quality risks are poorly addressed.

Figure 1.4 A low-fidelity test system.

Two other scenarios are possible. First, suppose that you have a test system with the same degree of coverage as test system B, but that the coverage area aligns with customer B's use of the product. In this case, your test team will do a fine job of catching critical defects—at least from customer B's perspective. You'll also be able to explain how those defects will affect the users, which is important in terms of establishing priority. If most customers, including your most important ones, use the product the same way customer B does, then test system B, coverage limitations notwithstanding, is a good test system.

Second, suppose that you have a test system with the same degree of coverage area as test system A, but that the coverage area does not align with customer A's usage of the product. In this case, you fail to test the features that customer A expects to use. In addition, the results of the testing you do perform can't be related back to real-world usage scenarios, which reduces the apparent priority of any defects you find. Since these features will probably reach the field buggy, customer A will be dissatisfied. If customer A is typical of your customer base—especially your important customers—you have a serious test coverage problem, even though the test system covers most of the product's features.

Figure 1.5 represents these scenarios. Of course, you can't test all of the quality risks and none of the customer uses, or vice versa. In Figure 1.5, these unlikely or unreachable zones are shown in the dotted-line enclosed areas in the upper left and lower right. The best test systems score on the right-hand side of the chart (covering customer usage), and the further up the right-hand side you get (the more quality risk you cover), the better your test system. Those quality risks that relate most closely to actual customer usage are the critical quality risks.

Figure 1.5 Test system coverage and its ability to assess quality.

The Classics and Beyond: Informal Methods for Assessing Quality Risks

So, how do I focus on the customer-critical quality risks? I want to address as many of these quality risks as possible, developing tests in an order consistent with customer priorities. Later in this chapter, I'll show you a formal approach for determining this priority, but I also use an informal method in which I outline the major quality risk categories and then refine and add details to that list with the help of my staff and colleagues who are especially customer-aware. (I refer to this approach in the exercises at the end of the chapter as the "informal risk analysis technique.")

The Usual Suspects

To develop the list of major quality risk categories, I start by breaking down the test process into the classic phases of component testing, integration testing, and system testing. Using the guidelines presented earlier in this chapter, you will have already determined which of these test phases you will run and which can be skipped because other colleagues are covering them. (In the following subsections, you might encounter some concepts that are new to you. Since this is a book on test management, not on test design, space and scope preclude me from explaining all these thoroughly. If you find yourself confused by a particular quality risk, please consult some of the books on test design listed in the bibliography.)

Component Testing

> **States.** In some computer systems, especially telephony systems, the components or some set of components implement what is called in computer science a *state machine*. A state machine is a system that moves through clearly defined states,

while the response (the associated output and the subsequent state) to an input depends on the current state and the input. State machines present a variety of quality risks that are related both to the state machine as a whole and to the individual states. Do the transitions from one state to another occur under the proper conditions? Are the correct outputs generated? Are the correct inputs accepted for each state? Consider an alarm card in the DataRocket server that sends SNMP information over the network if problems arise. This component spends most of its time in a quiescent state, but if it senses that the CPU is overheating, it transitions to a CPU Overtemp Warn state, during which it sends out alerts at regular intervals. If the problem does not clear up, the component transitions to a CPU Overtemp Critical state, at which point it initiates a system shutdown. You will need to verify that the transitions occur at the right points and that the component can't get "stuck" in a given state. For example, if the CPU returns to a normal temperature but the alarm card remains in a CPU Overtemp Warn state, the alarm card will continue to send (now spurious) alerts over the network and might do something dangerous, such as transitioning incorrectly to the CPU Overtemp Critical state. [8]

Transactions. Components that have transactions with the user or with other components present various risks. For example, creating a new file is a transaction in SpeedyWriter. Can the user select the appropriate file template? How does the product respond to illegal file names?

Code coverage. Untested code in a component presents unknown structural risks. These untested areas often handle unusual or hard-to-create conditions, which make it tempting to skip them. For example, simulating the CPU Overtemp Critical condition described earlier might result in damage to the test configuration. However, how else can you verify that the system shutdown will actually occur? If it is impractical—because of CPU placement, for example—to simulate the overheating using a hair dryer or a soldering iron, you might be forced to sacrifice one CPU to find out.

Data flow coverage. A data flow is the transfer of information—either through parameters, shared (global) data space, or a stored database—from one component of the system to another. In the past, the risks associated with data flows haven't received nearly the attention they deserve—which shows in today's software—but, with the advent of data warehouses and an increased focus on data quality, this is starting to change.[9] Increasingly, programs allow you to import, export, and link data from other programs, creating complex data flows. Users sometimes report strange and counterintuitive failures while using these features. If SpeedyWriter, for example, includes a component that reads and writes Microsoft Word files, testers must evaluate this feature across multiple Word formats (versions) and with files that include more than just text. In the hardware world, signal quality testing is a form of component-level data flow testing.

---

[8] Boris Beizer's, *Black Box Testing and Software Testing Techniques* provides ideas for behavioral and structural testing of state machines, respectively.
[9] See Larry English's book, *Improving Data Warehouse and Business Information Quality: Methods for Reducing Costs and Increasing Profits.*

Functionality. Each component exists to implement some set of functions, which are internal operations such as calculations and formatting. Functional quality risks are generally of two types: either the function is implemented incorrectly, or the function works but has undesirable side effects.

User interface. The quality risks in this area are similar to those encountered for functionality, but they also include questions of usability such as understandable prompts and messages, clear control flows, and appropriate color schemes and graphics. User interface testing during component testing often involves prototypes of the interface or uses lots of stubs as placeholders. The testers might not be able to exercise the whole system end to end, but each screen should be mocked up.[10]

Mechanical life. Any object that can be flexed or moved has a limit to the number of motions it can endure: keys on a keyboard break, hinges fatigue, buttons snap off, latches crack, and contacts fail.

Signal quality. Any circuit that processes data, whether digital or analog, is subject to the constraints imposed by signal quality. Lead times, lag times, rise times, fall times, noise, spikes, transients, and the like can be out of spec, causing a component to fail.

Integration Testing

Component or subsystem interfaces. Every API, every method, every function, every bus, every connector represents an opportunity for misunderstandings between the two (or more) component development engineers. These misunderstandings manifest themselves when two components that are otherwise correct fail together. In a sense, shared data files, and especially dynamic data such as configuration files and multi-user databases, are interfaces as well. In general, any place where data or control is transferred from one component to one or more components, either immediately or in a delayed fashion, an interface exists that can cause trouble.

Functionality. In integration tests, you again encounter the "wrong action" and "right action, wrong side effect" risks, but here I focus on functionality that requires the correct operation of two or more components or a flow of data between them.

Capacity and volume. Think of software, a computer, or a network of computers as a system of pipes for bringing in information, operating on it, storing it, and sending it out. The capacities (static) and volumes (dynamic) of these pipes must match the requirements of the application and the expectations of the user. From a structural test perspective, every buffer, queue, storage resource, processor, bus, and I/O channel in the system has a theoretical limit and a (lower) practical limit. For a single-user program on a PC, this might be a simple, well-bounded set of risks. For SpeedyWriter, the effects of network traffic and the speed of the typist

---

[10] As Steve McConnell points out in the *Software Project Survival Guide*, these mock-ups are an excellent time to get real users in front of the interface, and should actually be created during the requirements, design, or detailed design phase.

might be the only issues. For a network server such as DataRocket, however, a variety of risks can apply. Can the network card handle realistic traffic levels? Can the disk subsystem deal with realistic loads? Is the data storage capability sufficient? In integration testing, you can begin to evaluate these risks.

Error/disaster handling and recovery. Undesirable events happen. PCs lock up. Servers crash. Networks drop packets. Modem connections fail. Hard drives experience errors. Building air conditioners and heaters go out. Electrical grids have power surges, brownouts, and failures. It might be depressing, but you should construct a list of such situations and how they can affect your system. Increasingly, even common PC-based office applications and operating systems are being used in critical infrastructure. This implies a need for true disaster-recovery capability. Mostly, though, there are the mundane mini-catastrophes that will eventually afflict the system. You can start looking at these quality risks early in the integration test phase.

Data quality. If your product stores, retrieves, and shares significant amounts of data—especially data that has delicate links, relationships, and integrity constraints—you should consider testing whether the product can handle that data reliably. For example, I once used an expense-reporting program that had a serious data quality bug in the way it handled the expense report data file that it managed. Because I needed to analyze data across multiple reports, all reports had to reside in the same file. If the PC operating system crashed while the application had the expense-report file open, the application corrupted the file. The corruption was subtle; I could continue to use the file for quite a while afterward, but in the meantime, the corruption compounded itself. At some point, any attempt to add a new transaction caused the application to crash. The application did not include a file-repair utility. Because data storage and retrieval tend to be clustered in certain components or subsystems, you should start testing these areas as soon as these components are integrated.

Performance. As with capacity and volume, performance concerns apply to most subsystems or components in a product. For real-time and mission-critical applications, performance can be the most important quality risk. Even for systems that are not real-time, important performance issues exist. Most product reviews in computer magazines address performance. Performance is not only "how many per second," but also "how long." Consider the battery life of a laptop. As the system is integrated, you can begin to measure performance.

User interface. As more pieces of "real" functionality are integrated into the system, you might be able to test these through the user interface. (If the user interface is a true throw-away prototype, then you might not have this option.)

System and Acceptance Testing

Functionality. During system testing, you should consider functionality in terms of whole sequences of end-user operations (broad) or an entire area of functionality (deep). For example, with SpeedyWriter you might look at creating, editing, and printing a file, or at all the possible ways of creating a file, all the editing options, and all the printing options.

User interface. If you or the programmers have had a chance to work with a prototype in earlier test phases, usability testing during system test can focus on scrubbing out the irritating behaviors that crop up now that everything is connected to the interface. Regrettably, though, the system test phase is often the first time you will see the complete user interface with all the commands and actions available. (The prototyping I advocated earlier happens on the best projects, but not on all projects.) If so, you must address all usability issues at this stage. Either way, some usability testing is usually appropriate during the system test phase.

States. State machines can exist at the system level as well as at the component level. For example, a voice mail system is a complex computer-telephony state machine.

Transactions. Transaction handling can also occur at the system level. DataRocket, for example, handles transactions: printing a file, delivering a file (one chunk at a time), and so forth.

Data quality. During the system test phase, I revisit the data quality risks initially covered in integration testing, since the complexity of the data often increases once the entire product is integrated. For example, if SpeedyWriter supports embedded pictures and other nontext objects, this feature might not be dropped in until the end of the integration test. Working with such complex data makes problems more likely.

Operations. Complex systems often require administrators; databases, networks, and servers come to mind. These operators perform essential maintenance tasks that sometimes take the system offline. For DataRocket, consider the following quality risks: Can you back up and restore files? Can you migrate the system from Novell NetWare to Windows NT Server? Can you add an external RAID array? Can you add memory? Can you add a second LAN card?

Capacity and volume. During system test, I revisit the capacity and volume risks that were covered in integration testing, but this time, I use a more black-box approach. Rather than beating on individual buffers, queues, resources, and channels inside the product, I look at the capacity and volume limitations from a user's point of view.

Reliability, availability, and stability. Quality risks in this area include unacceptable failure rates (mean time between failures, or MTBF), unacceptable recovery times (mean time to repair, or MTTR), and the inability of the system to function under legitimate conditions without failure. MTBF demonstrations provide a typical example of reliability testing in the hardware world. In hardware, the theory and practice of measuring reliability are well established and widely practiced. In the area of software, there is a broader set of theories that are less uniformly applied on real projects.[11]

Error/disaster handling and recovery. As in the case of capacity and volume, I revisit error/disaster handling and recovery from a behavioral perspective. I focus on the external failures.

---

[11] For readers intrigued by this topic, you may want to read IEEE Standards 982 and 1061 which presents a number of reliability models. You can also check out Boris Beizer's essay, "Software is Different," (available in Software Research's "Software Test Techniques" electronic newsletter archive on www.soft.com).

Stress. This risk category is often an amalgam of capacity, volume, reliability, stability, and error/disaster handling and recovery. A single "stress test" suite can push the system in a way that provides information about all these areas.

Performance. First broached during integration testing, performance is another risk category that I revisit during the system test phase. Behavioral approaches are common, but mixed approaches with structural load generators coupled with behavioral probes have also worked well for me.

Date and time handling. The recent experience with the Year 2000 (Y2K) bugs raised the level of awareness about these types of quality risks. You might also need to take account of the fact that some countries—for example, Taiwan—base their calendars on events other than the birth of Jesus. Additionally, you might need to verify that your product works properly in different time zones, or even multiple time zones if it is a distributed system.

Localization. Localization typically refers to problems associated with different languages. Even Romance languages, which use the Latin alphabet, often include special letters, such as the ñ in Spanish, that can generate a quality risk if your product includes sorting or searching capabilities. Languages such as Chinese, Japanese, Russian, and Greek create bigger difficulties. Besides the software considerations, computers in these environments use different keyboards and different printer drivers. Moreover, language is not the only custom that changes at the border and can affect your system. Can your product handle 220 volts and 110 volts, 50 hertz and 60 hertz? How about the unique dial tones and ring signals found in Europe and Asia? Beyond the technical considerations, there are cultural issues, taboos, and "shorthands." What is considered an acceptable way of indicating something in one culture might be a rude or obscene gesture in another.

Networked and distributed environments. If your product works in a networked or distributed environment, you have some special quality risks to consider. For example, what if your system spans time zones? Can the constituent systems talk to each other without getting confused about Central Standard Time and Pacific Standard Time? If your systems must communicate internationally, will the telephone standards affect them?

Configuration options and compatibility. Most PC software these days supports various configuration options. SpeedyWriter, for example, might need to remember a customer's name, address, and company to generate letter outlines. DataRocket might allow various CPU speeds and multiprocessor settings. In addition, configuration options are now dynamic in a variety of ways that would have been unthinkable just years ago. On-demand loading and unloading of drivers (plug and play), libraries, and software; "cold," "warm," and "hot" swapping of devices; and power management can be seen as dynamically changing the configuration of software and hardware. Moreover, when you look out past the internal variables, the PC world includes a bewildering variety of software, hardware, and network environments that can create problems for your system. Will the system talk to all the printers your customers own? Do network drivers cause your system to fail? Can your software coexist with leading applications?

Standards compliance. In the hardware world, you might need to consider legal and market standards such as UL, FCC, CE, and others that might be required for your target market. In the software and hardware worlds, customers sometimes require compatibility logos such as Microsoft's "Designed for Windows." Seemingly innocuous bugs related to standards can have serious repercussions: your company might even find the product legally or effectively barred from the market.[12]

Security. Given your dog's name, your spouse's name, your children's names, and your birthday, I might be able to crack your computer accounts. On a larger scale, given a modem bank or a Web site, criminals might be able to break into your network. If security is a feature of or concern for your product, you will need to think about testing it.

Environment. Because hardware products must live in the real world, they are subject to environmental risks. What happens if you knock your laptop off the airplane's tray table? How do the shaking and bumping encountered during shipping affect a server? Can power sags and surges cause your system to crash and fail? What about the effects of temperature and humidity?

Power input, consumption, and output. All computers take in electrical current, convert some of it to heat or other electromagnetic radiation, and send the rest of it to attached devices. Systems with rechargeable batteries, such as laptops, might add some conversion and storage steps to this process, and some systems might use power in unusual modes such as 48 VDC, but ultimately the process is the same. This orchestration of electrical power can fail; insufficient battery life for laptops is a good example.

Shock, vibration, and drop. All computers will at some point be moved. I have never worked with a system that was assembled on the floor on which it would operate. In the course of this movement, the computer will experience shocks, vibrations, and, occasionally, drops. Some computers are subject to motion while on, others only while packaged. The system test phase is the right time to find out whether the system misbehaves after typical encounters with the laws of Newtonian physics.

Installation, cut-over, setup, and initial configuration. Every instance of a product has an initial use. Does the installation process work? Can you migrate data from an old system? Are there unusual load profiles during the first few weeks of use? These loads can include many user errors as people learn the system. In a multiuser situation, configuration will also include the creation of the initial accounts. Think about the entire process, end to end; individual actions might work, but the process as a whole could be unworkable. In addition, consider the possibility that someone might want to uninstall the product. If you've ever uninstalled a Windows application, you know how problematic that can be. Finally, don't forget to check out the licensing and registration processes.

---

[12] While standards are based on technical issues, politics and protectionism come into play due to the stakes. In an article called, "Standards Battles Heat Up Between United States and European Union" from the January, 1999 edition of *Quality Progress*, Amy Zuckerman writes, "The European Community . . . has reorganized to better use standards to take aim at what EC officials consider monopolistic high-tech manufacturers and consortia, mainly based in the United States." If standards can affect your company's ability to sell its product in the target markets, you should consider further research in this area. See Amy Zuckerman's book, *International Standards Desk Reference*.

Documentation and packaging. If your product includes documentation, you have risks ranging from the possibly dangerous to the simply embarrassing. Consider instructions in DataRocket's manual, accompanied by an illustration, that lead a user to set the input voltage selector for 110 volts in a 220-volt environment. On the less serious side, think of some of the humorous quotations from technical documentation that circulate on the Internet. Do you want your company singled out for such honors? Packaging, likewise, should be appropriately marked.

Maintainability. Even if your system is too simple to require an operator, you might still have maintainability risks. Can you upgrade software to a current version? Can you add memory to your PC? If your software works in a networked environment, does it support remote (possibly automated) software distribution?

Alpha, beta, and other live tests. For general-purpose software and hardware, no amount of artificial testing can cover all the uses and environments to which your customers will subject your product. To address these risks, I like to use a beta or early-release program of some sort.

Checking and Completing Your List

By the end of this exercise, I have an outline of the quality risks, broken down by phases and, within each phase, by test suite. My list almost certainly suffers from two defects, however. First, it includes some unimportant risks that customers won't care about. Second, and worse, it doesn't include some critical risks that customers *will* care about very much. My list is based on general categories of quality risks and my best educated guesses about how those categories apply to your product. It's a good start, but I need to refine it.

Peer Review

Assuming that I am not the entire test team, I review this list with my staff. Spending an hour or so working together on this list will improve it considerably; peer reviews often consist simply of putting one's work in front of a group.

The basic process of a peer review can be described as follows:

1. Circulate the draft document a few days in advance, and then schedule a conference room.

2. Invite anyone on your team who can contribute, and try to draw everyone into the discussion. Broad participation is important.

3. Take care to create a collegial review environment. If members of your test team are afraid to criticize your ideas, you won't learn anything interesting.

4. Walk through the document, spending sufficient time on the important details, while guarding against the natural tendency of meetings to become trapped in a "rat hole" or obsess on minor points. Take careful notes on comments and concerns.

5. Try to avoid spending longer than two hours in any one session. Although the duration of the meeting will depend on the level of detail that must be covered, most people find it hard to focus on highly technical material for more than a couple of hours.

After the review, I revise the document and recirculate it to the participants to ensure that I have adequately captured their ideas in my notes.[13]

Internal Experts

After getting my team's input, I consult with my coworkers. I start with sales, marketing, technical support, help desk people, and business analysts because they know and serve the customers. I usually set up meetings with the managers and get referred to others in the respective groups who have strong feelings about the product. I have found that most sales and marketing staff and business analysts are happy to explain what customers expect from the product and what the product should do.

Members of the technical support or help desk staff not only know the customers, but also know the product—often better, functionally, than the programmers and engineers who built it. They have probably talked with customers and users who treated them to frank and detailed analyses of product quality risks as they relate to customer dissatisfaction. I ask the technical support staff which product failures—past, present, and future—they lose sleep over. Which bug caused the most unpleasant support call? Technical support often tracks the details of the customer calls in a database, which is a treasure trove for you. By analyzing this data, you can learn where the product breaks and how customers use it.

I find it helps to keep in mind the story about the blind men and the elephant; people have different ideas about what's important and what's trivial. I try to cover everyone's "important" list, but I also remind people about reasonable limits if they give me an extensive wish list. In addition, if I encounter significant disagreements about the features and capabilities of the product, I discuss these with the project manager. I sometimes find myself in the middle of an unresolved dispute over product requirements or design.

External Sources

When I've worked with companies whose product or product line had a large number of customers, trade magazines helped me understand quality risks. For example, if you build Intel-based computers, you can read publications such as *PC Magazine, Byte,* and many others. The magazines often review hardware and software—not only yours, but also your competitors'. I read these reviews closely, especially the sections that describe how testing was performed. You can also join professional organizations such as the Association for Computing Machinery (ACM) and the Institute of Electrical and Electronics Engineers (IEEE) that publish journals on academic and commercial trends in the computer industry.

For some test areas, I consult experts. Reliability and security, for example, require specialized knowledge. If I wanted to measure the mean time between failure (MTBF) of the DataRocket server or the security of SpeedyWriter, I would retain professional help. If the system under test serves a unique customer base or has unique quality risks—for example, medical, banking, tax preparation, or accounting software—bringing in content experts and people who have experience developing similar systems makes sense.

---

[13] This process works best if people have some familiarity with the process and ground rules of peer reviews. For a good introduction, see Freedman and Weinberg's *Handbook of Walkthroughs, Inspections, and Technical Reviews.*

Finally, customer surveys can provide insight into how the system is used. If you are selling a product that includes a registration form, you might be able to add a section on quality and customer expectations that could help you to define the key quality risks. It might be a challenge to implement this quickly enough to help on a current project, but quality improvement is a process that takes time.

Proposing the Quality Risks

The last hurdle is ensuring that the project manager and the development managers buy into the list of quality risks. These individuals can suggest important additions and changes, and might raise pertinent questions about the relative priorities; getting their input will improve the list. In addition, by including them in the process, I build a level of comfort between these managers and me about what tests I plan to run. This mutual understanding prevents surprises and confrontations down the road, and assures the managers that I won't pull any "gotcha" maneuvers on them by running mysterious tests late in the game.

Finally, if my list contains any gross misunderstandings about what the product is designed to do, consulting with the project manager and the development managers will help me clear up the misunderstandings at this early stage. This avoids the lost time and the potential embarrassment of developing new tests for—and even reporting bugs against—"broken features" that don't exist.

After the other managers and I concur on the list of quality risks, I have a set of objectives for the test system I need. In other words, I have to create testware that targets the high-risk areas and put into practice a test process that employs this testware effectively to locate bugs in these areas. Table 1.1 shows an example of such a list, generated for SpeedyWriter. The table is broken down by test phase, by general category of risk, and then by specific risks. A priority—from 1 (highest) to 5 (lowest) in this example—is assigned to each risk.

Table 1.1   Prioritized Quality Risks for SpeedyWriter

QUALITY RISKS BY TEST PHASE	PRIORITY
Component Test Phase	
Code coverage	
Error handling	1
Importing/exporting	2
General	5
Data flow coverage	
Importing	2
Exporting	2
Hyperlinks	2

Table 1.1 *(Continued)*

QUALITY RISKS BY TEST PHASE	PRIORITY
Functionality	
File operations and dynamic data flows	1
Editing	1
Printing	1
Tables, figures, references, fields, and complex objects	1
Formatting	1
Spelling, thesaurus, grammar, change tracking, and other tools	1
Help	1
User interface	
Microsoft Windows 98/Me	3
Microsoft Windows NT/2000	3
Solaris OpenWindows (Sun)	3
Apple Macintosh	3
Linux Gnome	4
Integration Test Phase	
Component interfaces	
Toolbar-to-function	1
Menus-to-function	1
Display/preview	2
Printing	2
Event handling	2
Functionality (regression from component test)	1
System Test Phase	
Functionality (regression from component test)	1
User interface	
Microsoft Windows 95/98	1

Continues

Table 1.1 Prioritized Quality Risks for SpeedyWriter *(Continued)*

QUALITY RISKS BY TEST PHASE	PRIORITY
User interface *Continued*	
Microsoft Windows NT	1
Solaris OpenWindows (Sun)	1
Apple Macintosh	1
Linux Gnome	1
Capacity and volume	
Maximum file length	3
Maximum table size	3
Maximum number of revisions	3
Error/disaster handling and recovery	
Platform crash	3
Network failure	3
File space overflow	3
Performance	
Microsoft Windows Me/98	1
Microsoft Windows NT/2000	1
Solaris OpenWindows (Sun)	1
Apple Macintosh	1
Date handling	
Time zones	4
Leap years	4
Localization	
Spanish	2
French	2
German	2
Italian	5
Chinese	5
Japanese	5

Continues

Table 1.1   *(Continued)*

QUALITY RISKS BY TEST PHASE	PRIORITY
Networked environment	
Novell NetWare	5
Microsoft Windows NT/2000	5
PC NFS	5
Configuration options	
Preferences storage/retrieval	1
Available printer selections	1
Standards	
Microsoft Windows 98/Me	1
Microsoft Windows NT/2000	3
Sun Solaris	3
Security	
Password-protect files	4
PGP encrypt/decrypt files	4
Installation, setup, and initial configuration	
Microsoft Windows 98/Me	2
Microsoft Windows NT/2000	2
Solaris OpenWindows (Sun)	2
Apple Macintosh	2
Documentation	3

Failure Mode and Effect Analysis: A Formal Method for Understanding Quality Risks

The previous section outlined an informal approach to assessing quality risks. In this section, I'll present a formal technique for defining quality risks using an approach called *failure mode and effect analysis* (FMEA). I use this formal approach to map requirements, design specifications, and project team assumptions onto specific quality risks and effects. I can then rank these risks according to their risk priority and attack them in order.

DO COMPUTER USERS NEED A BILL OF RIGHTS?

Perhaps you, like I, have seen quality standards set high at the beginning of a project—when nothing is at stake—only for commitment to prove lacking when money and ship dates are at risk. This behavior highlights the fact that quality, unlike budget and schedule, is seen as both hard to quantify and of dubious business necessity. However, what if users were entitled to quality? In a 1998 article entitled "Guaranteeing Rights for the User," Dr. Clare-Marie Karat, a social psychologist and user interface designer at IBM's T. J. Watson Research Center, suggested the following computer user's bill of rights (reprinted with Dr. Karat's permission):

1. The user is always right. If there is a problem with the use of the system, the system is the problem, not the user.

2. The user has the right to easily install and uninstall software and hardware systems without negative consequences.

3. The user has the right to a system that performs exactly as promised.

4. The user has the right to easy-to-use instructions (user guides, online or contextual help, error messages) for understanding and utilizing a system to achieve desired goals and recover efficiently and gracefully from problem situations.

5. The user has the right to be in control of the system and to be able to get the system to respond to a request for attention.

6. The user has the right to a system that provides clear, understandable, and accurate information regarding the task it is performing and the progress toward completion.

7. The user has the right to be clearly informed about all system requirements for successfully using software or hardware.

8. The user has the right to know the limits of the system's capabilities.

9. The user has the right to communicate with the technology provider and receive a thoughtful and helpful response when raising concerns.

10. The user should be the master of software and hardware technology, not vice versa. Products should be natural and intuitive to use.

When thinking like Dr. Karat's becomes the common coin of software and hardware development, those of us who make a living testing new computer products will find ourselves living in a different world, both technically and politically.

I learned the FMEA technique by studying D. H. Stamatis' book *Failure Mode and Effect Analysis,* which contains a thorough presentation of this technique. In the following discussion, I have modified Stamatis' format and approach slightly.

Fundamentally, an FMEA is a technique for understanding and prioritizing possible failure modes (or quality risks) in system functions, features, attributes, behaviors, components, and interfaces. I have used it both structurally and behaviorally. It also provides a means of tracking process improvements such as closed-loop corrective actions, which makes sense as it came into existence in the Total Quality Management domain.[14]

---

[14] A closed-loop corrective action occurs when, after discovery of a problem, steps are taken to prevent the recurrence of that and similar problems in the future. For example, if you find that your room is full of flies, you might notice that they're coming in through the open window, which you then notice has a torn screen. Closed-loop corrective action refers neither to swatting the flies nor to closing the window but rather to repairing the screen.

	Failure Mode and Effects Analysis (Quality Risks Analysis) Form											
System Name: DataRocket			Supplier Involvement: Seven Lucky					FMEA Date: 5/20/2002				
System Responsibility: Jim Johnson			Model/Product: DataRocket					FMEA Rev Date: 5/28/2002				
Person Responsibility: Bob Chen			Target Release Date:									
Involvement of Others:			Prepared By: Lin-Tsu Wei									
					Initial FMEA							
System Function or Feature	Potential Failure Mode(s)- Quality Risk(s)	Potential Effect(s) of Failure	Critical?	Severity	Potential Cause(s) of Failure	Priority	Detection Method(s)	Likelihood	Risk Pri No	Recommended Action	Who/ When?	References
Video Subsystem												
Video Controller	Installation	Bad fit, blocked access to other cards, etc.	Y	1	PCI Slot Layout	1	Case/MB Design	1	1	Function Test	Test/ Product Test	Video Card Ref Guide, Pg 12 MB Ref Guide, Pg 15
	Palette Limit	Limited displays.	N	5	Memory size	5	Vendor HW Test	5	125	None		Video Card Ref Guide, Pg 10
	Performance	Slow screen displays.	N	4	Memory speed	5	Vendor HW Test	5	100	None		Video Card Ref Guide, Pg 10
	Reliability	Loss of functionality.	Y	1	Unreliable card, MB/card incompat	1	Vendor MTBF Test	3	3	MTBF Demo	Test/ System Test	Video Card Ref Guide, Pg 15
Novell Video Drivers	Incompatiblity	Loss of functionality	Y	1	Novell/Video chipset	2	Vendor driver test	3	6	Compat Test	Test/ Product Test	Video Card Ref Guide, Pg 11
	Resolution Limits	Partial loss of functionality	N	3	Novell/Video chipset	2	Vendor driver test	3	18	Function Test	Test/ Product Test	Video Card Ref Guide, Pg 11

Figure 1.6   A portion of the FMEA for DataRocket.

Figure 1.6 shows the top page of a sample FMEA chart for DataRocket. Let's go through each of the columns in detail.

System Function or Feature. This column is the starting point for the analysis. In most rows, you enter a concise description of a system function. If the entry represents a category, you must break it down into more specific functions or features in subsequent rows. Getting the level of detail right is a bit tricky. With too much detail, you can create an overly long, hard-to-read chart; with too little detail, you will have too many failure modes associated with each function.

Potential Failure Mode(s)—Quality Risk(s). For each specific function or feature (but not for the category itself), the entry in this column identifies the ways you might encounter a failure. These are quality risks associated with the loss of a specific system function. Each specific function or feature can have multiple failure modes.

Potential Effect(s) of Failure. Each failure mode can affect the user in one or more ways. I keep these entries general rather than trying to anticipate every possible unpleasant outcome.

Critical? In this column, you indicate whether the potential effect has critical consequences for the user. Is the product feature or function completely unusable if this failure mode occurs?

Severity. This column denotes the effect of the failure (immediate or delayed) on the system. I use a scale from 1 (worst) to 5 (least dangerous), as follows:

1. Loss of data, hardware damage, or a safety issue.
2. Loss of functionality with no workaround.
3. Loss of functionality with a workaround.
4. Partial loss of functionality.
5. Cosmetic or trivial.

Stamatis uses a reverse scale, in which larger numbers denote greater severity. However, I prefer to use the scale shown here, which is more in line with the typical use of the term *severity* as I've encountered it.[15]

Potential Cause(s) of Failure. This column lists possible factors that might trigger the failure—for example, operating system error, user error, or normal use. In my experience, this column is not as important as others when you are using an FMEA strictly as a test design tool.

Priority. While Stamatis uses the word *occurrence*, I prefer the term *priority*, by which I mean the effect of failure on users, customers, or operators. I use a scale from 1 (worst) to 5 (least dangerous), as follows:

1. Complete loss of system value.
2. Unacceptable loss of system value.
3. Possibly acceptable reduction in system value.
4. Acceptable reduction in system value.
5. Negligible reduction in system value.

These numbers are less precisely defined than severity ratings, which makes them difficult for test staff to estimate. I rely on input from sales, marketing, technical support, and business analysts.

Detection Method(s). This column lists a currently existing method or procedure, such as development activities or vendor testing, that can find the problem before it affects users, excluding any future actions (such as creating and executing test suites) you might perform to catch it. (If you do not exclude the tests you might create, the next column will be skewed.)

Likelihood. The number in this column represents the vulnerability, from 1 (most probable) to 5 (least probable), in terms of: a) existence in the product (e.g., based on technical risk factors such as complexity and past defect history); b) escape from the current development process; and, c) intrusion on user operations. I use the following 1-to-5 scale:

1. Certain to affect all users.
2. Likely to impact some users.

---

[15] This scale derives from the United States Department of Defense severity definition in MILSTD 2167A.

3. Possible impact on some users.

4. Limited impact to few users.

5. Unimaginable in actual usage.

This number requires both technical judgment and an understanding of the user community, which makes participation by programmers and other engineers along with business analysts, technical support, marketing and sales important.

RPN (Risk Priority Number). This column tells you how important it is to test this particular failure mode. The risk priority number (RPN) is the product of the severity, the priority, and the likelihood. Because I use values from 1 to 5 for all three of these parameters, the RPN ranges from 1 (most dangerous quality risk) to 125 (least dangerous quality risk).

Recommended Action. This column contains one or more simple action items for each potential effect to reduce the related risk (which pushes the risk priority number toward 125). For the test team, most recommended actions involve creating a test case that influences the likelihood rating.

Who/When? This column indicates who is responsible for each recommended action and when they are responsible for it (for example, in which test phase).

References. This column provides references for more information about the quality risk. Usually, this involves product specifications, a requirements document, and the like.

Action Results. A final set of columns (not visible in Figure 1.6) allows you to record the influence of the actions taken on the priority, severity, likelihood, and RPN values. You will use these columns after you have implemented your tests, not during the initial FMEA.

Stamatis recommends the use of a cross-functional brainstorming session to populate your FMEA chart. Gathering senior technical representatives from each team—development, testing, marketing, sales, technical support, business analysts, and so forth—you proceed to fill in the chart row by row. This is certainly the best way, but it requires a commitment from each group to send a participant to a meeting that could consume a significant part of a day. When I can't get people to attend a cross-functional session, I sometimes proceed with an FMEA anyway. To do so, I need written specifications, requirements, or other documents that describe how the system is supposed to work and what it is supposed to do. In this case, I must keep in mind the generic outline of quality risks described here, which helps me cover all the areas. It's definitely a poor second place to the cross-functional approach, but it works.

I have encountered a few pitfalls in using the FMEA method. In some cases, I have become distracted by quality risks that lie outside the scope of the test project. If I am working on SpeedyWriter, for example, I don't need to worry about operating system bugs or underlying hardware failures. For DataRocket, I needn't analyze possible low-level failures in drives or chips. If I find a bug related to a given failure mode, will the development team—or some other group—address it? If not, it's out of scope.

An FMEA document is large. Even when I develop it from specifications and requirements rather than from a brainstorming session, I nonetheless need to solicit comments from the rest of the project team. How do I convince these busy people to spend a couple of hours reviewing a dense document? I try circulating the document via email; asking for responses, questions, and concerns; and then scheduling a final review meeting. If I still have difficulty getting participation, I'll raise the issue with my manager. That doesn't always work, either, so I'm ready to move forward without outside feedback.

I have found that if I assign one person to go off and do the entire FMEA alone, I lose an essential benefit of the process: consensus on test priorities. It's preferable to divide the effort among multiple test engineers and then use frequent informal discussions to synchronize the effort, eliminate overlap, and keep the effort within the appropriate scope.

Finally, if I'm able to use the cross-functional meeting approach, I take care to ensure that all participants understand what they're in for. The meeting will take time, possibly all day.[16] Participants also need to agree on the scope of the meeting. I have used email to clarify these issues and to introduce all the participants to the FMEA form I intended to use.

What You *Can* Test: Schedule, Resources, and Budget

Whether I've used an informal approach or the more formal FMEA technique, I now have a prioritized outline of quality risks. This is analogous to the requirements for the overall project; the list of critical quality risks documents the essential requirements for my test effort. Now, I need to figure out a test schedule and a budget that will allow me to test the scariest risks.

One of my first managers was fond of this saying: "Schedule, cost, and quality—pick two." This pithy remark means that while for a given feature set you can freely select any two of these variables, doing so determines the third variable. I call this rule, which is illustrated in Figure 1.7, the "Iron Box and Triangle" of system development. The clockwise arrow indicates refinement during the planning stage. These refinements balance features, schedule, cost, and quality. Once implementation begins, the feature set becomes more rigid, the schedule more painful to change, and the budget increases less likely. Within the fixed "box" enclosing the feature set in Figure 1.7, the two lines that are drawn to select the schedule and the cost determine the placement of the third line (quality) that completes the triangle.

This creates a planning conundrum in that you have only a rough idea of what your test project is about, but the window of opportunity that might allow a realistic schedule and an adequate budget is closing. (And even this scenario assumes that you are on the project team during the planning phase. The situation is worse if you have joined the team later, during implementation, as you might have a fixed budget and schedule.) There's no perfect solution, but some project management techniques exist to help.

---

[16] Earlier, I mentioned that technical review meetings should be limited to a couple hours. In the case of FMEA reviews, though, I've often found it more productive to push ahead and try to conclude at all at once. Trying to restore context after a day or two off can be tough. If you need to break it up, I recommend holding the sessions daily until the analysis is complete.

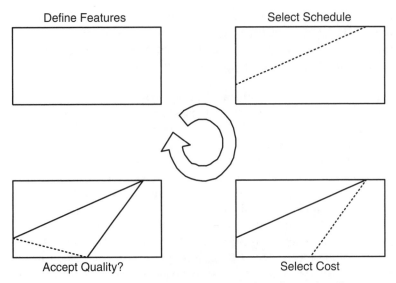

Figure 1.7 The feature, schedule, budget, and quality trade-offs.

Shoehorning: Fitting a Test Schedule into the Project

Often, software and hardware project schedules don't evolve according to any text-book approach. You might have to start with a ship date and a list of product features—the negotiability of both varies—and build the schedule from there. How can you construct a workable test schedule within these constraints?

I use a work-breakdown-structure, which is a top-down approach.[17] I find starting with big categories of work and iteratively decomposing them into discrete tasks intuitive, especially at the early stages when I don't have a lot of details. I start by breaking the test effort into major phases such as these:

- Planning (the work discussed in this chapter and the next).
- Configuration (getting the necessary hardware and other resources and setting up the test lab).
- Staffing (if applicable).
- Test development (building or deploying the test tools, creating the test suites and the test case library, putting the reporting tools in place, and documenting how the test process is to put these testware items into action).
- Test execution (running the tests, recording test status, and reporting results).

---

[17] When I was new to project management and work-breakdown-structures, I learned how to do them from *Effective Project Management* by Wysocki, et al., (Wiley, 2000) and *Winning at Project Management* by Gilbreath (Wiley, 1986).

Next, I divide each phase into activities. Within the planning category, for example, I set up activities such as defining quality risks, creating the schedule and the budget, writing test plans, and selecting test tools. Other activities might include getting bids from third parties for their help, or hiring test technicians, test engineers, and system administrators.

After that, I decompose each activity into tasks, and then subtasks if necessary. This decomposition continues until I have constituent tasks that are one or two days long and are the responsibility of one person. (I don't decompose the work-breakdown-structure this way for test execution; instead I use the test case estimating and tracking method illustrated in Chapter 5, "Managing Test Cases: The Test Tracking Spreadsheet.") These small task definitions allow me to ascertain whether I'm on track during the project. Big tasks can get dangerously out of control, and I won't find this out until a long period (a week or more) has slipped past me.

The activities in the configuration phase depend on the test environment I need. Even though I probably don't know all the details at this point, my list of quality risks usually has given me some ideas. Once I think through the quality risks, I have a "10,000-foot perspective" on the test suites I must create, which gives me a pretty good idea of my test environment needs.

For development, you must deploy your test tools and then develop the test suites themselves. I often list separate major tasks for each test phase and then enter the test suites as individual tasks within each phase. Test suite development should proceed in priority order. Developing test suites is a full-time job, so I'm careful not to set up work on various suites as parallel tasks unless I have multiple test engineers or can give a single engineer twice as long to finish. In addition, I take care to add a task for the test engineers to document how the test system works, both in terms of the design and functionality of the testware and the way the test process uses that testware to find bugs.

For test execution, there are two important questions to answer in coming up with a good estimate. First, how long will it take to run all the tests once (which I often refer to as a single "test pass")? Second, how many times will I need to run the tests against successive test releases to find all the important bugs and subsequently confirm the fixing of those bugs (which I refer to as the "number of test cycles")? Suppose I have six person-weeks of testing work defined for the system test phase and three testers allocated to run the tests. Then, each pass takes my test team two weeks. If I have found, on previous projects with the same project team, that we need to run six cycles to find and fix the important bugs, then I have six cycles, say one week each, with three passes in those cycles (see Figure 1.8).

The time required to run the tests is something a test manager can control and measure. As long as I can come up with solid estimates of how long and how much effort each test case requires, I can add up those numbers across the entire test set and use simple math to predict test pass duration. However, the number of cycles is dependent on many factors outside my control as a test manager. If the quality of the software is poor, then more cycles will be required. If the programmers are slow to fix bugs, then more cycles will be required. If bug fixes tend to break other areas of the product (i.e., to introduce regression bugs), then more cycles will be required.

If I have no historical data with the project team, I have to take a guess on the number of cycles. I've been pretty happy with six one-week cycles as a rule of thumb, although you'll need to consider your context carefully before adopting it. If the set of

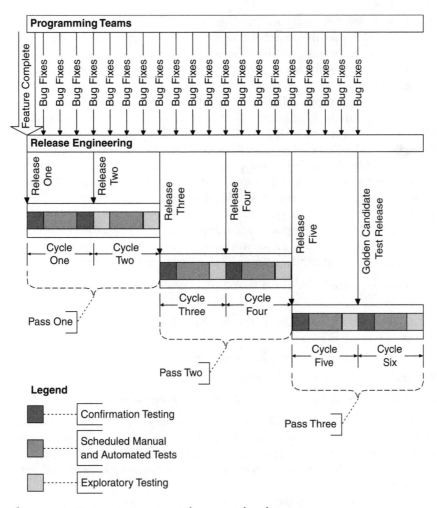

Figure 1.8   System test passes, releases, and cycles.

test cases (the "test set") is small enough, you can run a full pass in each cycle, which has benefits in terms of regression risk. (I'll talk more about test sets, suites, cycles, passes, phases, regression risks, and confirmation testing in Chapter 3.) More commonly, I estimate one week per test cycle, two or three cycles per pass, and three passes per phase. One of my clients, though, has a test set that requires about two person-decades of effort. The whole team runs each test case once as part of a year-long test pass. Complex projects might require two or three weeks per pass, with multiple cycles in each pass.

However the passes and cycles work out, I break the rules a bit on the work-breakdown-structure in the area of test execution, and assign the entire team to test tasks at the test cycle level of detail. I've found that trying to assign a single tester to a single test case in a work-breakdown-structure doesn't work well. For one thing, I generally don't know all the tests

I'm going to run during this early planning stage, so if I only account for the tests I know, I'll underestimate. Moreover, the project management tools I've worked with do a poor job of managing test cases as tasks. My usual rule of thumb is to estimate the test effort, increase it by 50 percent for the tests I don't know about yet, plan on between 20 and 30 hours of testing per tester per week, and just do the math.

In this first cut, I try to capture the basic dependencies. For example, I must develop a test suite before I can run it, and I can't start a test cycle until I receive something to test. Although some dependencies that loom far in the future won't jump out at me, my best effort will probably suffice. I try to build some slack and extra time into my schedule for the inevitable discoveries. Good project management process dictates that I track against and revise this schedule throughout my project, so I can add dependencies as they become apparent, but increases in schedule and budget numbers after the initial plan are often difficult to negotiate.

As I create the tasks, I also assign resources, even if I can't be complete at this point. I don't worry about staples such as desks, workstations, or telephones unless I have genuine concerns about getting an adequate budget for them. I focus on items such as these:

- Expensive resources such as networks, environmental test equipment, and test tools.
- Resources that require long lead times, such as lab space that must be rented and set up, or ISDN and T1 lines.
- Missing resources such as people I need to hire.
- External resources such as third-party labs.
- Scarce resources such as my test engineers and technicians.

I'm careful not to over-utilize resources that have limited "bandwidth" or availability. People, for example, can only do one thing at a time, and even shared resources such as servers, printers, networking infrastructure, and the like can be overtaxed. Certain types of tests, such as performance and reliability, require a dedicated set of resources for accurate results.

Accurate scheduling requires the participation of the actual contributors wherever possible. For example, it's better for the test engineer who'll design and implement an automated test suite to tell me how long it will take her than for me to guess myself, especially if she has experience doing test automation and I don't! The more experience with the task in question and the tool to be used the contributor has, the more accurate her estimate will be. There are also so-called Delphic oracle approaches where you poll multiple people on the team for best-case, worst-case, and expected-case task durations, then take the averages of those to come up with best-case, worst-case, and expected-case schedules. You might want to apply these types of approaches on long, complex projects where the consequences of error in the schedule are severe. No matter how careful you are, though, some studies have shown that initial estimates are off by 50 to 200 [sic] percent.[18]

---

[18] See Rita Hadden's, "Credible Estimation for Small Projects," published in *Software Quality Professional*. This includes a discussion of the Delphic oracle techniques.

One thing I do to improve the accuracy of my schedules is to refer to published rules of thumb to sanity check my estimates. Capers Jones, in *Estimating Software Costs*, includes an entire chapter of such rules. Martin Pol and Tim Koomen also include some rules for test estimation in *Test Process Improvement*. Effort and staffing ratios—for example, "X programmers on the project team requires a test team of Y testers"—are among the most common types of rules of thumb. Various papers that contain test estimation rules of thumb are published from time to time at conferences and in testing journals such as *Software Testing and Quality Engineering*, *The Journal for Software Testing Professionals*, and *Software Quality Professional*. You might want to accumulate a collection of estimation rules that you use to check your work-breakdown-structure.

Test estimation is hard to do perfectly, but not terribly hard to do well. If you follow good project management practices in preparing your work-breakdown-structure, don't forget key tasks, estimate conservatively, don't overload people and resources, involve your entire team in estimation, and focus on key dependencies and deliverables, you can construct a draft schedule for your test project that should prove relatively accurate. I also make sure that my milestone dates fit within the constraints of the project. As the project proceeds, I track progress against the schedule, adding details, adjusting durations, resolving resource conflicts, including more dependencies, and so on. Figure 1.9 shows an example of this approach, applied to testing for SpeedyWriter.

If you're new to management, you might feel a bit daunted by the prospect of doing a work-breakdown-structure. I encourage you to jump in with both feet, picking up a good self-study book first and then cranking out your first test project schedule with one of the project management tools on the market. My ability to schedule projects has improved—partly as a result of acquiring skills with the tools, although mostly as a result of experience—but I started with simple schedules and ran a number of test projects successfully. Scheduling and the project management tools are not trivial skills, so I recommend keeping it simple to start; your schedules might be less precise but are likely to be more accurate. If you try to create complicated 300-task schedules, you can get lost in the minutiae.

Estimating Resources and Creating a Budget

Given a work-breakdown-structure with detailed resource allocations, I can hammer out a budget in a couple of hours. Again, I use a top-down approach. I first create a list of resources, starting with general categories such as these:

Staff. This category includes permanent employees, contractors, and consultants.

Test tools. If I'm testing software, I might need code coverage analyzers, scripting utilities, GUI test automation systems, low-level diagnostic programs, and so forth. Hardware testing can involve oscilloscopes, shock and vibration tables, thermal chambers, CD-ROM burners, and other equipment. Don't forget basic utilities for hardware and software testing.

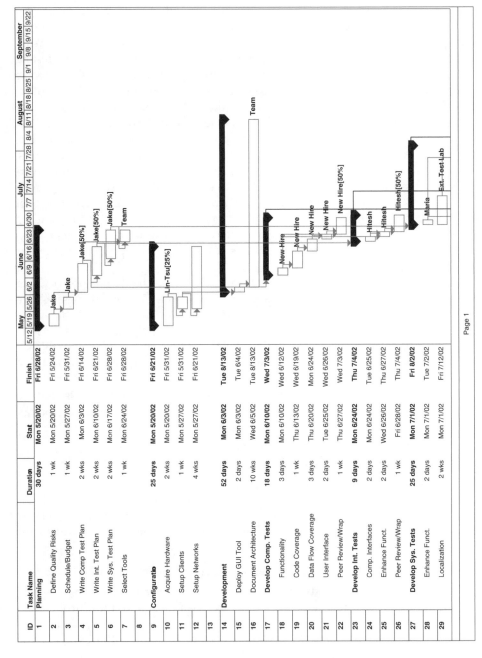

ID	Task Name	Duration	Start	Finish
1	**Planning**	**30 days**	**Mon 5/20/02**	**Fri 6/28/02**
2	Define Quality Risks	1 wk	Mon 5/20/02	Fri 5/24/02
3	Schedule/Budget	1 wk	Mon 5/27/02	Fri 5/31/02
4	Write Comp Test Plan	2 wks	Mon 6/3/02	Fri 6/14/02
5	Write Int. Test Plan	2 wks	Mon 6/10/02	Fri 6/21/02
6	Write Sys. Test Plan	2 wks	Mon 6/17/02	Fri 6/28/02
7	Select Tools	1 wk	Mon 6/24/02	Fri 6/28/02
8				
9	**Configuration**	**25 days**	**Mon 5/20/02**	**Fri 6/21/02**
10	Acquire Hardware	2 wks	Mon 5/20/02	Fri 5/31/02
11	Setup Clients	1 wk	Mon 5/27/02	Fri 5/31/02
12	Setup Networks	4 wks	Mon 5/27/02	Fri 6/21/02
13				
14	**Development**	**52 days**	**Mon 6/3/02**	**Tue 8/13/02**
15	Deploy GUI Tool	2 days	Mon 6/3/02	Tue 6/4/02
16	Document Architecture	10 wks	Wed 6/5/02	Tue 8/13/02
17	**Develop Comp. Tests**	**18 days**	**Mon 6/10/02**	**Wed 7/3/02**
18	Functionality	3 days	Mon 6/10/02	Wed 6/12/02
19	Code Coverage	1 wk	Thu 6/13/02	Wed 6/19/02
20	Data Flow Coverage	3 days	Thu 6/20/02	Mon 6/24/02
21	User Interface	2 days	Tue 6/25/02	Wed 6/26/02
22	Peer Review/Wrap	1 wk	Thu 6/27/02	Wed 7/3/02
23	**Develop Int. Tests**	**9 days**	**Mon 6/24/02**	**Thu 7/4/02**
24	Comp. Interfaces	2 days	Mon 6/24/02	Tue 6/25/02
25	Enhance Funct.	2 days	Wed 6/26/02	Thu 6/27/02
26	Peer Review/Wrap	1 wk	Fri 6/28/02	Thu 7/4/02
27	**Develop Sys. Tests**	**25 days**	**Mon 7/1/02**	**Fri 8/2/02**
28	Enhance Funct.	2 days	Mon 7/1/02	Tue 7/2/02
29	Localization	2 wks	Mon 7/1/02	Fri 7/12/02

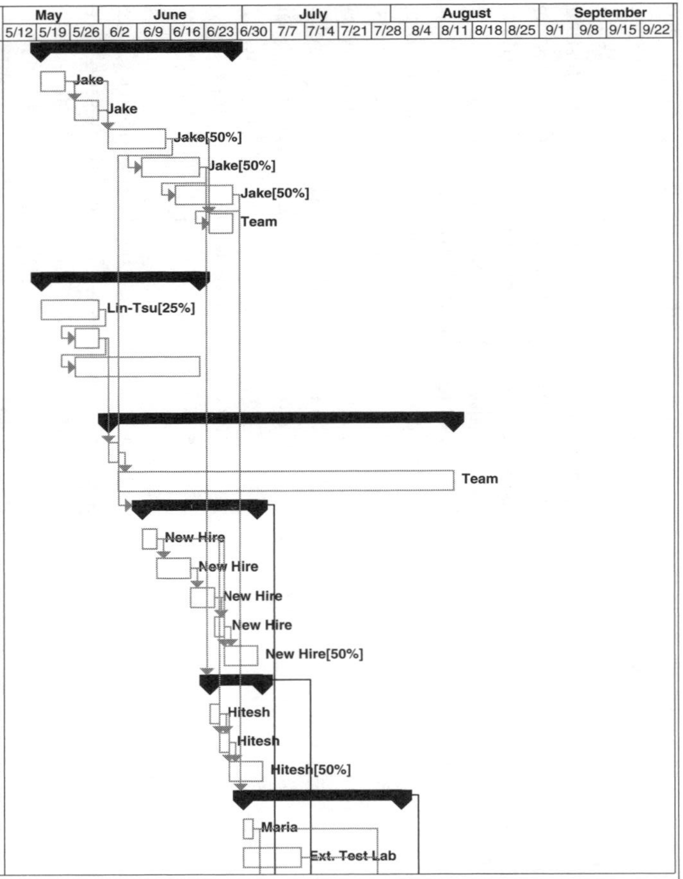

Page 1

Figure 1.9 A Gantt chart view of the work-breakdown-structure for SpeedyWriter.

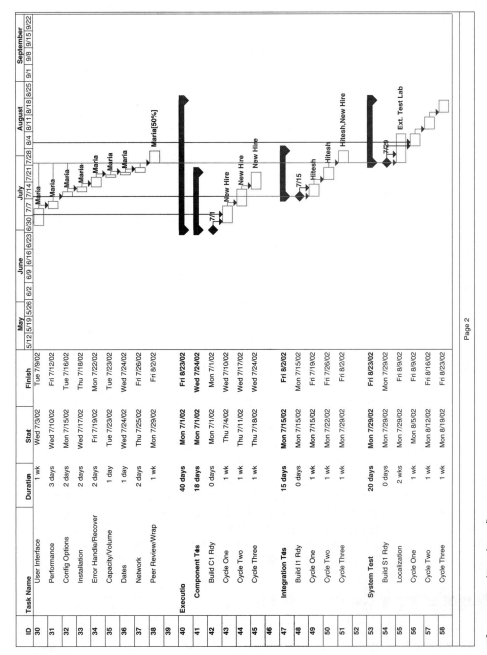

ID	Task Name	Duration	Stat	Finish
30	User Interface	1 wk	Wed 7/3/02	Tue 7/9/02
31	Performance	3 days	Wed 7/10/02	Fri 7/12/02
32	Config Options	2 days	Mon 7/15/02	Tue 7/16/02
33	Installation	2 days	Wed 7/17/02	Thu 7/18/02
34	Error Handle/Recover	2 days	Fri 7/19/02	Mon 7/22/02
35	Capacity/Volume	1 day	Tue 7/23/02	Tue 7/23/02
36	Dates	1 day	Wed 7/24/02	Wed 7/24/02
37	Network	2 days	Thu 7/25/02	Fri 7/26/02
38	Peer Review/Wrap	1 wk	Mon 7/29/02	Fri 8/2/02
39				
40	Executio	40 days	Mon 7/1/02	Fri 8/23/02
41	Component Tes	18 days	Mon 7/1/02	Wed 7/24/02
42	Build C1 Rdy	0 days	Mon 7/1/02	Mon 7/1/02
43	Cycle One	1 wk	Thu 7/4/02	Wed 7/10/02
44	Cycle Two	1 wk	Thu 7/11/02	Wed 7/17/02
45	Cycle Three	1 wk	Thu 7/18/02	Wed 7/24/02
46				
47	Integration Tes	15 days	Mon 7/15/02	Fri 8/2/02
48	Build I1 Rdy	0 days	Mon 7/15/02	Mon 7/15/02
49	Cycle One	1 wk	Mon 7/15/02	Fri 7/19/02
50	Cycle Two	1 wk	Mon 7/22/02	Fri 7/26/02
51	Cycle Three	1 wk	Mon 7/29/02	Fri 8/2/02
52				
53	System Test	20 days	Mon 7/29/02	Fri 8/23/02
54	Build S1 Rdy	0 days	Mon 7/29/02	Mon 7/29/02
55	Localization	2 wks	Mon 7/29/02	Fri 8/9/02
56	Cycle One	1 wk	Mon 8/5/02	Fri 8/9/02
57	Cycle Two	1 wk	Mon 8/12/02	Fri 8/16/02
58	Cycle Three	1 wk	Mon 8/19/02	Fri 8/23/02

Figure 1.9 (*Continued*)

Facilities and overhead. Items in this category can include travel allowances, lab space, workstations, and infrastructure such as cabling, routers, hubs, bridges, ISDN terminals, and so forth.

Test environment. This category includes the hardware, software, engineering samples, and experimental prototypes.

External labs. I include this category if I intend to use external labs for environmental testing, localization, performance, or other purposes (see Chapter 10, "Involving Other Players: Distributing a Test Project").

Within each category, I list the individual items I will need. I use placeholders to indicate where I might add items or quantities later.

To transform this resource list into a budget, I load it into a spreadsheet and line up columns to the right for each month of the project. For each item, I enter a cost figure—a monthly figure for variable costs or a one-time figure for fixed costs. Don't forget hidden or invisible costs such as burden rates for staff, agency markups for staff, application software, support contracts, and training.

If you find it difficult to estimate costs for tools, facilities, infrastructure, or the test environment, you can hit the Web or make some telephone calls. Estimating the cost of using an external lab might require an actual bid, although you can probably get a rough estimate by calling the lab. For unknown items—the placeholders on your resource list—you'll simply have to make an educated guess. Pick a comfortable figure with some wiggle room, but don't be so conservative that you'll be shot down when you approach management.

At this point, you can compare each line item against your schedule. When do you start using the resource? How long do you use it? Are ramp-up and ramp-down times associated with the resource? Answering these questions will tell you which months must absorb charges for each item, and what fraction of the charge applies in beginning and ending months. For fractions, I keep it simple; I find that halves and quarters are usually precise enough.

As I do for my schedules, I run a sanity check to ensure that all the numbers make sense. If allowed, I involve my staff in the process, making sure that they don't see each other's salary information. (Check with your management before circulating any proposed budget among your staff. Some companies don't allow individual contributors to see any budget information.) After coming up with the budget, I usually sleep on it and then review it the next day. I ask myself whether I've forgotten anything. If the budget contains a few gaping holes where I don't have enough information to even hazard a guess, I'll be honest and indicate that. Figure 1.10 provides an example of a budget for SpeedyWriter, assuming the schedule shown in Figure 1.9.

Negotiating a Livable Test Project

With a quality risks list, schedule, and budget, I have a concise package that I can take to management. By speaking management's language, I can address four key questions that will arise:

- What type of risk management are we buying?
- How long will it take?

	A	B	C	D	E	F
1		SpeedyWriter Test Budget				
2		May	June	July	August	Total
3	**Staff**					
4	Jake—Test Manager	$12,500	$12,500	$12,500	$12,500	$50,000
5	Lin-Tsu—Sys Admin.	3,516	3,516	3,516	3,516	$14,063
6	Hitesh—Test Engineer	0	3,750	7,500	7,500	$18,750
7	Maria—Test Engineer	0	1,875	7,500	7,500	$16,875
8	New Hire—Test Engineer	0	12,100	12,100	12,100	$36,300
9	Technicians	0	0	0	10,500	$10,500
10	Staff Materiel Overhead	7,000	0	0	0	$7,000
12	**Total Staff**	**$23,016**	**$33,741**	**$43,116**	**$53,616**	**$153,488**
14	**Travel and Training**	**$2,500**	**$2,500**	**$2,500**	**$2,500**	**$10,000**
16	**Tools**					
17	GUI	$5,000	$0	$0	$0	$5,000
18	Code Coverage	7,500	0	0	0	$7,500
19	Training	5,000	0	0	0	$5,000
21	**Total Tools**	**$17,500**	**$0**	**$0**	**$0**	**$17,500**
23	**Test Environment**					
24	Solaris Client	$1,500	$0	$0	$0	$1,500
25	Windows Me Client	1,200	0	0	0	$1,200
26	Windows 98 Client	1,200	0	0	0	$1,200
27	Mac Client	1,200	0	0	0	$1,200
28	Solaris Server	2,500	0	0	0	$2,500
29	Windows NT Server	2,500	0	0	0	$2,500
30	Novell Server	2,500	0	0	0	$2,500
31	Solaris x86	1,000	0	0	0	$1,000
32	Novell	700	0	0	0	700
33	Windows NT	500	0	0	0	500
35	**Total Test Environment**	**$14,800**	**$0**	**$0**	**$0**	**$14,800**
37	**External Labs**					
38	Localization	$0	$0	$5,000	$20,000	$25,000
40						
41	**20% Contingency Padding**	**$11,563**	**$7,248**	**$10,123**	**$15,223**	**$44,158**
42						
43	**Grand Total**	**$69,379**	**$43,489**	**$60,739**	**$91,339**	**$264,945**

Figure 1.10   SpeedyWriter budget.

- What will it cost?
- What's the return on investment (see Chapter 11, "Testing in Context: Economics, Lifecycles, and Process Maturity")?

Although each company has a different process for approving a test program, every project I've worked on has required some degree of discussion, explanation, and negotiation. I make a point of being flexible. If management insists on reduced costs or a faster schedule (or both), I eliminate tests in reverse priority order. If cost is the major concern but I can add a few weeks to the schedule, perhaps I can get by with one less employee. Outsourcing can also reduce costs when done wisely, as you'll see in Chapter 10. I make the case for what I believe needs to be done, but I'm prepared to do less. The only taboo is that I won't agree to do everything I initially proposed to do but in less time and/or for less money, unless management wants to cut out the contingency time (schedule slack) and money and run a high risk that later discoveries will break my budget or schedule. If I've created a realistic schedule and budget, then agreeing to some faster schedule and lower budget that fits management desire but not reality is hardly doing anyone any favors, and it certainly won't help my credibility. If handed a non-negotiable dictate—for example, "You will do this amount of testing in this period of time with this budget, end of discussion,"—then I simply agree to do the best job possible within those parameters and move on.

At the end of this negotiation, I have an approved budget and schedule and a mutual understanding of the scope and deliverables for my test project. Now it's time to move on to creating a detailed plan, building the testware, and putting the resources in place to carry out the project.

BUT WASN'T I JUST TALKING ABOUT A COMPUTER USER'S BILL OF RIGHTS?

You might ask me how I square focusing on quality with the difference between what I *should* and what I *can* test. Why quote Dr. Karat's "Bill of Rights" if I intend to knuckle under during budget and schedule negotiations?

I do think that things need to move in the direction Dr. Karat is pointing. Maybe we won't get to the final destinations she indicates. Business realities must be considered. However, let me end this chapter by saying that too many software companies ship software with either no testing at all, incompetent testing, or good testing but totally ignored findings. Just off the top of my head, I can spout off the following unforgivable "buggy software" stories:

- An expense reporting system that didn't have any data quality bugs at all...at least until the operating system crashed. (Gee, what are the odds of that?) Once the OS did crash, the file was randomly corrupted, and the corruption cascaded with subsequent use, so ultimately the entire expense report file was garbage. The vendor's technical support staff was aware of the problem, but rather than supply a patch or a file repair utility, they told me, "Email us your file and we'll fix it." Well, sure, there's nothing private or personal in that file. When I did send the file, I forgot to send the password, but they sent it back and explained that they knew how to get around the password. Wow, what security.

- The fact that some presentation files made with a major office automation suite, if corrupted in as much as a single bit in some cases, can become totally unreadable by the program. (See the first and last bullet for ways this might happen.) The software vendor knows about this bug, but they choose not to include recovery utilities in their applications. Instead, they send you to a software developer—who would be called a "highwayman" a couple centuries ago—who charges $400 for his recovery tool. Talk about turning the incompetence of others into a business opportunity!

- The Windows NT network driver that came with a very prestigious-name network card which, on two out of three boots, is unable to see the network. No diagnostic messages come up. Cold booting the system until communications are re-established is the only cure.

- The automatic update software in my laptop that recently "upgraded" the drivers for my built-in modem—without prompting me—resulting in the loss of all modem definitions in my Windows hardware profile. I wasted an entire day trying to get the drivers reloaded. My computer vendor's technical support was worse than clueless. Ultimately, I had to go out and buy a new modem, which also solved a bunch of connection speed and reliability problems I had been experiencing,

Case Study

On one project, we applied the Failure Mode and Effect Analysis (FMEA) technique to analyze possible ways that an application might fail. This application provided secure

> indicating that the buggy setup problem was only the tip of the iceberg, quality-wise, with this modem.
>
> ■ The printer I bought that didn't say anything on the box, in the manuals, or during the installation process about the fact that you couldn't install it on a networked PC and access it from other systems on the network. After a few hours of trying, I emailed tech support, only to get a response that boiled down to, "Oh, yeah, you can't do that." Oh, really? Why can't I do that? I have a 12-year-old dot matrix printer that was built before anyone had a small office network. I can share that printer just fine with every computer on my network. This whiz-bang color printer-scanner-copier that I bought in the day of ubiquitous small office/home office/home computer networking can't be shared with other computers? Pshaw!
>
> ■ The major-name graphics package I used to prepare figures for this book that lost hours of work over the course of the project by crashing during a routine file-save operation with the error message, "Error while saving file. This file may now be corrupted. Close this file and restart the operation." Silly me. I should know better than to do risky things such as save my files.
>
> ■ The daily (or more often) crash that my laptop computer subjects me to, generally without warning, usually losing a good 15 minutes' worth of work. I guess I should learn to save every 30 seconds? Or maybe that's risky...perhaps animal sacrifice would appease the software bug gods?
>
> If experienced people like me have problems like this, imagine the average computer user who has no idea whatsoever about what is going on when the system misbehaves. Moreover, why should users have to understand a computer to use it? Do you have to understand the four-stroke internal combustion engine, electronic fuel injection, and planetary geared, torque-converted automatic transmission systems to drive a car? Don Norman, in his book *The Invisible Computer*, discusses this situation at length. Ultimately, a computer is an implement that should help us get work done—nothing more, nothing less. I think we have a long way to go before we can claim levels of quality consistent with what the makers of almost every other useful implement sold on the market today. Perhaps rather than adding new features no one uses, bloating our software so that faster computers with more memory actually work more slowly than before, we could as system professionals focus on making practical tools that simply work, reliably, day in and day out, in obvious, self-explanatory fashion.
>
> Okay, diatribe aside, it's time to admit that the test manager's role is not necessarily to be the evangelist of this higher level of quality. We can do what we can, in small steps, to help our clients and employers ship better systems. I encourage you to hold systems to this standard when you're testing them. Put your reasonable user hat on and make reasonable comments about quality through your tests and your bug reporting system.

	A	B	C	D	E	F	G	H	I	J	K	L
1						**Failure Mode and Effects Analysis (Quality Risks Analysis) Form**						
2												
3	System Name: ********					Supplier Involvement: N/A					FMEA Date: 5/20/99	
4	System Responsibility:					Model/Product: ******* Rev ****					FMEA Rev Date:	
5	Person Responsibility: &&&& $$$$$$$					Target Release Date:						
6	Involvement of Others:					Prepared By: Rex Black						
7												
8						**Inital FMEA**						
9	System Function or Feature	Potential Failure Mode(s)- Quality Risk(s)	Potential Effect(s) of Failure	Critical?	Severity	Potential Cause(s) of Failure	Priority	Detection Method(s)	Detection	Risk Pri No	Recommended Action	Who/ When?
10	Shreds Deleted Files	Fails to Shred	Security Breach	Y	1	Program Error	1	Test; Debug Trace; Code Review	2	2	Test; Debug Tracing; Code Review	
11		Shreds Excessively	Data Loss	Y	1	Program Error	1	Test; Debug Trace; Code Review	2	2	Test; Debug Tracing; Code Review	
12	Temp File Recognition	Fails to Recognize	Security Breach	Y	1	Program Error	1	Test; Debug Trace; Code Review	2	2	Test; Debug Tracing; Code Review	
13		Recognizes Incorrectly	Data Loss	Y	1	Program Error	1	Test; Debug Trace; Code Review	2	2	Test; Debug Tracing; Code Review	
14	Internet Files Recognition	Fails to Recognize	Security Breach	Y	2	Program Error	3	Test; Debug Trace; Code Review	4	24	Test	
15		Recognizes Incorrectly	Data Loss	Y	1	Program Error	1	Test; Debug Trace; Code Review	2	2	Test; Rules Validation	
16	Shreds Swap Files	Fails to Shred	Security Breach	Y	1	Program Error	1	Test; Debug Trace; Code Review	1	1	Test; Debug Tracing; Code Review	

Figure 1.11   A case study FMEA.

file deletion functionality for PC users running some versions of the Windows operating system. We had a six-hour cross-functional meeting with the test team, the programmers, the project manager, a salesperson, and the marketing manager. In this meeting, we discussed ways in which the system might fail and possible approaches to mitigation. These included both testing and various programming process improvements. Figure 1.11 shows the top portion of this 100-item document. The full document is available at www.rexblackconsulting.com.

Notice that while the DataRocket example shown earlier in the chapter broke down failure modes based on major subsystems of the server, in this case the analysis starts with major functionality and expected behaviors. You can also use categories of quality risk as the starting point.

Exercises

1. Why is it impossible for testing to find all the bugs in a system? Why might it not be necessary for a program to be completely free of defects before it is delivered to its customers? To what extent can testing be used to validate that the program is fit for its purpose?[19]

---

[19] This exercise was contributed by Dr. Deepti Suri of Milwaukee School of Engineering.

2. Suppose that you go to an office supply store, buy a printer, and bring it back to your office. You connect it to one of the computers on the office network, and it works fine from that computer. However, when you try to share the printer with other systems on the network, you can't get the printer to work properly from the other workstations. After spending some time trying to figure it out, you find out from technical support that the printer does not support printing from a network, but only locally. Is this a bug (i.e., a quality problem) with the printer? Explain your answer in terms of reasonable customer expectations of quality.

3. Prepare a risk analysis for a calculator program, focusing on behavioral testing during a system test phase. (Suggestion: Imagine any of the popular PC operating systems such as Windows, Linux, and Solaris that include calculators.)

   ■ Use the informal risk analysis technique.

   ■ Use the formal Failure Mode and Effect Analysis technique.

4. Prepare a schedule and budget for testing the calculator based on the assumption that you will do the testing yourself.

   ■ Approximately what percentage of effort do you spend on each risk area? Does this resource allocation make sense?

   ■ If you had a bigger budget—including potentially more people—could you do the testing faster?

   ■ Did you develop your own test oracle (i.e., a way to determine whether the calculator was giving the right result), or did you use one or more reference platforms (in this case, other calculators)? Discuss the pros and cons of each approach.

   ■ Assume that your manager cuts your budget for testing the calculator by a quarter. What testing will you not do? Why did you pick those particular tests?

CHAPTER

2

Plotting and Presenting
Your Course:
The Test Plan

This chapter offers a practical approach to writing one or more test plans for your project. I'll walk through a sample template that I use to develop a solid test plan—and I'll look at the issue of getting the plan approved once I've drawn it up.

Why I Write Test Plans

In Chapter 1, "Defining What's on Your Plate: The Foundation of a Test Project," I discussed how I set the scope, schedule, and budget parameters for my test projects. Given a budget, resource commitments, and a schedule, can you claim that you have a test plan? Some people do. In my experience, however, you need more detail to successfully manage a test project. Below the objectives and estimates featured in Chapter 1 lurks another layer of complexity, right above the specific details of test suites—and it pays to consider this complexity in advance.

Writing a test plan gives you a chance to collect your thoughts, your ideas, and your memories. Undoubtedly you've learned a great deal throughout the course of your career. Writing a thorough test plan gives you a chance to crystallize that knowledge into a concrete way of tackling the tasks ahead.

I see the test plan also as an opportunity to communicate with my test team, my development colleagues, and my managers. The most intense discussion of what testing is all about often occurs when I hold a test plan review. I appreciate the chance to

45

have a forum focused solely on testing before a project enters the often-chaotic test execution periods, in which everyone can become so oriented toward minutiae that they lose sight of the big picture.

In some organizations, the test plan encompasses the entirety of the test effort, all the way down to defining all the individual test cases—often called the *test set* or the *test suites*—that the team will run. However, I recommend creating two distinct types of documents: first a test plan, and then an accompanying document detailing the test cases. The difference between a test plan and a test suite is a matter of strategy versus tactics: strategy consists of your overall plan for hunting down and identifying as many bugs as possible; tactics are the specific steps you will take to do this. This chapter focuses on the test plan itself; Chapter 3, "Test System Architecture, Cases, and Coverage," discusses the process of creating test suites, test cases, and other testware.

How Many Test Plans?

Suppose that you are working on SpeedyWriter. Further suppose that, as the test manager, you have responsibility for the component, integration, and system test phases, with an aggressive beta testing program during the system test phase. You thus have three distinct test subprojects to plan and manage. Do you write one plan or three? I favor using separate plans for test subprojects that are distinct in one or more of the following ways:

Different time periods. If the test planning, test development, test environment configuration, and test execution tasks for the subprojects start and end on different dates, I find that I have the information needed to plan some subprojects well before I get the necessary information for the other subprojects. (See Chapter 11, "Testing in Context: Economics, Lifecycles, and Process Maturity," for more information on system lifecycle models and test phase timing.) If I try to write only one test plan, I find myself forced to leave large sections of it marked "TBD" ("to be determined"), which can make the overall plan hard for people to understand and approve.

Different methodologies. Detailed discussions of code coverage instrumentation and platform-independent automated GUI test tools don't really go together. Likewise, in the case of hardware, discussions of thermal chambers, accelerometers, and business application compatibility testing can create a rather eclectic mix of topics in a plan.

Different objectives. If I'm trying to accomplish three different goals—in the current example, finding bugs in components, finding bugs in the relationships and interfaces between incrementally integrated components, and finding bugs in a fully integrated system—writing one plan each for component test, integration test, and system test allows me to focus my thinking on each goal in turn.

Different audiences. My test plan is not only my chance to inform my colleagues, my testers, and my managers of my vision, it is also a chance to discover their perspectives. This input is especially valuable to the extent that it gives me a better idea of how to focus my test efforts. If I write one lengthy test plan that addresses every issue, I might have trouble getting people to read it, not to mention getting them to participate in a three- or four-hour review. However, if I segment my planning, I'm better able to create documents that speak to the specific concerns of the individuals involved.

Multiple test plans can lead to overlapping content, though, which some people deal with by cutting and pasting shared sections such as test tracking, bug reporting and management, and revision control. Having the same information spread across multiple documents leaves you open to the possibility of inadvertent discrepancies or contradictory statements. When I have multiple test plans, I'll write a single master test plan that addresses these common topics and include references to them in the detailed test plans.

Using Drafts to Stimulate Discussion

I expect to release several versions of any test plan I write. Far from finding this frustrating, this sequence of drafts is a dialog that provides me an opportunity to pose questions to the readers. I use brackets in my plans (as opposed to colored fonts, which don't show up as well in hard copy) to indicate questions and open issues. My first drafts are always full of bracketed questions and statements such as these:

[TBD: Need to figure out what the hardware allocation plan is.]

[TBD: Need the Configuration Management team to define the revision numbering schema and the packaging.]

[TBD: Mary, please tell me how this should work?]

Although this might seem like "copping out," identifying and documenting open issues are among the most useful aspects of the planning exercise. Writing the plan forces me to think through the entire test effort—tools, processes, people, and technology—and to confront issues that I might otherwise miss. I then use the first few drafts of the plan as a method of bringing these issues to the attention of my peers and my managers.

That said, I do spend some time thinking about the questions, concerns, and issues I raise. If possible, rather than simply asking a question, I also include a suggested answer or a set of possible answers. A test plan that consists largely of notations about matters that are "to be determined" or issues that await resolution by someone else doesn't add a lot of value.

A Test Plan Template

The template presented in Figure 2.1 is one that I often use for developing test plans. (I have also used the IEEE 829 test plan template, which I'll discuss a little later in this chapter.) It isn't a tool for cutting and pasting a test plan in little time with little thought; rather, it is a logical set of topics that I've found I need to consider carefully for my test efforts. Feel free to add or delete topics as your needs dictate. The following sections examine the parts of the test plan template one by one.

Test Plan Template
Overview
Bounds
Scope
Definitions
Setting
Quality Risks
Proposed Schedule of Milestones
Transitions
Entry Criteria
Stopping Criteria
Exit Criteria
Test Configurations and Environments
Test System Development
Test Execution
Key Participants
Test Case and Bug Tracking
Bug Isolation and Classification
Release Management
Test Cycles
Test Hours
Risks and Contingencies
Change History
Referenced Documents
Frequently Asked Questions

Figure 2.1   A test plan template.

Overview

The overview section of a test plan allows me to introduce readers of the plan to my test project, including what's to be tested and the general test approach. What I've found is that oftentimes managers one or two levels above me don't really have a good idea of what testing buys them. In the overview, I present a concise explanation of my goals, methodologies, and objectives. Although this section should be fairly brief, it's often useful to include simple pictures or charts. You might want to illustrate concepts such as the architecture of the system under test, the decomposition or segmentation of the system for component or integration testing, or how this test effort fits into other test efforts that might precede, run concurrently, or follow.

Bounds

In this section, I set boundaries for the test plan by discussing what I will and will not test, by defining important terms and acronyms related to the testing I plan to perform, and by determining where and in what context the test efforts associated with this test subproject will take place.

Scope

Webster's Dictionary defines *scope*, in the context of a project or an operation, as the "extent of treatment, activity, or influence; [the] range of operation." When I describe the scope of my project, I am essentially demarcating what I will and will not pay attention to during the course of the project. I often use an "Is/Is Not" table to define the scope of testing, with the Is column listing the elements that are included within the scope of a particular test phase, and the Is Not column specifying elements that are not covered by this test effort. Table 2.1 shows an example of such a table, used to describe the scope of the system testing for SpeedyWriter based on the risk analysis shown in Chapter 1.

Table 2.1   Is/Is Not Format for Presenting Test Project Scope

IS	IS NOT
Functionality	File conversion
Localization (Spanish, French, and German only)	Localization (other than Spanish, French, and German)
Capacity and volume	Network compatibility
Basic file sharing	Network file sharing options
Configuration options	Security or privacy
Install, setup, initial configuration, update, and uninstall	Usability including any time and motion studies
Performance	Date handling
Windows, Unix (Solaris, Linux), and Mac compatibility and functionality	OS/2, Unix (beyond Solaris and Linux), or other platforms
Standards compliance	Structural testing
Error handling and recovery	
User interface (functional)	
Web browser compatibility	
Behavioral testing	
Beta testing by customers	

This compact form allows me to present a precise statement of scope. It's usually unnecessary to define each item at this point; the details about each aspect of testing belong in the test cases themselves.

Definitions

Testing, like other disciplines in the computer world, has its own terms and phrases. Therefore, I include a table of definitions in my test plans. Such a table can help to clarify terminology for those who are not experienced in the field of testing, and can also help to ensure that everyone on the test team is operating from the same set of definitions.

Feel free to use the glossary contained in this book as a starting point for compiling your own list. You should edit the definitions as necessary, deleting phrases that do not apply to your project. Putting a lot of extraneous verbiage in a test plan can lead to a severe case of MEGO ("my eyes glaze over") for readers.

Setting

This section of the test plan describes where I intend to perform the testing and the way those organizations doing the testing relate to the rest of the organization. The description might be as simple as "our test lab." In some cases, though, you might have testing spread hither and yon. I once managed a test project in which work took place in Taipei and Lin Kuo, Taiwan; in Salt Lake City, Utah; and in San Jose and Los Angeles, California. In cases such as this, I would present a table or diagram (such as the one shown in Figure 2.2) that shows how work will be allocated among the various participants. (For more information on managing distributed test efforts, see Chapter 10, "Involving Other Players: Distributing a Test Project.")

Quality Risks

If you followed the process discussed in Chapter 1, you already have the material you need for this section. Either you can summarize the quality risk documents you've prepared, or simply reference them in the test plan. If you suspect that many of your readers won't look at the referenced documents, it makes sense to summarize the quality risks here, given that your purpose is to communicate as well as to plan. However, if you know that people support your test planning process and will take the time to read your outline of quality risks or your *failure mode and effect analysis* (FMEA) chart, you can save yourself some work by referencing them.

I also like to cross-reference the test strategy and the test environments against the various risk categories. For example, if I know I'm going to use a particular configuration of a server and run primarily behavioral, manual tests to find potential functionality bugs (those mitigating the risks to quality in terms of functionality), then one row in my quality risks table might look as shown in Table 2.2.

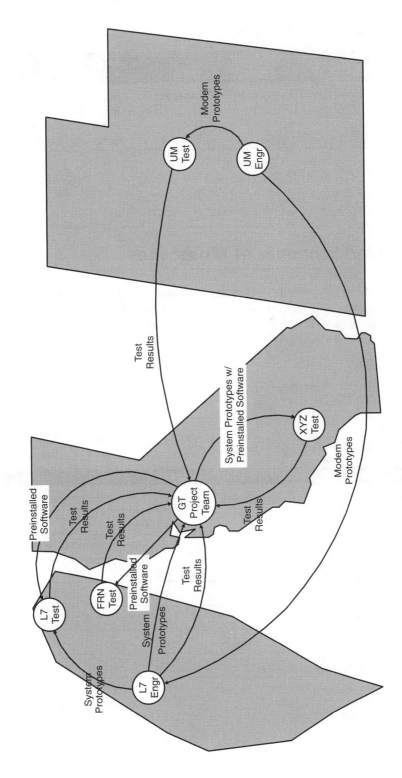

Figure 2.2 A context diagram for a distributed test effort.

Table 2.2   An Extract of a Quality Risks Table

QUALITY RISK CATEGORY	SERVER CONFIGURATION	TEST STRATEGY
Functionality	Solaris/Oracle/Apache	Manual Behavioral Primarily scripted Some exploratory

Proposed Schedule of Milestones

Most of my test plans contain a schedule for the test project's major milestones. You can extract these from the work-breakdown-structure, which I discussed in Chapter 1. I focus on the high-level milestones and deliverables that are visible to management. Table 2.3 provides an example of such a schedule.

Table 2.3   An Example Schedule from a Test Plan

MILESTONE	DATE
Test Development and Configuration	
Test plan complete	8/9/2004
Test lab defined	8/12/2004
FMEA complete	8/16/2004
Test lab configured	8/26/2004
Test suite complete	9/5/2004
Test Execution	
System test entry	9/2/2004
Cycle 1 Complete	9/16/2004
Cycle 2 Complete	10/3/2004
Cycle 3 Complete	10/13/2004
System test exit	10/13/2004

Transitions

For each test phase, the system under test must satisfy a minimal set of qualifications before the test organization can effectively and efficiently run tests. For example, it makes little sense to start extensive user-scenario testing of SpeedyWriter if the application cannot open or save a file or display text on the screen. Likewise, the DataRocket server can't undergo environmental testing—especially thermal testing—if you don't have even a prototype case. This section of the test plan should specify the criteria essential for beginning and completing various test phases (and for continuing an effective and efficient test process). I usually refer to these as *entry*, *exit*, and *continuation* criteria, respectively, but some test professionals use the terms *entry*, *stopping*, and *suspension/resumption* criteria.

As you write criteria for test phases and transitions, be aware of what you're actually saying: "If someone outside the test group fails to comply with these rules, I'm going to object to starting this phase of testing, ask to stop this phase of testing, or suggest that we not move this project forward." While these are technical criteria, invoking them can create a political firestorm. I only include criteria that I seriously believe will affect the test team's ability to provide useful services to the project. While test team efficiency is important to the project, making life convenient for the test team is not, so I'm careful to avoid criteria that could be construed as trying to shuffle make-work on to other departments. Finally, when test phase milestones—especially phase entry and exit meetings—occur, I explicitly measure the project against the criteria and report in those terms. I typically rate each criteria as "green" (totally satisfied), "yellow" (not entirely satisfied, but perhaps not a problem), or "red" (unsatisfied and creating a major problem), bringing the data I need to back up the criteria identified as "yellow" or "red."

The data to substantiate each violated criterion's status is critical, and should connect to an important business reality. What I've seen with entry, continuation, and exit criteria is that any reasonable-sounding criterion will usually pass muster in the test plan review, but, if that criterion isn't anchored in a solid business case for project delay, it will create all sorts of controversy when invoked.

Some people use hard-and-fast, bug-related exit criteria such as "zero open severity 1 bugs," "10 or fewer open severity 2 bugs," and so forth. I have found that these approaches can lead to counterproductive arguments about whether a bug is correctly classified in terms of severity, which ignores the bigger picture of quality and how quality fits into the other business issues such as schedule, budget, and features. However, in some contexts—for example, safety-critical systems, defense systems, outsource development, and so forth—using quantifiable exit criteria might be necessary.

Entry Criteria

Entry criteria spell out what must happen to allow a system to move into a particular test phase. These criteria should address questions such as:

- Are the necessary documentation, design, and requirements information available that will allow testers to operate the system and judge correct behavior?

- Is the system ready for delivery, in whatever form is appropriate for the test phase in question?[1]
- Are the supporting utilities, accessories, and prerequisites available in forms that testers can use?
- Is the system at the appropriate level of quality? Such a question usually implies that some or all of a previous test phase has been successfully completed, although it could refer to the extent to which code review issues have been handled. Passing a smoke test is another frequent measure of sufficient quality to enter a test phase.
- Is the test environment—lab, hardware, software, and system administration support—ready?

Figure 2.3 shows an example of entry criteria that might apply for SpeedyWriter.

Continuation Criteria

Continuation criteria define those conditions and situations that must prevail in the testing process to allow testing to continue effectively and efficiently. Typically, I find that the test environment must remain stable, the bug backlog manageable, the tests for the most part unblocked (e.g., by large bugs), installable and stable test releases must be delivered regularly and properly, and the change to the system under test must be known and controlled. Figure 2.4 shows an example of continuation criteria that might apply to SpeedyWriter.

Exit Criteria

Exit criteria address the issue of how to determine when testing has been completed. For example, one exit criterion might be that all the planned test cases and the regression tests have been run. Another might be that project management deems your results "OK," by whatever definition they use to decide such questions. (I'll look at some metrics that can shed light on product quality in Chapter 4, "An Exciting Career in Entomology Awaits You: A Bug Tracking Database," and Chapter 5, "Managing Test Cases: The Test Tracking Spreadsheet," along with examining some political issues associated with results reporting in Chapter 9, "The Triumph of Politics: Organizational Challenges for Test Managers.") In the case of System Test exit criteria—provided System Test is the last test phase on your project—these exit criteria often become the criteria by which the customer-ship or deployment decision is made. An example of a business-driven set of System Test exit criteria for SpeedyWriter is shown in Figure 2.5.

---

[1]In the component test phase (assuming that the test organization is involved at that point), I usually accept whatever development is ready to provide as long as it includes sufficient scaffolding, or harnesses to run my tests. Once I reach the system test phase, however, I ask for customer packaging, especially in the case of software, whose installation process has a significant impact on whether the system works at all.

System Test can begin when:
1. Bug tracking and test tracking systems are in place.
2. All components are under formal, automated configuration and release management control.
3. The Operations team has configured the System Test server environment, including all target hardware components and subsystems. The Test Team has been provided with appropriate access to these systems.
4. The Development Teams have completed all features and bug fixes scheduled for release.
5. The Development Teams have unit-tested all features and bug fixes scheduled for release.
6. Less than 50 must-fix bugs (per Sales, Marketing, and Customer Service) are open against the first test release slated. (50 being the number of bug reports that can be effectively reviewed in a one-hour bug triage meeting.)
7. The Development Teams provide software to the Test Team three business days prior to starting System Test.
8. The Test Team completes a three-day "smoke test" and reports on the results to the System Test Phase Entry meeting.
9. The Project Management Team agrees in a System Test Phase Entry Meeting to proceed. The following topics will be resolved in the meeting:
   • Whether code is complete.
   • Whether unit-testing is complete.
   • Assign a target fix date for any known "must-fix" bugs (no later than one week after System Test Phase Entry).

Figure 2.3   Entry criteria for SpeedyWriter.

System Test can continue if:
1. All software released to the Test Team is accompanied by Release Notes.
2. No change is made to the system, whether in source code, configuration files, or other setup instructions or processes, without an accompanying bug report. Should a change be made without a bug report, the Test Manager will open an urgent bug report requesting information and escalate to his manager.
3. The open bug backlog ("quality gap") remains less than 50. The average time to close a bug remains less than 14 days.
4. Twice-weekly bug review meetings (under the Change Control Board) occur until System Test Phase Exit to manage the open bug backlog and bug closure times.

Figure 2.4   Continuation criteria for SpeedyWriter.

System Test will end when:

1. No changes (design/code/features), except to address System Test defects, occurred in the prior three weeks.
2. No panic, crash, halt, wedge, unexpected process termination, or other stoppage of processing has occurred on any server software or hardware for the previous three weeks.
3. No client systems have become inoperable due to a failed update during System Test.
4. The Test Team has executed all the planned tests against the GA-candidate software.
5. The Development Teams have resolved all "must-fix" bugs per Sales, Marketing, and Customer Service.
6. The Test Team has checked that all issues in the bug tracking system are either closed or deferred, and, where appropriate, verified by regression and confirmation testing.
7. The test metrics indicate that we have achieved product stability and reliability, that we have completed all planned tests, and the planned tests adequately cover the critical quality risks.
8. The Project Management Team agrees that the product, as defined during the final cycle of System Test, will satisfy the customer's reasonable expectations of quality.
9. The Project Management Team holds a System Test Phase Exit Meeting and agrees that we have completed System Test.

Figure 2.5   SpeedyWriter System Test exit criteria.

Test Configurations and Environments

This section of the test plan is where I document which hardware, software, networks, and lab space I will use to perform the testing. For these various test systems, I'll describe whatever important configuration details bear mentioning as well. For a PC application or utility, this task can be as simple as listing the half-dozen or so test PCs, the two or three test networks (assuming that networking is even an issue), and the printers, modems, terminal adapters, and other accessories you might require from time to time. For commercial software or hardware, I find it useful to have competitors' systems available in my test lab as reference platforms. For example, when testing an Internet appliance (which provided Web and email features only), we had PCs configured with the various browsers and email clients so we could answer the question, "What happens when we run the same test using X (browser or email client)?" when confronted by potentially buggy behavior on the appliance.

Suppose, however, that you are testing a system with significant custom hardware elements (such as a new laptop or a server), one with many hardware elements (such as a network operating system or a network application), or one with expensive hardware elements (such as a mainframe, a high-availability server, or a server cluster). In these complex cases, using a simple table or a spreadsheet might not be sufficient. In Chapter 6, "Tips and Tools for Crunch Time: Managing the Dynamic," I'll introduce a database that can help you stay on top of complicated situations such as these. In Chapter 7, "Stocking and Managing a Test Lab," I'll show how to extend this database to include managing lab space and equipment. This database also models human resources and network needs. You can include the reports produced by this database in this section of the test plan.

When custom hardware is involved, you can present a scheme for hardware allocation in this portion of the test plan or in a separate document. Whatever the location, I've found it extremely important to prepare this allocation plan. Failing to establish a detailed plan for allocating hardware is tantamount to assuming that the hardware I need will magically make itself available, properly configured and ready for testing, at the very moment I need it. If you lead a charmed life, such things probably happen to you all the time, but they never happen to me. I always worry about hardware allocation, and work to have a hardware allocation plan in place around the time I'm finishing the test plan.

What goes into a test hardware allocation plan? I usually list the test purpose or use, the systems needed (including the quantities and revision levels), the infrastructure, the time period, the location, and any other hardware necessary for a particular test. Table 2.4 shows a prototype allocation plan for DataRocket's integration test and system test phases.

Test Development

In some cases, I find my test teams rerunning tests that were created in previous test efforts. In other cases, I've used a purely exploratory approach where I created the test data during testing and followed my muse in terms of procedures and specific test steps. Typically, though, my test projects include some amount of work to design and develop various test objects such as test cases, test tools, test procedures, test suites, automated test scripts, and so forth. Collectively, I refer to these objects as *test systems*.

In such cases, in this section, I'll describe how my test team will create each of those objects. (I'll look at some particulars of testware development in Chapter 3.) If we're going to use manual testing, then I'll let the readers know if we intend to write detailed test cases or use test charters.[2] If I need test data, then I'll explain how we're getting that data and why we picked those approaches. If we're doing test automation using existing (commercial or freeware) test tools, then I'll describe why we're using the particular tools we've chosen and how we intend to develop test scripts. If we're creating custom test tools or utilities, then I'll describe what those utilities are and how we intend to use them.

At some point, test system or testware development can become a software development project in its own right. I've worked on custom tool projects for clients where we created completely free-standing test automation and management tools. Some of my test projects have included test development efforts that involved person-decades of work. In such cases, my preference would be to have a separate plan that describes that development effort. Various good templates are available for software development plans.[3]

---

[2]Test charters are something I learned from James Bach in the context of his approach for exploratory testing. See his material on exploratory testing at www.satisfice.com.
[3]For example, see www.construx.com for templates drawn on Steve McConnell's *Software Project Survival Guide*.

Table 2.4 A DataRocket Hardware Allocation Plan

TEST USAGE	SYSTEM [QTY]	NETWORK	WHEN	WHERE	OTHER[QTY]
Integration Test Phase					
Component interfaces/ signal quality	Engineering prototype [2]	Novell NetWare, Network File System, Microsoft Windows NT	9/15–10/15	Engr lab	MS mouse, MS kbd, VGA mon, USB mouse, USB mon, USB kbd, 3COM LAN, USR mdm, Epson prn, Quantum HD, oscilloscope
Mechanical life	Engineering prototype [2]	None	8/1–10/1	Engr lab	None
Stress, capacity, volume	Engineering prototype [1]	Novell, NFS, NT	9/15–10/15	Test lab	MS mouse, VGA mon
Performance	Engineering prototype [1]	Novell, NFS, NT	9/15–10/15	Test lab	MS mouse, MS kbd, VGA mon, Quantum HD, IBM HD
System Test Phase					
MTBF demonstration	Validation prototype [4]	Novell	10/17–1/17	Engr lab	MS mouse, MS kbd, VGA mon, MUX
Functionality	Validation prototype [2]	Novell, NFS, NT	10/17–12/1	Test lab	MS mouse, MS kbd, VGA mon, USB mouse, USB mon, USB kbd, USR mdm, Epson prn, ISDN T. adptr
Stress, capacity, volume	Validation prototype [1]	Novell, NFS, NT	10/17–12/1	Test lab	MS mouse, VGA mon
Performance	Validation prototype [1]	Novell, NFS, NT	10/17–12/1	Test lab	MS mouse, MS kbd, VGA mon, Quantum HD, IBM HD
Compatibility	Validation prototype [3]	N/A	10/24–12/1	System Cookers, Inc.	MS mouse [3], MS kbd [3], VGA mon [3]
Environmental	Validation prototype [2]	N/A	10/24–12/1	System Cookers, Inc.	MS mouse [2], MS kbd [2], VGA mon [2]

Test Execution

This portion of the test plan addresses important factors affecting test execution. For example, in order to run tests, you often need to receive items from the outside world, primarily resources (or funding for those resources) and systems to test. In the course of running tests, you will gather data that you must track in a way presentable to your team, your peers, and your managers. In addition, you will run through distinct test cycles in each test phase. I find that the level of detail required here varies from team to team and project to project. With my more senior test teams on well-run projects, I can leave much of this section to the discretion of my crack team of testers. With junior testers, especially on chaotic projects, the more I can nail down the test execution realities during the planning phase, the more confusion I can anticipate and resolve ahead of time.

Key Participants

In this section, I identify the key participants in the test effort and the role they'll play in testing. I find it especially important to identify the external participants, the hand-off points, and each participant's contact information. Another useful portion of this subsection can be the escalation process; in other words, if some key participants do not or cannot fulfill their agreed-upon role, then what happens next? In the case of external participants, I work out the roles and hand-off points with the appropriate peer-level managers first, before putting that information in the test plan. Surprising fellow development-team managers with new and urgent assignments for their staff is unlikely to win any popularity points for the test manager who tries it.

Test Case and Bug Tracking

This section deals with the systems used to manage and track test cases and bugs. Test case tracking refers to the spreadsheet or database I use to manage all the test cases in the test suites and how I track progress through that listing. (If I don't track the tests I plan to run, how can I gauge my test coverage later on?) Bug tracking has to do with the process my team uses to manage the bugs we find in the course of testing. Since these systems form your principal communication channels inward to your own team, outward to other teams such as development, and upward to your management, you should define them well here. Chapters 4 and 5 deal with these topics in more detail. Even if you choose not to use the approaches described there, you might find some ideas in those chapters that will help you complete this section of the plan.

Bug Isolation and Classification

This section of the test plan is where I explain the degree to which I intend to isolate bugs and to classify bug reports. Isolating a bug means to experiment with the system under test in an effort to find connected variables, causal or otherwise. I find it's important to be explicit about bug isolation; otherwise, the test organization can end up involved in debugging, a developer task that can consume lots of my testers' time with very little to show for it in terms of test coverage (see Chapter 4.)

Classifying a bug report assigns the underlying bug to a particular category that indicates how the bug should be communicated and handled. For example, I've used classifications such as the following:

Requirements failure. The bug report concerns a failure of the system to meet its requirements. The appropriate party will resolve the problem.

Nonrequirements failure. The bug reported is not covered by the system requirements, but it significantly affects the quality of the system in unacceptable ways. The appropriate party will resolve the problem.

Waiver requested. The bug report does indeed describe a failure, but the developers request a waiver because they believe that it will not significantly affect the customers' and users' experiences of quality.

External failure. The bug report addresses a failure that arises from a factor or factors external to or beyond the control of the system under test.

Test failure. The developers believe that the test has returned a spurious or invalid error.

Rather than classifying bugs, some project teams use a single bug management process. Many successful development projects I've worked on used a bug triage process (sometimes as part of the change control board process) to assign bug priority and determine which bugs must be fixed prior to release. In that case, you might want to describe that process here.

Test Release Management

One of the major interfaces between the overall project and testing occurs when new revisions, builds, and components are submitted to the test team for testing. In the absence of a predefined plan for this, I have seen this essential hand-off point degrade into absolute chaos. On one project, a software development manager was emailing a new version of the software out to the entire project team, including the test team, every time any member of his team of programmers fixed a bug. We received a dozen test releases a day! I find that kind of anarchy unacceptable on my test projects, so in this section of the test plan I define the key elements of the test release process that can affect my effort. To revisit a figure from the previous chapter, in the ideal case, I try to create a test release process that looks as shown in Figure 2.6.

One element of that process is regular, predictable timing. How often will you accept a new test release into the testing process? My preference is usually once a week. On the one hand, once-a-week test releases give me ample time to complete plenty of scheduled testing and even do some exploratory testing as part of each test cycle, rather than just doing confirmation testing of the bug fixes in that test release. Test releases that show up once a day—or more frequently—leave my test teams little time for anything but confirmation testing the fixes. On the other hand, test releases that come every other week or even less frequently can introduce major regressions and other changes in behavior that I'd like to know about sooner. Therefore, the weekly test release strikes me as a reasonable balance in most contexts I've worked in, although your situation may differ.

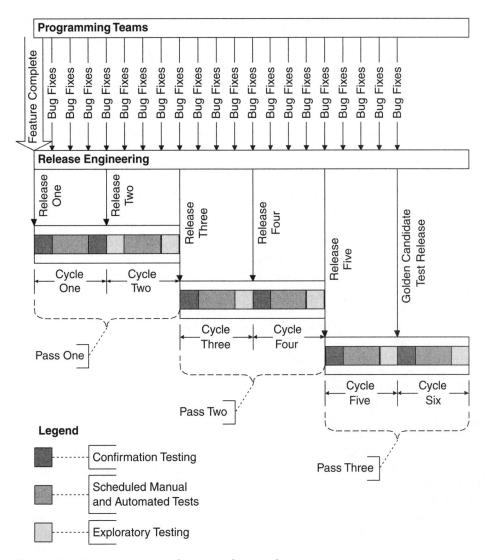

Figure 2.6 Test passes, test releases, and test cycles.

Every new release of a software or hardware component into the test lab should have a release (revision) number or identifier attached. This identifier is essential for determining which version of the system contains a bug, which version fixes that bug, which pieces are compatible with other pieces, and which versions you have tested.

You should also get release notes with the release. These release notes should specify which bugs were fixed, what changes were made, how the changes will affect system behavior, and so forth. This is especially true for complex systems that have to interface with other systems. For example, if an application accesses a database, you might need to change the schema of the database to accommodate changes in the program. This can be a real challenge if this database is shared across multiple systems, because plans must be in place to handle the ripple effects.

In addition, I need to be able to count on receiving new releases in a certain format. I specify for each test phase—and therefore in each test plan—a specific process and format for delivering new releases. For example, for software delivered during component and integration test phases, this format might be as simple as a tar or zip archive sent via email or posted to the network. Once I enter system testing, however, I usually want the software releases to arrive in the same format and with the same installation process as the initial customer release. I consider testing the installation process a key part of most System Test efforts, so I cover that here.

I also find I need a defined uninstall process for many projects. The reason is twofold. First, if an uninstall process exists and is accessible to users and/or customers, then I again need to test this capability. Second, if a test release comes along that, after installation, proves so unstable or nonfunctional that further testing is pointless, then reverting to a "known testable" release is the only way to return to making some type of forward progress. In the case of a simple application, an uninstall utility might be included, but complex systems—especially those that have shared databases—can have very complex installation and uninstallation processes.

In some cases, the proposed approach for accelerating a test process blocked or impeded by a bad test release is to install a new release. Therefore, you'll need to consider (for both software and hardware) whether you will accept new revisions in the middle of a test cycle. The key issues here are regression testing and the implications of the revision for the validity of your previous test cycle results. Will you have to do a complete reset and start the test cycle over if a driver, a configuration file, or an application build shows up midway? These unexpected arrivals can cause real problems, especially toward the end of the system test phase, if you are receiving new releases every few days or even every few hours. Without a completely automated regression test system that can repeat every test flawlessly in a day or so, you will never be able to eliminate the possibility that the new release has introduced a major new bug. (For a discussion of coverage problems and regression testing, see Chapter 3.)

This problem occurs even in hardware development. It is true that motherboards, cases, and so forth have long lead times and that engineering prototypes cost a lot to produce. Nevertheless, you might still receive the BIOS du jour or the daily "gold master" hard drive. My worst experiences with what I call "churn and burn" have occurred on laptop development projects. Because of the manual nature of PC testing, you will probably have time for little more than confirmation testing on new releases if they come daily, leading to dismal test escapes. (I'll talk more about test escapes in Chapter 3.)

These chaotic releases have affected the logistics and operation of a number of my test projects. Some amount of effort is required for flashing a BIOS, installing applications, or replacing a motherboard, especially when my lab contains half a dozen test platforms. If the process requires specialized skills, such as system administration, network administration, or database administration, I need to have the right person available to handle the job. Moreover, the system will be unavailable for test execution throughout the upgrade. Such abrupt, unexpected changes can also impose communication overhead and confuse testers. I have to inform everyone that a new release has dropped in, circulate the release notes (assuming that they exist), give my staff time to study them, and hope that everyone can keep straight just what the latest chunk of software is supposed to do.

As you can tell, I don't like midstream releases. However, it's also true that instituting significant, project-wide process changes from within the test team through the mechanism of the test plan can be difficult.[4] If your company's development "process" includes a system test phase comprised of 18-hour days, with a spinning disk containing the allegedly final test release landing on your desk hourly, you can't transform that by fiat in the test plan. However, you can—and I certainly would—attempt to convince people there is a better way, and, if I succeeded, I'd capture that in this section of the test plan.

Test Cycles

In Chapter 1, I used the phrase "test cycle" rather cavalierly, but perhaps a more formal definition is in order. By a test cycle, I mean running one, some, or all of the test suites planned for a given test phase as part of that phase. Test cycles are usually associated with a single test release of the system under test, such as a build of software or a motherboard. Generally, new test releases occur during a test phase, triggering another test cycle. For example, if test suites 3.1 through 3.5 are planned for a three-cycle system test phase, the first cycle could entail executing 3.1 and 3.2; the second cycle, 3.3, 3.4, and 3.5; and the third cycle, 3.1, 3.2, 3.3, 3.4, and 3.5.

Any given test phase involves at least one cycle through the test suites planned for that phase. (As I mentioned in Chapter 1, it's a challenge to estimate how many cycles will be needed in any given phase.) Each subsequent cycle generally involves a new release of one or more components in the system. This section of the test plan should spell out your specific assumptions and estimates about the number, timing, and arrangement of test cycles. A picture like Figure 2.6 can help.

Test Hours

In some cases, I find I need to define the specific hours of testing. In addition, on some projects I use multiple shifts to keep scarce resources humming 16 or 24 hours a day to accelerate the testing. In such cases, I'll define in this section the specific hours and shifts that will be used.

---

[4]Aesop's fables include the apt story about belling the cat. The mice are tired of scurrying about in fear of the cat, and they convene a council to decide how to deal with the problem. One suggests that they put a bell on the cat's collar so that they can hear him coming. All agree this is a capital idea, until one young whippersnapper asks, "But who will bell the cat?" When I'm tempted to push for a change in "the way things are done around here," I recall this tale and often think better of the effort.

Risks and Contingencies

I sometimes use the title "Open Issues" for this section. In it, I address potential or likely events that could make the test plan difficult or impossible to carry out. Topics might include training needs, the availability of additional development support for debugging if an exceptional number of bugs are found, and so forth. Alternatively, you can include this type of information when you discuss continuation criteria.

Strictly speaking, most advocates of good development processes encourage a global approach to risk management.[5] If you work on a project in which the entire team has a single risk-management plan, you might be able to omit this section by including these concerns in that plan.

Change History

This part of the document records the changes and revisions that have been made to the test plan itself to this point. Specifically, you can assign a revision number and record who made the changes, what those changes were, and when the revision was released.

Referenced Documents

As a rule, a test plan refers to other documents such as design specifications, requirements, the test suites, any quality-risk analysis documents, and other pertinent information. Listing these documents in this section lets me avoid extensive repetition of their contents (which can create complications when these documents change).

Frequently Asked Questions

On projects where I use neophyte test engineers and test technicians, I find that a frequently asked questions section is useful. Many of these questions entail describing the importance of the escalation process.

The IEEE 829 Template: Compare and Contrast

The test plan template presented previously complies with the IEEE 829 Standard in that it contains all the same information—at least as I use the template—but presents it in a way that I consider to be inherently lighter-weight; in other words, smaller. Let me describe each field in the template briefly and how the information in my template maps to the IEEE 829 template, shown in Figure 2.7.

[5]See, for example, McConnell's *Software Project Survival Guide*.

IEEE 829 Test Plan Template
Test Plan Identifier
Introduction
Test Items
Features To Be Tested
Features Not To Be Tested
Approach
Item Pass/Fail Criteria
Suspension Criteria And Resumption
  Requirements
Test Deliverables
Testing Tasks
Environmental Needs
Responsibilities
Staffing And Training Needs
Schedule
Risks And Contingencies
Approvals

Figure 2.7   IEEE 829 Standard test plan template.

The Test Plan Identifier is a just a unique name or document ID. I don't explicitly include this in my template, but rather follow whatever document naming and storage conventions are used by the project.

The Introduction is used in IEEE 829 test plans the same way I use the Overview section in my template.

The Test Items, Features to Be Tested, and Features Not to Be Tested cover the issue of scope. In most of my test plans, the implicit scope is the entire system, and testing will focus on the high-risk areas of that system, which are detailed in the Scope and Quality Risks sections. As discussed previously and as I'll show in the case study at the end of this chapter, my approach is to use a bullet item and tabular style of listing this information. The IEEE format is more narrative and more explicit.

The Approach section of the IEEE plan is where the tester presents the test strategies she'll use for specific tests. In my template, I present this information in the Quality Risks section.

The Item Pass/Fail Criteria and the Suspension Criteria and Resumption Requirements sections map back into the Entry Criteria and Exit Criteria, and Continuation Criteria sections, respectively. For lower-level testing, like component testing, the idea of defining discrete pass/fail criteria for test items in the test plan makes some sense, but I've found that all I can present is aggregate information during system testing.

To me, the Test Deliverables are bug reports and test case findings, along with aggregate-level metrics. (I'll examine bug and test tracking and metrics in Chapters 4 and 5.) In some cases, other deliverables might exist. The IEEE plan makes this discussion explicit, where I discuss deliverables in the various subsections of the Test Execution section. If deliverables other than bug reports, test results, and related metrics were required, I would define them in additional subsections of that section.

The Test Tasks section presents some of the same kind of information I present in Test Cycles; in other words, the procedures and activities that testers will need to undertake to make test execution happen. However, the IEEE plan can also deal with test development and environment configuration issues that I would discuss in the Test Development section.

The Environmental Needs section maps directly into the Test Configurations and Environments section in my template.

The Responsibilities and Staffing and Training Needs section correspond to my Key Participants subsection. I don't tend to discuss training within the context of my test plans, since I prefer to deal with the issue of training as a team-wide effort driven more by the long-term needs of the test organization rather than a reactive, project driven measure, but your approach might differ.

Both the Schedule and the Risks and Contingencies sections map directly into the corresponding sections in my template.

Finally, the Approval section in the IEEE template is where the key stakeholders in the test effort—and presumably the project as a whole—sign to indicate approval of the test plan. I'll talk more about my approach to getting approval in the next few pages, but suffice it to say that formal sign-offs is an approach I use infrequently.

Selling the Plan

After finishing a test plan, I want to obtain approval from project management and development peers. I have used the approach of attaching a formal sign-off sheet to the plan, a la the IEEE 829 template. The approach I usually prefer, though, is that of holding a review meeting with all the involved managers.

If your company tends to become mired in politics, a sign-off might be necessary to protect yourself. If such formalism is rare in your company, there are other ways to document approval, such as a circulation list that you keep. In any case, I recommend a tactful approach if you pursue a formal sign-off. Goose-stepping around the office with a document, requiring management signatures before you proceed with the test project, is not likely to endear you to your colleagues.[6]

I am often tempted to send the test plan via email, demanding that the recipients "speak now or forever hold your peace." After failing to receive any criticisms or concerns, you might assume that everyone has read your plan and agrees with it. This assumption is almost universally false. Lack of response usually means that no one has read it.

---

[6]You might want to consult the discussion on test plan approval in *Testing Computer Software*, by Cem Kaner, Jack Falk, and Hung Quoc Nguyen. These authors seem to have had positive experiences using a sign-off approach.

I find that review meetings are the best way to get people to read plans. One benefit of writing and circulating the plan is to provide a forum for discussing the test part of the project. What better way to achieve that than assembling the appropriate parties to hash out the plan?

Before I hold a review, I email the test plan with a note mentioning that we'll hold a meeting to review it in the next week. (Since email attachments are notoriously flaky, I offer to print a hard copy for anyone who can't open the file.) I invite every manager who is directly affected by the plan—usually the development manager, the project manager, the build/release manager, the technical support manager, the sales and marketing managers, the business analyst or other in-house domain experts, and my own manager—as well as the lead test engineer on the project. I send courtesy invitations to others who might have an interest, but I try to limit the total list to 10 or fewer. I then schedule the review.

At the meeting, I provide extra hard copies of the plan for forgetful participants. As the test manager, I lead the group through the plan section by section or page by page. If anyone has concerns, we discuss—and try to resolve—them on the spot. My goal is to leave the meeting with a marked-up copy of the test plan that will enable me to produce a "final" version. Shortly after the review, I make the requested changes to the document and recirculate it, this time marked as "Released for Execution" or "Release 1.0," to flag the fact that we intend to proceed according to this plan.

Clarity, Pertinence, and Action

One of my clients refers to long test documents as "shelfware." He has seen too many test managers and senior test engineers spend too much of their time filling enormous binders that then sit on shelves, untouched during test execution. My client's comments are a cautionary tale: veer off into a morass of documentation for its own sake—just to follow a standard or to "fill in the blanks"—and you can lose focus, relevance, and credibility.

The style of writing matters, too. Avoid passive verbs. Don't say that something "is to be done"; instead, say exactly who is to do what and when. Defining roles and responsibilities keeps you out of the trap I saw one client's test manager fall into when she wrote a test plan that was just a collection of statements of principle and pieties. ("Testing is good," "Bugs are bad," etc.) Keep jargon, buzzwords, and so forth limited to those appropriate for the audience, and use a Definitions section to promote further clarity.

I keep my test documents practical, focused, and short, and they work well for me. This approach to planning, customized to fit your particular needs, will help you write effective test plans that you can really use.

Bonus Test Planning Templates

A colleague of mine, Johanna Rothman, president of Rothman Consulting Group, has shared two of her own testing templates with me. They are included here by permission. Rothman tells me that she has her clients work through the strategy first (see Figure 2.8),

System Test Strategy
  1. Product, Revision and Overview
     Describe the product and revision designator.
     Describe briefly how the product works. Reference other material as appropriate.
  2. Product History
     Include a short history of previous revisions of this product. (3-4 sentences).
     Include defect history.
  3. Features to be tested
     List all features to be tested. Organize the list in the way that makes most
     sense—user features, or by level:
         Application
         Demo software
         Client substrate
         Server
         Network (this may be more layers)
  4. Features not to be tested
     Describe any features not to be tested.
  5. Configurations to be tested and excluded
     I recommend a table showing which hardware configurations will be tested
     with which software.
  6. Environmental requirements
     Enumerate hardware, firmware, software, networks, etc. required to carry
     out the testing.
  7. System test methodology
     Brief description of work items to be performed from the beginning to the
     end of the product development.
  8. Initial Test requirements
     Test strategy (this document), written by test personnel, reviewed by product
     team, agreed to by project manager.
  9. System test entry and exit criteria
  9.1 Entry Criteria
     The software must meet the criteria below before the product can start system
     test. Specifically enumerate any project-specific departures from the Generic
     Criteria. This list must be negotiated with and agreed upon by the project leader.

Figure 2.8 Rothman's test strategy template.

and then proceed to planning (see Figure 2.9). In the case where there is more than one
test subproject—for example, hardware and software subsystems that require testing
before overall system testing—then there will be a single strategy document that drives
the general testing strategy, with a test plan for each test subproject.

Which to pick, Rothman's or mine? That's a contextual question. Based on format, I
think Rothman's templates are more IEEE-like. Perhaps you don't like the IEEE template
but want to use another template that is clearly compliant. You can map between the sections of Rothman's template and the IEEE template more directly than with mine. In
addition, her process of having a single strategy document and a separate test plan for
each test subproject is IEEE-compliant. (The two sets of documentation are called a

Generic criteria:
1. All basic functionality must work.
2. All unit tests run without error.
3. The code is frozen and contains complete functionality.
4. The source code is checked into the CMS.
5. All code compiles and builds on the appropriate platforms.
6. All known problems posted to the bug-tracking system.
9.1 Exit Criteria
The software must meet the criteria below before the product can exit from system test. Specifically enumerate any project-specific departures from the Generic Criteria. This list must be negotiated with and agreed upon by the project leader.

Generic criteria:
1. All system tests executed (not passed, just executed).
2. Successful execution of any "Getting Started" sequence.
3. Results of executed tests must be discussed with product management team.
4. Successful generation of executable images for all appropriate platforms.
5. Code is completely frozen.
6. Documentation review is complete.
7. There are 0 showstopper bugs.
8. There are fewer than <x> major bugs, and <y> minor bugs.
9. Test Deliverables
   - *Automated tests in <framework>*
   - *Test Strategy and SQA project plan*
   - *Test procedure*
   - *Test logs*
   - *Bug-tracking system report of all issues raised during SQA process*
   - *Test Coverage measurement*
10. References
   Other documents referring the project or testing.

Figure 2.8   *(Continued)*

"Master Test Plan" and a "Level Test Plan" in Software Quality Engineering's IEEE 829-based testing course, "Systematic Software Testing.") Rothman's templates call for explicit content in terms of test deliverables, which might be helpful, especially if it's unclear how information and results will be transmitted to the rest of the project team.

My template, however, includes a section for quality risks and how those tie back to test strategies. In other words, if you are going to use the quality risk management concepts I discussed in Chapter 1, then my template specifically accommodates that. I also have explicit sections for details about the test execution processes and the organizational context of the test team.

Of course, there is no reason why you can't blend Rothman's template with mine and with the IEEE's. Just make sure that you resolve any redundancy issues; in other words, if you include sections that might possibly overlap, either merge them or change the headings and content of the sections to be clearly distinct. You can build

System Test Plan
1. Product purpose
   Briefly describe the product, why you want to produce it, what benefits accrue to the company, etc. (3-4 sentences)
2. History
   Include a short history of previous revisions of this product. (3-4 sentences)
3. Technical Requirements
   If you have a requirements document, reference it. Otherwise, include the bulleted list of functionality from the project plan. Be as specific as possible (this should be more in depth than the project plan.), Include features, performance, installation requirements.
4. System test approach
   Describe how much manual and automated testing you want to accomplish, and how you expect to use personnel (permanent, temporary, sqa, devo, etc.) Highlight issues from below that you think are problems!
5. Entry and Exit Criteria
   (If you have a small project, you can reference the entry and exit criteria from the system test strategy. If you have a large project of subprojects, create entry and exit criteria for each subproject.)
   Determine the objective criteria by which the software is known to be ready for entry into system test and exit from system test.
   For example, based on recent conversations, you already have entry criteria of:
1. Basic functionality must work.
2. All unit tests run without error.
3. The code is frozen and contains complete functionality.

Possible exit criteria:
1. All system tests execute (not pass, just execute).
2. Zero open priority 1 bugs.
3. Fewer than 20 priority 2 bugs.
4. Usability testing complete.

Include configuration issues for these next 6 items.
6. Features to be tested
7. Features not to be tested
8. Performance to be tested
9. Performance not to be tested
10. Installation to be tested
11. Installation not to be tested
12. Overall system test schedule

   Milestone   Expected date
   design test procedures for <feature a>
   review test procedures for <feature a>
   verify tests for <feature a> work
   install <feature a> tests in automated framework

Figure 2.9 Rothman's system test plan template.

your own template out of all three, provided you take care to avoid having your template turn into a hodgepodge of ill-fitting sections.

Case Study

On one project, my test team and I tested a browser-based program that provided home equity loan processing capabilities to call center banking agents. The project was somewhat quirky, since we executed tests developed by another team and didn't have a chance to do a formal risk analysis. However, this plan gives an example of how I applied the template shown earlier to a large in-house IT project. The document, "Case Study Loan Processing Test Plan.doc," is available at www.rexblackconsulting.com.

I thank my client on this project, a major mid-western financial institution, and the executive in charge of development for allowing me to share this example with readers of this book. I have purged all identifying and otherwise private information from this document. My client contact has asked that the organization remain anonymous.

Exercises

1. You are responsible for the System Test phase for a calculator program, as discussed in Chapter 1.

   - Assume that you are working in the same location (e.g., same cubicle or adjacent tables) as the sole programmer working on the calculator. How would you document the entry criteria, bug reporting, and test release process?

   - Assume that the development team is in another city. What are the entry criteria, bug reporting, and test release implications?

2. Based on the risk analysis, schedule, and budget you prepared in exercises 3 and 4 in Chapter 1, write a test plan following my template.

3. Translate the test plan you wrote in exercise 2 into the IEEE 829 format. Was there any particular information in one that was not accounted for in another? Which one do you prefer? Justify your answers.

Test System Architecture, Cases, and Coverage

Chapter 1, "Defining What's on Your Plate: The Foundation of a Test Project," and Chapter 2, "Plotting and Presenting Your Course: The Test Plan," provided a practical look at the process of defining a test organization's purview, understanding the risks to system quality that fall within that purview, and drawing up an overall plan for testing the most important of those risks. Now that you have a grasp of what's involved in these initial tasks, let's turn our attention to the specifics of building the test system itself.

First, we'll take a step back for a conceptual view of a test system and the relationships among the test system component parts. This section provides some definitions and describes the basic operation of a model test system. I use the phrase "test system architecture" to emphasize the fact that solid design and implementation are just as important for test systems as they are for the software and hardware we're testing.

After laying this foundation, I'll look at a method of defining test cases. This discussion presents a few test case templates that I find useful, and I also examine the level of detail required when writing test cases. Finally I'll analyze the issue of test coverage, discussing different approaches to measuring coverage, as well as appropriate steps you can take to fill the inevitable gaps.

Test System Architecture and Engineering

By "test system," I mean the organizational capability for testing created by the testing processes, the testware, and the test environment. The testing processes include both written and unwritten procedures, checklists, and other agreements about the way the test team does its testing. The testware includes all those tools, documents, scripts, data, cases, tracking mechanisms, and so forth that the test team uses to do its testing. The test environment includes the hardware, software, networking and other infrastructure, paper and other supplies, facilities, lab, and so forth that the test team procures, installs, and configures to host the system under test in order to test it. See Figure 3.1 for a pictorial representation.

A competent test team with a good test system can consistently provide effective and efficient test services to a (supportive) project. A good test system helps the tester focus her testing efforts on the key quality risks, and find, reproduce, isolate, describe, and manage the most important bugs in the software or hardware being tested, as well as capturing and analyzing key metrics.

Chapter 4, "An Exciting Career in Entomology Awaits You: A Bug Tracking Database," and Chapter 5, "Managing Test Cases: The Test Tracking Spreadsheet," focus on

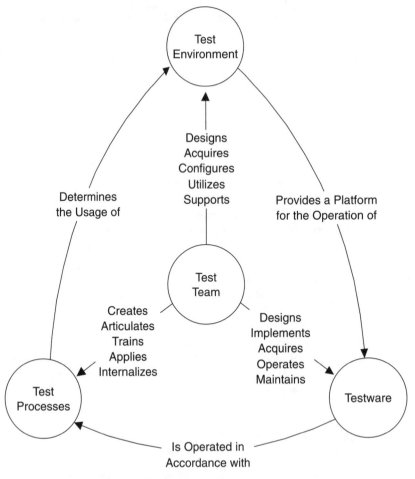

Figure 3.1 The composition of the test system.

the reporting and data management aspects of this system. Chapter 6, "Tips and Tools for Crunch Time: Managing the Dynamic," and Chapter 7, "Stocking and Managing a Test Lab," focus on the test environment, including the test hardware, software, and network and the test lab. In Chapter 11, "Testing in Context: Economics, Lifecycles, and Process Maturity," I discuss project context for testing, supportive and otherwise. In this chapter, I look at the principles and practices that underlie effective and efficient, integrated and maintainable test systems, especially the testware. Figure 3.2 is a visual representation of the testware, a model that I find useful in thinking about and communicating the structure and mechanics of test systems.

Let me explain the model shown in Figure 3.2 from the bottom up. Testware often involves one or more test tools—for example, operating systems, scripting languages, GUI test automation systems, API test harnesses, oscilloscopes, or thermal chambers. Using these tools produces result logs, which are either created automatically from the tool or logged manually by the tester.

Because the test team uses the tools to execute test cases, these tools support the test case library. The relationship between the two elements is "many-to-many"—that is, each tool can appear in multiple test cases, and any one test case can involve the use of multiple tools. Both the test case library and the result logs feed into reporting tools, with a greater or lesser degree of automation. Test engineers assemble test suites from the test case library; the relationship between cases and suites is also many-to-many. From the test suites and the reporting tools come test reports.

At the highest level, the test architecture is a document that defines the design principles, the structure, and the tools that apply for the testware and test environment, as well as the interrelationships between the constituent pieces; it is project-independent, but it reflects the system under test. The test plan harnesses the test system to the project.

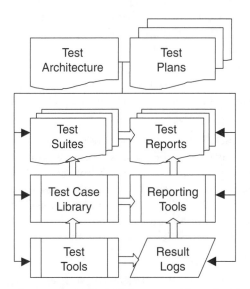

Figure 3.2   A logical decomposition of typical testware components.

The "Action" Components: Definitions

Figure 3.2 zeroes in on three elements of the testware: the test tools, the test case library, and the test suites. These are the "action" components, the testware parts that "do something." Figure 3.3 presents a hypothetical—and simplified—example of how these three components fit together. In reality, you might have a dozen or so test tools, a few hundred test cases, and a score or more test suites. Moreover, the lines between the test tools and the test conditions they create and measure are blurrier than those shown in Figure 3.3.

On the left side of Figure 3.3 are four test tools. In the software world, these might be a GUI test tool, a batch scripting language, a load generator, and an external performance monitor. In the hardware world, imagine an oscilloscope, a thermal chamber, a vibration table, and a "keyboard tapper."[1] A test tool can be any general-purpose hardware, software, or hardware/software system used during test case execution to set up or tear down the test environment, to create test conditions, or to measure test results. A test tool is also separate from the test case itself.

In the center of Figure 3.3 is the test case library, which is a collection of independent, reusable test cases. Each test case consists of a sequence of three stages:

- The *test case setup* describes the steps needed to configure the test environment to run the test case. Connecting a loopback device, making sure that a certain amount of disk space is available, and installing an application are examples of test case setup.

- The point of running a test case is to create a set of *test conditions;* the creation of these conditions allows the tester to assess the quality of the system in relation to particular risks to system quality and customer usage scenarios. Some of the conditions exist in parallel, and others exist in series. In the software world, running a test tool to consume all the buffers while submitting transactions is a specific condition that I might create as part of a performance test. In the hardware world, each cycle of the power switch is a test condition that might occur as part of a mechanical-life test. (I discuss the issue of the actions, data, and expected results associated with test conditions a little later in this chapter.)

- The *test case teardown* specifies the steps required to restore the test environment to a "clean" condition after execution of the test case (or test suite). Disconnecting a loopback device, deleting temporary files, and removing an application are examples of test case teardown.

Figure 3.3 also illustrates the role of test suites. Because test cases are reusable, I can incorporate each into various suites. In fact, in my testware, a test suite is simply a framework for the execution of test cases, a way of grouping cases. The advantage of a test suite is that it allows me to combine test cases to create unique test conditions. Test suite 2, for example, calls for the tester to run test cases 2 and 3 in parallel, which can lead to situations that neither test case could produce alone. As you can see in the figure, test suites, like test cases, can have setup and teardown activities associated with them.

---

[1]Undoubtedly those mechanical-life test tools for keyboards that can simulate years of typing have a more formal name, but "keyboard tapper" has always served me well.

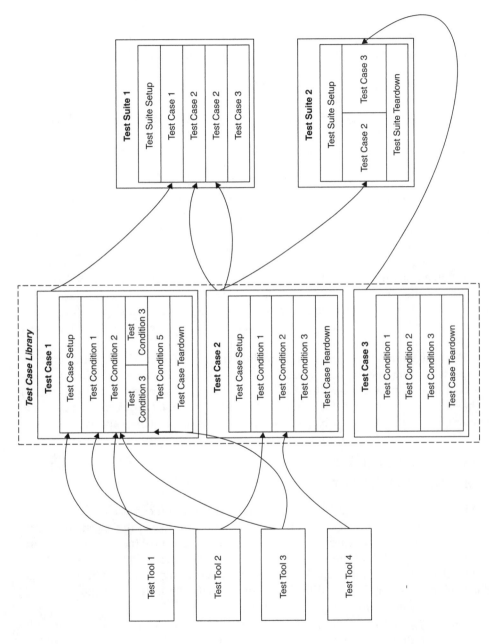

Figure 3.3 The "action components" of testware, and how they relate.

It's Not Saint Paul's, But...
Principles for Test System Architecture

One of the most stately, impressive buildings in Europe is Saint Paul's Cathedral in London. With understated elegance and restrained majesty inside and out, it has reliably provided a place of worship for generations of Londoners since its completion in 1710, shortly after the Great Fire of London. It withstood the savage Nazi bombing of South Britain in the early part of World War II, as well as the fearsome V-1 and V-2 rocket attacks as the war drew to its close.

Those of us who design test systems for a living could learn a lot from Sir Christopher Wren, the prolific architect who designed and built Saint Paul's Cathedral (as well as much of the rest of old London after the Fire). He built a cathedral that survived the German Blitz even though the structure was more than 200 years old at the time. How many of our test systems can withstand the tight deadlines and project pressure that occurs as the planned project end date approaches (often referred to as "crunch mode") on even three or four projects? The design and layout of London still work after all these years, although the city had a little trouble adjusting to the technological advance of the automobile. Do our test systems respond well to changes? Wren's works also have an elegance and simplicity that make them simultaneously powerful and obvious. Can we sit down with a typical test system and easily understand how to use it?

All too often, testware is a mess. When creating new test systems, I consider both function and form. Careful engineering creates the functions, and pervasive design decisions produce the form. Good test system architecture means well-designed testware and a well-designed test environment.

What constitutes good test system architecture? I can't offer specific statements that apply to all situations. If you use oscilloscopes, vibration tables, thermal chambers, and a hardware/software library to test PCs, you face a different set of test engineering challenges than if you need to automate the testing of a GUI application that runs on multiple operating systems. Nevertheless, some general principles apply.

Not an *Objet d'Art:*
Test System Quality

What would it mean for a test system to have quality? You can use the same quality risk analysis techniques discussed in Chapter 1 to try to answer this question for your specific test system, since test systems are usually a reflection of the software and hardware being tested. To state some general principles, I'll look to the ANSI/ISO 9126 characteristics for software quality: functionality, reliability, usability, efficiency, maintainability, and portability. I discuss usability specifically in the next subsection, but first let's look at the other five characteristics.

Most important, a well-designed test system provides the functionality you need for your testing projects. This might go without saying except that in reality, too many test systems don't meet this criterion. I find that developing testware with all the needed functions requires that I—like my engineering colleagues who must develop the right features in their software and hardware systems—focus on the tasks that the testers need to perform with the testware. This focus must inform the initial design of the test system and persist throughout its development and subsequent maintenance. Unfortunately, it's easy to get distracted by crises, minutiae, and the temptation to add bells and whistles. In fact, Dorothy Graham and Mark Fewster identify not providing a suitable tool for the most pressing test development and execution tasks as a leading cause of failure for automated testing efforts.[2]

What are these essential test tasks? Well, let's go back to the quality risk analysis I discussed in Chapter 1. In that analysis, I said that I try to identify the risks to system quality, prioritize those risks, and put an estimate in place for how much time and money I'll need to cover the critical quality risks. Therefore, quality test systems allow testers to cover all the critical quality risks effectively and efficiently. (I'll return to the mechanics of measuring this coverage later in this chapter.)

Another key element of test system functionality is a consideration I brought up in Chapter 1, test system fidelity. The test system should accurately model end-user hardware, software, and interface environments, and simulate end-user conditions. Low-fidelity systems introduce test artifacts, misleading system behaviors, or misleading results reported by the testware. For example, suppose that a SpeedyWriter test fails with the result *Can't open file*. That's a bug, right? Not if your tests caused the system under test to hit its open file limit immediately before trying to open the file in question.

Alternatively, test systems can cause the tester to fail to report real problems. Suppose that the tester in charge of environmental testing for a laptop computer reports that the computer passed the drop test. However, the test case specifies only a level drop on the bottom of the laptop. When the computer is dropped in the field on its edge, corner, or top, the case cracks or the LCD breaks.

Especially challenging types of fidelity and test artifact issues arise in performance, stress, capacity, error handling and recovery, and accelerated-life testing. In these types of tests, you will by necessity fake it: simulating failures by pulling power and network cables; trying to make a lifetime of use transpire by shaking, baking, sweating, pounding, and shocking a system; using scripts to generate loads; and using programs and instruments to measure cycle times. Numerous books on test case design devote attention to these topics. It's a good idea to consult the ones pertinent to your field before you spend a lot of time developing such tests.[3]

Moving beyond functionality, consider reliability. One attribute implied by a reliable test system is that you can produce the same result repeatedly, over an extended period of time. Repeatable, dependable test results are part of a reliable test system.

A low degree of coupling between test cases and activities is another attribute of reliability. The failure, blockage, or skipping of one test case shouldn't prevent you from running others. (However, a test case failure can indicate a problem in the *system under test* that is blocking other tests from running—a predicament quite different from one in which the *test system* is blocking test cases.) Imagine two unrelated features, A and B, in a system under test. Test cases TC_A and TC_B cover these features, respectively, and in that order in the test system. Feature B works, but A is broken. The test system should run TC_A and report the problem in feature A. It should then proceed to run TC_B

---

[2]For this and other important observations, see Graham and Fewster's book, *Software Test Automation*.

[3]Two of the best discussions are found in Boris Beizer's *Software System Testing and Quality Assurance* (for software) and Patrick O'Connor's *Practical Reliability Engineering* (for hardware).

TEST ARTIFACT FROM HELL

Although it's obvious that test artifacts are bad and test system fidelity is good, desirability does not always translate into implementation. This is especially true when the test artifact appears to be a small, harmless, simplifying assumption during design but hopelessly compromises your test results during execution.

My test team and I once designed a stress and performance transaction generator for a telephony system (an interactive voice response [IVR] server); it simulated lots of incoming phone calls. The telephony driver and utility software included a special program—a Unix daemon—to manage communication to the telephony hardware. We chose to invoke one instance of the daemon per simulated call to make the programming easy, although the daemon was designed to support approximately 24 callers. "So what?" we thought. "As long as the operation is legal, it shouldn't matter."

It *did* matter. When we started testing, we learned immediately that the daemon was a hungry little devil, devouring about 1 megabyte of memory per invocation. Consequently, we could simulate only 300 or so calls before the daemon filled the memory. We needed to simulate approximately 800 calls, but when we tried to do this, the resulting resource contention (swapping) created a ferocious test artifact that rendered our test results meaningless. We had to reengineer the test tool to multiplex 24 simulated caller programs into one daemon.

---

and report its results for feature B. However, if TC_A's success in finding a bug renders the test system incapable of executing TC_B, the test system is not reliable.

Because test resources and schedules are tight, efficiency matters. Continuing the preceding example, an efficient test system will allow the testers to run TC_B before TC_A if that's what makes sense, or even run TC_A without running TC_B. When creating any test system, but especially one that involves scalability, you should also consider test system performance. The system's performance is mostly a product of the speed of your tools, but it can also be determined by how efficiently you can schedule tests. Tests that must be run in sequence (for whatever reason) are less efficient than tests that can be run in parallel. Automated tests that can run (reliably) without human intervention for hours or even days are more efficient than those that require constant care, minor repair, and mid-course adjustment. If your test system takes weeks to run through all your defined tests, you will face a lot of hard choices about what to skip.

The test system should be portable to the same extent that the system under test is portable. External conditions that don't affect the operation of the system under test should not perturb or impede the operation of the test system or the results it reports. A classic example of this problem arises when you develop a test system that requires network access in order to run, even though the product, which is able to access network resources, is not inherently networked. If the network goes down, you can't test. Your painful alternative is to transfer a local copy to the marooned system and modify the tests to run in a standalone fashion.

Good test system architecture also implies maintainability. One aspect of this is flexibility over time. A minor change in the operating environment or an insignificant change in the behavior of the system under test should not topple the test system. For example, a networked test system that can't handle outside load on the network or file server bandwidth is inflexible. Similarly, the old capture-playback test tools for command-line and GUI programs often suffer from an inability to handle changes in screen resolution, a one-pixel shift in a window, or even changes in the date.

As a special case of flexibility, consider scalability, the extent to which the test system's parameters of operation can expand without necessitating major changes or fundamental redesign. If the system under test can support up to 60 transactions per second for the first release, your test system must be able to hit the upper boundary and simulate 60 transactions per second. However, you should design it to expand easily to accommodate 600 or maybe even 6,000 transactions per second for subsequent releases. Achieving such versatility might sound difficult, but you can often create it by devoting adequate care to design and initial implementation.

Maintainable test systems are consistent, which is significant in many ways. All the tools in your test system should work in as similar a fashion as possible. If you buy various tools that must work together, be sure that they do. Remember that off-the-shelf tools, like the tools you develop, have paradigms; they are based on assumptions about what you should and shouldn't do. These assumptions will of course enable or impede certain operations.

Reliability, efficiency, and maintainability are enabled by simplicity. The more bells and whistles you introduce into a test system, the wider its footprint. To stretch the metaphor a tiny bit, as objects become wider they lose the ability to fit into narrow spaces. In addition, a proliferation of test system features tends to result in tight coupling of the test system to particular operating environments, and can, if you're not careful, cause interdependence between test cases as well. Generality is usually desirable, but it's a smart move to make simplifying assumptions that don't impair the functionality of the test system.

That said, you'll often find a trade-off between simplicity on one hand and portability and functionality on the other. By making a test tool a bit more general (and thereby more complex), you might be able to get it to do double duty, saving the effort of developing another tool. In addition, two similar tools can be hard to maintain, especially if consistency of operation across the two is important.

No Test System Is an Island:
Testers and the Test System

Considerations of consistency and simplicity bring us to the human side of the equation. No matter how automated your test system, it does not create, use, or maintain itself; people do. I put the test team in the center of Figure 3.1 to emphasize this fact. Testers must set up the test environment, start the tests, interpret the results, reproduce anomalies manually, isolate bugs by experimentation, and restore the test environment to a known state at the end of the testing.

In addition, the testers will usually need to maintain the test system, especially the test cases and suites. This is especially true any time development adds new features to the product being tested, changes the definition of "correct" behavior for the product, or supports new configurations or environments. Maintenance is also necessary when you decide to enhance the test system to get better test coverage. My test teams have found a well-designed test system easier to maintain than one that is a mess.

In the area of consistency, it's helpful to limit your tool set. I once developed a test system that was implemented in four languages—TCL, iTCL, C, and Silk—running on Solaris and Microsoft Windows NT. The complexity made the development difficult. Technical challenges arose from getting the disparate interfaces to cooperate, while human difficulties ensued from the need to have such varied skill sets in a small team. Nevertheless, we were forced to use all four languages because of the architecture of the system under test. To preserve what little consistency we had left, we rejected a tool from an outside party that had been written in Perl. Although the tool would undoubtedly have been useful, the Tower of Babel was too high to add another level.

In contrast, my test team and I on another occasion supported a test system implemented almost entirely via Korn shell scripts, with only a few localized tests and utilities written in WinBatch and AutoTester. Nonetheless, the system ran on three or four variants of Unix, AS/400 (via network), DOS, and Windows, and it supported about 10 databases. The commonality of the test system components made maintenance technically straightforward and kept the team's skill set requirements simple. (We did, however, implement a shadow version of the test system in DCL to support VAX/VMS; most of our maintenance headaches came from this version.)

Simplicity of the test system is also essential to usability. The best test systems are easy to learn and easy to use. I also try to make the test system difficult to misuse, although I find I need to balance this objective against the costs of complexity. It shouldn't require a cabal of wizards knowledgeable in mystic scripting secrets and magical keyboard incantations to operate and maintain a test system. When outside people join your team, take advantage of the opportunity to quiz them about how easy—or how difficult—it is to learn the system.

Miscellaneous Good Practices and Principles for Quality Test Systems

In most situations, test systems need documentation. I like to cover three main topics: operations guide ("how do I use this beast?"); a functional design specification ("how does this beast work?"); and test system architecture ("why did you build the beast this way?").

The test system should also document itself. Largely, this happens through internal consistency. Filenames, result logs, and the like should be easy to read and should shed some light on their purpose. Plan to use intuitive and consistent variable names in programs and scripts, even if people won't read these files and logs during normal operation. When the test system doesn't work, a test engineer will have to figure out the problem, and obscure error messages such as *SYS40: Wrong at 252.351.37.92* and files with names like TST001.TXT will make the job difficult.

On the subject of files, try to ensure that your test system software doesn't become full of junk such as non-test-related documents, unidentifiable log files, output files associated with old bug isolation operations, and so forth. I once worked on a test system that tended to accrete "temporary" files with charming names like ZIT0009.PRN and other less printable garbage. To encourage cleanliness, I wrote a script that ran once a week, examining the test system and identifying every unexpected file, who created it, and when it was created. The script then mailed the list of junk files to the entire team, and I followed up with the owners of these extraneous files. If the files in fact represented new tests, I simply changed the script. Often, however, the testers had failed to clean up a test directory after running tests.

A well-designed test system promotes accountability. It should identify, usually through the logs and the result files, who ran specific tests. Using a generic *tester* login can cause frustration when you need to ask questions or investigate a problem. Testers should identify themselves when they log in so that the logs and the result files will bear date/time and owner information.

Finally, if your test organization develops special tools, you'll want to avoid two mistakes that are archetypal in software development. First, don't forget the importance of configuration management and release engineering. The software and documentation portions of the test system should be checked in, checked out, and managed just like any other software. Second, remember to test the tests. A standard test plan and suite should exist for the test system. A tester should revise and execute the plan any time changes are made to the test system.

To close on the topic of test system architecture, let me point out that the quality of the test system, like the quality of software and hardware systems, follows from a good underlying test system design. Test system quality is a key factor in the number of result interpretation errors your testers will make. While test team competence and diligence are also factors, quality guru W. E. Deming's famous red-bead/black-bead experiment is, in fact, designed to demonstrate that system capability results in some amount of unavoidable variation in results. As test managers, we are responsible for putting the most appropriate and capable systems in place for our test projects.[4]

The Bricks and Mortar of the System: Test Cases

In a sense, everything in the test system—the test processes, the test tools, the reporting formats, the test environment, and so forth—exists to support the execution of test cases. The test case—at least in my model of the test system—is where actions are taken on the system under test, data are supplied to and acted upon by the system under test, and the system under test ends up in some state or states, with resulting outputs and behaviors that testers can compare to expected results. The set of three values—action, data, and expected results—is where the testing happens; where the test conditions are created.

Creating Test Conditions

How exactly are test conditions created? At the highest level, I think of test cases as consisting of a sequence of actions, each action having potentially some associated test data and some associated expected result. Figure 3.4 gives a graphical illustration of the process, which I'll walk through in detail in the next few paragraphs.

---

[4]This exercise is described in Mary Walton's book, *The Deming Management Method.*

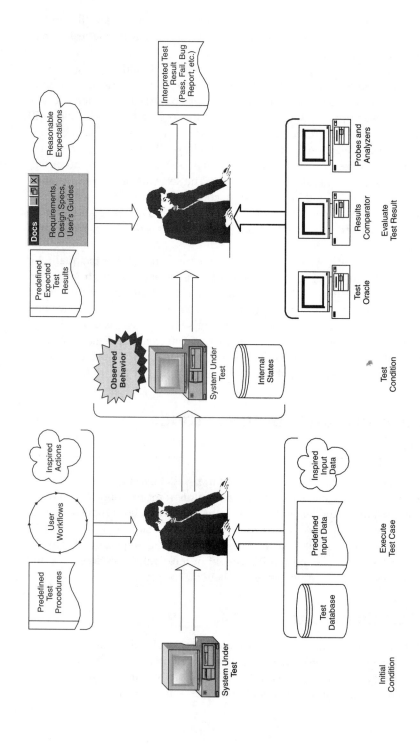

Figure 3.4 Creating test conditions through test case execution.

Assume that we start at step one of a test case, the first action to be taken. The system is in whatever initial condition is reached from the test suite and test case setup steps. Following our test procedures, system documentation, or inspiration, we deliver some data to the system under test. Some of that data comes from persistent databases, some from various input devices, including from our creative fingers on keyboards, mice, and so forth. The test condition is created. The system under test responds. It processes this data, going through whatever computation steps occur. Output is generated and the system enters some subsequent state. The output, the subsequent state, and the way in which the system behaves during its response comprise the results. At this point, we can evaluate the results, using automated tools, documented expected results, system documentation, and our own reasonable expectations about how our system should respond (i.e., our sense of what quality is for our product). After we make our determination, we can proceed to the next test step or substep.

Let's move from the general to the specific—that is, from the architecture of the overall test system and generic test cases to the construction of specific test cases. Since I find examples most compelling in illustrating specific points, I'm going to present a couple of templates in this section that I use to create test cases. I'll examine each part of each template and then look at an example of its use.

A Basic Testing Template

Figure 3.5 shows a basic test case template that can be used for either manual or automated testing. It complies with the IEEE 829 standard for test documentation, assuming

	A	B	C	D
1	Test Case Name:	Mnemonic identifier		
2	Test ID:	Five-digit ID, XX.YYY: XX suite number, YYY test number.		
3	Test Suite(s):	The name of the test suite(s) that use this test case.		
4	Priority:	From coverage analysis		
5	Hardware Required:	List hardware in rows		
6	Software Required:	List software in rows		
7	Duration:	Elapsed clock time		
8	Effort:	Person-hours		
9	Setup:	List steps needed to set up the test		
10	Teardown:	List steps needed to return SUT to pretest state		
11				
12	ID	Test Step/Substep	Result	Bug ID
13	1.000	Major step		
14	1.001	Minor step (substep)		
15	1.002	Minor step (substep)		
16	2.000	Major step		
17				
18	Execution Summary	Status		
19		System Config ID		
20		Tester		
21		Date Completed		
22		Effort		
23		Duration		

Figure 3.5   A basic test case template.

that each test step includes the action to be taken, the associated data, and the expected results. Let's look at each piece a little more closely.

I refer to the first 10 rows of the template, which identify and describe the test case, as the "header" section. It's a good idea to name the test case with both mnemonic and numeric identifiers. The mnemonic name is a short description that conveys the essence of the test—for example, Stress, 1m Drop, or Network Performance. For the numeric identifier, I use a Dewey decimal–style notation: for example, a test case that is used in the fifth test suite and that is the second test case is assigned identifier 05.002. Alternatively, you can use a pure sequential numbering, to emphasize the many-to-many relationship between test cases and test suites.

The next entry in the header lists the name of the test suite (or suites) in which the test case will be used. Because a given test case might be used in multiple suites, this entry could get a bit unwieldy. However, in practice, most test cases are used in only one test suite, so including the name of the suite provides some useful information with only infrequent confusion.

Sometimes I assign a priority to each test case. Prioritizing is most useful when I need to determine how many times a given test should be run. I've assigned priority based on intuition; the opinions of the sales, marketing, technical support, and development teams; my coverage and quality risk analyses; or all of these. Test coverage analysis, for example, allows you to assign the highest priority to those test cases that cover the most important quality risks, requirements, and functions. (Later sections of this chapter discuss test coverage and the use of priority to drive test scheduling.)

The next entries in the header address resource requirements. For two of these entries, I list, row by row, the hardware and software needed to run the test. You might want to restrict these lists to the nonobvious: for example, if you are testing a Windows-based application and the standard test environment includes Microsoft Windows Me, Microsoft Office XP, Norton AntiVirus, and LapLink, you needn't duplicate that listing for every test case.

The entries for Duration and Effort specify how long it will take to run the test, in clock time and in person-hours, respectively. In creating these estimates, you have two alternatives: you can assume that the test passes, or you can make assumptions about the time impact of typical failures. (I used to prefer the former approach, but I now use the latter. I try to estimate how much bug reporting will happen in a given week, and then drive that back into the test case effort estimates.) The estimate of person-hours specifies the human resources needed to run the test. For example, do you need two people to run the test, one in front of each terminal? You would if you were testing the Death Match feature in a game such as *Doom*.

In the final two entries of the header, I specify the setup procedures and the teardown procedures. Sometimes there are none, but typically, two or three steps, such as installing or uninstalling an application, are needed at the beginning and end of a test. For example, when a test is completed, you might need to delete sample files that were created during the test in order to return the system under test to its original state.

With the preliminaries out of the way, let's move on to the test case proper. A test case is fundamentally a sequence of actions, performed serially, in parallel, or in some combination, that creates the desired test conditions. It might involve the use of special test data, either entered as part of running the test step or prior to starting the test case.

The test condition is associated with some expected result, which might be in an output, a system state, a timing or sequencing result, or some other observable behavior. The template breaks down these actions into steps and substeps.

Each step or substep has a numeric identifier. Again using a Dewey decimal–style notation, I number steps sequentially starting from 1 and then number their subordinate substeps decimally (1.001, 1.002, and so forth). This numbering allows me to refer to specific test steps by combining the test case's numeric identifier (from the header) with the test step identifier—for example, the second substep of step 5 in test case 9.010 can be unambiguously identified as 9.010.5.002. This method is useful in bug reports and in discussions with testers. (The bug tracking database defined in Chapter 4 includes a field that captures this value.)

To the right of the list of steps are two columns that allow testers to record the results of their testing. Following the execution of a test case, one of three statements will typically hold true for each step:

- The tester ran the test step or substep and observed the expected result, the whole expected result, and nothing but the expected result. The test step or substep did not locate any bugs. The tester should record *Pass* in the Result column.

- The tester ran the test step or substep, and the outcome was, to a greater or lesser extent, unexpected. The test case was a success because the tester has identified some untoward behavior that can now be reported in your bug tracking database (as mentioned previously). How to classify the test case? If the unanticipated result was something along the lines of a CPU catching fire or a program crashing with a General Protection Fault or a system lockup, the tester should enter *Fail* in the Result column. However, what if the unexpected result is immaterial to the correct operation of the functionality under test? Development might see your team as unfair and alarmist if the tester throws this test case into the "failure" bucket. It is important, however, to keep track of the test case that did find a new bug, so I don't want my testers to record it as a *Pass*. Entering *Warn* as a result is usually a good solution. A *Warn* entry can also cover some of the gray areas between complete failure and tangential failure—for example, if the functionality under test works correctly but causes an incorrectly spelled error message to be displayed.[5]

- The tester did not run the test step or substep. If running the step was impossible— for example, because the test was impeded by a known bug in the system or by the lack of essential resources—the tester should record *Block* in the Result column. If the tester chose not to run the test step or substep, it should be marked *Skip*. In either case, the tester should explain this omission.

If a test step is marked *Fail* or *Warn*, the tester should also indicate, in the Bug ID column, the identifier for the bug report filed as a result of the observed failure. Chapter 4 covers this topic in depth; for now, suffice it to say that you need a facility for recording bugs, and that each bug report so logged needs a unique identifier.

---

[5]Not to split hairs too much further, but I would record a *Fail* for an incorrect message or a display that included offensive language, obscene images, or libelous statements.

At the bottom of the template is a summary section in which the tester indicates an overall assessment of the test case. The Status entry should be marked *Pass*, *Warn*, or *Fail*, depending on the success—or lack thereof—of the test case. (Remember, successful test cases find bugs.) The tester might also record *Block* or *Skip* if applicable. Since test cases consist of multiple steps, I find that I need a hierarchical rule for assigning test case status based on test step status, such as:

If any test step or substep is in progress, then the entire test case is "IP."

Else, if any step or substep is blocked, then the entire test case is "Block."

Else, if any step or substep failed, then the entire case is "Fail."

Else, if any step or substep warned, then the entire case is "Warn."

Else, if all steps pass, the entire case is "Pass."

I don't have a rule for "Skip" because generally this decision is made at the test case level. The tester should next note the specific system configuration used for the test. (Chapter 5 introduces the idea of assigning an identifier to different system configurations.)

In the final part of the Summary section, the tester should record his or her name or initials (depending on your custom), the date on which the test case was completed, the actual effort expended in terms of person-hours, and the duration. The latter three pieces of information allow you to track progress and understand variances from the plan that result from fast—or slow—test progress. Be careful, though, not to use these duration and effort numbers as a cudgel. Testers are not likely to find motivational an angry boss who yells at them for not achieving (possibly unrealistic) targets. Instead, they quickly learn to manipulate these numbers, which prevents you from seeing a realistic picture of your test operation in this area.

A Stress Test Case for DataRocket

Let's look at a brief example of how you might use the test case template. Figure 3.6 shows a test case designed to evaluate DataRocket's response to CPU and memory loads while running under Sun Solaris, Microsoft Windows NT, and Novell NetWare. (This example is, of course, a bit contrived; in reality, you would perform the installation for each operating system and then run all the load and capacity suites before installing the next OS.) A tester (initials LTW) has run the test case and recorded the results.

Suppose that, when LTW installed the test tool from the CD-ROM for Windows NT, the CD-ROM failed to read on the first two tries. The third try succeeded, but this ratio of two failures out of every three tries held up on subsequent retests. Because the failure doesn't materially affect the CPU or the memory subsystem, LTW classified it as a *Warn*.

Worse, however, Solaris, a key network operating system in the target market, did not install or run reliably. About half the time, the system panicked during the installation; the rest of the time, it panicked later, sometimes under load, sometimes just sitting there. This result is a *Fail*, as it obviously does materially affect the CPU and memory response to stress.

In the Summary section, the overall test case result is marked *Fail* because of the failure of the Solaris installation. System configurations B, A, and C are not identified in Figure 3.6, but you can assume that a separate lookup table maps these IDs to specific systems. Also note that the Solaris bug seems to have consumed a lot of LTW's time; the Effort and Duration entries are well over the allocated times.

CONFESSIONS OF AN OVERZEALOUS TEST MANAGER

I once worked at an organization where the testers, who were mostly contractors, had their billable hours capped by the planned effort of the test cases they ran. If they tried to bill more hours than the total effort allocated to their assigned test cases, the project leads rejected their time cards. The leads had an incentive to enforce these limits because they received bonuses based on budget underruns incurred on their projects. Since this organization worked primarily with fixed bids, this method effectively aligned the test technicians with a key corporate objective: meeting or exceeding the profit margins for each project. What you measure is what you get.

Conversely, what you *don't* measure is what you *don't* get. In the absence of corresponding quality assurance pressures such as audits of test results, some testers adopted a "see no evil" attitude. Successful tests—ones that fail—take longer to analyze and complete than unsuccessful (passed) tests. Remarkably, most testers remained conscientious and spirited trackers of bugs.

In addition to the quality problems caused by linking pay to planned test effort, it was unfair to penalize the testers so heavily. Test case delays and time overruns have more to do with the management hierarchy, the support organizations, and the developers than with lackadaisical or featherbedding attitudes on the part of test technicians. Furthermore, there was nothing but downside for the test technicians, while the project leads were motivated to hoard hours in an attempt to make their bonuses as big as possible. I admit to being an exacting enforcer of hour limits in those days, but I wouldn't make the same mistake today.

	A	B	C	D
1	Test Case Name:	CPU and Memory		
2	Test ID:	2.001		
3	Test Suite:	Load, Capacity and Volume		
4	Priority:	High		
5	Hardware Required:	One DataRocket Server		
6	Software Required:	Load, Capacity and Volume Test Tool		
7		Windows NT		
8		Solaris		
9		Novell		
10	Duration:	3		
11	Effort:	4		
12	Setup:	Install Windows NT		
13		Install Novell		
14		Install Solaris		
15	Teardown:	None necessary.		
16				
17	ID	Test Step/Substep	Result	Bug ID
18	1.000	Test CPU load on Windows NT.		
19	1.001	Install Windows NT. Confirm proper install.	Pass	
20	1.002	Install LCV Test Tool from LCV CD-ROM. Confirm proper install.	Warn	009
21	1.003	Run LCV Test Tool, CPU Module, for one hour. Check log file for failures on exit.	Pass	
22	2.000	Repeat steps 1.001-1.003 for Solaris.	Fail	010
23	3.000	Repeat steps 1.001-1.003 for Novell.	Pass	
24	Execution Summary	Status	Fail	
25		System Config	B,A,C	
26		Tester	LTW	
27		Date Completed	7/14	
28		Effort	6	
29		Duration	5	

Figure 3.6   The basic test case template used for a DataRocket stress test.

Other Test Case Templates

Some test cases involve entering data into fields on a well-defined sequence of screens. This is especially the case with transactional components or systems. Registration screens, application wizards, and many e-commerce Web sites follow very specific sequences of screens that implement the potential workflow with few if any opportunities for variation, except where the values entered on one screen determine which of two or more subsequent screens will be followed. (In other words, where the system has a tree-type workflow.) A typical word processor is an example of a test that's very much *not* that way, as there are an almost infinite number of workflows, each very different, that could result in an identical document.

In the case of screen- and field-oriented systems, I have used a test template such as the one shown in Figure 3.7. In this template, you can put many test cases on a single worksheet, because the screen and field names remain the same. I once managed a test project for a bank where we tested a browser-based home-equity-loan application-processing system. The software had six or seven screens, each with well-defined, invariable fields that had to be filled in before the user could proceed to the next screen. Our test case definitions consisted of a sequence of columns in the worksheets that identified the inputs for those fields, and, below each input, the expected result, if appropriate.

Suppose that one of the tests we need to run against DataRocket is configuring the server with any one of three bundled operating systems. An "easy-start" disk is included with the server that gathers the user's information into memory, and then drives the OS installation process. At the end, upon rebooting, the system is to call a server at Winged Bytes offices to register the product and the bundled OS. The test case we develop for these three sets of related test conditions is shown in Figure 3.8.

	A	B
1	Test Case Name:	Mnemonic identifier
2	Test ID:	Five-digit ID, XX.YYY: XX suite number, YYY test number.
3	Test Suite(s):	The name of the test suite(s) that use this test case.
4	Priority:	From coverage analysis
5	Hardware Required:	List hardware in rows
6	Software Required:	List software in rows
7	Duration:	Elapsed clock time
8	Effort:	Person-hours
9	Setup:	List steps needed to set up the test
10	Teardown:	List steps needed to return SUT to pretest state
11		
12	**Screen/Field**	**Test Step/Substep**
13	Screen1	Screen name
14	Field1	Input value for field1.
15	Field2	Input value for field 2.
16	Screen2	Screen name.
17	Expected Results	The result at the final (test condition) input.
18		
19	**Execution Summary**	
20	**Status**	
21	**Bug ID**	
22	**System Config ID**	
23	**Tester**	
24	**Date Completed**	
25	**Effort**	
26	**Duration**	

Figure 3.7   A screen- and field-oriented test case template.

There are many, many different ways to document test cases. Myriad templates have been developed and used by various test teams. The industry standard, IEEE 829, is shown in Figure 3.9. What's not important is the particular templates you choose, if any; what is important is that if you do choose templates for your test cases, it is suitable for the kind of system you're testing.

How Detailed? The Effects of Precision

An important decision when thinking about documenting test cases is how much detail should be included? How precisely the actions, data, and expected results should be documented? I've found that there is always a trade-off. On the one hand, an extensive, detailed, precise test case assumes less knowledge on the part of the testers, which often allows me to use testers with lower levels of skill than I might otherwise require. It also supports reproducibility: if nothing is left to the judgment of an individual tester, I usually see less variability in two evaluations of the same test by two different people, or even by the same person at different times. In addition, if development is involved in

	A	B	C	D
1	Test Case Name:	Configure/Register NT	Configure/Register Solaris	Configure/Register Novell
2	Test ID:	3.001	3.002	3.003
3	Test Suite(s):	Basic Functionality	Basic Functionality	Basic Functionality
4	Priority:	High	High	High
5	Hardware Required:	One DR Server	One DR Server	One DR Server
6	Software Required:	Windows NT	Solaris	Novell
7	Duration:	8	8	8
8	Effort:	4	4	4
9	Setup:	Install blank HD.	Install blank HD.	Install blank HD.
10	Teardown:	Save "clean" NT drive.	Save "clean" Solaris drive.	Save "clean" Novell drive.
11				
12	**Screen/Field**	**Test Step/Substep**	**Test Step/Substep**	**Test Step/Substep**
13	Welcome Screen			
14	Welcome Message	Check against docs.	Check against docs.	Check against docs.
15	Operator Name	Enter first, MI, last.	Enter first, MI, last.	Enter first, MI, last.
16	Company Name	Enter name (min/max).	Enter name (min/max).	Enter name (min/max).
17	Company Address	Enter various options.	Enter various options.	Enter various options.
18	Next Button	Mouse or tab/enter.	Mouse or tab/enter.	Mouse or tab/enter.
19	Install Screen			
20	Select OS	Windows NT	Solaris	Novell
21	Enter Disk Registration	Try invalid, then valid.	Try invalid, then valid.	Try invalid, then valid.
22	Confirm CD-ROM Insert	Try no, see CD request, then try yes w/o CD, see error message, then try yes w/CD.	Try no, see CD request, then try yes w/o CD, see error message, then try yes w/CD.	Try no, see CD request, then try yes w/o CD, see error message, then try yes w/CD.
23	Confirm Install Start	Confirm no start if "YES" not entered exactly as spelled.	Confirm no start if "YES" not entered exactly as spelled.	Confirm no start if "YES" not entered exactly as spelled.
24	Complete Screen			
25	Success Message	Check against docs.	Check against docs.	Check against docs.
26		Reboot; verify NT load. Verify automatic call to reg server.	Reboot; verify Solaris load. Verify automatic call to reg server.	Reboot; verify Novell load. Verify automatic call to reg server.
27	*Repeat above using a bad disk.*	Verify failed install, "Fail" message, no registration.	Verify failed install, "Fail" message, no registration.	Verify failed install, "Fail" message, no registration.
28				
29	**Execution Summary**			
30	**Status**	Warn	Fail	Pass
31	**Bug ID(s)**	009	010	
32	**System Config ID**	B	A	C
33	**Tester**	LTW	HS	LTW
34	**Date Completed**	7/19	7/20	7/21
35	**Effort**	8	8	8
36	**Duration**	3	3	2

Figure 3.8   A screen-oriented registration test case.

IEEE 829 Test Case Specification Template
Test Case Specification Identifier
Test Items
Describe features and conditions tested
Input Specifications
Data Names
Ordering
Values (with tolerances or generation procedures
States
Timing
Output Specifications
Data Names
Ordering
Values (with tolerances or generation procedures
States
Timing
Environmental Needs
Hardware
Software
Other
Special Procedural Requirements
Inter-Case Dependencies

Figure 3.9   IEEE 829 test case template.

the review process for test cases as my team constructs them, spelling out the details serves to communicate, clearly and unambiguously, what types of failures we're looking for and what behaviors we'll consider buggy.

On the other hand, writing a precise, detailed, unambiguous test case can involve considerably more work than writing a laconic one—and it's not simply twice as much work; in fact, it's usually closer to 10 times as much. Obviously, you have to write more, but you also must "unlearn" information that seems obvious to you and your test engineers but could mystify or confuse the test technicians and any others who might become involved in testing. If you've ever tried to explain what testing is all about to someone with no experience in the field, you already know that this can be quite difficult. Understanding the level of detail required for the test team you have assembled (or intend to assemble) is, I find, the key toward writing effect test cases. At some point, I have to assume that my test team is not staffed entirely with clueless technophobes.[6]

Beyond the effort required to write unequivocal test cases, consider the effort needed to maintain them. In one example test case, step 1.001 tells the test technician: *Install Windows NT. Confirm proper install.* The instruction *Install Windows NT 5.0. Confirm proper install* might have been better, but it would require me to update the OS version before using this test case in the future. Or, suppose that I had launched into an exposition, dozens of steps long, about how to install Windows NT 5.0 and then how to confirm the

---

[6]Actually, there are projects where I *wanted* one or two clueless technophobes available for usability testing, due to the target market for the system under test. For example, as part of system testing for a consumer product that includes advanced computing features driven by voice commands.

proper install. As soon as the next version of Windows NT comes out and totally changes the installation procedure (say), the test case will require an extensive rewrite.

There is a style of testing called *exploratory* testing, which I alluded to briefly in Chapter 1. In exploratory testing, testers design, develop, and execute tests during test execution. This is the other end of a continuum from what is often referred to as *scripted* testing; in other words, tests that are not highly ambiguous. Purely exploratory testing is a technique that can work well for skilled, experienced testers. To capture coverage information, I have used exploratory testing in combination with what James Bach refers to as *charters*, which are high-level (i.e., imprecise, ambiguous, rough) directions to the tester on what area of functionality or what type of behavior to test over the course of a *session*. These sessions are usually between 60 and 180 minutes long, and the charters a few (three to 10) words long.[7]

There is no single "right" answer. Every test operation has different constraints in terms of the resources and time available to develop test cases, the technical and product expertise possessed by the engineers and technicians, the concern with strict reproducibility, traceability, and auditability, and the effort that can be spent maintaining test cases. (I seldom choose a single approach for my entire test effort, but rather I allow some of my skilled test engineers to use chartered exploratory test techniques while I make sure that test technicians have ample guidance in scripted test cases.) Decisions about level of detail, like much of management, must move on a continuum (see Figure 3.10). The test case presented in this case study is simplified, but its level of detail and precision is consistent with the test cases I usually use and have seen in some of the best test organizations.

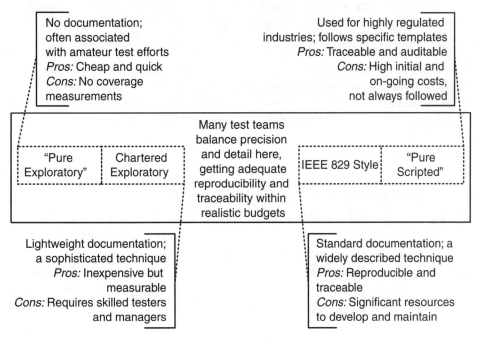

Figure 3.10 The exploratory/scripted test case continuum.

[7]For more information on this form of structured exploratory testing, see James Bach's Web site, www.satisfice.com.

**DANGERS ON THE EXPLORATORY/SCRIPTED
TEST CONTINUUM EXTREMES**

In the first edition of this book, I wrote, "I approach the topic of ad hoc testing (also called ad lib testing) as I would approach a South Texas rattlesnake. I worry that if I say anything good about ad hoc testing, some poor reader will assume that I am giving my blessing to 'guided exploratory testing' as a primary technique. Just so there's no confusion: in my opinion, testing without written test cases and documented expected results has a lot in common with the Hispanic party tradition of letting blindfolded children pummel a hanging piñata with a stick to get at the candy inside. Would you bet your job and the quality of your company's product on this methodology?"

I was too harsh and too sweeping in my comments. I have seen people use exploratory testing successfully. I have, since I wrote that uncharitable paragraph, had a chance to work with James Bach at his Workshop on Heuristic and Exploratory Testing (WHET). He's convinced me that the approach, applied intelligently in the right context, is one that has many benefits.

However, it is possible to do it wrong. I've seen it plenty of times, usually due to poor skill on the test team or poor guidance from the manager. I saw one client adopt this as primary technique without the proper skill level in the test team. They couldn't keep track of what was going on with the system they were testing, so they wrote bug reports that consisted solely of single sentences such as, "Blue screen of death observed," and other less-than-profound observations.

I've seen and heard of people going wrong on the other extreme, too. Sometimes considerable effort is expended on heavily scripted test cases that are then a constant burden to update and use. The client I mentioned in Chapter 1 who called test plans and test cases "shelfware" had seen one too many examples of this approach.

There are rattlesnakes all across the continuum, but I'd guess there are more at the extremes. While I have seen a few organizations use approaches at the extremes of the continuum successfully, and I understand that context plays a huge role in this decision, I would caution you that I have seen test organizations founder on the rocks of sloppy exploratory testing, and have also seen test teams squander precious resources on intricate documents seldom referenced after they were written.

Avoiding the Dreaded "Test Escape": Coverage and Regression Test Gaps

Whatever measurements your manager applies to your performance, one key criterion indicates whether you are doing your job well: the number of *test escapes*—that is, the number of field-reported bugs that your test team missed but could reasonably have detected during testing. This is quantifiable using the following metric:

$$DDP = \frac{bugs_{test}}{bugs_{test} + bugs_{customer}} \times 100\% ,$$

where "DDP" stands for "defect detection percentage." We'll look at this metric again in a little more detail in Chapter 4 when we have a database in place for gathering the underlying data.

Note the word *reasonably*. If your testers could have found the bug only through unusual and complicated hardware configurations or obscure operations, that bug should not count as a test escape. Moreover, the count of the bugs found in the field does not include bugs previously detected by testing; in other words, if the testers found the bug during testing, but it was not fixed because of a project management decision, it doesn't count. Finally, note that in many environments one can assume that most field bugs are found in the first three months to a year after deployment, so DDP can be estimated after that period.

Test escapes usually arise through one or a combination of the following types of problems:

- **A low-fidelity test system.** While a low-fidelity test system might cover a significant chunk of the product's features and operations, it doesn't cover the ones most important to your customers, usually as a result of poor engineering.

- **A regression test gap.** The test suite does contain test cases covering the operation in which the bug surfaced, but the test cases were last run before the fault was introduced in the system under test. Regression test gaps arise from schedule or resource limitations or from planning errors.

- **A test result interpretation error.** A tester fails to detect or report incorrect system behavior, assigns an excessively low priority or severity to the bug, or otherwise understates the significance of the problem.

Chapter 6 discusses result interpretation errors in more depth; for now, let's look at how low-fidelity test systems and regression test gaps create test escapes. Imagine for a moment that defects are fish (not bugs), that tests are fishnets, and that testers are the crew on a fishing boat. When you have a low-fidelity test system, the fish (the defects) are escaping by swimming through holes in the fishnets. When regression test gaps occur, the fish are swimming under a fishnet that is only half deployed. Prosperous fishing crews have an efficient fishing system. Flourishing test teams have powerful test systems and use them effectively. The following sections discuss some ways to maximize your catch. First, though, a cautionary tale to illustrate the stakes.

Bad Coverage Decisions with the Best Intentions

Coverage mistakes are easy to make, even if you spend time thinking about the issue. Some years ago, I took over as a test manager in a company that had developed a neat way of automating testing, using a portable scripting language and the command-line functionality of the system under test. For two years my team and I worked with that test system, polishing it to a bright luster. We wrote an intelligent output comparison program. We had clean, maintainable test tools, under strict revision control. The system was robust, reliable, and fast. Furthermore, we analyzed test coverage in terms of the crucial databases and operating systems supported by the system under test, and we had most of them nailed. Nevertheless, we had significant test escapes, and the customers were unhappy. Accordingly, my managers were unhappy, and they made my team and me very unhappy by liquidating the test organization.

What happened? I let the test tool determine my decisions about test coverage. As Gerald Weinberg has pointed out, "The child who receives a hammer for Christmas will discover that everything needs pounding."[8] We had only two test suites that evaluated the user interface. We barely tested the utilities included with the package. We spent insufficient time understanding the unique uses and the special boundary conditions that plagued our customers.

I took a couple of lessons away from this experience. The most important was to be sure that my consideration of coverage is driven by the quality risks that matter to my customers, my end users, and my colleagues in such areas as marketing, technical support, sales, business analysis, the help desks, and any others who are close to the users (i.e., the key testing stakeholders). I also learned that coverage is not a one-time consideration, so I'm sure to constantly revisit my coverage goals.

Are You Testing What Development Is Building?

If you are lucky enough to get written requirements and design specifications for your product, you probably already use them as a basis for test planning and test system development. You should also close the loop and ascertain the coverage. You can use a numeric approach, such as the one outlined for quality risk coverage in the following section, or you can use a cross-reference approach. (This approach is sometimes called a *functional tracing* or *function-test matrix*.) To create a cross-reference document, carefully go through the requirements or specifications, and note (in a soft copy) the specific test cases that verify each requirement or specification. For those not paired with a test case, decide whether there's a good reason to skip testing in that area. If there isn't, you have found a coverage problem you need to address. Apply this approach iteratively until you are happy with your test system's coverage. You can also circulate this marked-up cross-reference to your peers, especially those key testing stakeholders, to be sure they're comfortable with what you plan to test.

You can apply this approach even if you don't have requirements or design specifications documents. By listing the functional areas of the product at a general level and then subdividing them into more specific areas, you have a black-box decomposition of what the system is supposed to do. (This is analogous to building the requirements and design specifications documents from the product itself, which is reverse-order but not unusual.) Then proceed as just described, using either a numeric or a cross-reference approach. Iterate until you're satisfied, and circulate the document for review.

Remember two caveats about using such a functional coverage approach, however. First, it measures testing of what the system *does*. Don't forget about what it *doesn't* do, *shouldn't* do, and *should* do—these factors are equally important to your customers. Second, if you are focused narrowly on functions, you can easily overlook factors such as stability, performance, data quality, error handling and recovery, and other such

---

[8]Gerald Weinberg, *Secrets of Consulting*, p. 53. This book is recommended reading for consultants and contractors and is full of pithy, memorable rules of thumb like this.

"system" problems. My mistake in the cautionary tale related earlier was, at least in part, that of depending solely on a narrow functional coverage analysis to validate my testing approach. As your coverage analyses move further away from customer requirements and more into the minutiae of system functionality, you need to augment your approach by looking at what the customers care about.

Relating Quality Risks to Test Cases

Chapter 1 introduced (or maybe reintroduced) you to a list of generic risks that apply to the quality (i.e., quality risks) of many computer systems, and I used that list to develop a prioritized set of quality risks for our SpeedyWriter case study. That chapter also explained the use of an *failure mode and effect analysis* (FMEA) approach for defining quality risks. Whichever approach I use for test case development, I need to ensure quality risk coverage. After I have generated my list of quality risks, I benchmark my test system against it.

One way to do this is to list test case identifiers as column heads to the right of the FMEA chart itself. In each cell where a quality risk row intersects a test case column, I enter one of the three values shown in Table 3.1.. (In Chapter 5, I'll show you a variation on this technique that also ties coverage to test case status, providing data for a very interesting chart we can create to measure test coverage during test execution.)

In addition to rating individual test case and quality risk intersections, I aggregate this information. When I total the numbers by quality risk category and by test suite, I am measuring, respectively, whether I'm covering particular risks and whether tests are providing an adequate return on investment. Remember, though, to relate these numbers to the risk priority numbers. High coverage numbers should correspond to high risk, low coverage numbers to low risk.

Figure 3.11 shows an example of quality-risk coverage analysis for the video subsystem of DataRocket. As you can see from the rightmost column, our coverage for each risk is Spartan; increased coverage for this area might be warranted.

If you were careful to capture the pertinent data in the References column of the FMEA (as explained in Chapter 1), you could also generate the coverage analyses for requirements and design specifications discussed in the previous section. You could then use this cross-reference to prepare a set of documents that, because they are less information-dense than an FMEA, will allow your peers to review your coverage. It is sometimes difficult to get people outside test to review FMEA charts, but requirements, specifications, and functional decompositions are easier to digest.

Table 3.1 Quantitative Test Coverage Analysis

VALUE	COVERAGE MEANING
0 (Or blank)	The test case does nothing to address the quality risk.
1	The test case provides some level of indirect coverage for the quality risk.
2	The test case provides direct and significant coverage for the quality risk.

System Function or Feature	Potential Failure Mode(s)- Quality Risk(s)	1.001	1.002	1.003	1.004	1.005	1.006	1.007	1.008	2.001	2.002	2.003	2.004	2.005	2.006	2.007	2.008	3.001	3.002	3.003	3.004	3.005	3.006	3.007	3.008	3.009	4.001	4.002	4.003	Total
Video Subsystem																														
Video Controller	Installation																								2					2
	Palette Limit																								2					2
	Performance																								1					1
	Reliability									1															1					2
Novell Video Drivers	Incompatiblity									1															2			2		5
	Resolution Limits																								2			2		4
	Performance																								1			1		2
	Installation																								2			2		4
NT Video Drivers	Incompatiblity									1															2			2		5
	Resolution Limits																								2			2		4
	Performance																								1			1		2
	Installation																								2			2		4

Figure 3.11   Analyzing the quality risk coverage of DataRocket's video subsystem.

These quality-risk coverage numbers are relative and subjective. No hard-and-fast rule separates a 0 rating from a 1, or a 1 from a 2. However, as long as you and your engineers use the ratings consistently, and you use peer reviews to ensure agreement, the numbers have meaning. Be careful, though, to avoid bias in one direction or the other. If your team is consistently too optimistic, assigning 1s and 2s gratuitously, you overestimate your coverage. Conversely, you can also underestimate it.

Configuration Coverage

Let's suppose that you are testing SpeedyWriter, and your manager tells you to run only the installation and file-open tests. You not only will be allowed to retain your current level of staff and resources, but also will be given even more resources—an unlimited hardware budget. In return, all you have to do is test SpeedyWriter against every possible combination of client computer, platform (Web browser, operating system, and network), and I/O peripheral. Would you do it?

For purposes of illustration, let's assume 20 possible variations of each variable: 20 different client computers; 20 operating system, browser, and network combinations; and 20 combinations of printers, mice, keyboards, scanners, and video controllers. Figure 3.12 shows the "test space" created by this scenario.

As you can see from Figure 3.12, you would have to test 8,000 different configurations, give or take a few hundred "impossible" configurations, such as the use of a particular peripheral with an operating system that doesn't support it. If the two tests (installation and file-open) take about an hour, including setup and teardown time, you have about 2.75 person-years of work ahead of you. In addition to the time, imagine the expense. This simple example could easily cost $100,000 in hardware, operating systems, and server software alone. (Chapter 10, "Involving Other Players: Distributing a

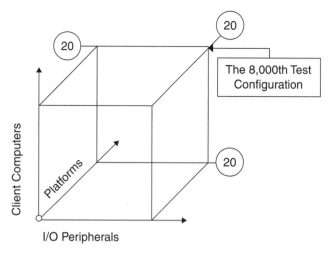

Figure 3.12 An intractable configuration coverage problem.

Test Project," discusses how to reduce the expense of covering multiple configurations by leveraging the capital expenditures of external test labs.)

Even this discouraging example simplifies the matter. In reality, the platform and I/O peripheral dimensions are themselves multiple dimensions. In general, any time you confront the issue of configuration coverage, you are faced with a truly ugly N-dimensional matrix of configuration combinations that you have no hope whatsoever of covering completely. What to do?

Three techniques can be effective in managing this problem. The first is to be sure that you pick the key configurations. For each configuration variable, identify a handful of hardware, software, or infrastructure items that you really care about. Factors to consider in this decision include customer usage, the risk to the product if that particular item does not work, and your gut feeling for where the bugs are. You should also consider the long-term usefulness of the item in your lab and, naturally, its price. Expect to spend some time negotiating your list with management, and be ready to justify each purchase. In addition, keep in mind that configuration testing is but one of the many classes of testing you must do. By trying to cover too many configurations, you might end up with too little time and money and too few staff resources to test other important quality risks.

Even if you had only five variations of each configuration variable in the Speedy-Writer example, completely covering the matrix would take three person-weeks. That's probably a significant chunk of time in your project unless configuration testing is your main quality risk. Rather than trying to cover every single cell in the matrix, you might choose a second technique, known as *shotgunning*, in which you simply distribute your tests randomly across the cells. (I'll show you another useful way to apply shotgunning later in this chapter.)

The third technique offers an opportunity to increase test configuration coverage through careful use of test cycles. By reshuffling the configuration used with each test in each cycle, you can get even closer to complete coverage. Continuing our Speedy-Writer example, suppose that you had 250 test cases to run and three test cycles. You could test each configuration combination against six cases. This isn't exhaustive, but at least you've sampled each one.

Finally, a last technique you can apply is the use of widespread beta testing. By picking potential customers who can, collectively, help you cover many of the key configurations, you should be able to locate many of the remaining configuration-specific bugs that matter to your customers and users. This also provides the benefit of testing in the customer environment and with customer data, although this added level of complexity can make isolating bugs challenging. Finally, you'll need to find beta testers who will stay engaged enough in the process to provide good feedback, which also implies that beta testing must happen only when the product is stable enough not to frustrate and drive away your beta testers.[9]

Bug Coverage

So far, we've discussed several ways to analyze coverage: by requirements specifications, by design specifications, by functional areas, by quality risks, and by configurations. All these methods address the question, "Have we tested X?" However, when you consider the objective of testing—to find bugs—the real question is, "What bugs *haven't* we found?" The approaches we've covered provide indirect information, since bugs usually relate back to one or more of these areas. However, what we really need to know about is bug coverage.

Unfortunately, we can't know what we don't know. If it were possible to know all the bugs in advance, the entire test effort would be unnecessary. Suppose, though, that you could estimate the total number of bugs in the system under test. Or, perhaps you could measure the bug-finding effectiveness of your test system. The literature on testing and quality assurance suggests three techniques for solving these problems.

The most commonly cited and, in my experience, commonly used technique for estimating bug numbers relies on historical data. Based on the size of the current project, the sizes of past projects, and the number of bugs found in past projects, the test manager can estimate the number of bugs in the current project. Suppose the current project is estimated at 5,000 lines of code. Further, suppose that historical data indicates one bug found in system test or in the first six months following release for every 100 lines of code. In this case, we can estimate that either we find 50 bugs during system test or resign ourselves to the remainder surfacing after release. Line-of-code estimates being notoriously unreliable early in the project, though, I would expect this estimate to be subject to considerable error.

Alternatively, we might measure project size in function points, which is said to be more reliable as an estimating tool. Suppose we expect—based on the requirements—that we'll implement 100 function points. Suppose further that we expect 1.5 bugs per

---

[9]When Microsoft first released Windows 95, the need for backward compatibility with Windows 3.1 and 3.11 hardware created many of the last-minute schedule slips. This requirement opened up a truly massive configuration matrix that it took Microsoft months to cover, even with the help of beta testers

function point, so 150 bugs would escape into the system test phase. We can either find about 150 bugs during system test, or deliver those bugs to the customers and users.

This technique—which has many variants—is called a *defect removal model*. The model assumes that, during each phase of the project, some number of defects are *injected (inj)* into the system by developer error, some number of defects are *removed (rem)* through testing and quality assurance, and the difference *escapes (esc)* to the next phase of the project. Suppose we have a "V" model type of development effort (see Chapter 11 for a discussion of lifecycle models) with six phases, requirements *(req)*, design *(des)*, implementation *(imp)*, component test *(ct)*, integration test *(it)*, and system test *(st)*. If we have historical data not just for the effectiveness (i.e., DDP, as discussed earlier) of system testing, but also for all the previous phases, we can estimate the bugs delivered to our users as the number of bugs that escape at the end of the system test phase.

$$bugs_{esc,st} = bugs_{inj,st} + bugs_{esc,it} - bugs_{rem,st}$$
$$bugs_{esc,it} = bugs_{inj,it} + bugs_{esc,ct} - bugs_{rem,it}$$
$$bugs_{esc,ct} = bugs_{inj,ct} + bugs_{esc,imp} - bugs_{rem,ct}$$
$$bugs_{esc,imp} = bugs_{inj,imp} + bugs_{esc,des} - bugs_{rem,imp}$$
$$bugs_{esc,des} = bugs_{inj,des} + bugs_{esc,req} - bugs_{rem,des}$$
$$bugs_{esc,req} = bugs_{inj,req} - bugs_{rem,req}$$

These types of sophisticated defect removal models tend to be accurate (+/− 10 percent according to one of my clients who uses a lines-of-code model), but do require good defect and project management metrics. Furthermore, changes in the process, technology, and the team can invalidate these models for future projects.[10]

A couple of theoretical techniques have been developed as well. One is *error seeding*, which involves the deliberate introduction of bugs into the system under test. Because the bugs are known to the people (outside the test team) who planted them, they can be removed manually at the end of the test process. Since the test team remains unaware of the seeding, the extent to which the test system reveals the known bugs allows you to infer the extent to which it found unknown bugs. Suppose that the system under test contains N bugs, and K bugs are seeded. At the end of system testing, the test team has found n unseeded and k seeded bugs. Error seeding theory asserts the following:

$$\frac{k}{K} \approx \frac{n}{N}$$

Solving for N, you find the following:

$$N \approx n\frac{K}{k}$$

Some important cautions apply to this technique. You must remember that these are approximations. If you have found 95 unseeded bugs and 19 out of 20 seeded bugs,

---

[10]For a good discussion on defect removal models, see Pankoj Jalote's *CMM in Practice*, Stephen Kan's *Metrics and Models in Software Quality*, and Capers Jones' *Estimating Software Costs*.

you can't assume that exactly five unseeded bugs remain to be found. The technique simply gives you an estimate against which you can gauge a measure of effectiveness for your test system and a level of confidence in your results. Additionally, in order for this approximation to hold, the bugs seeded must be representative. The technique measures only the test system's ability to find *seeded* bugs, and you must infer its effectiveness against real bugs based on that. Also keep in mind that bugs don't exist in a vacuum. Because they often interact, the seeding itself can create test artifacts that lessen the strength of your inference.

Like error seeding, *fault injection* provides a way of measuring the effectiveness of your test system. In this technique, errors are created dynamically in the system under test by deliberately damaging, or perturbing, the source code, the executable code, or the data storage locations. For example, the fault injection process might create a so-called mutant system by flipping a bit in a data storage location immediately prior to the execution of a test case. The test results against these mutant systems allow you to make certain estimates of the quality of the system under test as well as the quality of your test system. While this technique shows promise, it currently remains in the experimental stage. The key challenges are to simplify it in such a way that a reasonable amount of mutants deliver statistically meaningful results and to automate the creation of mutants.[11]

A problem with both fault injection and error seeding is that one can't inject defects into code that doesn't exist. So, bugs that came about during the requirements and design phases can't be found. That is, if we have a missing requirement, then no code will be implemented, and no errors can be seeded or faults injected into code that's not there.

Regression Test Gaps

The concept of regression is straightforward but sometimes misunderstood. Formally, you can say that if, as a result of a change in the system under test, a new revision of the system, S_{n+1}, contains a defect not present in revision S_n, the quality of the system has regressed. Plainly speaking, regression occurs when some previously correct operation misbehaves. (If a new revision contains a new piece of functionality that fails without affecting the rest of the system, this is not considered regression.)

Usually, you'll detect regression when test cases that passed previously now yield anomalies. Some regression, though, is so obvious that no test is required to find it—flaws in a system's case or a glitch in software installation, for example. Or, you can have Zen regression: if a bug crawls into the system but no one detects it, you will find this regression, like the sound of the unattended falling tree, hard to prove!

In an ideal setting, the test team would have the time needed to execute all the test cases during each cycle of each test phase. This would ensure that within days (or even hours) you would catch any regression in a new release. However, running all the test suites in such a way that every configuration is covered could take forever, stretching test cycles into weeks, months, or even years rather than days. Few organizations (except those developing safety-critical systems) have such luxurious time frames; pesky realities such as budgets and deadlines tend to compress test phases.

---

[11]If you are interested in pursuing these topics further, I recommend *Software Fault Injection*, by Jeff Voas and Gary McGraw, which provides extensive references to the pertinent research.

In addition to the "do it all by tomorrow" urgency that prevails on most development projects, you can become a victim of your own success. When you first start developing tests, you'll probably be able to hit only the most critical items. As your test system and your team grow and mature, however, you'll find that you have more tests to run than time in which to run them.

One or both of these factors usually forces me to select a subset of the test suites for each test cycle. Yet each test case omitted might create a regression test gap. (If you can drop a test case without affecting test coverage, you should consider deleting the test case from your test suite. It is probably redundant, assuming that your measurement of coverage is valid.) Unless you execute every test case in every test suite against every revision and configuration, you are exposed to regression test risks—to follow an earlier analogy, some fish will swim around a partially deployed fishnet. What can you do?

Is Automation a Complete Solution?

Some people suggest test automation as a solution to this problem, and it can be—at least partially. An automated test system runs more tests in a given period than a manual system does, and, consequently, the regression test gap is reduced. Nevertheless, automation is not a panacea. As a test manager, you will receive lots of brochures touting (expensive) test automation tools, so bear the following in mind when you read them.

For a stable system, you can develop automated tests and run them repeatedly, with some minor modifications to one or two test cases each time. However, when interfaces, major functions, or supported environments evolve and change rapidly, automated tests require significant maintenance. Because these changes occur in the course of a fast-paced development project, you will discover these problems in the thick of test execution, when you don't have the resources to fix them. This might tempt you to wait until the product is released to develop automated tests for maintenance, but systems in development run the highest risk of regression. (In my experience, most regression test "failures" during maintenance turn out to be unintended, but correct, consequences of other changes. Trying to anticipate these expected-result changes prior to running the tests against the maintenance release is often impractical.) Just a cruel irony of life in a test organization, I'm afraid. That said, the most practical approach is, in my experience, to focus most functional automation efforts on functionality introduced in the previous release, as this will tend to remain stable from one release to the next.

Furthermore, test automation only automates the creation of test conditions, not the setup and teardown of test cases and suites, nor the analysis of the results. Testers can spend a significant amount of time getting the test environment, test data, and test tools configured. Moreover, glitches encountered in setting up the tests usually come from the test system itself, not from the system under test. Any time spent setting up the tests or chasing down test artifacts disguised as bugs is time not spent testing. Large numbers of failed test cases can result from a single bug, leading to extensive analysis efforts beyond what would be required in the case of manual testing, where test failures are noted, isolated, reproduced, and reported in real time.

In the hardware world, automation can help only in certain areas. For stress, capacity, and performance testing, for example, automation is essential. However, when you test multiple applications—imagine compatibility testing Windows-based applications against a new desktop computer—the time needed to install the application and verify the installation can make up the bulk of the test. You can't effectively automate these operations. Even in the software world, installation of the program and its ancillary utilities, followed by configuration and verification of the install, are by necessity manual activities for most systems. (I have worked on a few projects in which automated distribution of the software and the test system itself made these costs of automation low. Most test projects, however, involve a manual installation, configuration, and verification process as the first—and often nontrivial—step of a new test cycle.) You can automate the testing of the application itself, but this might save you only a few dozen hours per project. Test automation won't help if installation and configuration eat up half the time in your test cycle.

I don't mean to disparage test automation. It is useful, and it will often help to reduce regression test gaps. Testing for certain quality risks, such as performance, stress, capacity, and volume almost always requires the assistance of automated test tools. Despite some claims to the contrary by test automation tool vendors, though, it is not a silver bullet for functional regression testing.

Four Ways to Spread Tests Across Cycles

Test automation or no, the time will probably come when you will be forced to select only a subset of the test system for certain test cycles—or even test projects. When this happens, these four alternative tactics can be useful in minimizing regression test gaps:

- Assigning a priority in advance to each test suite, and then running the test suites in a way that favors the higher-priority tests.

- Assigning priorities dynamically to each test suite as each test cycle begins, and then running the test suites in priority order.

- Shotgunning the test suites across the test cycles.

- Running the entire set of test suites straight through as many times as possible (definitely more than once), which I call *railroading* the tests.

SILVER BULLETS OR SOLID ENGINEERING?

In his book, *The Mythical Man-Month*, Fred Brooks includes a chapter entitled "No Silver Bullets," in which he argues that the quest for universal cures to the "software crisis" is counterproductive. This year's be-all-and-end-all always turns into last year's incremental improvement. RAD, object-oriented programming, 4GLs, structured programming, FORTRAN, and COBOL all have had their moment in the sun. Test automation, likewise, is useful within the limits of the problems it can solve. Nevertheless, it will not cure cancer, remove warts, feed the dog, or promote world peace.

Richard Gisselquist, a senior programmer at Silicon Graphics, makes a similar point in a 1998 article entitled "Engineering in Software." He writes that hot programming trends "and CASE [tools] are not engineering." He claims that solid engineering consists of managing expectations and the development team, properly designing and implementing the system (whatever the language and the CASE environment), and promoting the proper use of the system. I believe this is just as true for testing as it is for the project as a whole.

The next few pages use a DataRocket example to illustrate each of these approaches, demonstrating practical ways of slicing and dicing the test suites in a test phase under tight—but not quite unreasonable—schedules. Of course, if you are receiving releases of software every few hours, all these means of partitioning tend to fall into the "rear-ranging deck chairs on the Titanic" cliché. (The most chaos-resistant technique is rail-roading, as you'll see.) Remember, too, that although these scheduling methods might appear clever and efficient, they are nevertheless only fancy ways of making compromises: I'm trading added risks for saved time and resources. Any time I plan a test cycle that includes anything less than a full pass through every test suite in the current test phase, I create a regression test gap.

For our example, let's assume that you have one month to run system testing for DataRocket. During that period, you are scheduled to receive two motherboard revisions and 10 BIOS releases. You plan to run 10 cycles, the first and the tenth lasting one week and the intervening cycles lasting two days. The entire system test takes about four days to run, depending on the number of bugs you find. Table 3.2 shows the test schedule with milestones.[12]

Prioritizing

Let's start by using the priority approach. Based on a three-level division of priority, let's suppose that the high-priority subset of the test system consists of test suites STS1, STS2, STS5, and STS7, and takes two days to run. The medium-priority subset containing STS3 and STS6 takes one day. The low-priority portion containing STS4 and STS8 also takes one day. Figure 3.13 shows a road map for running these tests in priority order. (The higher-priority tests are shown with darker shading.)

Table 3.2 A Frenetic DataRocket System Test Schedule

CYCLE	START	END	MB REV	BIOS REL	% TESTS
1	7/1	7/7	A	X1	100
2	7/8	7/9	A	X2	50
3	7/10	7/11	A	X3	50
4	7/12	7/13	A	X4	50
5	7/14	7/15	B	X5	50
6	7/16	7/17	B	X6	50
7	7/18	7/19	B	X7	50
8	7/20	7/21	B	X8	50
9	7/22	7/23	B	X9	50
10	7/24	7/30	B	X10	100

[12]This is not a recommended schedule. A four-day system test is probably not exhaustive, given typical staffing levels in a test organization. A two-day test cycle gives you time to hit only the high points. Nevertheless, schedules resembling Table 3.2 are hardly atypical, unfortunately.

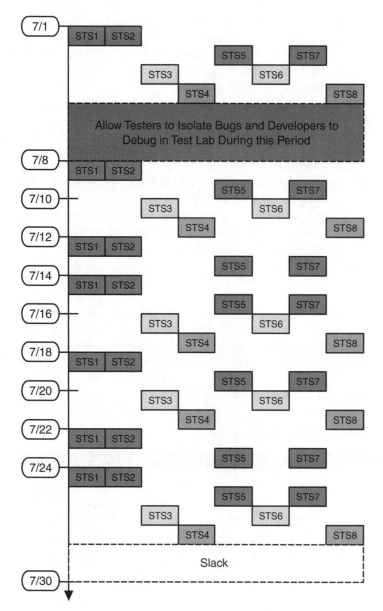

Figure 3.13   A road map for test selection based on priority order.

Notice that the road map in Figure 3.13 starts and ends with a complete pass through the test system. The complete first pass provides a baseline for the rest of the testing and alerts development to every bug I can find in the system right from the start. The three-day hiatus from organized test suite execution allows testers to isolate all the bugs revealed by the first run of the test suites and gives the developers access to the test lab for debugging purposes. (See Chapter 7 for some tips on how to do this without invalidating subsequent tests.)

The complete last pass gives you a chance to yell "Stop!" before your organization embarrasses itself with a buggy release. Of the two complete passes, the last pass is the most important in terms of preventing test escapes. It is also the one most likely to receive short shrift as a result of resource redirection and project fatigue. I try to run a complete last pass even if management declares the final cycle formally complete. Because of the ramp-up time, I usually still have a chance to stop a bad release before it hits the customers.

In the middle of the road map, you can spread your test suites across the other test cycles. The high-priority test suites are run seven times in total, while the medium- and low-priority test suites are run five times. This arrangement comes fairly close to totally rerunning all of the test suites in every cycle, yet it is 14 days shorter.

Of course, this road map suffers from two obvious defects. The first is that it is simplified to make a point. In the real world, you won't have eight test suites that divide into three neat groups of four, two, and two, with each suite taking exactly a day to run. Life seldom works out as neatly as this example. The second problem is the absence of slack except at the end. On real projects, deliverables slip frequently. (At the risk of sounding inordinately cynical, I can't remember a single project in which every single major deliverable into test hit its target date.) This road map won't handle those slips well. Instead, I would hide a day of slack in each cycle, or at least insist on keeping the weekends. (Think of weekends as "hidden slack" that you can draw on every now and then if you have a motivated team.)

Dynamic Prioritizing

The priority-order approach might have raised a question for you: how do you know in advance which test suites should have a high priority? You can guess, based on past experience or the quality risks covered, but the odds are pretty good that you will be proven partially or totally wrong. Suppose that you assign a high priority to DataRocket's thermal test (STS1) because an early engineering evaluation unit caught fire at one point. Also suppose that you assign a low priority to the USB, FireWire, serial, and parallel port test (STS4) because development has found no problems in this area.

By the end of July 4, though, you discover that you have the priorities backward: the thermal test passes with headroom to spare, but the USB test is a target-rich environment. It turns out that the developers forgot to test the interaction of power management with USB hot plugging and hot unplugging, and the system crashes when you try this. Now, suddenly, STS4 is a high-priority suite, and STS1 is a low-priority suite.

You can handle this situation by conceding in advance that the priorities you come up with ahead of time won't mean much. With this concession, you simply plan to run four test suites, selected based on the priorities of the moment, during the second through ninth test cycles (with complete passes at the beginning and the end, as before). See Figure 3.14 for a road map of testing under this plan.

I'm not a big fan of this approach, although I know successful test managers who use it. It strikes me as dangerously close to an ad hoc, "figure it out as we go along" test methodology. (Chapters 4 and 5 discuss the use of bugs metrics and test metrics, respectively, to estimate test suite priority. I use these metrics to select tests that yield the most important bugs. For purposes of this discussion, I have assumed a visceral approach to test case importance, but I'd apply a more rigorous technique to make this approach a lot less subjective if I used it.) Maybe you can't foresee everything or assign the priorities perfectly, but refusing to plan leaves you totally crisis-driven. Caught up in the

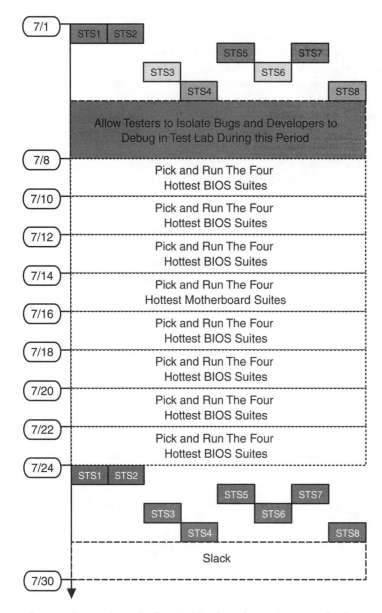

Figure 3.14   A dynamically prioritized road map for test selection.

emergency du jour, you could easily reach the end of the test phase and find that you have spent all your time running fewer than half of your test suites. If you then run all the test suites in the last cycle (which you should) and find a slew of nasty bugs, you deliver a Hobson's choice to the project team: fix the bugs and slip the schedule, or ship the bugs and keep the schedule.

Shotgunning

Suppose that you want to have a plan in place, to help impose some discipline, but you find the concept of selecting the priorities in advance laughable. In essence, you are considering all test suites equally important, and therefore you can simply distribute the suites randomly in test cycles 2 through 9. (Cycles 1 and 10 remain "total coverage" cycles as always.) Figure 3.15 shows the road map for this scattering of test cases.

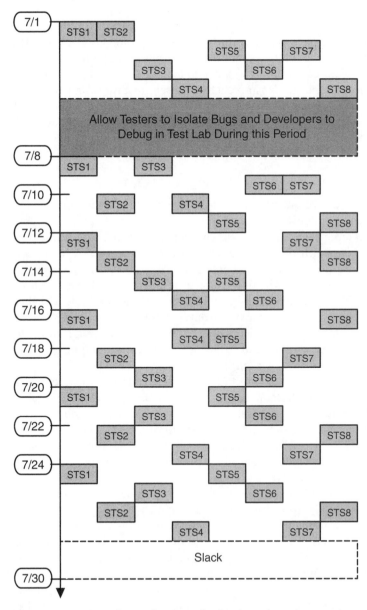

Figure 3.15   A road map for test selection based on shotgunning.

This shotgun approach is more robust than the others. Since you are decoupling your test suite selection from the specific test deliverables, a change in those deliverables doesn't affect your plan. What if the BIOS release doesn't show up on July 10? With the previous schedules, you might have wondered what to do next. With a shotgun road map, however, four test suites have not yet been run against the X2 BIOS release, so you can simply continue with your plan to run those tests.

Railroading

The shotgun approach looks clever on paper, but the premise might strike you as flawed. After all, if the test suites are equally important, why go to the trouble of randomizing their run order? You could just as easily use the test suite numbering—STS1 through STS8—as the sequence. In this case, the testing rolls on regardless of what's going on in the project. Figure 3.16 shows a road map for this railroad approach.

Like the shotgun method, the railroad approach to test selection is resistant to slips in delivery dates. For example, if the X3 BIOS release arrives on July 11 instead of July 10, you needn't be concerned; you can just install the new BIOS on the test systems and run STS7 and STS8. If a deliverable slips by a long enough period, you can go to exploratory testing. (In the real world, running out of things to test happens rarely indeed.)

Avoiding Mistakes

What I most want to avoid is a situation in which I never get to run an entire set of tests—or in which I run them only once early on and never return to them—because they keep getting preempted by new releases. This can happen if I run in test suite order, as in the railroad approach, but start over with the first test suite every time a new release shows up. Figure 3.17 shows the result of this approach. Obviously, large regression test gaps are created in the middle of the system test phase, while the test team repeats STS1 through STS4. The bill for this mistake comes due around July 27, when STS5 and STS6 are run for the first time in about 20 days. These tests, as well as STS7 and STS8, are likely to reveal significant problems that, because of the looming ship date, give management the unpleasant choice of delaying the product or shipping known bugs. People will blame the test manager for this situation, and rightly so.

Two additional points are key to good test selection. First, for every new release of software or hardware, I have my testers perform thorough *confirmation testing* against each bug that has allegedly been fixed in the release—and I have them do this first. (Confirmation tests check for bugs related to the failure of a bug fix to address the reported issue fully, and they usually involve rerunning the test procedure and isolation steps, per the bug report.) The fixes are where the new and changed stuff lives. In software, for example, bugs abound in new and changed code. The parts not changed, although perhaps not directly tested, at least have been subjected to incidental tests along the way. The new stuff is truly untested and unseen.

Second, I take into account the inevitable ups and downs of the process. When my plan encounters reality, I want it to bend, not break. I try to create robust plans that handle changes well, which is why I prefer the shotgun or the railroad approach when I have to choose. Be flexible, though, when your plan is forced to change, and remember that you can mix and match the test suite selection methods—for example, you can use the railroad approach and still preempt some of the test suites for others you feel

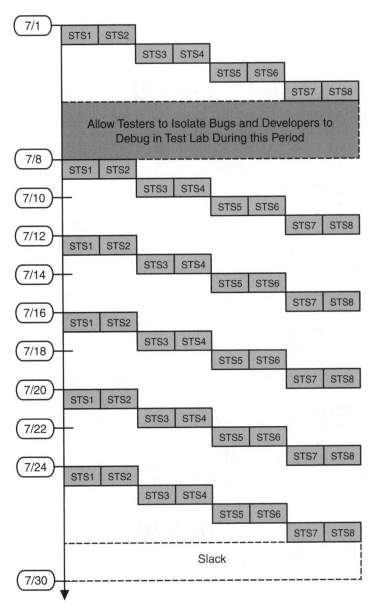

Figure 3.16 A road map for test selection based on railroading.

are more important. Plans are good, but keep the goal in mind and be ready to adapt to changes as they happen. (Chapter 6 provides a tool to help you track and manage those changes effectively.)

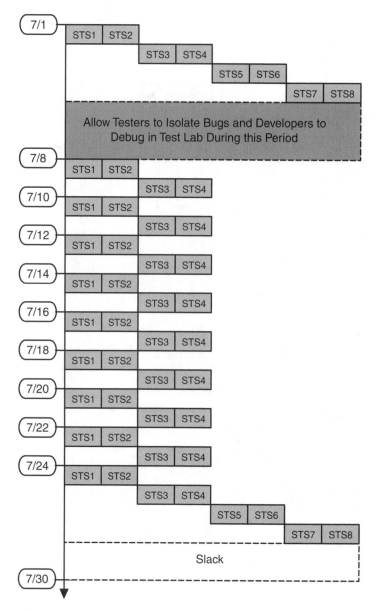

Figure 3.17 A road map for bonehead test selection.

What If I Can't Repeat All the Tests? Alternative Regression Risk Mitigation Strategies

The standard technique—you might say the " brute force" technique—to mitigate regression risk is to repeat the tests you have, over and over, against each release into the test organization (i.e., each test cycle) and against each release to the customers or users. This is the technique illustrated in the last few sections. Extensive automation or simple products with simple feature-sets make this possible, but in some cases such test repetition is impractical.

One of my clients tests geological modeling software, an extremely complex application with an almost unlimited potential number of data sets and workflows. The entire set of tests used for system test takes about two person-decades to run. With a 20-person test team, they have no time to repeat tests, with the exception of some very basic functionality tests that don't even come close to exercising a thousandth of the possible workflows and data sets. What to do?

One simple approach is, in each test cycle, to rerun every test case that failed the last time it was run, whether in the last cycle, the cycle before that, or even in the first test cycle if the test effort is spread that thin. (A slightly more risk-averse approach would be to rerun every test that has ever failed during the entire test phase during every test cycle or every other test cycle, even if it passed the last time it was run.) The rationales here are that the tests that have failed before are likely to fail again, that bugs tend to cluster together, and that changes tend to be localized and break features that are "nearby."

But is it really true that failures are localized? Imagine a client/server family of applications with a shared database. The development team might change a table in the database to accommodate a new report. Testing might find a bug or two in the new report, but, if we don't regression-test broadly enough, fail to find a huge set of bugs in another application that also uses that same table. To handle this problem, some test teams resort to change analysis.

In change analysis, we sift through what we know about the system as it exists now and what we know about the proposed changes. We look at our risk assessments, our coverage information, and our past bug logs. Based on this data, we conclude that the changes increase the level of risk attendant to some set of quality risks in the system. We rerun the tests that cover those risks.

But what a luxurious amount of data and time I need for this process! While I've done this informally, based on gut, I've never—nor have any of my employers, clients, or seminar attendees— been able to do the kind of detailed analysis that would be required to draw solid, logical, quantifiable inferences about what to test and what to ignore.

This leaves me with the approach my geological modeling software client uses. Start by assuming that the system is a minefield, and each mine a bug. Testing detects some of the mines—by hitting them—but each subsequent change can—and many changes definitely will—introduce new mines. If we create test cases that are limited and isolated in their test conditions, then each test case is like walking gently through the minefield. But what if our tests are broad in coverage—for example, based on various workflows, usage scenarios, and data sets—then wouldn't each test case be more like dragging a wide iron bar across the minefield? This is exactly my client's experience. They use structural coverage—in other words, "How much of the code have we tested?"—as their key metric for assessing regression risk. By measuring structural coverage, they find they cover 60 to 70 percent of the modules in a given four-week period (i.e., the rolling four-week average test structural coverage is between 60 and 70 percent). Over the course of the year-long test period, coverage is close to 100 percent. Are there regression risks? Certainly, but this method of test design and their metric for checking up on regression risks assures them that the level of risk is acceptable, given that the alternative is to multiple the test team size by 25 or so to achieve a complete test pass against every other (weekly) test release.

"There's a Lesson to Be Learned Here...": Test Case Incremental Improvement

No matter how good a job I do on my first crack at developing test cases and suites, my test systems always have holes. Budget and time pressures, along with human mistakes, result in incomplete testing. Some test cases won't cover conditions they should, or some test suites won't include important test cases, or the overall test system won't have all the test suites it needs.

In the case of most consumer software and hardware products, a few omissions won't prove fatal to the product, provided you are careful to test the critical features. (The issue of test escapes takes on a different meaning when you are dealing with safety-critical systems such as traffic-light, medical, or power-plant control computers or with situations that involve people's privacy and security. A higher standard of quality is required in safety- or mission-critical systems.) Nonetheless, I attempt to improve my test system for each subsequent release. A few techniques for doing this involve responding to the failures in the shipping product, incorporating the practices of others into your test system, and using exploratory testing.

Responding to Failures

One obvious way of enhancing a test system is to plug gaps that come to light when some poor customer or user is whacked in the forehead by a test escape. Of course, this doesn't mean that you or anyone else in your company will celebrate test escapes; you'd rather your customers were dazzled by your product's quality. However, a bug found in the field is the perfect candidate for inclusion in the test system. You know that it's important to your customers, or to at least one of them, because they wouldn't bother to report it if it weren't. Assuming that development is fixing the problem, it's also important to your management. As an added bonus, the test case should be relatively easy to write: given a field report, you should have the steps to reproduce the bug and any ancillary test data at hand.

In addition to learning from your own test escapes, how about learning from someone else's? As the saying goes, "any fool can learn from his (or her) own errors, but a wise person learns from the mistakes of others." Reading trade journals, keeping up on pertinent Internet newsgroups and Web sites, and networking with your peers in the test profession and your niche of the computer business will allow you to learn from their blunders.

Adopting Best Practices

Beyond merely learning from others' mistakes, you also want to learn from their successes. I'm not suggesting industrial espionage, but rather research. For example, simply by reading this book you are learning new test techniques, even though the book is primarily about *managing* testing. Likewise, trade journals might print articles that evaluate your competitors' products, often including sidebars on "how we tested" that you can use to benchmark your own testing.

Training sessions, conferences, and seminars provide great opportunities to expand your test system as well as your skills. If you purchase test tools, you almost certainly have training options. Even if you believe that your team understands the use of a purchased tool, it might make sense for one person to attend the training session and bring back good ideas. Likewise, seminars are opportunities for cross-pollinating your test system with your peers. Every presenter at a reputable conference or training session is an expert chosen by the organizers of the event to offer unique knowledge and skills.

Some practicing test professionals write off the academic world. It's true that research literature is not always practical. However, today's research is tomorrow's state-of-the-art product or process. I try to read at least one or two advanced books every year, as well as pertinent articles in the monthly *Journal of the Association for Computing Machinery.*

Using Exploratory Testing

Some people have a knack for rooting out errors, like a fine bird dog on a quail or a pig after truffles. Glenford Myers, in *The Art of Software Testing,* refers to this process as "error guessing." This might sound like a precise technique, but Myers admits that no technique exists—it's simply intuition. Part of what I want to do as a test manager is to find bugs, so exploratory testing is great for that—provided I have the right people— but I'd also like reproducibility for subsequent test cycles.

My challenge as a test manager is to convince my intrepid exploratory testers to write down their brilliant ideas. Many of these testers tend to have a problem understanding the value of documentation. I, however, know when they've come up with a particularly good test: they find a bug. Since I capture defect data in my bug tracking database, I can ensure that any problems found during exploratory testing turn into a documented test case.

You Can't Do It All: Deciding What Not to Do

As a final note on test cases, let me revisit a point made in earlier chapters: as much as it pains me to do so, I must make choices about what I will and won't test. With luck, I can get others to help you make those choices, thereby making my life easier and providing you with some political cover at the same time. (External support for my test goals, and the management backing it brings, is something I can't have too much of.)

Nonetheless, at times I have to make tough decisions. On most projects, eventually, someone asks me whether, in my professional judgment, a feature needs to be tested. What they are asking me is a question about bug coverage: "Do you think we will find critical bugs in this if we test it?"

There is no magical heuristic that will prevent me from making the wrong decisions. Hard choices are hard because no solution is obvious and the stakes are high. When faced with these types of choices, I approach them with an open mind. I question my assumptions about what "has" to be tested. Why do I feel that way? I trust my gut, but I confirm my intuition. Then I talk it over. I ask my test team what they feel is essential, and why. I consult test stakeholders, peers, and colleagues. I quiz my development associates on the project. I review any pertinent references in books and articles.

After going through the exploratory process with an open mind, I make my decision. I document what I intend to keep and what I intend to drop. I'm prepared to answer why. When I feel confident in my decision, I communicate it. And then I'm prepared to start all over again if need be.

Case Study

In this section, I illustrate two styles of test case documentation. The first follows the screen-oriented template introduced earlier, which my team and I used for testing the browser-based program for home equity loan processing described in the case study for Chapter 2. Note that the test procedure (actions taken) is implied by the flow of the screens, but that the input data and the expected results are defined very precisely. The document, "Case Study Loan Processing Test Cases.xls," is available at www.rexblackconsulting.com.

I thank my client on this project, a major mid-western bank, and the executive in charge of development for allowing me to share this example with readers of this book. I have purged all identifying and otherwise private information from this document. My client contact has asked that the organization remain anonymous.

The second set of tests show a data-driven approach used for a custom automated test harness. This test harness sent the data to the subsystem under test—in this case, small programs running across a network providing security and access control—and then checked the return values. Note the use of HTML-style "tags" to define stanzas that control the harness. The documents, "Case Study Functionality.suite" and "Case Study AddValidUser.case," are available at www.rexblackconsulting.com.

Bonus Case Study

Ross Collard, principal consultant of Collard and Company and fellow testing expert, provided me with the following interesting case study that examines degrees of test case documentation details and precision. In this case study, Ross enumerates five points on the precision spectrum I showed as Figure 3.10, with an additional level for automation. Note that Ross uses the phrase "test specification" where I would probably use "test case."

LEVELS OF DETAIL IN A TEST SPECIFICATION*

A test specification can be detailed at several different levels:

Level 0: No documentation is prepared before trying the test case: "Just do it."

Level 1: A brief description of the overall purpose and nature of the test. Typical length of the documentation: one or two lines.

Level 2: A list of the conditions and items to be tested, with the description of each condition limited to one line. Typical length: a quarter page to a full page.

Level 3: An outline of how to test each condition on the list in level 2. The outline includes the input data, initial conditions, and expected results for each condition. Typical length: a quarter to a half page for each condition, for a total of one to three pages.

Level 4: A step-by-step description of how to perform the test manually, including every action, click, and keystroke. Typical length: a half page to two pages for each condition, for a total of three to 20 pages.

Level 5: An automated test program. The typical length varies based on the conciseness or density of the test scripting language: if the language is concise, there typically can be 10 to 100 lines of code (instructions) in the test script language, but if it is wordy, there can five to 50 pages of source code in this language.

An example of these various levels of detail follows.

Example of Test Spec. Levels of Detail

Level 1

Verify that the search function works correctly in the ABC system.

Level 2

Verify that the search function works correctly in the ABC system, by testing these conditions:

1.1	Click the search button without entering any search parameters.
1.2	Attempt to enter invalid search keys.
1.3	Enter a valid search key for which no matching records are found.
1.4	Enter a valid search key for a record which the user is not authorized to access.
1.5	Enter a full or partial search key which is unique, and ensure that the matching record is displayed for this search key.
1.5.1	Full last name, all other parameters blank.
1.5.2	Full last name, first initial.
1.5.3	Full last name, first initial, date of birth.
1.5.4	Full last name, first initial, age range (from - to).
1.5.5	Partial last name, all other parameters blank.
1.5.6	Partial last name, first initial.
1.5.7	Partial last name, first initial, date of birth
1.5.8	Partial last name, first initial, age range.
1.5.9	Soundex (sound-alike name) retrieval, e.g., "Smythe" is considered a match for "Smith."

Continued

LEVELS OF DETAIL IN A TEST SPECIFICATION* (Continued)

1.5.10 Full customer ID#.

1.5.11 Partial customer ID# (an asterisk can be used as a "wild card" for one or more digits in the customer ID#).

1.6 Enter a full or partial search key that is not unique, and ensure that a list of all matching records is displayed for the search key.

1.6.1 Full last name, all other parameters blank.

1.6.2 Full last name, first initial.

1.6.3 Full last name, first initial, date of birth.

1.6.4 Full last name, first initial, age range (from - to).

1.6.5 Partial last name, all other parameters blank.

1.6.6 Partial last name, first initial.

1.6.7 Partial last name, first initial, date of birth.

1.6.8 Partial last name, first initial, age range.

1.6.9 Soundex retrieval.

1.6.10 Full customer ID#.

1.6.11 Partial customer ID#.

1.7 Enter a partial search key that matches more than the maximum number of records that are allowed to be retrieved (let's say, more than 1,000 matching records), and ensure that the response is the message: "Too many matches to display."

1.8 Refresh the search window after a search has been completed (by pressing the Alt-F4 key combination), change the value of one search parameter, and initiate a new follow-on search.

1.9 Terminate a search after it has been initiated but before it has been completed and before the responding matches have been displayed.

Level 3

For brevity, these next levels of detail are limited to one condition (1.5.1) from the prior list.

1.5.1 Enter a full last name as the search key that is unique, all other search parameters blank, and ensure that the matching record is displayed for this search key.

Description: Search based on complete last name, with no first name and no suffixes, with one matching record in the search database.

Initial Conditions: ABC system running under Win2000, with the search window open.

Input: Full last name, followed by Enter key.

Expected Results: Search results window opens, and displays the customer that matched the search key on the last name.

Continued

LEVELS OF DETAIL IN A TEST SPECIFICATION* *(Continued)*

Level 4

1.5.1   Enter a full last name as the search key that is unique, all other search parameters blank, and ensure that the matching record is displayed for this search key.

Initial Conditions:
Platform: Win2000
ABC system running, version: 5.06.04
No other applications running
Blank screen
Search window open
No other windows open
Initial location of cursor is in the first position of the last name.
All parameters in the search window are set to blank or null values.
Test database: SSIMENU
Test case table: Y2KAPL3, with the table pointer set to the correct next test case.
Customer SMITH, JOHN exists and is the only SMITH entry in the test database.
Caps Lock is not set and is assumed to have no effect (i.e., upper- or lowercase data entry does not matter).

Input search key:
Last name: SMITH
Enter key
Process (to run the test case)
Retrieve the next set of inputs (last name: SMITH) from the table of test cases.
Edit the test case to ensure the inputs are valid.
Enter the data from the table (last name: SMITH) in the appropriate data entry fields of the search window.
Click on the Search key or press the Enter key (either should work).
Verify the correct list of customers is displayed in the search results window.
Press Escape, Cancel, or Ctrl-C to terminate the search.
Return to the search window ready for the next search.

Expected behavior:
Search results window appears.
List of the matching customers with the specified search parameters appears in the window.
For this test case, the list should contain only one member: SMITH, JOHN.
After pressing the Escape or Cancel key, the search results window disappears and the search window reappears with the cursor in the last name field

*I thank Ross Collard for permission to share this case study with the readers of this book.

Exercises

1. You are responsible for the System Test phase for a calculator program, as discussed in Chapters 1 and 2. Write a test case for the multiplication feature (assume standard rather than scientific mode) in three formats:

   a. The sequential-step template.

   b. The screen-oriented template.

   c. The IEEE 829 template.

   How do the three test cases compare?

2. The other dyadic operators (those that take two operands like addition, division, and subtraction) can be tested using the same format. How would you change your approach for the unary operators (those that take one operand like square root, inverse, and change sign)?

3. The expected result for a calculator must be known very precisely to ascertain pass or fail status for tests of mathematical correctness. What if we were testing the user interface (appearance, functionality, etc.) of the calculator? Can we describe precisely all the attributes that make a user interface good? Comment on whether we can describe precise pass and fail criteria for user interface tests, and whether pass or fail status is an absolute for user interface tests.

1

CHAPTER

4

An Exciting Career in Entomology Awaits You: A Bug Tracking Database

You now have a thorough test program put together. Time to relax, exchange the quadruple espressos for a few nice cold Warsteiners, and coast, right? After all, the only work that remains is executing the test plan, and surely your test technicians, with a little guidance from the test engineers, can handle that.

Definitely not. Your job as test manager remains as important as ever when you move into the stage of implementing the test plan and gathering data related to that plan.

Once test execution begins, even the most organized approach will not save you from the excitement of the project going on around you. A test plan, test cases, test tools, test architecture, measures of test coverage, and all the other program components you've developed are proactive and, when completed, relatively static objects.[1] Welcome now to the world of the reactive and the dynamic. Following a test plan diligently and using a test system properly but flexibly require continual adjustments in your priorities, meticulous attention to details both clear and subtle, and adaptation to the endless changes in the project.

You will soon find yourself awash in the data generated by your shiny new test system. This is good, because this is the objective. Testing should generate useful information about the quality of the system. Testing is about risk management, and you can't manage risk without data.

---

[1]This is not to say that a test system should not change. But major improvement of a test system is a matter of incorporating the lessons of a project into the system deliberately, generally at the end of the project.

Raw test data, however, tend toward the amorphous, the confusing, and the hard to categorize. Moreover, the quality of the system under test is a moving target during test execution. Therefore, there's a real challenge ahead for you in terms of extracting information from all that data.

Worse yet, remember all those commitments people made in terms of entry criteria, system delivery dates, acceptable turnaround times for test results, and so forth? Be prepared for otherwise honest and upstanding citizens to go back on their word shamelessly. This is not because they are out to get you. Eagles and sharks live at the end of the food chain, and every toxin that trickles into the ecosystem ends up sickening or killing the hapless predators disproportionately. Likewise, test is at the end of the development schedule, and every failure, delay, and slip-up can manifest itself in test, concentrated along the way into a noxious slime of confusion and missed dates that can make you very ill indeed.

Clearly, you need a way to track, analyze, and present what's going on in your once-peaceful test domain. The following three chapters provide some tools and techniques that will keep you on top of the test results and help you minimize the damage from the inevitable bombshells.

As a start, this chapter introduces a tool that supports a critical and visible role played by test organizations: the finding, documenting, and tracking of product defects (a.k.a., bugs). The role is critical because, if it is done right, many of the bugs you find will be fixed, making test a direct contributor to increased product quality. Because bug reports provide tangible evidence of quality problems, they are visible not only to developers, but also often all the way up to the executive level. I have used a variety of bug tracking systems and have seen the task done well and not so well by clients, vendors, and test labs. The approach outlined here handles the necessary tasks, is easy to implement, and provides information appropriate to all levels of an organization.[2]

Why Bother?
The Case for a Formal Bug Tracking System

To start, let me explain some of the terms I'll use to be sure you can understand what I'm talking about. By *defect* or *bug*, I mean some problem present in the system under test that would cause it to fail to meet a customer's or user's reasonable expectations of quality. To tie back to Juran's definition of quality in Chapter 1, "Defining What's on Your Plate: The Foundation of a Test Project," a bug is a potential source of product dissatisfaction.

A bug report is a technical document that describes the various symptoms or failure modes associated with a single bug. A good bug report provides the project management team the information they need to decide when and whether to fix a problem. A good bug report also captures the information a programmer will need to fix and debug the problem. Because a bug report is so specific and discrete, it is the most tangible prod-

---

[2]For other ideas on bug tracking databases, see Chapters 5 and 6 of *Testing Computer Software*, by Cem Kaner, Jack Falk, and Hung Quoc Nguyen. I don't agree with everything these authors say, but they make some excellent points about writing good bug reports and managing bugs.

uct of testing and represents a well-defined opportunity for the project team to make a decision to increase the quality of the system. (Because we want to focus on problems in the system under test, not in the development or maintenance process, testers should not file bug reports against process breakdowns such as late delivery of test releases. We'll look at a database you can use for that purpose in Chapter 6, "Tips and Tools for Crunch Time: Managing the Dynamic.")

A bug tracking system is some program or application that allows the project team to report, manage, and analyze bug reports and bug trends. Functionally, most bug tracking systems provide a form that allows us to report and manage specific bugs, a set of stored reports and graphs that allow us to analyze, manipulate, and output this bug data in various ways, and a customizable workflow or life cycle that provides for orderly bug management. (I'll talk more about each of these items later in this chapter.) Architecturally, bug tracking systems run the complexity gamut (see Figure 4.1). Sophisticated systems allow clients to connect to the corporate network, intranet, or Internet, and communicate with databases on a server or set of servers, depending on the exact implementation. Simple systems run on a single, standalone PC or workstation. I'm going to use the simple architecture to illustrate the ideas in this chapter, but those ideas scale to the most complex of networked, distributed systems.

Perhaps you don't see the value in having a bug tracking system. You might be thinking, "Spending all that time and effort documenting bugs is too much hassle, especially with the developers right across the hall." It's true that creating, evolving, and using a bug tracking database take significant effort and discipline. However, don't skip this chapter yet. I think you'll find that a systematic approach to bug tracking provides some important benefits:

- A bug tracking database facilitates clear communication about defects. Well-written, standardized reports tell the story much better than free-form emails or shouts across a hallway or to the next cubicle.

- Using a database allows automatic, sequential bug numbering (a useful way to keep track of and refer to bugs), and it provides a number of analysis and reporting options that are not available with a flat file. If you have never looked into the various types of product and process metrics that can be derived from defect information, be ready to be surprised.

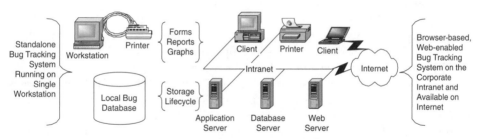

Figure 4.1 Simple and sophisticated bug tracking system architectures.

- A bug tracking database allows the development team to fix problems based on importance to the project team, project management, the customers, and the users. With a more informal approach, the tester who has the best rapport with the most developers is often the one whose bugs get fixed.

- You can manage bugs throughout their life cycle, from the initial report to the final resolution. This ensures that bugs don't fall through the cracks, and it keeps attention focused on the important bugs that need to be fixed as quickly as possible.

- As bugs progress through their life cycle, developers, testers, and managers learn new information. A well-designed bug tracking database allows you to capture this history and then refer to it later when you are looking at the status of the bugs.

- Every bug report that is closed in your database is a defect that might otherwise be included in a shipping product, causing support calls, bad reviews, and lost sales. Every bug report that is not closed when the product ships provides technical support with useful advance warning and proves that your testers found the bug in the event that it crops up in the field. (We'll look at how this data can help us measure the return on the testing investment in Chapter 11, "Testing in Context: Economics, Life Cycles, and Process Maturity.")

In this chapter, I'll present a simple bug tracking system that realizes these benefits. (This database complies with IEEE Standard 829 in terms of content, although its format differs considerably from that shown in the standard.) You can use this database, which is included with the templates for this book, or use the ideas in this chapter to develop a requirements list for a bug tracking system you build or buy yourself.

So, What Seems to Be the Problem? The Failure Description

Bug tracking systems allow you to capture a lot of information about each bug. Some of this information is classifying data, generally selected from some set of values. For example, severity and priority ratings for bugs often run from 1 (most serious) to 5 (least serious). Other information is more narrative, describing what happens when the bug symptoms appear, how the bug was fixed, and so forth.

I'll discuss all of these possible pieces of information in detail, but let's start with the narrative data that captures the account of the problem as told by the report's author. This is the heart of any bug tracking and reporting system, the *failure description*. This is the message of the bug report. The failure description is the tester's first and best opportunity to communicate clearly with the programmers and the project team about a problem. Done properly, it captures in simple prose the essentials of the bug. Done poorly, it obfuscates the bug and misleads the reader.

What does a good failure description look like? Figure 4.2 shows the failure description for a nasty bug in the SpeedyWriter product. The failure description contains three basic sections: summary, steps to reproduce, and isolation.

The *summary* is a one- or two-sentence description of the bug, emphasizing its impact on the customer or the system user. The summary tells managers, developers, and other

Summary
Arial, Wingdings, and Symbol fonts corrupt new files.

Steps to Reproduce
1. Started SpeedyWriter editor, then created new file.
2. Typed four lines of text, repeating "The quick fox jumps over the lazy brown dog" each time.
3. Highlighted all four lines of text, then pulled down the font menu, and selected Arial.
4. All text converted to control characters, numbers, and other apparently random binary data.
5. Reproduced three out of three tries.

Isolation
New to build 1.1.018; same test case passed against builds 1.1.007 (System Test entry) through 1.1.017.
Reproduced with same steps using Wingdings and Symbol fonts.
On vague suspicion this was a formatting problem, saved file, closed SpeedyWriter and reopened file, but data corruption remained.
Saving file before changing font prevents bug.
Bug does not occur with existing files.
Only happens under Windows 98, not Solaris, Mac, or other Windows flavors.

Figure 4.2 A good SpeedyWriter bug report.

readers why they should care about the problem. The sentence "I had trouble with screen resolutions" is a lousy summary; the sentence "Setting screen resolution to 800 by 1024 renders the screen unreadable" is much better. A succinct, hard-hitting summary hooks the reader and puts a label on the report. Consider it your one chance to make a first impression.

The *steps to reproduce* provide a precise description of how to repeat the failure. For most bugs, you can write down a sequence of steps that recreate the problem. Be concise yet complete, unambiguous, and accurate. This information is critical for developers, who use your report as a guide to duplicate the problem as a first step to debugging it. I heard one team of programmers complain bitterly about the poor job the test team was doing; in the final analysis, their complaints centered around the poor quality of the steps to reproduce.

Reproducibility varies considerably. In many cases, failures are reproducible 100 percent of the tries only for simple functional bugs. When repeating a test case three times reproduces the identical (incorrect) behavior three times, the bug is certainly reproducible. Nevertheless, the possibility remains that the next run of the test case will produce a different symptom or perhaps no failure whatsoever. Moving to a different environment—from the test lab to the development lab, for example—often affects reproducibility, as can seemingly unrelated version changes. (I'll discuss the use of a test lab to provide a controlled test environment in Chapter 7, "Stocking and Managing a Test Lab.") Thus, it's important for the author of the bug report to verify reproducibility. Good bug reports include statements such as "I tried the above steps four times and observed the error three times."

Isolation refers to the results and information the tester gathered to confirm that the bug is a real problem and to identify those factors that affect the bug's manifestation. What variations or permutations did the tester try in order to influence the behavior? For example, if the problem involves reading the CD-ROM drive on DataRocket, what happens when it is set to a different SCSI ID? Did the tester check the SCSI termination? If SpeedyWriter can't print to a laser printer, can it print to an inkjet? Good isolation draws a bounding box around a bug. Documenting the isolation steps performed will assure the programmers and the project team that the tester isn't simply tossing an anomaly over the wall, but is instead reporting a well-characterized problem.

More Like Hemingway than Faulkner

Two of the great writers of the early twentieth century, Ernest Hemingway and William Faulkner, allegedly hated each other. Like their personalities, their prose differs dramatically. Hemingway created a muscular style of prose that used short sentences, focused on actions, and spelled out events clearly and sequentially. Faulkner, conversely, wrote long sentences, made the prose the point as much as the story, used metaphors, and changed points of view. A remarkable capacity and appetite for alcoholic beverages is one of the few known common interests between them.

Had he tried his hand at computer testing, I suspect that Hemingway would have written great bug reports (as long as he was sober). I doubt that Faulkner would have. It's not simply a matter of style, though. Even if you write like Hemingway, it takes concentration, practice, and discipline to describe bugs well. Over the years, I have read literally hundreds of bug reports that had significant problems.

How can you write better descriptions? Most important, remember that good bug reporting starts with good testing. Testers who have an ad hoc, disorganized approach to testing tend to write rambling, confusing bug reports. Testers who follow a sequence of test steps carefully, apply thoughtful exploratory testing techniques, take detailed notes, and isolate bugs using a methodical process tend to write concise, clear bug reports.

On a similar note, bug reports should be written concurrent with or immediately following testing. A tester who runs many tests, takes notes on various bugs that arise, and then waits to write a report until a dozen or so problems have piled up not only endangers the overall schedule—delaying the day the bugs are reported delays the day the bugs are fixed—but also tends to write poor reports. The tester is likely to forget pertinent details and might lose access to the test configuration needed to repeat the test. If the test must then be rerun to gather more information on the bug, you're out of luck.

When it comes to writing the report, make sure that it's accurate, complete, and concise. A report that gets major details wrong is embarrassing at best. A report that omits important information is misleading. A report that takes 400 words to describe a bug won't be read. After the report is written, invest a little extra time and effort in a review. As the test manager, you can either review all the reports yourself or use a peer review process. Peer review works well when everyone on the test team agrees about how reports should be written. If you're having consistency problems, though, you might want to do all the reviewing yourself.

Summary
SpeedyWriter has trouble with Arial.

Steps to Reproduce
1. Open SpeedyWriter.
2. Type in some text.
3. Select Arial.
4. Text gets screwed up.

Isolation
   N/A

Figure 4.3   A vague, incomplete bug report.

Finally, good bug reports tell the reader what the tester found, not what the tester did. Some organizations do use a "test report" approach, documenting every step taken, every behavior observed. There's a place for this level of detail, but it's the test case description itself, not the bug report. When I write reports, I document the minimal number of reproduction steps, and I include only isolation information that yielded an interesting data point. If I run one test and see two independent bugs, I write two reports.

Figure 4.3 and Figure 4.4 show two failure descriptions that might describe the same bug reported in Figure 4.2. The report in Figure 4.3 is vague and incomplete, with a

---

Summary
I ran SpeedyWriter for Solaris, Windows 98 and Mac, and with certain fonts it seems to screw up some data.

Steps to Reproduce
1. I opened SpeedyWriter on Windows 98, then edited a couple existing files. These files contained a mix of fonts.
2. Printing of the files worked fine.
3. I created and printed a graphic, which worked okay. Some of the lines aren't real sharp, though.
4. After this, I created a new file.
5. Then, I typed in a whole bunch of random text.
6. After I typed the text, I then highlighted a few lines of it. Next, I pulled down the font menu and picked Arial out of the list.
7. The text I changed got screwed up.
8. I was able to reproduce this problem three times, which was every time I tried it.
9. I reran steps one through six on Solaris and didn't see any problems.
10. I reran steps one through six on Mac and didn't see any problems.

Isolation
I tried selecting a few of the different fonts, but only Arial has this bug.
However, it might still occur in the other fonts I didn't test.

Figure 4.4   A verbose and confusing bug report.

misleading summary, missing steps, and no isolation. The report in Figure 4.4 babbles on and on, with a rambling summary, extraneous steps, and information on isolation that doesn't help the reader understand the bug.

Ten Steps to Better Bug Reports

I once heard someone at a conference say that in his organization, programmers kicked back almost half of the bug reports filed to the test team as irreproducible, no-fault-found, works-as-designed, or otherwise not actionable. If I saw such a rate of bug report rejection on one of my projects, I would take that as indicating a process break-down requiring immediate resolution: All that time wasted writing those bug reports; the frustration and damage to team cohesion between programmers and testers; and, worst of all, no opportunity to improve product quality.

Some number of bug reports will always be irreproducible or contested. Some bugs exhibit symptoms only intermittently, under obscure or extreme conditions. In some cases, such as system crashes and database corruption, the symptoms of the bug often destroy the information needed to track down the bug. Inconsistencies between test environments and the programmers' systems sometimes lead to the "works fine on my system" response. On some projects without clear requirements, there can be reason-able differences of opinion over what is "correct" behavior under certain test condi-tions. Sometimes testers misinterpret test results and report bugs when the real problem is bad test procedures, bad test data, or incorrect test cases. We'll look at all of these non-bug-report related causes of non-actionable bug reports in the next few chapters, but in the meantime I'll just say that, on my projects, less than 20 percent of bugs fall into such categories. If I saw that 50 percent of my team's bug reports were ending up in the garbage can, I'd suspect a bad bug reporting process.

To prevent such problems, I have developed a 10-step process that I use as a guideline and checklist for experienced testers, and as a training tool for people new to testing.

1. **Structure:** Test thoughtfully and carefully, whether you're doing exploratory or scripted, manual or automated testing.

2. **Reproduce:** My usual rule of thumb is to try to reproduce the failure three times. If the problem is intermittent, report the rate of occurrence; for example, one in three tries, two in three tries, and so forth.

3. **Isolate:** See if you can identify variables—for example, configuration changes, workflow, data sets—that might change the symptoms of the bug.

4. **Generalize:** Look for places that the bug's symptoms might occur in other parts of the system, using different data, and so forth, especially where more severe symptoms might exist.

5. **Compare:** Review the results of running similar tests, especially if you're repeat-ing a test run previously.

6. **Summarize:** Write a short sentence that relates the symptom observed to the customers' or users' experiences of quality, keeping in mind that in many bug review or triage meetings, the summary is the only part of the bug report that is read.

7. **Condense:** Trim any unnecessary information, especially extraneous test steps.

8. **Disambiguate:** Use clear words, avoiding especially words that have multiple distinct or contradictory meanings; for example, "The ship had a bow on its bow," and "Proper oversight prevents oversights," respectively.

9. **Neutralize:** Express yourself impartially, making statements of fact about the bug and its symptoms and avoiding hyperbole, humor, or sarcasm; remember, you never know who'll end up reading your bug report.

10. **Review:** Have at least one peer, ideally an experienced test engineer or the test manager, read the bug report before you submit it.

The point of this process is not to produce homogeneous bug reports, but rather to ensure that every bug report that comes out of my team is accurate, concise, well-conceived, and of the highest quality. By working through this process with my test teams, I instill a focus on writing good bug reports. By applying this process on my projects, my testers consistently produce bug reports that are clear to project management, actionable by the developers, and quickly repaired.

Because of the quality of our bug reports, my test teams enjoy improved communication to senior and peer management, which enhances credibility, standing, and our access to needed resources. My testers have excellent relationships with their programmer peers, because we are providing the programmers with useful information as well as avoiding pointless arguments over bug reports. The faster, more efficient bug life cycles mean quicker fixes, fewer reopens, and thus less time spent retesting and quicker conclusion to each test phase. All together, I think that focusing on writing good bug reports is one of the most important things the test manager can do to support increased product quality.[3]

Flexible Reporting: Beginning to Construct a Database

You could implement every piece of advice in the previous section in a bug reporting system that relies on email or a flat file. I have seen projects that use spreadsheets or word processors to track bugs, but the reporting options were sparse, limited to little more than a printout of the worksheet or document. (Spreadsheets can summarize and graph data, as discussed later in this chapter, but with poor text reporting capabilities. Word processors have good text formatting, but poor analysis and graphical abilities.) To store, manipulate, search, analyze, and report large volumes of data flexibly, you need a database.

There are certainly many options for commercial and freeware bug tracking databases you could buy. However, many companies do build their own. Therefore, this section explains how to build a bug tracking database using what we've discussed so far. Later sections of this chapter build on this foundation to enhance the database's capabilities. I used Microsoft Access for the database shown here, but you can use StarOffice, FileMaker, Oracle, or any other relational database application. In the course of these discussions, you'll see not only how to build a bug tracking database, but what fields you should look for in a commercial bug tracking system if you decide to buy one.

---

[3]I benefited from an online discussion with Bret Pettichord on the SWTEST-Discuss newsgroup when I was thinking through these ten steps. Pettichord is the coauthor, with Cem Kaner and James Bach, of *Lessons Learned in Software Testing*, an expert on test automation, and all around nice guy.

Minimally, a bug tracking database stores failure descriptions—summary, steps to reproduce, and isolation—together with identifying information such as a sequential ID number, the project name, the author of the report, and the date the report was filed. Figure 4.5 shows the design view of an Access table (*tblBugs*) that stores this basic information. I've used the memo data type in Access for the *Steps to Reproduce* and *Isolation* fields because entries in these fields can be rather long. If you want to restrict these entries to a particular size to prevent excessive verbiage, you can use a text field rather than a memo field. The *Bug ID* identifier is a sequential number assigned by the AutoNumber feature in Access. The *Date Opened* field uses the standard Access date/time data type, formatted as a short date because you don't need to capture the specific time when the bug report was filed.

Because entering text directly into an Access table is cumbersome, you can set up a form for entering bug reports. I used the Access 2000 Form Wizard to create the bug entry form shown in Figure 4.6, and then entered the SpeedyWriter bug report you saw earlier in Figure 4.1.

Once you've put a bug report into your database, you'll probably want to get it out at some point. I used the Access 2000 Report Wizard (with a few design adjustments) to create two reports in about five minutes. The simplest is the bug detail report, which prints all the information about the bug; Figure 4.7 provides an example. I usually produce a more compact report for management that has just the summary, the tester, and the date opened, too.

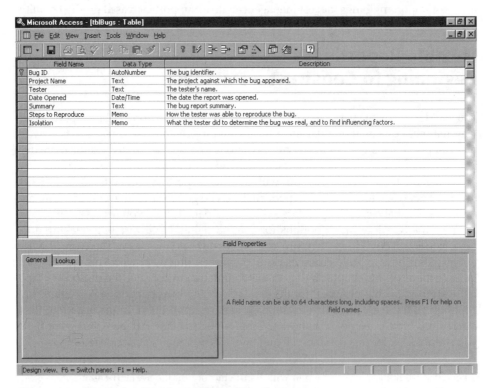

Figure 4.5 The design for a basic bug tracking database.

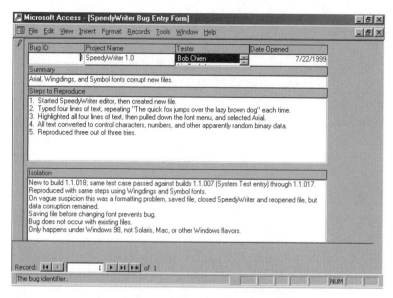

Figure 4.6 A bug report in the SpeedyWriter bug database, using a bug entry form.

The Vital Few and the Trivial Many: Ranking Importance

This database can capture details about bugs found by test, but it doesn't yet contain a mechanism that allows you to assign levels of importance to bugs. To solve this problem,

SpeedyWriter Bug Detail

Bug ID	Project Name	Tester	Date Opened
1	SpeedyWriter 1.0	Bob Chien	7/22/1999

Summary

Arial, Wingdings, and Symbol fonts corrupt new files.

Steps to Reproduce

1. Started SpeedyWriter editor, then created new file.
2. Typed four lines of text, repeating "The quick fox jumps over the lazy brown dog" each time.
3. Highlighted all four lines of text, then pulled down the font menu, and selected Arial.
4. All text converted to control characters, numbers, and other apparently random binary data.
5. Reproduced three out of three tries.

Isolation

New to build 1.1.018; same test case passed against builds 1.1.007 (System Test entry) through 1.1.017.
Reproduced with same steps using Wingdings and Symbol fonts.
On vague suspicion this was a formatting problem, saved file, closed SpeedyWriter and reopened file, but data corruption remained.
Saving file before changing font prevents bug.
Bug does not occur with existing files.
Only happens under Windows 98, not Solaris, Mac, or other Windows flavors.

Figure 4.7 A bug detail report.

you can add two metrics of importance—severity and priority—and then aggregate them to create a third, compound metric.

The first metric is *severity*. By severity, I mean the impact, immediate or delayed, of a bug on the system under test, regardless of the likelihood of occurrence under end-user conditions or the affect such a bug would have on users. I often use the same scale I used for failure mode and effect analysis (see Chapter 1):

1. Loss of data, hardware damage, or a safety issue.
2. Loss of functionality with no workaround.
3. Loss of functionality with a workaround.
4. Partial loss of functionality.
5. Cosmetic or trivial.

The second metric is *priority*. I use priority to capture the elements of importance not considered in severity, such as the likelihood of occurrence in actual customer use and the subsequent impact on the target customer. When determining priority, you can also consider whether this kind of bug is prohibited by regulation or agreement, what kinds of customers are affected, and the cost to the company if the affected customers take their business elsewhere because of the bug. Again, I find a scale like the priority scale used in the FMEA useful:

1. Complete loss of system value.
2. Unacceptable loss of system value.
3. Possibly acceptable reduction in system value.
4. Acceptable reduction in system value.
5. Negligible reduction in system value.

Priority and severity are not completely independent, but it is possible to have low-priority, high-severity bugs, and vice versa. If DataRocket, for example, doesn't pass the Microsoft Windows standards certification test, the product's advertising, promotional materials, and sales pitches can't use the "Designed for Microsoft Windows" logo. This can be the kiss of death for a computer system, since logos are often checklist items for corporate purchasers. Even if the bug that crops up in the Windows NT certification test is entirely cosmetic—a severity 5—it is a priority-1 bug if it blocks certification.

Conversely, suppose that to recreate SpeedyWriter's hypothetical bug, the tester had to type one line of Arial text, followed by one line in a symbol font and then another line of Arial. The problem is a severity-1 bug because data is lost. However, what are the odds of a user typing exactly three lines of text, formatting the first as Arial, the second as symbols, and the third as Arial without saving at any point in the process? Despite its severity rating, I would assign this bug a priority of 4 or 5.

What you need is a single number that captures the overall importance of a bug. We created a similar number in Chapter 1 as part of the FMEA approach to ranking quality risks: in FMEA, you multiply severity by priority by likelihood to create a risk priority number. For purposes of the bug tracking database, you can ignore the likelihood factor (since the bug was likely enough that it occurred during testing) and simply multiply severity by priority to calculate a risk priority number (RPN) for the bug.

Using this approach, the RPN can range from 1 (an extremely dangerous bug) to 25 (a completely trivial bug).

The database modifications associated with adding these metrics of importance are straightforward. In the bug table, you can add three fields: *Severity*, *Priority*, and *Risk Priority Number*. I use numeric fields of the "byte" type, not so much to save space as to emphasize the appropriate range.

Next, you should make the corresponding changes in the bug entry form, adding the three fields and then automating the calculation of the risk priority number. (The automation of the calculation can be tricky, depending on your expertise with the database package you're using. Since this is a book on testing, not on database programming, I've omitted the details of exactly how it's done in Access, but you can look at the sample database available at www.rexblackconsulting.com for examples.) To include the measures of importance in the detail and summary reports, simply insert the appropriate fields. Of course, if you include these fields in your table from the beginning, the Report Wizard can pick them up automatically.

Putting the Tracking in Bug Tracking: Adding Dynamic Information

So far, you have a database that is fine for *reporting* bugs but not for *tracking* them. It still lacks a way to include dynamic information, a mechanism to trace the steps through which a bug must move on its way to resolution. Having this information available would allow you to answer questions such as these: Who is currently responsible for pushing the bug toward closure? Is the resolution process "stuck" or moving forward smoothly? When will the bug be fixed?

Using States to Manage Bug Life Cycles

The aim of reporting problems is to bring them to the attention of the appropriate people, who will then cause the most important bugs to be fixed—or will at least attempt to have them fixed. The test organization then must either confirm or rebut the possible fixes. Other possible outcomes for a particular bug report include its cancellation as a nonproblem, its closure as redundant, or its indefinite dormancy because of a lack of interest. In other words, a bug report should go through an identifiable lifecycle, with clear ownership at each phase or state in its life cycle.

While the appropriate life cycle for your organization might vary, here's one life cycle I've used:

Review. When a tester enters a new bug report in the bug tracking database, the bug tracking database holds it for review before it becomes visible outside the test team. (If nontesters can report bugs directly into the system, then the managers of those nontesters should determine the review process for those nontester bug reports.)

Rejected. If the reviewer decides that a report needs significant rework—either more research and information or improved wording—the reviewer rejects the report. This effectively sends the report back to the tester, who can then submit a revised report for another review.

Open. If the tester has fully characterized and isolated the problem, the reviewer opens the report, making it visible to the world as a known bug.

Assigned. The appropriate project team member(s) assign it to the appropriate development manager, who in turn assigns the bug to a developer, or assigns the bug to the test team for further research and isolation. (See *Guiding the Bug Life Cycle: The Bug Triage Process* later in the chapter.)

Test. Once development provides a fix for the problem, it enters a test state. The bug fix comes to the test organization for confirmation testing (which ensures that the proposed fix completely resolves the bug as reported) and regression testing (which addresses the question of whether the fix has introduced new problems as a side effect).

Reopened. If the fix fails confirmation testing, the tester reopens the bug report. If the fix passes confirmation testing but fails regression testing, the tester opens a new bug report.

Closed. If the fix passes confirmation testing, the tester closes the bug report.

Deferred. If appropriate project team member(s) decide that the problem is real, but choose either to assign a low priority to the bug or to schedule the fix for a subsequent release, the bug is deferred. Note that a bug can be deferred at any point in its life cycle. (See *Guiding the Bug Life Cycle: The Bug Triage Process* later in the chapter.)

Figure 4.8 shows these states and the flows between them. Terminal states—in other words, states in which a bug report's life cycle might terminate and the bug report become legitimately inactive with no further action required or expected—are shown with heavy lines. Flows out of such states are shown with dotted lines, since they are optional. The exception is the case of a previously closed bug report whose symptoms are found to have returned. In this case, the closed bug report should be reopened.

Emphasizing Ownership and Accountability

While the state of a bug gives hints about what needs to happen next, tracking the assigned owner of a bug as well as the intended fix date provides a rudder to keep the process sailing toward a conclusion. Emphasizing personal ownership of a problem and setting an estimated fix date serve to cement commitments and support accountability. In addition, a bug sometimes blocks forward progress in the testing effort, and having some idea of its fix date allows you to plan the resumption of the blocked tests.

As the state diagram in Figure 4.8 shows, bugs can be reassigned, and such changes often shift the estimated fix date. If this is a problem in your organization, you can institute an assignment history, similar to (or part of) the status log discussed in the next section. (I haven't had that much trouble with "bouncing ball" bug reports, however, so I normally don't track at this level of detail.)

The bug tracking system should track not only developer ownership, but also tester ownership. When a bug returns to the test organization, the bug tracking system

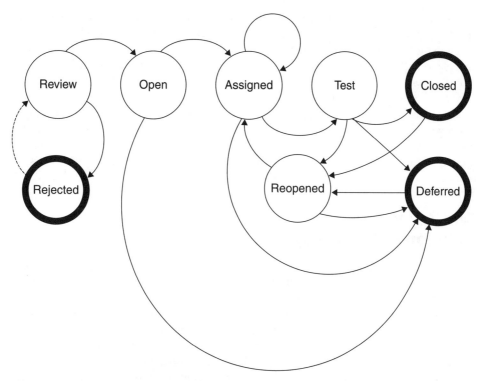

Figure 4.8 A bug report life cycle or workflow.

should assign a tester to perform the confirmation and regression tests. In other words, as soon as the fix arrives in the next build or test release, the tester verifies the fix and then closes or reopens the bug. The tester might also open a new bug report if regression testing indicated that the programmer has broken something new in the course of attempting the fix. This use of ownership in the test organization helps the test manager track expeditious resolution of bugs, and identify and resolve any blockages that arise in the bug life cycle.

Good bug tracking systems often allow owners and stakeholders to log notes and history for a bug report as it progresses along its life cycle. That is, the appropriate testers, programmers, and managers can add a log entry to the bug report, especially when a bug reports goes through a state change. After a bug is assigned, for example, the development manager might note to whom it was assigned, when, and under what circumstances. When the fix comes back to the test organization, the test manager might enter a comment that development believes the problem is resolved. However, don't feel compelled to make a log of everything. The status entry *7/16: Muhammad assigned the bug to John* is useful; the entry *7/17: Had a five-minute discussion in the lunchroom with John about how the bug manifests itself* is not. The status log should capture significant events in the life cycle of the bug, not serve as a diary.

Ultimately, the states in a bug report life cycle or workflow represent the key players in the bug find and repair cycles that arise naturally on most development and maintenance efforts. The transitions between states represent handoffs between those key players. A good bug tracking system should allow you to implement whatever workflow would be appropriate in your particular development or maintenance context. The more automation the tool can provide—for example, sending email to the stakeholders when a bug changes state—the better the tool can support the workflow. However, process automation is only half the battle. Each project team member, the project managers (including the test manager), and the appropriate people in charge of the bug triage process must all play their parts with diligence and alacrity to ensure that each bug report moves expeditiously through the life cycle to a terminal state.

One Key Handoff: Isolation to Debugging

One key bug reporting handoff exists between the tester and the programmer when the underlying bug report goes from being isolated to being debugged. The responsibilities of the test organization and the developers meet at this boundary. (In terms of the state diagram in Figure 4.8, this is the line connecting the open and assigned states.) Because of the frequency with which this handoff occurs during most test projects, and because of the opportunity for miscommunication over the boundary between isolation and debugging, the sharpness of the distinction you draw between the two has a lot to do with the control you have over your scarce test resources.

Any time a tester observes a difference between actual and expected results or behavior (what some test experts call an *anomaly*), that observation should set in motion the appropriate bug life cycle. Along this life cycle, a series of questions must be answered:

1. What is the exact and minimal sequence of steps required to reproduce the symptoms of the bug? How often do these steps successfully reproduce it?

2. Does the failure indicate a test bug or a system bug? In other words, does the anomalous result originate from a test artifact or a tester error, or from system misbehavior that could affect customers?

3. What external factors influence the symptoms? In the SpeedyWriter example, one way the tester looked for influential factors was by trying different fonts.

4. What is the root cause of the problem, in the code, the electronics, the network, or the environment? Root causes are internal factors.

5. How can the problem be repaired without introducing new problems?

6. Are the changes properly debugged?

7. Is the problem fixed? Does it now pass the same test it failed before, and does the rest of the system still behave properly?

Step 1 proves that the bug is not a fluke and refines the experiment. Steps 2 and 3 isolate the bug. Steps 4, 5, and 6 are debugging tasks. Step 7 involves confirmation and regression testing. Figure 4.9 shows these questions in the context of players and handoffs.

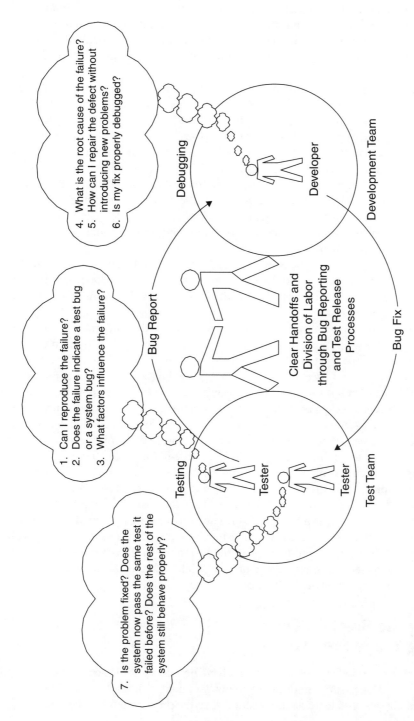

Figure 4.9 Questions, players, and handoffs in the bug life cycle.

In moving through the life cycle, the bug moves through and out of the test team (steps 1, 2, and 3), into the programming or engineering team (steps 4, 5, and 6), and then back into test (step 7). While this flow of responsibility might seem straight-forward and obvious, defining and consistently observing it, especially the bound-ary between steps 3 and 4, can involve a significant amount of rigor, discipline, and will power.

In the excitement and pressure of test execution, the first four steps can get mixed up. Testers sometimes fail to characterize and isolate bugs completely, which results in uncertainty about the reproducibility, veracity, and nature of the bugs. The programmers and engineers—quite correctly—then get the testers involved in ongoing question-and-answer sessions as part of their debugging work. The testers, who have plenty of other work on their plates, are sucked into debugging, which is a development responsibility. The developers are forced to ask the testers a lot of central questions that the testers should have answered when they wrote their reports. As a result, person-hours, the most precious resource on any project, are squandered. Through failure of clear handoffs, the productivity-enhancing tactics of division of labor and specialization of roles are defeated. To me, that's unacceptable.

When you review bug reports, or when you have your staff review one another's reports, be sure that the answers to the questions in steps 1, 2, and 3 are crystal clear. This way, you can draw the line between isolation and debugging distinctly and keep your testers focused on testing.

It is true, however, that testers must sometimes assist developers in debugging activities, especially when the test team has unique hardware items tied up in the test network, when the test system—tools, scripts, and environment—requires special expertise to operate and is essential to reproducing the bug, or when a bug, for what-ever reason, proves irreproducible in the development lab. Most of the time, though, when I have observed testers become involved in debugging it was for dysfunctional reasons. In some cases, it was my fault as the test manager for not adequately commu-nicating the difference between isolation and debugging to the project team. In other cases, the tester wrote a poor bug report (this set of circumstances became less of a problem for me when I implemented the bug reporting process and techniques out-lined in this chapter). Sometimes, programmers or engineers don't accept bugs reports as complete and accurate even though they are. These three cases are typically process problems that I can resolve as a test manager. The fourth case is a motivational or per-sonnel management issue that arises when testers find it more interesting to work with the programmer or engineer on debugging than to move on to other testing. For all these cases, you must either limit the extent to which this happens or accept the signif-icant drain it will impose on your resources.

Guiding the Bug Life Cycle: The Bug Triage Process

For some of the states in Figure 4.8, you might have noticed multiple arrows coming out of a single state. These represent decision points happening within the state. One of the most interesting sets of state transitions occurs when the project team decides whether to defer work on a bug report, especially in that initial decision when the bug report moves either from: open to assigned; or, open to deferred. How does this decision get made?

In some cases, this is a small, obvious decision. If a bug's symptom is obviously a high priority (e.g., very visible and/or dangerous to many users), if the bug is obvious in its fix (e.g., a misspelled message or a simple logic error) and the impact to the tester and programmer of fixing the bug is minimal (e.g., 15 minutes to repair the code and five minutes to confirm the fix in the next test release), then some number of bugs can be resolved at the discretion of the testers and programmers involved. At some point, a large number of these types of bugs becomes a management issue, but often I've seen this be a process that can proceed in the background with minimal management attention.

However, some bugs have unclear priority, might well require an unknown and possibly extensive effort to fix, might require significant effort (including build and test effort) to integrate and confirm, or some combination of these three factors. In such a case, the project management team must intervene in some fashion to make the fix/defer decision. There are two common approaches that I've seen, and both can work. One is the bug triage or bug review committee, and the other is a change control board (CCB).

A bug triage or bug review committee is a subset of the overall project team. Typical attendees include the test manager, the project manager, the development manager, the release engineering or build manager, and some senior technical experts. There are often attendees to represent the users and customers. On a mass-market system, these might include the sales, marketing, and technical support managers. For an in-house IT project, the project sponsor and senior users of the system might attend. In custom development efforts, I have often seen the client send attendees.[4]

The committee meets regularly—as often as once a day—to review the bugs opened or reopened since the last meeting, and decide, for each bug, whether and when to fix it. The primary driver of this decision is the bug's priority, which might be adjusted upward or downward by the committee. However, schedule and budget implications are also considered. For example, a bug that blocks significant chunks of testing will usually be scheduled for repair ahead of other bugs, because finishing text execution is on the critical path for finishing the project.

A CCB serves a similar function, but has a broader scope. Not only will a CCB decide on whether bugs should be fixed, but they generally also decide on changes proposed for the requirements, design, user interface, supported configurations, and other significant adjustments to the project plan. CCBs sometimes have broad powers to decide on changes in budget and schedule, too, although in some organizations these decisions are reserved for senior managers. CCBs are often comprised of the same sort of people as a bug triage committee, although more powerful CCBs tend to include more senior managers, too.[5]

There are plenty of possible variations to the bug triage process. I am not a partisan for any particular approach, because each organization needs to adopt a bug triage process that works in its context. The important aspect to me is that the bug triage

---

[4]Even though it's a book ostensibly for children, Robert Sabourin's *I am a Bug* includes an insightful discussion of the bug life cycle, including the triage process.
[5]A good discussion of change control boards can be found in Steve McConnell's *Software Project Survival Guide*.

process includes the input of the major stakeholders. (The people who participated in the quality risk analysis discussed in Chapter 1 might be a good place to start.) Part of keeping all these busy professionals involved is having a CCB or bug triage meeting duration and frequency that works for the entire team. Keeping the meeting focused on bugs and moving quickly through a tight list of bugs is essential. To help with that, I have three suggestions:

- All participants should come to the meeting either prepared to make a recommendation on any particular bug, or prepared to abstain from discussion about that bug. These meetings will end up lasting too long if extensive Q&A sessions are required to explain each bug to the participants.

- Try to limit the discussion on each bug to five minutes or less, and discuss only bugs and the direct ramifications of bugs. Schedule the meetings frequently enough that the meeting takes an hour or less. This should be possible for any project where the bug find rate does not exceed 60 per week.

- Make the decision to fix or defer each bug exactly once and in the first meeting in which that bug is addressed. Avoid the temptation for "analysis paralysis" or a Hamlet-like debate ("to fix or not to fix, that is the question") that allows a single bug report to eat up an hour of the team's time over the course of a dozen meetings.

Like all rules of thumb, exceptions will arise, but in my experience, few bugs really need an exception to one or more of these rules. If you find that more than, say, 10 percent of the bugs require extensive discussion, Q&A sessions, or revisiting during the project, ask yourself if there's not a change you could make to some other process to reduce that number. Bug triage committees and CCBs are powerful techniques for balancing quality, schedule, budget, and features on a project, but they can easily become bureaucratic, time-wasting tar pits. Once that happens, people will find (rightfully so) convenient excuses not to attend.

Putting the Dynamic Fields in Place

You can easily add all this dynamic information to your bug tracking database. You'll need to add four fields to the table and the form: *State*, *Owner*, *Estimated Fix Date*, and *Log*. *State* and *Owner* are text fields, with the entry selected from a list box. *Estimated Fix Date* uses a standard Access date/time data type, formatted as a short date. It's probably most useful to define *Log* as a memo field, although you can, for reasons of space, use a text field. (You could also use an external table linked through a foreign key with a separate row for each entry. Implementing such a database, however, involves database programming, which is beyond the scope of this book.)

Figure 4.10 shows the bug entry form with the four new fields; Figure 4.11 shows the updated version of the bug detail report. I include all four of these fields in all my reports, including the bug summary report. Doing so crowds the detail report a bit, but it's worth it because I use that report as a management tool, and the addition of these fields makes the report even more valuable.

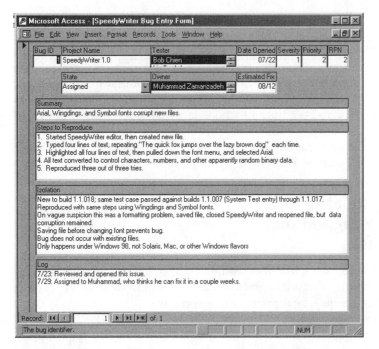

Figure 4.10 A bug entry form with dynamic information.

SpeedyWriter Bug Detail

Bug ID	Project Name		Tester	State	Date Opened
1	SpeedyWriter 1.0		Bob Chien	Assigned	7/22/1999

Severity	Priority	Risk Priority Number	Owner		Estimated Fix
1	2	2	Muhammad Zamanzadeh		8/12/1999

Summary

Arial, Wingdings, and Symbol fonts corrupt new files.

Steps to Reproduce

1. Started SpeedyWriter editor, then created new file.
2. Typed four lines of text, repeating "The quick fox jumps over the lazy brown dog" each time.
3. Highlighted all four lines of text, then pulled down the font menu, and selected Arial.
4. All text converted to control characters, numbers, and other apparently random binary data.
5. Reproduced three out of three tries.

Isolation

New to build 1.1.018; same test case passed against builds 1.1.007 (System Test entry) through 1.1.017.
Reproduced with same steps using Wingdings and Symbol fonts.
On vague suspicion this was a formatting problem, saved file, closed SpeedyWriter and reopened file, but data corruption remained.
Saving file before changing font prevents bug.
Bug does not occur with existing files.
Only happens under Windows 98, not Solaris, Mac, or other Windows flavors

Log

7/23: Reviewed and opened this issue.
7/29: Assigned to Muhammad, who thinks he can fix it in a couple weeks.

Figure 4.11 A bug detail report with dynamic information.

Finishing Touches: Capturing Bug Data for Analysis

You now have a fully adequate bug tracking database that you can use to manage bugs through their entire lifecycle, to produce summary reports for management and detail reports for developers, and to keep track of who is responsible for moving bugs forward. You might want to design additional reports or make some cosmetic changes, but the database is essentially complete. To gather some additional data that can bring bugs into sharper focus, however, I recommend that you add a few more fields.

What the Bug Relates To: Subsystem, Configuration, and Quality Risks

Some of the data you might want to gather would help you understand what the bug is related to. In other words, what is the context for the bug? There are a number of data elements you could gather here, but I prefer to focus on three.

Adding a *Subsystem* field allows you to captures which component of the system bears the brunt of each bug's symptoms. In our DataRocket case study, for example, subsystems might break down as follows:

Mainboard. The CPU, the motherboard, the memory, the on-board fans, and common built-in controllers for the USB, parallel, serial, mouse, and keyboard ports.

Video. The video card and, if bundled, the video cable and monitor.

SCSI. The SCSI adapter, the internal cables, the external cables, the RAID hardware, the tape drive, and the CD-RW drive.

Network. The controller configuration, which can involve one or more cards.

Telecommunications. The optional bundled modem(s), the ISDN terminal adapter, or the computer-telephony-integration hardware.

Other hardware. The case, the power supply, the mouse, and the keyboard.

BIOS. The features controlled by the BIOS, especially power management and boot-up passwords.

Other software. Any custom drivers, such as bundled custom network drivers, as well as any preinstalled network operating systems that might ship on the system.

For SpeedyWriter, you might choose to decompose the subsystems this way:

User interface. The behavior of the graphical user interface (GUI), including video, mouse, and keyboard aspects, such as screen painting, print previews, windowing, and all command selection sequences.

Tools. The ability to check spelling, use a thesaurus, track revisions, create tables, display graphs, insert files and other objects, draw pictures, and so forth.

File. Create, open, save/save as, and export and import features.

Edit engine. The formatting, editing, font selection, footnote/endnote features, and so on.

Install/config. The installation, configuration, reconfiguration, and upgrade processes.

Docs/packaging. The documentation, help files, or packaging.

In addition to system-dependent components, you might include three catchall subsystems to deal with exceptional situations:

Other. The bug affects a particular subsystem, but not one that is listed.

Unknown. The bug doesn't appear to have anything to do with any subsystem.

N/A. No subsystem applies.

Usually a small fraction—less than 5 percent on most of my projects—of the total bugs will fit into each of these three categories. If the number is larger, the Other category is probably picking up too many bugs that should have their own subsystem category.

As you've probably noticed, the division of a system into subsystems is arbitrary. In some cases, especially projects in which different teams work on each subsystem, the task is easier. Regardless, you need to establish a subsystem breakdown that is meaningful for each project, because you can't categorize if everyone decides for themselves what subsystems exist in the system under test.

Moving on to the next data element, consider adding a *Configuration* field or fields to tracking the test release and test environment in which the bug was observed. Projects usually involve multiple revisions of software and hardware, many of which must operate in multiple software, hardware, LAN, WAN, and database environments. Capturing configuration information in the bug tracking database can help you understand the setting in which failures occur.

I often employ multiple configuration fields. These parallel the subsystem values, but it's seldom a complete overlap. For example, with DataRocket you might track the BIOS revision, the mainboard revision, the case version, and the bundled software version.

Alternatively, you can use a lookup table approach. For SpeedyWriter, you might use a combination of letters and numbers to indicate software revisions and the test environment. Suppose that the SpeedyWriter internal revisions are identified in *X.YY.ZZ* format, such as 0.01.19. The systems in the test lab are labeled A, B, C, and D; the three networks (Novell NetWare, Sun Solaris, and Microsoft Windows NT) are assigned the identifiers X, Y, and Z, respectively. A test configuration of an NT workstation connected to a Solaris server with the second major and thirty-third minor revision might thus be designated A.Y.0.2.33. Of course, you must be careful to record details about how to decode or "read" these designations; such a sequence of letters and numbers doesn't exactly explain itself.

The third data element traces the bug back to the test basis that it relates to. (The test basis is foundation for the testing we intend to do.) I generally use quality risks as the basis of my testing, as discussed in Chapter 1. Therefore, I have added a field for this in the bugs table. Both the Failure Mode and Effect Analysis and the informal risk analysis approaches can yield two-level risk categories for quality; in other words, there's the category such as functionality, then the detailed risk element within functionality, such as file operations, editing, printing, and so forth. You should keep this decomposition of risk breakdowns so you can aggregate at the higher level or focus on the lower levels at will.

Some people use requirements, designs, implementation details, and other data as the test basis. In some test approaches, the test basis is derived from these items by creating an inventory of test objectives. In such a situation, you could trace back to the test objective inventory instead of quality risks.

Either way, if you have prioritized the risks, the test objectives, or whatever your chosen test basis, you can set up the database to suggest the associated priority of the basis as the default priority for the bug report. This can help your testers decide what the bug priority should be.

Where the Bug Came From: Resolution and Root Cause

The simplest way to keep track of where bugs come from is to ask the programmers and other engineers who fix the bugs to take a note. By adding a *Resolution* field, this note can be entered to describe how the problem was solved. (Alternatively, you could use the *Status* field for this purpose, but a separate field is more useful for reports.) You can also force completion of this field using Visual Basic for Applications or whatever automation tools your database environment provides. Any time a bug is closed, some notation should be made.

The problem with free-form resolution fields is that it's hard to do analysis on them. In addition, if people forget to write anything down—or write something so cryptic that no one but the engineer who wrote it can figure it out—then you might be missing data for many bugs. The solution to this problem is for the project team—specifically, the development or project manager—to institute a root cause analysis process and a bug taxonomy.

If you are the first test manager your company has ever had, with no exposure to root cause analysis, and your development process consists of hacking and flailing away until the product appears to work, root cause analysis is probably beyond the level of process maturity at your company. (See Chapter 11 for more on development processes and process maturity.) You might want to read this section as information only. Doing root cause analysis is not a trivial undertaking. Furthermore, it requires the assistance of the developers and the support of management.

Simply put, a root cause is the underlying reason for a bug. When you are doing behavioral (black-box) testing, a bug makes its presence known through an observed behavior, a symptom, an anomalous output, data transformation, slow response time, a system crash, an inexplicable delay, or some other visible program transgression. (During structural [white-box and gray-box] testing, you can observe bugs that don't involve program output or behaviors because you have access to internal program states and other information that tells you whether something has gone awry.) Therefore, when a tester doing behavioral testing observes a bug, he sees only the symptom. Taking cough medicine to stop hacking or aspirin to lower a fever doesn't cure a cold because it doesn't address the root cause, the virus that is making you sick.

Some test experts model the connection between root causes and bugs with the sequence of events shown in Figure 4.12. An anomaly occurs when a tester observes an unexpected behavior. If the tester's actions were correct, this anomaly indicates either a system failure or a test failure. The failure arises from a fault in either the system or the test. The fault comes from an error committed by a software or hardware engineer (while creating the system under test) or a test engineer (while creating the test system). That error is the root cause.

This model illustrates the connection between bugs and their root causes in an elegant way, but it suffers from some flaws. First, errors, faults, and failures don't have one-to-one relationships. The trickiest bugs—stability problems, for example—often arise from complex interactions of components, any one of which is not necessarily an error. Next, the conditional language points out that while many events might possibly transpire, sometimes nothing happens at all. Errors don't always cause faults, faults occasionally remain hidden in programs, and failures aren't always observed. Therefore, the model has limitations, but it does create a useful mental picture. That intellectual image can help you think about root causes.

Usually, the aim of performing a root cause analysis isn't to determine the exact error and how it happened. Other than flogging some hapless engineer, you can't do

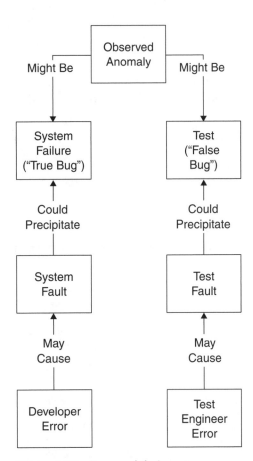

Figure 4.12 Bugs and their root causes.

much with such information. Instead, root cause analysis categorizes bugs into a taxonomy. For DataRocket, you might, in a root cause analysis, assign hardware bugs to one of three categories: design, production, or material. A design bug results from the misuse of a component, a failure to understand the limitations of a chip, inappropriate air flow, or other such "should have/could have known better" failures. A production bug ensues from a failure on the production line—for example, a CPU is improperly inserted and falls out during shock and vibration testing. A material bug occurs when a component misbehaves or fails. (These categories are relative to whether your company buys or sells the failed item. A producer's design failure can cause the consumer to experience a material failure. For example, the Pentium floating-point bug was Intel's design failure, but computer makers experienced a component failure.) In addition to these hardware failures, you need to include at least one category for software failures arising from BIOS bugs.

For software, you might consider the following bug taxonomy, which is based on one originally published by Boris Beizer.[6] While retaining the essentials of the original, I have added two features to the list: explanations and examples associated with the various root causes, and a few bookkeeping categories that will help you deal with unusual cases (Duplicate, NAP, Bad Unit, RCN, and Unknown).

Functional

Specification. The specification is wrong.

Function. The specification is right, but implementation is wrong.

Test. The system works correctly, but the test reports a spurious error.

System

Internal Interface. The internal system communication failed.

Hardware Devices. The hardware failed.

Operating System. The operating system failed.

Software Architecture. A fundamental design assumption proved invalid.

Resource Management. The design assumptions are OK, but some implementation of the assumption is wrong.

Process

Arithmetic. The program incorrectly adds, divides, multiplies, factors, integrates numerically, or otherwise fails to perform an arithmetic operation properly.

Initialization. An operation fails on its first use.

---

[6]This taxonomy is based on the appendix "Bug Taxonomy and Statistics," in *Software Testing Techniques,* 2d ed., by Boris Beizer. Copyright © 1990 by Boris Beizer. Reprinted by permission of the author. Another form of root cause analysis that is becoming quite popular is orthogonal defect classification, created by Ram Chillarege at IBM. See Chillarege's papers on the topic on his Web site, www.chillarege.com. Finally, there is also the IEEE Standard Classification for Software Anomalies, Std 1044-1993 and Std 1044.1-1995.

Control or Sequence. An action occurs at the wrong time or for the wrong reason.

Static Logic. Boundaries are misdefined, logic is invalid, "can't happen" events do happen, "won't matter" events do matter, and so forth.

Other. A control-flow or processing error occurs that doesn't fit in the preceding buckets.

Data

Type. An integer should be a float, an unsigned integer stores or retrieves a negative value, an object is improperly defined, and so forth.

Structure. A complex data structure is invalid or inappropriate.

Initial Value. A data element's initialized value is incorrect. (This might not result in a process initialization error.)

Other. A data-related error occurs that doesn't fit in the preceding buckets.

Code

A typo, misspelling, stylistic error, or other coding error occurs that results in a failure.

Documentation

The documentation says the system does X on condition Y, but the system does Z—a valid and correct action—instead.

Standards

The system fails to meet industry or vendor standards, follow code standards, adhere to naming conventions, and so forth.

Other

The root cause is known, but fits none of the preceding categories.

Duplicate

Two bug reports describe the same bug. (This can happen when two testers report the same symptom, or when two testers report different symptoms that share the same underlying code problem.)

NAP

The bug as described in the bug report is "not a problem" because the operation noted is correct. The report arises from a misunderstanding on the part of the tester about correct behavior. This situation is distinct from a test failure (whose root cause is categorized as *functional/test*) in that this is *tester* failure; that is, human error.

Bad Unit

The bug is a real problem, but it arises from a random hardware failure *that is unlikely to occur in the field.* (If the bug indicates a lack of reliability in some hardware component, this is not the root cause.)

RCN

A "root cause needed"; the bug is confirmed as closed by test, but no one in development has supplied a root cause.

Unknown

No one knows what is broken. This root cause usually fits best when a sporadic bug doesn't appear for quite awhile, leading people to conclude that some other change fixed the bug as a side effect.

Why go to the trouble of capturing this information? First, gathering root cause data allows you to apply the Pareto Principle—focus on the vital few, not the trivial many—when the time comes to try to improve your development process. For example, if most DataRocket failures result from bad components, you should revisit your choice of suppliers. Next, if you use industry-standard bug taxonomies, you can compare root cause statistics for your projects against the averages. You can also accumulate historical data over the course of your projects that you can use for in-house comparisons. Finally, if you know where bugs are apt to originate, you can tailor your test effort to hit those areas particularly hard. By combining root cause data with subsystem breakdowns, you can get a good idea of what breaks in which parts of the system.

How Long Was the Bug Around? Close Date and the Injection, Detection, and Removal Phases

In addition to tracking where the bug came from, it's useful to know how long it was in the system. We can capture a couple of different sets of data to answer this question. The easiest is to keep track of the length of time the bug is known active—in other words, the time from initial discovery to confirmation of closure or deferral—which we can do by capturing not only the open date but also the date on which the bug report entered a closed or deferred state. Entering this date in the *Close Date* field is more than simply tidying up your records; you'll see how this piece of information comes into its own later in this chapter, when we discuss extracting metrics from your database.

The more sophisticated set of data we can track has to do with when the bug was originally created, when we found it, and when we confirmed it fixed. While we could do this by date, the more typical way to handle this is by project phase. The specific phases that you have in your projects will vary depending on your system life cycle (see Chapter 11), but for the moment let's assume that your projects consist of eight phases:

Requirements. The activities in which the project team figures out what the system is to do.

Design. The activities in which the project team figures out how the system will do what it does.

Implementation. The activities in which the project team implements the requirements according to the design.

Component Test. The activities in which the project team looks for and repairs bugs in the constituent pieces of the system.

Integration Test. The activities in which the project team looks for and repairs bugs in the interaction of components.

System Test. The activities in which the project team looks for and repairs bugs in the entire system, fully integrated.

Acceptance Test. The activities in which the project team demonstrates that the system meets requirements.

Post-Release. The activities in which the project team supports the system in the field.

A *defect removal model* analyzes, for all eight phases, the bugs *injected* (or created), the bugs *detected* (found through testing or quality assurance), and the bugs *removed* (through repair, confirmation testing, and regression testing) in each phase of testing. The concept of defect removal models is a sophisticated one, well beyond the scope of this book.[7] However, in order to support the data collection needed, the bug management process will need the engineering team to identify the *Phase Injected*, and the test team to identify the *Phase Detected* and *Phase Removed*. The bug tracking system will need to capture these three values for each bug.

The reason for capturing these two sets of data is to look for opportunities to improve our processes. It turns out that bugs found and fixed in the same phase in which they're created are much less dangerous to the project in terms of schedule and budget. Therefore, defect removal models allow us to analyze the number of bugs that *escape* from one phase to the next. Keeping this metric small reduces the likelihood of schedule slips and budget overruns. Similarly, within a phase, the shorter the period of time the bug is open, the less risk there is of delay in meeting the exit criteria for that phase. I'll show you ways to present the "bug lifetime" metric in the last section of this chapter, but first, let's finish up our bug tracking database.

The Finalized Bug Tracking Database

The data-capturing fields that we'll add now all allow us to categorize a bug report. In a database, we can do this a couple of ways. One is to pick from a fixed list of possible items. This works for values that won't change over time. In this case, the *Phase Injected*, *Phase Detected*, *Phase Removed*, *Severity*, *Priority*, and *Root Cause* fields won't change, so we can implement them as Microsoft Access combo boxes that present a list of valid values to the user.

For values that will change over time, having the database look up the valid values and present that list to the user is the way to go. This involves providing a separate table and using a query to retrieve the information from that table. For our database, there are five fields that fall into this category: *Tester*, *Owner*, *Configuration*, *Subsystem*, and *Quality Risk*. Let's look at *Subsystem* for an example of how this works, as all five work in substantially the same fashion.

---

[7] Pankoj Jalote's *CMM in Practice* and Kan's *Metrics and Models in Software Quality* address this topic in details, including the schedule and budget implications of these metrics.

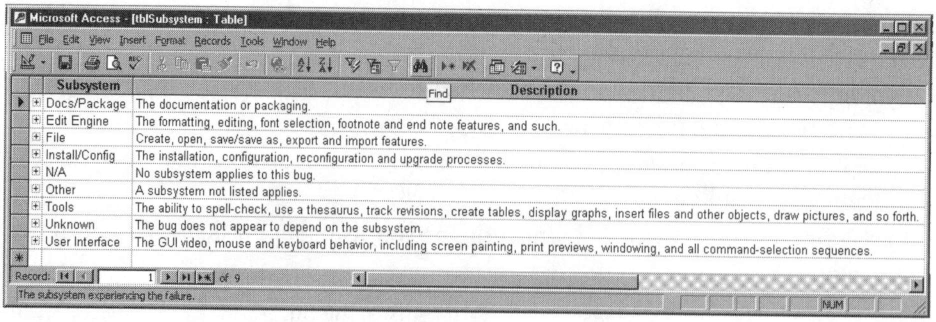

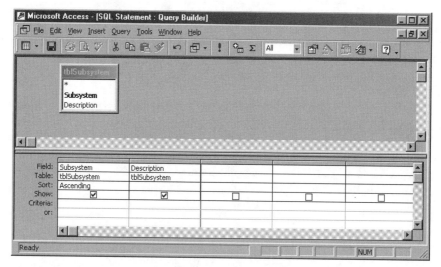

Figure 4.13   The subsystem lookup table.

Figure 4.13 shows the subsystem lookup table. It's just two text fields, one with the subsystem mnemonic, the other with a more complete description of the subsystem. Figure 4.14 shows the query that is used to get these values for bug entry form, and Figure 4.15 shows the definition for the subsystem combo box on the bug entry form. Finally, you can see the added fields in Figure 4.16, which shows the completed bug entry form. (Try it on your own system to see how the table lookup shows up in the pulldown combo box.) I include all of these fields in the bug detail report, but might leave them out of the bug summary report for brevity.

Figure 4.14   Subsystem lookup query.

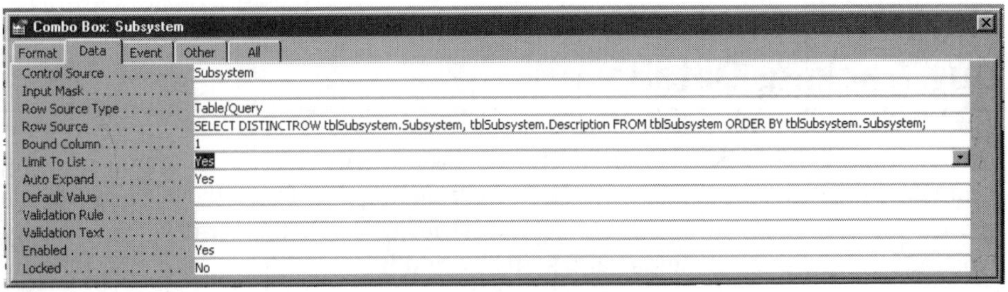

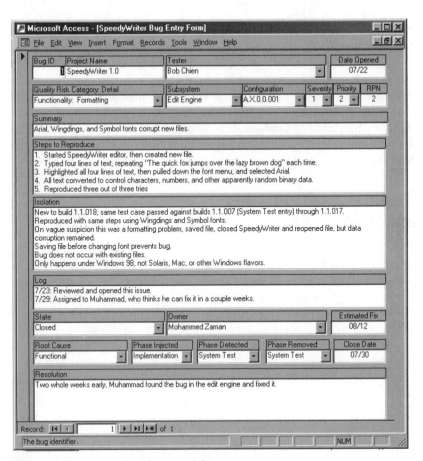

Figure 4.15   Subsystem combo box definition on bug entry form.

Figure 4.16   A complete bug entry form.

Extracting Metrics from the Bug Tracking Database

The bug reports just described are useful in and of themselves, but the bug tracking database can be a source of even more information. Bug data forms the basis of various quality control charts in a number of industries (though the term *bug* is usually replaced by *defect* in other fields), and software and hardware are no exception. Using this bug tracking database, you can generate bug analysis charts that allow you to see patterns your bug data. These charts are also excellent for communicating with management because they highlight and illustrate test results that are difficult to explain with raw data.

The following sections introduce some powerful and easy-to-generate charts. These charts will allow you to communicate testing status related to bugs in terms of trends. By communicating in terms of trends, you can summarize key facts. This allows you to get your points across quickly and visually. It also promotes management of the project by key indicators, rather than whatever crisis happens to be going on at the time. These defect charts make up a key part of what I refer to as the *test dashboard*, which I'll discuss again in the Chapter 5, "Managing Test Cases: The Test Tracking Spreadsheet," and Chapter 9, "The Triumph of Politics: Organizational Challenges for Test Managers."

I create these charts typically by exporting data from a bug tracking database into a spreadsheet. I set up the example spreadsheets for these charts using the Access bug tracking database we built in this chapter. I've populated the sample spreadsheets with various dummy data sets to create these charts. The data is manipulated to illustrate points, so please don't assume that these charts necessarily represent a "typical" project. If you already have a bug tracking database, or have bug data in some other format that you can easily get into a spreadsheet, I'd encourage you to load your own data into the *Bugs* worksheet of the spreadsheet and see what these charts look like for your projects.[8]

How Defect Removal Proceeds: The Opened/Closed Chart

The most basic defect analysis chart plots the cumulative number of bugs opened against the cumulative number closed or deferred on a daily basis. For brevity, I refer to it as the *opened/closed* (or the *found/fixed*) chart. Figure 4.17 presents a sample chart, which offers a general view of the development project's status, taken during the middle of the System Test phase.

This information-rich chart provides answers to a number of questions. First, are you ready to ship the product? Since the number of bugs in a given program is unknown but is essentially a fixed number once development ends, test projects eventually hit a point at which further testing produces diminishing returns.[9] When the

---

[8] For more charts that might be useful, see Kan's *Metrics and Models in Software Quality Engineering*, or Chapter Nine of Beizer's *Software System Testing and Quality Assurance*.

[9] I have, however, worked on projects in which the incidence of regression was so high that it seemed as if each fix release closed six bugs and caused a dozen new ones.

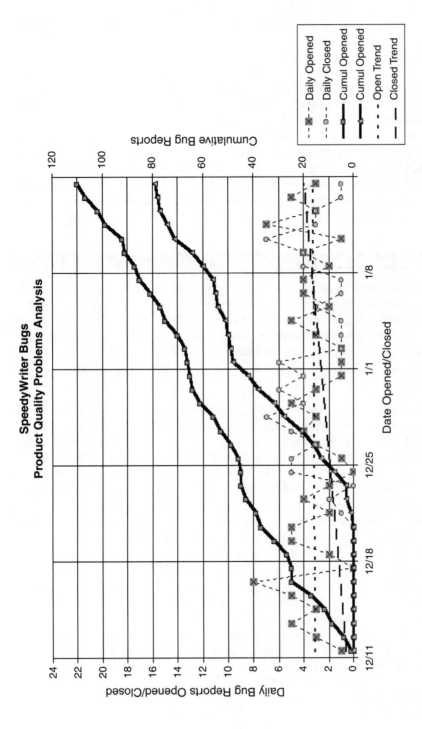

Figure 4.17 An opened/closed chart for SpeedyWriter.

cumulative opened curve—the top curve on the chart in Figure 4.17—levels off at an asymptotic limit, testing is usually considered complete, at least for the phase currently under way. (The asymptote actually indicates the fading of the test system's ability to find bugs in the current phase. Given a good test system, the bugs found represent the bugs most likely to torment the customer, and the fading of the test system is consistent with customer indifference.) Conversely, a cumulative opened curve that refuses to flatten indicates that you have plenty of problems left to find. The chart in Figure 4.18 shows that we are not through finding bugs.

Next, have you finished fixing bugs? Once development winds down, developers usually start to catch up with the problems. Shortly afterwards, the opened curve should start to flatten. Consequently, the cumulative closed curve—the lower curve on the chart in Figure 4.18—begins to converge with the cumulative opened curve. (Both *Deferred* and *Closed* bugs are counted as *Closed* for purposes of this chart.) Figure 4.18 shows a project where, barring any other worrisome metrics or findings, we are ready to ship.

THE FIX DATE PRECEDES THE CLOSE DATE

If you were to draw a "fix curve" based on the dates when developers actually repaired bugs, you would see that the closed curve lags behind it by a week or so. This lag results from delays incurred in getting the fix into the next test release, delivering that release to the test team, and testing for confirmation and regression. These various delays cause the convergence at the last day of testing shown in the sample chart in Figure 4.18.

At a more general level, is the bug management process working? It is working well in both Figure 4.17 and Figure 4.18: the closed curve follows right behind the opened curve, indicating that the project team is moving the bugs quickly toward resolution.

Finally, how do milestones in the project relate to inflection points, changes in the slope of the opened or closed curves? The overlapping of the phases in these examples obscures this relationship somewhat, but often when you move from one test phase to the next, you will see a spike in the cumulative opened curve. Such rises are gentle in our idealized example, but these transitions can be dramatic and even downright scary on some projects. As developers move from writing new code or engineering new hardware to fixing bugs, you should see an upward turn in the cumulative closed curve. Sometimes, when the bug triage process falls behind, a "bug scrub" meeting, where the technical and management leaders of a project gather to decide the fate of all known bug reports, can result in a discontinuous jump in the cumulative closed curve.

To explore the use of opened/closed charts, let's look at three nightmare scenarios that represent those unpleasant projects in which all test managers eventually participate. Assume that, in each case, we're working on a project where the scheduled ship or deployment date is September 13. For the first nightmare, imagine that during the system test phase, the bug find rate remains high and refuses to level off. The opened/closed chart that results appears in Figure 4.19. Notice the deceptive leveling in the second cycle (8/23 through 8/29), where the opened curve appears to flatten, only to leap up sharply in the third cycle (8/30 through 9/5). If the project team ships the product as scheduled, they can expect many failures in the field.

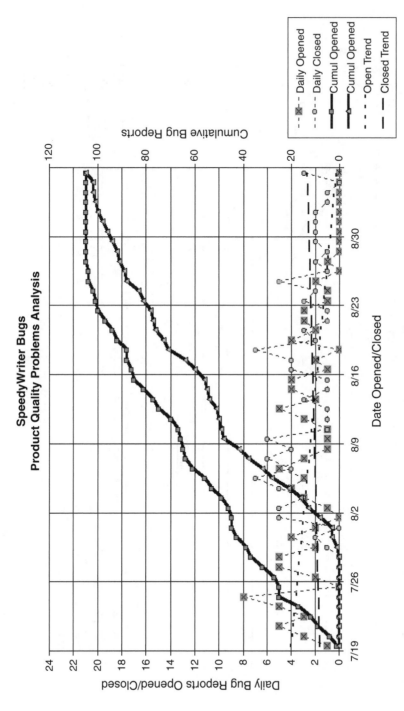

Figure 4.18 A good-looking opened/closed chart.

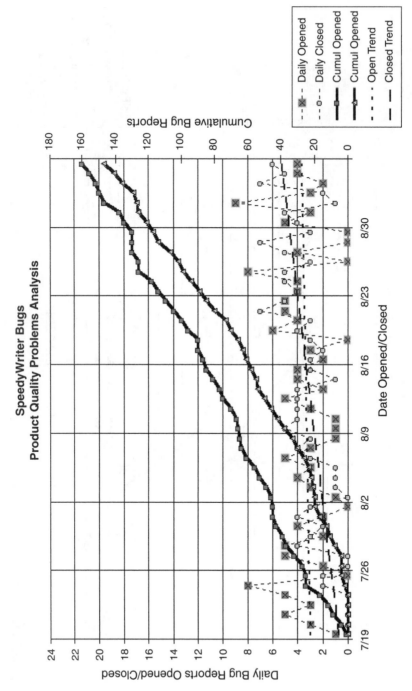

Figure 4.19 The nightmare of endless bug discovery.

For the second nightmare, which is a bit milder, let's assume that development is ignoring some of the bugs. The developers have convinced themselves that about 25 of the bugs that test has reported are not really problems and can be disregarded. Figure 4.20 shows the opened/closed chart for this scenario. Until about August 20, the chart in Figure 4.18(the idealized example) and the chart in Figure 4.20are not radically different: on that date, the opened/closed gap is about 20 in the former chart, whereas it is about 30 in the latter. Ten bugs out of 100 one way or the other three weeks before the first customer ship is not a catastrophe. However, as the final two cycles of system testing unfold (8/23 through 8/29, and 8/30 through 9/5, respectively), it becomes clear that the gap is not narrowing. Unless you bring the pernicious bugs to project management's attention around August 23, the development team will deliver a *fait accompli*. Overturning their decision to ignore these bugs even a week later will require a slip in the delivery date.

As a final nightmare—well, okay, just a disquieting dream, actually—let's suppose that the developers and the testers are both doing the right things at a technical level, but the bug management process isn't working. The development manager doesn't notify you when bugs are fixed and ready for retesting, and you don't follow up with your testers to make sure they close bugs that they have retested. In addition, testers don't bother to report bugs when they find them, but instead wait until Thursday or Friday each week. Then they enter their findings, some dimly remembered, into the bug tracking database. Figure 4.21 shows how the opened/closed chart looks in this example. The trouble here is that you can't tell whether a jump in a curve represents a significant event or simply indicates that some people are getting around to doing what they should have done earlier. If you use this chart as part of your project dashboard or scorecard, your vision is blurred.

Why Bugs Happen:
The Root Cause Chart

Root cause data is most interesting in the aggregate. Listing the closure of one bug with a specific root cause might not mean much, but seeing the breakdown for 100—or 1,000—bugs can tell an engaging story. Figure 4.22 presents a root cause breakdown for the SpeedyWriter example, showing the contribution of each type of error to the total number of bugs found and fixed so far. (During test execution, many bugs will not have root causes assigned to them because they are still under investigation.) As discussed earlier, analyzing a breakdown of root causes can serve to focus not only test efforts, but also development attention on those areas that are causing the most serious and frequent problems. As you might imagine, a chart such as the one in Figure 4.22 grabs management's attention more effectively than a table would.

How Development Responds:
The Closure Period Chart

Closure period (a.k.a. *closure gap*) is complicated to calculate, but it has a simple intuitive meaning: the closure period gauges the programming and engineering teams' responsiveness to the test team's bug reports. *Daily closure period* refers to the average number

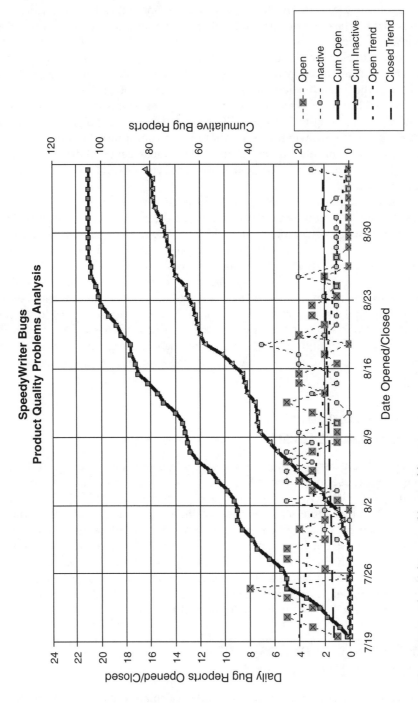

Figure 4.20 The nightmare of ignored bugs.

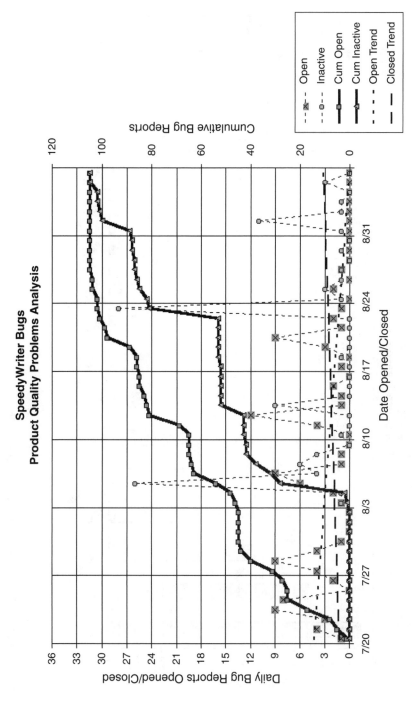

Figure 4.21 The nightmare of mismanaged bugs.

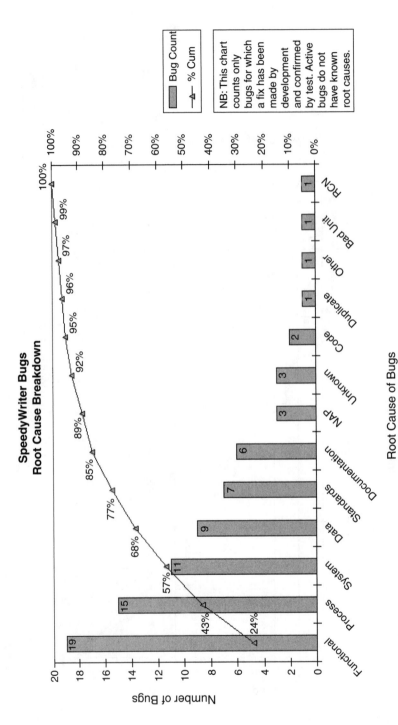

Figure 4.22 A root cause breakdown for SpeedyWriter.

of days between the opening of a bug and its resolution for all bugs closed on the same day. *Rolling closure period* is the average for all closed bugs, including the current day and all previous days. Figure 4.23 shows the closure period chart for the SpeedyWriter project. As you can see, the daily plot tends to pull the rolling plot toward it, although the ever-increasing inertia of the rolling average makes it harder to influence as the project proceeds.

It's useful to look at closure period in terms of stability and acceptability. A stable closure period chart shows a relatively low variance from one day to another, with the slope of the rolling closure curve remaining almost constant and close to 0. In addition, to the extent that the daily closure period changes, it fluctuates randomly around the rolling closure curve, staying within a few days in either direction.

On an acceptable closure period chart, both the daily and rolling closure curves fall within the upper and lower limits set in the project or test plan for bug turnaround time.[10] Although the pressures of the typical project make it hard to believe, there is indeed a lower limit for an acceptable closure period. Bugs deferred the day they are opened pull the daily closure curve toward zero, but the bug remains in the product. I audited a project once where the team took test releases two or three times a day for bugs identified just hours before. Although the closure period was very quick (a little over a day), that project had a significant number of bug reports that had been re-opened multiple times, one of them 11 times. Haste makes waste, as the cliché goes. Finally, an acceptable daily closure curve does not exhibit a significant trend toward either boundary.

A closure period chart that is both stable and acceptable indicates a well-understood, smoothly functioning bug management process. The ideal is a low number with a downward or level trend, since an efficient bug management process drives bugs through their state transitions to closure with all deliberate speed. The closure period in Figure 4.23 is stable and, if management is realistic in its expectations, acceptable. Bugs tend to get fixed and confirmed closed in about a week and a half, which is a good pace if you assume one-week cycles and don't admit experimental bug fixes into the lab during cycles. (For a discussion of the danger of midstream changes in the system under test, see Chapter 2, "Plotting and Presenting Your Course: The Test Plan," specifically the sections on release management and test cycles.) Note that if the developers could fix bugs instantly, the lower bound on the process is four days, given weekly releases into the test environment and about a day of confirmation testing per test release. This is shown on the graph by the dashed lines above and below the horizontal four gridline.

In Exercise 5 at the end of the chapter, I'll show you a variation on this chart that displays the data as a histogram rather than averages on a timescale. This format of presenting this data might be more interesting to you, especially if stability isn't a concern but long lag time for bug fixes is. This data can also be very useful in creating simple models for predicting the length of time required for a test phase to find and confirm fixed all important bugs, which is something else I'll show you how to do in that exercise.

---

[10]To emphasize this, you might add draw these lines to the chart, but don't confuse them with the upper and lower control limits on a control chart. For more information on control charts and other statistical quality control techniques, see Kaoru Ishikawa's *Guide to Quality Control*, published 1982 by the Asian Productivity Organization.

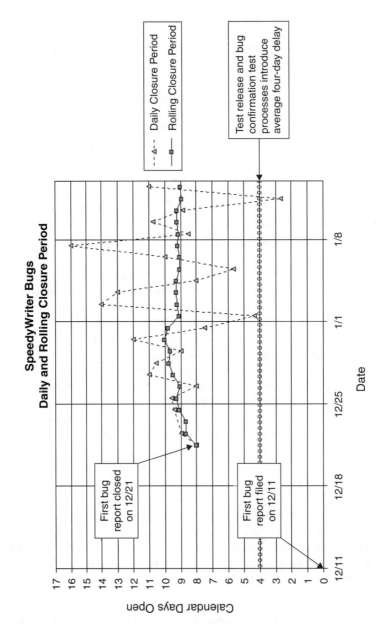

Figure 4.23 A closure period chart for SpeedyWriter.

What Was Broken: The Subsystem Chart

Like the root cause breakdown, the subsystem breakdown is a simple chart with an important message: it tells you which subsystems experience the most bugs. Like the root cause chart, it's useful to format this as a Pareto chart, as shown in Figure 4.24, because usually two or three subsystems suffer the most problems.

You can use a subsystem chart in the same way you use a root cause chart, to focus process and product improvement efforts. The fact that the user interface and the edit engine account for two out of every three bugs found in SpeedyWriter, for example, indicates that an effort to make fewer mistakes in these areas would pay off handsomely. Moreover, if you are dividing your test effort evenly among the six subsystems, you should consider spending most of your testers' time on these two problem areas.

This conclusion might seem counterintuitive—after all, if you didn't find many bugs in the other four subsystems, maybe you should have spent more time looking in those four categories. And you certainly should do this if post-release field problems indicate a disproportionate number of test escapes in these four areas. However, as Glenford Myers points out in *The Art of Software Testing*, where you find many bugs, you will find more bugs. Therefore, you can predict from the SpeedyWriter data that most of the field bugs will also come from the user interface or the edit engine. For subsequent SpeedyWriter releases, you should spend even more time and resources looking for bugs in these subsystems.

However, this advice comes with a caveat. Let's suppose that we know, through a magic crystal ball, that a given release of SpeedyWriter contains 400 bugs. Further, suppose we have two test teams, Test Team A and Test Team B, each running SpeedyWriter system test. After the first test cycle, Test Team A looks at Figure 4.24. They decide to focus the rest of the testing effort on the user interface and the edit engine, and they succeed in finding all the bugs in those subsystems. Conversely, Test Team B decides that the current test approach is fine, and they end up finding the same percentage distribution across the subsystem in the rest of the bugs they find. Both teams find 238 bugs (see Table 4.1). Which team did a better job?

The answer depends on risk. If the user interface and the edit engine are the highest-risk subsystems, and bugs in other subsystems will cause little if any trouble to users, operators, and other system stakeholders, then Test Team A is doing the right thing. However, in the case of a typical mass-market application like a word processor, users do care about file operations, installation and configuration, tools, documentation, and even packaging. In this case, what we know about the risks for mass-market applications tells us that Test Team B is on the right track. Therefore, while Figure 4.24 can tell you about technical risk—where the most bugs live—it doesn't tell you about business risk, which is an important consideration in my approach to using testing to help manage the risks to the quality of the system.

An After-the-Fact Metric: Defect Detection Percentage

So far, we've been looking at metrics and charts that we generate during the project, but there is one very important defect metric that you might want to examine shortly

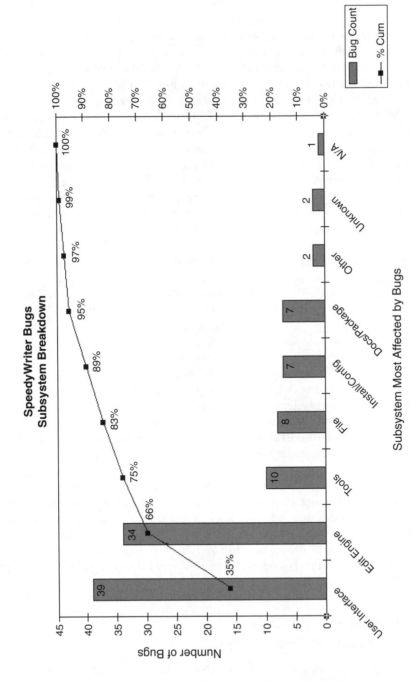

Figure 4.24   A subsystem breakdown for SpeedyWriter.

Table 4.1   A Tale of Two Test Teams

SUBSYSTEM	ACTUAL BUGS	TEST TEAM A	TEST TEAM B
User Interface	100	100	74
Edit Engine	100	100	66
Tools	50	10	20
File	50	8	28
Install/Configuration	50	7	28
Documentation/Packaging	25	7	12
Other	10	2	4
Unknown	10	2	4
N/A	5	2	2
Total	**400**	**238**	**238**

after the project concludes. This metric is variously called the *defect detection percentage* or *defect removal efficiency*, and was briefly mentioned in Chapter 3, "Test System Architecture, Cases, and Coverage." Remember that I said that mathematically, the defect detection percentages is defined as

$$DDP = \frac{bugs_{testers}}{bugs_{testers} + bugs_{customers}} \times 100\% \, .$$

In this equation, $bugs_{testers}$ represents the count of all unique, true bugs found by the test team. This number excludes duplicates, nonproblems (NAPs, WADs, etc.), test and tester errors, and other spurious bug reports, but includes any bugs found but not fixed due to deferral or other management prioritization decisions. $bugs_{customers}$ represents unique, true bugs found by customers after release that were reported to technical support and for which a fix was released; in other words, bugs that represented real quality problems. Again, this number excludes duplicates, nonproblems (NAPs, WADs, etc.), customer, user, and configuration errors, and other spurious field problem reports, and includes any bugs found but not fixed due to deferral or other management prioritization decisions. In this case, excluding duplicates means that $bugs_{customers}$ does not count bugs found by customers that were previously detected by testers, developers, or other prerelease activities but were deferred or otherwise deprioritized, because that would be double-counting the bug. In other words, there is only one bug, no matter how many times it is found and reported. (For mathematical purists, these variables really represent the cardinalities of the sets of bugs found by testers and the bugs found by testers and by customers, as use of set math would cause the nonunique elements to drop out naturally.) Since there is no effort variable involved in calculating this metric, I prefer to call this the *defect detection percentage* rather than *defect removal efficiency*.

To calculate this metric, we need to have the bug tracking system discussed in this chapter, but we also need a way to track bugs found in the field. Most help desk or technical support organizations have such data, so it's usually just a matter of figuring out how to sort and collate the information from the two (often) distinct databases. We also have to decide on a time window. That depends on how long it takes for your customers to find 80 percent or so of the bugs they will find over the entire post-release life cycle of the system. For laptop computers, for example, the rate of customer encounters with new bugs (unrelated to new releases, patches, and so forth) in a release tends to fall off very close to zero after the first three to six months. Therefore, if you perform the calculation at three months, adjust upward by some historical factor—say 10 to 20 percent—you should have a fairly accurate estimate of $bugs_{customers}$, and furthermore one for which you can, based on your historical metrics, predict the statistical accuracy if need be.

Note that this *is* a measure of test effectiveness, and a very pure one at that. Finding bugs and giving the project team an opportunity to fix them before release is exactly what we want a test team to accomplish. Ideally, this metric would be 1 (or 100 percent), because we'd like to find all the bugs before release. Realistically, though, we have to distinguish between what we *should* test and what we *can* test, as discussed in Chapter 1. To adjust for that, we can eliminate customer-identified bugs that are outside the scope of testing as defined in Chapters 1 and 2. In other words, we only count bugs found by the customer if they could have reasonably been found by the test team during the test project agreed to with the project management team.

A Note on Metrics and Charts

As you accumulate historical defect data—on both good and bad projects—you can compare charts from your current projects with charts from previous projects. Such comparisons can be enlightening. Even within a single class of projects such as laptop computer development, I have seen variances of 600 percent in the total number of bugs found. Beyond the simple totals, the shapes of the curves can also differ. If you use these charts consistently across a few projects, you will soon recognize "virtuous" and "evil" shapes.

Avoid blind faith in your charts, though. One key assumption of the opened/closed chart is *ceteris paribus* (all things held equal). You can arbitrarily flatten any cumulative opened curve by stopping the test effort. You can cause the opened and closed curves to converge by deferring bugs rather than fixing them. You can "spoof" opened and closed dates in the database to make the opened/closed chart fit any profile you choose (as I did to create the sample charts in this section). You can easily rig the closure period chart, too. Breakdowns in the bug triage process, recording phony opened and closed dates, opening new bug reports rather than reopening existing ones when fixes fail in confirmation testing, and other manipulation of the opened and closed dates will defeat your purpose. Finally, carelessness when assigning subsystems and root causes to bugs renders these charts worse than pointless. Nothing good can come of making resource allocation decisions based on phony data.

Similar cautions apply to any other analysis of defect or test data. For your analyses to have meaning, the underlying data must be accurate, complete, and free from gerrymandering. Only honest data yields worthwhile information.

The reports, charts, tables, and forms presented in this chapter are just starters. With a little imagination, you can extract all types of useful data and reports from a bug tracking database. Start with simple tasks, learn the tool, and then expand it to meet your needs. In Chapters 5 and 9, we'll revisit this topic, augmenting bug data with test result data to build what I call a balanced scorecard or dashboard for the test operation.[11]

BUILDING VERSUS BUYING

Instead of developing your own bug tracking database, you might want to consider buying one of the many excellent packages on the market. Which alternative—building or buying—is better? In J. R. R. Tolkien's *Lord of the Rings* trilogy, one character says to the protagonist, "Go not to [us] for advice, for [we] will tell you both yes and no." I'm afraid I must do the same.

On the one hand, several arguments favor purchasing a package. These packages represent the collected thoughts of many experienced testers. Most commercial software packages are professionally executed and documented. The developers have considered in advance many of the problems that you will run into later if you decide to create your own system. Buying is also a cheaper approach; a widely sold commercial package leverages the entire customer base. You might spend many hours developing your own package, and you should take into account what those hours are worth.

On the other hand, creating your own bug tracking system has its advantages. You know best what you need to track and what data is pertinent to your operation. A general-purpose package, no matter how customizable, won't be exactly what you need. Remember, too, that tools have paradigms, and test tools have embedded notions about the development process that might not fit the way your organization does business. The poorer the fit, the harder you will have to work to make the bug tracking system work for you. Finally, if you discover that your commercial system contains bugs, you must work with the vendor to get them fixed—if the vendor will fix them. When you create and control your own system, you can always fix the bugs (provided you can find the time).

The question of buying versus building is not trivial. You will have to live with the decision for some time, so be sure you consider all the angles.

Managing Bug Tracking

When projects are in a test execution phase, I probably spend 10 to 20 percent of my time working with bugs, either those already reported or those about to be reported. Because testing should mitigate quality risks, and because a bug report documents the transition of a quality risk into a failure mode, I consider bug reports the most important "product" of the test effort. Time devoted to understanding and managing bug data is time well spent.

---

[11]For further information about possible metrics and the need to manage by a limited set, see the discussion on quantitative methods in Beizer's *Software System Testing and Quality Assurance*. Chapters 3 and 4 of Kan's *Metrics and Models in Software Quality Engineering* can help you take your metrics program to the next level once you've mastered the tools outlined in this chapter.

The preceding section on metrics might have given you the impression that managing bugs consists mostly of analyzing data and gleaning meaning. I wish it were! You'll soon discover two other areas of concern. The first is staying aware of the politics and potential misuse of the bug data. The second is dealing with certain types of problematic bug reports that can consume a disproportionate share of your time.

Politics and Misuse of Bug Data

Chapter 9 deals with management considerations and the politics of the test manager's position in detail. Here, however, we should briefly examine political issues that are specifically related to bug data. From the most adversarial point of view, for example, you can see every bug report as an attack on a developer. You probably don't—and certainly shouldn't—intend to offend, but it helps to remember that bug data is potentially embarrassing and subject to misuse. Candor and honesty are critical in gathering clean bug data, but developers might distort the facts if they think you might use the data to slam them with the bug reports. Think of the detailed bug information your database captures as a loaded revolver: an effective tool if it's in the right hands and used with caution, but a dangerous implement of mayhem if it's treated carelessly.

Don't Fail to Build Trust

Most experienced developers support bug tracking efforts. Nevertheless, some individuals—especially those who have experienced highly adversarial test/development relationships—won't disclose any more information to you than required, and they might do so with an uncooperative attitude.

I once worked with a development manager who wanted to argue over every bug report. Bug triage meetings with this guy were a misery of semantic arguments punctuated with repeated assertions that any bug he had succeeded in ignoring for the past three or four weeks had probably been fixed in some recent release and should be retested by my team. In his mind, our relationship was by nature purely adversarial. There was no trust.

Some situations are irretrievable. Developers who are convinced that a written bug report is one step removed from a written warning in their personnel files probably will never trust you. Most developers, though, approach testing with an open mind. They understand that testing can provide a useful service to them in helping them fix bugs and deliver a better product. How do you keep the trust and support of these developers?

- Don't take bugs personally, and don't become emotional about them. The times I have anointed myself the "defender of quality" and acted holier-than-thou with my colleagues are moments in my professional life that I look back on with embarrassment and regret. Even if you're right on the issue, you're doing the wrong thing because you end up alienating people with whom you need to maintain a professional and trusting relationship.

- Submit only quality bug reports: a succinct summary, clear steps to reproduce, evidence of significant isolation work, accuracy in classification information, and a conservative estimate in terms of priority and severity. Also try to avoid "cheap shot" bug reports that can seem like carping.

- Be willing to discuss bug reports with an open mind. No matter how convinced you are that a program or a computer is malfunctioning, you should listen to developers when they explain that the bug is actually correct behavior. If you make the extra effort to discuss their opinions, it goes a long way toward keeping the flow of information moving.

- If developers want you to change something in your bug reporting process, be open to their suggestions. They are, after all, some of the key customers for your bug report product. If they want reports delivered in a different fashion, advance warning before summaries go to management, or additional information in the reports, try to accommodate them whenever it's practical to do so.

Most of these suggestions are simple common courtesy and professionalism. You don't have to compromise your role in order to keep reasonable developers satisfied that you aren't grinding an ax.

Don't Be a Backseat Driver

The test manager needs to ensure that testers identify, reproduce, and isolate bugs. It's also part of the job to track the bugs to conclusion and to deliver crisp bug status summaries to senior and executive management. These roles differ, though, from managing bug *fixes*. In most of the organizations I've worked in, managing the bug fix process was the development manager's job; ensuring that this process moves at a satisfactory pace was the program manager's job. Even if some managers encourage you, don't get sucked into doing either.

If you, as an outsider, make it your job to nag developers about when a specific bug will be fixed or to pester the development manager about how slow the bug fix process is, you are setting yourself up for a highly antagonistic situation. Reporting, tracking, retesting, and summarizing bugs are your worries. Whether any particular bug gets fixed, how it gets fixed, and when it gets fixed are someone else's concerns.

Don't Make Individuals Look Bad

It is a bad idea to create and distribute reports that make individuals look bad. There's probably no faster way to guarantee that you will have trouble getting estimated fix dates out of people than to produce a report that points out every failure to meet such estimated dates. Creating reports that show how many bug fixes resulted in reopened rather than closed bugs, grouped and totaled by developer, is another express lane to bad relationships.[12] Again, managing the developers is the development manager's job, not yours. No matter how useful a particular report seems, make sure that it doesn't bash individuals.

---

[12]See Chapter 6 of *Testing Computer Software*, by Kaner, Falk, and Nguyen, for an expansive discussion of this and other ways to create bad blood between test and development using a bug tracking database.

Sticky Wickets

Challenging bugs crop up on nearly every project. The most vexing are those that involve questions about correct behavior, "prairie dog" bugs that pop up only when they feel like it, and bugs that cause a tug-of-war over priority.

Bug or Feature?

Although a perfect development project provides you with clear and unambiguous information about correct system behavior in the form of requirements and specifications, you will seldom have such good fortune. Many projects have only informal specifications, and the requirements can be scattered around in emails, product road maps, and sales materials. In such cases, disagreements can arise between development and test over whether a particular bug is in fact correct system behavior.

How should you settle these differences? Begin by discussing the situation with the developers, their manager, and your testers. Most of these disagreements arise from miscommunication. Before making a Federal case out of it, confirm that all the parties are clear on what the alleged bug is and why your team is concerned.

Suppose that everyone understands the problem the test team is reporting, but the development team insists that the system is behaving properly, while you remain unconvinced. At this point, you might want to get other groups involved. Technical support, help desk staff, marketing, business analysts, sales, and the project manager might have strong opinions. Even if consulting with other people doesn't resolve the dispute, it at least escalates the problem to the proper level of attention.

If, after all the jawboning is over, you are the lone skeptic, now what? Insisting that the bug remain assigned to the recalcitrant developer won't help. If the bug remains active, you'll be forced to rehash this discussion every time you circulate your bug list. My preference is to cancel the bug—in other words, in the bug database I introduced in this chapter, put it in a *Closed* state with a root cause of *NAP*—but make a notation on the record that I disagree.

Irreproducible Bug

This challenge with irreproducible bugs comes in two flavors. First, some bugs simply refuse to reproduce their symptoms consistently. This is especially the case in system testing, in which complex combinations of conditions are required to recreate problems. Sometimes these types of failures occur in clusters. If you see a bug three times in one day and then don't see it for a week, has it disappeared, or is it just hiding? Tempting as it is to dismiss this problem, be sure to write up these bugs. Random, intermittent failures—especially ones that result in system crashes or any other data loss—can have a significant effect on customers.

The second category of irreproducible bugs involves problems that seem to disappear with new revisions of the system, although no specific fix was made for them. I refer to these as "bugs fixed by accident." You will find that more bugs are fixed by accident than you expect, but that fewer are fixed by accident than some project Pollyannas suggest. If the bug is an elusive one, you might want to keep the bug report active until you're convinced it's actually gone.

Deferring Trivia or Creating Test Escapes?

While bug severity is easy to quantify, priority is not. Developing consensus on priority is often difficult. What do you do when bugs are assigned a low priority? Bugs that will not be fixed should be deferred. If you don't keep the active bug list short, people will start to ignore it. However, there's a real risk that some deferred bugs will come back to haunt you. For this reason, a bug triage committee or CCB should make the final call on priority and deferral. In many cases, though, I didn't have the benefit of a bug triage committee, and so had to build consensus around bugs via email and face-to-face discussions. In these cases, when a bug was assigned a low priority and then ignored, I pressed for a clear decision about whether the bug would be fixed or deferred rather than discussing it repeatedly. What if a deferred bug pops up in the field as a critical issue? Is that a test escape? Not if my team found it and then deferred it on the advice or insistence of the project manager.

After you institute a bug tracking system, including the database and metrics discussed here, you will find yourself the keeper of key indicators of project status. As I've emphasized, *fairness* and *accuracy* should be your watchwords in this role. Your peers and your managers will use your database and charts to make both tactical (day-to-day) and strategic (project-wide) decisions. If you take these activities seriously and apply the tools introduced in this chapter conscientiously, you and your test organization will provide invaluable assistance to the project team in creating the best possible product.

Case Study

Prior to my team getting involved in the loan processing application project discussed in the case study for Chapter 2, another team ran a test project against a previous release of the application. The test project ran from August 20 to November 12. The case study bug metrics document, "Case Study Loan Processing Bug Metrics.xls," is available at www.rexblackconsulting.com. Please note that, due to a lack of root cause data, only three of the four charts mentioned in this chapter are shown.

The opened/closed chart in Figure 4.25 resembles Figure 4.19, and this was indeed the situation: the bug reports just never stopped coming. A number of factors contributed to the inability of the project team to stabilize the system's quality. One was frequent change in the requirements. Another was excessive regression; for example, one bug report was re-opened 10 times. Another was too-frequent (daily and sometimes hourly) test releases, which prevented the test team from getting through the planned tests. Ultimately, the release was cancelled in lieu of the subsequent project, which was the one my team worked on.

I thank my client on this project, a major mid-western financial institution, and the executive in charge of development for allowing me to share this example with readers of this book. I have purged all identifying and otherwise private information from this document. My client contact has asked that the organization remain anonymous.

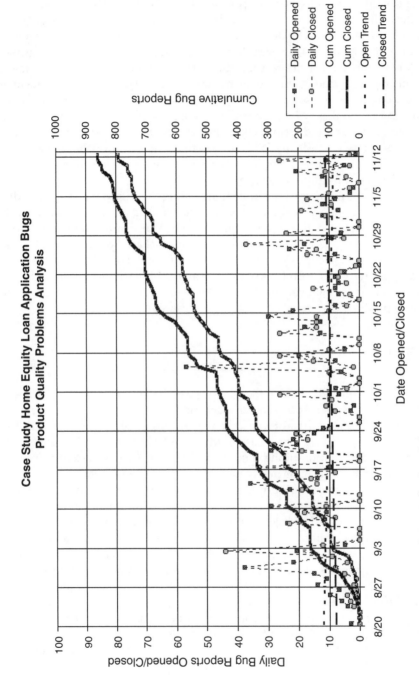

Figure 4.25 Case study opened/ closed chart.

Exercises

1. Refer to Figure 4.26.

   ■ What isolation steps should you perform?

   ■ In addition to missing isolation, there are at least three improvements needed to bring this report in line with the 10-step process outlined earlier. Identify them.

   ■ The calculator is exhibiting this behavior in the binary, octal, and hexadecimal modes because it apparently works in an integer-only fashion in these modes. (Note that division causes truncation of the remainder, too.) If the decimal key (".") were properly grayed out, would that be a sufficient indication of an integer-only mode? Explain your reasoning.

   ■ What is the appropriate severity and priority for this bug?

   ■ If you have two or more people available, have a bug triage discussion about this bug.

2. Using either exploratory testing or the test cases you created in Chapter 3, find a functionality bug in an application or utility running on your PC or workstation. (Sadly, this will not be hard.)

   ■ Write a bug report following the 10-step process outlined in this chapter.

   ■ Have a colleague or fellow student review your bug report. How many changes did you make based on the review?

   ■ Repeat steps 2.a and 2.b for a user interface or usability bug.

3. Figure 4.27 shows a fancy workflow (life cycle) from an automated bug tracking tool.[13] A well-suited bug reporting workflow fits into the organizational context in which the project occurs, and therefore looking at the workflow can tell you a lot about the organization's team structure (i.e., org chart) or at least the roles played by people within the project team.

   ■ Based on the bug tracking workflow shown in Figure 4.27, identify the different teams or roles that exist in this project team.

   ■ Based on your organizational context, draw a bug tracking workflow for your project.

4. In the case study, I mentioned three factors outside the test process that contributed to the failure of the case study system to achieve stable quality. (Frequent requirements change; excessive regression; frequent test releases interfering with timely planned test completion.) Refer to Figure 4.28 and note that almost 20 percent of the bug reports are opened more than once. What

---

[13] I thank Sheri McAdoo for allowing me to reprint this diagram. Sheri has worked in Testing and Quality Assurance for over 15 years and works as an independent consultant based in Denver, Colorado. Questions or comments can be sent to smcadoo@testing.org.

Summary
Inconsistent indication (chime versus gray-out) of key availability in calculator.

Steps to Reproduce
1. Start Windows Me calculator.
2. Select Scientific mode from the View menu.
3. Cycle the calculator through hexadecimal, decimal, octal, and binary modes.
4. As you go into these modes, note that certain value keys in the rightmost set of keys become blue or gray ("grayed out") depending on whether the key is available in this mode. For example, the "A" through "F" keys are blue only when the calculator is in hexadecimal mode.
5. However, note that the decimal point (".") key remains blue in all modes, not just decimal mode.
6. Go into the hexadecimal mode and press the decimal point (".") key. Note that the key depresses, then a chime sounds indicating the key is unavailable. Repeat for octal and binary modes. Note same behavior.
7. Go into decimal, octal, and binary mode. Press a gray ("grayed out") unavailable key. Note that nothing happens and no sound is made.

Isolation
    ???

Figure 4.26   A bug report needing isolation—and some other work.

change to the test process could we make to help the development team spend less time in rework?

5. One important—and difficult—part of estimating for a test project is predicting how long it will take to find and fix all the important bugs. Notice that, if we can predict when the cumulative opened curve will flatten and when the cumulative closed curve will intercept the cumulative opened curve, then we can predict this key indicator of quality. Given enough historical bug tracking data, along with information about the size of the project, you can develop models using a spreadsheet to make these predictions in your organization, provided the teams and processes remain stable over time. These models are simple but effective forms of defect removal models, which I referred to earlier in this chapter. While such a model is not 100-percent accurate, such a model is at least based on data, not on wishful thinking, and can be improved over the course of multiple projects.

■ To know when we'll be done finding bugs, we have to know how many bugs we are going to find. Suppose we know that during system test we find two defects per person-month of estimated team effort on average for our projects. If we have 150 person-months of effort estimated for this project, how many bugs do you expect to find? (Note: While thousands of source lines of code [KSLOC] and function points [FP] are often considered to be more accurate units for sizing projects, estimated person-months of effort is perhaps the most easily gathered metric of project size.)

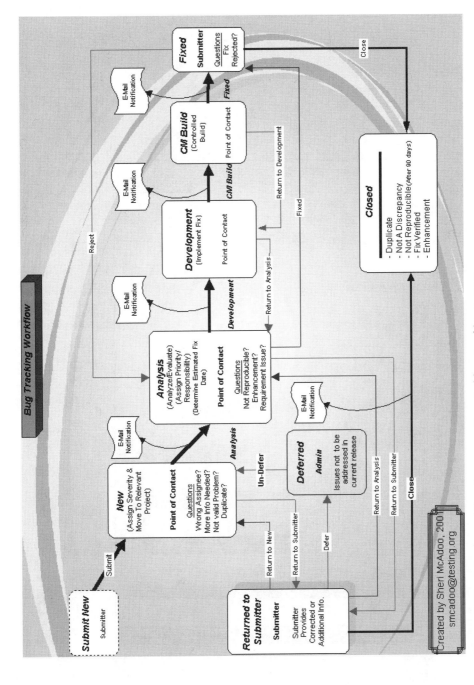

Figure 4.27 A fancy workflow from an automated bug tracking system.

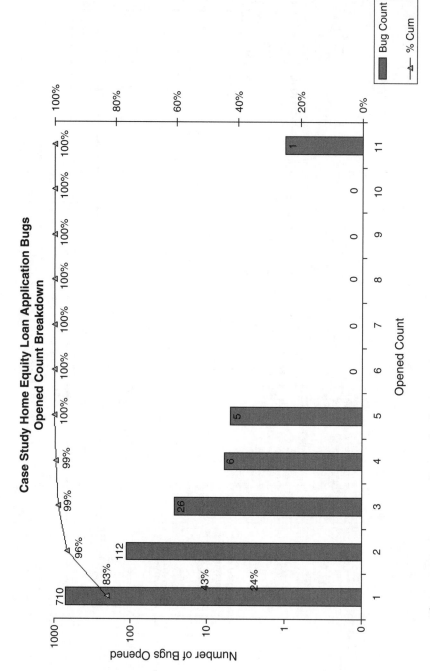

Figure 4.28 Bug opened count for the case study.

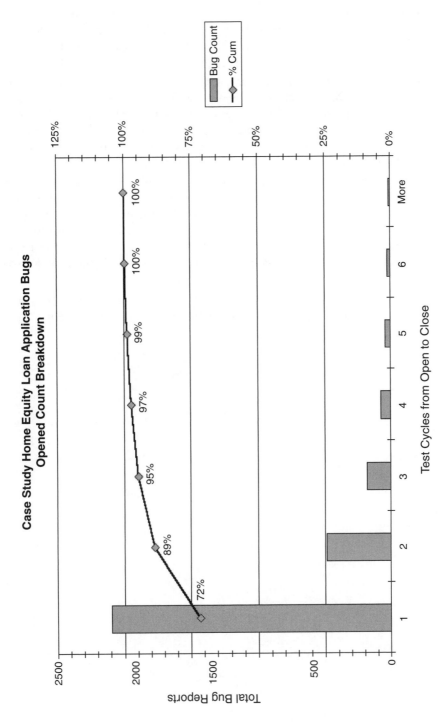

Figure 4.29 Closure period distribution for exercise 5.

- Suppose we find on average 1.25 bugs per tester day, and you have eight testers assigned. How many working days will it take to find all the bugs you'll find in system test? Assuming weekly test cycles, how many test cycles is this?

- Suppose half of the bugs in each test release are found during each test cycle that covers that test release. Suppose that the remaining predicted bugs are found in the last test cycle. In other words, the first test cycle finds half of the bugs that will be found in system test, and each subsequent cycle finds half the remaining bugs, until the last cycle finds all the remaining bugs. Calculate and graph the expected cumulative opened curve.

- Based on a histogram of closure periods from previous projects such as the one shown in Figure 4.29, suppose that roughly three-quarters of the bugs found in the previous test release are fixed in the next test release. Further suppose that three-quarters of any bugs remaining from any previous test release are likewise fixed in each release. Assume that the last test cycle results in the closure of all remaining bugs. Calculate and graph the expected cumulative closed curve.

- Based on this model, how long will it be before you are ready to exit system test, assuming the exit criteria include finding and closing all bugs?

Managing Test Cases:
The Test Tracking Spreadsheet

Quick! For your last three test projects, answer the following questions:

- How many test cases did you plan to run?
- How many test cases did you actually run?
- How many tests failed? Of those, how many later passed when the bug was fixed?
- Did the tests take less or more time, on average, than you expected?
- Did you skip any tests? If so, why?
- Did you tests cover all the important risks to system quality?
- Did your management ever ask for a cumulative summary of test results, both passed and failed? If so, did you provide an accurate summary, or did you take a SWAG (scientific wild-ass guess)?

On any given project, I can answer these questions by checking my test tracking spreadsheet, a tool I use to manage test execution. This chapter shows you how to create and utilize this tool.

In its most basic form, the test tracking spreadsheet is a "to do" list, with the added capability of status tracking. Using DataRocket as a case study, this chapter demonstrates how to build an abbreviated test tracking spreadsheet for system testing. We'll begin our example with a minimalist, or stripped-down, model of the spreadsheet. As you learn to add enhancements and to adapt this tool to fit your own needs, you should eventually be able to implement a complete set of test tracking and reporting capabilities using the spreadsheet as the foundation. As you'll see, you can also integrate individual test cases constructed with the approach outlined in Chapter 3, "Test System Architecture, Cases, and Coverage." Finally, we'll pull in the bug metrics discussed Chapter 4, "An Exciting Career in Entomology Awaits You: A Bug Tracking Database," combine them with some important test metrics, and build a simple but powerful and balanced test dashboard.

Building a Minimalist Test Tracking Spreadsheet

Let's start by building a very simple test tracking spreadsheet, and then see how we can adapt it to our case study.

The Basic Spreadsheet

To keep our sample worksheets relatively small, let's suppose that you have defined a simple four-suite system test phase. You intend to run these four test suites:

- Environmental
- Load, Capacity, and Volume
- Basic Functionality
- Standards

You want to track the status of each test case, the configuration against which the test was run, and who ran the test. You also want to summarize the test status numerically.

Figure 5.1 shows an example of a test case summary worksheet as it might appear halfway into the first cycle of system testing. The first column of the Excel worksheet (Test Suite/Case) contains the names of the test suites and, within each suite, the test cases. The names are short mnemonics that convey an idea of the test's purpose. In the second column (State), you can record the state of each test case. A blank entry in this column means that the test case is still queued for execution. A *Pass* entry signifies that the test case did not identify any bugs; *Fail* indicates that one or more bugs were found.

The *System Config* column lists an identifier for the system configuration used in each test case. A separate worksheet that serves as a lookup table, shown in Figure 5.2, allows you to record important details about each configuration, such as the motherboard revision, the BIOS level, the operating system, the specific network setup, and any additional software or hardware involved in the test.

Returning to the test case summary worksheet in Figure 5.1, notice the *Bug ID* column. For any test case that finds a failure, this column should contain the bug identifier from the bug tracking database. If a test finds more than one failure—in other words, more than one bug is reported based on the test's outcome—then I use one extra row per additional bug report directly below the test case row to track the bug IDs. I find this approach more elegant than letting the Bug ID column get wider and wider to accommodate a few test cases that have five or 10 bugs reported against them.

	A	B	C	D	E	F	G	H	I
1		DataRocket System Test Tracking							
2			System	Bug			Roll Up		
3	Test Suite/Case	State	Config	ID	By	Comment	T	F	P
4	*Environmental*								
5	Operating Thermal Profile	Pass	D		HS		1	0	1
6	Operating Temp/Humid Cycle	Pass	D		HS		1	0	1
7	Nonoperating Temp/Humid Cycle	Fail	D	017	HS		1	1	0
8	Nonoperating Drop	Pass	D		HS		1	0	1
9	Nonoperating Shock	Pass	D		HS		1	0	1
10	Nonoperating Thermal Shock	Pass	D		HS		1	0	1
11	Packaging Drop					Package not ready yet.	1	0	0
12	Packaging Shock					Package not ready yet.	1	0	0
13	**Suite Summary**						8	1	5
14									
15	*Load, Capacity, and Volume*								
16	CPU and Memory	Pass	A,B,C		JR		1	0	1
17	FDD/Jaz/CD-ROM/DVD	Fail	A,B,C	020	JR		1	1	0
18	RAID	Pass	A,B,C		JR		1	0	1
19	Tape	Fail	A,B,C	020	JR		1	1	0
20	Network	Pass	A,B,C		JR		1	0	1
21	Modem Bank	Pass	A,B,C		JR		1	0	1
22	USB/Parallel/Serial	Pass	A,B,C		JR		1	0	1
23	**Suite Summary**						7	2	5
24									
25	*Basic Functionality*								
26	Configure/Register NT						1	0	0
27	Configure/Register Solaris						1	0	0
28	Configure/Register Novell						1	0	0
29	FDD/Jaz/CD-ROM/DVD						1	0	0
30	RAID						1	0	0
31	Tape						1	0	0
32	Network-NT						1	0	0
33	Network-Novell						1	0	0
34	Network-PC-NFS						1	0	0
35	Modem Bank						1	0	0
36	USB/Parallel/Serial						1	0	0
37	UI (Video/Kbd/Mouse)						1	0	0
38	**Suite Summary**						12	0	0
39									
40	*Standards*								
41	Solaris Logo						1	0	0
42	Windows NT Logo						1	0	0
43	Novell Logo						1	0	0
44	**Suite Summary**						3	0	0

Figure 5.1   A test case summary worksheet, halfway through the first cycle of system testing.

The *By* column on the worksheet contains the initials of the tester(s) who ran the test, and the *Comment* column allows you to enter text to provide more information on the test case status.

	A	B	C	D	E	F	G
1							
2	System Config ID	MB Rev	BIOS	OS	Network	Other SW	Other HW
3	A	ST-01	X.015	Solaris	IP/NFS		
4	B	ST-01	X.015	Windows NT	IP/NT		
5	C	ST-02	X.016	Novell	IPX/Novell		
6	D	ST-01	X.015	Windows NT	N/A		

Figure 5.2   A configuration lookup table in the *System Config* worksheet.

The last three columns of the worksheet in Figure 5.1, which I refer to as the *Roll Up* columns, help you summarize the status information. Each test case can be assigned three numeric values based on its state:

- The T column contains the value 1 if the row lists a test case. For example, in Figure 5.1, there is a "1" in cell G5 because cell A5 contains the name of a test case, "Operating Thermal Profile, and the rest of the information in row 5 concerns that test case. Conversely, cell G4 is blank because cell A4 contains the name of a test suite, "Environmental," not a test case.

- The F column contains a formula that computes the value 1 if the test case in that row has a *Fail* state (and computes the value 0 otherwise). For example, in Figure 5.1, there is a "1" in cell H7 because the corresponding test case, "Nonoperating temp/humid cycle," has the word *Fail* in cell B7 (column B is the State column). Conversely, Cell H6 contains a "0" because the corresponding test case, "Operating temp/humid cycle," has the word *Pass* in cell B6.

- The P column contains a formula that computes the value 1 if the test case in that row has a *Pass* state (and computes the value 0 otherwise). To turn the preceding example around, in Figure 5.1 there is a "1" in cell I6 because the corresponding test case, "Operating temp/humid cycle," has the word *Pass* in cell B6. Conversely, Cell I7 contains a "0" because the corresponding test case, "Nonoperating temp/humid cycle," has the word *Fail* in cell B7.

In the suite summary rows—rows 13, 23, 38, and 44 in Figure 5.1—you can add these three columns to see how many test cases are in the test suite and how many test cases are in each state. For easiest reference, you should also set up a third worksheet that will display the test case counts for each test suite. Figure 5.3 offers an example of such a test suite summary worksheet.

At this point, you have a simple but informative test tracking spreadsheet that provides test case details, with a reference to the bug tracking database for more data on failures. (Adventuresome types might want to use advanced features to allow you to "click through" the bug ID on the test case summary worksheet to the database. In the bug

	A	B	C	D	E
1	DataRocket System Test Suite Summary				
2					
3					
4		Total			In
5	Suite	Cases	Fail	Pass	Queue
6					
7	Environmental	8	1	5	2
8	Load, Capacity, and Volume	7	2	5	0
9	Basic Functionality	12	0	0	12
10	Standards	3	0	0	3
11					
12	Total	30	3	10	17
13	By Pct		10%	33%	57%

Figure 5.3   A test suite summary worksheet.

tracking database, you could even add the ability to track the test cases associated with a particular bug, and "click through" from the bug tracking database to the test case summary worksheet.) This spreadsheet offers, in the test suite summary, a management-level perspective of the test execution results. The spreadsheet also contains information about the test environment that will be useful in attempting to reproduce failures, in debugging, and in analyzing root causes. In addition, the spreadsheet identifies the tester(s) in case you need to follow up with questions about the testing performed.

Using the Test Tracking Spreadsheet on Test Projects

You may recall in Chapter 1, "Defining What's on Your Plate: The Foundation of a Test Project" (see *Shoehorning: Fitting a Test Schedule into the Project*), and Chapter 2, "Plotting and Presenting Your Course: The Test Plan" (see *Test Release Management*), that I discussed the concepts of test passes, test releases, and test cycles. I refer to one complete execution of all the planned test cases as a *test pass*, while a *test cycle* is the subset of the test pass run against a single test release. I've reproduced that illustration from Chapter 1 as Figure 5.4 for convenient reference. In this figure, you can see that the test team intends to run each test three times during the test phase shown there, with half the tests run in each of the six cycles against the six test releases. How does this plan affect the test tracking spreadsheet?

There are a few ways you can handle it. The most obvious way is to have one test case summary worksheet and one test suite summary worksheet for the entire test phase. The problem with this approach is that test case status will change at least with each pass, and you will lose information about how tests behaved in the first two passes as you update the worksheets. Therefore, another approach is to have one pair of worksheets (test case summary and test suite summary) for each test cycle. However, now you'll see that only half of your tests are planned to be run in each worksheet, which can create some problems with gathering metrics and summarizing results. (I'll talk about test case metrics and charts toward the end of this chapter.)

My preference is to have one pair of worksheets for each pass. That way, each test case summary shows all the test cases ready to run for that pass. Based on the date on which the test was run—which I'll discuss in the next section—I can tell which test release I ran each test against, although you could also add a column to track release IDs if you'd prefer. The downside to this approach is that test case status is not really a snapshot of an assessment of quality, since I've accepted a new test release in the middle of the pass if I'm following the approach just described. (If you think of testing software as analogous to testing a new drug, accepting a test release before you've run all the tests is similar to changing one or two ingredients in the drug during your drug trial before you've finished assessing the drug's safety and efficacy.) However, I've found that I can deal with that situation provided the new release doesn't destabilize the test environment too much; I just take a calculated risk that I can wait to catch any regressions in the next cycle. If, by having a compact test set, lots of testers, or good automation, I can make my pass and cycle lengths the same, this problem goes away.

In terms of how I use this tool, my approach is to have a once-a-day test team debriefing, usually at the end of the day, where I sit down with each tester one-on-one.

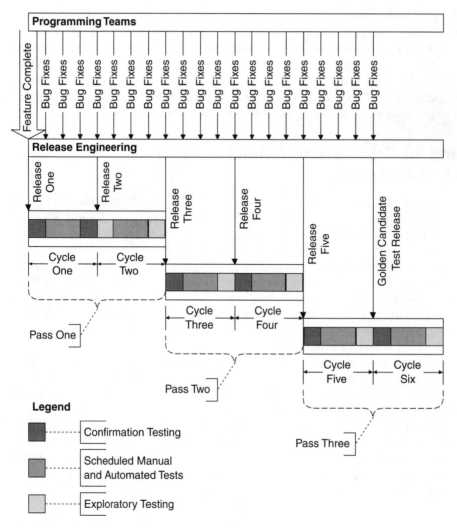

Figure 5.4   Test passes, test releases, and test cycles.

In this debriefing, I ask about the tests run over the course of the day, the findings of those tests, and what tests remain to be run. I review each bug report filed. As I go through the debriefing, I update the test case summary worksheet. That way, that worksheet serves as a structured agenda for my debriefing session. If I have too many people reporting to me on a project to make this practical, I assign two or more lead test engineers to do the debriefing. I ask them to report significant findings that affect the outcome of the test project to me after their debriefing sessions. I generally find that if the end-of-day debriefing includes five or less people, it can be done in an hour or less.

Making Enhancements

Although the basic test tracking spreadsheet you've just seen is useful, you can certainly improve it to record and analyze even more information. Figure 5.5 and Figure 5.6 show an extended version of this tracking spreadsheet, with lots of useful enhancements that I've added over the years. The following sections describe how these data items help me manage my test projects. You might want to incorporate some of them (or come up with others on your own).

Assigning Identifiers and Testers to Test Suites and Cases

In addition to using short names for test suites and test cases, you can assign a Dewey decimal–style ID number to each. In a *Test ID* column, inserted to the left of the *Test Suite/Case* column, you can number each test suite, starting with 1.000, then 2.000, and so on. Each test case carries the suite number to the left of the decimal and its own sequential ID to the right of the decimal. For example, in the test case summary shown in Figure 5.1, the Load, Capacity, and Volume test suite would have the test ID 2.000, and the test ID for the CPU and Memory test case would be 2.001; likewise, the test ID for the Tape test case in the Basic Functionality test suite would be 3.003.

	A	B	C	D	E	F	G	H	I	J	K	L	M	N	O	P	Q	R	S	T	U	V	W
1			DataRocket System Test Case Summary																				
2					Parr One																		
3		Test			System	Bug	Bug		Plan	Act	Plan	Act	Plan	Act		Roll Up Columns							
4	Owner	ID	Test Suite/Case	Status	Config	ID	RPN	By	Date	Date	Effort	Effort	Dur	Dur	Comment	T	S	P	F	FV	Q	I	B
5	System Cookers, Inc.																						
6		1.000	*Environmental Test*																				
7		1.001	Operating Thermal Profile	Pass	D			SC	7/13	7/14	4	4	72	72		1	0	1	0	#	0	0	0
8		1.002	Operating Temp/Humid Cycle	Pass	D			SC	7/13	7/14	4	4	72	72		1	0	1	0	#	0	0	0
9		1.003	Non-Operating Temp/Humid Cycl	Pass	D			SC	7/13	7/14	4	4	72	72		1	0	1	0	#	0	0	0
10		1.004	Non-Operating Drop	Pass	D			SC	7/13	7/14	2	2	2	2		1	0	1	0	#	0	0	0
11		1.005	Non-Operating Shock	Pass	D			SC	7/13	7/14	2	2	2	2		1	0	1	0	#	0	0	0
12		1.006	Non-Operating Thermal Shock	Pass	D			SC	7/13	7/14	2	2	72	72		1	0	1	0	#	0	0	0
13		1.007	Packaging Drop	Pass	D			SC	7/13	7/14	2	2	2	2		1	0	1	0	#	0	0	0
14		1.008	Packaging Shock	Pass	D			SC	7/13	7/14	2	2	2	2		1	0	1	0	#	0	0	0
15			**Suite Summary**						**7/13**	**7/14**	**22**	**22**	**296**	**296**		**8**	**0**	**8**	**0**	**0**	**0**	**0**	**0**
16	**Winged Bytes**																						
17	LTW	2.000	*Load, Capacity and Volume*																				
18		2.001	CPU and Memory	Fail	A,B,C	009	2	LTW	7/10	7/6	4	6	6	7		1	0	0	1	1/2	0	0	0
19						010	6													1/6			
20		2.002	FDD/Jaz/CD-ROM/DVD	Pass	A,B,C			LTW	7/10	7/6	4	4	4	4		1	0	1	0	#	0	0	0
21		2.003	RAID	Pass	A,B,C			LTW	7/10	7/6	4	4	4	4		1	0	1	0	#	0	0	0
22		2.004	Tape	Pass	A,B,C			LTW	7/10	7/7	4	4	4	4		1	0	1	0	#	0	0	0
23		2.005	Network	Pass	A,B,C			LTW	7/10	7/7	4	4	4	4		1	0	1	0	#	0	0	0
24		2.006	Modem Bank	Pass	A,B,C			LTW	7/10	7/8	4	4	4	4		1	0	1	0	#	0	0	0
25		2.007	USB/Parallel/Serial	Pass	A,B,C			LTW	7/10	7/8	4	4	4	4		1	0	1	0	#	0	0	0
26		2.008	All Subsystems	Pass	A,B,C			LTW	7/10	7/10	4	4	4	4		1	0	1	0	#	0	0	0
27			**Suite Summary**						**7/10**	**7/10**	**32**	**34**	**34**	**35**		**8**	**0**	**7**	**1**	**0.6667**	**0**	**0**	**0**
28																							
29	JC	3.000	*Basic Functionality*																				
30		3.001	Configure/Register NT	Pass	A,B,C			JC	7/9	7/7	2	2	2	2		1	0	1	0	#	0	0	0
31		3.002	Configure/Register Solaris	Pass	A,B,C			JC	7/9	7/7	2	2	2	2		1	0	1	0	#	0	0	0
32		3.003	Configure/Register Novell	Pass	A,B,C			JC	7/9	7/7	2	2	2	2		1	0	1	0	#	0	0	0
33		3.004	FDD/Jaz/CD-ROM/DVD	Pass	A,B,C			JC	7/9	7/7	2	2	2	2		1	0	1	0	#	0	0	0
34		3.005	RAID	Pass	A,B,C			JC	7/9	7/7	2	2	2	2		1	0	1	0	#	0	0	0
35		3.006	Tape	Pass	A,B,C			JC	7/9	7/7	2	2	2	2		1	0	1	0	#	0	0	0
36		3.007	Network-NT	Pass	A,B,C			JC	7/9	7/7	2	2	2	2		1	0	1	0	#	0	0	0
37		3.008	Network-Novell	Pass	A,B,C			JC	7/9	7/9	2	1.5	2	1.5		1	0	1	0	#	0	0	0
38		3.009	Network-PC-NFS	Pass	A,B,C			JC	7/9	7/9	2	1.5	2	1.5		1	0	1	0	#	0	0	0
39		3.010	Modem Bank	Pass	A,B,C			JC	7/9	7/9	2	2.5	2	2.5		1	0	1	0	#	0	0	0
40		3.011	USB/Parallel/Serial	Pass	A,B,C			JC	7/9	7/9	2	2.5	2	2.5		1	0	1	0	#	0	0	0
41		3.012	UI (Video/Kbd/Mouse)	Pass	A,B,C			JC	7/9	7/10	2	1	2	1		1	0	1	0	#	0	0	0
42			**Suite Summary**						**7/9**	**7/10**	**18**	**17**	**18**	**17**		**12**	**0**	**12**	**0**	**0**	**0**	**0**	**0**
43																							
44	HL	4.000	*Standards*																				
45		4.001	Solaris Logo	Pass	A			HL	7/8	7/7	8	8	16	16		1	0	1	0	#	0	0	0
46		4.002	Windows NT Logo	Pass	B			HL	7/8	7/5	8	8	16	16		1	0	1	0	#	0	0	0
47		4.003	Novell Logo	Warn	C	005	25	HL	7/8	7/10	8	8	16	16		1	0	1	0	1/25	0	0	0
48			**Suite Summary**						**7/8**	**7/10**	**24**	**24**	**48**	**48**		**3**	**0**	**3**	**0**	**0.04**	**0**	**0**	**0**

Figure 5.5 An extended test case summary worksheet.

When more than one person will be running tests, I find it useful to add an *Owner* column to the test case tracking worksheet. The owner might be the organization responsible for running the test, the engineer writing the test, or the test technician running the test. A test can have multiple owners over time; for example, a different tester might run each test in each test pass to get multiple perspectives.

Adding Date and Hours Information: Plan versus Actual

Your overall schedule is based in part on projected test completion dates, and one important component of your budget is projected effort (person-hours) per test case. Adding information about completion dates and effort to your test tracking spreadsheet can help you perform a "reality check" if your test project starts to deviate from the schedule or budget.

You can add two date columns, *Plan Date* and *Actual Date*, to the test case summary. The plan date comes from the schedule, based on when you expect the test case to be completed. For simplicity, my practice is to assign every test case in a test suite the same planned completion date. Actual Date, the second date column, indicates when the tester actually completed the test.

You can also track actual and planned effort. I do this in person-hours. If you estimated that a test case would require five person-hours, but instead it took 10, that bears explaining. Conversely, you might find that another test case takes less effort than predicted. By accumulating these numbers and analyzing them, you can refine your plans for test cycles, improve your test cases, and figure out which test cases are consuming the most effort.

Now, two questions often come up in this context. One is whether you should count time spent on writing bug reports as part of the test execution effort. Another is whether to count time spent on rerunning a test if you do run a test more than once in a given test pass. (You might choose to rerun a test in the second cycle of a test pass because the new test release fixed a bug found in the first cycle, and you want to confirm that the affected test[s] now passes.) Typically, I would count both, so I include a little extra time in the planned test effort to allow for these categories. The correct amount of time will depend on how many bugs you think you'll find—especially in your first test pass—and how many tests you have. I spread the time evenly over all the tests. Those tests that pass should come in under time, and those that fail should tend to go a little over.

	Total	Planned Tests Fulfilled				Weighted	Planned Tests Unfulfilled				Earned Value			
Suite	Cases	Count	Skip	Pass	Fail	Failure	Count	Queued	IP	Block	Plan Eff	Act Eff	% Effort	% Exec
Environmental Test	8	8	0	8	0	0.00	0	0	0	0	22.00	22.00	100%	100%
Load, Capacity and Volume	8	8	0	7	1	0.67	0	0	0	0	32.00	34.00	106%	100%
Basic Functionality	12	12	0	12	0	0.00	0	0	0	0	18.00	17.00	94%	100%
Standards	3	3	0	3	0	0.04	0	0	0	0	24.00	24.00	100%	100%
Total	31	31	0	30	1	0.71	0	0	0	0	96.00	97.00	101%	100%
By Percentage		100%	0%	97%	3%		0%	0%	0%	0%				

DataRocket System Test Suite Summary — Pass One

Figure 5.6   An extended test suite summary worksheet.

A neat trick you can do when you add tracking of actual and planned person-hours is to look at *earned value*. To illustrate the concept of earned value, suppose that you offered to wash 10 cars for $100. You plan on spending half an hour per car, so you'll make $20 per hour. However, at the end of four hours, you've only washed five cars. While you've expended 80 percent of the planned effort, you've only achieved 50 percent of the milestones. The idea of earned value allows you to see that you will not finish all 10 cars in the remaining hour, because it's taking you 48 minutes per car. At this rate, you will actually earn $12.50 per hour rather than $20.

To return to the testing world, consider test cases instead of cars to be units of work, and that you planned to get 75 test cases done by five testers in two weeks, assuming 30 hours of testing time per tester per week. (In my experience, this is a pretty good rule of thumb on my test teams, although some test managers have told me they have productivity rates more like 20 hours per tester per week.) If your team has completed 30 test cases but all told, they've expended only 100 person-hours of effort, your earned value situation is good. You are 40 percent through the planned test execution, but have used only 33 percent of your planned effort. I'll show you more ways to track whether you're on schedule with earned value in the section *Putting the Test Tracking System in Motion*.

Using test cases as a unit of work assumes that the effort and duration of each test case are relatively uniform. It doesn't matter if some test cases are a little longer and some a little shorter, but if some test cases are an hour long and others are 10 hours long, that can make the results misleading. If you finish all the hour-long tests first, it might look like you're making great progress in terms of milestones, but you might not have time left over for the 10-hour tests.

Understanding How Long Tests Run

In some cases, the amount of effort required to run a test is less than the time the test takes to run. For example, if you use automated tools for functional regression or performance testing of your software, you might start the tests, leave them, and then return later to analyze the results. In the case of hardware, life tests, reliability demonstrations, and burn-in tests are the same way. To know how long tests take to run, it's a good idea to gather duration information as well. Adding a *Test Hours* column that captures the duration in the test tracking spreadsheet is a relatively straightforward way to do this.

In addition to the planning benefits of knowing how long tests take to run, test duration time is commonly used when testing hardware to generate mean time between failures (MTBF) figures. It is also used similarly in various reliability models for software. While I've done hardware reliability testing using MTBF statistical models, I've not worked on any software projects where we needed to make sure predictions.[1]

---

[1] For good information about software reliability, see Chapters 7 and 8 of Stephen Kan's *Metrics and Models in Software Quality Engineering*. Chapter 9 of Boris Beizer's *Software System Testing and Quality Assurance* contains an excellent discussion of techniques and problems with them, while Beizer's article "Software Is Different" (found at the Software Research archives at www.soft.com) points out the reasons such calculations are questionable. You can also refer to IEEE Standard 982.1 and 982.2. Finally, John Musa is another published authority on the topic, though many of his books are now out of print.

Increasing the Precision of Test Case State

The basic test suite summary introduced earlier records three possible states of a test case: *Pass*, *Fail*, or *In Queue*. (The *In Queue* state is indicated by the lack of an entry in the *State* column of the test case summary.) However, I prefer to be much more precise about the life cycle of a typical test case. While the appropriate life cycle for the way you test might vary, here's a test case life cycle I've used:

Queue. The test case is ready to run, assigned to a tester for execution in this test pass.

In Progress. The test is currently running and will probably continue to do so for a while. (If a test takes less than a day, I don't bother to mark a test *In Progress* since I track test case status daily.)

Block. Some condition—such as a missing piece of functionality or a lack of a necessary component in the test environment—has prevented the tester from executing the test to completion. (I usually document the blocking condition in the *Comments* column of the test case summary worksheet.) One way to think of the *Block* state is: I wanted to run the test, but I couldn't.

Skip. You've decided to skip the test for this pass, perhaps because it's a relatively low priority. (Again, the *Comments* column of the test case summary worksheet should reflect why the test is not run.) One way to think of the *Skip* state is: I could have run the test, but I didn't want to.

Pass. The test case ran to completion and the tester observed only expected results, states, and behaviors.

Fail. In one or more ways, the tester observed unexpected results, states, or behaviors that call into question the quality of the system with respect to the objective of the test. One or more bugs were reported.

Warn. In one or more ways, the testers observed unexpected results, states, or behaviors, but the underlying quality of the system with respect to the objective of the test is not seriously compromised. (I usually count *Warn* in the *Pass* category in the test suite summary rather than adding another column to that worksheet.) Another way to think about this is that *Warn* means that the bugs were either trivial in nature or not material to the feature under test. One or more bugs were reported. A handy rule of thumb I use is that a test associated only with deferred and non-must-fix bugs (per the bug triage committee) should be marked as *Warn*, not *Fail*.

Closed. After being marked as *Fail* or *Warn* in the first cycle of a test pass, the next test release included a fix to the bug(s) that afflicted this test case. Upon rerunning the entire test case, no bugs were observed. Marking such tests as *Closed* rather than *Pass* allows you to track the fact that the test did fail against one of the releases tested in the test pass. (As with *Warn*, I count *Closed* test cases in the *Pass* category in the test suite summary.)

Figure 5.7 shows this life cycle. Dotted lines indicate uncommon flows, while heavy circles indicate states that are typically final for the test case in that pass (i.e., a *terminal state*). From a point of view of the mechanics of the test case tracking worksheet, you'll

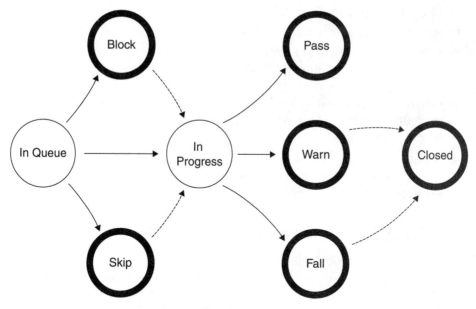

Figure 5.7 One possible test case life cycle.

need to add a few more columns for the extra roll-up fields, which I'll illustrate in the section *Putting the Test Tracking System in Motion.*

Note that this life cycle is tightly coupled with the entire test pass, test release, and test cycle approach shown in Figure 5.4. For example, suppose that you are less regression-averse than I am on most projects. You decide not to rerun tests after they have passed. In other words, you'll rerun failed or warned tests against subsequent releases, but only until they pass. Once all the tests are marked *Pass*, *Closed*, or *Warn*, you declare victory. In that situation, you would have a test case life cycle that applied to the entire test phase, rather than pass-by-pass, and it would include arcs from *Fail* and *Warn* to *In Progress*. In my approach, whatever state the test case is in at the end of the pass, it remains in that state. In subsequent passes, it starts anew with an *In Queue* state. I bring this example up to encourage you to consider how your testing strategies and test project realities will affect your use of this tool.

One possible complication is that, as I discussed in Chapter 3, a test case is an amalgamation of test steps and substeps. Test cases generally cover multiple test conditions. If one test condition fails and the rest pass, what to do? At one point, I tried having compound states such as *Block/Fail* and so forth, but found that made the test suite summary and other metrics very hard to gather. Do I count the test as *Block*, as *Fail*, or as both? It was too confusing for me, and impossible to explain to the rest of the project team. Therefore, I use the simple hierarchical rule introduced in Chapter 3:

■ If any step or condition in the test case is underway, I mark the test *In Progress*.

■ Else, if any step or condition was blocked, I mark the test *Block*.

- Else if any step or condition failed, I mark the test *Fail*.

- Else, if any step or condition resulted in a warning, I mark the test *Warn*.

- If the test was marked *Fail* or *Warn* in the first cycle, was rerun in the second cycle, and the tester must have observed only expected results, states, and behaviors, I mark the test *Closed*.

- Otherwise, it must be the first time the tester ran the test in this pass, and further, the tester must have observed only expected results, states, and behaviors, so I mark the test *Pass*.

Since I usually make the decision to skip tests at the test case level of granularity, I don't need a rule for handling skips. My testers and I discuss test findings and assign these test states during the daily debriefing.

Prioritizing Test Suites and Cases

Our discussion of regression gaps in Chapter 3 (see *Avoiding the Dreaded 'Test Escape': Coverage and Regression Test Gaps*) raised the issue of how to select or prioritize test suites to be rerun in multiple-pass situations—that is, how to select the test suites that find the most important bugs. A numerical technique for doing this can be found in the concept of *test suite yield*. This method considers not only the number of bugs found by the suite, but also the severity and priority rankings of the bugs (the risk priority numbers from the bug tracking system). By calculating a weighted failure number for each suite, you obtain a numeric yield that you can use to select test suites.

It's easy to add such a feature to your test tracking spreadsheet. Begin by inserting a column in the test case summary worksheet to store the risk priority number (RPN) for the corresponding bug ID. Then, in the Roll-Up area, insert a column named FW (for Failure Weight) that holds a formula calculating the reciprocal of the RPN in each row. Finally, add a column in the test suite summary worksheet that references the sum of the reciprocals for each suite. Now you have a test suite summary column that starts at 0 and increases as the yield—RPN weighted—of the test suite increases. You can now figure out at a glance which test suites in your test system are most effective.

If you want to look at efficiency as well as effectiveness, then you might want to use a normalized value.[2] You can use the number of test cases in the suite, if test case effort and duration are relatively uniform as I mentioned earlier in relation to earned value. If they are not, then you can normalize by effort or duration, depending on which is more meaningful in your situation. For heavily automated test regimes, for example, duration is likely to be more meaningful.

For the purists out there, you might question my choice to add the inverse RPNs rather than, say, multiplying them, squaring the sums, or using another more exotic function. If you believe that such an approach is more appropriate, try it. I would argue

---

[2] I use the word "normalized" in the mathematical sense of dividing by a factor that ensures "apples-to-apples" comparisons. For example, when speaking of automobile mileage, we don't talk about how many miles or kilometers are traveled per tank of gas—which varies from one vehicle to the next—but rather in terms of miles per gallon or liters per hundred kilometers.

that multiplying overstates the importance of RPN 1 bugs while downplaying the importance of other bugs. Is a test suite that yields one RPN 1 bug eight times better than a suite that yields three RPN 2 bugs? I would deem the latter test suite better, a conclusion that supports the additive approach. Squaring the sums also emphasizes the bugs with smaller RPNs, although in a more appropriate way; but it makes the number more difficult to explain, without adding much information. As always, however, follow your muse; if you have a better idea, go ahead and implement it.

As with the subsystem breakdown chart in Chapter 4, failure weight is a measure of technical risk; in other words, where are the bugs most likely to occur. Again, any method of prioritizing that relies strictly on technical risk ignores the very important aspect of business risk. Business risk derives from what the users will do with the system, what value the customers are paying to receive from the system, and so forth; basically, what it would mean for the system to have quality as discussed in Chapter 1. Therefore, you might want to add a Priority column to the test case summary worksheet to track and manage this aspect. By analyzing which risks to system quality are covered by each test, you can assign a priority based on your quality risks assessment priority.

Scrutinizing the Roll-Up Columns

Rather than create this spreadsheet from scratch, I encourage you to download it from my Web site and adapt it to your use. One of the reasons I suggest that is that the roll-up columns on the rightmost side of Figure 5.5, along with the test suite summary worksheet, can be a bit inscrutable for novice spreadsheet users. However, if you want to understand how these work, download the spreadsheet and follow along with me for a moment.

The "T" roll-up column is just a constant value, either "1" if the cell to the left in column C—the "Test Suite/Case" column—is a test case, not a test suite, a blank line, or a suite summary. The "S," "P," "F," "Q," "I," and "B" columns, however, all contain formulas that check whether the "Test State" column contains the text "Skip," "Pass," "Fail," blank (for "In Queue"), "IP" (for "In Progress"), or "Block," respectively. If correct text is found in that column, then the formula returns a "1"; if not, then a "0" is returned. (I count "Warn" as a "Pass"; if you don't like this, you might want to add another roll-up column to count the warns separately, or change the formula to count "Warn" as "Fail.") These columns are summed in the "Suite Summary" rows and then referenced in the suite summary worksheet.

If you prefer to use other names for the same states, abbreviations for the states, or a different set of states entirely, you'll need to change these roll-up columns, both the headings and the formulas. I encourage you to spend some time studying how the current formulas work before you start hacking on them, because they're fragile and not exactly self-documenting. You'll also need to change the test suite summary worksheet to reflect any states you add or rename.

The "FW" column contains the failure weight, which, as discussed earlier, is the inverse of the RPN for any bugs found by that test case. This is also added up in the "Suite Summary" rows and referenced in the suite summary worksheet.

One important part of using this tracking spreadsheet is keeping the formula references correct, especially in the "Roll Up" columns and in the suite summaries. It's not too hard after a little practice, but the first few times you get bitten by a broken cell reference it does eat up some time. As the carpenter's adage goes, "Measure twice and cut once." Check the references often when you first start using this tool, and you'll learn how to avoid stubbing your toe on spreadsheet quirks.

Other Ways to Summarize and Group Data

Beyond just summarizing by test state and failure weight, you can analyze more of the data you're gathering. For example, I usually include an earned value section of the test suite summary worksheet that looks at planned versus actual test effort and associated test case completion. You can also look at planned versus actual dates or durations, assigned owner versus tester, and so forth. The test tracking spreadsheet is a flexible tool, and it lends itself to extensions. Just remember that the more bells and whistles you attach, the bigger the file gets, the slower the updates become, and the more impenetrable the data seems to many managers and developers.

You also might want to think twice about certain types of metrics—in particular, those that address questions such as "Who found the most bugs overall?", "Who spent the most time testing?", and "Who found the most bugs per hour spent?" I find these numbers dangerous, and I don't generate them. As soon as you begin analyzing employee performance data, you take risks. If people know you are measuring them this way, they will soon figure out how to manipulate the numbers. In addition, if you use such data to rank employees for a layoff or to fire laggards, you might believe that you're being fair, but you could find yourself in court responding to a lawsuit.[3]

The test case summary worksheet shown earlier grouped data primarily by test suite. Alternatively, you could use test phases, owner, or organization as major groups. (Multiple organizations are sometimes involved in test efforts, especially those that include outsourcing. Chapter 10, "Involving Other Players: Distributing a Test Project," discusses applying the test tracking spreadsheet to such "virtual test teams.") The grouping can be as flat or as hierarchical as you want. If you use too many levels, you'll make the chart difficult to read. If you use too few—for example, 1,000 detail rows but no grouping—the chart will be monotonous and hard to scan. If in doubt, try out a few different arrangements and see what looks most readable and accessible.

Extending the Spreadsheet by Including Test Case Details

Chapter 3 provided a template for writing test cases, constructed with a spreadsheet. It has probably already occurred to you that you can integrate the test cases with the test tracking spreadsheet. By doing so, you gain automatic summaries of the test cases as you update them with test results. You can use links or references between worksheets to automatically transfer information such as the test ID, the test case name, and so forth from the test case template to the test case summary, or vice versa.

---

[3]Cem Kaner, Jack Falk, and Hung Nguyen mention this possibility in terms of misuse of testing metrics in *Testing Computer Software*. The same concerns would apply here.

By creating a separate worksheet for each test case, you can include all the tests, along with the summaries, from a given test phase in a single spreadsheet. By establishing links up to the test case summary and down into each test case worksheet, you can create a complete, self-summarizing test tracking system. The feasibility of building such a system depends on how many test cases you intend to run. If you have too many to fit into a single spreadsheet, you can link them across multiple files. For very large projects, however, in which you would need to tie together a great many spreadsheets, this effort might prove too complex, and the system might be too difficult to maintain.

If you decide to use this approach, you'll need to establish a process for updating the worksheets. An approach I've used is to print the test cases and test case summary worksheet, have test engineers and technicians make notes on the hard copies, and input the results myself as part of the daily debriefing. This ensures that the data is more consistent, and it prevents mistakes in using the formulas. Personally, I find that staying intimately acquainted with test execution at a test case level makes a lot of sense. However, if your management style is better suited to focusing at a higher level, let your testers update the test case worksheets, and then you can audit the test case summary and test suite summary after the updates.

Tracking Coverage

In addition to using the test case summary to track test case information, we can also use that worksheet to tie test cases back to the test basis. This is similar to including the *Quality Risk* field in the bug tracking database as discussed in Chapter 4. In the test case summary worksheet, I can include a set of columns to the right of the roll-up columns that I can use to assess quality risk coverage.

Figure 5.8 shows the test coverage analysis for our DataRocket case study. I've identified seven broad categories of risks to system quality, plus a catchall category "Other." In each category, I look at planned and actual coverage. The planned coverage, as in Chapter 1, is a "2" if the test case directly addresses the risk, a "1" if the test case indirectly addresses it, and blank (counted as zero) if there is no coverage. The actual coverage uses the same weighting, but counts only if the test has been run and resulted in a Pass, Warn, or Fail. (It looks at the "Pass" and "Fail" roll-up columns to do this.) Blocked, skipped, and queued tests don't count toward actual coverage.

If you remember the DataRocket Failure Mode and Effect Analysis (FMEA) chart from Chapter 1, you can see that I'm tracking test coverage using broad categories of quality risks, not the type of low-level details shown in the FMEA chart. This makes sense here, because I intend to use this data to look at coverage at a high level for results-reporting purposes. If I wanted to analyze the test execution in detail to look for gaps in coverage and the related risks to system quality, then I'd need to use the FMEA chart level of detail. In my experience, if you need tracing that level of detail, you're better off doing the test and quality risks tracking in a database (see this chapter's *Case Study*).

Putting the Test Tracking System in Motion

To illustrate how the test tracking spreadsheet can work for you, this section presents three short case studies, using the DataRocket information shown earlier. In all scenarios,

Test Suite/Case	Install		Functionality		Reliability		Performance		Compatibility		Environmental		Standards		Other	
	Pln	Act	Pln	Act	Pln	Act	Pln	Act	Pln	Act	Pln	Act	Pln	Act	Pln	Act
Environmental Test																
Operating Thermal Profile					1	1					2	2				
					0	0					0	0				
Operating Temp/Humid Cycle					1	1					2	2				
					0	0					0	0				
Non-Oprtng Temp/Humid Cycle											2	2				
Non-Oprtng Drop											2	2				
Non-Oprtng Shock											2	2				
Non-Oprtng Thermal Shock											2	2				
Packaging Drop											2	2				
Packaging Shock											0	0				
Suite Summary	**0**	**0**	**0**	**0**	**2**	**2**	**0**	**0**	**0**	**0**	**16**	**16**	**0**	**0**	**0**	**0**
Load Capacity and Volume																
CPU and Memory			1	1	2	2	2	2	1	1						
			0	0	0	0	0	0	0	0						
			0	0	0	0	0	0	0	0						
			0	0	0	0	0	0	0	0						
			0	0	0	0	0	0	0	0						
FDD/Jaz/CD-ROM/DVD			1	1	2	2	2	2	1	1						
RAID			1	0	2	0	2	0	1	0						
Tape			1	1	2	2	2	2	1	1						
Network			1	1	2	2	2	2	1	1						
Modem Bank			1	1	2	2	2	2	1	1						
USB/Parallel/Serial			1	0	2	0	2	0	1	0						
All Subsystems			1	0	2	0	2	0	1	0						
			0	0	0	0	0	0	0	0						
Suite Summary	**0**	**0**	**8**	**5**	**16**	**10**	**16**	**10**	**8**	**5**	**0**	**0**	**0**	**0**	**0**	**0**
Functionality																
Configure/Register NT	2	0	2	0					2	0						
Configure/Register Solaris	2	0	2	0					2	0						
Configure/Register Novell	2	0	2	0					2	0						
FDD/Jaz/CD-ROM/DVD			2	2					2	2						
RAID			2	0					2	0						
Tape			2	2					2	2						
Network-NT			2	2					2	2						
Network-Novell			2	2					2	2						
Network-PC-NFS			2	0					2	0						
Modem Bank			2	2					2	2						
USB/Parallel/Serial			2	0					2	0						
UI (Video/Kbd/Mouse)			2	2					2	2						
Suite Summary	**6**	**0**	**24**	**12**	**0**	**0**	**0**	**0**	**24**	**12**	**0**	**0**	**0**	**0**	**0**	**0**
Standards																
Solaris Logo	1	0			1	0			1	0			2	0		
Designed for Windows Logo	1	1			1	1			1	1			2	2		
Novell Logo	1	1			1	1			1	1			2	2		
Suite Summary	**3**	**2**	**0**	**0**	**3**	**2**	**0**	**0**	**3**	**2**	**0**	**0**	**6**	**4**	**0**	**0**
Test Pass Summary	**9**	**2**	**32**	**17**	**21**	**14**	**16**	**10**	**35**	**19**	**16**	**16**	**6**	**4**	**0**	**0**

Figure 5.8   Tracking test coverage.

assume that you are about halfway through the scheduled system test phase. The first two scenarios represent test projects in some amount of trouble, one with a minor problem, and the other in serious difficulty. The third scenario describes a successful project.

Little Trouble

It's July 16. Life is pretty good on the test project. All the systems showed up on time—a small miracle—and you have yet to run into any major bugs. You sent the systems out to an external test lab named System Cookers, and most of the environmental tests finished almost a week early; this was a major stroke of luck since these tests were considered the most risky. Nevertheless, you do have a few problems, as your current test case and suite summary worksheets (shown in Figure 5.9 and Figure 5.10) indicate.

First, and worst, the standards testing is taking longer than planned. Hitesh, the test engineer in charge, is deluged with other systems in the lab and probably won't wrap up that work for a few more days. This isn't a big deal—assuming that all the tests pass. Given the difficulty of predicting *that*, however, you're a little nervous.

Second, you seem to have underestimated the size of the effort. All of these tests are taking longer, in person-hours, than you expected. You are incurring some overtime

				System	Bug	Bug		Plan	Act	Plan	Act		Roll Up Columns							
Owner	Test ID	Test Suite/Case	State	Config	ID	RPN	By	Date	Date	Effort	Effort	Comment	T	S	P	F	FV	Q	I	B

DataRocket System Test Case Tracking Spreadsheet — Pass Two

Owner	ID	Test Suite/Case	State	Config	Bug ID	Bug RPN	By	Plan Date	Act Date	Plan Effort	Act Effort	Comment	T	S	P	F	FV	Q	I	B
System Cookers, Inc.																				
	1.000	*Environmental Test*																		
	1.001	Operating Thermal Profile	Pass	D			SC	7/16	7/10	4	5		1	0	1	0	0	0	0	0
	1.002	Operating Temp/Humid Cycle	Pass	D			SC	7/16	7/10	4	6		1	0	1	0	0	0	0	0
	1.003	Non-Operating Temp/Humid Cycle	Pass	D			SC	7/16	7/10	4	4		1	0	1	0	0	0	0	0
	1.004	Non-Operating Drop	Pass	D			SC	7/16	7/10	4	6		1	0	1	0	0	0	0	0
	1.005	Non-Operating Shock	Pass	D			SC	7/16	7/10	4	6		1	0	1	0	0	0	0	0
	1.006	Non-Operating Thermal Shock	Pass	D			SC	7/16	7/10	4	3		1	0	1	0	0	0	0	0
	1.007	Packaging Drop	Block					7/16		4		Package redesign IP.	1	0	0	0	0	0	0	1
	1.008	Packaging Shock	Block					7/16		4		Package redesign IP.	1	0	0	0	0	0	0	1
		Suite Summary						7/16	7/10	32	30		8	0	6	0	0.00	0	0	2
Winged Bytes																				
	2.000	*Load, Capacity and Volume*																		
LTW	2.001	CPU and Memory	Pass	A,B,C			LTW	7/10	7/10	4	5		1	0	1	0	0	0	0	0
LTW	2.002	FDDI/Jaz/CD-ROM/DVD	Pass	A,B,C			LTW	7/10	7/10	4	5		1	0	1	0	0	0	0	0
LTW	2.003	RAID	Pass	A,B,C			LTW	7/10	7/11	4	5		1	0	1	0	0	0	0	0
LTW	2.004	Tape	Pass	A,B,C			LTW	7/10	7/11	4	5		1	0	1	0	0	0	0	0
LTW	2.005	Network	Pass	A,B,C			LTW	7/10	7/12	4	5		1	0	1	0	0	0	0	0
LTW	2.006	Modem Bank	Pass	A,B,C			LTW	7/10	7/13	4	5		1	0	1	0	0	0	0	0
LTW	2.007	USB/Parallel/Serial	Pass	A,B,C			LTW	7/10	7/14	4	5		1	0	1	0	0	0	0	0
LTW	2.008	All Subsystems	Pass	A,B,C			LTW	7/10	7/14	4	5		1	0	1	0	0	0	0	0
		Suite Summary						7/10	7/14	32	40		8	0	8	0	0.00	0	0	0
	3.000	*Basic Functionality*																		
JC	3.001	Configure/Register NT	Pass	B			JC	7/5	7/5	4	8		1	0	1	0	0	0	0	0
JC	3.002	Configure/Register Solaris	Pass	A			JC	7/5	7/6	4	8		1	0	1	0	0	0	0	0
JC	3.003	Configure/Register Novell	Pass	A			JC	7/5	7/7	4	8		1	0	1	0	0	0	0	0
JC	3.004	FDDI/Jaz/CD-ROM/DVD	Warn	A,B,C	005	6	JC	7/9	7/16	2	4		1	0	1	0	1/6	0	0	0
JC	3.005	RAID	Pass	A,B,C			JC	7/9	7/16	2	4		1	0	1	0	0	0	0	0
JC	3.006	Tape	Pass	A,B,C			JC	7/9	7/16	2	4		1	0	1	0	0	0	0	0
JC	3.007	Network-NT	Pass	A,B,C			JC	7/9	7/16	2	4		1	0	1	0	0	0	0	0
JC	3.008	Network-Novell	Pass	A,B,C			JC	7/9	7/16	2	4		1	0	1	0	0	0	0	0
JC	3.009	Network-PC-NFS	Pass	A,B,C			JC	7/9	7/17	2	4		1	0	1	0	0	0	0	0
JC	3.010	Modem Bank	Pass	A,B,C			JC	7/9	7/17	2	4		1	0	1	0	0	0	0	0
JC	3.011	USB/Parallel/Serial	Pass	A,B,C			JC	7/9	7/17	2	4		1	0	1	0	0	0	0	0
JC	3.012	UI (Video/Kbd/Mouse)	Pass	A,B,C			JC	7/9	7/17	2	4		1	0	1	0	0	0	0	0
		Suite Summary						7/5	7/17	30	60		12	0	12	0	0.17	0	0	0
	4.000	*Standards*																		
HL	4.001	Solaris Logo	IP	A				7/8		8			1	0	0	0	0	0	1	0
HL	4.002	Windows NT Logo	IP	B				7/8		8			1	0	0	0	0	0	1	0
HL	4.003	Novell Logo	IP	C				7/8		8			1	0	0	0	0	0	1	0
		Suite Summary						7/8	1/0	24	0		3	0	0	0	0.00	0	3	0

Figure 5.9 A worrisome test case summary.

costs associated with your contractor, Jim, and an irritated employee, Lin-Tsu, who has had to work overtime for two weeks. (You can see this most clearly in the earned value section of the suite summary.)

Third, the packaging was given a last-minute facelift, delaying that portion of the environmental testing. Fourth, the floppy drive doesn't read 1.2MB (Japanese) formatted disks. You mark this as a *Warn* because this problem might delay shipment in Japan, although nowhere else.

The latter two problems, of course, are system-related issues, which you can't really affect. However, you do have two lessons to learn. The first is that you should cross-train your staff on standards testing, so that you don't get held up there again. Next, you should be careful to adjust your planned effort for the next test project.

Big Trouble

It's July 26. You have big problems. Engineering samples showed up for testing a week late, but the project release date remains unchanged. You lost a week from your first test cycle. You don't have all the drivers you need for the supported operating systems, which blocks three very important test cases. On top of that, Solaris, an important network

	A	B	C	D	E	F	G	H	I	J	K	L	M	N	O
1					DataRocket System Test Suite Summary										
2						Pass Two									
3															
4			Total	Planned Tests Fulfilled				Weighted	Planned Tests Unfulfilled				Earned Value		
5	Suite		Cases	Count	Skip	Pass	Fail	Failure	Count	Queued	IP	Block	Pln Hrs	Act Hrs	% Effort	% Exec
6															
7	Environmental Test		8	6	0	6	0	0.00	2	0	0	2	32.00	30.00	94%	75%
8	Load, Capacity and Volume		8	8	0	8	0	0.00	0	0	0	0	32.00	40.00	125%	100%
9	Functionality		12	12	0	12	0	0.17	0	0	0	0	30.00	60.00	200%	100%
10	Standards		3	0	0	0	0	0.00	3	0	3	0	24.00	0.00	0%	0%
11															
12	Total		31	26	0	26	0	0.17	5	0	3	2	118.00	130.00	110%	84%
13	By Pct			84%	0%	84%	0%		16%	0%	10%	6%				

Figure 5.10 A worrisome test suite summary.

operating system for your customers, won't install or run reliably with DataRocket. The system panics during installation in nearly half the tests; at other times, it panics under load. This bug, which is referenced in the test case shown in Figure 5.11, blocks completion of most tests.

You also have problems with the Environmental test suite. The CPU exceeded its temperature specification in the thermal profile test. The CPU vendor tells you that the chip will suffer a serious degradation in its MTBF at this temperature, making the sys-

	A	B	C	D	F
1	Test Case Name:	CPU and Memory			
2	Test ID:	2.001			
3	Test	Load, Capacity and Volume			
4	Priority:	High			
5	Hardware	One DataRocket Server			
6	Software Required:	Load, Capacity and Volume Test Tool			
7		Windows NT			
8		Solaris			
9		Novell			
10	Duration:	3			
11	Effort:	4			
12	Setup:	Install Windows NT			
13		Install Novell			
14		Install Solaris			
15	Teardown	None necessary.			
16	ID	Test Area/Condition	Result	Bug ID	Bug RPN
17	1.000	Test CPU load on Windows NT.			
18	1.001	Install Windows NT. Confirm proper install.	Pass		
19	1.002	Install LCV Test Tool from LCV CD-ROM. Confirm proper install.	Warn	9	3
20	1.003	Run LCV Test Tool, CPU Module, for one hour. Check log file for failures on exit.	Pass		
21	2.000	Repeat steps 1.001-1.003 for Solaris.	Fail	10	1
22	3.000	Repeat steps 1.001-1.003 for Novell.	Pass		
23	Overall	Status	Fail		
24		System Config	B,A,C		
25		Tester	LTW		
26		Date Completed	7/14		
27		Effort	16		
28		Duration	16		

Figure 5.11 A test case showing a serious problem.

tem prone to failure in a few months. In addition, the motherboard cracked during the temperature/humidity cycle test. Although the system still ran after the test, the damage indicates that the board is improperly mounted. To add insult to injury, the cardboard box, the padding, and the system case suffered cosmetic damage during the packaging drop test, indicating a need to redesign the package. All of these difficulties are reflected in the test case summary worksheet shown in Figure 5.12.

These problems are very serious. Does it even make sense to move on to the third pass of system testing? Probably not. You are effectively blocked until you have a fix for the Solaris bug, and you can't finish all the tests until the rest of the missing drivers show up. The environmental test—an expensive operation—will need to be rerun, but only after the mounting and temperature problems are resolved. You almost certainly won't exit the system test phase until weeks after the scheduled date, delaying first customer shipment. The severity of the problems is evident in the test suite summary worksheet shown in Figure 5.13. In my experience, this is the type of situation that arises when too little component and integration testing was done prior to starting system test. A few large, functionality- and test-blocking bugs come up right away, preventing further progress. Once these bugs are resolved, a whole host of serious bugs affecting finer-grained areas of functionality and behavior will become visible.

	Test			System	Bug	Bug		Plan	Act	Plan	Act	
Owner	ID	Test Suite/Case	State	Config	ID	RPN	By	Date	Date	Hrs	Hrs	Comment
DataRocket System Test Case Tracking Spreadsheet												
			Pass Two									
		System Cookers, Inc.										
	1.000	*Environmental Test*										
	1.001	Operating Thermal Profile	Fail	D	005	1	SC	7/16	7/19	4	5	
	1.002	Operating Temp/Humid Cycle	Fail	D	006	1	SC	7/16	7/19	4	6	
	1.003	Non-Operating Temp/Humid Cycle	Pass	D			SC	7/16	7/19	4	4	
	1.004	Non-Operating Drop	Pass	D			SC	7/16	7/19	4	6	
	1.005	Non-Operating Shock	Pass	D			SC	7/16	7/19	4	6	
	1.006	Non-Operating Thermal Shock	Pass	D			SC	7/16	7/19	4	3	
	1.007	Packaging Drop	Fail	D	012	5	SC	7/16	7/19	4	2	
	1.008	Packaging Shock	Pass	D			SC	7/16	7/19	4	2	
		Suite Summary						7/16	7/19	32	34	
Winged Bytes												
	2.000	*Load, Capacity and Volume*										
LTW	2.001	CPU and Memory	Fail	B,C	010	1	LTW	7/10	7/21	4	16	Solaris panics.
					009	3						
LTW	2.002	FDD/Jaz/CD-ROM	Block	B,C			LTW	7/10		4		Solaris panics.
LTW	2.003	RAID	Block	B,C			LTW	7/10		4		Solaris panics.
LTW	2.004	Tape	Block	B,C			LTW	7/10		4		Solaris panics.
LTW	2.005	Network	Block	B,C			LTW	7/10		4		Solaris panics.
LTW	2.006	Modem Bank	Block	B,C			LTW	7/10		4		Solaris panics.
LTW	2.007	USB/Parallel/Serial	Block	B,C			LTW	7/10		4		Solaris panics.
LTW	2.008	All Subsystems	Block	B,C			LTW	7/10		4		Solaris panics.
		Suite Summary						7/10	7/21	32	16	
	3.000	*Basic Functionality*										
JC	3.001	Configure/Register NT	Block					7/12		4		Not all NT drv avail.
JC	3.002	Configure/Register Solaris	Block					7/11		4		Not all Sol drv avail.
JC	3.003	Configure/Register Novell	Block					7/10		4		Not all Nvll drv avail.
JC	3.004	FDD/Jaz/CD-ROM	Block	B,C			JC	7/9		2		Solaris panics.
JC	3.005	RAID	Block	B,C			JC	7/9		2		Solaris panics.
JC	3.006	Tape	Block	B,C			JC	7/9		2		Solaris panics.
JC	3.007	Network-NT	Pass	B			JC	7/9	7/16	2	1.5	
JC	3.008	Network-Novell	Pass	C			JC	7/9	7/16	2	1.5	
JC	3.009	Network-PC-NFS	Block	A	010	1	JC	7/9		2		Solaris panics.
JC	3.010	Modem Bank	Block	B,C			JC	7/9		2		Solaris panics.
JC	3.011	USB/Parallel/Serial	Block	B,C			JC	7/9		2		Solaris panics.
JC	3.012	UI (Video/Kbd/Mouse)	Block	B,C			JC	7/9		2		Solaris panics.
		Suite Summary						7/12	7/16	30	3	
	4.000	*Standards*										
HL	4.001	Solaris Logo	Block	A	010	1	HL	7/13		8		Solaris panics.
HL	4.002	Windows NT Logo	IP					7/13		8		
HL	4.003	Novell Logo	IP					7/13		8		
		Suite Summary						7/13	1/0	24	0	

Figure 5.12   A test case summary indicating major problems.

	Total	Planned Tests Fulfilled				Weighted	Planned Tests Unfulfilled				Earned Value			
		DataRocket System Test Suite Summary												
				Pass Two										
Suite	Cases	Count	Skip	Pass	Fail	Failure	Count	Queued	IP	Block	Pln Hrs	Act Hrs	% Effort	% Exec
Environmental Test	8	8	0	5	3	2.20	0	0	0	0	32.00	34.00	106%	100%
Load, Capacity and Volume	8	1	0	0	1	1.33	7	0	0	7	32.00	16.00	50%	13%
Basic Functionality	12	2	0	2	0	1.00	10	0	0	10	30.00	3.00	10%	17%
Standards	3	1	1	0	0	1.00	2	0	2	0	24.00	0.00	0%	0%
Total	31	12	1	7	4	5.53	19	0	2	17	118.00	53.00	45%	37%
By Pct		39%	3%	23%	13%		61%	0%	6%	55%				

Figure 5.13 A test suite summary reporting major problems.

No Problem!

It's July 15, and the living is easy. You received a telephone call this morning from the lab manager at System Cookers informing you that DataRocket passed all the environmental tests as of yesterday. This is only a day late, which is good, since the systems got to the lab three days late. The first pass of system test is now finished. The only problem found was a minor glitch during Novell standards testing, for which you just received a waiver. Your test suite summary worksheet shows that 100 percent of the tests have been run, with 100 percent passing. Better yet, you were within 1 percent of your estimated effort. The test suite summary worksheet (see Figure 5.14) also reflects this smooth sailing.

Based on these fantastic results, you have the enviable job of walking down to the project manager's office today and waiving the second and third passes of system testing, as DataRocket now satisfies the system test exit criteria. The product will ship about a month early, provided all goes well during pilot testing.

Extracting Metrics from the Test Tracking Spreadsheet

Like bug reports, test cases are important details for test managers to stay on top of. However, the test case summary worksheet is probably not something you'll want to

	Total	Planned Tests Fulfilled				Weighted	Planned Tests Unfulfilled				Earned Value			
		DataRocket System Test Suite Summary												
				Pass One										
Suite	Cases	Count	Skip	Pass	Fail	Failure	Count	Queued	IP	Block	Pln Hrs	Act Hrs	% Effort	% Exec
Environmental Test	8	8	0	8	0	0.00	0	0	0	0	32.00	32.00	100%	100%
Load, Capacity and Volume	8	8	0	8	0	0.00	0	0	0	0	32.00	32.00	100%	100%
Basic Functionality	12	12	0	12	0	0.00	0	0	0	0	30.00	31.00	103%	100%
Standards	3	3	0	3	0	0.04	0	0	0	0	24.00	24.00	100%	100%
Total	31	31	0	31	0	0.04	0	0	0	0	118.00	119.00	101%	100%
By Pct		100%	0%	100%	0%		0%	0%	0%	0%				

Figure 5.14 A test suite summary for a product that will ship soon.

present to managers—there's just too much data there. Unless you're fortunate enough to work for a former test manager, the odds are that your manager will find the detail either confusing, or, in some cases, an irresistible temptation to micromanage your work.

Therefore, as with bug reports, extracting a set of metrics is a good idea. The test suite summary is one possible way to present this data. It is clearly management oriented, summarizing the key details of test execution.

The problem with the test suite summary is that it's just a snapshot; it doesn't tell us much about how things have gone and where the trends are headed. (The earned value does, to some extent, capture trend information, but not every manager I've worked with has been able to interpret that easily.) Therefore, I generally don't include the test suite summary as part of my testing dashboard. Instead, I graph three sets of data that are easy to extract daily using the test management tools we've already developed.

Can We Get Any Work Done? Charting Test Progress

The first of these charts is the test progress chart, which looks at how many test hours have been achieved daily. By *test hours*, I mean the actual effort measured against all the tests. Based on my "30 hours per tester" rule of thumb that I quoted earlier, I can multiple six times the number of testers assigned to my test project and come up with a planned number of test hours per day. I might see some variation around that number one way or the other—tests sometimes take longer than planned because of bugs, and shorter than planned when things go smoothly—but I should see a regular pattern of achievement of planned test hours every day. If not, then I can only assume that serious stability problems with the system under test, some logistical problems with the test environment, or other issues are interfering with my ability to get testing done. If I can't get through my testing, why should management think that the users would be able to use the system to get real work done?

Figure 5.15 shows an example of this chart for a two-tester effort. This team is clearly having trouble getting through the tests. Because test hours are only claimed when the test cases they're associated with are completed, this chart seems to indicate a lot of tests going over schedule. In addition, we have a couple of weekdays in the test schedule where no testing gets done at all. Most likely, the test environment is out of action or a bad test release has brought the testing down. Finally, you can see testing happening over the weekend, which is always a sign to me as a manager that a project is out of control. Whenever projects start to eat into people's personal time, you can be sure that burnout and staff turnover are not far behind, leading to even greater losses in efficiency.

Are We Getting as Much Work Done as Planned? Charting Planned Test Fulfillment

The second chart is the test fulfillment chart, which looks at whether we're getting through all the tests we planned. Given some stable number of test cases and a fixed period to complete a test pass, we can plan how many tests should get done, on average, every day. For example, if we have 50 test cases planned for the test phase, the

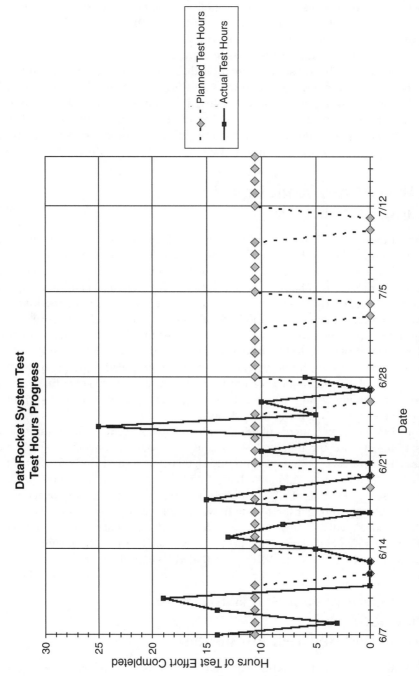

Figure 5.15 A chart of system test progress (test hours achieved)

phase is eight weeks long, and we intend to run four test passes for this phase, we have to complete five test cases per day to stay on track. Even if I'm achieving the test hours, if I can't get through all my tests, then that tells me that tests are taking longer than planned. That could be because I underestimated, but it could also be because the tests are finding more bugs than anticipated. If so, is it likely the system will be ready for customers on the planned ship date?

Figure 5.16 shows an example of this chart. This test team has 31 tests planned per pass, spread across 10 days as four tests on the first day and three tests every day after. The first pass didn't go too well; we didn't make it through all the planned tests. Pass two looks better, except that you can see we've planned on skipping eight of the tests, which hopefully does not include any of the four tests we didn't get to in pass one. In pass one, also, more tests failed than passed, which is a bad sign if our tests are well aligned with customer usage. (Remember that in Chapter 1, I said aligning tests with customer usage was essential.) If Figure 5.15 and Figure 5.16 are the same project, then as a test manager I would probably go to the project manager and explain to her why the project was in trouble.

As a matter of fact, Figure 5.15 and Figure 5.16 *are* from the same hypothetical test project. Now, to illustrate the point I was making earlier about the test suite summary, see Figure 5.17. This doesn't look too bad, does it? We're behind schedule in the earned value area, but hey, just make your testers work over the weekend. We've gotten through 64 percent of the tests, and only around 10 percent are failing, so surely we can fix that. This is the problem with snapshots. Figure 5.17 creates the illusion that there's only a temporary problem that a little extra effort can resolve, while Figure 5.15 and Figure 5.16 show that we have a long-term trend that has played out over three weeks that indicates the project is in trouble.

Are We Testing What We Promised? Charting Test and Bug Coverage

So far, in Chapter 4 and this chapter, we've looked at metrics that measure findings and results. Test cases, test effort, and bug metrics are all interesting sets of data, but they really only tell us something to the extent that our testing is an accurate assessment of quality. In other words, to understand what these metrics and the bug metrics in Chapter 4 really mean, we have to look at how they tie back to the risks to system quality risks we said we would address in Chapter 1. By using the quality risks coverage information I set up earlier in this chapter, and extracting the quality risk field from the bug tracking data discussed in Chapter 4, I can create the chart shown in Figure 5.18.

This chart includes a set of dark gray bars that plot the percentage of planned coverage we've achieved against each of the quality risk categories. This data set is based on the weighted coverage figures shown in Figure 5.8. Since we plan on three passes, the total planned coverage is three times the numbers shown in the "Pln" columns along the bottom of that figure. Dividing the totals from the "Act" columns for the passes run so far by that total planned coverage yields the percentage for each category shown in the graph. If we have to add subsequent passes because of schedule slips, then the percentage we achieve either can exceed 100 percent or you can refigure the planned coverage. The problem with the latter approach is that people will be con-

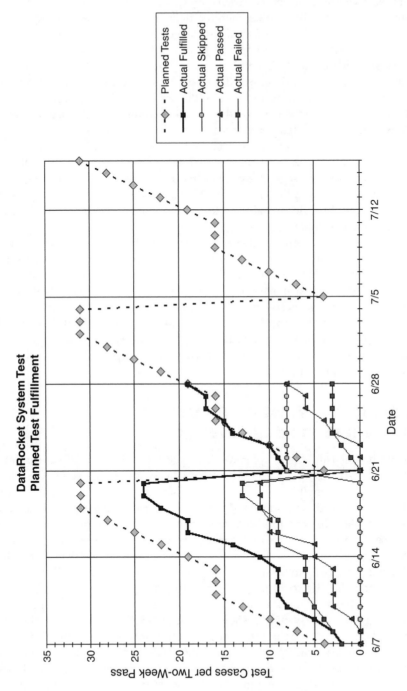

Figure 5.16 A chart of system test fulfillment (completion of planned tests).

	A	B	C	D	E	F	G	H	I	J	K	L	M	N	O
1					DataRocket System Test Suite Summary										
2						Pass Two									
3															
4		Total	Planned Tests Fulfilled				Weighted	Planned Tests Unfulfilled				Earned Value			
5	Suite	Cases	Count	Skip	Pass	Fail	Failure	Count	Queued	IP	Block	Pln Hrs	Act Hrs	% Effort	% Exec
6															
7	Environmental Test	8	8	8	0	0	0.00	0	0	0	0	0.00	0.00	0%	0%
8	Load, Capacity and Volume	8	6	0	5	1	2.45	2	2	0	0	32.00	30.00	94%	75%
9	Functionality	9	2	0	1	1	1.30	7	5	1	1	18.00	6.00	33%	22%
10	Standards	3	2	0	1	1	1.25	1	0	1	0	24.00	19.00	79%	67%
11															
12	Total	28	18	8	7	3	5.00	10	7	2	1	74.00	55.00	74%	50%
13	By Pct		64%	29%	25%	11%	N/A	36%	25%	7%	4%				

Figure 5.17   A snapshot of the system test effort in tabular form.

fused when they see coverage go down—perhaps dramatically—after you've added more test passes. I prefer to let the coverage exceed 100 percent, because I measure my percentage against the baseline or original planned test coverage.

Next to each coverage bar you see a gray bar. These bars are calculated looking at the percentage of bugs found in each quality risk category. As the testing proceeds, a project on a path to success will show the taller dark gray bars next to the taller lighter gray bars; this means that testing is effective at finding bugs where it looks. (We'll need to look at other charts such as the opened/closed chart from Chapter 4 to know whether those bugs are getting fixed.) Taller dark gray bars near shorter lighter gray bars are a trouble sign, because that might well indicate that many more bugs lurk in an area not

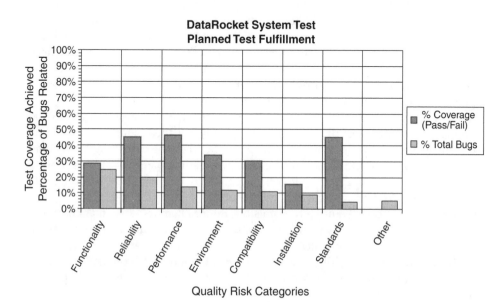

Figure 5.18   Relating bugs and tests back to the risks to system quality.

fully tested yet. At the beginning of a test phase, note that test coverage will be low, but the total percentage of all bugs found will always add up to 100 percent, so the dark gray bars might look kind of scary towering over the stubby little light gray ones. If that chart unduly alarms management, you can plot bugs and test coverage on two different scales, and perhaps use a count rather than a percentage for bugs.

Note that there is a many-to-many relationship between tests and quality risks. Tests generally cover multiple conditions. (See this chapter's *Case Study*.) I have a one-to-one relationship between bugs and quality risks because bugs reports should deal with a specific symptom. If you decide that bugs actually can relate to multiple quality risks, then be aware that the total of all the bug bars in this chart will exceed 100 percent.

From the chart in Figure 5.18, we can draw a number of conclusions. We can see that functionality is only partially tested but very buggy. Adding some new test cases, doing some exploratory testing, and accelerating the planned testing in that area if possible would be good ideas. Since standards testing is mostly complete but not finding many bugs, perhaps we can shift some of the resources planned for further standards testing in the immediate future to functionality? Notice that once again, though, as with focusing on affected subsystems based on the chart discussed in Chapter 4, we have to consider business risk. If nonconformance to standards is the highest risk and functionality is the lowest, then perhaps you don't want to reallocate resources based on this chart.

Test Status in a Nutshell: Building a Balanced Scorecard or Dashboard

The three charts I just introduced, together with the opened/closed chart discussed in Chapter 4, often make up my dashboard—what some refer to as a *balanced scorecard*—for a test project. These are referred to as "balanced" because any misleading trend or data in one chart will be balanced out or further explained by another chart.

In Chapter 4, I said that, in an opened/closed chart like Figure 5.19, we want to see the opened curve flatten out and the closed curve turn up to intercept the opened curve from below. Suppose we saw such a trend? That could be because we're almost done testing, but it could also be because all the testers are spending all their time on confirmation testing bugs being fixed and released to the test team hourly.

However, if that was the case, Figure 5.15 would catch that, because we wouldn't be achieving any hours of test progress. (I only count hours spent against planned test cases, not against overheads such as installing new builds, confirming bug fixes, going to meetings, and so forth.) Still, it could be that I was getting plenty of planned testing hours done, but not finding many bugs due to a bunch of pernicious existing bugs that made every test take twice as long as I had planned.

However, in that case, Figure 5.16 points out the problem, because that chart will show that I'm not fulfilling my planned test cases. If we have a bunch of bugs making us unable to test areas of the system, then those blocked test cases will show up as a gap between planned and fulfilled tests. Remember, though, that I count skipped tests as fulfilled, because I planned to skip them. If I skipped a bunch of tests and declared victory, wouldn't that fake out the charts?

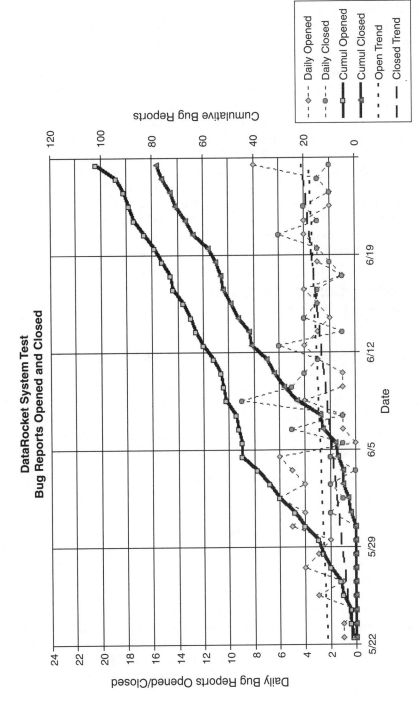

Figure 5.19 An opened/closed chart for DataRocket, completing our dashboard or balanced scorecard for system test.

Nope. If I do that, then Figure 5.18 gives me away, because my achieved coverage measured against the quality risks will be low. If it is low in particular areas while a disproportionate number of bugs have been found there, I know that the charts together—far from telling us that we're about to ship as the opened/closed chart might have misleadingly done—tell me that some specific area or areas of quality are severely hindered by bugs.

As you've seen in these two chapters, this balanced scorecard doesn't require buying any complex or expensive test management tools—you can build it with a spreadsheet and a database. If you want to get fancy, you can post these charts on the company intranet via some automated refresh schedule. If so, you'll need to have a way to get the bug and test data into the appropriate repositories at regular intervals and in sync with each other so the charts match up. Because the dashboard is balanced, discrepancies between source datasets can show up as conflicting figures on two charts. Such mismatched charts will at best lead to questions, and at worst can damage the test team's credibility. One of the nice things about buying test management tools is that the good ones can generate these reports for you, post them to the intranet, and keep the data sets in sync, all automatically.

Questioning Dashboards: Dissent and Disputes

As you've probably guessed by this point in the book, I'm a numerical, analytical type of manager. A "what gets measured gets done" sort of guy. I like metrics, charts, and data. Chapters 4 and 5 of this book were fun for me to write, because I got to crawl around in a bunch of test data, hypothetical and real, and tease meaningful information out of it. Many of the managers I've worked for have also been inclined toward these types of charts and graphs, so these charts have served me well. However, there are dissenters out there, and I would be doing you a disservice if I didn't point you in their direction so you can hear the other side of the story.

Charts, graphs, and numbers tend to give people—especially managers—a feeling of mastery, control, and insight. If the dashboards are well constructed, I would argue that those are not just feelings, those are realities. We are in control. However, how do we know that the dashboards are well constructed? Perhaps we're fooling ourselves, our peers, and our managers, driving multimillion-dollar projects with faulty gauges? Perhaps gathering all these numbers is a distraction from real testing work?

Two notable test-world dissenters from the type of charts I'm advocating are James Bach and Cem Kaner, two people whose opinions I respect quite a bit. Bach advocates a "low tech" dashboard, using a white board to quickly summarize where we've tested, where we haven't tested, and what we've found. Kaner has suggested that perhaps we don't know what we're counting with all these fancy metrics. His critiques of testing metrics appear in a paper entitled "Yes, But What Are We Measuring?" and in an article on software metrics entitled "Rethinking Metrics." I encourage you to check out Bach and Kaner's thoughts as part of deciding on whether and how to use metrics.[4]

---

[4]James Bach's paper on dashboards can be found at www.satisfice.com. Kaner's paper and article are at www.kaner.com.

While most of my experiences with dashboards are good, I have had some problems with them that I should mention as cautionary tales. I have worked with a few managers that used test metrics as a means to achieve political ends, often against the test team. In one case, a development manager explained away an enormous bug backlog by saying, "Those bugs aren't customer-facing. The test team is just wasting everyone's time filing all these trivial bug reports." After release, it turned out he was wrong, but by that time the damage was done—to the project and to the test team! One project manager took up valuable project status time—the time I was supposed to spend explaining to everyone what the test status was—talking about how confusing he found the test charts. What a coincidence that those charts, interpreted correctly, showed the project to be in serious trouble and nowhere near on track to hit the current schedule!

Sometimes people find these charts confusing, especially if they don't know much about testing. One project manager was very perplexed by why the test case count changed from one test pass to the next. I explained that we were adding new test cases as we found areas needing further testing. This wasn't okay from her point of view, as she was thinking of the test project in terms of, "Okay, we have 247 test cases; as soon as all of those pass, we can ship." It's more complicated than that, of course, and her confusion indicated that I needed to do a better job of explaining testing and the charts to her.

At this point, it's time for me to admit that I've gone about this entire discussion backwards. Rather than starting with the neat charts and graphs, maybe I should have started with the goal of the test project: to provide the project team with information that helps the team manage the risks to the quality of the system. This includes especially an accurate, meaningful, and timely assessment of system quality, along with data about the project. I create this information by developing tests that address the important quality risks, deploying the system under test in the test environment, running the tests I developed, and reporting my findings in a way that communicates effectively with the project team.

So, what questions would I need to be able to answer for management to serve that goal? Often times, the questions are:

- How is the quality of the system? Are we fixing the quality problems we know about?

- How is the progress of the test effort?

- Are we running all the planned tests?

- Did we address the important quality risks, and what did we find related to those risk?

What trends are developing in these four areas, and what does those trends tell us about when we'll get to an acceptable level of quality?

If these are the questions management has, then the four charts I've just outlined—or variations on them—should suffice. However, your manager might have different questions. Or, you might find that these charts, for whatever reason, don't help you communicate effectively with your colleagues. Charts, metrics, and reports are a means of providing information. Since providing information is the service that testers are rendering, it is incumbent on us to find ways to deliver information that is not only accurate and timely, but also in a format and presentation that our colleagues can understand.[5]

The process of developing usable metrics is an iterative one. I find that there's a continual process of:

1. Reassessing the questions that need to be answered, and putting together charts that answer those questions.

2. Making sure that people understand what the metrics mean—and what they don't mean.

3. Getting buy-in to use the metrics as useful information, even when that information is not good.

4. Managing the perceptions people have about the usefulness, accuracy, credibility, and timeliness of the information.

Only part of the first step involves the technical tasks we've looked at in Chapter 4 and in this chapter. We'll return to the bigger, interpersonal and managerial issues associated with this process in Chapter 9, "The Triumph of Politics: Organizational Challenges for Test Managers."

First, though, let's move on to a few more tools and techniques. The next chapter will examine what you need to know to manage the dynamic period of test execution, and some tools that can help you plan and track some of the moving parts.

Case Study

On the loan processing application project discussed in the case studies in Chapters 2 and 4, it was very important to ensure that various specific conditions were evaluated. Banks have lots of business rules about who can and can't get a loan, as well as being heavily regulated by individual states and the United States Federal government. Failure to test all these conditions could have resulted in situations such as making loans to bankrupt or unemployed applicants, getting sued for not being able to prove a legitimate business reason for denying a loan to an applicant, and so forth. Therefore, the test team built an Access database to keep track of all these conditions, and to trace the conditions back to specific test cases that covered them. The case study test coverage tracking database, "Case Study Loan Processing Test Coverage Tracking.mdb," is available at www.rexblackconsulting.com.

This database contains two tables, TestCases and TestConditions, with a one-to-many relationship between the two based on the "Sequence" field, which was one unique test case identifier (see Figure 5.20). The tests were built to cover all the conditions. Various queries exist in the database to check that all conditions were covered, to verify that most test cases mapped to a condition, to identify the test cases that covered

---

[5]Dr. Victor Basili has described the process of developing good project metrics as "Goal-Question-Metric." A good paper explaining this process is Rosenberg's and Hyatt's "Developing a Successful Metrics Program," posted by the Software Assurance Technology Center on their web site at stsc.hill.af.mil.

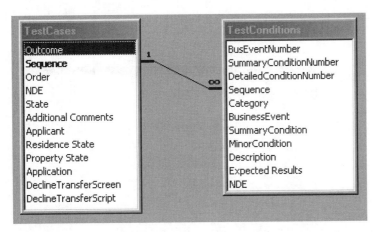

Figure 5.20   Two database tables tracking test case coverage.

particularly high-risk conditions, and so forth. This database could easily be extended with result and bug tracking information, which would then allow an integrated view of the test status, including coverage, in a single database.

However, such integrated test management databases are a major undertaking to construct. (My team and I built a test management system for one client that also included an automated API-testing harness, and the entire application required more than two person-years of effort.) Therefore, on this project I used my usual test tracking spreadsheet. The case study test tracking document, "Case Study Loan Processing Test Tracking.xls," is available at www.rexblackconsulting.com. Please note that I do not have an integrated dashboard in this spreadsheet, as I used the separate bug metrics spreadsheet that was the topic of Chapter 4's case study. Also note that I did not import data from the coverage tracking database to analyze coverage into this spreadsheet, although that would not be terribly difficult to do (see exercise 3). Finally, note that the layout and format is a little less polished than the examples in this chapter. Sometimes, polish is sacrificed for utility and speed on real projects, so you shouldn't feel bad if your spreadsheets, reports, templates, and tools don't look as fancy as many of the ones in this book!

A few noteworthy details bear discussion. Notice in Figure 5.21 that the planned and actual effort hours (columns L and M) are very small numbers. Most test cases involved submitting a single loan application into the system, which took between 15 and 30 minutes. This is really about the finest-grained level of detail you can effectively track using this technique. If you start tracking one- and two-minute tasks, you'll spend as much time updating the worksheets as getting any work done. My usual rule of thumb is to build test cases between one and four hours long, though, as in this case, that rule has to bend sometimes. For this system, the test case duration was driven by the workflows being tested.

	Owner	Test ID	Test Suite/Case	Test State	System Config	Bug ID	Bug RPN	Bug State	By	Plan Date	Act Date	Plan Hrs	Act Hrs	Comment
			Some Loan App Release 1.0 System Test Case Tracking Spreadsheet											
				Pass 3										
		2.000	*UAT Scripts*											
49	HD	2.001	1.1.0 More than 4 Stips Approved	Varn	018994/Train	1009		2 Assigned	HD	5/18	5/14	0.50	0.50	
50	HD	2.002	1.1.1 Basic App / Co App	Varn	018994/Train	1009		2 Assigned	HD	5/18	5/14	0.50	0.50	
51	HD	2.003	1.1.2 Direct mail, No ID	Varn	018994/Train	1009		2 Assigned	HD	5/18	5/14	0.50	0.25	
52	HD	2.004	1.1.2.2 Collateral for sale	Pass	018994/Train				HD	5/18	5/14	0.50	0.25	
53	HD	2.005	1.1.3 Collteral Type is 2-4 Dup/Tri/Quad	Varn	018994/Train	1009		2 Assigned	HD	5/18	5/14	0.50	0.25	
54	HD	2.006	1.1.4 Property is located in California	Varn	018994/Train	1009		2 Assigned	HD	5/18	5/14	0.50	0.25	
55	HD	2.007	1.1.5 Discharged BK < 36 months	Pass	018994/Train				HD	5/18	5/14	0.50	0.25	
56	HD	2.008	1.1.5.2 Non-discharged bankruptcy	Pass	018994/Train				HD	5/18	5/14	0.50	0.25	
57	HD	2.009	1.1.6 Joint	Varn	018994/Train	1009		2 Assigned	HD	5/18	5/14	0.50	0.50	
58	HD	2.010	1.1.7 Varm Transfer	Pass	018994/Train				HD	5/18	5/14	0.50	0.25	
59	HD	2.011	1.1.7.4 Co-App is under 18 years old	Pass	018994/Train				HD	5/18	5/14	0.50	0.25	
60	HD	2.012	1.1.8 CA cond. Approve < 1 acre	Varn	018994/Train	1009		2 Assigned	HD	5/18	5/14	0.50	0.50	
61	HD	2.013	1.1.8.2 CA cond. Approve 5-25 acres	Varn	018994/Train	1009		2 Assigned	HD	5/18	5/14	0.50	0.50	
62	HD	2.014	1.1.8.3 SLA calculates DTI factoring in	Fail	018994/Train	1067		2 Review	HD	5/18	5/15	0.50	0.50	
63	HD	2.015	1.1.9.4 Applicant has rental income	Varn	018994/Train	1009		2 Assigned	HD	5/18	5/15	0.50	0.25	
64	HD	2.016	1.1.10 App has Non-Discharged BK	Pass	018994/Train				HD	5/18	5/15	0.50	0.25	
65	HD	2.017	1.1.11 Co-App Self Empd < 12 months	Pass	018994/Train				HD	5/18	5/15	0.50	0.25	
66	HD	2.018	1.1.13 DTI to High	Varn	018994/Train	1067		2 Review	HD	5/18	5/15	0.50	0.50	
67	HD	2.019	1.1.14 DTI to High	Fail	018994/Train	1069		2 Review	HD	5/18	5/15	0.50	0.50	
68	HD	2.020	1.1.15 > 25 acres and > $100,000	Varn	018994/Train	1068		2 Review	HD	5/18	5/15	0.50	0.25	
69	HD	2.021	1.2.1 App has Non-Discharged BK	Pass	018994/Train				HD	5/18	5/15	0.50	0.25	
70	HD	2.022	1.2.2 App has suspected Bureau Fraud	Pass	018994/Train				HD	5/18	5/15	0.50	0.25	
71	HD	2.023	1.2.4 App score is below minimum	Pass	018994/Train				HD	5/18	5/15	0.50	0.25	

Figure 5.21   Case study test case summary for pass three.

In Figure 5.22, you can see that most of the passes were defined as one week. This corresponded to the test release cycle, which was weekly. However, the first pass took three weeks, and seems to have been planned that way. In actuality, that "plan" was really in response to the fact that we violated the entry criteria in terms of having a stable system. As a result, we were unable to get any real testing work done until the middle of the second week, and even then it was slow. (This inefficiency also shows up in the Test Progress chart, which is in the spreadsheet if you care to look at it.)

Notice also that the test case counts changed from 274 in passes one and two to 299 in passes three through five. This happened primarily because we added some new test cases for debt consolidation in pass three. This was related to a change in the system's functionality.

I thank my client on this project, a major mid-western financial institution, and the executive in charge of development for allowing me to share this example with readers of this book. I have purged all identifying and otherwise private information from this document. My client contact has asked that the organization remain anonymous.

Exercises

1. Assume that you are working on a large development project, leading a test team, and reporting to a project manager. Because of the large number of bugs found in the latest test cycle, your colleague, the development manager, thinks

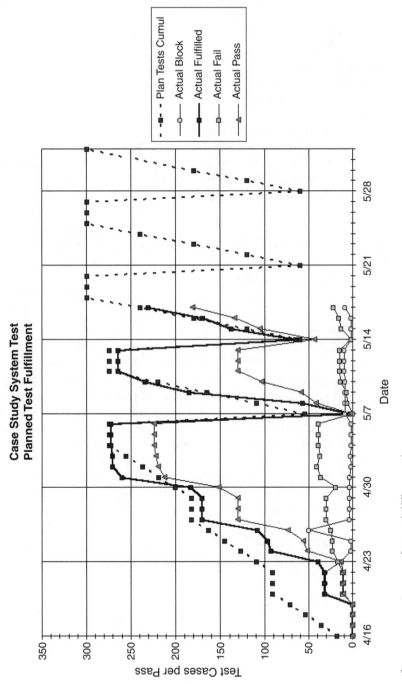

Figure 5.22 Case study test fulfillment chart.

that the testing effort was not started in earnest until recently. You believe that the increase in the number of bugs is because the quality of fixes put in this release of the software is not good, specifically that there are many regressions. Can you use the test tracking spreadsheet to demonstrate this? If so, sketch a test tracking spreadsheet that might illustrate this point.[6]

2. Suppose that your project's regression testing strategy is to rerun only test cases that have failed against previous releases, rather than rerunning every test case in the test set for the test phase as shown in this chapter. In other words, in each cycle you have an ever-increasing (hopefully) number of tests that you skip because they have already passed. If you use the tracking spreadsheet shown in this chapter, this growing number of skipped tests will eventually distort the test summary and the planned test fulfillment chart, because skipped tests are counted as fulfilled. (A further complication is that skipped tests are not counted in earned value calculation, because they do not involve any planned or expended effort.) How could you modify this technique to accommodate tracking such a project?

3. Export the coverage tracking data from the TestConditions table in the case study coverage tracking database into a worksheet in the case study test tracking spreadsheet. Match the sequence numbers in the test conditions table against the sequence numbers embedded in the test case names in most of the test suites. (You can ignore test cases that don't map to specific test conditions for this exercise.) Produce a chart that shows coverage of these conditions, similar to the chart shown in Figure 5.18 but without the bug data. In any of the three passes for which the test tracking spreadsheet contains test results, do any conditions remain uncovered? Is there any explanation of this in the test tracking spreadsheet?

4. In the templates and case studies provided with this book, there are three files that have test tracking data from multiple test passes:, "Case Study Info Appliance Client Test Tracking.xls," "Case Study Info Appliance Server Test Tracking.xls," and "Case Study Loan Processing Test Tracking.xls." For the passes for which you have data on each project, produce a single graph that shows how the total weighted failure counts from the Test Suite Summary worksheets behaved during the project. Compare this chart with the find-fix charts found in "Case Study Info Appliance Bug Metrics.xls" and "Case Study Loan Processing Test Tracking.xls." Do you think that charting the total weighted failure from one pass to the next might serve as an equally good or better measure of quality and project progress? Explain.[7]

[6]This exercise was contributed by Dr. Deepti Suri of Milwaukee School of Engineering.
[7]I thank Ken Sommerville of XLR8 Technology for asking the perceptive question that led me to create this exercise.

Tips and Tools for Crunch Time: Managing the Dynamic

If you've been through a test project once or twice, you know that "crunch mode" is both hectic and confusing: facts are often cloudy, plans are in flux, and dependencies, once unclear, jump into sharp relief the moment they are not met. To some extent, the planning, preparation, and structured information gathering I've recommended in previous chapters can help you alleviate these problems. However, test execution is always a challenge, and you can't document your way out of whatever amount of chaos exists on the project, because it will by nature leak into the test project.

This chapter offers two new tools specifically geared toward managing the goat rodeos that can consume your life during test execution. One is a logistics database that tracks the locations, configurations, and test requirements for hardware, software, infrastructure, and staff. The other is a simple change management database that helps you respond to the inevitable course corrections, both smooth and jerky, that occur on any test project. First, though, let me offer some observations on crunch mode that might aid you in maintaining your professionalism and sanity during this high-pressure period.

Do Sweat the Details: Staying on Top of Everything

The common thread running through all the tips in this section is the importance of remaining in control of the details swirling around you. During test execution, you will have many items to attend to, all of them urgent, but you should be sure to set aside some time to look at where your testing is taking you. Are you on track? What risks and roadblocks loom? In that spirit, here are some suggestions that should help you survive crunch time.

Moving Forward While Getting All the Facts: The Desire for Certitude, the Imperative of Progress

Imagine that you and I have two conversations. In the first, we're standing near a brick house, and you point to the wall and say, "Look at that chameleon! It changed color to match the brick." I look, I see the lizard, I notice its red hue, and I agree. In the second, you say, "Did you know that my golden retriever Gertrude can talk?" In the absence of hearing the dog talk myself, I'm not likely to believe you.

Often, the most interesting bug reports start out along these lines: *I did X, and everything seemed to be going fine. Then, all of a sudden Y happened, and the system crashed.* Sadly, you then discover that repeating the action X doesn't repeat the consequence Y. You try it a dozen times, but you can duplicate it only once or twice. You change some variables that might be related, and you can't reproduce the problem. But maybe it's not gone. It's hard to tell these types of stories to developers without triggering incredulity.

A solid bug report is satisfying and goes a long way toward building credibility with developers. Certitude—"this is the truth, and I can demonstrate it"—is a good feeling. A clean, reproducible bug report is indisputable. In many cases, though, the price of certitude is too high. If you've ever had to perform a reliability test of software or hardware, you know how time-consuming such demonstrations of statistical confidence can be. If you tried to investigate every bug to the level of certitude, you'd never find half of them. It's important to keep in mind the need to progress. Testing computers, like all engineering, is not a search for truth—that's science. Engineering is about producing things, about making useful objects. Often as not, close enough must be good enough.

This is not to say that sloppy work or a lack of attention to details in developing test systems, running test cases, or writing bug reports is acceptable. As I pointed out in the case study in the last chapter, though, there are certain levels of polish that can be skipped in the interests of time. If you're writing a bug report about a low-priority problem, you should certainly write a good report, as described in Chapter 4, "An Exciting Career in Entomology Awaits You: A Bug Tracking Database." However, you needn't try every single possible isolation step or reproduce the bug a dozen times.

Dependencies, Schedules, and Reminders: The Importance of Follow-Up

One of the more daunting challenges of managing a test project is that so many dependencies converge at test execution. You can often kludge your way through test development, but you can't execute tests unless all the myriad details and external components come together at the right time. One missing configuration file or hardware device can render all your test results meaningless. You can end up with a entire platoon of testers sitting around for days.

This type of incident is hardly the test manager's fault. You probably have your hands full managing your own team, and you can't be expected to manage others. This is cold comfort, however, when you are spending a weekend in the lab with your testers. All too often, missing components show up or prerequisite tasks are completed at 5:00 on a Friday afternoon, followed by a pep talk from a manager who stresses that it's the responsibility of the team players in the test organization to help compensate for the schedule hit. It's true that you can't manage other groups, but you should try to keep an eye on project-wide events and trends that can negatively impact your test schedule, and make sure you clearly communicate the potential or pending difficulties to your management.

Beyond simply staying in the loop concerning other parts of the project, it's essential that you learn to manage time and to set reminders and milestones for yourself. I've used scheduling programs such as Outlook, PDAs, and paper systems such as Day-Timer. The particular tool you choose doesn't matter much, as long as you set reminders about when external events that affect testing are scheduled to occur, and then follow up with the appropriate person:

Phone switch should be configured today. Check with John.

Three systems due to ship from Lucky Bit today. Check with Lin-Tsu and then verify customs broker with Jack.

Muhammad's team to deliver first cut of the XYZ software today. Follow up.

Keeping apprised of schedule slips, feature changes, and other modifications to the plan allows you to react in advance, which gives you more options. Wouldn't you rather know at 4:00 on Wednesday afternoon that you have to line up staff for weekend coverage, instead of finding out at 4:00 on Friday afternoon? By being proactive, you will earn some recovery or contingency time.

It Won't Deliver Itself: Revisions and Release Processes

Between the completion of a hardware or software subsystem and its delivery to test lie various degrees and types of heavy lifting. Software must be assembled into a package of some sort, either physical or electronic. Hardware must be configured, packed up, and sent. Shipping and customs clearance might be issues. People don't tend to volunteer to carry out these activities, which are not heroic, rewarding, or easy to keep straight.

Because you are on the receiving end, it behooves you to drive the definition of the process. For each subsystem or system, you should ensure that someone is on the hook for delivering usable, testable items to your test group. I'm not suggesting that you take ownership of such tasks—far from it; you have enough to do. Often a well-worded email, sent to your manager and some of the people you suspect *might* be appropriate owners, will suffice.

In extreme cases, you might need to develop and promulgate a plan yourself. Such a plan would assign ownership of various stages of the delivery process to specific people, based on your understanding of their roles. This is dangerous ground politically, however; be sure that you have sufficient clout before you attempt it.

As discussed in earlier chapters, you'll also face the issues of frequency and configuration management as new builds are released. Within a few weeks of initial delivery, you should seek renewed commitments from your development counterparts that they intend to adhere to the release plan agreed upon previously.

It Won't Install Itself, Either: Configuring the Test Environment

In some cases, testing covers the process of installing software or hardware components. When you test operating systems or applications, for example, the first step of testing a new build is to test the installation or upgrade procedures, which should result in a configured test environment. Unfortunately, however, it often leaves you with a broken mess, especially at the beginning, so you must have contingency plans in place whenever possible. One way to do this is to keep hard drive images of "known good" systems either on the network, on tape, or on spare drives. There are also commercial configuration management tools available for complex networks.

You can't always put such plans in place, of course. Obviously, access to a stable, completely installed version of the system under test is essential for effective testing. If you can't install the software or you can't get an operating system running on the computer you're testing, you are blocked. Since you'll find such announcements unpopular with management, always double-check to make sure you have your facts straight.

Sometimes the task of installing and configuring the test environment is too complex for a typical tester to handle. In such instances, you have two alternatives: either have the necessary level of system administration support available within your team, or have the expertise available on call from the project team, information systems, technical support, or another appropriate group.

My preference is the former. The best way to ensure that someone's priorities are aligned with yours is to have that person on your team. If you do use external system administration support, do your best to get a guarantee of response times and a clear process for escalating problem situations up the management chain to prevent them from festering. I have worked with some excellent support staff, but I have also had some negative experiences with relying on outside help. These problems were usually not the other team's fault. When a limited set of people must support half a dozen groups, eventually your request will languish in a queue. That will not happen if the support resource works on your team.

"The Hobgoblin of Small Minds" Is Your Friend: Auditing and Updating Test Results

Testing can be a confusing environment. Except for the simplest of functional bugs, it's seldom clear exactly what has gone wrong when an anomaly first comes to light. Significant time might elapse between the first muttered, "What the heck?" and the completion of a bug report. Of course, since a bug report is often just a description of symptoms, further discovery is usually needed. A certain lack of clarity comes with the territory. Indeed, since tests are experiments, you could say that testing is about *creating* a lack of clarity, about raising questions in people's minds, about challenging "facts" people "know" that just ain't so.

When you are challenging preconceived notions, you must back up your assertions with data. This requires spending a lot of time keeping your internal data—especially bug tracking and test tracking—as consistent and current as possible. When you're asked about status, you'll want to provide management with clear answers.

Chapters 4 and 5 introduced two linked tracking mechanisms, for bugs and for test cases. The linkages exist in both directions: the bug reports reference test case identifiers, and test cases—at both a detail level and a summary level—reference bug reports and their risk levels. The test project dashboard summarizes information from both, creating another set of linkages. Figure 6.1 provides a visual representation of these linkages.

By going through the bug reports, the test tracking worksheets, and the dashboards at the same time to ensure consistency, you can keep these documents consistent. Because bug reports and the status of test cases change over time, the two will get out of sync if you don't review the linkages regularly. This can happen quickly. When test execution is at full bore, you should audit the spreadsheets and the reports once or twice a week. I find that the daily debriefing process I described in Chapter 5, "Managing Test Cases: The Test Tracking Spreadsheet," allows me to integrate this work into my daily routine.

Admittedly, auditing all these documents, charts, graphs, and data can be a painstaking exercise. The truly motivated among you might decide to implement a complete integrated test management system as I discussed in Chapter 5. This system could automate the linkages. However, reconciling the bugs, the tests, and the charts manually actually provides an interesting side benefit: by forcing yourself to crawl through the details of every active bug, every planned test, and every chart and metric, you become intimately aware of what's going on. The ritual can reward you by identifying a number of important issues that need to be addressed.

You might start by going through the spreadsheet. If testers are making notes on hardcopy test cases, you should enter this data in the worksheets. If testers are doing the updates themselves, you should review the results in the test case summaries and the test suite summaries. If you have questions, drill down to the test case level or across to the bug tracking database. For each test case that has identified a bug, check the status of the bug report: Is it still open? Is the risk priority number correct? Does the configuration and tester information in the bug report match the test case summary?

After checking the spreadsheet, move on to the bug reports. Although you would have already audited many of the reports as part of auditing the spreadsheet, it's a good idea to walk through the bug reports at the detail level. Seeing a bug report might remind you to follow up on an item with a colleague or to schedule a confirmation test that you somehow missed.

Defining a Test Execution Process

You've probably seen an assembly line on TV, in a newspaper or magazine article, or perhaps even in person. On early automotive assembly lines, cars were built in one spot, with workers moving around to assemble them. Henry Ford revolutionized not

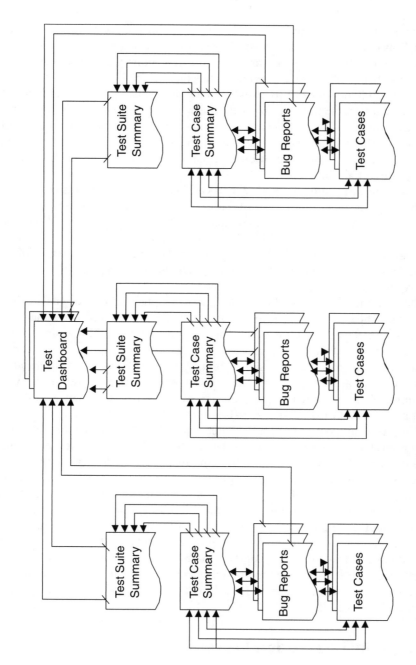

Figure 6.1 The linkages between test tracking and reporting documents.

just car assembly, but the entire manufacturing process when he introduced the idea of bringing the car to the worker on a moving line. All the tools were ready at hand in the right places, the parts came to the worker as needed, and the workers built the car piece by piece as it moved along the line.

Now, test execution is more creative that working on an assembly line, true. However, you'll need some process for assigning tasks, gathering results, recognizing and intervening in process breakdowns, and collecting metrics on how effective and efficient your process is. This means that you and your team need to come up with a process, and as a test manager you'll need to manage it.

Even exploratory testing involves some type of process. James Bach, a pioneer in that field, has come up with the concept of chartered exploratory testing. Using this technique, testers are assigned a test charter; for example, "test the printing capabilities." Each charter is allocated a certain amount of time for exploration, say 90 minutes. At the end of the period, the test manager debriefs the tester, gathering details about what was tested and what was found. At that time, the tester either is told to continue exploring that area for another set period of time, or is assigned a new charter.[1]

When Test Fails: Minimizing Test Result Interpretation Errors

Despite your best efforts, it sometimes happens that the test system itself produces errors. On the one hand, testers sometimes report correct system behavior as a bug, assign an excessively high severity or priority to a bug, or otherwise overstate the significance of a problem. Although they don't jeopardize product quality, such errors can damage the credibility of the test organization; developers and project managers tend to adopt a "boy who cried wolf" attitude toward the test team after enough false alarms. On the other hand, testers sometimes fail to detect or report incorrect system behavior, assign an excessively low priority or severity to a bug, or otherwise understate the significance of a problem. This type of error often leads to a test escape, which is a direct risk to system quality.

One cause of both types of errors is MEGO, the affliction in which "my… eyes…glaze…over." Very detailed written test cases are notorious for this problem. A tester running a test will always notice if the system catches fire or the program causes the blue screen of death, but an inattentive tester can miss subtle signs of system failure. Likewise, a lack of attention to specifications or other system documentation during bug isolation can cause correct behavior to be mistaken for a bug.

Test automation provides a partial solution to this problem. Automated tests, unlike testers, never get too bored to notice that an error message is misspelled or a transaction takes 50 milliseconds too long. (Bill Perry and Randy Rice, in their fine book *Surviving the Top Ten Challenges of Software Testing,* make a similar point when discussing test automation.) It is, however, quite possible—indeed, all too common—for a test developer to embed result interpretation errors in automated tests.

---

[1]For more information on this, see the Satisfice web site, www.satisfice.com.

Even if your testers don't suffer from shrinking attention spans after 12 grueling hours of running tests, they can misinterpret test results by guessing wrong about what was supposed to happen. As I mentioned in Chapter 3, "Test System Architecture, Cases, and Coverage," you don't want your test case library to turn into a groaning bookshelf of totally unambiguous—and totally unmaintainable—pages stuffed into binder upon binder. Nevertheless, if you leave questions of correct behavior to the judgment of testers, they will make some mistakes. There is no perfect solution to this quandary, but appropriate automation, continual test case enhancement in response to test escapes, avoiding working people beyond their limits of concentration, and careful assignment of team members for test execution all help.

On the topic of assigning testers, one of your jobs as a manager is to know the strengths and weaknesses of your team members. One of the most important variables in preventing errors is skill level. If, for example, you assign the Microsoft Windows logo certification test to a tester who has no experience with Windows, the poor fellow will probably not succeed in running it. If you ask a software test engineer to run a shock and vibration test on DataRocket, don't be surprised when she botches the job. I'm not arguing for career stultification; assigning new tasks keeps testers challenged and ensures a well-rounded test team. When you do cross-training, though, it's important not to set up the tester—and the project—for failure. Provide adequate instruction first, and then supply support from an experienced engineer during cross-training.

In addition to skill levels, you need to consider less tangible attributes when assigning testers. If the test is complicated and somewhat tedious, can the tester focus? If the test is a group effort, do the assigned testers work well together? If you suspect that the tester will need to contact a developer at some point, will the tester be able to make that contact?

Of course, in the real world, you'll have to make many test assignments based on who's free. Like any team, yours will contain some stars and some solid but unspectacular performers. As much as you want star-quality work on all the jobs in your bailiwick, there's only so much star power to go around. Moreover, demand for a tester's particular skills can vary depending on the types of tests you need to run. When these realities force you to select a less-than-perfect tester, be sure to put safety nets such as peer reviews and the support of experienced engineers in place.

WHEN TEST ESCAPES TURN DEADLY

If you are not familiar with the Therac story, brace yourself. The Therac 25 nuclear medicine device was designed to administer precise dosages of radiation to hospital patients. Because of a software glitch that made it to the field, the device overdosed a number of patients, some of whom died as a result. Incidents such as this have fueled efforts by some in the computer industry to institute mandatory licensing or certification programs for computer professionals.

For a complete discussion of this and other dangerous test escapes, check out Peter Neumann's book *Computer-Related Risks*. You might also want to subscribe to the online forum *Risks Digest*, available through the *comp.risks* Usenet newsgroup and via email at *risks-request@csl.sri.com*.

Here I must also inject a note of business reality. In some fields, any failure to detect a bug is totally unacceptable. If you are in charge of testing a system such as the Therac nuclear medicine device (see the sidebar *When Test Escapes Turn Deadly*), every test engineer and technician on your team must be top-notch, experienced, and deeply knowledgeable about the system under test. In contrast, if you test a typical consumer software or hardware product, you will probably have to accept a few result interpretation errors on both sides of the coin as part of the business. Of course, at some point, the business model for computer hardware and software could change if customers, legislatures, or regulatory agencies decide that buggy products are unacceptable.[2] However, the reality today is that you won't have the time, the budget, the staff, or the management focus to achieve perfect testing or perfect products.

"I Wish You a Merry Dragon Boat Festival..." When Crunch Time, Holidays, and Cultures Collide

Remember to consider holidays when you schedule crunch periods. Needless to say, you'll encounter major impediments to getting work done during holidays. Your testers will be both reluctant and less able to work long hours. Even if everyone on the team does come in to the office on a holiday, they won't be working the 60- to 80-hour weeks that are common during crunch mode. Holidays mean time spent with family, which implies a break from 14-hour days. Even more important, those people who carry the most water for your team—the men and women who consistently pull the all-nighters when the going is tough—have a debt to repay to themselves and their families during holidays. Not coming home on an ordinary Wednesday night during a big push is making a sacrifice, but not coming home for Passover or Christmas Eve can create serious issues in a tester's family life.

Testers are not the only ones who face these problems. Chapter 11, "Testing in Context: Economics, Lifecycles, and Process Maturity," discusses what I call "gas pedals" and "brake pedals" for test operations. One major class of brake pedals is lack of proper system administration, infrastructure, and development support. Convincing system administrators and developers to wear pagers and give out their home telephone numbers is difficult enough under any circumstances; during holidays, people might well refuse the request. Even if you do have contact information, it might not do you any good. A system administrator who is visiting relatives in Buffalo, New York, without a laptop computer isn't much help when your test server goes down at 8:00 P.M. on December 31 in San Jose, California, even if you do find that individual near a telephone and sober.

If you do business internationally, you also need to consider cultural issues related to crunch periods. The most obvious is that different countries observe different holidays.

---

[2]See Cem Kaner and David Pels book, *Bad Software*, for a look at the legal and societal implications of bugs. In *After the Gold Rush*, Steve McConnell discusses the concepts of licensure and certification for software engineers.

Asking a Taiwanese testing lab to squeeze in a rush test job from December 22 through December 31 might not create a problem. However, you might get an education about the Chinese (Lunar) New Year if you schedule a month of crunch time at the same lab in January or February. Calendar software such as Microsoft Outlook often includes support for foreign holidays.

In addition, you will find that the workaholic traditions that seem to accompany high-tech jobs in some countries do not apply the world over. Asking people to work until midnight or come in over a weekend can be a cross-cultural *faux pas*. Indeed, in France, overtime is against the law. I have often been struck by the extreme demands of American work habits in comparison with the "gotta live a little" attitudes prevalent in some of the foreign countries where I have worked. Also bear in mind that in some countries, formal work hours end strictly on time so that informal work—building relationships with colleagues over dinner or drinks and solving the problems of the day in a frank and relaxed environment—can occur regularly.

Before you begin to conduct business internationally, I encourage you to study the cultures and work styles of your new foreign colleagues. (One of my clients organized an off-site "culture course" for employees and consultants working in Taiwan—a valuable experience.) Such study can help you build more productive working relationships, and you will also enjoy a unique chance to immerse yourself in the culture of another country without the artificiality that comes with seeing that country as a tourist.

A Spider's Web of Connections: Managing Test Hardware and Software Configuration Logistics

If your system under test is used in a limited setting with a tightly defined list of possible hardware peripherals and software applications, the management of test hardware and software configuration is simple. I once consulted with a client who was working on a Microsoft Windows CE computer for an automobile. The system was installed in the dashboard, connected to only three or four peripherals, had a very simple BIOS, ran only one operating system, and supported a small set of applications. From the point of view of hardware logistics and software configuration management, the test organization merely needed to track BIOS levels, Windows CE releases, the hardware revision levels of the handful of peripherals, and the motherboard and chassis releases. A few very simple tables, implemented in Microsoft Word, were sufficient.

Not all projects are this straightforward, however. Whether you work on software or hardware development projects, you might find yourself managing a complicated and changing array of hardware devices, especially during test execution. In addition, the software installed on these devices can vary. You must allocate this hardware, make sure that the right software is deployed on it, track its movements, understand who needs it and for what, and ensure that all the appropriate connections are available.

Perhaps your system supports many different configurations or is deployed in a large setting, but you only test with a basic setup. For example, if you have an e-commerce application, maybe you only test with one or two clients browsing the site at once. Alternatively, if you have a client server system that supports 100 clients in a call center, perhaps you test only with one client talking to the servers.

While this might suffice for functional testing, some bugs only show up in more complex configurations. Performance, data quality, reliability, load, and error handling are some of the risks to system quality that really can only be effectively explored in configurations that are as close to "real world" as possible.

The topic of test hardware is connected to software configuration management—which is a major issue during crunch time. Chapter 7, "Stocking and Managing a Test Lab," expands this discussion by focusing on test lab management, but for now, we'll take a look, using SpeedyWriter as a case study, at a database that will help you manage hardware logistics and software configuration for your project. This database tracks the following:

- Hardware installation, locations, and moves.
- Current, historical, and planned software configurations.
- Hardware interconnections and networking.
- Test locations.
- Test infrastructure.
- Test engineer assignments and locations.
- Human resource deployment.

The Pieces and How They Connect: An Entity-Relationship Diagram

Because this database is complex, it's useful to begin with a conceptual overview of the elements and how they relate. Figure 6.2 shows an entity-relationship (E-R) diagram for the database. Those of you who have some familiarity with database design or administration probably recognize this format. However, if it's new to you, don't worry; you don't have to understand database design to use this tool.

The rectangles in Figure 6.2 represent entities, which are objects of some kind. Each entity has a set of properties, represented by labeled lines. One (or more) of these properties, called the *key*, uniquely identifies an individual entity. In Figure 6.2, lines with solid endpoints indicate key properties, whereas lines with open endpoints indicate nonkey properties. For example, *Name* is a key property of the *Hardware* entity, while *Quantity* is a nonkey property of this entity.

The diamonds represent relationships between pairs of entities. Relationships can also have properties. (Not all relationships have properties, though; relationships are identified by the entities they associate.) There are three types of relationships: one-to-one, one-to-many, and many-to-many. In a one-to-one relationship between entities X and Y, any one Y can have a relationship with one and only one X at any given time, and vice versa. A one-to-many relationship between X and Y would allow any one X to have relationships with multiple Ys, but each Y could have a relationship with only one X. For example, you can have a number of coins in your pocket, but a given coin can only be in one pocket at one time. In a many-to-many relationship, both X and Y are unrestricted in terms of the number of associations that can exist between them. A

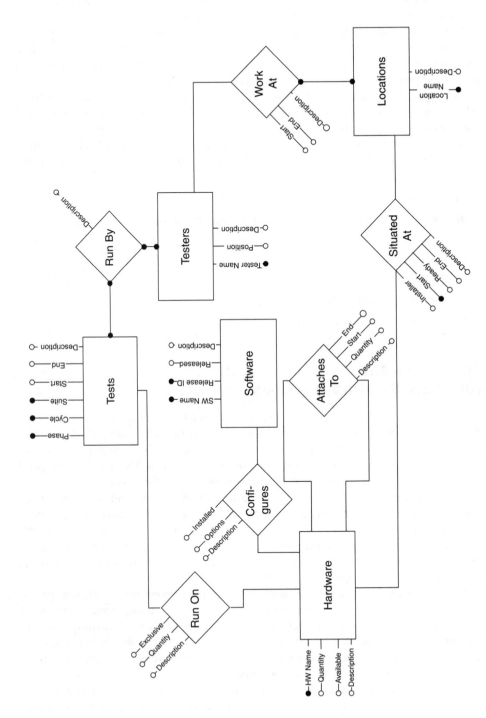

Figure 6.2 An entity-relationship diagram for test logistics.

corporation can have many shareholders, and a person can own stock in many companies at once. In the case of this database, all the relationships are many-to-many, as I'll explain in detail later on.[3]

Let's look more closely at each entity and relationship in Figure 6.2. The *Tests* entity, with six properties, appears at the center top of the chart. The value of the *Phase* property can be Component, Integration, or System. *Cycle* is the sequence number of the test cycle in that phase; I use cycles rather than passes because we're going to track software revisions with this tool, which are the basis of test cycles in my approach. The *Suite* property is the name of the suite. (Alternatively, you could use an ID number for the *Suite* property, although a number is less descriptive.) These first three properties taken together uniquely identify an individual test, as in Integration Test, 2, GUI/Edit Engine. The *Start* and *End* properties indicate the scheduled run dates for that suite in that cycle. *Description* includes any other pertinent information; there is a description field included for free-form notes with each entity and relationship.

Proceeding clockwise around the diagram, you can see that the entities *Tests* and *Testers* are linked by the relationship *Run By*—in other words, tests are run by testers. Testers are uniquely identified by their names. Testers have a position, generally either a test engineer or test technician. Because each test is run by one or more testers, and each tester runs one or more tests, the relationship is many-to-many.

Testers work at locations—that is, the *Testers* and *Locations* entities are linked by the *Work At* relationship. In some cases, locations are temporary, within the time frame of the project, so the relationship includes start and end dates. Testers might work at more than one location during a given period of time. Furthermore, a single location might have 0, 1, or more testers working at it at any given time. Therefore, the relationship is many-to-many.

Let's return to the top of the diagram and work our way counterclockwise and down. Tests run on one or more items of hardware, each of which in turn runs one or more tests. A test requires a given quantity of each hardware item, usually one but sometimes more, and the test's relationship with the hardware can be either exclusive or nonexclusive, depending on whether the test requires dedicated use of that piece of hardware during its execution. For a hardware item, the properties of interest are *HW Name*, *Quantity*, *Available* (the date of availability), and *Description*.

Software configures most hardware items—that is, the particular combination of one or more software items installed on a piece of hardware, and the way in which they are installed, determines the hardware's functionality. The same piece of software might be installed on multiple hardware items, too; for example, you might run Linux on multiple servers in your server farm. The *Software* entity has four properties of interest: *Name*, *Release ID* (the release number), *Released* (the release date), and *Description*. The software configures the hardware on the date on which it is installed with particular options.

In a networked or telecommunications environment, a given piece of hardware attaches to one or more other pieces of hardware. Routers, hubs, and switches attach to many devices at once; modems, keyboards, and mice attach to one computer at a time. Such attachments have start and end dates, and the quantity required is also relevant.

---

[3]For a complete explanation of entity-relationship modeling of databases, targeted at beginning database users, data modelers, and business analysts, see *Conceptual Database Design*, by Carlo Batini, Stefano Ceri, and Shamkant Navathe.

Finally, hardware items are situated at a particular location during certain periods of time. In the *Situated At* relationship, an installer sets up the hardware, starting on a particular date. The hardware will be ready for test on a date shortly thereafter, and the hardware will end its sojourn at that location at a later date. More than one piece of hardware might well be situated at a particular location, and a piece of hardware might move around during the course of the test effort.

From Diagram to Schemas: Implementing the Logistics Database

To implement the logistics database, I have used Microsoft Access, but you can use any relational database. Begin by creating a table for each entity. Each table should contain a field for each entity property.

Because each relationship is many-to-many, the relationships in the diagram also translate directly into tables. A table for a many-to-many relationship includes the keys from the two related tables, with the combined keys and possibly some relationship properties used as the key for the relationship table. The relationship table also contains fields for each property in the relationship.

I have not provided the design details for each table, but they are not complex. Most of the fields are basic text, integer, or date fields, except for the *Exclusive* field in the *Run On* table, which is a *yes/no* field. Figure 6.3 shows the tables and their relationships.[4]

Budgeting and Planning: Using the Logistics Database Ahead of Time

One of most important uses of the logistics database is as a planning tool. The following sections walk through an example of how to use the database, based on a case study of SpeedyWriter test logistics. The example illustrates how you can enter data in the database's tables and then display it in simple but powerful reports. This database does not support form-based data entry, although you might want to add this and other enhancements if you choose to make the logistics database part of your standard toolkit. To keep the data minimal in this example, I have omitted test development, but you might need to allocate hardware and people for test development on most of your projects. Although this case study is a simplification, I have used this database to plan hardware, software, network, and human logistics for test projects much more complex than this.

[4]Database purists and data modeling professionals might not like this translation. Access, with its cascading update feature, allows me to avoid the use of surrogate keys for the joins while retaining the ability to change values in key fields without having to do extensive database updates. If you use a database without cascading update capabilities, however, you might be stuck with surrogate keys.

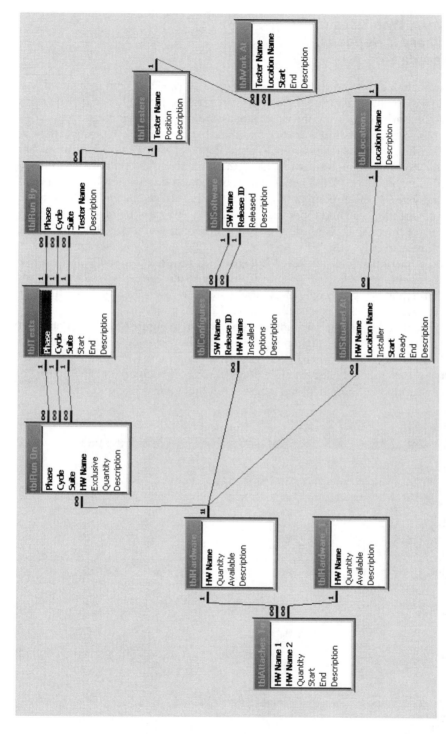

Figure 6.3 Microsoft Access view of tables and relationships in the logistics database.

The Work, Who Does It, and Where It Happens: The People Side

To begin planning the SpeedyWriter test project, you can start with individual tests and who will run them. Figure 6.4 shows the table created for the *Tests* entity, detailing the test suites to be run during the various phases, along with their constituent cycles. A table of testers appears in Figure 6.5, and the table in Figure 6.6 represents the *Run By* relationship, which matches testers to tests. Note that some tests require more than one tester, and that some testers run more than one test. Also note that two of the "testers" aren't people. STC is a fictional but not atypical external test lab that specializes in software/hardware compatibility testing. Sales/Marketing refers to the internal sales and marketing staff and those special users they choose to involve in testing.

Alone, the three tables don't do a good job of telling you who's doing what and when. Why manually cross-reference the three tables when you can create reports based on a query that joins all three? In Figure 6.7, for example, you'll find a report titled Tester Assignments that documents which tester performs which tests, and when. This report is organized by phase, cycle, and start date, and also shows the overall length of time the tester is scheduled to work on the project.

An alternative view of the same information, shown in Figure 6.8, documents when and who runs each test. You might notice that in this Test Schedule report, the tests run finish-to-start with no downtime in between. This is fine if you have built slack into the duration of each test suite; for example, three days are scheduled for the Edit Engine test suite during the component test phase, even though it is likely to take only two

Phase	Cycle	Suite	Start	End
Component	1	Edit Engine	7/19	7/21
Component	1	User Interface	7/22	7/23
Component	2	Edit Engine	7/26	7/28
Component	2	File	7/26	7/27
Component	2	Tools	7/28	7/28
Component	2	User Interface	7/29	7/30
Component	3	File	8/2	8/3
Component	3	Tools	8/4	8/4
Integration	1	Edit Engine-UI	8/2	8/4
Integration	2	Edit Engine-File	8/9	8/10
Integration	2	File-UI	8/11	8/12
Integration	3	Edit Engine-UI	8/16	8/18
System	1	Documentation/Packaging	8/16	8/20
System	1	Install/Configure	8/16	8/20
System	1	Performance	8/16	8/18
System	2	Beta	8/23	9/5
System	2	Compatibility	8/23	8/29
System	2	Error Handling/Recovery	8/23	8/24
System	2	File Sharing	8/25	8/27
System	3	Compatibility	8/30	9/5
System	3	Documentation/Packaging	8/30	9/3
System	3	Error Handling/Recovery	8/30	8/31
System	3	File Sharing	9/1	9/3
System	3	Install/Configure	8/30	9/3
System	3	Performance	8/30	9/1

Figure 6.4   The SpeedyWriter tests.

Tester Name	Position
⊞ John Goldstein	Technician
⊞ Lin-Tsu Woo	Engineer
⊞ Liz Campbell	Technician
⊞ Muhammad Zamanzadeh	Manager
⊞ Sales/Marketing	Sales, Marketing, and Users
⊞ STC	Test Lab

Figure 6.5   The SpeedyWriter testers.

days. However, if you use a best-case estimate for each suite and pack the tests as shown here, you will find yourself either slipping the schedule or requiring lots of weekend work from your testers when expectations aren't met.

Next, you need to address the question of where the test work happens. The *Locations* table is populated with four places where testing will occur or where test hardware will be located. "JG Home" is John Goldstein's home, where he works between bouts on the road. "SC Engr" is the Software Cafeteria engineering offices. "SC SM" is the Software Cafeteria sales and marketing offices. Finally, "STC Lab" is the independent test lab.

The table in Figure 6.9 represents the *Work At* relationship, which matches testers with locations. (I've used *1/1/1900* to indicate, "as far in the past as is relevant to this project" and *12/31/9999* to indicate, "for the duration of this project," although you can't see the years in this report format. Rest assured that Lin-Tsu, Liz, and Muhammad will not spend 8,100 years at Software Cafeteria, although on some late nights it

Phase	Cycle	Suite	Tester Name
Component	1	Edit Engine	Lin-Tsu Woo
Component	1	User Interface	Lin-Tsu Woo
Component	2	Edit Engine	Lin-Tsu Woo
Component	2	File	Liz Campbell
Component	2	Tools	Liz Campbell
Component	2	User Interface	Lin-Tsu Woo
Component	3	File	Liz Campbell
Component	3	Tools	Liz Campbell
Integration	1	Edit Engine-UI	Lin-Tsu Woo
Integration	2	Edit Engine-File	Lin-Tsu Woo
Integration	2	File-UI	Lin-Tsu Woo
Integration	3	Edit Engine-UI	Lin-Tsu Woo
System	1	Documentation/Packaging	John Goldstein
System	1	Install/Configure	Lin-Tsu Woo
System	1	Install/Configure	Liz Campbell
System	1	Performance	Lin-Tsu Woo
System	2	Beta	Sales/Marketing
System	2	Compatibility	STC
System	2	Error Handling/Recovery	Lin-Tsu Woo
System	2	File Sharing	Lin-Tsu Woo
System	3	Compatibility	STC
System	3	Documentation/Packaging	John Goldstein
System	3	Error Handling/Recovery	Lin-Tsu Woo
System	3	File Sharing	Lin-Tsu Woo
System	3	Install/Configure	Lin-Tsu Woo
System	3	Install/Configure	Liz Campbell
System	3	Performance	Lin-Tsu Woo

Figure 6.6   The SpeedyWriter test assignments.

Tester Assignments

TesterName	Position	Phase Cycle Suite		Start		End
John Goldstein	**Technician**					
		System Test				
		1	Documentation/Packaging	8/16		8/20
		3	Documentation/Packaging	8/30		9/3
		John Goldstein works on this project from		8/16	to	9/3
Lin-Tsu Woo	**Engineer**					
		Component Test				
		1	Edit Engine	7/19		7/21
		1	User Interface	7/22		7/23
		2	Edit Engine	7/26		7/28
		2	User Interface	7/29		7/30
		Integration Test				
		1	Edit Engine-UI	8/2		8/4
		2	Edit Engine-File	8/9		8/10
		2	File-UI	8/11		8/12
		3	Edit Engine-UI	8/16		8/18
		System Test				
		1	Performance	8/16		8/18
		1	Install/Configure	8/16		8/20
		2	Error Handling/Recovery	8/23		8/24
		2	File Sharing	8/25		8/27
		3	Error Handling/Recovery	8/30		8/31
		3	Performance	8/30		9/1
		3	Install/Configure	8/30		9/3
		3	File Sharing	9/1		9/3
		Lin-Tsu Woo works on this project from		7/19	to	9/3
Liz Campbell	**Technician**					
		Component Test				
		2	File	7/26		7/27
		2	Tools	7/28		7/28
		3	File	8/2		8/3
		3	Tools	8/4		8/4
		System Test				
		1	Install/Configure	8/16		8/20
		3	Install/Configure	8/30		9/3
		Liz Campbell works on this project from		7/26	to	9/3

Saturday, December 22, 2001   *Page 1 of 2*

Figure 6.7   The Tester Assignments report.

might feel that way.) The real globetrotter of the team, you can see, is John Goldstein, the resident technical writing evaluator. He spends the first week testing at the Engineering office, stays for a week of meetings related to another project, returns to his home office for what he hopes will be a final review of the documentation, and then jets off to the Sales and Marketing office to help with the product launch.

Rather than putting together a report that merely correlates testers and locations—the table is simple enough, after all—you can generate two reports that tie together tests, testers, and locations, as shown in Figures 6.10 and 6.11. The first is location-oriented, organized by place; the second is test-oriented, providing the location last. As you can see, these reports can replace the previous reports, unless you find the location information distracting.

Test Schedule

Phase	Cycle	Suite	TesterName	Start		End
System Test						
	1					
		Documentation/Packaging		8/16		8/20
			John Goldstein			
		Install/Configure		8/16		8/20
			Lin-Tsu Woo			
			Liz Campbell			
		Performance		8/16		8/18
			Lin-Tsu Woo			
		System Test, Cycle 1 runs from		8/16	to	8/20
	2					
		Beta		8/23		9/5
			Sales/Marketing			
		Compatibility		8/23		8/29
			STC			
		Error Handling/Recovery		8/23		8/24
			Lin-Tsu Woo			
		File Sharing		8/25		8/27
			Lin-Tsu Woo			
		System Test, Cycle 2 runs from		8/23	to	9/5
	3					
		Compatibility		8/30		9/5
			STC			
		Documentation/Packaging		8/30		9/3
			John Goldstein			
		Error Handling/Recovery		8/30		8/31
			Lin-Tsu Woo			
		File Sharing		9/1		9/3
			Lin-Tsu Woo			
		Install/Configure		8/30		9/3
			Lin-Tsu Woo			
			Liz Campbell			
		Performance		8/30		9/1
			Lin-Tsu Woo			
		System Test, Cycle 3 runs from		8/30	to	9/5
		System Test runs from		8/16	to	9/5

Figure 6.8 The Test Schedule report.

Tester Name	Location Name	Start	End
John Goldstein	JG Home	1/1	8/8
John Goldstein	JG Home	8/21	9/3
John Goldstein	JG Home	9/6	12/31
John Goldstein	SC Engr	8/9	8/20
John Goldstein	SC SM	9/4	9/5
Lin-Tsu Woo	SC Engr	1/1	12/31
Liz Campbell	SC Engr	1/1	12/31
Muhammad Zamanzadeh	SC Engr	1/1	12/31
Sales/Marketing	SC SM	1/1	12/31
STC	STC Lab	1/1	12/31

Figure 6.9 The testers at their locations.

Tests by Location and Tester

Location	TesterName	Start	End	Phase		CycleSuite
JG Home						
	John Goldstein	8/21	9/3			
		8/30	9/3	System Test	3	Documentation/Packaging
SC Engr						
	John Goldstein	8/9	8/20			
		8/16	8/20	System Test	1	Documentation/Packaging
	Lin-Tsu Woo	1/1	12/31			
		7/19	7/21	Component Test	1	Edit Engine
		7/22	7/23	Component Test	1	User Interface
		7/26	7/28	Component Test	2	Edit Engine
		7/29	7/30	Component Test	2	User Interface
		8/2	8/4	Integration Test	1	Edit Engine-UI
		8/9	8/10	Integration Test	2	Edit Engine-File
		8/11	8/12	Integration Test	2	File-UI
		8/16	8/18	Integration Test	3	Edit Engine-UI
		8/16	8/18	System Test	1	Performance
		8/16	8/20	System Test	1	Install/Configure
		8/23	8/24	System Test	2	Error Handling/Recovery
		8/25	8/27	System Test	2	File Sharing
		8/30	8/31	System Test	3	Error Handling/Recovery
		8/30	9/1	System Test	3	Performance
		8/30	9/3	System Test	3	Install/Configure
		9/1	9/3	System Test	3	File Sharing
	Liz Campbell	1/1	12/31			
		7/26	7/27	Component Test	2	File
		7/28	7/28	Component Test	2	Tools
		8/2	8/3	Component Test	3	File
		8/4	8/4	Component Test	3	Tools
		8/16	8/20	System Test	1	Install/Configure
		8/30	9/3	System Test	3	Install/Configure
SC SM						
	Sales/Marketing	1/1	12/31			
		8/23	9/5	System Test	2	Beta
STC Lab						
	STC	1/1	12/31			
		8/23	8/29	System Test	2	Compatibility
		8/30	9/5	System Test	3	Compatibility

Saturday, December 22, 2001   Page 1 of 1

Figure 6.10   The Tests by Location and Tester report.

A certain amount of magic is required in the query for the reports shown in Figures 6.10 and 6.11. That query is shown in Figure 6.12. The database join by itself does not restrict the testing by location, since it is the date on which the tester performs the test, together with the tester's location at that time, which determines where the testing happens. Therefore the two date-matching criteria shown in the join are essential to making the query—and the reports that use it—work.

Locations by Test and Tester

Phase	Cycle	Suite	Tester Name	Start		End	Location
System Test							
	2						
		Beta					
			Sales/Marketing	1/1		12/31	
				8/23		9/5	SC SM
		Compatibility					
			STC	1/1		12/31	
				8/23		8/29	STC Lab
		Error Handling/Recovery					
			Lin-Tsu Woo	1/1		12/31	
				8/23		8/24	SC Engr
		File Sharing					
			Lin-Tsu Woo	1/1		12/31	
				8/25		8/27	SC Engr
			System Test, Cycle 2 runs from	8/23	to	9/5	
	3						
		Compatibility					
			STC	1/1		12/31	
				8/30		9/5	STC Lab
		Documentation/Packaging					
			John Goldstein	8/21		9/3	
				8/30		9/3	JG Home
		Error Handling/Recovery					
			Lin-Tsu Woo	1/1		12/31	
				8/30		8/31	SC Engr
		File Sharing					
			Lin-Tsu Woo	1/1		12/31	
				9/1		9/3	SC Engr
		Install/Configure					
			Lin-Tsu Woo	1/1		12/31	
				8/30		9/3	SC Engr
			Liz Campbell	1/1		12/31	
				8/30		9/3	SC Engr
		Performance					
			Lin-Tsu Woo	1/1		12/31	
				8/30		9/1	SC Engr
			System Test, Cycle 3 runs from	8/30	to	9/5	
			System Test runs from	8/16	to	9/5	

Figure 6.11   The Locations by Test and Tester report.

The Assets, How You Use Them, and Where They Live: The Hardware and Infrastructure Side

Let's move on to the issue of managing hardware and infrastructure, starting with hardware. Chapter 2, "Plotting and Presenting Your Course: The Test Plan," introduced the idea of a hardware allocation plan. (See *Test Configurations and Environments* in that chapter.) Now you can expand this concept by using the logistics database to plan for the hardware, software, and infrastructure items you need, to organize how these items will be assigned and shared, and to track various configurations.

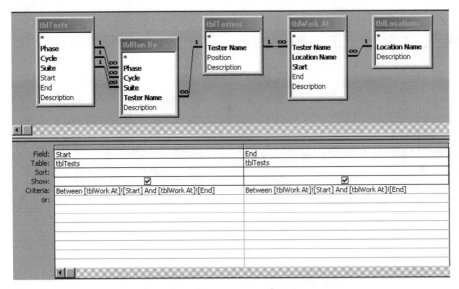

Figure 6.12   A query to show locations, tests, and testers.

For the SpeedyWriter case study, hardware and infrastructure come in three flavors: clients, servers, and networking/telecommunications devices. Let's assume that you want to cover five operating systems on the client side: Mac OS, Windows 98, Windows Me, Windows NT, and Sun Solaris. As noted earlier, SpeedyWriter testing starts in mid-July and runs through early September. Suppose that three client systems are available in the test lab during this time: a Sony laptop, a Macintosh, and a Dell desktop. By purchasing two other clients—say, a Hewlett-Packard and a Micron—you can cover all five target client platforms.

Two questions might occur to you at this point. First, why not simply plan to use the testers' workstations as test platforms? Sometimes you should do this. In our example, John Goldstein uses his PowerBook to do the documentation and packaging testing. Testers will undoubtedly install SpeedyWriter on their workstations and use these for isolation. Usually, however, you want your test clients to be "clean" configurations. Using an individual's workstation can create questions about bugs. For example, did the software under test corrupt the Registry, or does the problem stem from the old shareware game the user installed six months ago that never would completely uninstall?

Second, could you save money by allocating only two or three systems and using partitioning and multiboot utilities to install and select multiple operating systems on each? Again, this is sometimes a good idea. When testing software, you indeed might want to be able to boot different operating systems on a single platform to determine whether bugs are hardware-related. However, don't plan on saving money by getting too clever with your test hardware allocation. Do you want one bug on a single platform/operating system combination to bring other scheduled testing to a halt because you have a platform shortage? How many wasted hours of a tester's time will pay for a $2,500 computer? Of course, when you're talking about $250,000 servers, the story is different, but those servers can frequently support multiple users simultaneously. A

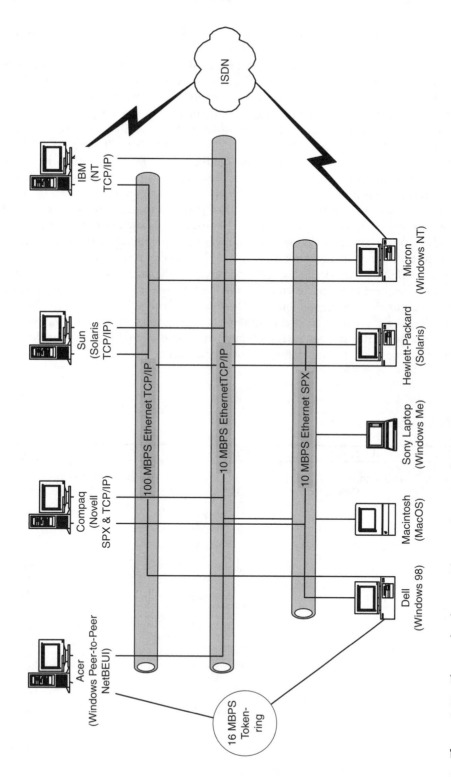

Figure 6.13 The test hardware and network environment for SpeedyWriter testing.

235

client computer running tests is generally exclusively allocated for those tests for the duration of the tests.

Let's assume that you want to cover four logical network types: Microsoft peer-to-peer (NetBEUI), Novell (SPX and TCP/IP), Solaris (NFS with TCP/IP), and Windows NT (TCP/IP). Suppose that everything except the Microsoft peer-to-peer server is already up and running in the building; you can then budget an inexpensive Acer system to serve as the cooperating host. The systems attach, variously, to five different physical network types: 100 Mbps Ethernet TCP/IP, 10 Mbps Ethernet TCP/IP, 10 Mbps Ethernet SPX, 16 Mbps token-ring NetBEUI, and ISDN dial-up networking TCP/IP. (It's important to include different physical network types because different network connections require different drivers on the client side, which can intersect with application operations—even though they're not supposed to do so.) Figure 6.13 shows the test lab configuration with these clients, servers, and network types.

Although you have now defined a test network without much regard to the specific tests you will run on it, this is not a case of putting the cart before the horse. Your test network definition grew out of your coverage goals for the clients, servers, and network types. Having met these goals, you can now distribute test suites across the various client configurations, either randomly or based on which ones you think are most likely to find bugs against a particular configuration. Notice that by spreading the testing over the clients, you can also cover the servers and networks easily, provided you make sure that tests actually do exercise all the network connections available to the clients.

Hardware Assignment

Client	Network	Server	Phase	Cycle	Suite	Exclusive	Start	End
Dell W98 Client							7/15	
	10 Mbps SPX						7/19	
		Compaq Novell Server					1/1	
			Component Test					
				1	Edit Engine	Yes	7/19	7/21
				2	User Interface	Yes	7/29	7/30
			Integration Test					
				1	Edit Engine-UI	Yes	8/2	8/4
				2	Edit Engine-File	Yes	8/9	8/10
				2	File-UI	Yes	8/11	8/12
				3	Edit Engine-UI	Yes	8/16	8/18
			System Test					
				1	Install/Configure	Yes	8/16	8/20
				1	Performance	Yes	8/16	8/18
				2	Error Handling/Recovery	Yes	8/23	8/24
				2	File Sharing	Yes	8/25	8/27
				3	Error Handling/Recovery	No	8/30	8/31
				3	File Sharing	No	9/1	9/3
				3	Install/Configure	No	8/30	9/3
				3	Performance	No	8/30	9/1
	100 Mbps TCP/IP						7/19	
		IBM NT Server					1/1	
			Component Test					
				1	Edit Engine	Yes	7/19	7/21
				2	User Interface	Yes	7/29	7/30

Figure 6.14 The Hardware Assignment report.

Test Hardware

Phase Cycle Suite Client Network Server	Exclusive	Start	End
Component Test			
1			
Edit Engine		7/19	7/21
Dell W98 Client	Yes	7/15	
10 Mbps SPX		7/19	
Compaq Novell Server		1/1	
100 Mbps TCP/IP		7/19	
IBM NT Server		1/1	
Sun Solaris Server		1/1	
16 Mbps Token-Ring		8/2	
Acer MS Server		8/13	
User Interface		7/22	7/23
HP Solaris Client	Yes	7/14	
10 Mbps TCP/IP		7/19	
Acer MS Server		8/13	
Compaq Novell Server		1/1	
IBM NT Server		1/1	
Sun Solaris Server		1/1	
100 Mbps TCP/IP		7/19	
IBM NT Server		1/1	
Sun Solaris Server		1/1	
2			
Edit Engine		7/26	7/28
Mac Client	Yes	7/12	
10 Mbps TCP/IP		7/19	
Acer MS Server		8/13	
Compaq Novell Server		1/1	
IBM NT Server		1/1	
Sun Solaris Server		1/1	
File		7/26	7/27
Sony WMe Client	Yes	7/19	
10 Mbps SPX		7/19	
Compaq Novell Server		1/1	
Tools		7/28	7/28
Micron NT Client	Yes	7/6	
10 Mbps TCP/IP		7/19	
Acer MS Server		8/13	
Compaq Novell Server		1/1	

Sunday, December 23, 2001   *Page 1 of 12*

Figure 6.15 The Test Hardware report.

Your next task is to set up some reports. You can begin by creating tables based on the *Hardware* entity and the *Run On* and *Attaches To* relationships from Figure 6.3. In much the same way you created reports for the tests and the testers, you can create two reports for tests and hardware, including the attached hardware in this case. Figure 6.14 shows the Hardware Assignment report, organized by hardware; Figure 6.15 shows the Test Hardware report, organized by tests. The former is useful for system administrators and for preparing budgets, while the latter helps testers and test managers understand what hardware they will use to run tests (and also helps you spot missing hardware).

You will also need to situate the hardware. In the Situated At table in this case study, I've shown all the hardware located at the Software Cafeteria Engineering headquarters in Austin, Texas (see Figure 6.16). Typically, I use a finer granularity for locations than this example allows, which enables me to track places such as "Second Floor

HW Name	Location Name	Installer	Start	Ready	End
10 Mbps SPX	SC Engr	James Sakayeda	7/17	7/19	12/31
10 Mbps TCP/IP	SC Engr	James Sakayeda	7/17	7/19	12/31
100 Mbps TCP/IP	SC Engr	James Sakayeda	7/17	7/19	12/31
16 Mbps Token-Ring	SC Engr	James Sakayeda	7/31	8/2	12/31
3COM TA	SC Engr	James Sakayeda	7/24	8/1	12/31
Acer MS Server	SC Engr	Sharif al-Hassan	8/12	8/13	12/31
Compaq Novell Server	SC Engr	N/A	1/1	1/1	12/31
Dell W98 Client	SC Engr	Rajesh Gupta	7/15	7/15	12/31
HP Solaris Client	SC Engr	Rajesh Gupta	7/14	7/14	12/31
IBM 16 Mbps TR	SC Engr	James Sakayeda	8/8	8/10	12/31
IBM NT Server	SC Engr	N/A	1/1	1/1	12/31
ISDN Line	SC Engr	Rajesh Gupta	7/24	8/2	12/31
John's Powerbook	SC Engr	N/A	8/16	8/16	12/31
Mac Client	SC Engr	Rajesh Gupta	7/12	7/12	12/31
Micron NT Client	SC Engr	Sharif al-Hassan	7/6	7/6	12/31
Sony WMe Client	SC Engr	Rajesh Gupta	7/19	7/19	12/31
Sun Solaris Server	SC Engr	N/A	1/1	1/1	12/31

Figure 6.16   Where the hardware is situated.

Lab," "Thermal Chamber," and so forth. If you want to use this database to manage tight or limited spaces, you should consider this level of detail. In addition, you might want to include footprint areas and overall dimensions for servers and other lab equipment so that you can compare the space taken up by the hardware in a lab to the space available in the lab (see Chapter 7 for more on this idea.)

As a final note, let me point out another simplification contained in this section. This example does not account for the hardware that the sales and marketing beta sites will provide, nor does it include the STC lab's hardware. To use this database to ascertain hardware coverage, you would certainly need that level of detail. However, I usually capture that type of data in the test tracking spreadsheet.

What's Running Where?
Tracking Software Configurations

In general, you can use the logistics database to track all types of software configurations on test hardware. You can trace the BIOS, operating system versions, applications, virtual machines and interpreters, compilers, utilities, test tools, test scripts, and other software revisions. To keep our case study simple, though, this section shows only SpeedyWriter software revisions.

Unlike the hardware and human logistics planning discussed in the preceding sections, this section focuses on a dynamic aspect of the database. (After all, this chapter is about crunch mode!) In this example, software is arriving according to a release schedule but rather unpredictably within a one- or two-day window. Table 6.1 shows the planned release schedule for each flavor of SpeedyWriter (that is, for each of the five host, or target, client systems: Mac OS, Windows 95, Windows 98, Windows NT, and Solaris), with the associated test phase and cycle. In addition, releases of Speedy-Writer for each host system are planned for the same day.

Table 6.1   Planned Releases for Target Platforms

REVISION IDENTIFIERS	RELEASE DATE	PHASE	CYCLE
C.1.Mac C.1.W95 C.1.W98 C.1.WNT C.1.Sol	7/19	Component	1
C.2.Mac C.2.W95 C.2.W98 C.2.WNT C.2.Sol	7/26	Component	2
I.1.Mac I.1.W95 I.1.W98 I.1.WNT I.1.Sol	8/2	Component Integration	3 1
I.2.Mac I.2.W95 I.2.W98 I.2.WNT I.2.Sol	8/9	Integration	2
S.1.Mac S.1.W95 S.1.W98 S.1.WNT S.1.Sol	8/16	Integration System	3 1
S.2.Mac S.2.W95 S.2.W98 S.2.WNT S.2.Sol	8/23	System	2
S.3.Mac S.3.W95 S.3.W98 S.3.WNT S.3.Sol	8/30	System	3

The plan shown in Table 6.1 looks good, but it probably won't survive its first encounter with reality. Good tests will find bugs, which often delay releases. Some bugs hold up the releases to the point that entire revision levels will be skipped for certain cycles. Logistical problems—lack of proper build platforms, compiler glitches, and so forth—will also detain releases. Every now and then, releases will come in early; and some releases might be skipped because the previous test cycle did not find any bugs in them.

Let's take a hindsight view of what actually happens. Figure 6.17 shows a snapshot of a table based on the *Software* entity. If you are using the railroad method of spreading test suites across configurations (see Chapter 3), you can assume that delayed and even skipped releases do not affect the planned execution of tests. Figure 6.18 shows the Tested Configurations report, which cross-references tests against hardware and the software running on those platforms. (Of course, you could also produce a report that was organized by software and showed the tests run against the software configurations.) Since SpeedyWriter runs on the client side, this report does not show the networks or servers.

You can also expand this database to track hardware changes as they occur. In order to do that most effectively, you would need to bifurcate every date field into *Planned Date* and *Actual Date* fields. You can even use "deleted" and "added" flags to indicate those records that were dropped or inserted after the initial plan was formulated. Such an approach might constitute the beginnings of a very precise change management database for testing. I prefer, however, to use the more flexible approach introduced in the following section.

SW Name	Release ID	Released
SpeedyWriter	C.1.Mac	7/19
SpeedyWriter	C.1.Sol	7/20
SpeedyWriter	C.1.W95	7/19
SpeedyWriter	C.1.W98	7/19
SpeedyWriter	C.1.WNT	7/19
SpeedyWriter	C.2.Mac	7/26
SpeedyWriter	C.2.Sol	7/30
SpeedyWriter	C.2.WNT	7/28
SpeedyWriter	I.1.Mac	8/2
SpeedyWriter	I.1.W95	8/3
SpeedyWriter	I.1.W98	8/1
SpeedyWriter	I.1.WNT	8/1
SpeedyWriter	I.2.Sol	8/9
SpeedyWriter	I.2.W95	8/10
SpeedyWriter	I.2.W98	8/11
SpeedyWriter	I.2.WNT	8/8
SpeedyWriter	S.1.Mac	8/16
SpeedyWriter	S.1.Sol	8/17
SpeedyWriter	S.1.W95	8/17
SpeedyWriter	S.1.WNT	8/17
SpeedyWriter	S.2.Mac	8/23
SpeedyWriter	S.2.Sol	8/23
SpeedyWriter	S.2.W95	8/25
SpeedyWriter	S.2.W98	8/26
SpeedyWriter	S.3.Mac	8/30
SpeedyWriter	S.3.W95	8/31
SpeedyWriter	S.3.W98	9/1
SpeedyWriter	S.3.WNT	8/30

Figure 6.17 Release of software for SpeedyWriter.

Tested Configurations

Phase	Cycle	Suite	Client	Software	Release ID	Released	Installed
Component Test							

1

    Edit Engine: Starts on 7/19 and ends on 7/21
      Dell W98 Client (Available 7/15)

				SpeedyWriter	C.1.W98	7/19	7/19

    User Interface: Starts on 7/22 and ends on 7/23
      HP Solaris Client (Available 7/14)

				SpeedyWriter	C.1.Sol	7/20	7/21

2

    Edit Engine: Starts on 7/26 and ends on 7/28
      Mac Client (Available 7/12)

				SpeedyWriter	C.2.Mac	7/26	7/26

    File: Starts on 7/26 and ends on 7/27
      Sony WMe Client (Available 7/19)

				SpeedyWriter	C.1.WMe	7/19	7/19

    Tools: Starts on 7/28 and ends on 7/28
      Micron NT Client (Available 7/6)

				SpeedyWriter	C.1.WNT	7/19	7/19

    User Interface: Starts on 7/29 and ends on 7/30
      Dell W98 Client (Available 7/15)

				SpeedyWriter	C.1.W98	7/19	7/19

3

    File: Starts on 8/2 and ends on 8/3
      HP Solaris Client (Available 7/14)

				SpeedyWriter	C.2.Sol	7/30	7/30

    Tools: Starts on 8/4 and ends on 8/4
      Mac Client (Available 7/12)

				SpeedyWriter	I.1.Mac	8/2	8/2

Integration Test

1

    Edit Engine-UI: Starts on 8/2 and ends on 8/4

Monday, December 29, 2001   *Page 1 of 6*

Figure 6.18 The Tested Configurations report, which relates tests, hardware, and the software running on the hardware.

Expect the Unexpected:
A Change Management Database

No matter how well you plan, no matter how carefully you follow up, no matter how effectively you work with your testers, colleagues, and managers, you will have to respond to the unexpected. Change is unavoidable, and not all changes can be foreseen. Last-minute course corrections, external errors, and internal omissions occur on every development project.

Change is often a manifestation of the learning process. As the development team—including test—proceeds through design, implementation, and testing toward the released product, individuals, groups, and the entire team learn more about how the product should function and behave. Changes related to such acquired wisdom are opportunities to be welcomed, since these changes result in a better product.

Sometimes changes are the result of someone's mistake. A failure to plan or follow up in one group can cause problems in other groups. Because test is on the receiving end of many project deliverables—and also because it needs extensive infrastructure, hardware, and software resources and support—your team is probably more susceptible to the vagaries of the unexpected than other development teams. (In fact, Bill Perry and Randy Rice, in *Surviving the Top Ten Challenges of Software Testing*, identify responding to change as one of the top 10 challenges facing test organizations.) Thus, you might find yourself in need of a way to track and manage incoming changes that threaten to rock—if not tip over—your boat.

Change management is seen by most system professionals as a project-wide functional, not the role of the test organization. For example, Steve McConnell recommends that the project manager or the project management team establish a change control board (CCB). This board manages—monitors, assesses, and accepts or rejects—alterations in any portion of the project plan that is under change control, which includes the test plans and the schedule. (See Chapter 6 of McConnell's *Software Project Survival Guide* for an excellent discussion of how such a CCB should work and what it should do.)

If you are fortunate enough to work on a project that has a formal CCB, you can use that mechanism to track both deliberate and accidental alterations in the test plan and the schedule. However, if you work in environments such as those I'm most used to, where change management is an informal or even nonexistent process, the following sections might help you find a way to track the changes that affect your team, the consequences and the impact of those changes, and the recovery plans you put in place.

So What?
Using (and Misusing) Change Management Data

By gathering data on changes, impact, and recovery plans, you can fulfill several important communication and planning responsibilities. Gathering this data provides a structured way to communicate to project management the consequences that certain decisions and events have for the test organization. Using a database also allows you to assemble persistent data that is especially helpful in post-project analysis meetings (a.k.a., "post-partums"). In addition, committing recovery plans to writing helps to ensure that you aren't simply reacting on the spur of the moment—and it can also save you from having to formally update the test plan, the schedule, and other documents in the midst of crisis conditions. (Significant unexpected changes often rule out spending an hour checking out documents from the repository, modifying them, and then recirculating them for comments, sign-off, or approval.)

Bear in mind, however, that a change management database is not a place to record a laundry list of complaints. You will probably want to track only those changes that gain or cost a person-day, a calendar-day, or more. Note that you should include gains.

Some changes are for the better: deliverables show up a day early, software is so good that test cycles are dropped, external support is beyond expectations. The database described here supports capturing the good as well as the bad and the ugly.

Simple Is Good: The Change Management Database

This change management database is actually quite simple because the needs it serves are straightforward. Figure 6.19 shows the underlying table definition in Access, including a brief description of each field. You can insert data directly into the table using the Access datasheet view, but if you find lengthy text (memo) fields difficult to work with in this view, you can use a form such as the one shown in Figure 6.20, which presents a sample entry for DataRocket.

The *Change Type* field captures information that categorizes the changes. Your list of possible values might include categories such as these:

Early Deliverable. Some piece of hardware or software—a part of the system under test—showed up early.

Late Deliverable. The converse of the preceding category: the piece of hardware or software showed up late.

Feature Addition. A new feature that will, presumably, require testing, was added to the product.

Feature Change/Deletion. An existing feature was dropped or significantly changed. Any test tools, cases, or suites written primarily or partially for this feature must either change (requiring more time) or be dropped (meaning that the time already spent was wasted).

Test Addition. An existing feature, not previously planned for testing, must now be tested. Such a reversal is often a result of a change in test priorities: what was once a "don't care" area suddenly became an important feature in the product.

Test Change/Deletion. An existing test is dropped, not because the feature was omitted, but because someone decided that time or resources should be spent otherwise.

Schedule Slipped. You have been granted more time to complete testing. Note that project schedule slips that do not move the planned ship date actually result in an opposite type of change from the test team's point of view, since testing starts later but must conclude at the previously agreed time.

Field Name	Data Type	Description
ID	AutoNumber	Unique identifier for the change.
Project Name	Text	Name of project on which the change occurred.
Date Noted	Date/Time	Date on which the change was first noted.
Impact Date	Date/Time	Date on which the change will first affect testing.
Change Description	Memo	Short summary of what changed.
Change Type	Text	Type of change that is affecting testing.
Cross-References	Memo	List of the specific test documents that are affected by the change, with page and paragraph numbers.
Impact Description	Memo	Short description of what this change will mean for testing.
Schedule Impact	Number	Number of calendar-days delay or advance as a result of this change.
Resource Impact	Number	Number of person-days lost or saved as a result of this change.
Other Costs/Savings	Currency	Other costs/savings associated with this change.
Test Impact	Memo	Short list of the test case IDs affected by this change.
Recovery Plan	Memo	Short description of how we intend to accommodate this change, including any contingency plans identified in the test or project plan.
Status Log	Memo	Log of progress toward recovering from this problem.

Figure 6.19 A simple table for capturing test changes.

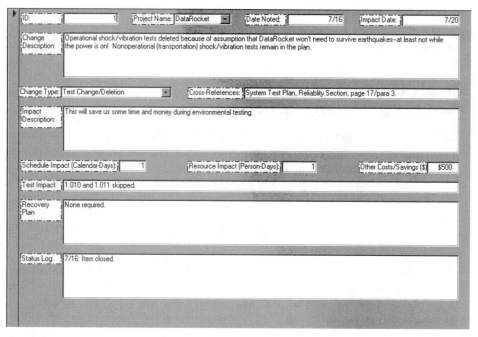

Figure 6.20 A form for entering change data, with a DataRocket sample.

Schedule Shortened. You have less time to complete testing. This often results when you are unable to start testing on time, but planned test exit dates remain unchanged.

Dependency. Some dependency (a factor other than the system under test) was not available or did not perform as expected.

Budget Increased. You received additional funds for testing, which, for example, allow you to purchase additional tools or hire more staff.

Budget Reduced. You lost funds previously committed.

Quality Exceptional. The system under test arrives with such a high level of quality that exit criteria are met ahead of schedule, allowing a planned cycle or pass of testing to be skipped.

Quality Problem. The system under test arrived on time, but with such abysmal quality levels that the stopping criteria in the test plan must be invoked, large numbers of tests are blocked, tests identify many bugs and take longer than planned, and so forth.

Because this tool is primarily text-based, it is certainly possible to use a word processing program to maintain it. However, I find that I value the reporting, categorizing, and analyzing options available in a database. I can produce a report that summarizes positive and negative impacts and adds up hours gained and lost. I can also export this data to a spreadsheet for analysis by date, category of change, and so forth.

Often, keeping track of changes is the best you can do during crunch time. This chapter's tips and tools notwithstanding, you will probably find yourself responding to events for the most part. Project crunch times can be managed by the entire project team when the project managers are careful to consider the effects of changes, overtime, pressure, and deadlines on the project team. We'll look at what those types of project teams look like and how they behave in Chapter 11. You can play a more effective role within any project team, chaotic and reactive or orderly and mature, by developing and exercising the "softer" management skills involved in working with your team, your peers, and your managers. During crunch-time especially, personal attributes such as grace under pressure, respect for your colleagues, and an even temper will serve you well, too. I'll discuss these skills in Chapter 8, "Staffing and Managing a Test Team," and Chapter 9, "The Triumph of Politics: Organizational Challenges for Test Managers." First, though, let's look at stocking and managing a test lab, which will build on the discussion of test logistics in this chapter.

Case Study

On one project, my test team and I tested an interactive-voice-response (IVR) network connected to a central call center. The IVR network allowed people to access and exchange information and interact in various local communities. The call center gave these people access to technical and personal help with their use of the IVR network. The project involved building a large test IVR/call center network.

For this project, I used a variation of the test logistics database introduced in this chapter. The database, "Case Study IVR Network Test Logistics.mdb," is available at www.rexblackconsulting.com.

In the hardware table, notice that we have a specific system administrator assigned to install each piece of equipment (see Figure 6.21). This might be necessary when multiple people are involved in supporting the test environment.

When I discovered hardware availability issues or problems with this database, I would work with the project management team to resolve them somehow, and then update the database. This is why you don't see a lot of issues with hardware not ready in time for a given test, testers unavailable or double-booked for assignments, or any of the other issues mentioned in this chapter. If you wanted to track such problems, you'd need to add tables that tracking historical status as well as current status.

If you look at the "Test Hardware Usage by Hardware" report, you'll see on pages 8 through 11 and 13 that we had an on-going problem with getting sufficient PRI ISDN and T1 lines for testing. The database isn't completely up to date, as we did finally resolve those problems partially—enough to complete testing. On page 26, you'll also notice that we did not have the live agent workstations to perform the CSA System Test (CSA stood for "Customer Service Application"). We ended up running those tests in a simulated agent workstation environment, and then running the Integration Tests that involve the agent workstations in a real environment. Because those tests revealed bugs in the agent workstations' interaction with the CSA database, it would have been preferable to find those bugs a few weeks earlier. This illustrates the danger of running high-level test phases in simulated environments.

Hardware Name	Location Name	Administrator	Start	Ready	End
10 MBPS E'net 1860 B1	1860 B1	James McIntyre	7/1/1998	7/1/1998	12/31/9999
10 MBPS E'net 1860 H3	1860 Heat Lab	James McIntyre	7/1/1998	7/1/1998	12/31/9999
1860 Network	1860 B1	James McIntyre	7/1/1998	7/1/1998	12/31/9999
Beta	1860 B1	James McIntyre	7/15/1998	7/15/1998	12/31/1999
Cisco 3810/1010	IRU	Todd Harrington	10/9/1998	10/19/1998	10/19/1998
Cisco 3810/1010	IRU	Todd Harrington	12/1/1998	12/15/1998	12/15/1998
Cisco 3810/1010	STC	NTS	10/26/1998	10/26/1998	11/30/1998
Dev Agent	1860 Test	Barbara Jefferson	9/23/1998	9/23/1998	12/31/9999
Dev IVR #1	1860 B1	James McIntyre	8/23/1998	8/23/1998	12/31/9999
Dev SVR	1860 B1	Natasha Illyanov	6/22/1998	6/22/1998	12/31/9999
ES 3500 CSA	1777 Windy City	James McIntyre	12/28/1998	1/1/1999	12/31/9999
ES 3500 CSA	1860 B1	James McIntyre	9/28/1998	9/28/1998	12/27/1998
ES 4500 CDR	1860 B1	James McIntyre	9/28/1998	9/28/1998	12/31/9999
Full MAN	1777 Windy City	James McIntyre	11/1/1998	11/1/1998	12/31/9999
Full MAN	1860 B1	James McIntyre	11/1/1998	11/1/1998	12/31/9999
Full WAN	1325 Capone	James McIntyre	11/20/1998	11/20/1998	12/31/9999
Full WAN	1777 Windy City	James McIntyre	11/20/1998	11/20/1998	12/31/9999
G3 "R" PBX	1777 Windy City	James McIntyre	11/20/1998	11/20/1998	12/31/9999
Half WAN	1860 B1	James McIntyre	11/16/1998	11/16/1998	12/31/9999
Live PRI ISDN 1325-V	1325 Capone	James McIntyre	12/31/9999	12/31/9999	12/31/9999
Live PRI ISDN 1860 B1	1860 B1	James McIntyre	12/31/9999	12/31/9999	12/31/9999
Live T1 1325-V	1325 Capone	James McIntyre	12/31/9999	12/31/9999	12/31/9999
Live T1 1860 B1	1860 B1	James McIntyre	12/31/9999	12/31/9999	12/31/9999
Lucent Open IVR	1777 Windy City	James McIntyre	12/31/9999	12/31/9999	12/31/9999
Null WAN	1860 B1	James McIntyre	10/7/1988	10/7/1988	12/31/9999
PCS PBX	1860 B1	James McIntyre	9/23/1988	9/23/1998	12/31/9999
PL 3000 (WF)	1777 Windy City	James McIntyre	12/28/1998	1/4/1999	12/31/9999
PL 6500 CM/CSA	1777 Windy City	James McIntyre	12/28/1998	1/1/1999	12/31/9999
PL 6500 CM/CSA	1860 B1	James McIntyre	10/15/1988	10/15/1988	12/27/1998
Prod 1	1860 B1	James McIntyre	8/3/1998	8/3/1998	12/31/9999
Prod 10	1325 Capone	James McIntyre	12/7/1998	12/14/1998	12/31/9999
Prod 11	1325 Capone	James McIntyre	12/7/1998	12/14/1998	12/31/9999
Prod 12	1325 Capone	James McIntyre	12/7/1998	12/14/1998	12/31/9999
Prod 2	1860 B1	James McIntyre	12/7/1998	12/14/1998	12/31/9999
Prod 4	1860 B1	James McIntyre	10/14/1998	10/19/1998	12/31/9999
Prod 5	1860 Heat Lab	James McIntyre	10/14/1998	10/19/1998	12/31/9999
Prod 6	1860 Heat Lab	James McIntyre	10/14/1998	10/19/1998	12/31/9999
Prod 7	IRU	Todd Harrington	10/9/1998	10/19/1998	10/19/1998
Prod 7	IRU	Todd Harrington	12/1/1998	12/15/1998	12/15/1998
Prod 7	STC	NTS	10/26/1998	10/26/1998	11/30/1998
Prod 9	1325 Capone	James McIntyre	12/7/1998	12/14/1998	12/31/9999
Prod Agent	1777 Windy City	James McIntyre	12/28/1998	1/4/1999	12/31/9999
Prod IVR 1	1777 Windy City	James McIntyre	12/28/1998	1/1/1999	12/31/9999
Prod IVR 1	1860 B1	James McIntyre	10/7/1988	10/7/1988	12/27/9999
Prod IVR 2	1777 Windy City	James McIntyre	12/28/1998	1/1/1999	12/31/9999
Prod IVR 2	860 B1	James McIntyre	10/30/1988	10/30/1988	12/27/9999

Figure 6.21   Installed hardware table with explicit supporting system administrator assignment.

Some of the tables in this database are not populated; for example, those related to specific projects and hardware attachment. I have left these in the database in case you want to experiment with them.

For this project, I also used the change management database introduced in this chapter. The database, "Case Study IVR Network Test Change Management.mdb," is available at www.rexblackconsulting.com.

As you page through the Changes report or the Changes form, you'll see that this project was significantly affected by a variety of changes. You might at first surmise that this reflects poorly on the project teams involved, but the truth is much more subtle than that. It's true that some players did drop the ball on certain tasks, and those problems rippled through to the test team. However, the project was based entirely on cutting-edge technology, which, as we'll discuss in Chapter 9, is always risky. In addition, the project had three major subsystems and a number of smaller and constituent subsystems that had to come together, meaning lots of interconnections and dependencies that affected the project—and testing. Finally, there were significant conversion issues that arose from the legacy data. All in all, this was one of the most complicated systems-development undertaking I've ever worked on, lasting over two years, executed by teams in about 10 different companies involving dozens if not hundreds of person-months of effort, and charged with achieving a huge leap in technology using brand-new components. This database reflects the type of change and fast-thinking that is involved when smart people work on complex systems development projects. If I had one thing to do over again on this project, I'd have built more resilience and robustness into my test plan so that changes rippling through the project didn't have a more significant impact on testing than they should have.

I thank my client on this project, a regional entertainment services firm, and the project managers in charge of development for allowing me to share these examples with readers of this book. I have purged all identifying and otherwise private information from this document, including changing the names of the participants in a random fashion. No client confidential information or information covered by nondisclosure agreement is contained in these documents. My client contact has asked that the organization remain anonymous.

Exercises

1. Identify the days on which you are unavailable for cultural, religious, or personal reasons. (There are no wrong answers here.) Compare your list with a peer's list, ideally someone with a different cultural or religious background. Describe at least one way that diversity in a project team can accelerate the schedule.

2. In exercise 1 in Chapter 3 and exercise 2 in Chapter 4, how much time did you decide to spend on each exercise? Discuss the time-management decision you made in terms of certitude versus progress. Note that there is no "right" answer in terms of time spent on either exercise, and that the right answer for this question depends not on justifying how much time you did spend, but rather on whether

you might or might not make those decisions differently on a real project where certitude/progress trade-offs are more acute.

3. Using the change management data in the case study, find the "vital few" changes types through a Pareto chart as shown in Chapters 4 and 5.

- Based on the number of changes.
- Based on the schedule impact.
- Based on the resource impact.
- Based on the other cost.

Stocking and Managing a Test Lab

In many organizations, the test manager is responsible for stocking and managing the test lab. If you are taking over an existing operation, this might not present much of a challenge; once you've seen a test lab in action, it's fairly obvious how to run one. However, for a first-time test manager in a new organization, getting a test lab up and running can be something of a mystery.

Simply put, a test laboratory is a place where testing is conducted. I use the word *laboratory* deliberately to emphasize that testers must perform controlled experiments, dealing with measurements and known quantities. They must be equipped with solid tools and a skeptical outlook in their attempt to establish facts. The test lab is an engineering laboratory, of course, not a scientific research laboratory, so the testers are seeking practical knowledge. Nevertheless, like a research laboratory, the test lab should be a place where structured, methodical, calm approaches prevail, not the center of a maelstrom where chaos reigns. (Don't underestimate the psychological effect of having people put on lab coats before entering the test lab!)

A test lab is also a physical location—or locations. When you have more than one test lab, it's useful to assign a name to each lab: a designation indicating its location ("B1"), a meaningful description ("the heat lab"), or just a whimsical name ("Gretchen"). When you conduct distributed testing (more on this in Chapter 10, "Involving Other Players: Distributing a Test Project"), you might even have multiple labs spread out over several continents.

This chapter describes the process of planning, establishing, and running a test lab. We'll look at questions such as these: Do you need a test lab? How do you select and plan the physical space? How do you outfit the lab? What about security? How do you manage the configuration of the test lab? What about the human factors? Before we begin, however, let me point out several considerations to keep in mind.

First, remember that testing can be conducted in settings other than test labs. You might recall John Goldstein, the documentation tester from the SpeedyWriter example in Chapter 6, "Tips and Tools for Crunch Time: Managing the Dynamic," who performed tests at his home, at the engineering office, at the sales and marketing office, even on an airplane in transit. Beta testing often takes place at customers' sites. Testing is still testing when it occurs outside the lab—although a less calm and collected atmosphere often prevails in a setting other than the lab.

Second, this chapter focuses on garden-variety test labs: labs that test hardware for environmental factors, reliability, electromagnetic radiation, sound, and software compatibility; and labs that test software for hardware compatibility, performance, system behavior, and the like. This discussion does not deal with setting up clean room environments, testing battlefield conditions, dealing with toxic chemicals, doing radiation hardness testing, or working in other such exotic or dangerous settings. If your job requires you to test in these situations, you'll need to consult other references.

Finally, note that throughout the chapter I use the phrase "test platform" to refer to any piece of hardware on which testers run tests. In the case of hardware testing, this is often the system under test, but this is not always so. For example, a hub can be a test platform when you are testing server connections to a network. In the case of software testing, the test platform is the host for the system under test (the software).

Do You Need a Test Lab?

Not every test organization needs a test lab. Some organizations need a lab only at certain times; others are immobilized without one. Because setting up and (especially) maintaining a decent test lab is an expensive proposition, you should carefully evaluate whether or not you actually need a lab.

Let's look at our two hypothetical companies. If you are the test manager for Winged Bytes, working on DataRocket and other servers, you will want a test lab. Environmental testing often requires thermal chambers and tables for shock and vibration tests. Electronic testing involves oscilloscopes, spectrum analyzers, and voltage meters. Reliability testing requires keyboard tappers and accelerated-life test chambers. Compatibility testing calls for a library of hardware and software. These types of test tools—especially bulky tools such as chambers and space-consuming collections of software—require a home of their own, away from general circulation.

If you are the test manager for Software Cafeteria, working on SpeedyWriter, however, you might not need a test lab. Your setup involves only a few workstations and some operating system software in open areas. The network infrastructure and servers are probably hidden away in a server room (or at least in a wiring closet) and thus don't require a separate lab.

The following questions can help you decide whether to establish or to forego a test lab:

- Do you need large test tools such as chambers? Are some of your test tools nonportable ones—an oscilloscope, for example—that need a special permanent location?

- Is a special environment required? If your test platforms have strict environmental requirements (as servers do) or unusual voltage needs (as telephone switches do), you will need at least a server room, if not a separate test lab.

- Is security an issue? For example, when testing new software or hardware, confidentiality is a big concern. Secrets stay secret only when as few people as possible know about them. Moreover, if you perform compatibility testing with a variety of software packages, the CD-ROMs and disks are valuable, as are the CPUs, tape drives, hard drives, and the like. Keeping them in a restricted-access test lab—especially in a locked cabinet—can save thousands of dollars in shrinkage (from loss, damage, or theft) over the years.

- Do you need to prevent nontesters from fiddling with your test environment? You might find that some individuals from other teams can't help themselves; they insist on loading quick patches or trying to hook up some device to the test platform "just to see if it works." They then forget to undo whatever they did. If you work with people like this, the formalism of a test lab might deter such well-intentioned but counterproductive hacking on your test platforms.

- Do you need access to the test facility for an extended period of time? Can multiple projects—concurrent, sequential, or both—leverage the cost of the lab to lower the total cost to the organization? Better yet, can you make the test lab a profit center by selling tools and services from the lab to outside, noncompeting companies? (This is less unlikely than you might expect. For example, if you have a printer compatibility test lab for SpeedyWriter, you might sell printer compatibility test services to other companies.)

If you really need a test lab, you will be able to make a business case for it based on these (and possibly other) factors. Try preparing a budget specifically for the test lab; you'll be surprised at how much it can cost. Remember, too, that money and effort are required not only to set up a lab, but also to maintain it. If the costs seem prohibitive, you almost always have alternatives. By carefully using external resources such as third-party test labs and your vendors, as described in Chapter 10, you can leverage their investments in labs and lab materiel to minimize or eliminate the need for your own. Even expensive testing budgets might prove wise investments, though, as we'll see in Chapter 11, "Testing in Context: Economics, Lifecycles, and Process Maturity."

Selecting and Planning a Lab Area

Once you've decided that a test lab is necessary, you'll need to select a location for the lab and plan its configuration. As you consider the factors outlined here, try to sketch a scaled floor plan of the lab, along the lines of the example shown in Figure 7.1. Make this floor plan as large as possible if you sketch it on paper, or use graphing or drawing software such as Visio. Either way, you should count on developing the floor plan iteratively; you might even need to start all over if you discover that the space you initially selected is unsuitable.

Size. Is the potential lab space large enough? When the shape of the room is anything other than square or rectangular and wide, you must consider size in conjunction with layout—that is, you must look at the actual working space. Also consider the height of the ceiling; I have seen racks of equipment as high as eight feet. Pay attention to the doors—everything in the lab must come in and, eventually, go out through them. Begin your sketch of the lab by drawing the lab area, including the location of the doors and the direction in which they open.

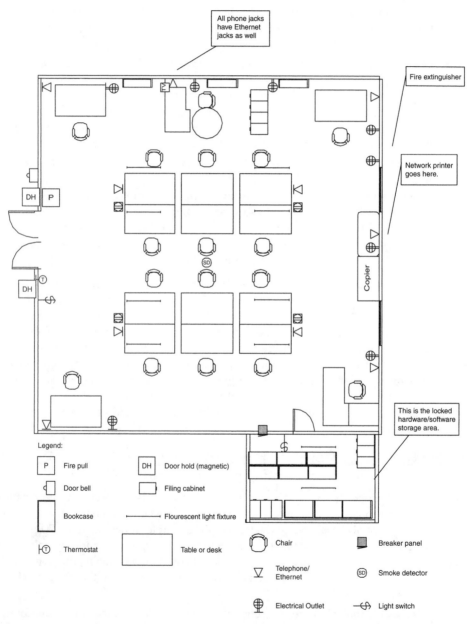

Figure 7.1 An example of a floor plan sketch for a test lab.

Lighting. Windows can provide both aesthetic benefits and a welcome break for testers. Some of the most pleasant test labs I ever worked in had high-rise views, one of downtown Taipei and the other of Santa Monica. Unfortunately, these same labs were also quite unpleasant when the afternoon sun came streaming into them in the summer. Beyond the heat it generates, direct sunlight can make screens difficult to read and damage valuable equipment. All windows in your lab should be tinted and should have effective shades installed. Also note the level of the windows: if they are at ground level or close to it, they can create a security problem.

As for artificial lighting, fluorescent lights are the most common type and are probably the best. Incandescent lights, although not associated with headaches and eyestrain as fluorescents are, tend to throw light in limited areas. Spot lights, track lights, and the like look cool, but they are a better choice for conference rooms than for labs, again because of the type of light they give off. Even and consistent lighting is important when testers are reading documents and screens or evaluating the quality of a display. On your floor plan, indicate the locations of both lighting fixtures and windows (if any).

Layout. When you select a lab space, keep in mind the types of tables and equipment racks you need to install. If you rack-mount most of your equipment, or if it is freestanding, a square room might work very well. If you use tables or desks, a rectangular room might be a better choice, as long as it is wide enough. Remember to leave enough open space to allow people to come and go freely. Populate your floor plan sketch with a scale layout of the chairs, desks, cabinets, shelves, tables, racks, and equipment you intend to install. To keep your floor plan less cluttered, you can use a legend to describe some of these objects.

Climate control. The test lab must have sufficient air conditioning and heating to preserve a stable, normal operating temperature and humidity for your equipment and your testers. Although the testers might go home, the equipment does not—which means continuous (24-hour, year-long) climate control. Your lab might also need automated shutdown capabilities if temperature or humidity limits are exceeded. If you have multiple labs or workspaces on the same system, ensure that each lab has its own thermostat. Locate the thermostat on your floor plan.

Fire safety and prevention. Every workplace should have a smoke or fire detector, either battery-powered or backed up by a battery (and this detector must be tested regularly). To control a fire, a test lab must have, ready at hand, portable fire extinguishers that are electrically safe and rapidly effective. If the lab contains large equipment such as mainframes or telephony switches, you will also need sophisticated, automatic fire suppression equipment that can put out a large electrical fire on its own while staff members attend to their personal safety. Include the fire detection and extinguishing equipment in your sketch, and make sure that your layout doesn't impede access to these devices or impede their use or flow. If objects in the lab get in the way, you should revisit your layout.

Power. Electrical power in one form or another (120 VAC, 240 VAC, 480 VAC, 48 VDC, and so on) must be provided in all test labs, and it must be available in the right places. In addition, the incoming power must be conditioned and uninter-

Field Name	Data Type	Description
Location Name	Text	The name of the location
Description	Text	The description of the location.
Length	Number	Length of the lab in feet.
Width	Number	Width of the lab in feet.
Height	Number	Height of the lab in feet.
Entrance Width	Number	Width of the entrance.
Entrance Height	Number	Height of the entrance.
Lights	Text	The type and wattage of the lighting.
Floor Plan	OLE Object	An image file picture of the floor plan.
Climate Control	Text	The air conditioning and heating facilities.
Fire Control	Text	The fire detection and suppression facilities.
Power	Text	The power available in the lab (120 VAC, 240 VAC, 480 VAC, 48 VDC, etc.) including number of each.
Connections	Text	Phone (PSTN, BRI ISDN, PRI ISDN, T1, OC3, etc.), network (Ethernet, Token Ring, ATM, etc.), others.

Figure 7.2   Extending the logistics database to include test lab locations.

ruptible, immune from the spikes, surges, sags, brownouts, and blackouts that plague the power grid. If it isn't, you will need to provide such conditioning and backup power in the lab, or be prepared to suffer the consequences. Indicate all the various power outlets on your floor plan.

Static. If you decide to carpet your lab, you will need to take extra precautions to inhibit static. Tile, linoleum, cement, and raised floors tend not to suffer from this problem to the same degree, but even clothing can generate static. The lab should contain static mats and other grounded metal objects to help testers dissipate static when they accumulate it.

Facilities. Facilities for your staff, such as restrooms, stairways, elevators, and so forth (including handicap accessibility) are important not only because you might be legally obligated to provide them, but also because they affect the productivity of the team. In addition, remember that you will need to connect the lab to the outside world using telephone lines (PSTN, BRI ISDN, PRI ISDN, T1, OC3, and so on); network cables such as category 3 Ethernet, category 5 Ethernet, token ring, optical, or ATM; and possibly other connections. If the proposed lab site does not already have the appropriate wiring installed, you will need to build it in, possibly at considerable expense. (A raised-floor configuration can make wiring within the lab painless, but the wiring must still be brought into the lab space, either through a wall or through a crawl space above the ceiling or below the floor.) You should also identify connections for running water if your planned tests require water for cooling or heating. Indicate all facilities and connections on your drawing.

To track many of the factors listed here, you can enhance the logistics database introduced in Chapter 6. Figure 7.2 shows a Locations table that can capture descriptive data about an individual lab site. As shown in Figure 7.3, a Hardware table can track the requirements and specifications of the lab's hardware.

The Test Lab Inventory

What items will you need to operate your test lab? Every test lab has different needs, depending on the systems under test. In addition, the importance of any specific item depends on the importance of the particular tests it supports.

Field Name	Data Type	Description
HW Name	Text	Short name of the hardware item.
Quantity	Number	Number of these items available in this lot.
Available	Date/Time	The date on which this lot of these items becomes available for configuration.
Length	Number	Length in inches.
Width	Number	Width in inches.
Height	Number	Height in inches.
Min Temp	Number	Minimum (operating) temperature.
Max Temp	Number	Maximum (operating) temperature.
Min Humidity	Number	Minimum (operating) humidity.
Max Humidity	Number	Maximum (operating) humidity.
Power Requirements	Text	Input power (120 VAC, 240 VAC, 480 VAC, 48 VDC, etc.).
ESD Safe?	Yes/No	Can withstand ordinary electrostatic discharges?
Connections	Text	Phone (PSTN, BRI ISDN, PRI ISDN, T1, OC3, etc.), network (Ethernet, Token Ring, ATM, etc.), others.
Description	Text	Any other information for this hardware item.

Figure 7.3 Extending the logistics database to include test lab hardware.

Suppose that you are setting up a test lab for Winged Bytes in order to perform testing not only for DataRocket, but also for the entire line of servers, desktops, and laptops produced by the company. You will use System Cookers, a third-party test lab, to do the environmental testing, so you don't need to buy thermal chambers, shock and vibration equipment, or HALT chambers.[1] Assume that your team will focus primarily on behavioral (black-box) tests. Based on this information, let's try to put together a list of the things we'll need for the lab.

A Sample Inventory Template

The following sections might represent a first pass at developing a "shopping list" for equipping the Winged Bytes test lab. You would need to buy one or more items in each category listed below. For software and hardware items, the choice of which specific ones to buy could be driven by sales and marketing staffs projections about the target customers, technical support's input on what the current customers use, and the test teams ideas on what is most likely to find bugs, design and requirements statements about support configurations, and so forth.

Software

Operating systems. You will need a wide representation of significant operating systems, which will be used primarily for compatibility testing.

Applications. A variety of software applications will be needed for compatibility testing and for use on tester workstations.

Test tools and utilities. Items such as these will be useful for diagnosing problems, creating simple automated tests, and sending faxes and files, making system images (i.e., snapshots of system hard drives), backing up critical data, measuring system performance, and generating background loads on systems.

---

[1]HALT is an acronym for *highly accelerated life testing*, which, through a combination of software operation and extreme environmental stress, simulates an entire lifetime for a computer. Some leading-edge computer vendors use HALT testing to predict the failures that will occur in the system under test as well as the life expectancy of the system. See *HALT, HASS & HASA Explained: Accelerated Reliability Techniques* by Harry McLean.

Hardware

PC Cards. PC Cards (formerly PCMCIA cards) tend to expose a lot of bugs in laptop systems, especially those that arise in conjunction with power management.

Monitors/video cards. The video subsystem is a frequent source of headaches. Consider using a variety of monitors and video cards.

Printers/scanners. Printers and scanners are not typically a source of hardware trouble, but you will find these items useful for verifying the functionality of USB, parallel, serial, and infrared ports

Modems/network cards. You will need a fairly wide variety of modems and network cards to test servers. The SpeedyWriter example in Chapter 6 showed five physical network types, counting ISDN, four servers, five clients, and 18 different network cards or adapters. Each card should be different to get as much test coverage as possible.

Data storage. In addition to items such as external hard disks, external removable storage, and external tape drives, you will need a fairly complete contingent of hard drives and other options.

Surge protectors/UPS units. In a good test lab, the wall current should be conditioned and backed up, but sometimes you have to make do with whatever power you can get. Surge protectors and uninterruptible power supply units can help.

Reference platforms. When you are conducting tests, the priority assigned to a bug often depends on whether the same failure occurs on multiple industry-standard platforms. In many cases, a reference platform is not just hardware, but also a particular PC with a particular OS and set of applications installed.

Cables. Because cables are relatively expensive for such small items, it's tempting to skip them. However, the first time an engineer wastes an hour trying to copy a group of files from one system to another because you don't have the right cable to use for a network or file-copy utility, cables will start to look like a bargain. At the very least, you'll need cables such as:

- Ethernet
- Token ring
- Parallel printer
- Serial printer
- Serial cross-over
- USB
- Telephone

Networking. In order to avoid testing on the corporate network, you will need to set up temporary networks in your test lab. Hubs and switches are fairly inexpensive, but make sure you pay the extra money to get a reliable brand. I had a cheap Ethernet hub once that would crash when new systems were added to the network—

either by plugging them in or just powering them on—and tremendous amounts of my time went up in smoke trying to figure out the problem.

Consumables

Be sure to have a plentiful supply of all consumables on hand. This saves time and prevents the loss of focus that occurs when your staff members become embroiled in wild goose chases searching for supplies. Remember that a missing $50 tape can cost you double that amount in an engineer's wasted time.

Computer media. This category includes such basics as floppy disks, removable storage device media, and DAT tapes.

Desk necessities. These items are the old standbys: notebooks, paper, pens, pencils, transparent tape, sticky notes, staplers, and paper clips.

Printer supplies. For all the printers involved in either testing or reporting results, you will need the appropriate types of toner, printer paper, printer cartridges, and ribbons.

Furnishings

Copiers and printers. Every test lab needs its own printer; you shouldn't count on using your test printers. Having a small copier isn't a bad idea, either.

Shredder. A shredder is a good idea if you work with confidential papers.

Benches, desks, stools, and chairs. It goes without saying that you will need places for your team to sit and work, but you'd be surprised how many labs have uncomfortable or inappropriate furniture.

Mouse pads. These often allow more precise, smooth motion than moving a mouse across a Formica lab counter. Even optical mice can have problems with certain color or texture surfaces.

Static pads. You should provide a few of these in every lab, to minimize the occurrence of static-discharge damage to hardware.

Tools

Specialized hardware. For basic electrical testing in the hardware test lab, you will need certain specialized hardware, such as an oscilloscope or a voltage meter.

Test management software. If you decide not to create your own systems for bug tracking, test tracking, estimating, and similar management tasks, you should plan to buy commercial software packages that implement such systems.

Computer toolkit. A fully stocked computer toolkit—including screwdrivers, wrenches, chip-pullers, and so on—is a necessity in every test lab.

Reference Materials

The classics. For every type of testing, a small set of books define the current best practices; be sure to have copies of these books on hand.

Standards. If industry or government standards apply to any of the systems under test, you will need to have up-to-date editions of these standards available.

Telephone books. Current telephone books are useful for many reasons, not the least of which is that sooner or later you will need a late-night take-out or dinner delivery for the test team.

Using Risk Analysis to Pick the Right Inventory

In some cases, the potential inventory for your test lab can be enormous. If you're testing a PC application such as a video game or accounting software, there are literally millions of potential supported configurations. (I covered this issue in Chapter 3, "Test System Architecture, Cases, and Coverage," in the section *Configuration Coverage*.) Even for a browser-based application, you have dozens of different browsers along with many different possible back-end configurations. Problems related to configuration can arise in just about any quality risk category. I've seen variations in configuration lead to the discovery of bugs related not just to functionality, but also to performance, reliability, data quality, the user interface, and operations, among others. I once saw variations in the firmware on an embedded modem lead to a significant difference in connection stability on otherwise identical versions of an information appliance.

In Chapter 3, I said that picking the key configurations was a function of the impact to the system if a particular configuration doesn't work, customer usage of that particular configuration, and the likelihood of problems in that particular configuration. (The same idea applies to any inventory item you would need to set up one of these configurations.) If you think back to my discussion of risk analysis in Chapter 1, "Defining What's on Your Plate: The Foundation of a Test Project," you'll recognize that these three factors map to the three variables in a Failure Mode and Effect Analysis: Severity, Priority, and Likelihood. Therefore, if you have used this risk analysis technique, you can add a section analyzing the various inventory items you might purchase.

Given a risk priority number (RPN), you now have an assessment of the importance of including an particular item in your inventory. However, you also need to consider cost. An item might be relatively high risk, but if it's so expensive that it consumes the entire lab budget, then you'd be foregoing all other configuration coverage to address just this one item. That's not likely to be an intelligent risk-management decision. You might want to add a cost column to your Failure Mode and Effect Analysis chart, and then sort by RPN first and cost second, both on an ascending scale. The high-, medium-, and even some low-risk items that are low cost you might as well buy, the high- and medium-risk items that are of medium cost you probably should buy, and the high-risk items that are highly expensive you should try to buy if possible.

Your cost factors should take into account depreciation across multiple or subsequent projects, too. In other words, the potential for re-use of an item should be an important consideration in whether you decide to purchase it. If you buy an item that you can use across 10 different projects, only one-tenth of the purchase price should accrue as a cost to your project. (This is one reason why buying lots of telephone and networking cables makes sense; not only are they cheap in general, they can be leveraged across hundreds or even thousands of projects, making their cost per project well under a penny.) Of course, depreciation is all well and good, but you are dealing with a fixed amount of money to outfit your lab. Just because you can depreciate a $100,000 supercomputer across 100 projects doesn't relieve your budgetary problems if you only have $100,000 to outfit your lab.

Since the number of potential items could be enormous, you might want to group equivalent items together in a class. For example, you could consider all models of laser printers from a single vendor equivalent. To pick a specific item out of this class, you can look at the risk, cost, and potential for re-use factors for that specific item compared with other items in the same class. Your sales, marketing, business analysts, users, technical support, and help desk staff might have strong opinions about which specific items represent certain classes, too. It is a good idea to take their ideas into account if practical.

Again, remember that configuration testing is but one of the many classes of testing you must do. Even if you have an almost unlimited budget for lab inventory, you probably don't have an unlimited number of people you can fit into that lab. By trying to cover too many configurations, you might end up with too few people to test other important quality risks.

Finally, keep in mind that beta testing and the use of third-party test labs (discussed in Chapter 10) can help keep your inventory costs down. A third-party test lab can re-use even expensive items with short lifespans—servers, for example—across multiple projects in a fairly short period of time, due to their volume of testing business. If you can get enough beta copies into the hands of a representative subset of customers, you might be able to cover an enormous variety of items.

Further Thoughts on Stocking Your Lab

No matter what you are testing, some general observations about your lab's inventory apply. Most important is that you must be certain to maintain some extra money in your test lab budget. You can't foresee everything, and you are sure to be caught off guard by a sudden need at some stage of the project. When that need arises, it might well be urgent and unavoidable. It's easier to include $5,000 in a "rainy day fund" during budgeting than to go begging to management for another $2,500 in the middle of crunch mode—when everyone has innumerable other crises to attend to.

Along these lines, don't forget to budget for maintenance. Some companies will give you free upgrades to software and firmware for life, but most will not. If your hardware is three, four, or more firmware revisions out of date, and your software one or two major releases in the past, how well are you modeling the real world in your test lab? Even one revision can make a big difference in software or hardware behavior. (As a tester, you know this implicitly for your own products, but it's easy to forget that we're all in the same boat.)

Finally, as you estimate quantities for certain test equipment such as mice, keyboards, printers, and monitors, remember that these items are often shared. You must have a sufficient number of these items on hand so that people don't waste time waiting to use them. When working with software, make sure to have enough licenses for every concurrent user.

Security and Tracking Concerns

Over time, you can spend millions of dollars outfitting a test lab. With accumulated assets worth that much, you need to protect your investment from damage, theft, and other losses. In hardware testing, for example, your assets might include some big-ticket items such as thermal chambers and oscilloscopes. A thermal chamber isn't terribly easy to steal, but one person with a car can easily make off with an oscilloscope. In software testing, you often use test platforms such as laptops that anyone with a decent-sized briefcase could sneak out of the building.

No matter how honest your team and your other colleagues might be, the concept of *due diligence* requires that you, as the responsible manager, make efforts to prevent theft and the loss of valuable assets.[2] With that said, you also don't want your security system to impede your team's productivity. A happy medium might be the use of a library system, in which one or more people fill the role of asset librarian. The asset librarian assumes responsibility for ensuring that every valuable materiel asset is secured when it is not in use, possibly in a locked cabinet or safe (for small hardware and software items) or a locked room (for larger items). When a tester needs to use an item for testing, for example, the tester checks it out from the librarian and then checks it back in when the test is completed. As you'll see in the next section, a simple database can track assets as they are checked in and out.

The beauty of this system is that one person is always accountable for each article at any given time. (You might need several asset librarians if you have multiple test shifts.) Economists refer to the "tragedy of the commons" as that situation in which everyone mistreats a shared set of resources because no one has ownership. In a library system, signing out a piece of equipment indicates ownership, and the individual who has signed it out must take special care that the item doesn't become lost or damaged.

You should also consider the issue of insurance as the value of your lab assets increases. Even if your company has corporate insurance, you might need to declare these lab assets specifically in order to protect them. Understand the terms of coverage. For example, if your lab is in a location that is subject to floods, are you insured against such events?

In addition to considering theft, loss, or damage to physical property, you must also worry about intellectual property. I once worked at a third-party testing company where most clients had their own separate labs, each accessible only with a card key. Each tester

---

[2]Informally, the phrase "due diligence" refers to the requirement that responsible employees, contractors, and consultants, especially managers, not be negligent of the consequences of their decisions and the attendant risks to their employers or clients. This means managers must think of ways to protect your employer or client from harm resulting from both acts and omissions.

had an individual card key, and a printer in a locked room logged the use of that card to enter a lab. Only staff members who were actively working on a client's project had card key access to that client's lab. Some clients insisted on labs without windows. Locked filing cabinets held specifications and other confidential documents. Even people not directly involved in testing, such as the sales staff and the bid writers, had to clean off their desktops and lock up the contents of their desks before leaving each day.

Managing Equipment and Configurations

The sample test lab inventory for Winged Bytes, presented earlier in this chapter, contains categories of items that can be classified as either consumable or durable. Most of the consumable items don't need any serious management—it's silly to try to keep track of pencils, for example. For such items, the only management concern is ensuring an adequate supply. However, for durable items such as desks, hubs, software, and the like, you'll need to manage them individually.

A common approach is to use asset tags. A sticker or plaque emblazoned with a unique identifier is affixed to each valuable item. (Your company might already use this method for managing desks, chairs, and other durable office furnishings.) Such durable items can be either portable or nonportable. A desk, for example, is fairly nonportable; once you place it, it is likely to stay put. In contrast, a laptop computer or a hub that your team uses for testing might move around. In this case, the ownership concept discussed in the preceding section becomes important. It is immaterial to you, for example, which asset tag is on the chair on which Lin-Tsu sits, but you do care which of the three copies of Microsoft Office she has at her workstation.

Note, however, that it makes sense to consider value when using this approach. Cables are a perfect example. Putting asset tags on telephone wires, and then trying to track who has them, is absurd; it'll cost you more in time than it would cost to replace the cable. In this case, I recommend that you accept some shrinkage of your cable inventory, whether from loss, damage, or even theft, rather than descend into incidents reminiscent of Captain Queeg's farcical inquisition into "who ate the strawberries" in *The Caine Mutiny*.

In addition to asset management issues, the question of asset configuration is important for some items. In the case of an oscilloscope, for example, you probably don't need to worry about revisions of the component boards. However, for each DataRocket in your lab, you must know not only the revisions for all the boards, but also the BIOS releases, the software installed, the disk drives present, and so forth. This is also true if you test software: because you test it on test platforms, you'll need to know exactly how each platform is configured.

You might be able to adapt the logistics database introduced in Chapter 6 to meet your configuration and asset management needs as well as for test lab logistics. Figure 7.4 shows the entity-relationship diagram for an adapted database. The *Hardware* entity you saw in Figure 6.2 now becomes the *Asset* entity, with the asset tag number (*Asset ID*) as its key property. In practice, serial numbers make decent asset identifiers, or you can use your own system. This entity also has a *Make* property, for the manufacturer name,

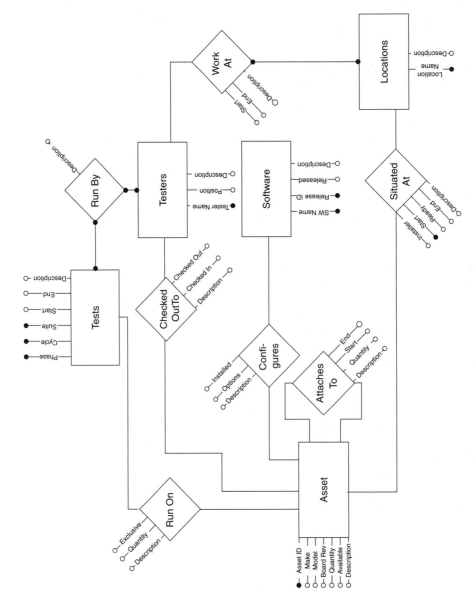

Figure 7.4 An entity-relationship diagram for managing logistics and lab assets.

a *Model* property for the specific model name, and *Board Revs* property for the board revisions in the hardware. Adding a *Project* property to the *Tests* entity enables you to manage multiple projects in this one database. With the addition of the *Checked Out To* relationship, you can also track responsibility for assets as your testers check hardware and software assets in and out of the library.

Beyond software and hardware configurations, another important dimension exists for test platform configuration, that of data (see Figure 7.5). The data dimension includes items such as databases and configuration files (the Windows Registry, for example, or Unix cron tables) as well as test input, output, and log files. Data can affect the behavior of the system as much as the software and the hardware can. Moreover, data presents a unique challenge in that the data configuration of the test platform is often changed, both deliberately and inadvertently, over the course of test execution.

Figure 7.6 shows the various data configuration states through which a test platform might move. These different states can be extremely complex. For each data state D_i, every byte of storage in system memory, video memory, the hard drive, networked storage, and any other secondary storage available to the test platform can be significant. In addition, the actions that cause data transformation are discrete keystrokes, mouse movements, network transactions, and so forth. Literally millions of such actions take place as part of a fairly straightforward test. Given this complexity, scaling up to, say, a 72-hour reliability test run on a network of two dozen servers and clients, means that you have reached the point where capturing all data configurations in any meaningful sense is impossible.

Fortunately, being able to recreate any arbitrary data configuration D_i doesn't add much value. The two data states you care most about are D_0 and D_n. D_n is particularly important if you are testing data quality. D_0 is important because, if you want to rerun a set of test suites against a particular configuration, you must restore all three dimensions of that configuration, data included. For this reason, it is often helpful to use tape, stored networked images, or removable storage media to take a "snapshot" of the test platform's data configuration before you begin to test. This step might add a few minutes to test suite setup time, but it is very helpful if you need to reproduce a particular result.

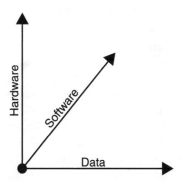

Figure 7.5 The dimensions of test system configuration.

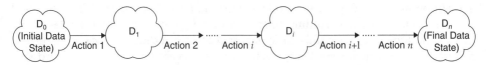

Figure 7.6   Data configuration changes resulting from setup and test actions.

Keeping the Test Environment Clean

As I've stressed before, it is important to know precisely what is on each test system at any given time during test execution. Otherwise, bugs can become irreproducible and bug reports will be inaccurate. Although this might sound obvious, many people underestimate the importance of strict configuration management in test environments.

In my experience, the fastest way to let your test environment deteriorate into a mysterious state is to allow someone with a "hacker mentality" to work on your test systems. Just one letter altered in one configuration file, one cable disconnected, one software package installed can change the whole demeanor of a bug. Unless everyone working on your test system logs all changes to every test platform, your test environment will quickly become uncertain. The frustration engendered by bugs that change shape daily has made me a firm believer in scrupulous configuration management.

Most developers want to be able to make changes and try quick experiments when they're debugging; having to document every single step they try slows them down. Unfortunately, this often puts the goal of preserving test platform configuration in conflict with the goal of rapidly debugging a problem. From the test perspective, the best possible solution to this problem lies in preventing any debugging activities from taking place on the test platforms. In a perfect world, the development team has its own development labs—or at least development systems and networks—which reduce or eliminate the need to work in the test lab.

As a practical matter, however, some bugs will occur only in the test environment. Remember that the test environment is as "user-like" as possible, while the development environment tends to be less controlled, with a narrower range of systems available. If a SpeedyWriter bug occurs only on a PowerBook computer, and the test team has the only PowerBook in the company, the developers must use test's hardware to debug the problem. Likewise, a performance problem on a token ring network will likely have to be verified in the test lab if all the development networks are Ethernet.

I'm afraid there is no simple solution here. On the one hand, dogmatically clinging to the notion that all debugging must happen outside the test lab can have a dangerous impact on a product's ship schedule. On the other hand, letting any developer who needs to track down a bug start hacking away on the test environment is an invitation to chaos. Loaning test equipment to developers isn't much of a solution, either. On occasion, I have "loaned" hardware to development tiger teams for debugging, only to find it "borrowed" on a nearly permanent basis. Don't assume that there is such a thing as "test's hardware"; project management can reassign it at a moment's notice. So, before you decide to let another group use your hardware "for a while," consider the possibility that "a while" might be the remainder of the project.

If you do have a situation where you share the test lab with the development team, and you can make this work in terms of shifting the use of the hardware, the tape or network drive image strategy discussed previously for capturing useful data configurations can help you and the development manager. You can accumulate a library of useful tape snapshots. You might want D_0, while the developers want D_i and D_j. This is certainly no panacea, and conflicts will arise, but you can at least prevent chaos in terms of the data state of the lab hardware.

Human Factors

Although the focus of this chapter has been on material objects and information related to them, you need to remember that *people* test in the test lab. The safety of the people who work in your lab must be of special concern to you as a manager. In addition, you need to consider the issues of how testers interact with your lab equipment (including possible damage to the equipment), and how to run the lab so that the testers are as productive as possible.

A Safe Lab Is a Productive Lab

As noted earlier, I assume that you are working in a typical test lab, where no extraordinary chemical, electrical, radiological, or mechanical hazards exist. If your staff must handle, use, or store dangerous chemicals; radioisotopes; radiation-emitting devices; sharp or heavy test probes or tools; high-voltage or high-current components; mechanical presses, punches, or drills; extremely hot or cold articles; or any other compound or object that can injure, electrocute, burn, blind, deafen, sterilize, poison, genetically damage, cut, or kill, you will need to take precautions beyond those discussed in this book.

Most of the test labs I've worked in were less dangerous than the typical garage, bathroom, or kitchen. Nevertheless, everyone working in the lab must understand basic safety considerations and practice common sense. Thoughtless or careless behavior can result in harm to personal property, injury to oneself or others, or damage to the tools, systems, and facilities in the lab.

For example, if your testers work on the interior portions of computers, with computer peripherals, or with add-on devices, you might want to have them wear lab coats. If lab coats are considered excessive, at least make sure that people do not wear billowy or very loose clothing, and insist that they tuck in or bind any loose items such as ties, bandannas, and scarves. (I once ran into a colleague who was wearing a silk tie that looked as if a puppy had used it for a chew toy for about a week. When I asked about it, he explained that he had been leaning over an open computer and had failed to notice that his tie had become entangled in protruding pins on the back of an ISA card. When he straightened up, the little wires shredded the end of the tie like razors.)

Hair and jewelry can cause similar problems. Beards, long hair, and handlebar mustaches can, under certain circumstances, get caught in a computer or in moving parts. Moist or sweaty hair can also create a short circuit on a live board. Loose necklaces can be snagged; rings (especially if they are large or numerous) can catch on notched and hooked items. In addition, dangling earrings, nose rings, and other uncovered jewelry stuck through sensitive body parts can get snared, leading to painful or dangerous injuries.

Speaking of painful and dangerous injuries, keep in mind that the inside of a computer often has sharp edges and is certainly not sterile. I have taken more skin off my knuckles and the back of my hands while working inside a computer than I care to recall. Gloves might help, but it is cumbersome to work on small chips, jumpers, and screws while wearing any glove thick enough to make a difference. Testers must be extremely careful and should wash cuts thoroughly and immediately.

Many test labs include eye wash stations. Drilling, machining, or filing any metal or plastic component can create shards that can lodge in the eye. Broken glass is always a possibility when working with computer monitors. A reversed capacitor, an overworked resistor, or a chip pushed beyond its specifications can smoke, snap, or even explode. Eye protection is an especially good idea when working with prototype hardware.

Earlier in this chapter, I discussed the need for smoke detectors and fire extinguishers in the lab. At the risk of belaboring the point, make sure to test those smoke detectors as specified in the owner's manuals if appropriate. In addition, a fire extinguisher does no good if no one knows where they are or how to use them. Finally, people should know the evacuation route if a serious fire breaks out.

As a last note on safety, keyboards and mice must be positioned to minimize the risk of repetitive stress injuries. Likewise, work surfaces, chairs, and stools need to be set up so that people can work at comfortable angles, with proper wrist support and proper posture.

Damage to Lab Equipment

Working on computers can cause injury to a person, but a person can also inflict damage on software and hardware. In a lab where I worked, someone spilled an entire cup of coffee on a keyboard. The keyboard survived, but it required a complete disassembly and cleaning. On another occasion, I saw someone destroy a laptop computer by allowing a few drops of condensation to drip from the outside of a water bottle directly onto the mainboard through the keyboard. Greasy fingers can render a laptop's touchpad unreliable. If you decide to allow food in your lab, be sure that people understand the need to keep it away from the equipment, and institute rules against working on the equipment while eating or drinking.

Other objects that require caution in the lab include magnets, which can wipe out removable magnetic media such as floppy disks quite easily. Paper clips, pins, and other small objects can be dropped and become lodged in a computer, which will eventually cause a short and damage the unit. Should this occur, the tester must power off the unit immediately and retrieve the lost item before powering it on again.

Shock, vibrations, and drops are also concerns. Be sure that equipment is not perched precariously in positions from which it can fall. Badly placed wires can trip and injure a tester, but they can also bring an attached component crashing to the ground or tear out a part of the system. (I seriously damaged an integrated modem in a laptop by inadvertently yanking the RJ-11 cable attached to it.) On a similar note, I once saw someone attempt to seat a recalcitrant computer board using a two-by-four and a ball peen hammer. This type of activity, along with slapping, pounding, or kicking any delicate electronic object, is always a bad idea. And, while you can hurl a pen or pencil at a VDT in a fit of pique, doing the same to an LCD panel is likely to damage or destroy it.

When working on a computer, a tester or engineer must have the proper tools available. Trying to use a flathead screwdriver to tighten a Phillips-head screw might strip the head of the screw, leaving the component improperly seated and impossible to remove. Pliers or the wrong wrench can round the edges of a nut. Removing a chip without the proper chip-puller invites damage to a very valuable piece of equipment. If partial or complete disassembly is a possibility, you should provide trays to hold and categorize screws, jumpers, and other small components that can easily get mixed up or roll off the table.

In addition to providing proper tools, you should also train your staff to apply the carpenter's adage "measure twice, cut once"—that is, paying proper attention to each task and double-checking before taking action. When I first started working with computers, before the days of flashable EEPROMs, I installed a one-of-a-kind ROM backward in its socket. When I powered up the computer, I fried the chip and had to wait two days for a replacement. The client was not amused. Proper grounding when working on any electronic equipment is also a must, of course. Be sure to provide grounding straps and static pads liberally throughout the lab.

Finally, you need to take care when cleaning computers, test tools, and the like. Spraying ammonia-based window cleaners on display screens might not be a good idea, depending on what the screen is made of and where the overspray ends up. Cleaning a laptop keyboard requires special attention because excess moisture can easily work its way into the system enclosure.

Productivity in the Lab

The setup of your test lab can be an important factor in the productivity of the people working in it. Tools and workstations should be set up to minimize the need for people to move around the lab. Having all the necessary components for completing a task close at hand helps avoid breaking the tester's concentration (or the concentration of colleagues). During an intricate test, any interruption can cause the tester to lose a critical train of thought, thereby omitting an important step or missing an indication of an error.

The idea of breaking one's concentration raises the issue of radios, TVs, and CD players. If all the denizens of the lab agree on a definition of "good music," allowing some low-volume background music can make for a pleasant environment. However, the more people who are involved, the more likely it is that a conflict will ensue about what is tolerable. In addition, although listening to music can be enjoyable and improve morale, it doesn't necessarily improve productivity.

Radios, of course, play more than just music. Listening to talk radio might contribute to stimulating debate among those in the lab, but it is almost certainly a distraction. Even worse, a television, especially when tuned into those daytime "spectacle shows," is nothing but an electronic attention magnet; people simply aren't focused on testing if they're watching TV. In general, it's probably best that people use headphones and that the listening be confined to music.

Finally, your lab setup can contribute to productivity by ensuring that at least two network workstations are available to those working in the lab. This workstation should provide testers with access to the bug tracking database, the test tracking spreadsheet, the system configuration tracking database, and any other reporting and information resources the testers need to execute the tests and report results efficiently.

Case Study

In the course of various projects, I've had the opportunity to see a number of medium-to large-sized hardware and software test labs. In the next few paragraphs and figures, I'll describe and sketch some common layouts for test labs, including some key features, pros, and cons of each layout. To keep the figures simple, I've omitted the furniture, facilities, and other details shown in Figure 7.1. The dimensions are fairly arbitrary, so please don't use these as floor plans for your test lab without making sure the layouts make sense for you.

Figure 7.7 shows a software test lab layout that would be fairly typical for an independent test lab that was organized based on technology areas. The main lab areas are classified by the type of testing that goes on in each location: Windows, Unix, and Networking. The test engineers and technicians work in one of these labs, depending on the skills and assignments. (Chapter 8, "Staffing and Managing a Test Team," will discuss tester skills and ways of organizing test teams.) I also have shown a dedicated lab for one client. Clients often request dedicated labs when they will have ongoing testing happening and need a secure, separate space, away from the potentially prying eyes of competitors visiting the company (see Chapter 10). The overall space also includes some work areas for visiting clients and for the salespeople, who might need private spaces to meet with clients or have conference calls. The reception area will include a receptionist's workstation and a waiting area, and often letters of appreciation from clients. The common area might include shared printers, a copier, a workstation or two, and, in some companies, a Ping-Pong table or some other games. Finally, there is a software/hardware library, probably under control of one or more librarians, a kitchen and lunch area, and the managers' cubicles.

Figure 7.8 shows the same overall lab space for a company that has chosen a project-centric way of organization. The left and right sides at the top of the figure are now common lab areas where one or more projects will occur at one time. There's no privacy or separation for the clients, but this is economical in terms of space usage. The large lab space on the center right is split into two dedicated project labs. These labs aren't dedicated to any one client permanently, but they are dedicated to a single project for the duration of that project. This gives the client some of the benefits of the dedicated client lab space, but that does not include the ability to store prototypes, software, and documents long-term at the lab facility.

For labs that do a lot of hardware testing—by this I mean primarily various types of hardware reliability testing—the layouts tend to be test-type centric, as shown in Figure 7.9. The building is split into two main areas, the office area and the testing area. For safety and noise reasons, these areas will be separated by sound-proof, fire-proof, smoke-proof, and possibly projectile-proof walls and doors. (Hardware testing always has the possibility of resulting in physical failure of the system under test, which, if catastrophic, can result in fire, toxic vapors, and flying chunks of the system.) Walls also

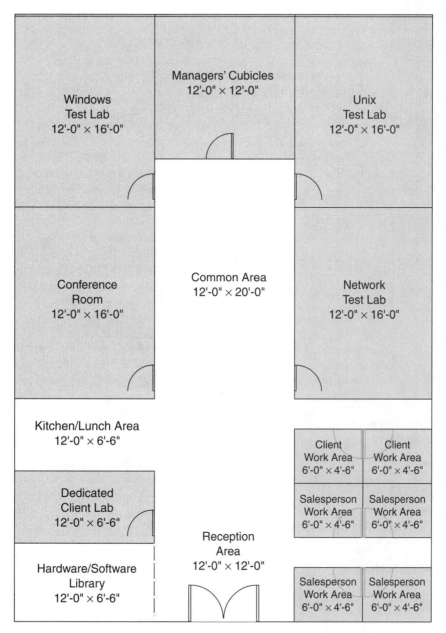

Figure 7.7   A technology-centered lab layout.

separate the main testing area into smaller areas dedicated to particular types of tests. Sliding garage-type doors—typically quite tall, say 10 or 12 feet—allow large pieces of equipment such as mainframes and telephone switches to be offloaded directly into the appropriate lab space from a truck.

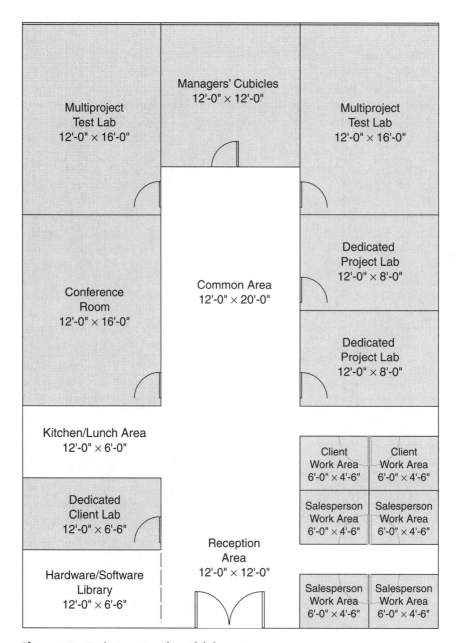

Figure 7.8 Project-centered test lab layout.

I saw a very interesting variation on these types of labs when visiting Satisfice, Inc., the test lab and consultancy run by my colleague and fellow test professional James Bach. Satisfice's lab space was primarily composed of open areas, including one particu-

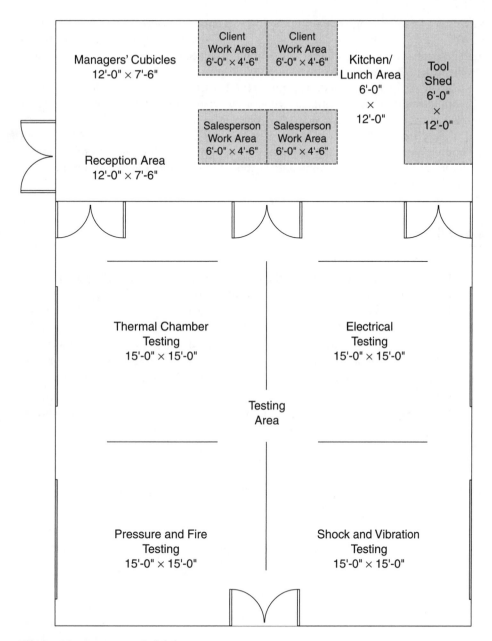

Figure 7.9 A test-centric lab layout.

larly large room with about a dozen movable, kidney-shaped tables. On each table was a laptop computer wired into a network that served as a workstation. Any testing could be set up on any table and have access to the network through the laptop. This space also served as a large training area, since training was another service offered by Satisfice. A projector and various whiteboards—again, mobile—made the space instantly reconfigurable to suit a variety of testing, training, or meeting needs. In the back of the room was a well-stocked library of books on testing.

I acknowledge my sources of inspiration for this section, which includes every independent testing company, client, and vendor I've visited that had a test lab. Significant in this list are, in alphabetical order, American Megatrends, Compal Computer, Compaq, Dell, Gateway, Hewlett-Packard, Hitachi, NSTL Taiwan, NTS/XXCAL, Quanta Computer, Satisfice, and Sun Microsystems, among others. I especially thank James Bach for permission to share some details about Satisfice's innovative and unique test lab configuration.

Exercises

1. Draw a lab space sufficient for the test environment shown in Chapter 6 as Figure 6.13. (Reproduced here as Figure 7.10 for convenience.) Draw your figure to the same level of detail as Figure 7.1. Make sure to show power and networking connections along with space for testers to set.

2. All the other relationships in the entity-relationship diagrams in Chapters 6 and 7 have been many-to-many. However, what type of relationship must the "Checked Out To" relationship be to implement the asset tracking database discussed in this chapter?

3. Not all asset tracking systems are high-tech. Implement an asset tracking system with index cards. What information goes on each index card?

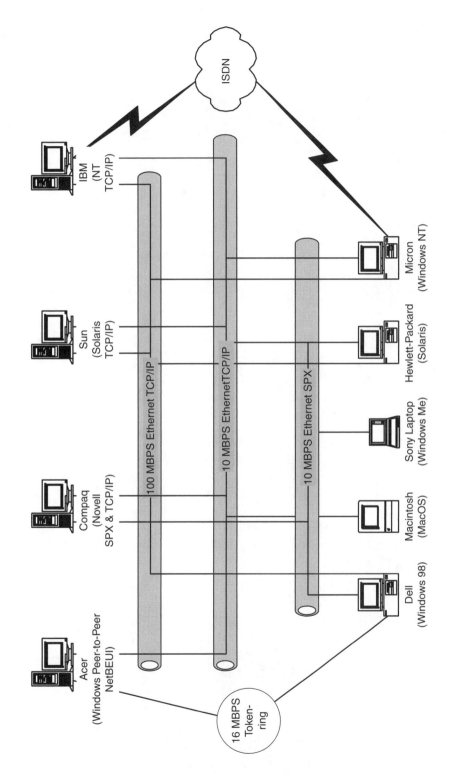

Figure 7.10 SpeedyWriter test environment.

Staffing and Managing a Test Team

Hiring, motivating, and retaining an excellent staff are among the most important tasks any manager performs. The extent to which a manager does a good or poor job at these tasks largely determines the extent to which he or she is a good or poor manager. Although these are survival issues for all managers, from those at the neighborhood steak house to corporate CEOs to successful politicians, staffing and managing a test team has its own unique quirks. This chapter offers some pointers on a few of the issues that are particularly deviling:

- What personal attitudes, behaviors, and work styles make for good testers?
- How do you avoid hiring the wrong people for your test team?
- How many people do you need, what skills should they have, and what positions do they fill?
- Do you want to organize your staff by projects or by areas of test specialization?
- How do you find, interview, and hire good test team members?
- What motivates test staff, and what demotivates them?
- How can you use interim staff such as temporaries, contractors, and consultants to help your team over the tough stretches?

The Right Person for the Job: What Kind of People Make Good Test Engineers

Let's start with personal traits for testers, because there's no point in worrying about someone's skills, position, or career goals if that person just isn't cut out to be a tester. The following are some traits I look for—and look out for—when I interview potential testers. After hiring someone, I encourage and cultivate these qualities in my team during test projects.[1]

Professional Pessimism

A Pollyanna attitude is the wrong attitude on a test team. In fact, testers are professional pessimists. Management pays them to explore the dark side of the project. One development engineer told me that he "felt very depressed" after reading the FMEA chart my test staff had prepared. I find it more depressing, however, to ignore the possibility of failure during development, only to live with the reality of preventable failure after release. Testing involves anticipating the worst of all possible worlds in order to achieve the best possible situation, given realistic project constraints.

Everyone wants to release products of the highest quality. I have heard project managers comment that testing budgets are a waste of money because those development scoundrels should be building software or hardware that works in the first place. Those managers do care about quality, but they don't understand the process of software development.[2] Development engineers, especially the good ones, want to practice a craft and to create products of elegance and quality. You will encounter very few "just a paycheck" hacks in the computer business.

Nevertheless, a test team must foresee and evaluate the ways in which a product might fail. I believe that this pessimistic, depressing function should live in an independent group— mostly because it *is* depressing and pessimistic, at least to developers. Having constructed a beautiful piece of software or hardware, developers can hardly be expected to turn around and beat it, torture it, subject it to cruel boundary conditions, stress it, and force it to handle "unlikely" errors.

The test organization plays this difficult and, in many ways, noble role. One computer consultant referred to testing as the point in the project at which people's "depraved mind[s]…can be usefully employed." A good test engineer does not mind thinking about ways the product can fail. You might hope that nothing will go wrong, but relying on this

---

[1] Bill Hetzel, in Chapter 11 of *The Complete Guide to Software Testing*, identifies the "five Cs" as important characteristics of a good testing specialist: controlled (organized and systematic); competent (aware of proper test techniques); critical (focused on finding problems); comprehensive (attentive to details); and considerate (able to communicate well with development peers).

[2] Scott Adams's series of Dilbert cartoons about testing put the following words into a development manager's mouth: "If a tree falls in the forest, and we've already sold it, does it have quality?" Actually, I've never heard anything quite that cynical. I believe that most failures to understand and appreciate the value proper testing brings to a project arise from ignorance, not apathy.

hope denies the entire history of computing. Thus, the tester creates failures in a safe environment, allowing the project team to fix them. Testing requires a pessimistic mindset in the pursuit of a lofty goal: company success through better products.

That said, professional pessimism differs from obnoxious behavior. A tester should focus on catching bugs in the product, not on catching the project team member who might have introduced the bug. Furthermore, the tester must be sensitive to the possibility that a developer will see negative test results as a personal attack. Pointing out specific flaws in a balanced, fair way is helpful. Attacking the product categorically and in general terms is not.

It is essential for everyone on the test team to maintain open, frank, and courteous relationships with the entire project team. If, through repeated conflicts, you reach the point where influential players on the project team refuse to listen to you, disbelieve what you say, or bear a grudge against you, the effectiveness of your test operation will suffer. Being a tester is not a license to be offensive. It is a challenge to be positive, pleasant, and the bearer of bad news, all at the same time.

Balanced Curiosity

During test development, a tester must spend time learning to understand the system under test in order to write high-yield test cases. During test execution, bug isolation—fully identifying the factors that affect the behavior of bugs—is an essential part of creating good reports. However, it's important to differentiate between a tester who takes the time needed to develop a thorough test or write a good bug report, and one who goes off on a snipe hunt.

A good test engineer develops test cases the way an expert spelunker goes into a cave. Dead ends abound, but the test engineer understands the situation and writes test cases that lead to bugs. This requires curiosity. The test engineer must read the specifications, discuss "what-if" scenarios with the developers, and mentally twist and turn the system under test, examining all the angles. Without curiosity, a fascination with the goal, the engineer will write superficial test cases.

A good test engineer also knows how to chase down a problem, trying the smart variations first, with an innate sense of what levers affect the anomalous behavior. Such an engineer willingly spends an hour or two rerunning a test case with minor variations to get at the essence of a bug, if that's appropriate.[3] This same type of curiosity leads scientists to spend time in a lab looking through a microscope or in an observatory staring at stars. A person who possesses this trait and uses it wisely is an irreplaceable asset.

However, if a tester becomes engrossed in unlikely failure modes and spends hours writing test cases to expose them, you end up with low-yield test cases. A tester who spends long hours investigating trivial bugs is squandering a precious resource: the test team's time. Curiosity motivates a tester to perform otherwise tedious isolation steps against bugs, to research obscure and possibly undocumented aspects of the system

[3]Myers, in *The Art of Software Testing*, refers to the ability to write high-yield test cases and to isolate bugs as "error guessing."

under test, and to sift through ambiguity for understanding. A tester who rushes to write up a serious and complex bug report after reproducing the symptom once, without additional work, probably isn't curious enough. In contrast, a tester who spends hours on each bug, trying dozens of variations to find the root cause, is going too far.

What divides "curious enough" from "not curious enough" and "too curious?" Good judgment. Some testers are able to balance the need to finish developing the test suite in time for test execution with the thrill of writing a clever, effective test case. They can balance the pressure to move forward with the desire to know why a bug occurs.

Focus:
No Space Cadets

One Saturday morning I went into the test lab and found absolutely no progress being made. A test engineer had brought everything to a standstill by pulling the two other engineers in the lab into isolating a problem. He had found a serious bug, but it didn't require the attention of three test engineers, and it really didn't need to hold up restarting the stress test, whose completion gated the product release. No one could question this engineer's dedication—he frequently spent the night in the lab, curled up in a sleeping bag—but his lack of focus put schedules in danger. He had also managed to defocus two other test engineers.

This situation exemplifies two types of focus problems. First, the engrossed engineer pursued the bug before him so narrow-mindedly that he lost sight of the more important priority. He should have realized after a few minutes that he needed to take a break, restart the stress test suite, and then continue analyzing the failure. Imagine a cook who produces perfect, lump-free gravy while the roast in the oven becomes the culinary equivalent of shoe leather. He was too focused. Second, the distracted engineers broke away from their tasks to gaze upon this wondrous bug, just for a moment. The moment passed, but they forgot what they were supposed to be doing until I arrived. They weren't focused enough.

Testers should reevaluate the appropriateness of their choice of tasks every so often. Testers need quiet, focused periods to solve difficult problems, so you don't want to encourage scatterbrained behavior. However, especially during test execution, every tester should frequently examine whether the task on the table is the most important way to spend time at the moment.

Most testers will go off on a tangent from time to time. As the test manager, you must stay on top of your staff's activities to ensure that the tester who strays is herded back quickly. Recognize that the dynamic nature of the project can lead to frequent shifts in priority, making the task that was right yesterday the wrong task today. If your entire team has problems focusing on the right tasks, ask yourself whether you are communicating priorities clearly and effectively.

Some testers need more redirection—either from the task at hand to more pressing issues, or from the chimera back to their assignments—than others do. At the least, these people shouldn't hold leadership roles in your organization because they misdirect others as well as themselves. For the most hardened offenders, you might need to consider whether they should remain in the test group. Someone who consistently makes the wrong decision about which task to focus on might not be someone you can change.

Avoid the Aspiring Hero

Part of the problem with getting good test engineers lies in the fact that so few people choose this as a specialty. Test work is perceived—wrongly, I believe, but widely nonetheless—as unglamorous drudgery in many companies, which creates two problems for you. First, you might end up hiring people who view the test organization as an extended "Hell Week" they must endure in order to join the fraternity of developers. These folks can work out, providing that the would-be programmer or motherboard designer is qualified for a development position, is on a career path toward that goal, and has skills you need. However, this type of situation gets ugly when it becomes obvious to everyone except the employee that a future as a developer isn't in the cards. Second, you might find that some of your test staff deal with formal or informal caste systems by adopting an inappropriate attitude toward the development staff, who sometimes treat testers with disdain in companies that foster an exaggerated pecking order. This situation can turn into a feeding frenzy of recrimination and backstabbing that will make your life difficult and damage your team's productivity. Be sure that candidates for test positions understand their prospects and can deal with their place on the company totem pole.

Shun the Sloth

I worked with a test engineer who was intelligent and capable of good work, but who had no drive. He would sit in the lab and browse the Internet for hours, neglecting important test tasks. In response, some of his colleagues wrote a program that checked whether he was running Internet-related processes on the test network; if he was, the program would kill the offending process and send a message to his screen that read: "Get back to work." In addition to his Internet vice, he had an aversion to hard work. He would work an eight-hour day, no more and often less when he could get away with it. I liked the guy personally, but he did not add a lot of value to the test organization. Eventually, he quit and moved on to a different job.

Don't misunderstand—a test operation shouldn't be run like the Bataan death march, nor does blowing off steam by playing a video game or surfing the Web cause an immediate schedule slip. Moreover, people who put in eight solid hours of work at a high level of productivity and then leave the lab are not shirking. They are engaged in what is sometimes called "having a life." Some high-tech companies have a reputation for demanding ridiculous hours and slavish devotion, to the exclusion of a normal existence. In my experience, tired people do poor-quality work, and unrealistic schedules are seldom met.

Nevertheless, testing does involve hard work. Tight schedules, last-minute slip-ups, late hours, and weekend test runs call for people who will go the extra mile. If you find that a tester consistently misses deadlines, or sets individual deadlines that allow far more time than required, or evades every bit of overtime or weekend work on flimsy pretenses, you have a sloth on your hands and should set about reforming this employee if possible. Of course, if you see any indication during the hiring process that a person won't work hard, you're better off not hiring that individual in the first place. Slothful test engineers force their colleagues to carry their weight.

Reject Casper Milquetoast

The flip side of the obnoxious, confrontational jerk discussed earlier is the tester who is just too mild-mannered. Rather than becoming ineffective by being in everyone's face, this engineer is too retiring, too confrontation-averse. Such a person will have real difficulties in testing. In order to promote quality, a tester must advocate, argue, assert, and defend, without hesitating to bring problems to the attention of management. A tester who files a bug report and then backs down at the slightest hint of controversy can't contribute to the quality of the product.

Although it's important to avoid undue obstinacy, testers must have the courage to make waves when the situation calls for it. As a colleague once said, "If you're not making people upset, you're not doing your job." This is different from saying, "Your job is to upset people." Rather, it means that testers necessarily cause controversy and distress when they uncover problems that have negative implications for project schedules, resource requirements, and so forth—or when they point out the possibility of those problems. A person afraid of upsetting others makes a poor test engineer. Test engineers should never go out of their way to upset people, but should be willing to deliver and defend bad news in spite of the reaction it might cause.

Defining the Test Team: How Many Whos Do What?

Now that we've looked at testers as individuals, let's expand our perspective and look at how testers fit into a test team. If you were assembling a sports team, the game you intended to play would define the team: you would know how many players were required, what skills they needed to possess, and what positions they would play. When assembling a development team, you can base your decisions on certain models that indicate how many coders, engineers, architects, and so forth you will need. These various models don't all agree on every point, but you can pick an approach secure in the knowledge that someone—if only the author of the book or paper that explains the model—has successfully applied it to one or more projects. The following sections outline some workable methods of defining a test team.

Size

If you are running a one-off test project—in other words, you intend to assemble a team that lasts only for the duration of the current project you're running—then sizing is pretty simple. Use the estimation techniques discussed in Chapter 1, "Defining What's on Your Plate: The Foundation of a Test Project," and then go out and hire however many contractors you will need for the duration of the project, taking into account any outsourcing you can do as discussed in Chapter 10, "Involving Other Players: Distributing a Test Project." (Hire contractors, not employees, because you don't intend to keep anyone long-term, right?) However, because most companies and IT organizations are going concerns in that they intend to produce and maintain systems over time, most of us have to think longer-term.

There is a range of possibilities for sizing the test team long term. At one extreme is a very deliberate, structured approach. In this technique, you look at the long-range (18 months, two years, three years, etc.) plan for the company's system projects (in many high-tech companies, this is called the "product road map"). Based on this road map, you can do rough estimation following the discussion in Chapter 1, including plenty of caveats for unforeseen overlap, scope creep, and missing projects. You hire however many testers for your test team as are needed to handle the heaviest project load that will exist at any one time.

A variation on this approach is to staff for the valleys in workload rather than the peaks, and then staff to the peaks using contractors. You have a lot more flexibility this way, because unforeseen changes in scope, slips in schedules that cause overlap, and so forth aren't the cause of huge logistical dilemmas and painful "quality versus schedule" tradeoffs. Instead, we trade off money for quality by hiring short-term contractors. However, this does tend to reduce test team effectiveness and efficiency during projects, because these contractors will need to go up the learning curve for each project.

Another variation is using a rule of thumb such as the tester-to-developer ratio discussed in Chapter 1. Based on the size of the development team, the test team is established. The theory here would seem to be that, since testers will only have to test what the developers build, we can piggy-back off the development manager's estimates. Any variation in workload due to the natural error inherent in ratios will "come out in the wash" over enough projects. This is a common approach, but it tends to break down when outsourcing or integration of commercial off-the-shelf components is involved. However, if the test manager has latitude to augment the test team with contractors, this should work as well as the previous approach.

At the other extreme, the approach that is most painful and generally demonstrates the lowest level of management commitment to the test team as an organization—and often to quality products—is the approach summed up in the words of many of my seminar attendees. "We don't estimate how many people we need. Management tells us how many people and who exactly we can have, and then tells us what to do with those people." These same people are often the ones telling me about how their managers keep loading them down with extra work because they have lots of free time in their groups. We'll discuss these interrelated phenomena further in Chapter 11, "Testing in Context: Economics, Lifecycles, and Process Maturity."

Now, just about any staffing level can work, provided you clarify expectations through the "might test, should test, can test" process outlined in Chapter 1. You'll need to have at least enough people to make some tangible contribution—I would guess that absolutely no less than one tester per 10 developers would probably be a good rule of thumb for this threshold in most contexts I've worked in—but from that point up, you can do some meaningful testing, find some dangerous bugs, and help get them fixed. Be careful about that expectation thing, though: I have seen test managers get themselves into serious, deep, irreparable trouble when management anticipated dramatic, immediate improvements in product quality because of their team's efforts in spite of minimal staffing levels. It's also true that, while test team size can be reduced through orderly processes, solid support, and quality deliverables, assuming that these and other facilitative traits will exist in the project without any effort is wishful thinking (see Chapter 11).

If you don't receive all the staff you need the first time around, don't give up hope immediately. Your logic might not have won this time, but it might well have sensitized management to your real staffing needs. As I mentioned, you should look at ways to accomplish some of your test tasks without relying on permanent staff. The last section of this chapter (*Extending Your Talent: Using Temps, Contractors, and Consultants*) offers some ideas on retaining temporary staff to get through busy periods, and Chapter 10 discusses external resources. Use of temporary or external resources can resolve your real problem—getting the work done—while addressing management's concern that a test organization, once grown, will become a big, unproductive black hole.

Skills

Skills can be thought of as falling into four categories. The first, general professionalism, I see as most important in the areas of basic skills such as reading, writing, and mathematics.

Testers must know how to *really* read—not superficially but with intense focus, meticulous attention to detail, and nearly masochistic capacity. Engineering prose is often dense, sometimes takes liberties with the mother tongue, and occasionally does a poor job of pointing out salient topics. Test case development involves a thorough reading of the specifications, the requirements, the product documentation, and myriad other detailed references. Test engineers and technicians often read hundreds of pages over the course of a project. Furthermore, these product documents often contradict one another. Whether trying to develop tests or looking for documentation bugs, testers must find and report these discrepancies, which is a painstaking process.

As email becomes the primary communication channel in the high-tech world, people on a hot project—testers, developers, and managers alike—can receive dozens of project-related emails each day. Especially during the period of test execution, they must read these messages with care and comprehension if they are to act on them with due speed. Test execution also requires the ability to understand possibly ambiguous instructions, grasp the goals, and take the right actions. A tester can't run tests without being able to read a test case, test tool documentation, and output logs.

Test personnel must also know how to write. I'm not talking about perfect grammar and spelling, although poor use of language can certainly distract and confuse readers. The most important issue is the ability to communicate effectively in writing. When testers find a problem, they must communicate the symptoms they observe. This is the essence of testing, and it requires writing a good bug report. The bug report is the most tangible product of testing and the foundation of most quality metrics. Just as you wouldn't hire a chef who can't cook, you shouldn't hire test staff who can't write bug reports. The task of communicating blockages and breakdowns in the test process itself, often via email, also requires writing ability. Poor written communications can cause you, as a test manager, some real heartburn.

Interestingly, I have found the ability to communicate clearly in writing to be nearly independent of whether the tester is using his or her native language. I've worked with some Taiwanese test engineers who were tough to communicate with in spoken English, but who nevertheless wrote excellent bug reports in perfectly clear, if not always grammatically correct, English. I've also known some American test engineers whose bug reports, in English, required extensive editing. The difference lies more in the degree of care taken in expressing one's thoughts than in knowledge of the language.

The application of metrics in testing, such as a reliability growth model for software or MTBF calculations for hardware, can entail a sophisticated understanding of statistics and mathematics. If your test organization uses such metrics, you will need at least one person—in addition to yourself—who understands how these metrics work. For the rest of the team, a simple understanding of some basic mathematical and statistical concepts will suffice. It's not possible to give hard-and-fast rules for which specific concepts testers need to know in all cases, but you'll usually want the engineers on your staff to be familiar with statistical concepts such as distribution functions, means and standard deviations, and the like.

Beyond basic professionalism, there are three other specific categories of skill to consider:

Technology. Since bugs often are technology-dependent—or at least influenced by the technology the system was built with—it's often helpful for testers to understand how systems are built, so having a grasp of the underlying programming languages, system architectures, operating system features, networking, presentation layers, database functionality and implementation, and so forth.

Application domain. Other bugs arise less from how the system was built than from what the system is supposed to do. Especially when it's most difficult to predict what a correct result would look like, testers need to understand the business, technical, or scientific problem being solved by the system.

Testing. In addition to knowing where bugs live and what they look like, testers need to know how to find them, effectively and efficiently. In some cases, this is just a matter of sitting down in front of the system with adequate technological or application domain insight, but often it is not. I once saw a multimillion-dollar project fail in no small part due to the lack of knowledge of some otherwise-talented technical people who tried to perform load and performance tests that were well beyond their knowledge of that art. When test engineering and execution requires special skills, the test team must have ample numbers of people with such skills.

The first two categories are well recognized, but I find the third category of skill, testing, to be often under appreciated as a unique, distinct skill that must be well represented within a strong test team.

This disconnect strikes me as somewhat strange, because I'm hardly the first person to note the importance of test-specific skills in a test team. Glenford Myers, author of *The Art of Software Testing* and a pioneer in the field, makes a case for having a test staff comprised of "system test experts"—that is, people whose careers are focused on testing as a specialty. However, I think the devaluation of test expertise might arise from a gap in testing as practiced in some organizations.

I've reproduced Figure 1.1 here as Figure 8.1. In some organizations I've seen or talked to testers from, there is very little true behavioral testing done. In these organizations, whatever independent testing occurs—in other words, testing outside of the unit testing done by developers—happens under the monikers of "system test" or "integration test," but it applies primarily live testing techniques and is a variant of acceptance testing. In these cases, those people doing testing are either technologically savvy programmers and developers unit-testing their own code, or application-

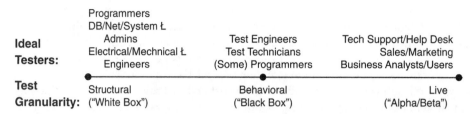

Figure 8.1   The test granularity spectrum, from a skills perspective.

domain experts testing the system under end-user conditions. The application-domain experts are often temporarily assigned from the marketing, sales, help desk, business analyst, or technical support ranks.

Please don't misunderstand me, because I definitely do see understanding the technology and the application domain as important for testers. However, it's important to recognize that testing does have its own set of special skills, especially nonfunctional tests such as error handling, capacity, performance, and so forth. Just because you have a test organization now that includes only technology and application domain experts doesn't mean that's necessary a good idea. Revisit the list of critical risks to system quality that you put together back in Chapter 1. Are there any high-priority risks you're not testing because you don't have the right skills in your test team? If so, the odds are good that you need to revisit the importance of testing skills in a balanced, effective, and efficient team.

What are the critical skills for your projects and your test team? That's a question only you can answer. What I like to do is to look at the tasks that I identify on the work-breakdown-structure for my projects and ongoing maintenance efforts. Based on these tasks, what skills do I need in my test team to perform those tasks competently? Given a list of these critical skills, I can then assess the current team's capabilities against those skills—or better yet, have people self-assess.

Figures 8.2 and 8.3 show a quantitative skills assessment for the SpeedyWriter test team, based on the project schedule shown in Chapter 1. As you can see, the rightmost column defines the critical skills, grouped into the four categories discussed in this section. The next-rightmost three columns define desirable and required levels of experience for positions within the test team (more on positions in the next section). The middle five columns define where the various test team members stand on those skills, from no knowledge ("0") to expert knowledge ("3"). The leftmost two columns show the team minimums and averages in each skill and in each skill category, allowing me to see relative strengths and weaknesses.

I find that doing this skills analysis on a spreadsheet is nice. I like the quantitative—although admittedly subjective and of limited precision—measurement of skills at the individual and team level. This makes an excellent hiring tool, as you'll see in a minute. I can also set goals for team skills growth as part of a quarterly or yearly team skills assessment, and then use education, training, and task assignment options to help the team and each person on it grow in their skills over time.

Software Cafeteria Test Team
Skills Assessment and Management Worksheet

Legend										
0 = No Knowledge		1 = Some Knowledge		2 = Knowledgeable		3 = Expert Knowledge				
R = Required		D = Desirable								
TT=Test Technician		TM = Test Manager		MTE = Manual Test Engineer		ATE = Automated Test Engr				

Skills and Qualifications	TT Minimum Ratings	ATE Minimum Ratings	MTE Minimum Ratings	TM Jake	MTE Lin-Tsu	ATE Bob	MTE Hitesh	STE Mania	Team Minimum	STeam Average
General Qualifications										
Education										
Bachelor Science Degree (or +)	D	D	D	BS (CSE)	Ph.D. (CS)	BS (Math)	MA (Psych)	BS (Bus)		
Test Training or Certification	D	D	D	CSQE	ISEB					
Other							LFC	CPA		
Work Experience (Years)										
Test Roles	D	5R	5R	7	5	6	11	12		
Non-Test, Computer	D	D	D	3	2					
Non-Computer, Domain	D	D	D							
Non-Computer, Non-Domain							10	6		
Total/Any/Other	1D	5R	5R	10	7	6	21	22		
Professionalism										
Oral Communication	1R	2R	2R	3	1	2	3	2	1	2.2
Written Informal Communication	1R	3R	3R	3	3	2	3	3	2	2.8
Written Formal Communication	D	D	D	3	0	1	3	1	0	1.6
Continuing Education	D	R	R	Yes	Yes	Yes	Yes	Yes	Yes	Yes
Test Team Building/Cross-training	D	2R	2R	3	2	1	3	2	1	2.2
Cross-functional Relationship Building	D	2R	2R	3	2	1	3	2	1	2.2
Reading (Retention, Reasoning, and Analysis)	1R	2R	2R	3	2	2	3	2	2	2.4
Business/Technical Trends (Journal Reading)	D	1R	1R	3	1	3	1	1	1	1.8
Testing Skills										
General										
Testing Standards	D	2R	2R	3	3	3	3	3	3	3.0
Software Development Life Cycles	D	2R	2R	3	3	3	3	2	2	2.8
Testing/Development Processes/Maturity	D	1R	1R	2	2	3	1	1	1	1.8
Change Management	D	1R	1R	2	2	3	1	1	1	1.8
Relating Testing to Business/SDLC	D	1R	1R	3	3	3	2	1	1	2.4
Planning										
Estimation		D	D	3	1	1	2	1	1	1.6
Documentation		D	D	3	1	3	2	1	1	2.0
Cost of Quality		D	D	3	2	2	1	1	1	1.8
Quality Risk/Failure Mode and Effects Analysis		D	D	3	2	1	1	1	1	1.6
Quality Risk Analysis and Management		D	D	3	2	1	1	1	1	1.6
Design and Development										
Behavioral (Black-box)	D	2R	2R	2	3	3	3	2	2	2.6
Structural (White-box)	D	D	1R	1	3	2	1	2	1	1.8
Static (Requirements, Specifications, Documentation)	D	D	2R	2	3	1	3	2	1	2.2
Reliability (Statistics)		2R	D	1	1	3	1	2	1	1.6
Performance (Modeling/Simulation/Testing)		2R	D	1	2	3	1	3	1	2.0
Code/Dataflow Coverage		2R	2R	2	3	1	3	3	1	2.4
Quality Risk/Requirement Coverage (Traceability)		1R	2R	3	2	3	1	1	1	2.0
Automation (Development)										
COTS Execution (Silk, Validor, etc.)		3R	D	1	1	3	1	3	1	1.8
COTS Test Management		D	D	3	1	2	1	1	1	1.6
Custom Toolsmithing		3R	D	3	1	3	1	3	1	2.2
Configuration										
Test Data Generators		1R	D	1	1	2	1	2	1	1.4
Version Control		1R	1R	2	2	2	1	3	1	2.0
Configuration Management		D	1R	1	2	2	1	1	1	1.4
Integration Testing		D	1R	3	2	2	1	1	1	1.8
Execution										
Manual Scripted	D	D	3R	3	3	1	3	1	1	2.2
Manual Exploratory	D	D	3R	3	3	1	3	1	1	2.2
Automated		3R	3R	1	1	3	1	3	1	1.8
Bug Isolation	D	3R	3R	3	3	3	3	3	3	3.0
Bug Reporting	D	3R	3R	3	3	3	3	3	3	3.0
Test Status Reporting	D	2R	2R	3	2	3	3	2	2	2.6
Test Metrics (Dashboard)	D	1R	1R	3	2	3	1	3	1	2.4
Average Testing Skills				2.4	2.1	2.3	1.7	1.9	1.3	2.1

Figure 8.2   The first page of a skills assessment worksheet.

Software Cafeteria Test Team
Skills Assessment and Management Worksheet

Legend:
0 = No Knowledge	1 = Some Knowledge	2 = Knowledgeable	3 = Expert Knowledge
R = Required	D = Desirable		
TT=Test Technician	TM = Test Manager	MTE = Manual Test Engineer	ATE = Automated Test Engr

Skills and Qualifications	TT Minimum Ratings	ATE Minimum Ratings	MTE Minimum Ratings	TM Jake	MTE Lin-Tsu	ATE Bob	MTE Hitesh	STE Maria	Team Minimum	STeam Average
Domain Knowledge										
Word Processing										
Windows Applications	D	1R	2R	3	3	2	1	3	1	2.4
Unix Applications	D	D	D	1	1	3	3	2	1	2.0
Macintosh Applications	D	D	D	0	1	0	3	3	0	1.4
Graphics and Figures	D	1R	2R	2	2	3	2	1	1	2.0
Tables	D	D	1R	1	2	3	2	1	1	1.8
Mathematical/Engineering	D	D	1R	1	3	3	0	0	0	1.4
Document Management										
Windows Applications		D	D	1	2	1	0	2	0	1.2
Unix Applications		D	D	0	0	0	1	1	0	0.4
Macintosh Applications		D	D	0	0	0	1	1	0	0.4
Other		D	D	0	0	0	0	1	0	0.2
Hierarchical Storage Management		D	D	1	2	0	0	3	0	1.2
Document Interchange										
Windows Applications		D	D	1	2	1	0	3	0	1.4
Unix Applications		D	D	1	0	0	1	3	0	1.0
Macintosh Applications		D	D	0	0	0	1	3	0	0.8
Domain Knowledge										
Printing										
Color	D	D	D	0	0	1	1	2	0	0.8
Laser	D	D	D	1	1	1	1	2	1	1.2
Inkjet	D	D	D	1	1	1	1	2	1	1.2
Publishing/Binding		D	D	0	0	0	1	2	0	0.6
Web Publishing										
HTML	D	D	D	1	3	3	2	3	1	2.4
XML		D	D	1	3	3	0	2	0	1.8
Other		D	D	1	1	3	0	2	0	1.4
Average Domain Knowledge				0.8	1.3	1.3	1.0	2.0	0.3	1.3
Technical Expertise										
Programming										
C/VB (3GL)	D	1R	D	2	2	3	2	3	2	2.4
Java/C++ (OO)	D	1R	D	0	1	3	2	2	0	1.6
Shell (Tcl/Ksh) Scripting	D	2R	D	3	2	3	2	2	2	2.4
Code Complexity and Metrics		1R	D	2	0	0	2	2	0	1.2
Operating Systems										
Windows	D	1R	1R	2	3	2	1	2	1	2.0
Linux	D	1R	1R	2	2	1	3	2	1	2.0
Solaris	D	1R	1R	2	1	1	1	2	1	1.4
Mac OS	D	D	D	0	2	0	3	3	0	1.6
Other	D	D	D	1	1	0	3	3	0	1.6
Networking/Internetworking										
TCP/IP, FTP, RCP (Internet Architecture)		1R	1R	2	1	1	1	1	1	1.2
Browsers (NS, IE, etc.)	1R	1R	1R	2	3	2	2	1	1	2.0
Network Application Architecture (Tiered)		1R	1R	2	3	2	1	1	1	1.8
Network Hardware		1R	1R	2	3	2	1	1	1	1.8
Systems and Servers										
Java-based Web Servers		1R	1R	1	3	1	1	3	1	1.8
Database Servers		1R	1R	2	3	1	1	3	1	2.0
Mainframe		1R	1R	1	2	1	1	3	1	1.6
Average Technical Expertise				1.6	2.0	1.4	1.7	2.1	0.9	1.8

Figure 8.3 The second page of a skills assessment worksheet.

Education and Training

The topic of education and training for testers is something of a briar patch, and I'm sure to brush up against some thorns in the next few paragraphs. In general, we in the testing world are plagued by a number of problems in this area, which harken back to some comments I made in the Introduction. One is that there is no generally accepted, standard body of knowledge for testing. Another is that, with a few notable and satisfying exceptions, testing is not widely taught in colleges and universities. Furthermore, some people don't believe that we know enough about testing at this point to adopt the types of licensure and certification options that doctors, lawyers, and other professionals have. Therefore, the best I can do here is comment briefly on the state of education and training for testers, and hope that the offerings in this area ultimately catch up with the need.

In terms of formal education—in other words, through colleges and universities— the options are few but the trends are heartening. For example, as I am writing this, I am privileged to be working with Professor Patricia McQuaid of California Polytechnic State University and Professor Deepti Suri of the Milwaukee School of Engineering to develop their testing courses. Professors Cem Kaner and James Whittaker are offering a software engineering degree with a specialization in software testing at Florida Institute of Technology. A few other professors in the United States and Canada have approached me about using this book as a testing textbook, which I hope indicates a growing awareness of the need for educational programs in this area. Nevertheless, for the foreseeable future, most people with college degrees who come to us looking for jobs as testers will not have degrees in software testing, or even have taken a single course in software testing as part of their curriculum.

Considerable debate exists around the need for a degree in the first place, too. In some places where I've taught my test management course—most notably, India— people have told me that no one even gets in the door for an interview without a degree. However, in most places in the United States and Europe, non-degreed people are considered for positions in the test team, provided that skills and experience make up for the lack of a degree. In certain organizations, though, this is not appropriate. For example, some of my course attendees and clients make very complex systems that require a high degree of domain knowledge; my oil exploration software client requires test engineers to have degrees in geology, geophysics, petrochemistry, and the like. My usual rule of thumb is that engineers should either have a degree or an extra two or more years of experience, while test technicians I'm willing to hire without degrees under most circumstances.

Don't get me wrong, a degree is always a nice thing to see on a résumé —but what kind of degree to look for? That depends on which of the three specific categories of skill is most important in your organization. You might want to focus on technology, in which case software engineering, computer science, and other engineering degrees might be a fit. You might want to focus on application domain expertise, like my oil exploration client, in which case a degree related to the problem the system solves is more important. However, you might think that testing is about how systems and people relate to each other and how we can "know" anything about the quality of a computer system, in which case psychology, logic, philosophy, math, and other fields might be more appropriate. You might choose to mix up your team, striving for diversity in educational backgrounds. A degree generally indicates an ability to persevere and to dedicate oneself to a rigorous and prolonged endeavor, which is something you want in a tester, too.

There are many different types of degrees and diplomas floating around out there, too. I find that many of my test technicians tend to hold technical or trade school certificates, or two-year degrees from junior or community colleges. At the test engineer level, the four-year bachelor's degree and beyond tend to predominate. I have had a few people working for me in various capacities with advanced degrees as well, although this is uncommon.

I've also found some atypical forms of education that some of my best testers have had. Some people have learned about computers in high school or in continuing education ("night school") courses. More importantly, though, I've had great success with former military people, especially retired noncommissioned officers. Noncoms spend their careers welding young people straight from boot camp into effective teams for disparate activities, from working on electronics to maintaining a submarine to charging into a dangerous field of battle with courage, a gun, and supreme confidence in their noncom's leadership. These human skills can be invaluable in building a test team, especially one that will include lots of inexperienced test technicians.

Training courses and seminars are another popular way for people to learn about technology, the application domain, and testing. These have grown to include certification programs. Certification programs generally include some course of study along with standard exams to demonstrate mastery of the material. There are various programs in the area of test tools—most of the big automated test tool vendors seem to offer certification programs these days—along with certification in the area of tester skill. The American Society for Quality, the British Computer Society, the Quality Assurance Institute, and the International Institute for Software Testing all offer certification programs that I'm aware of, and soon, Software Quality Engineering will join the ranks.[4]

All of these certification and other training programs can be beneficial adjuncts to real-world experience. I have, however, seen some technical recruiters misuse certification programs by representing to their clients that the mere possession of the appropriate brightly stamped sheet of paper made a candidate an expert in the field. These programs can give attendees useful knowledge and expose them to a broader set of ideas than they would encounter in day-to-day experience, but they are not a substitute for hands-on performance of testing roles.

Finally, conferences are also a good place for testers to get education and training on testing, technology, and the application domain, both from known experts in the field and from each other. The best conferences I've attended included lots of experienced practitioners telling other attendees about what's worked—and what hasn't worked—for them. From most of the conferences I've attended, I have brought back at least one idea that paid for the cost of the conference by itself.

Steve McConnell, in *After the Gold Rush*, discusses training and education in the area of software engineering as part of a trend toward professionalization of the field. The same is probably true for testing, although we have a long way to go before (de facto or legally required) mandatory training, education, licensure, or certification solve all of our hiring problems. Additional organizational questions exist in this area, too. Is it reasonable for an employee or employer to expect or demand some level of education and training, including support for ongoing education? Is it reasonable for employers to worry about employees taking advantage of tuition-reimbursement or training course opportunities, and then leaving or demanding steep raises? Picayune though such questions might seem in the bigger scheme of things, these questions nonetheless

---

[4]By way of full disclosure, I have been involved in both for-profit and non-profit activities related to each of these organization's certification programs.

are significant barriers to training and education in many organizations, which dampens the overall supply of trained, education testers in the job market.

Positions, Experience, and Goals

If you automate most of your testing, or if most of your testing involves the use of complex tools, your staff might be comprised entirely of test engineers. A test engineer is the technical peer of a programmer, a mechanical engineer, or an electrical engineer. Having chosen testing as a specialty, test engineers write tests; create, customize and use advanced test tools; and have unique skills such as test design, bug reporting, and problem isolation.

If your testing involves simple manual operations such as loading floppy disks in response to a prompt, installing and checking PC Cards, and configuring systems according to a simple checklist, you should also have some test technicians on staff. Such straightforward, rote tasks tend to distract test engineers from their more challenging duties. In addition, some engineers do a poor job with tasks they find boring or "beneath" them. Having test technicians, who are less skilled, handle these easier chores might well improve the quality of your test operation.

Local colleges, universities, and technical schools provide good sources for test technicians. One or two postings on their job boards can often identify a few qualified computer science students. These students enjoy working in their chosen field, usually work hard, and are likely to be bright, so you'll get excellent value for the wages you pay.

Not every student is a good fit. You should try to hold out for computer science, computer engineering, or at least engineering students. The deeper level of computer knowledge these engineers-in-the-making bring to the test organization will make a difference. Watch out, however, for hacker types, who often have trouble focusing, following a process, and staying on task.[5] Worse yet, in spite of their need for guidance, these folks like to work from nine to five—but that's usually 9 P.M. to 5 A.M. For all students, monitor their work behavior for a while, especially if they have never held a job. Before turning student technicians loose on the midnight shift, make sure that they can work effectively and professionally with minimal supervision.

Speaking of late-night testing, moonlighters can be another good source of technicians who can keep your test resources utilized all night long. Most dual-job types are motivated. In addition, they might bring experiences from their day jobs that could make them better testers. Use caution with moonlighters, though. Since you don't provide their sole—or even main—source of income, and your project might not be their first priority, you should give them tasks that can slip a bit in the schedule without causing disaster. With individuals who are moonlighting expressly to build an outside consulting career, you can be a little freer about moving them into key positions, provided they have proven track records. (Regardless of who is on the night shift—seasoned test engineers, students, or moonlighters—keep a close eye on your night crew's productivity. Some people overestimate their ability to work effectively with little sleep; others get stuck or veer off track without guidance.)

---

[5]The term "hackers" might call to mind kids who use computers with criminal intent. But I'm using the word in its original meaning: semiprofessional computer wizards who can achieve great results but tend to follow their own muse a bit too frequently.

Finally, keep in mind that your team might need to contain other positions in addition to test engineers and test technicians. In some cases, for example, you might have a release management or configuration management engineer in your organization. As Chapter 9, "The Triumph of Politics: Organizational Challenges for Test Managers," describes, a variety of nontest tasks often migrate into test organizations.

The position you can put people into depends to some extent on their level of experience. Test engineering jobs will generally require someone who has experience. My rule of thumb—which varies from project to project—is two years for degreed engineers and four years for non-degreed engineers. My preference is usually that the experience be in the area of testing, although application domain knowledge or technical skill might be more important, depending on the needs of the project and the current strengths and weaknesses of the team.

You should also consider not only where people have been, but also where they want to go. In other words, what is the career goal of each person on the test team, and how do his or her past, current, and future positions fit into that goal? The alignment of a person's aspirations with his or her position makes the difference between an inspired, dedicated, brilliant tester and a lackadaisical, bored, clock-puncher.

There's a special risk for the test manager in the area of goals. Some people see testing as a temporary stepping stone, a way to gain insight into the company's products and services and a place to gain exposure to the underlying technology. Some organizations explicitly define testing as the "farm team" for the rest of the organization. I have a number of concerns about these approaches. For one thing, is someone likely to have the requisite critical skills and pursue growth in those skills if those skills are not aligned with that person's career path? Second, having artificially high turnover in the test team means that the team will always be weak, the test manager will always be hiring, and the few experienced testers will always be training new hires. This leads to reduced efficiency and effectiveness in the test team.

Specialists or Project Resources? Organizational Models

In a very small company or on a dedicated project effort, everyone works on a single project, and the question of organizational models does not exactly dominate the discussion. Suppose, however, that you have two, three, or a dozen projects going at one time. Do you break your team members into groups based on the projects they are working on, or based on the special skills they have?

Let's look at an example. You are the test manager at Winged Bytes. Two systems are in the test lab at the same time, the DataRocket server and the PortaByte laptop. Organization by skills assigns John to the BIOS, Hemamalini to Windows 95, Sandra to Windows NT, Gordon to PC Card and PCI add-on cards, Crystal to networks, and Shao-Lin to environmental and reliability testing. Organization by project assigns John, Hemamalini, and Sandra to the DataRocket team, while Gordon, Crystal, and Shao-Lin work on the PortaByte. Figure 8.4 shows an organizational model based on skills, while the model shown in Figure 8.5 is based on projects.

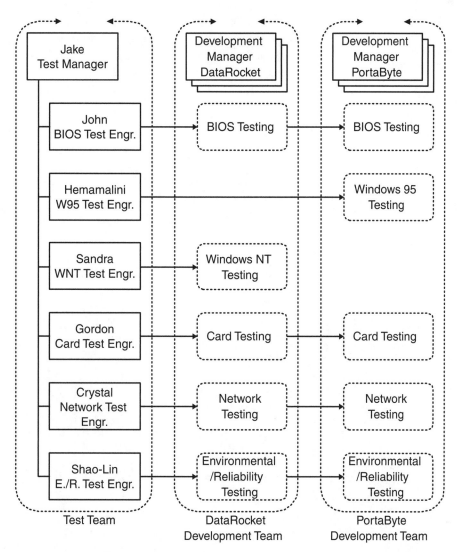

Figure 8.4   A skills-based test organization.

The skills-based model has a lot to recommend it, especially in the high-technology world. Instead of everyone having to keep up with many topics, each member of your test staff can focus on the quirks and subtleties of his or her own area of specialization. In some cases, the complexity of the tools and technology the tester must master demands a skills-based organization. The skills assessment worksheet, by the way, will tend to focus on relative strengths and the number of people strong in each skill, rather than relative weakness, because the idea is that the team be rounded as a whole, but that each team member be focused on a few critical skills.

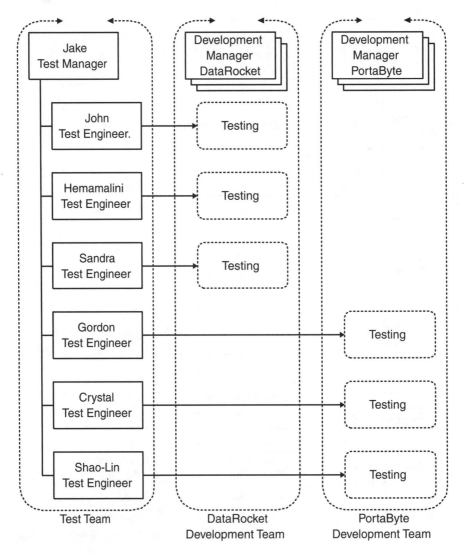

Figure 8.5 A project-based test organization.

While the skills-based approach provides a test manager with a great deal of flexi-bility, project managers might not like it. As one project manager told me, "I don't want to hear about anyone working on anything other than my project." In an organization in which project managers are rewarded for delivering a quality product on time, such an attitude is consistent with the company's incentive structure. A skills-based organi-zation deprives project managers of control over the allocation of test resources.

If you encounter such resistance, you have to decide whether you can persist with a skills-based approach—and whether you *want* to persist. Don't choose a skills-based model without consideration for the feelings and interests of project managers. Maintaining a positive relationship with the project managers to whom your test team provides services will boost your career and make your workday go smoothly. (Chapter 9 discusses the importance of working well with project managers in more detail.)

Besides, the second approach—a project-based organization—can have advantages for a test manager. If you have some otherwise excellent staff members who just don't focus very well, a skills- based organization might exacerbate the problem because it would force these people to jump from one project to another during the week. Assigning them to a single project, in a project-based organization, cuts down on the interruptions and shifting tasks. In addition, if your company tracks hours spent on projects, having each person billing time to only one project makes your reporting job less confusing.

One risk posed by the project-based approach deserves mention, however. Although the test personnel report to you, they also, in a sense, work for the development managers. They probably have more contact on a daily basis with the development team than with you. Assuming that they can maintain positive, open working relationships with the developers, this contact reduces the need for you to micromanage the activities for each project. However, development managers with a strong will or lots of political clout can sometimes prevail upon your test engineers to do things they shouldn't—closing bugs that aren't confirmed as fixed, for example, or compromising test processes. If your test engineers don't have much experience with a formal test organization, they can easily "go native," acting more like a developer than an independent tester. You need to monitor this situation closely.

When first setting up a test team, few test managers can use either a skills-based model or a project-based model exclusively. Some situations require experts, especially when a task involves mastery of a tricky test tool. For example, if you use capture/playback (a.k.a., "screen scraper") types of automation tools for GUI testing, your team should include a GUI test engineer or two. Of course, your GUI test experts must understand how their expertise fits into the overall test architecture. However, using a GUI tester to write API tests in C++ is probably not the best deployment of that individual's skills. Plan on using a mixed approach as your team grows. Once your organization reaches a certain size and maturity level, you will be able—and will need—to pick one or the other.

Hiring Testers

In the first half of this chapter, we looked at somewhat static and dry topics, which are necessary to lay the foundation for the test team. For the remainder of this chapter, let's look at the dynamics of test team management, starting with how we hire people to fill out that test team we've spent the last few pages characterizing and defining.

Defining the Job

To start hiring, you'll first need permission from management to hire people. This is sometimes referred to as "having a req," meaning that a hiring requisition has worked its way through the process at your company and is now approved. If you have a human resources department, they have likely defined this process and the various forms and approvals required. As there can be legal ramifications associated with offering a job that doesn't exist, this is a hurdle that I recommend you clear before you proceed.

Either before, during, or immediately after the requisition phase, you'll need to define a job description. Job descriptions generally serve two purposes. One is as a recruiting tool. It can be posted on the Internet and job boards, given to recruiters, and so on. The other purpose is as a formal definition of the new-hires roles and responsibilities.

A job description should address the following issues:

- What tasks and responsibilities are involved?
- What and how much experience?
- What specific skills are needed?
- What training, education, certification, security clearances, or licenses are required?
- What are the hours and the dress code, is a drug test required, when is the starting date (if not immediately), what career path is compatible with the position, and so forth?

These issues should be covered at whatever level of specificity is required for you—and the candidates—to determine fitness for the job. You don't want to scare off applicants who could make excellent testers, but you also don't want to receive résumés from people who are clearly unqualified. For this reason, it's also a good idea to distinguish between required ("must have") and desirable ("nice to have") credentials.

Your skills assessment spreadsheet can help you prepare a job description. In the estimate prepared in Chapter 1, the SpeedyWriter test manager identified a need for a new test engineer to work on component test development and execution, something that requires a focus on technology and the internals of the system. Figure 8.6 shows the job description for this position. Note that this document, while useful both as a recruiting and a personnel-file document, would need to be condensed if you intend to post this on a job board or in the classified ads.

Another subject you have to consider as part of defining the job is what you intend to pay the new hire. Various sources publish salary survey information, such as *Contract Professional* magazine, the American Society for Quality's journal, *Quality Professional*, and staffing and recruiting Web sites such as salary.com. Remember that the free market for labor works, and it will continue to work tomorrow. This is especially important to keep in mind during recessions and economic hard times when the temptation to low-ball is the greatest, but any time you try to hire at "bargain basement" prices you can count on one of three outcomes. First, you might get exactly what you paid for; in other words, the person was not as competent as you thought during the hiring process for whatever reason. Second, you might get a bargain, but sooner or later that person will realize his true market worth and fly the coop, possibly in the middle of a tight project. Third, the person might realize that the pay is a raw deal, but consider herself stuck for whatever reason, leading to disgruntlement or poor performance.

You might have noticed that I set the bar pretty high in my job description in Figure 8.6. A person with these qualifications is a technical professional peer of a programmer, a system administrator, or other skilled technical professional. I believe in building

---

Test Automation Engineer

Roles and Responsibilities

Participate in a test automation tool selection process for an automated component testing harness in a Java/EJB/Ant environment.

Participate in project-wide reviews of requirements, system architecture, and detailed design documents.

Develop and execute automated tests using the selected tool, which will likely require programming in C, C++, Java, or some scripting language.

Perform static analysis of source code using complexity metrics.

Effectively communicate testing activities and findings in oral and written formats.

Integrate the test suites into the test management system and custom test harnesses.

The ability to participate effectively in estimation, planning, cost-of-quality, and quality risk analysis is desired.

Education

Four-year degree in computer science, computer engineering, electrical engineering, or software engineering desired; or add two additional years experience.

Certification in testing tools or testing skills desirable.

Experience and Skills

Five or more years experience in test automation, with at least one year of that experience in a Unix Web/database/application server-side browser-based application environment.

Familiarity of the underlying architecture of a multi-tier browser-based application is required, including operating systems, servers, networking, clients, and browsers.

Programming, system administration, or database administration experience is a plus.

At least some knowledge of word processing is required, and more extensive experience with word processing, content management, and document management systems is a plus.

Career Path

A demonstrated career commitment to testing and/or quality assurance is preferred. The candidate should show a familiarity with the latest testing theory and practice, a commitment to on-going learning about the field, and a history of applying useful testing concepts in previous positions.

Other

Dress is business-casual and hours are flexible. Some weekends and evenings will be required.

A demonstrated ability to work effectively and harmoniously as part of an independent test team within a project-service-organization context is required.

Figure 8.6 A job description for a SpeedyWriter automated test engineer.

teams of tester where the engineers are at that level, and I believe in paying them at that level, too. If a senior software engineer in your company makes $80,000 per year, say, then a senior test engineer with the same number of years of experience, education, and training should make that amount, too.

Finally, don't forget to think about the career path for your candidate. What advancement opportunities exist? How do you intend to promote growth in skills during this person's tenure in the test team, and how does that match up with potential career paths? Can you accommodate someone who wants to spend some time in testing, and then move into another area of the company such as technical sales, marketing, programming, management, or system administration? How long would that person need to stay in testing to be a net positive to the test team? These are important questions that a serious candidate will need you to be able to answer. A test position should be a fondly remembered step on someone's professional ladder, not a bear trap that someone will have to escape to progress.

Gathering and Screening Résumés

With your proverbial ducks in a row on the job definition front, it's time to start collecting and screening candidate résumés. Candidates can be found in a number of ways, including classified ads, college job boards, agencies and recruiters, for-profit and not-for-profit Internet sites and newsgroups, and, not least of all, your peers. (Another benefit of going to conferences and training programs is that you meet bright, involved people you might want to hire.) You can also recruit current and former contractors, but keep in mind that usually there are conversion fees payable to that contractor's agency that can range as high as 50 percent of the annual salary.

As résumés come in, check them against the job description. Separate—but don't discard—the qualified from the unqualified. (You might decide to rethink your qualifications or consider the less-qualified for test technician roles.) Circulate the qualified candidates' résumés to other people on the test team and possibly to other peer managers. Have one or more of the team do a telephone interview of the candidates. Ask for references if they weren't provided, and check them if appropriate. In some companies, the human resources department does all reference checks and even preliminary telephone interviews, so check with them on the precise process to follow.

During telephone (and on-site) interviews, I'm looking for people to tell me about what they've done on past projects that relates to the job description. I go down the résumé before the telephone interview and make notes about past tasks and activities that could have taught them important skills useful for my efforts. I ask people questions such as, "Tell me about what kind of test harness you built for the XYZ system," "Talk to me a little about one or two bug reports you wrote on project ABC," and "The last time you ran a test case that was somewhat ambiguous about the expected results, how did you decide whether it passed or failed?" (This type of open-ended questioning about past actions is called "behavioral interviewing" because you are trying to explore past behaviors and the motivations behind them.) I also ask basic knowledge questions about testing, the technology, and the application domain. For example, "What is the difference between behavioral and structural testing?"

Sad but true, not all résumés are sterling examples of truthful self-presentation. Somewhere along the way, it became acceptable in the United States and in some countries in Europe to inflate your qualifications on your résumé. (Anecdotally, I have heard fewer stories about this happening in my conversations with peers from India, Taiwan, and other parts of Asia.) Therefore, part of the screening and telephone interview process must be looking for red flags. Does a buzzword on the résumé indicate mastery of a topic, or just exposure to it? Can all claims be backed up in terms of actual, meaningful work done on a project? Are the degrees, licenses, certifications, publications, and other professional qualifications substantiated?

Other warning signs include excessive job changes. This might indicate a candidate's ability to talk his way into jobs for which he's not qualified, or it might indicate an inability to get along with people, leading to rancorous departures. (Note that contractors will tend to change jobs every time their contracts end, although they should stay until they've finished their engagement.) Gaps in employment history can indicate personal or health problems—which you should steer away from discussing for legal reasons—but it could also indicate a stint in jail or other voluntary but odd choices in ways to spend one's life that might make you reconsider hiring someone. (Caveat: Criminal convictions, especially those long past or which have been expunged, set aside, or pardoned generally do not disqualify candidates, and considering such convictions as part of the hiring process can expose you and your employer to legal liability.) Frequent changes in career can indicate a flightiness and flippancy that might make you worry about someone's tendency to bolt from your project right when the pressure is highest.

While the threat of legal action has clamped down on what many past employers are willing to say about people during reference checks, most managers will *want* to help you hire their best former employees and avoid hiring their worst. Listen carefully to the words these people use—and don't use—and connect the dots. One of my course attendees told me that she replied to every question a manager asked her about a former employee (not a superstar, for sure) with the following deadpan words: "He was very punctual." The manager hired this person all the same! Don't bring a tin ear to the reference-checking process.

By the end of the screening process, you should be able to decide whether the person fits the basic qualification as laid out in the job description. You should also have a basic feel for whether you like the candidate, whether she'll fit into the team, and whether you think you're likely to hire her. If the answer to any of these questions is "no," then set the résumé aside and move on. The last thing you need to do during a busy test project is spend time interviewing someone who is unlikely to be a positive contributor to the project team. The best thing that can happen if you do is that you just waste a few hours of everyone's time, which is hardly good, but the worst thing that can happen is that you talk yourself into making a hiring mistake, which can cost you literally months of time later, damage test team credibility, and lower test team productivity.

On-Site Interviews

Interview processes tend to vary. Here's one that I've seen work well:

1. The human resources manager or the equivalent person orients the candidate to the company, salary, and benefits, and "how things are done around here."

2. The test manager and other members of the test team, including test engineers and test technicians, determine the candidate's fitness for the position, including personality. This includes some mixture of one-on-one and group interviews, usually, or a group lunch.

3. Other managers might interview senior, lead, or management candidates. If a candidate will be working closely with someone in marketing, sales, business analysis, technical support, programming, or another team, then that person should probably interview the candidate. (People outside the test team should not, however, have veto power over test hiring decisions unless that's a reciprocal company policy and you likewise have veto power over other team hires.)

4. Sometimes, the HR manager will debrief the candidate at the end, just to see how the interview went.

In some high-tech companies, before the interview even starts, the candidate must sign a nondisclosure or confidentiality agreement. Sometimes, the company has a standard form for this, which you should use if it does.

Interviewing styles tend to vary considerably. My primary focus during an interview is to decide whether a person will fit into the test team personally, professionally, and capably. I start with describing the project at a high level, and then I start asking questions, again, that relate past project tasks and activities to what the person will be doing should he or she get the job. You might want to consider questions such as the following as a starter:

- For the last test you ran, did you expect it to pass or fail? Why?
- Tell me about the manner and tone you used to discuss a recent bug report with other members of the project team.
- Tell me about a controversial bug report that you advocated.
- Talk to me a little about what, in general, you find rewarding about working.
- Tell me about your experiences on a project where you worked XX hours per week. ("XX" being the peak number of hours I expect people to have to work during this project.)
- On your last project, how did you decide the right amount of time to spend writing a test case or isolating a bug?
- Tell me about how your past managers have helped you maintain proper focus.
- Tell me about what you learned on project XYZ that you think can help us test our product.
- Tell me about a previous test project that you really enjoyed. What did like the most?
- Describe the career you see for yourself in testing.

Each of these questions is actually just the start of a line of related questions that I pursue. As during the telephone interview, I will also ask questions to probe a person's knowledge of the critical skills. The line of questions continues until I've explored the topic fully and satisfied myself as to the person's experience and qualifications in that regard.

I have my "BS antennae" set to their highest level of sensitivity during the process, and I drill down on any answers that I find unfulfilling, wishy-washy, or vague. This can often indicate an area of weakness that a candidate is trying to paper over. If this is a weakness I can live with, I'll tell the candidate up front that I'm looking for a desirable qualification but not a required one. Whatever the case, I always react better to someone who says, "I don't know the answer to that question," than I do to someone who tries to snow me. I sometimes hire people whom I think will grow into a job, but I never hire people I think are trying to con their way into a job.

One way to give a person a chance to demonstrate competence is to use audition interviews. What we've done on my teams is to ask each candidate to run a scripted test case we know will fail. Now, we don't tell the candidate the test will fail, and we also pick a test whose failures are appropriate in complexity and subtlety for the candidate's level of experience. We put the candidate in front of the system under test, provide whatever basic orientation is necessary, and then ask the candidate to run the test. We provide the candidate with a clipboard and notepad to write on to report any bugs or other interesting observations. This has been a tremendously effective technique for identifying qualified testers. Of course, some wags have told me that, if you schedule enough audition interviews, you might never actually have to hire anyone, but I don't recommend audition interviews as a primary testing technique!

Making the Hiring Decision

I prefer to have a debriefing session together with all the interviewers at the end of the interview, to compare notes. Don't just use a checklist or form circulated via email or on paper, but actually sit down together and talk about the candidate, too. One course attendee told me once that everyone came to this debriefing meeting very positive about a candidate, but found when they discussed specific questions, that the candidate had given substantially different answers to each interviewer about what he had done on specific projects!

After all the candidates have been interviewed, you should make the hiring decision as quickly as possible, while people's recollections are still fresh and the best candidate is still available. (Remember, the good ones don't stay in the job market for very long, even in tough times.) Offers of employment can be extended by telephone or through an offer letter; your HR department probably has a standard process for this.

Sometimes, candidates want to negotiate the salary. I'm usually willing to do this, although I try to come to the table with my best offer up front. One thing I'm very loathe to engage in is a bidding war. This happens when a candidate takes your offer letter to another potential employer, asks them to beat it, and then comes back to you with *that* offer letter and asks you to beat it. This is the type of thing that is appropriate when buying a car or a house, because ultimately it's a zero sum game. However, I don't see hiring someone as a zero sum game, and I don't really want to hire someone who sees it that way, either. The flip side of setting a fair salary based on prevailing and historical market value for a person's skill and experience is that I know my offer is fair. If someone wants to play games with me during the hiring process, then I'll let the other bidder win the bidding war, and good luck to both parties.

Avoiding—and Undoing—Hiring Mistakes

I am advocating that you be tough in your approach to hiring. The objective of the hiring process is to separate the qualified from the unqualified, the willing from the unwilling, the interested from the uninterested; in short, to make judgments about people and their skills, experiences, and personalities. In some ways of thinking prevalent today, it's not nice, it's not okay, it's not politically correct to judge. It's true that you shouldn't be unduly harsh. I know of a few managers who use intimidation and "good cop, bad cop" routines to interrogate interviewees. This just scares people off, the good along with the bad. It's also true that you should only consider factors relevant to the job at hand, and, of course, you should avoid breaking the laws that govern hiring in your local, state, and Federal jurisdiction. (The HR department should be able to advise you about what interview questions are disallowed, or you should consult an employment-law attorney.) I'm absolutely not recommending that you be discriminatory—as anyone who's worked with me or on my test teams will attest—or that you hold against people past mistakes, personal or professional, from which they've learned valuable lessons. To paraphrase Nietzsche, any really bad mistake is also a really important learning opportunity, so you might find that some of your best test team members have made some pretty big mistakes on past projects.[6]

As much as it's nice to be nice, though, we must keep in mind that the essence of hiring is to choose teammates. We all probably remember physical education period from our school days, so the kindest souls will know that it hurts sometimes when you're not chosen. However, you have a fiduciary responsibility to your employer or client to pick only the very best people for your test team, so you must steel yourself to that duty. To hire the wrong person is to set that person, yourself, your team, and your employer up for a failure—which isn't doing anyone any favors—but to hire the right person promotes the success of all involved.

To go back to our dour philosopher friend Nietzsche, though, sometimes you will—just as I certainly have—create learning experiences for yourself by making hiring mistakes or inheriting someone else's hiring mistake. Dealing with a problem employee is a test of your leadership skills and your character. Don't fail the test by trying to ignore it or pretending it will go away. It won't. Yes, it's a big unpleasant waste of time to fire someone, but just one or two inappropriate test team members can make a tough situation untenable. I will admit to having kept some testers around long after they had demonstrated their negative impact on team morale and performance. I have learned my lesson and won't repeat that mistake. Keeping a problem employee on board does no one any good. Here's why.

The rest of your staff suffers most when you keep dead weight around. The team has to compensate for this person's blunders and mistakes. Furthermore, one individual's poor work can result in a perception that the entire test team is incompetent and careless, which leads to the project team looking askance at your bug reports, metrics, and

---

[6]Nietzsche's aphorism is, "The only learning experiences are bad experiences." I think Nietzsche underestimates the learning possibilities in good experiences, but is right on the money about the need to learn from bad experiences.

other test data. Most damaging, an individual who is not contributing usually knows it and adopts various defensive postures to camouflage the failure—for example, denigrating the work of the other team members. In such cases, productive and motivated contributors suffer disparagement to salve the ego of the inept one. Others get tired of pulling the other person's load. In both cases, qualified testers might resign rather than work with someone who is offensive, incompetent, or both. All of these outcomes are unfair to you and your team.

Your human resources department will likely have a process by which people undergo coaching, reprimands, and ultimately involuntary separation (firing). If you are a good manager—in other words, someone who cares about the people who work for you and who wants to do right by the team—you will probably feel awful throughout this process. Nevertheless, it is *because* you are a good manager that you must do it. The person you fire might find the experience quite painful in the short run. Still, a smart person will take the opportunity to assess what he or she did wrong, and decide to do better next time. Follow the process, coaching the employee and then gradually moving up the ladder from verbal to written warnings. Once you hit the second or third written warning, it's time to make a change. You obviously aren't getting through, and after the third warning you won't be taken seriously if you don't let this person go.

Bringing the New Tester On-Board

When someone accepts an offer—and sometimes even when someone already in the company becomes part of the test team temporarily or permanently—you should get moving on the logistics of having a workstation, a badge, a telephone extension, and other perquisites of employment arranged for the new hire on her first day. Are there forms to fill out? Security hurdles to leap? A drug test, fingerprints, background checks, or other such details to attend to? Nothing shouts out chaos and disorder to me like showing up on my first day at a job or an engagement and finding that no one was ready for me to arrive.

You should also think about training and orientation, especially if there's no standard program offering by the human resources department. Many people use a variant of "sink or swim" for training. Some people can handle this, while others can't, and in all cases I think it sends a questionable message to new hires that could sour them on the job from the start. I have a one-day training that I provide to all my new testers that addresses issues such as how to design and write a test case, how to do exploratory testing, how to write a bug report, what goes in a test plan, the context of testing, and so forth. I also generally assign a mentor to new hires. The mentor will orient the new hires and review all their work for the first few weeks. Yes, this does lead to a productivity hit, but it also leads to consistent levels of quality in test team output and sends a message to new hires that they are important members of the team whose success is instrumental to the success of the team as a whole.

Looking back on this section, you might say, "Gee, Rex, this is a pretty involved process you've laid out here, and you know, I've got a lot of testing work to do." It's very easy for me to sit here and write about spending all this time on hiring, and hard for you—and for me—to actually do it when all that other stuff is going on. Trust me, though, of all the topics addressed in this book, hiring the right people might very well be the most important one.

You can do everything else right, but if you have the wrong team, your test projects will feel like swimming through freshly poured concrete. Conversely, you can make a lot of mistakes, even some big ones, and come out smelling like a rose with the right team in place. I know it's hard to do under conditions of pressure, but do make sure you allocate plenty of time for the hiring process and use it. Rushing a hiring decision because of some externally perceived sense of urgency is a mistake. Having the wrong person on your test team can lead to tremendous problems, as discussed previously. Conversely, hiring the right people leads to nonlinear gains in effectiveness, efficiency, and credibility, because the whole can be greater than the sum of the parts when you build your teams from carefully selected individuals.

Giving a Damn: Motivating Your Test Team

Maintaining morale and motivation on a test team takes some doing. In my experience, the traditional "team building" exercises don't work too well with test folks, since we tend to be a cynical lot. There are, however, some management styles you can adopt that will do what no amount of ersatz group bonding exercises can: convince your team members that you value their time and contributions, respect their opinions, and will stand up for them when they need you. The following sections offer tips about some techniques that have worked for me, and some that I try to avoid.[7]

Be On Your Team's Side

As noted earlier, some people regard testing as low-caste work. You might not be able to change this perception, and often the perception is a political reality. However, you can take some steps to minimize the extent to which this situation demotivates your team.

One of these steps is to make sure your testers know that you respect their intentions and will defend their actions, even the occasional boner. Every now and then, someone on your staff will put a cherry bomb in a wasp's nest. The resulting swarm of angry critters, looking to sting the perpetrator, can overwhelm the poor tester. These types of incidents usually arise from high-visibility bug reports, although hallway conversations about the tenuous connection between reality and the latest delivery date run a close second. These situations are even worse when your test engineer has in fact made a mistake. I have seen bug reports given legalistic scrutiny, and I pity the engineer who mischaracterizes a bug.

---

[7]There are a number of excellent ideas in Rick Craig and Stefan Jaskiel's book, *The Systematic Software Testing Handbook*, but the chapter on test management, which addresses many of the issues in this chapter and especially being a good leader, is worth the purchase price by itself. Especially if you are new to being a manager—but even if you're a seasoned veteran—I recommend that you read their book, and particularly that chapter. Tom DeMarco's allegorical novel, *The Deadline*, is also chock full of great management ideas, including my favorite leadership aphorism, "lead with the heart, trust your gut…build soul into the organization, [and] develop a nose for [untruth]."

When faced with angry attacks on one of your team members, never upbraid or criticize the hapless tester publicly, no matter what the mistake. You should, however, acknowledge the problem, perhaps saying something along these lines: "Yeah, we probably could have done a better job. I guess I goofed when I reviewed that report. But let's talk about this bug." This approach allows you to admit the mistake, take the blame yourself, and move to the matter at hand. (Of course, if you have staff members who habitually shoot off their mouths or write up "omigawd" bug reports without checking the facts, you must deal with this problem on a long-term basis.)

In addition, what testers do wrong should not distract focus from what they do right. If an offending bug report lacks a few isolation steps, but the bug is undeniable, don't let people lose sight of that fact. If a tester's manner is inappropriate in the course of escalating a serious problem, shift the focus back to the problem. Do this with the tester present. Visibly stand up for your employee in public, and then do whatever coaching is needed later, in private, after you both have had a chance to blow off steam and reflect calmly. You'll build real loyalty among your staff by displaying this type of solidarity under fire and by dealing with their failures in private.

Another step is to make sure that the "goodies" get doled out fairly to your team. Some years ago, a test network administrator I supervised wanted to attend a networking conference, which made good sense to me. It was appropriate for his career path, he could learn something of immediate importance, and the timing was good. We did the whole "trip request" tango, which also involved my manager.

Several development engineers had also signed up for the same conference. As the date approached, a senior manager started complaining about the large number of attendees, suggesting that perhaps some attendees should cancel. Guess who made the short list of extraneous attendees? I responded reasonably, explaining the original justifications—still valid—for sending the network administrator on this trip. I became a bit less reasonable when my own manager hopped on the dog pile. I fired off an email to my manager implying that management was singling out my engineer because of his position in test. I also asked pointedly whether she cared about this employee and about the effect that canceling the trip would have on his morale. My engineer attended the conference.

Make sure that your staff members get an equal crack at all the perks. The following list should help you keep an eye on the situation and restore a level playing field if need be. A word of warning, though: before you accuse anyone of stacking the deck against your test team, have your facts in order. You'll look paranoid if you can't document inequities.

Salaries. If the pay scale for test engineers is below that of the other engineers in your company, work with the human resources department to ensure pay parity for equal levels of responsibility, experience, and education. The old wisdom that testers should make less than developers is just that: old. Use salary surveys, as discussed earlier, to bolster your case. Be aware, however, that this is a tough nut to crack if you have inherited an existing test team.

Job titles. If the ladder of job titles in development has more rungs, with more prestige, than the one in test, do whatever you can to resolve the inequity. Again, you'll probably need to enlist the cooperation of the human resources office. Argue for a parallel set of technical titles, such as Member of the Technical Staff, Senior Member of the Technical Staff, Principal Member of the Technical Staff, and so forth. If these parallel rungs already exist, but the test staff hold only the Member of the Technical Staff titles, not the more senior titles, investigate whether test employees are being given a lower rank than their history with the company, their years in the industry, and their levels of responsibility warrant.

Hours. If testers are expected to work unusual hours, or if they get stuck testing over the weekend to meet a schedule target while the rest of the development team has the weekend off, ask for compensatory time off for your staff—or just give it to them. If testers must cede test's hardware to developers for debugging during regular business hours and consequently must perform testing after hours, discuss the matter with your development manager colleagues. Point out the unfairness, and ask to work out a schedule for debugging access that "spreads the misery." If they refuse, go to your manager.

Training sessions, off-sites, seminars, and conferences. If developers frequently attend plum events in exotic locations, while testers seldom do, find a particularly useful and particularly attractive event for your best staff person to attend, and sell it to your manager. Repeat this tactic as needed to help redress any imbalance. Budget freezes sometimes restrict the number of employees who can be sent to conferences and training seminars. If these freezes affect test attendees but not development attendees, ask your manager or the human resources office to establish a training budget for each department, including yours, with demonstrable equity.

Support a Reasonable Workstyle

Hard work, unrealistic schedules, and the occasional strange hours come with the test territory—and this lifestyle burns people out. You might encounter testers whose previous employers have overworked them ferociously; not surprisingly, this usually makes them unwilling to be taken advantage of again.

To help alleviate some of the stress involved in testing, be sure to pace your team. You might be pressured to inflict undesirable work conditions on the team as soon as test execution begins. Resist it. A test project is always a marathon; never start with a sprint. Testing often begins behind schedule, has too few people allocated to it, and seldom ends on the date originally planned. Under these circumstances, you should avoid pushing too hard too early.

Also try to break up the work whenever possible. On one of my jobs, test builds for the monthly maintenance releases usually showed up on Friday afternoon around 4:00. As the build and development teams headed out for their weekends, test staff installed these builds and started automated tests, sometimes working well into the evening. Next came the weekend work to keep the tests going so that we could report on test status on Monday afternoon. Everyone loved this arrangement except us. You should pay your staff back for extra efforts like this. If people work over the weekend, give them a Friday or a Monday off. Let them go early during the week after a rough session. Try to give them breathing spells between crunches.

Clearly, one reason for the feelings of stress and overload is that most test organizations are understaffed. When your best efforts to achieve a realistic staffing level fall short, you might try shifting gears by remembering that "understaffed" can be synonymous with "overtasked"—a perspective that allows you to consider other options for reducing your team's load. Try to get support from other groups in the company for chores that might not be part of your core mission but are essential to accomplishing it. For example, you might be able to use an administrative assistant to do some of the tedious data entry work, freeing up some of your testers' time.

A second problem is that test organizations often start participating in projects too late. Ideally, one or two test people should be involved in a project right from the beginning. You'll need to assign someone to start preparations for a new project up front rather than waiting until a few days before component, integration, or system test execution is scheduled to begin.

As a manager, you obviously must be involved in planning the test effort, but you also need an engineer to attend to the technical details. This engineer can plan the reuse and adaptation of the existing test system (tools, cases, and suites), select whatever new tools are needed, define the changes to the test architecture, and so forth. The test engineer should also participate in technical reviews and have detailed discussions with the developers. You might not be able to spare someone full-time, but it's important enough to set aside a few hours every week. If you don't take the time to do this, you and your team will be forced into a reactive mode when test execution starts and will be chronically unable to get solid test execution under way.

Early test involvement in new projects has another benefit that feeds back into the issue of understaffing. The commencement of any new project reopens discussion of appropriate staff levels. As you demonstrate your organization's ability to add value to the delivered product, management is likely to approve more realistic staffing levels for subsequent projects.

In companies that have no experience with formal testing or with early test involvement in development projects, some care is required in implementing this up-front participation. Begin by selling the project manager on the benefits of more effective, less hectic testing. If the two of you approach management, you're more likely to succeed, especially since the project manager—as a person who will bring a saleable product to the company's portfolio or deliver a working system to the users—will usually have a lot more pull than you do.

A more subtle source of overload in the test organization is change. Changes in the project plan do not smite developers and test staff alike. Take scope creep, for example. Adding a few simple APIs to a program can generate a whole slew of new test work, because now you need to test other programs (and maybe even hardware devices) that use those APIs. In hardware, changing the design of a moving part—say, a PC Card bay door—might call for not only re-executing that lengthy 10,000-repetition mechanical-life test, but also reworking your fixtures and test tools.

Scope shrink is just as bad. This type of change can make it hard to distinguish between time well spent and a perfectly good day squandered. Suppose that one of your engineers spends 12 hours implementing a particularly nifty test tool for generating network load, which seems like a good investment. Two days later, management pulls network support from the system under test as part of a decision to trim features in order to hit a marketing window. Sure, it will be nice to have that test tool in the next product cycle, but in the meantime, you've let two or three other tasks languish, and those jobs are now much more important.

In addition, keep in mind that test execution occurs in the most "change-rich" portion of the project. As people begin to perceive how unrealistic the schedule is and yet make frantic efforts to adhere to it anyway, you'll see abrupt deletions in product functionality, reorganization of some or all of the project teams, dropping of entire test suites from the plan, and other such corrections. These changes aren't always constructive or carefully considered. "Do something! Do anything!" often becomes the project slogan as schedules start to slip, and schedule slip is most noticeable during test execution, simply because test happens to be the caboose on the project train.

Without exaggerating or overreacting, never let significant changes to the project go unremarked or undocumented. If the change is big, bring it to management's attention—not as a complaint but as a matter that should be understood and acknowledged. If someone suggests adding support for BeOS to DataRocket, your response should be along these lines: "Great! We anticipate that will cost $1,500 in new software for our lab, require one additional engineering sample, and consume 50 person-hours. Let's talk about how we get these new resources."

Whether the change is small or large, it must be managed. Chapter 6, "Tips and Tools for Crunch Time: Managing the Dynamic," introduced you to a simple database that can help you track changes (see *Expect the Unexpected: A Change Management Database*). While best practices call for all changes to be managed at a project-wide level, you should plan on tracking and managing them yourself until your organization reaches that level of maturity.

When you are faced with too few people, too much work to handle at once, and an environment of constant change, the rush to keep up can tempt you and your team to devise kludges. A kludge is any ill-advised, substandard, or "temporary" bandage applied to an urgent problem in the (often misguided) belief that doing so will keep a project moving forward. However, the reality is that these hasty little shortcuts usually serve only to transfer pain from the present to the immediate future—and add more pain to it in the bargain.

It often seems that performing an ad hoc, undocumented test on some "one-shot feature that will never come up again" almost ensures that testing this feature will become enshrined in the regular routine. Once you have a workable process in place, don't deviate from it at the drop of a hat. An engineer who devises a new test case needs to write it down. A technician who alters a test case should document the change and the reason for it. A tester who changes a system configuration must record the new setup. The cliché "more haste, less speed" is a cliché because it's true.

Foster Career Development for Each Tester

The old military recruiting slogan in the United States read, "It's not just a job, it's an adventure." Testing is sometimes an adventure, and it should be a good job, but it should also be something else: an integrated part of each test team member's career path.

This means that it is up to us as test managers to ensure skills growth in a way that is consistent with each tester's career needs as well as with the needs of the team. As I mentioned before, I like to use the skills assessment worksheet for this purpose. Have people set quarterly skills-growth goals that meet their career needs and help fill in weaknesses in the test team. (This is another reason why aligning candidates' career paths with testing is so important, because it prevent wide mismatches between your teams skills-growth needs and those of your team members.) Provide formal and informal training opportunities as well as work assignments to help people meet these skills-growth targets.

Informal training opportunities can include mentoring from strong team members. It can also include "book clubs" where the entire team reads a book on testing and then discusses it over weekly lunches provided by management. Formal training includes off-site and on-site seminars and training courses provided by experts, as well as some computer-based and Internet-based training courses.

As managers, we need to work with our testers to get them deserved promotions and raises. Yearly performance appraisals are the usual vehicle for this. At some point, too, it will be time for someone to leave the test team to pursue her career. A good manager doesn't stand in the way, even though we always hate to see good people leave. Look at it this way, though: If you don't help the person pursue her career within the company, then she'll just leave and pursue her career somewhere else. A good manager should work with the "receiving" manager to help set up the erstwhile tester for success in her new job.

Don't Offer Bonuses Based on Meeting a Schedule

Promising bonuses to staff based on whether a schedule is met is a bad idea, especially for a test team. Testing, when done properly, finds bugs, often more than expected. If the project team ignores the bugs in order to meet the schedule, the money spent on testing is wasted (see Chapter 11 for a discussion of testing return on investment). However, if the project team takes the time to fix the bugs, the test team's collective bonus can disappear. Project-wide, every test case that finds a bug reduces the odds of getting a bonus for everyone. What type of motivation does this provide? Such obvious common sense notwithstanding, these bonus arrangements do occur.

Schedule-based bonus plans usually descend from above. If the project manager proposes a scheme like this, explain the perverse incentives it will create for the testers and the negative dynamic it will set up between test and the rest of the project team. If the development team gets a bonus for meeting a schedule, that's fine (although you should remind management of the tension this will generate as the test team succeeds in finding bugs). However, the test team should have a different bonus plan, one that emphasizes the role of testers as quality advocates. How about a bonus based on a high defect detection percentage, adjusted for test project scope and calculated three months after product release (see Chapter 4, "An Exciting Career in Entomology Awaits You: A Bug Tracking Database")? Admittedly, this arrangement will not be implemented without some effort on your part, but the path of least resistance—going along with a plan that provides an incentive for your team to do the *wrong* thing—makes no sense.

Don't Buy Bugs Like Sacks of Rice

I once heard a rumor about a test contractor who got paid by the bug and by the hour, earning over $500,000 in one year from one project. This story, while apocryphal, probably contains elements of truth.

Bug reports are not commodities. The importance of bugs and the quality of reports vary. If you want to generate a huge volume of bug reports—many of them lousy and many detailing unimportant bugs—you can award bonuses based on the sheer number of reports. If you want good bug reports, don't do this.

Expecting Thanks for Saturday Night's Pizza

When your team is working late nights and weekends, plan to pay for some meals during these overtime periods. Get approval to submit an expense report. And when you buy meals, remember that people get tired of pizza. Most American-style pizza is just about the least healthy food around. Vary the menu, and offer your staff options they'll find palatable. Instead of getting irritated when employees have special meal requests, remember that you are not doing them a favor by buying them a meal—they are doing you and your company a favor by giving up their own time. Some companies foster a "macho geek chic" centered on late nights, early mornings, and pizza feasts during midnight bull sessions. What exactly is the prize for winning a sleep-deprivation or junk-food-consumption contest? This seems neat for the first five or so years you're in this business, but after that it becomes obvious for what it is: a cheap way to take advantage of the employees.

Promoting an Us versus Them Mentality

In my opinion, the worst motivational technique is whipping up confrontational attitudes between testers and developers. This type of "mock duel" might inspire testers to find more bugs in the short run. However, for the same reasons that being a jerk isn't among the traits of a good test engineer, fostering mistrust and ill will between the test and development organizations won't work either.

So, What Are People Actually Doing?

It's all very well and good for me to sit here and write, "Do this, don't do that," but what are people actually doing in the field? Good question. In an interesting discussion on the Internet testing discussion SWTEST-Discuss, the following ideas came up most frequently.

Some people are using management by objectives, usually in the form of yearly performance appraisals, to reward testers. Management by objectives has the risk of perverse incentives—what the total quality management people refer to as "the false customer"—that can create motivation problems for testers. For example, one of my peers was rated on the quality of the product being shipped and hitting the schedule. He found so many bugs that, even with the delay in schedule, they couldn't fix them all, so he ended up getting a 0-percent raise that year. He quit and went somewhere else where expectations were more reasonable. In another situation I'm aware of, the management dictate went down, in the form of an email memo to senior managers, that no one was allowed to achieve more than 80 percent of their objectives because they needed to cap salary expense growth at 2 percent that year. This memo became public knowledge in record time and contributed to immense dissatisfaction with the company. One of many people who quit—in the middle of a recession, by the way—explained, "Better to be unemployed in a lousy economy than to spend one more day at [that company]."

I have used management by objectives successfully when I align the objectives with what you actually want and can expect from the test team—in other words, an accurate and meaningful assessment of system quality before release, communicated in an effective and timely manner to the project management team. I also require people to actively participate in the skills assessment and growth program, although I do not set numerical targets for skills growth over the year.

Some people use metrics based on test cases run versus planned or the number of bugs found. As mentioned in Chapter 3, "Test System Architecture, Cases, and Coverage," paying people for hitting the planned number of test cases is tantamount to paying them to ignore bugs, so I don't believe this is a good idea. Paying people for bug reports means you'll get lots of bug reports, but will they be good ones? Those who report success with these approaches go to great efforts to remove the weird incentives.

The most success seemed to be claimed by those who used defect detection percentage as a metric of quality achieved. Some people mentioned that they used defect detection percentage, schedule achievement, budget containment, and feature delivery all together across the entire project team. The idea is to put everyone on the same incentive plan and reward them for what the market would reward the company for: delivering a good enough product that offered the essential features early enough and cheaply enough. Although I haven't seen this approach in action, this is the one that makes the most sense to me.

Extending Your Talent: Using Temporary Experts and Implementers

Sometimes the list of tasks that simply must be done by a given date exceeds the capability of the test team. Sometimes you need to ramp up the test team for some peaks in workload. You might need additional expertise or just help in implementing some test development or execution effort. These situations are usually transitory and you can phase out the extra help after a period of days, weeks, or months. (For circumstances where long-term outsourcing is appropriate, see Chapter 10.) The remainder of this chapter discusses such temporary help and its use and misuse.

The Roles Temporary Workers Play

Let me start by defining the type of extra help I'm talking about. During the era of the organization man, this would be an easy exercise. Temporary agencies supplied clerical workers and other low-level interim staff to meet rush-period needs, while academia, industry alumni, and consulting companies supplied consultants to transfer expertise into the organization.

These days, though, especially in high technology, applying simplistic models such as this no longer works. Temporary agencies still exist, but they don't just supply data entry clerks, they also place six-figure-a-year programmers, test engineers, and business analysis. Some of the people who bring expertise to a company are these same test engineers, while others are the more traditional experts.

Not only is the model no longer applicable, the labels by which you could once identify the various players have become meaningless. A "temp" might very well have experience with advanced office-automation tools and software that makes him or her quite different from yesterday's typist. Not all those who call themselves "consultants" work for consulting companies or bring dozens of years of unique experience and research to their assignments.[8]

Instead of relying on labels, let's break down the contributions of temporary staff along two axes: implementation and expertise. The diagram in Figure 8.7 shows the different types of assistance that temporary staff can bring to your organization. Let's go counterclockwise around the triangle to understand what each of these possible roles entails.

Toward the left apex, you find people who are best suited as temporary test technicians. They will play an important, but not critical, role in implementation and execution. They might bring special skills to your team, but they have no role in teaching those skills to your staff. Indeed, to the extent knowledge is transferred, they will spend time learning your processes and test system.

As you move toward the lower apex, you start to find the types of people who qualify as what one might call "consultants" in the traditional sense. On the mid-point of the line, perhaps, you would encounter on-site trainers who spend a few days working with your staff on a particularly tricky test automation tool, solving a few implementation problems, and then leaving. People who work near the lower apex will spend their time teaching and training exclusively. (These are people about whom Edwin Meese, a former United States Attorney General who now makes a living as an expert, quipped, "An expert is somebody who is more than 50 miles from home, has no responsibility for implementing the advice he gives, and shows slides.") For example, someone who comes on-site to teach you to perform a failure modes and effects analysis on your products performs this role.

Moving toward the upper apex, you find highly knowledgeable professionals who, in addition to transferring that expertise to their clients, help their clients apply their knowledge to the implementation of technology. For example, I often work side by side with my clients to implement a test program while I train the client's employee test manager to take over after I have left. Once I leave, I have trained my clients to execute an ongoing process, implemented by my associates and me.

Finally, moving back toward the left apex, some temporary staff, while possessed of great expertise, focus their efforts on implementing. The client might secure a "black box" from them—a test tool, for example—but receive little or no training in how it works internally. The sole instruction might consist of how to use the tool.

---

[8]In *The Computer Consultant's Guide*, Janet Ruhl, in her helpful guide to temporary staffing in the high technology world, acknowledges the confusion that exists in the use of words like "temp," "contractor," and "consultant."

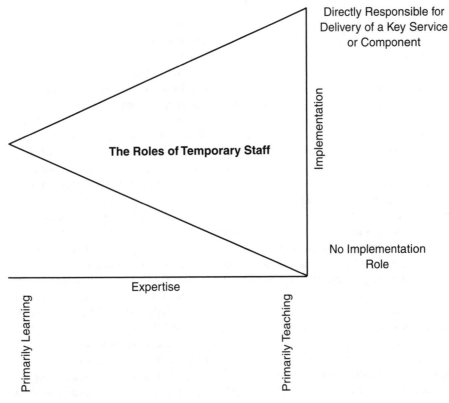

Figure 8.7 Roles of temporary staff.

Long-Term Temporary Workers

Notice that, to a great extent, you can place your permanent staff within this triangle as well. Your team members will probably operate more near the center than at the apexes, or perhaps along the upper edge (from left to right, think test technicians to test engineers). One important distinction will apply, though: you are not the temporary worker's employer, you are the client. This can have powerful implications in terms of how you relate to these folks.

Since we are talking about temporary workers, many of the people who fit this description will be on-site for only a few days. A trainer who teaches your engineers how to use a testing tool, for example, will probably be on-site only for a week or less. A traditional consultant who counsels you on overcoming a particular challenge might likewise spend only a few days. However, there has grown up a class of professionals who work on a contractual, rather than an employee, basis with companies for a few weeks, months, or even years. These workers are temporary in that they have no career path at your company, and will probably leave when their project or assignment is over. They look and act much like typical employees, with some important differences.

Some companies, and people within those companies, adopt dysfunctional outlooks toward these types of temporary workers, from blindness to the distinction to outright resentment at the transitory nature of their engagement. To use long-term temporary workers effectively, it's important to separate emotion and wishes from reality.

First, let's define the terms of the relationship. I'll refer to these long-term temporary workers as "contractors" in the following discussion. In this case, I mean a person who works on a contract, rather than an employee agreement, for some long period of time, usually working as an implementer as much if not more than a change- or knowledge-transfer agent within the company. Contractors are paid by units of time, often hourly, although sometimes by the day or the week. They frequently work on-site, and side by side with employees, in a similar capacity. A contractor is generally brought on for a specific project, and his stay at the company is generally delimited by the duration of the project as well as by his contract. (By this I don't mean to imply that a contractor is not necessarily a consultant, but to emphasis the contractual rather than employee nature of his relationship.) It's usually the case that a contractor's idea of the perfect workplace differs from that of the average permanent employee. While every temporary worker is a human being with unique wants and needs, some generalizations do apply.

One is that money is a different type of motivator for temporary staff than for the average salaried employee. I realize that sounds crass, but the distinction is important. A contractor who works long hours for less than his usual rate will find it difficult to get work at his previous rate once he leaves. One implication of this is that you usually get what you pay for. If you go looking for a bargain, you might find one; perhaps a skilled contractor is new to the temporary world and doesn't know his or her own worth. More likely, though, people who have been around for a while know what they're worth. If you're paying them that much, you're not getting a bargain. If they're taking less than their usual rate because they need the money, they'll probably stick around longer than they should, but eventually they'll leave.

Unless your company works with temporary personnel directly as subcontractors, you should also be aware of agency fees and how they fit into the financial equation. Some agencies collect up-front fees as high as 50 percent of the billing rate. In other words, you might find a contractor's rate of $100 per hour to be steep, but the contractor might be getting only $50 of that rate. Again, you get what you pay for. The $50 per hour you pay to the agency is strictly to cover its profits, the risks that your company will not pay, and the costs of marketing, maintaining an office, and insurance, only the last of which does you any good. (Please note that I'm not talking about testing consultancies, test labs, and other organizations that back up their test teams with knowledgeable consultants who can help with the project—see Chapter 10—but rather "body shops" that provide a contractor from their résumé database based on a keyword match.) In the United States, the only other benefits to your company is protection from retroactive reclassification of subcontractors as employees, either at the instigation of the Internal Revenue Service and from the contractors themselves through a lawsuit. The $50 per hour the contractor receives is for the skills that the individual brings to the job, and that's the skill level you should expect.

Suppose, however, that you are paying $100 an hour to an agency for a contractor whose skills are really worth that amount. In this case, you're actually in worse shape than in the previous example. Temporary workers talk to one another, and they either know the agency's billing rate coming in, find out about it later, or at least have a good idea of what it is. Your contractor, who is not stupid, will discern the situation and will soon leave as a result of being underpaid by the agency. You'll suffer when a key resource disappears in the midst of a project because of a conflict that has nothing to do with you.

If you feel that an agency is offering you a contractor at such a low rate that he will feel short-changed, you might want to consider other candidates, or at the least make sure that this person is not going to be the linchpin of some critical project. You should also ask yourself whether the agency in question makes a practice of such behavior. If so, their placements will probably be an endless source of grief to you. The obvious solution, rectifying the inequity to the contractor, is, unfortunately, quite difficult. First and most importantly, your management will assume you have rocks in your head, or worse, if you negotiate your contractors' rates upward. Second, the agency might increase its rate to you at your request, but pass none of that on to the contractor. (Your contract with the agency might well prohibit you from discussing the contractor's net pay with the contractor.) It might seem like simple greed for an agency to place someone at a low rate, but there are business reasons beyond money. Cheaper contractors are easier to place, and, once they've moved into a higher rate, they often resist moving back down.

Assuming that the pay rate is appropriate, good contractors will stick out almost any assignment, provided that you don't change the rules in the middle of the game or subject them to inhuman harassment. Because these workers don't care about advancement in the company, you don't have to worry about the usual motivators, and you might find that temporary personnel will work hard on assignments that might demotivate or drive out permanent employees. Two factors, however, distinguish acceptable assignments from the ones contractors will fight to keep: intellectual challenges and lots of billable hours. The first applies to all employees, of course; everyone likes to learn and grow on the job. The second, though, is unique to temporary workers. Permanent salaried workers, paid by the week, will put in a certain number of hours willingly and then begin to grumble. If they're too overworked, they'll leave. However, hourly temporary workers usually welcome as many billable hours as you can provide.

You should structure your relationship with contractors (and their agencies) to take account of this situation. On the one hand, if your main concern is meeting a deadline, and you can hire only one contractor, make sure that person is paid hourly and is very motivated by money. To the extent that hard work and long hours can keep your project on schedule, you'll get results. On the other hand, if your main concern is staying within budget, set up a daily or weekly rate. That way, even if the contractor works seven days, you will pay for only 56 hours per week. (Unfortunately, too many managers try to have it both ways: they negotiate a daily or weekly rate and then try to have contractors work 12-hour days. This might work with some temporary staff or for a little while, but, again, you get what you pay for. Eventually, a sharp contractor will understand that seven hours is closer to a full day than 12—so guess what you'll get for your money.)

Contractors' lack of concern with advancement in the company has a downside. Many of these folks pursue a bohemian work style because of their distaste for the office politics needed to make it in many firms. Thus, they often display a real disinclination to participate in any event or exercise that smacks of office intrigue or maneuvering. Team picnics or company dinners are usually safe, but pointless meetings, "face time" with management, and pain-sharing exercises aren't. Let the contractors skip these. You'll get more work out of them, and you'll keep them happy.

Speaking of keeping contractors happy, one school of thought asks, "Why bother? After all, they're leaving eventually." Temporary workers of all stripes are used to "engagements from hell," but you'll get better work from happy people than from unhappy ones, regardless of their employment status. You will also earn whatever loyalty is possible under the circumstances, which you just might need some day.

Speaking of keeping people happy, treating contractors with disrespect or showing envy toward their above-employee pay rates is a mistake. I knew of one manager who openly referred to his contractors as "software whores." He was smiling when he said it, but, needless to say, some of them found it offensive. What type of work and commitment do you think he received from these people?

Should you try to "convert" your best contractors—that is, try to hire them as permanent employees? When I worked as an employee in management roles, I was often under pressure to convert contractors. As a contractor, I have also felt the pressure from the other side, having turned down a number of job offers. And, of course, some temporary workers sign on with a company *hoping* to get an offer.

If you want to convert someone—or if you are under pressure from management to do so—a subtle approach is best. Contractors who want job offers won't need an engraved invitation. They might even bring up the issue themselves. However, some of them would consider an offer insulting and would resent any repeated efforts. These folks usually perceive a job offer as the company's way of saying, "We are paying you more than you are worth." Indeed, saving money is usually management's primary motivation in converting temporary staff. The oft-stated purpose, making sure that the contractors stay around because everyone loves their work so much, is less frequently the real reason.

If an interim staff member turns down a job offer, it doesn't necessarily mean that the individual is getting ready to leave. Many temporary workers are happy to have serially monogamous relationships with clients. Just letting them know that they have a home for as long as they want it will minimize the odds that they will look for other work.

Hiring Contractors

Hiring a contractor is easier than hiring a person for a permanent staff position. It's a lot easier to get permission from management to bring on temporary help because the budget impact is less and the commitment level minimal. If you make a hiring mistake, you can easily let the temporary worker go. That said, any hiring decision should be taken seriously.

The first step in hiring temporary help is realizing that you'll need it. Most project management software, for example, allows you to see your staffing needs during project planning. To revisit the SpeedyWriter project, suppose that you examine the time that will be required from Lin-Tsu to accomplish the tasks that have been assigned to her for this project. As you can see in Figure 8.8, she will be over-allocated for three weeks in the middle of the test effort. This problem needs to be resolved, and bringing on a contractor would make sense.

Although contractors can be brought on board fairly rapidly, you do need to allocate sufficient lead time. If you need someone with basic data entry skills to sit in front of a keyboard and follow a manual test script, you can usually have this person on site in a week or less. However, if you need an experienced test engineer, finding the right con-

Software Cafeteria Test Team
Skills Assessment and Management Worksheet

Legend	0 = No Knowledge	1 = Some Knowledge	2 = Knowledgeable	3 = Expert Knowledge
	R = Required	D = Desirable		
	TT=Test Technician	TM = Test Manager	MTE = Manual Test Engineer	ATE = Automated Test Engr

Skills and Qualifications	TT Minimum Ratings	ATE Minimum Ratings	MTE Minimum Ratings	TM Jake	MTE Lin-Tsu	ATE Bob	MTE Hitesh	STE Maria	Team Minimum	STeam Average
Domain Knowledge										
Word Processing										
Windows Applications	D	1R	2R	3	3	2	1	3	1	2.4
Unix Applications	D	D	D	1	1	3	3	2	1	2.0
Macintosh Applications	D	D	D	0	1	0	3	3	0	1.4
Graphics and Figures	D	1R	2R	2	2	3	2	1	1	2.0
Tables	D	D	1R	1	2	3	2	1	1	1.8
Mathematical/Engineering	D	D	1R	1	3	3	0	0	0	1.4
Document Management										
Windows Applications		D	D	1	2	1	0	2	0	1.2
Unix Applications		D	D	0	0	0	1	1	0	0.4
Macintosh Applications		D	D	0	0	0	1	1	0	0.4
Other		D	D	0	0	0	0	1	0	0.2
Hierarchical Storage Management		D	D	1	2	0	0	3	0	1.2
Document Interchange										
Windows Applications		D	D	1	2	1	0	3	0	1.4
Unix Applications		D	D	1	0	0	1	3	0	1.0
Macintosh Applications		D	D	0	0	0	1	3	0	0.8
Domain Knowledge										
Printing										
Color	D	D	D	0	0	1	1	2	0	0.8
Laser	D	D	D	1	1	1	1	2	1	1.2
Inkjet	D	D	D	1	1	1	1	2	1	1.2
Publishing/Binding		D	D	0	0	0	1	2	0	0.6
Web Publishing										
HTML	D	D	D	1	3	3	2	3	1	2.4
XML		D	D	1	3	3	0	2	0	1.8
Other		D	D	1	1	3	0	2	0	1.4
Average Domain Knowledge				0.8	1.3	1.3	1.0	2.0	0.3	1.3
Technical Expertise										
Programming										
C/VB (3GL)	D	1R	D	2	2	3	2	3	2	2.4
Java/C++ (OO)	D	1R	D	0	1	3	2	2	0	1.6
Shell (Tcl/Ksh) Scripting	D	2R	D	3	2	3	2	2	2	2.4
Code Complexity and Metrics		1R	D	2	0	0	2	2	0	1.2
Operating Systems										
Windows	D	1R	1R	2	3	2	1	2	1	2.0
Linux	D	1R	1R	2	2	1	3	2	1	2.0
Solaris	D	1R	1R	2	1	1	1	2	1	1.4
Mac OS	D	D	D	0	2	0	3	3	0	1.6
Other	D	D	D	1	1	0	3	3	0	1.6
Networking/Internetworking										
TCP/IP, FTP, RCP (Internet Architecture)		1R	1R	2	1	1	1	1	1	1.2
Browsers (NS, IE, etc.)	1R	1R	1R	2	3	2	2	1	1	2.0
Network Application Architecture (Tiered)		1R	1R	2	3	2	1	1	1	1.8
Network Hardware		1R	1R	2	3	2	1	1	1	1.8
Systems and Servers										
Java-based Web Servers		1R	1R	1	3	1	1	3	1	1.8
Database Servers		1R	1R	2	3	1	1	3	1	2.0
Mainframe		1R	1R	1	2	1	1	3	1	1.6
Average Technical Expertise				1.6	2.0	1.4	1.7	2.1	0.9	1.8

Figure 8.8 An example of resource over-allocation for the SpeedyWriter project.

tractor will take at least a month—or, more likely, two months if you have exacting skill requests such as the ability to use GUI automation tools, if you need someone with an advanced technical degree, or if you require specific content expertise in areas such as security or usability.

Once you find the perfect person, establishing a business relationship between your employer and the temporary worker can be quite complex, as illustrated in Figure 8.9. (The following information is primarily applicable to the United States. Janet Ruhl's book contains similar information for Canadian and British contractors.) The top two circles and the upper arrow show a test manager's relationship with the company—in this case, the manager is a permanent employee of the firm. The rest of the drawing shows the various business relationships that can be set up between temporary personnel and a client. At least one of these relationship paths must exist before the temporary worker can do one billable minute's work for you.

The simplest relationship appears in the center of the figure, directly below the client company. The temporary worker is self-employed as the sole proprietor of his or her own business. Your company, the client, has a direct relationship with this business. If you are in the United States, at the end of the year, your company sends the worker a 1099 Federal tax form, not the W-2 form the test manager and other perma-

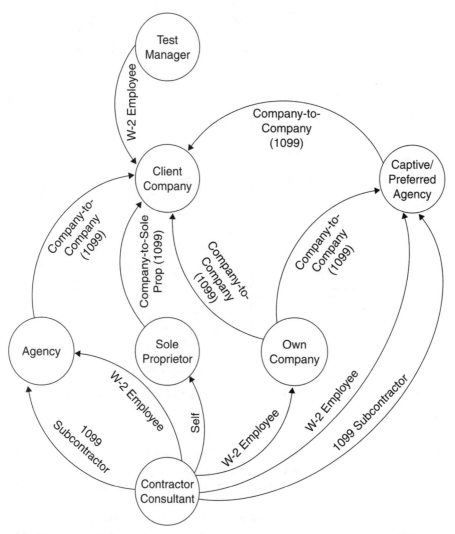

Figure 8.9 Typical business relationships between a temporary worker and a client company.

nent employees receive. Consequently, this worker is often called a "1099 subcontractor." This relationship is much like the one a homeowner might have with a house painter, or the one a car owner might have with an individual (independent) mechanic.

To the immediate right of this relationship is a variation in which the temporary worker's business is incorporated. In that case, he or she works for the business as an employee. At the end of the year, your company sends the worker's business a 1099.

The indirect relationship shown at the far left of the figure is probably the most common. Here the individual works for an agency, either as a 1099 subcontractor or a W-2 employee. It's likely that the agency received your job requirements, matched them to the contractor's résumé in its database, and sent the person to see you. If you hire that worker, your company pays the agency, and the agency—after pocketing its margin—pays the worker.

You might ask, "What's the point of the middleman?"—especially when you consider that margins can run as high as 50 percent. There are several advantages for the contractors. For example, they receive marketing services: they don't have to go out looking for clients; instead, the agency finds the clients for them. Temporary workers can also receive other benefits such as group insurance, a 401(k) plan, and an employer-of-record, which can help with getting credit. (Especially if you have no track record, being self-employed can make buying a car or a house difficult.) Finally, contractors working for some temporary agencies are guaranteed payment on a regular schedule, regardless of when and whether the client pays.

Your company also receives benefits, in the form of three safeguards. The first is protection from the United States Internal Revenue Service. If your company works directly with temporary personnel, the IRS can, under some circumstances, retroactively classify those people as employees and then fine your company heavily for not withholding taxes from their pay. The second is protection from the temporary personnel themselves. In the past, some of these workers have sued past clients, claiming that they were really employees and thus were entitled to participate in benefit programs, especially stock option programs. The client companies have sometimes lost these lawsuits, to the tune of considerable sums of money. (This is an unfortunate situation whereby the litigants have, basically, taken millions of dollars out of the pockets of their fellow contractors and deposited it into the pockets of temporary agencies.) People who are the employees of an agency during their work with your company have less chance of successfully bringing such a suit. The third protection is that the agency generally carries insurance on its contractors, which can mean that if a clumsy contractor slips and breaks a bone, your company isn't facing an expensive lawsuit. (Your employees are probably covered under your workman's compensation plan and your corporate liability insurance, but contractors might not be.)

To the far right in Figure 8.9 is a variation on the worker/agency/client model. In this case, your company works only with a single, internal "captive" agency or a small set of preferred agencies. All temporary workers must be employed through these agencies, whether the worker operates as a sole proprietor or as an incorporated business. This arrangement provides all the advantages of the agency model just described, but with the added benefit of allowing your company to keep the accounts payable simple and, if desired, to control or at least curb the agencies' margins.

This arrangement has its drawbacks, however. It's usually true that people who don't have to compete for a client's business soon take it for granted. By limiting the pool of agencies, your company will pay a price in terms of service. The temporary workers also pay a price in that the agency, while collecting a margin from fees that arguably belong to the workers, has done little or nothing to market these people and has no incentive to keep them happy in order to place them at other companies later. Moreover, by limiting the pool of agencies, this arrangement limits the pool of available candidates. An agency's database is its most prized possession, and agencies do not all have access to the same pool of talent.

As if all this weren't complicated enough, you should be aware that the business relationship between the temporary worker and the client is often not immaterial to the contractor. Some temporary personnel work only on a 1099 basis; others work only as W-2 employees. Some will not work through agencies at all; others work only through agencies. Sometimes workers prefer or avoid specific agencies because of positive or negative past experiences. All these factors can complicate and even scuttle your attempts to hire the best temporary help.

Bringing on the Experts

On occasion, you will find yourself confronted by a situation beyond your ability. You don't need extra hands to accomplish a task; rather, you need extra knowledge. In these cases, you need someone who fits into the right sector of the triangle in . This person would be a "consultant" in the traditional meaning of the term. How do you pick the right one? How do you find someone who can actually solve your problem?

First and foremost, it's important to be clear about the problem you want the consultant to help you solve, and how you expect her to help you solve it. In some cases, you want the consultant to assess your difficulties and advise you on possible solutions. Alternatively, you might want the consultant to train you or your team. For example, I work with an accountant in my consulting business, and I often call him with questions about how to stay out of trouble with the United States' Internal Revenue Service. He tells me what I need to do, and I do it. This type of activity is *consulting* in the original sense of the word, transferring knowledge, teaching me. I also use this same accountant to do my corporate and personal taxes. In this case, he is acting as a practitioner. He is still bringing special expertise to my needs—I have no aptitude for or desire of mastering the intricacies of tax law—but he is applying that knowledge directly to benefit me, rather than teaching me to help myself.

A consultant on a software or hardware development project likewise can be heavily involved in implementation or not at all. In my practice, most of consulting does involve implementation as well as teaching my clients. On some projects, I have come on board ostensibly to teach, and then found that I actually needed to help the client build and manage their test team. I consider myself a "consultant" regardless.

Whatever you call an expert, the distinguishing quality is exactly that: expertise. This person brings knowledge to your relationship that you don't have, and that's exactly what you want. However, it is essential that you figure out whether this person or consulting group is bringing the *right* knowledge.

Making this determination is not easy. A consultant might have as much trouble figuring out how to help you as you have trouble figuring out what help you need. (Gerald Weinberg's book, *The Secrets of Consulting*, can help you resolve this and other consulting paradoxes.) Most consultants want to avoid having clients that, for some weird reason, "just didn't work out." However, the high fee you paid an inappropriate consultant without any tangible benefit could doom your test operation.

This requires some advance thinking. You need to define in your mind the problem you want solved. If it's an implementation problem, make sure you define it that way. I once hired a consultant to work with me on an MTBF demonstration plan without taking this important first step. He did not expect actually to have to write the plan, which was exactly what I needed him to do. It was an engagement that "just didn't work out," and I had to replace him.

Given a definition of the problem, you can assess what type of expertise you need. It also has implications on what type of person you need. A knowledge-transfer problem, such as training you to use a new test tool, requires not just a person skilled in the use of the tool, but also a person who is an effective communicator of ideas. In contrast, an implementation problem, such as building an automated test suite using a new test tool, requires the same type of skill in terms of the tool, but you can retain a person less suited to communicating if you find someone who can produce such a test suite in a short period of time.

With the problem clearly defined, you must extensively interview any prospective experts, expensive or not, before signing a contract. In addition to getting to the bottom of the softer side, such as teaching abilities and fit with the company culture, you will need to satisfy yourself that they do indeed have the right level of proficiency in terms of any tools that will be used or technology that will be involved. Because they are the expert, not you, you might not know enough about the topic at hand. In that case, you'll need to complement your discussions with them by talking to their references. If they can provide you with the name and telephone number of a past client for whom they solved a similar problem, you can satisfy yourself that they can solve your problem by talking to this person.

Interviewing an expert is different from interviewing a contractor or permanent employee. A prospective consultant might want to put on a presentation, have you visit his site, or meet with some of his associates. All these are good ideas, but it's important that you stay focused on the problem, as you've defined it in your mind, and how the expert or experts can help.

When interviewing consultants for implementation engagements, you should also be on guard against bait-and-switch tactics. Ask the person doing the pitch, "Are you the consultant who will actually do the work?" If someone else will be brought in, this might not be a problem, but you should reserve the right to talk directly to that person. Don't allow a situation in which the consulting business can put anyone who needs a few billable hours on your job. This might be just another project to the consulting company, but it's your livelihood.

Another danger is the overpaid neophyte. You might have seen the advertisements by a Big Six consulting firm that compared their competitors' staff to elementary school children in terms of their innocence and lack of experience. This is humorous in the abstract, but you won't find it funny if you discover one day that you are paying $200 an hour for the "expertise and experience" of someone who just graduated from college. Insist that the consultants on your project have a proven record of accomplishment in solving the types of problems you're facing. Again, reserve the right to interview every consultant who will work on your project.

After all, whether your staff is comprised of temporary or permanent employees, technicians, or senior engineers, they are part of your test team. Far from being interchangeable bit players, each of them, and all of them together, hold the success of your test organization in their hands as much as you do. While effective management cannot be discounted, neither can the importance of any participant in a team effort. Leadership is the art of getting work done through others.

Case Study

On one project, my associates and I tested an information appliance. This system was comprised of set of a back-end servers to which the clients would connect, giving the users access to the Internet, email, and other services. See Figure 8.10 for an illustration of the system under test, its basic architecture, and the test team.

Starting from the left side of the figure, one thing we wanted to test was actual user experience in the field. For this reason, one of the test engineers worked on usability testing from various outside locations.

Another thing we needed to test was scalability and performance of the servers. As commercial tools were not available to do the type of load generation and probing we needed, we had to write some of the load and performance tests, which talked directly to the servers. The two test toolsmiths were in charge of this effort.

Finally, most of the test execution was actually done by test technicians against the appliances themselves in the test lab. We used primarily scripted manual tests—albeit some were actually manual probes done while performance and load tools hit the servers hard, letting the manual testers know what the user experience would be like at full look. We also did some amount of exploratory testing. For example, the test manager (me) and the appliance and server lead test engineers would spend an hour a day each following our hunches to find bugs and simply using the system the way we thought users would. We often managed to find bugs that had eluded scripted tests this way.

Now look at Figure 8.11. Notice how the organization chart follows the architecture of the system under test and the test work being done. I believe this is fairly typical of a well-structured test team. You can achieve this type of flexibility using either the skills-oriented or project-oriented model discussed in this chapter.

I thank my client, who wishes to remain anonymous, for permission to discuss this project here. I also thank my client contacts for their excellent support and steady leadership on this project. Finally, thanks to my test team for their professionalism and excellence on this project.

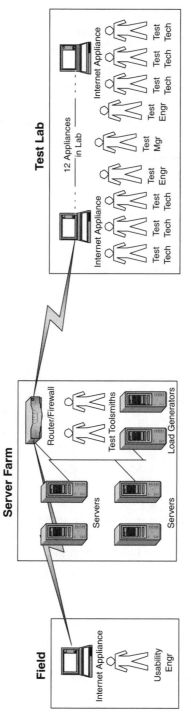

Figure 8.10 System architecture and test team.

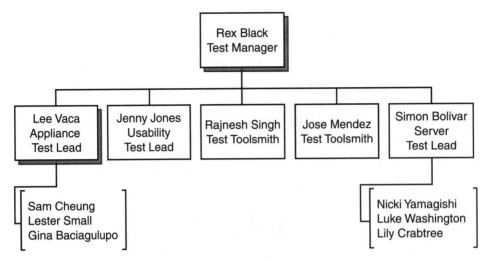

Figure 8.11   The information appliance test team organization.

Exercises

1. Discuss how well your personal attitudes fit into the qualifications of professional pessimism, balanced curiosity, and ability to focus.

2. Sketch a critical skills worksheet for testing a video game. Sketch the worksheet for testing control software for an automated factory. Compare and contrast, commenting on the similarities and differences.

3. Calculate the defect detection percentage for your test team on a recent project, using three months as the time window for 90 percent of the customer-discovered bugs to arrive. (See Chapter 4 for a refresher on how to calculate this metric.)

   ■ Calculate without adjusting for scope limitations. In other words, every unique, true bug found by customers in the first three months counts "against" the DDP.

   ■ Recalculate, eliminating from the customer-discovered bug count any bugs that were out of scope or could not have reasonably been found during the test effort.

   ■ Propose and describe a reasonable bonus system based on one of these DDP calculations.

4. Find a partner and practice some of the interviewing techniques discussed in this chapter. Figures 8.12 through 8.17 present a sequence of job descriptions and

---

Test Automation Engineer

Roles and Responsibilities

Participate in a test automation tool selection process.

Develop and execute automated tests using the selected tool.

Integrate the test suites into the test management system and custom test harnesses.

Education

B.Sc. in computer science, computer engineering, or electrical engineering, or two additional years experience, or tester certification.

Experience and Skills

Five or more years experience in test automation.

Unix test experience required, ideally including development of custom automated test systems using scripting languages like ksh, csh, tcl, etc.

Internet test experience highly desirable, including development of automated test tools.

Expertise Required

A demonstrated career commitment to testing and/or quality assurance is preferred. The candidate should show a familiarity with state-of-the-art testing theory and practice, and be able to discuss how she applied the ideas in her previous positions.

Other

Dress is business-casual and hours are flexible. Some weekends and evenings will be required.

Figure 8.12   Test automation engineer job description.

résumés; each résumé matches or is a fit for the preceding job description. (These materials are available for your convenience on the Web site.) Pick a job description/résumé pair with your partner and try out some of the ideas in this chapter. If you have access to a computer and the test cases and bug reports from previous chapters, use those for an audition exercise. If you want to make it interesting, have the interviewee exhibit positive or negative behaviors related to the job. Positive behaviors include appropriate humor, a friendly demeanor, genuine enthusiasm, active questioning, and an organized approach to the interview. Negative behaviors include lack of interest, greed, tiredness, jitters and nervousness, disorganization, and outright dishonesty. At the end of the exercise, make the hiring decision and explain why.

Test Automator

Professional experience

2000 - Present   Denial180   Buffalo, NY
Senior Test Engineer, Consultant
- Developed testware for proprietary SDK. Developed a test system to dynamically generate test cases for a web-based app. Developed data driven GUI automation test tool using Segue SilkTest.Set up initial load tests using Segue SilkPerformer.

1999 - 2000   DefunctBank   Providence, RI
Senior Test Engineer, Consultant
- Evaluated and implemented testing tools, specifically test automation, incident tracking and SCM. Developed functional, load, and performance tests for a web-based financial application using Mercury Interactive LoadRunner.

1999   Ford Motor Credit   Detroit, MI
Senior Test Engineer, Consultant
- Develop testing and quality assurance processes for client/server application development environment. Evaluated automated test tools, made recommendation for purchase and defined test automation infrastructure.

1998 - 1999   Star69   Calgary, Alberta
Senior Test Engineer, Consultant
- Develop test plans and automated and manual test procedures for client/server application used in a proprietary telephony system. Test environment is QA Partner on NT 4.0.

1998 - 1999   BFSP Software＊   Wimberdoodle, PA
Quality Assurance Engineer
- Develop test plans and automated and manual test procedures for database migration, update, and conversion utilities. Test environment was QA Partner on NT 4.0 and Windows 98 clients.

1996 - 1998   DefenseGiant   Seattle, WA
Quality Assurance Engineer
- Develop test plans and automated and manual test procedures for an military records system and supporting utilities. Evaluated defect tracking systems to select Test environment was Windows NT 4.0/3.51 and Windows 9x clients with HPUX Oracle servers using QA Partner.

1994 - 1996   BigTestCompany   Orlando, FL
Quality Assurance Engineer
- Develop test plans and automated and manual test procedures for various Intersolv PVCS products, including Version Manager and Tracker. Test environment was QA Partner on Windows NT 4.0 and 3.51 and Windows 95 and 3.1.

1989 - 1994   DenseByte   Albuquerque, NM
Quality Assurance Engineer
- Develop, maintain, and perform test procedures on Density, a database retrieval and report generation system. Test environment was AutoTester, UNIX shell scripts, VMS DCL, and C on UNIX, VMS, DOS, and Windows.

1988 - 1989   DenseByte   Albuquerque, NM
Programmer Analyst
- Developed software using proprietary pattern recognition utilities. Applications included database research system. All development was done using C on PCs.

Figure 8.13   Test automator engineer résumé.

| 1988 - 1988 | Depends | Albuquerque, NM |

Programmer Analyst
- Developed enhancements and performed system maintenance on PCs for life insurance illustration application. Converted application from FORTRAN to C.

| 1986 - 1988 | Big Massive Utility | Albuquerque, NM |

Programmer Analyst
- Developed interprocessor communication control software, using FORTRAN on VAX./VMS, for a SCADA gas and electrical operations system. Communications applications included graphic display, remote transmission unit, and user application support for system services.

| 1986 - 1986 | Scorpion Tech | Albuquerque, NM |

Programmer Analyst
- Participated in development of a point of sale system controlled by a SWTPC 68010- based processor.

| 1985 - 1986 | Labyrinth, Inc. | Albuquerque, NM |

Programmer Analyst
- Assisted in the design and coding of a fourth generation language and applications development system for PCs. Developed user documentation.

| 1984 - 1985 | TelComSwitch | Albuquerque, NM |

Programmer Analyst
- Developed and maintained user interface software for the host computer of a telecommunications system. Designed and developed software to support the Distributed Architecture ACD86 1.3. Coordinated with technical writers to ensure completeness and accuracy of the user documentation.

| 1981 - 1984 | DatumSphere | Albuquerque, NM |

Software Certification Specialist
- Certified software for telecommunication systems; established requirements and procedures for testing, reviewing and analyzing design and functional specifications; designed and coded test systems.

| 1979 - 1981 | Chaos Computing | Phoenix, AZ |

Programmer Analyst
- Developed and maintained software for an interactive mapping graphics system. Designed and developed software to access the graphical and non-graphical databases and reformat information for reporting.

| 1979 - 1979 | Forko | Albuquerque, NM |

Programmer Analyst
- Developed and maintained software for academic use, principally interactive programs for scientific and business applications. Consultant to faculty and students.

| 1978 - 1979 | Brianiac Univ. | Wimberdoodle, PA |

Programmer Analyst
- Developed a real-time data acquisition program for heart research. Developed data analysis software to support the acquisition program.

| **Papers** | November, 1996 | EuroConference | Paris, France |

"Integrated Test Automation" co-authored with Bob Jones, Jenna Brucker, and Hemamalini Chowdry.

| **Education** | 1975 – 1977 | Brianiac Univ. | Wimberdoodle, PA |

BA Criminology

Figure 8.13 *Continued*

Lead Test Engineer

Roles and Responsibilities
Lead test case development and execution by less-experienced test engineers and technicians in a Windows/Web environment.

Assist the test manager in reporting test results to management and technical staff.

Education
B.Sc. in computer science, computer engineering, or electrical engineering, or two additional years experience, or tester certification.

Experience
Four+ years experience in test engineering, developing and executing test cases, test tools, and test suites, including lead roles.

Windows test experience and knowledge of Windows technology required.

Familiarity with Internet technologies like HTML, streaming audio/video, browsers, etc., required.

Internet test experience highly desirable.

Experience with e-commerce highly desirable.

Expertise Required
A demonstrated career commitment to testing and/or quality assurance is preferred. The candidate should show a familiarity with state-of-the-art testing theory and practice, and be able to discuss how she applied the ideas in her previous positions.

Other
Dress is business-casual and hours are flexible. Some weekends and evenings will be required. Lead may need to provide direction to evening or graveyard test shift.

Figure 8.14 Lead test engineer job description.

Test Lead

OBJECTIVE To acquire a position as a **Test Engineer.**

WORK EXPERIENCE

Aug 2000 to
Present

Starsearch
Test Engineer (Software)
- Responsible for interviewing, hiring and placing candidates in various test positions within the company.
- Develop and managed manual test cases for astrological software.
- Manage a team of technicians in their daily duties.
- Attend meetings with developers and managers for risk assessment of product.
- Ensure that specific elements of the product are thoroughly tested per the Test Plan documentation.
- Review bug reports from the test technicians for errors prior to them being entered into the tracking software.
- Revise current test cases to reflect changes made to the Test Plan documentation for new functionality and performace issues..

Jun 1999 to
Aug 2000

Radio.com Inc.
Test Engineer (Hardware/Software)
- Develop, execute and manage manual test cases.
- Manage a team of test technicians in their daily duties.
- Attend meetings with developers and managers for risk assessment and candidate release of product.
- Ensure that all elements of the product are thoroughly tested per the requirements documentation.
- Maintain a tracking matrices containing relevant information as it pertains to the test cases and suites.
- Review bug reports from the test technicians for errors prior to them being entered into the tracking software.
- Revise current test cases to reflect changes made to the requirements documentation for new functionality.
- Provision test devices using Linux operating system for use in a systems test lab.

Jan 1999 to
May 1999

Wigglewham Computer Corporation
System Test Engineer (Portables)
- Responsibilities include testing all components of Wigglewham Longitude and Depresion computers for functionality with all operating systems.
- Refer problems and possible solutions with the system to the proper department
- Send and receive bug reports to and from Microsoft and to work with them to resolve problems with the Operating system as it relates to Wigglewham systems.
- Troubleshoot all aspects of the operating system for possible conflicts.
- Attend meetings with other heads of department for "brain storming" possible ways to correct problems with the systems.

May 1996 to
Dec. 1998

Bumblediddle USA CORPORATION
Mobile Computing Team Leader
- Performed phone support for end users owning the Bumblediddle HomelyPCs and Limitias as well as the Bumblediddle HomelyPC 72 and Limitia 89 series notebook computers along with all Bumblediddle models.

Figure 8.15 Lead test engineer résumé.

- Handled escalated customers from the team level as well as Corporate Escalations that have contacted Bumblediddle USA's Corporate Facilities.
- Conducted failure analysis of software and hardware issues and instructs end users on the proper resolution.
- Hands on repair of escalated issues that the Technicians in our Repair Depots have been unable to duplicate.
- Assisted Team Members under my supervision in the resolution to technical issues.
- Provided direct communications between the Customer Service Line and Advanced Product Support on the resolution to issues unresolvable by associated Analyst.
- Tracked subordinates phone statistics: consisting of call times as well as quality assurance of each Team Members obligations under my management.
- Additional training includes HomelyPC 7000 New Product Training, Limitia 610 New Product Training, Networking and Supporting Windows NT core Technologies.
- Advanced Product Support Liaison for the Call center. Troubleshooting problems with the systems that the analyst find are reoccurring and take them up with engineers to find answers.

Jan. 1976 to
Jan. 1996   **U. S. Army**
- Provided direct supervision for 155 soldiers in an Air Defense Battery.
- Was responsible for accountability and maintenance of over 1.7 billion dollars worth of equipment.
- Trained new recruits in the proper ways and values of the military way of life.
- Was required to submit a 6-week training schedule to my superiors for my battery.
- Received numerous awards for best-maintained and trained battery within the Division.

EDUCATION & TRAINING
Extensive experience in Solaris 2.5, 2.6, 2.8, Irix, Oracle, Windows, NT, Windows 2000, Dos, Linux 6.1, SQL 7, and Perl. I also have some knowledge of TCL and Exceed.

August 1997   Tex-R-Us Education Centers
Supporting Windows NT 4.0 core technologies.
Philadelphia, Pennsylvania

Mar 1997   Microsoft
Windows 95 Certification
Wimberdoodle, Pennsylvania

Mar 1999   Microsoft
Microsoft MCSE
Wimberdoodle, Pennsylvania

July 1983 to   University of Wyoming (correspondence)
Jan 1996   Information Technology (BA)
Business Administration. (AA)

REFERENCES   Will be furnished upon request.

Figure 8.15   *Continued*

Test Technician

Roles and Responsibilities
Participate in test case development and execution in a Windows/Web environment.

Assist the lead test engineer in gathering and formatting information for test results reporting.

Education
Degree or technical certification desirable but not required.

Experience
Previous experience in test engineering, developing and executing test cases, test tools, and test suites is a plus.

Windows test experience or knowledge of Windows technology required.

Familiarity with Internet technologies like HTML, streaming audio/video, browsers, etc., required.

Internet test experience highly desirable.

Experience with e-commerce highly desirable.

Expertise Required
Ideal position for new-career or second-career person looking to enter the software business. Be organized, responsible, able to take and follow directions, and eager to learn.

Other
Dress is business-casual.

Position may require some evening or graveyard test shift work.

Figure 8.16 Test technician job description.

TEST TECHNICIAN

OBJECTIVE: To obtain a position that will utilize my current and future computer skills while allowing me to learn and grow as a productive member of the organization.

SPECIAL
SKILLS:

General: Typing 75 WPM, ability to work on own, ability to learn quickly, organizational skills.

Software: Windows NT, 95, 98 and 3.1, DOS, HTML, PERL, UNIX, Linux CorelDraw, TCP/IP, Adobe PhotoShop, Illustrator, Pagemaker, Freehand Quark XPress, C++, SQL, Front Page.

Hardware: Microtek, UMAX & Epson Scanners, IBM AT & PC, Macintosh Plus & Power PC, IBM Laser 4019, HP Lasers, IBM Proprint, Epson

ACHIEVEMENTS:

February 26th 1998 – Wigglewham Certificate of Completion of XYZ Training
February 1999 – Wigglewham Recognition of Outstanding Service Award
FY '99 Q3 and Q4 Wigglewham's Service Roundtable

Built a successful business with only a $2000 Student loan for the past 10 years and still maintain my first client to whom utilized my services.

Learned the Software required to create my own virtual website for my business in less than two weeks.

During the lean beginning years and after deciding to close business, worked for several temp agencies around town, and became known as the person they could send out on any job and their customer would be satisfied with my work performance.

WORK EXPERIENCE:

March 2000 – Present
Graphic Designer/Typesetter
Printy-Pro
Wimberdoodle, Pennsylvania
Responsible for color separating customer's artwork; designing of logos; page layouts and design for press ready art. Website development and troubleshooting. Technical support for in-house computers, both Mac G3 & G4 and PC.

February 1998 – December 1999
Sr. XYZ Technician
Wigglewham Computer Corporation
Wimberdoodle, PA
Responsible for customer's satisfaction by effective resolution Wigglewham's major account customer's of computer related problems. Identified and recognized the CIH virus prior to the publication of it's existence in the United States. Ensure proper escalation procedures are followed. Perform assigned functions according to standardized policies and procedures. Analytical ability is required in order to re-

Figure 8.17 Test technician résumé.

solve technical issues. Works on routine and semi-routine assignments requiring basic analytical ability to resolve routine to moderately complex technical issues. Normally receives little instruction on routine to moderately complex technical issues. Designed and created the logo for group's identification. Have received numerous accommodations from both customers and Wigglewham for identifying problems with systems that other technicians had not. Designed and maintained the group's website and the website for SelectCare services.

March 1989 – November 1999
Owner
Ingenious Abacus
Wimberdoodle, PA
Built 386, 486 and Pentium computers for business use; maintained, troubleshot and researched all systems, printers and other equipment necessary for the daily operations of business; installed and troubleshot all OS and software programs; creation and maintenance of virtual website; programmed web pages using HTML and PERL codes; creation of web forms and CGI-bin manipulations; creation of advertising design layout, graphic design and computer fonts via CorelDraw, LviewPro and Microtek scanner for clientele and business related uses; customized Quicken financial software, Personnel management of up to 3 employees; extensive word processing and database management for creating and management of clientele's wedding invitations using Onfile and WordPerfect 5.1; Sales; Office organization; Payroll; Bookkeeping; Customer Relations; etc

Aug 1998 – Dec 1998
Computer Illustrator
Brainiac University
Wimberdoodle, PA
Graphic design of Engineer's schematics and documentation for publication Technical writing adaptation, editing for the multiple required formats of technical publications

Dec 1996 - Feb 1998
Cohiba Staffing Services
Wimberdoodle, PA
Temporary service; worked in Law firms, as graphic designer and various other offices and positions.

Nov 1988 – March 1990
Rent-A-Geek Staffing
Wimberdoodle, PA
Temporary service.

EDUCATION: Wigglewham's Professional Course work (Computer architecture, MS SQL & NT Core)
1998 – Present: Brainiac University – Pursuing CS BS Degree
Wimberdoodle Community College
1988-90 Raleigh Dole-Jackson Business College
1984 Poorsville Sr. College
North Pine Sr. High School

Figure 8.17 *Continued*

The Triumph of Politics: Organizational Challenges for Test Managers

"Office politics." We all use the phrase, usually to connote something negative about a coworker, department, or company. At one time or another, we've all undoubtedly made a comment such as this: "Oh, you know Jim—he's so *political.*"

To some extent, I hesitate to use the term *politics*—the euphemisms *management considerations* or *soft skills* seem less negative— but the word is apt for three reasons. First, as a manager, you must be sensitive to political realities, some of which are unique to test management. Second, politics in the electoral sense is described as "the art of compromise," and that is certainly an art you must master in a typical hardware or software development organization. Finally, politics is also the art of managing relationships that involve power, authority, and responsibility.

Don Quixote, Champion of Quality: What's Your Job, Anyhow?

Don Quixote, the immortal character created by Miguel Cervantes, is a minor Spanish nobleman who decides that he is by birth a knight-errant. Venturing forth on a quest with his squire Sancho Panza, he stumbles into a series of misadventures, jousting with a giant who is actually a windmill, and defending the honor of a maiden named Dulcinea who turns out to be a prostitute.

I admit that I've held some quixotic positions in my career. The most notable came with the title "Quality Assurance Manager." I considered myself the test manager, while everyone else drew his or her own conclusions about what I was to do. With the budget I had, I was lucky to do a passable job of testing. One of my development manager peers suggested that I focus on working with the programmers to build a higher level of quality in the product, but I wasn't appropriately staffed for that role. What my managers wanted me to do, specifically, and how I would know that I was succeeding—in other words, the scope of my job—remained undefined. This was a political error on my part.

I have drawn my own boundaries too widely once or twice as well. It's tempting to decide that you, the test manager, are the lone defender of product integrity. From the point at which you make this decision, it's but a short ride to the windmill and Dulcinea. Looking back on these events, I feel vaguely embarrassed that I took myself so seriously while playing Don Quixote. Again, the error was political, in that I didn't clarify with my management what purpose my organization and I served.

The role and responsibilities of a test manager must be unambiguous. I have had the most success when I defined my role clearly and specifically with my managers and then communicated those boundaries to my peers and to my team. Whenever an issue arose that started to blur the boundaries, I reconfirmed my understanding.

The title you hold and the name of your group are important to drawing these boundaries. Titles and names are organizational shorthand, code words that have real implications. These abbreviations signify: the missions the management team expects a person or group to serve; the benefits the company expects to accrue from that person's or group's activities; and the strategic reason for the presence of that person or group. Your title and the name of your group are short answers to the question, "What do they pay you to do?"[1]

If your title is "Test Manager" or some variant of that designation, the boundaries are partially drawn right away. In such a situation, once you ensure clear ownership of the various phases of testing—unit, component, integration, and system, for example—you should know exactly what tasks you own. By reinforcing these perimeters in your test plans, using "Is/Is Not" tables and entry, continuation, and exit criteria (as discussed in Chapter 2, "Plotting and Presenting Your Course: The Test Plan"), you clarify what the test team will do. And, just as important, you clarify what your team will *not* do.

Be aware, though, that people sometimes use the word *test* to reach beyond the typical scope of writing and evaluating test cases against live, executable systems, hardware or software. One test authority, Bill Hetzel, defines requirements reviews, design reviews, and code reviews as tests.[2] It makes sense to investigate expectations in this regard. If your managers and peers think along the lines of Hetzel's definition, this expanded scope will have significant implications for the minimum skill set your test engineers must possess. The increased critical skills in the areas of application domain and technological expertise

---

[1]For an excellent discussion of this issue, see Johanna Rothman's article, "What Do They Pay You to Do," in Software Testing and Quality Engineering magazine, Volume 3, Issue 3 (September/October 2001), pages 64 and 63, which can now be found on www.stickyminds.com.
[2]In Bill Hetzel's *The Complete Guide to Software Testing*, Chapters 4, 5, and 6 specifically discuss reviews, requirements, and designs.

should show up in your critical skills assessment worksheet (discussed in Chapter 8, "Staffing and Managing a Test Team").

If your title contains the word *quality*, be careful. The title "Quality Control Manager" is safe, because most people understand quality control to mean testing to find defects. However, the title "Quality Assurance Manager" leaves many questions open, as I discovered. Quality assurance (QA) is not only the location of bugs through testing—it also involves the prevention of bugs. Some might say that in addition, it includes actively ensuring the continuous improvement of product quality. In the strictest sense, quality control is concerned with product, quality assurance with process.

The IEEE Standard 610.12-1990 points out this difference. Quality assurance is defined as, "(1) A planned and systematic pattern of all actions necessary to provide adequate confidence that an item or product conforms to established technical requirements. (2) A set of activities designed to evaluate the process by which products are developed or manufactured. Contrast with: quality control." The first definition includes testing, but also other activities, such as code reviews or inspections, which contribute to and measure product quality. The second definition is entirely procedural, with the emphasis on processes that enable quality. This implies that the quality assurance group has a role in ensuring conformance to best software or hardware development practices throughout the organization, often well beyond the development team itself. Quality control, conversely, is defined as "A set of activities designed to evaluate the quality of developed or manufactured products. Contrast with: quality assurance." (A caveat, though, is that IEEE's definition for quality control includes the following: "Note: This term has no standardized meaning in software engineering at this time.")

I won't make a blanket statement warning you never to take a job as a QA manager. If you accept such a job, however, be sure to work carefully with your managers and peers up front in an effort to understand and guide their expectations. In the beginning, you will probably find that their expectations are not congruent with each other's or with yours. Moreover, if you are the first QA manager the company has ever had, management's expectations of your ability to affect product quality will very likely be inconsistent with its forecast of your budgetary needs.

Suppose that you are offered a job with the title "Director of Quality" or "Chief Quality Officer." However you slice it, such a job entails corporation-wide management of product and service quality. To succeed, you'll require sufficient authority and standing to work with the entire organization in defining processes, and sometimes this will involve cajoling and even dictating to your peers that process will be followed. You will also need sufficient staff and other resources to do a thorough, professional job of testing as well as the not insignificant amount of quality management work. Don't plan on shoehorning the quality roles into the workload of your existing test engineers and technicians. Besides not having time for such tasks, they might not be qualified, either.

If I held the title "Quality Assurance Manager" but believed that my authority and resources supported only test activities, I would try to change my title. I would gather some case studies about what a true quality management role entails, which would provide some ammunition to convince my manager that my role didn't match this description. If my managers insisted that I keep the title but didn't give me the requisite authority and resources, I would resign. I see no point to holding a position in which I'm bound to fail.

Finally, an aside on ethical implications: If you do accept a role that has wide-ranging quality assurance responsibilities, make sure you know enough about formal quality management. For example, I spent time in the early 1990s studying Total Quality Management, and stay current on the topic just in case. You will also need to understand the entire development process and current best practices in your industry. However, a few weeks of training will not qualify you to implement a company-wide quality program. It is, at the least, unprofessional to promote yourself as competent to perform jobs that you know are beyond your capacity. Indeed, it's a violation of the Association for Computing Machinery's Code of Ethics. This might strike you as trifling, but if your company becomes involved in a lawsuit, wearing a hat that's three sizes too big will at best make you look silly in court.

Where You Fit: The Test Group in the Organization

With the scope of your job defined, let's place the test group in its organizational context. A number of possible organizational models can apply. Figure 9.1 shows one basic model for a test group, in which the test manager reports to the development manager. In this case, a lead test engineer typically manages the team. (Test groups tend to be small when they service a single development team.) This lead engineer communicates test results directly to the development manager.

Some people have reported success with this model, but I've seen—and heard of—too many problems where it's used. What's wrong with including the test organization in the development team? First, it is often difficult to preserve the notion of an independent test organization giving unbiased information to the project when the test manager reports to the development manager. It's too much to expect that managers will pursue an agenda contrary to *their* manager's interests—but this model requires that test managers do just that if they are to be independent in any sense. (In most situations I've seen, the development manager is held primarily accountable for the delivery of a particular set of functions within a predetermined time frame, which sets up a schedule-versus-quality tradeoff that tilts the field against the test organization.) Second, testing does not receive access to the resources it needs. The development

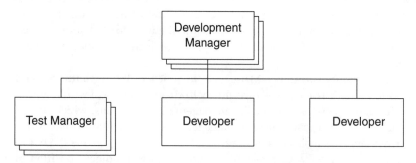

Figure 9.1   The test organization as part of development.

manager is often forced to choose between purchasing tools for development or for testing, between hiring developers or testers. Third, testing might not even be able to keep the resources it has. In crunch mode, testers will be pulled into debugging activities, tool creation, and even coding. Finally, the test team's clout is at an absolute minimum. Developers are often free to treat testers' bug reports as suggestions, and most testers aspire to become developers. As a practical matter, integrated test organizations often disappear over time, melting back into the development teams.

Nevertheless, this model makes sense in some situations. If you are working in a small startup with, say, a dozen or so engineers, other models can put too many layers in place. You don't want to negate the advantages of a small organization, such as shared vision and low communication overhead, by imposing unnecessary layers of management. If your company uses the approach illustrated in Figure 9.1, just keep in mind that it will require special care to preserve a separate test team.

Figure 9.2 shows another common model, in which the test manager and the development manager both report to the project manager. This is not a perfect solution, but it is an improvement over the previous model. The test group is still not independent in a real sense, because the test manager answers to the project manager. A project manager's agenda and interests usually more closely resemble those of a development manager than those of a test manager. However, a project manager, being less involved in the creation of the system under test, can usually bring a more dispassionate outlook to the discussion of problems than a development manager can.

Under the arrangement shown in Figure 9.2, the development and test organizations usually have separate headcounts and budgets, which reduces the resource contention encountered in the first model. You must still compete for the same pool of money, but now the development manager is a peer, not your superior. Likewise, test's "cookie jar" can't be raided without at least the project manager's blessing, thus minimizing situations in which you lose resources yet are expected to meet the original schedules and scope of testing. Moreover, the test organization has more stature, as bug reports and other test status reports go directly to project management.

Despite these advantages, you should count on being considered a project resource and expect to participate in all the panics and crunches, even if test's involvement does not add value. For example, if the implementation falls behind schedule, your team will probably be required to commiserate with the tardy developers by suffering through the same six-day weeks, long hours, abrupt changes of priority, and all the

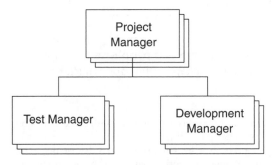

Figure 9.2 The test organization as a development project resource.

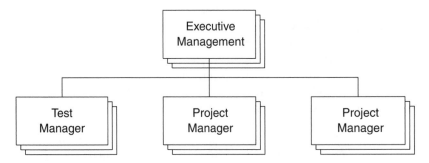

Figure 9.3 The truly independent test organization.

rest. This is especially the case if your company practices the "kiddie soccer" approach to project management.[3]

Figure 9.3 shows my preferred model. Here, the test team is truly independent. Executive management's agendas and interests promote the good of the company. (If they don't, you have bigger problems.) Therefore, management will listen to test status reports with a completely open mind. You might burst management's bubble in terms of the quality of the product, but in this situation it is most likely that the management team will see the quality problems as arising in the project manager's domain rather than being somehow "your" problem. Clout, budget, and staffing problems are minimized, for the most part. You have a budget based on how many projects you will be asked to support—and if your project load increases, you will be able to obtain more resources.

Of course, there is no paradise on Earth. Market-driven companies make money by selling products, not by building them. IT departments must put working systems on users' desks. Deployment dates are often more closely related to marketing windows, contractual obligations, and user needs than to assessments of quality, independent or not. You will be subject to project pressures, sometimes very strong ones. This third model, however, unlike the others, is at least structured in a way that does not actively undermine you.

What Else Fits?
Adding Other Functions to Test

In part because testing is often a misunderstood function, you might be invited to take charge of all sorts of additional duties that are more or less peripheral to testing. Test managers, in their copious free time, sometimes discharge other duties such as:

---

[3]In real soccer, everyone plays a specific position, and the whole team plays with grace, cohesion, and a sense of trust that each player knows his or her part. When young children first play soccer, though, the whole complement of players on both sides run around in a disoriented mob, chasing the ball around the field. There are no real positions and no sense of direction. Everyone is excited and much energy is expended, but little is accomplished.

- Configuration management and release management.
- Customer support.
- Operations such as system administration and disaster recovery.
- Quality management—for example, code reviews, inspections, and process.
- Management of the development lab.
- Creation of training data and procedures for operations staff.

The list of duties that might be attached to the test function is probably endless. However, does placing these functions in the test organization make sense?

In my opinion, the answer is usually—but not always—"no."[4] Some of the specific situations in which I recommend against such arrangements include the following:

The test team shares some responsibility for product development, or is completely integrated into the development team. There are well-documented reasons why developers can't test their own code, in terms of subjectivity and bringing the same blindspots to the testing as to the creating; in addition, they don't have the test expertise to test other developers' code at a system level. It is also true that many developers tend to dislike testing and give it short shrift when forced to do much of it.

Management assigns additional duties to the test team because the group is perceived to have the bandwidth. This perception is nearly always wrong: I have never managed, seen, or heard of an overstaffed test group. The extra duties will assuredly weaken the team's ability to focus on testing.

Specific tasks are assigned to a member of the test team who possesses a relevant skill set. Such assignments might make sense as temporary duties, but if the role is ongoing, your test team has been effectively downsized.

A member of the test team wants to take on additional responsibility as part of individual career growth. This might make sense for the individual, but does it make sense for your test team? This person probably belongs in another group; perhaps now is a good time for the transition?

Even in the best-case scenario, assigning additional roles and responsibilities to the test team distracts everyone from the main mission: finding bugs. In the worst-case scenario, you might find yourself unable to fulfill test responsibilities competently, although you are still being held accountable both for testing and for the new duties. To avoid such a situation, be sure to draw your test group's organizational boundaries—your team's "Is/Is Not" table—as a first step in your tenure as test manager. If you are asked to take on additional responsibilities, be sure to clarify whether these duties are permanent or temporary and to explain their impact on your ability to test.

All that said, you may have to accept certain expansions of your test group's role in order to help the company succeed. On a purely Machiavellian basis, the last thing you

---

[4]A specific case that seems to make sense is having a senior test engineer or the test manager serve as the project's "risk officer." Steve McConnell makes this suggestion in Chapter 7 of his *Software Project Survival Guide.*

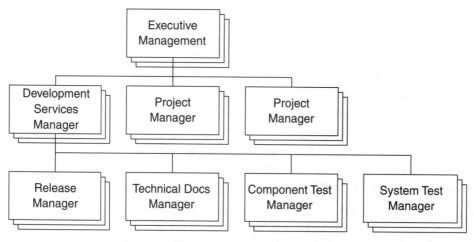

Figure 9.4 A development services group.

want is to be branded "not a team player" or "inflexible"—unless you truly don't care about advancement or permanent tenure within the company. And it's certainly true that an arrangement in which the test team works with other teams, all under the same manager, needn't be a disaster. Such an arrangement can work well when the teams are grouped together because of synergy in the kinds of tasks they perform and the kinds of expertise each group needs, as opposed to a desire to get something for nothing or to throw undesirable duties over the wall into the test ghetto. If you are faced with the suggestion that the test team take on other responsibilities, you might consider proposing an approach like the one shown in Figure 9.4. This model illustrates the structure of a development services group in which I once worked, an organization that performed very well.

Working with Other Managers: Directions of Test Management

Test projects must be managed in three directions:

Inward. Managing inward means defining your test team, hiring its members, organizing the team's structure, and supervising and motivating your employees.

Upward. Managing upward means summarizing the status of the test process and escalating urgent problems to the attention of the project management team, setting expectations, responding quickly but prudently to changes in direction, participating in management meetings, and "selling" your test effort.

Outward. Managing outward means communicating test results, clarifying problem reports, and discussing test needs and services with your management peers.

These three directions are represented in Figure 9.5. Chapter 8 focused on managing inward; here we'll look at the other two directions.

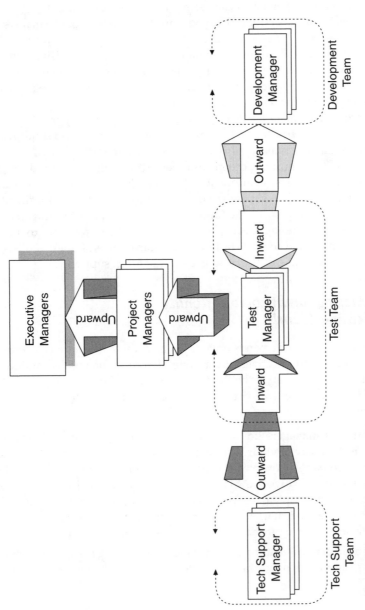

Figure 9.5 The three directions of test management.

Managing Upward

Managing upward is often a difficult challenge, especially when you are communicating to people who have only a dim understanding of what testing is all about. Managing upward requires that you spend a significant amount of time preparing reports, focusing on process, and devising an effective set of test indicators or metrics—the test dashboard—that your management can use to understand test status.[5]

As part of this effort, it is critical that you learn to "manage your managers" effectively. Perhaps this concept seems strange. It doesn't imply that you will tell your bosses what to do; rather, it means that your effectiveness in supervising your team's interactions with your superiors will determine your success as a manager in many ways. If you think about it, your ability to handle such interactions probably had a lot to do with why you became a manager in the first place.

Poor upward management leads to a perception among the upper echelons of the company that your team has "failed." As much as the paperwork and status reporting can seem tedious and disconnected from critical tasks, remember that your managers are, in a real sense, your most important customers. (After all, we are producing information—an assessment of system quality—that should be useful to our managers, right?) From your immediate supervisor on up to the corporate vice president, these are the people who must provide the funds you need to carry out testing. Help them understand what you're doing. Clearly explain the benefits of testing. Provide useful information in a timely and accurate fashion. If you can do these things, you'll be much more successful in obtaining critical resources and political support.

Bringing Management to Your Reality: Communicating Clearly

One of the most important demands of your job is that you communicate with upper management clearly and effectively. Every one of your managers has an individual management style, and this style should determine exactly how you approach the task of managing upward. In general, however, it's useful to keep the following considerations in mind:

Ensure that your managers do not hold you personally responsible for product quality. It should be obvious that the test organization doesn't write the code or build motherboards. However, it is hardly uncommon for unenlightened senior managers and executives to blame test managers when low-quality systems under test don't complete test phases on time. Likewise, managers of customer support or sales and marketing too frequently consider every field bug a test escape, whether testing that area was in scope or not.

Help your managers understand testing. If they lack a testing background, they might not grasp the reasons why you do (and don't do) certain things. Avoid focusing on

---

[5]For another, similar perspective on managing upward (and outward), see Chapter 6 of Bill Perry and Randall Rice's *Surviving the Top Ten Challenges of Software Testing,* which focuses on the need to sell management on what test can contribute and to establish clear communication and reporting.

minutiae such as boundary conditions, state machines, and load generators, which are simply a means to an end. Instead, talk about risk management and about the impact of serious test escapes on the reputation and revenues of the company.

Think ROI—return on investment—which we'll discuss further in Chapter 11, "Testing in Context: Economics, Lifecycles, and Process Maturity." Your managers will regularly go to bat for your budget with other managers (their bosses). If you can't explain to your superiors the business benefits gained by spending tens of thousands of dollars for GUI test automation tools or a thermal chamber, how will they explain the payoff to *their* managers?

Be ready to measure your results. The charts and reports introduced in Chapters 3, 4, and 5 provide the tools you need to summarize test coverage, the status of testing, and the quality of the system under test. Being crisp and quantitative will help your managers understand and support what you're doing. Remember, though, that we need to understand the information needs of our managers and tailor our metrics, charts, and reports to provide that information.

Another aspect of useful results reporting involves keeping test data, information, and reports accurate and timely. Inaccurate reporting can damage your team's credibility, making your managers' lives—as well as your own life—more difficult. Reports that show trends only when it's become too late to take remedial action will likely be more frustrating than enlightening.

Communicate in terms of moving the project forward. Most project managers aren't interested in test theory or test as an abstract idea, but with the ways in which testing can advance the project. If you try to understand what your managers need to accomplish and then attempt to connect test's contributions to those goals, you can keep your communications with them relevant and on target. (A colleague once described our mutual manager as the kind of guy who "if you told him you had a flat tire, would offer to help change your shoe." Taking actions that do nothing to promote the success of the project—or that might even actively impede it—and focusing on solving problems that are extraneous to the ones that urgently need solving will not endear you to other participants.)

Be ready to participate in the dog and pony shows. I have spent many an hour putting together snazzy presentations for management meetings or searching through various CD-ROMs for a graphic to enliven a slide—even though my spiel was sometimes cancelled at the last minute. These activities are part of your managerial "selling" role, so learn to enjoy them and do them well.

Address both the urgent and the important. Urgent matters require immediate action to prevent a major crisis or even the total failure of the project—for example, you are unable to install the system under test in the lab. Important matters need focused, deliberate attention. Addressing important matters usually leads to improvements in process efficiency, quality of product, clarity of communication, and order in the workplace. Often, the two types of issues are related. On one project, we continually received builds of abysmally poor quality. We could usually install them, but they had major regressions from previous functionality. The urgent matter, repeatedly, was to get a new build to the test lab so that we could proceed with testing. The important matter, often lost in the accompanying fire drill, was that development needed to run a short regression or smoke test before delivering the product to the test group.

Remember that you are the interface between the test group and the project. For a tester, success means finding bugs; the worse the better. You want your team members to be diligent about finding problems and to feel a sense of accomplishment when they do. For everyone else on the project, however, news of a nasty bug is nothing to smile about. As the test manager, you must maintain a somewhat two-faced display of positive encouragement and near-celebration of bugs inside your team, while understanding the negative effect that bugs have outside your team. One talented test manager, Reynolds MacNary, uses the phrase "optimistic on the outside, pessimistic on the inside" to capture this dichotomy.

Don't let bad news wait. If there's anything a manager dreads more than bad news, it's bad news that's two days old. The business impact of a problem almost always grows more severe as the problem festers. Nevertheless, do take the time to make sure you've gotten your story straight; reacting and managing are different behaviors.

On that note, escalate deliberately. Before you bring a problem to your managers' attention with a request for help, ask yourself whether they can and will make the situation better, not worse. I had a client who, when informed of a problem, would immediately begin making irate telephone calls to anyone he saw as responsible or culpable. Occasionally this solved the problem, but often it merely enraged those who were the targets of the telephone calls. In another situation, a colleague referred to the escalation process by snorting that "escalation is just another way of saying 'Get information to Joe' [named changed to protect the guilty] so he can micromanage you." If you work for such managers, use caution.

Admittedly, managing upward can involve tedious activities, especially when it feels like you're trying to communicate with people who speak another language. How many presentations can you put together on the same topic, especially while your team is doing real work? Wouldn't you rather spend time managing your test engineers, who understand what you're talking about and admire your advanced knowledge and skills, instead of working with a bunch of managers who just don't get it? When you get caught up in one of these "leave me alone and let me work" funks, remember that upper management must either buy the end product—if it's in-house—or sell it to customers and clients. And these managers are the people who make what you and your team do possible. Although their different perspectives make communication challenging, they are paying for your test operation. In Chapter 11, we'll return to the topic of test budgets, specifically on ways you can explain the financial benefits of releasing quality systems.

"How about a Third Shift, and Weekends, and...": The Effects of Lateness on Test

In addition to budgets, another major management concern is hitting scheduled project end dates. However, in the high-tech world, schedule delays are a way of life. Some argue that these delays result from the incredible pace at which technology evolves and from the fact that anything new is, by nature, somewhat unknown and unknowable. Some technical staff and development managers say that delays are simply the effects of reality biting down hard on unrealistic schedules imposed by uninformed or overly aggressive managers, salespeople, and marketers, who correspondingly often blame lazy and disorganized developers and technical people. Others hold poor planning and estimation techniques responsible. Who's right? Who cares! Although discussing culpability makes for a nice venting exercise over drinks after a long day of trying to catch up on a schedule everyone but senior management admits is unachievable, it doesn't accomplish much.

High-tech projects very often run late vis-à-vis the official schedule. As the test manager, your moment in the spotlight comes during test execution, at the end of the project—which means that, much of the time, you will be running tests just as the schedule's disconnection from reality becomes painfully obvious to all involved. Unfortunately, you are likely to suffer the consequences of management's rude awakening well out of proportion to the degree to which your team contributed to the delay.

As a schedule begins to slip, managers often impose a crunch mode regimen, in an attempt to make up time through sheer effort: this thinking assumes that if the schedule is off by 20 percent, making everyone work 50 hours a week instead of 40 will allow them to catch up. This sounds reasonable, but I have never seen it work. In addition, the test effort might well be chugging along just fine on a 40-hour-per-week schedule; it's often the case that only 40 hours or so of work can be done on a given deliverable, especially when quality is poor. Trying to impose extra hours on your team could actually have a negative effect in the long run, by draining energy that will be needed later.

Nevertheless, failing to participate in these exercises, or arguing openly against them, displays disloyalty to your managers and can destroy your advancement opportunities at the company. If you truly can't contribute anything by working hard, and want to conserve the test team's strength, have its weaker players put in the extra hours during the "show trial" periods of the crisis, and then bring the stronger players into the overtime mix as soon as they can be productive. If you feel absolutely compelled to dispute the intelligence of the crisis mentality, do so one-on-one with your managers; a general email or a public comment that rails against management is, politically, a suicidal maneuver.

Schedule delays tend to result in scope shrink and sometimes even in product redesign. If you begin to see significant, perhaps ill-advised changes being made to the product in an attempt to meet the schedule, it is critical that you communicate the effect of these changes to your managers. Again, though, diplomacy is important. Greeting news of an alteration by telling everyone who will listen, "That's the stupidest idea yet for rescuing this hare-brained schedule," won't win you friends in high places if the change was proposed by executive management.

If the schedule slips so far that no one—not even project management—is able to pretend that it can ever be rescued, replanning often begins. This is the rational choice, but it is not painless. You'll have to participate in planning exercises all over again, which can seriously distract your attention from managing your team.

Sometimes, management takes out its frustrations on the people involved. Employees can be fired, especially those perceived as malcontents or flagrant contributors to the project delay. Since testing is usually just beginning, you and your team are not likely to be pegged as responsible for the delay, but if you've spent a lot of time maligning the schedule or the management in the hallways, you are a prime candidate for malcontent status.

Along with firings, you could face a mass reorganization. A client of mine once proposed, in all seriousness, that breaking up the independent test group and having each lead test engineer report directly to the respective subsystem development manager would get us back on schedule. I had to muster a significant effort to defuse this initiative, and even then I lost about a quarter of my team to the development managers who claimed to need help with unit, component, and string testing for which they were responsible. Weird ideas become the theme as the consequences of missed schedules start to sink in.

Of course, scapegoat firings and reorganizations do not address the underlying causes of delays. Indeed, they create dysfunctional dynamics, such as fear, defensiveness, confusion, and miscommunication that actually exacerbate the fundamental problems and produce further delays. You will gain nothing by pointing this out publicly, however. If these types of actions are proposed or implemented, work behind the scenes to mitigate the damage to your team.

Even more frustration can accompany a slipping schedule if senior management succumbs to the siren song of ad hoc testing by unskilled staff, often on loan from other parts of the organization. This can happen when managers see all forms of testing as equivalent in terms of effectiveness and value. From this mistaken context, such ad hoc testing looks like a bargain: no test development is needed—just hurl a bunch of warm bodies at the product, let them bang away like monkeys, and soon enough you'll find all the bugs. In such a case, you must convince your managers that although ad hoc testing might do a decent job of finding bugs on a single release, it cannot improve product quality in the long term.

It's annoying when managers scrap best practices the moment schedules slip. Don't take it personally, however, and don't see it as a mark of irredeemable failure on the part of your managers. Remember that the end goal is to deliver a working system to users and customers—that's how we all get paid—and that management might deem it necessary to cut some corners to accomplish that goal. It's unfortunate that the corners being cut are yours in this instance, but you might still be able to make a difference at your company, so don't overreact to the crisis. We'll return to this issue of process maturity—adopting and sticking with process improvements that make long range sense—in Chapter 11.

Managing Outward

Let's assume that you work in an organization such as those modeled in Figures 9.2 and 9.3. The development managers, and perhaps the project managers, are your peers, sitting laterally across from you on a standard organizational chart.[6] Additional peers might include the information technologies (IT), management information systems (MIS), operations, or facilities manager; the sales manager; the marketing man-

---

[6]In this era of New Age organizational charts that show customers at the center or managers "under" their individual contributors, you might have to tweak your chart a little before the political realities become clear. Don't fall for the hype: the old pyramid organization charts represent the true power relationships.

ager; business analyst manager; the help desk, customer or technical support manager; the technical documentation manager; and the configuration and release engineering manager, among others. These are the people who see your test group as a team of professionals who affect their work, as opposed to seeing you simply as colleagues, coworkers, or people who happen to pick up paychecks in the same office.

Your Partners in Building Quality Systems: Development Peers

The toughest peer relationship to manage well is that between testers and developers. This relationship is often seen as inherently adversarial, but ideally is a partnership in building a quality system, just as an editor works with a writer to create a better book. The bug reports that testers write are assertions that the system under test is not perfect. When a healthy peer relationship exists, developers will see these bug reports as helpful suggestions for quality improvement and fix the bugs. In less healthy organizations, programmers sometimes react defensively: they take umbrage at the tests themselves, considering them "unfair"; they claim bug reports are poorly written or unclear; or that they consider the bug in question too trivial to waste precious time on.

Testers and developers must have fundamentally different outlooks to do their jobs properly. Developers must be optimistic to succeed. Why work long hours, give up weekends, and make other sacrifices to create something if you fear that the only result will be a raft of bugs? Testers, however, must pursue bugs with vigor and enthusiasm. Chapter 8 described testers as "professional pessimists," who must think about ways to break the product in order to find these defects.

These differences of professional perspective can descend into rancor if you're not careful. Gloating over bugs, trying to "catch" developers, or making a point of embarrassing development colleagues will poison the well. Even though most developers and development managers do not take every bug report as a personal attack, the situation can devolve into a highly polarized one.

Despite these potential problems, there is no peer relationship in which it is more important for you to maintain open, collegial communications. Don't forget that the test team and the development team will either succeed together or fail together. A development project is like a boat headed for a port, with the entire team aboard. If the test group wastes time taking potshots at developers, they might succeed in wounding a few, but they will primarily succeed in shooting holes in the boat and sinking it.

Don't draw the definition of "developer" too narrowly, either. Anyone who provides you with products to test is a developer. A technical writer or a release or configuration engineer is also a developer. Testing finds their mistakes, too, and you must handle these relationships with care as well.

All these developers also receive a product from you: your bug reports. Most enlightened developers entertain a well-written, clear, conscientiously researched bug report with professionalism. Like your team, though, they are affected by the quality of the product they receive. A lousy bug report slows the debugging process just as an unstable, buggy system under test slows down the test cycle. Unlike your team, however, developers' jobs do not involve helping you improve the quality of your bug reports. As Chapter 4, "An Exciting Career in Entomology Awaits You: A Bug Tracking

Database," stressed, you and everyone on the test team must strive to provide high-quality bug reports to your development colleagues.

Be careful to keep your development peers honest about which test tasks *they* own and which tasks *you* own. As you begin to build an independent test organization, some development managers and staff tend to disengage from testing, assuming that your group, operating in parallel, is somehow redundant to their efforts. A colleague of mine describes this behavior as development becoming "addicted" to the new test organization, relying on you to perform tasks that in reality are the responsibilities of developers. Once development stops doing its own testing, an unfortunate scenario results, in which the presence of the test organization actually worsens product quality because the structural testing at which developers excel—and which complements the behavioral testing performed by most independent test organizations—disappears from the overall test program. A dysfunctional situation, indeed, but it occurs frequently. Proactive discussions with your development management peers can keep such a misfortune from befalling your company.

The Supporting Cast: Internal Service Providers

Some of your management peers are involved in providing services—usually some type of logistical or administrative support—to the test organization. If you are tempted to think of these service providers as in some sense lower on the political totem pole than the test group, don't. Because you must depend on these organizations to get, maintain, and use critical resources, managing these peers effectively is essential to your success.

The logistics database introduced in Chapters 6 and 7 can help you work with your management peers who are responsible for computer equipment, networking, and facilities. Don't be the tail trying to wag the dog, however. Before you put together a complete hardware, software, infrastructure, and staffing logistics plan using this database, be sure that the IT or MIS manager will agree to execute it. The plan you devise might conflict with the manager's other priorities, or the staff might not be available to make it happen. I have occasionally found that although I could propose a detailed plan, implementing that plan was not on the MIS manager's "to do" list.

The human resources or staffing manager is another key person among your peer relationships, especially if you are building a new test organization. HR managers sometimes hold outmoded but still too common ideas about testers being low-paid button-pushers rather than skilled professionals. You will need to change this thinking before the HR manager can help you effectively. In addition, as Chapter 8 stressed, you might need the HR manager as an ally to remedy inequities that exist in your company between developers and testers.

Administrative staff and their managers are also invaluable resources. They can help with travel arrangements, procure necessary supplies for your team, and be an extra set of hands for reports, presentations, and the like. Moreover, in the more Byzantine sense of the word *politics*, don't forget that administrative assistants and secretaries often know all sorts of interesting facts. I'm referring not to gossip but to pertinent questions about staffing assignments, upcoming projects, and meeting agendas.

Help Desk, Customer or Technical Support: Often Overlooked

A good relationship with the help desk, customer support, or technical support manager serves both preventive and corrective purposes. Effective, proactive communication with the customer support manager and team during the test design and implementation phases can add a lot of value to your tests. Most customer service managers have been on the receiving end of the fallout from a bad system, shipped way too early, with too many unknown (and even known) bugs. Many of these field failures can be translated into a useful test case. (To get an idea of how motivated these folks are to help you do a good job in preventing field problems, imagine the churn-and-burn atmosphere of an understaffed support organization dealing with a deluge of angry customers who just spent an hour on hold in addition to suffering some critical system failure.)

The customer support manager also has a nonacademic interest in your test results. Bugs found during testing, if fixed, are bugs not reported in the field. The key phrase, of course, is "if fixed." It's important, therefore, that you work closely with the customer support manager to communicate bugs found and bugs fixed, and that you set the manager's expectations properly. If you include customer support in your circulation list for bug reports and metrics, you give the manager an invaluable opportunity to sound off if it seems that the project is on track to lay an egg.

This level of interest is a double-edged sword. If you don't include the customer service manager in discussions of bugs and test coverage, he might come to the conclusion, especially if significant field problems remain, that the test organization is incompetent. A politically well-connected customer support manager in this position might well agitate for the dissolution of the existing test team and its replacement by an organization internal to his group. I have seen such moves succeed, so beware.

This is another reason why adopting the defect detection percentage (discussed in Chapters 4 and 8) as the measure of test team effectiveness makes so much sense. This metric is based on two numbers, the bugs your team finds and the bugs that are reported to the technical support manager. The scope-adjusted defect detection percentage takes into account that management might reduce what's in scope for your test project, but either way, the customer support manager should be your partner in achieving the ideal defect detection percentage for your organization.

Business Analysts, Sales, and Marketing: Vital Allies

Like customer support managers, business analysts, sales and marketing managers tend to have strong feelings about what you should test and what your results should be. In general, you should manage your relationship with these peers similarly. There are, however, two key differences, one negative, one positive.

On the negative side, some business analysts, sales, and marketing experts, even those with considerable experience in high-tech fields, don't really understand the complexity of testing. They might not understand your bug reports unless you are careful to describe the possible impact on customers in the summary. Even if you are, not all failures lend themselves to concise, straightforward impact assessments, especially sporadic but dangerous ones. It takes a technically sophisticated person to understand why "sometimes" is worse than "always" in such cases. In addition, sales and marketing people don't always understand why testing takes as long as it does. The "how hard can it be?" mentality can easily take root in organizations that are removed from the technical realities.

To a misguided few sales and marketing types, every field failure is a test escape. No matter how obscure a customer's problem, you and your team of knuckleheads should have found it during testing. I once took considerable heat for a bug that caused a loss of network connection on a computer running Microsoft Windows 95. The failure occurred only in heavily loaded 16-Mbps token ring environments with one particular brand of PC Card adapter connecting to one type of network server. Even when I pointed out that we couldn't very well run stress and capacity tests on every single PC Card network adapter/NOS combination, since these combinations would surely number in the thousands, one salesperson continued to rail against my organization's lousy testing. The bug did cost the company a large sale, but this individual's unreasonable expectations about what it was possible to test were out in the stratosphere.

I could have diffused this problem politically, though, had I been more careful to involve all the salespeople in discussions of test scope, which brings me to the plus side of the equation. Business analysts, sales, and marketing can provide useful support in terms of budgeting and scope. Strategically, if sales and marketing managers agree that high quality is an important brand differentiator in your market niche, and if you can then convince them that thorough testing is essential to achieve this distinction, you will have powerful backing for an effective, wide-ranging test operation, adequately staffed and funded. Business analysts who understand the mission-criticality of certain systems can help you achieve sufficient resources for complete testing of these crucial applications. Tactically, for any particular product, discussing with the business analysts, sales and marketing people what's in and what's out of the scope of testing (and why) could spark a reconsideration of the project plan that would allow test to have a bigger impact.

Handle these opportunities with care, though. Reciting to the sales manager a tale of woe about the sorry budget you have and the screwed-up system that will be shipped or delivered because of poor testing will, at best, come off as whining. Assuming that the sales manager is not your direct superior, it could also come across as backstabbing your boss, with predictable consequences. A diplomatic opening through a telephone call or email—"Hi, I'm the new test manager, and I'd like to get your input on what we should be testing"—is much more positive. Be forthright in telling your own managers that you intend to have such a conversation to get concurrence on test priorities for the project in question. You don't have to declare your intentions to lobby business analysts, sales and marketing managers for their strategic support of your test organization, because you're going to be subtle and indirect about that, right?

Testing in the Dark: Should You Proceed without Documentation?

In order to design, develop, and run tests, you need what's often referred to as an *oracle*, something that tells you what the expected, correct result of a specific test should be. Specifications, requirements, business rules, marketing road maps, and other such documents frequently play this role. However, what if you receive no formal information that explains what the system under test should do?

In some organizations with mature development processes, the test department will not proceed without specifications. Because everyone expects to provide a specification to the test team as part of the development process, you are seen as reasonable and within the bounds of the company's culture when you insist on written specs.

Trouble arises, however, if you stiffen your neck this way in a company that operates in a less mature fashion. Depending on your company's readiness to embrace formal processes (and also on your personal popularity, tenure, and political clout), any one of a spectrum of outcomes could occur:

- Your management, recognizing the need to formalize processes, backs you up 100 percent and institutes formal requirements and design specification processes throughout the organization as part of the planning phase of every new development project. Industry-standard templates for internal product documentation become the norm, and consultants are brought in to train people.

- Your management, not knowing quite how to handle this odd demand, assumes that you must know what you're talking about. The dictate goes out to all the organization's groups to support you, but since no one has any training in formal development processes, the effort produces poor-quality documents that don't help. Furthermore, because the effort is (rightly) seen as a waste of time, people are upset with you for bringing it up.

- Your management listens to your demand but then explains that the company just isn't ready for such cultural and process shifts. Perhaps things will change after the next few products go out, they speculate, but right now, process just isn't on the to-do list. Besides, this product is really critical to the success of the company, and taking big chances on unproven ways of doing things would be too risky. You are told to get back to work.

- You are fired.

The moral of this story is that you should carefully consider whether your company is ready for formal processes before you insist on requirements or design specifications and other accoutrements of mature development projects.

If you are willing to compromise, you might consider the following options for testing without specifications:

If you are testing a commercial product, remember that you have the benefit of competitors. Because your customers will expect your product to behave substantially like the products of your competitors, these competitive products are, in a sense, your oracle. In compatibility test labs, for example, most projects have a "reference platform"—a competitor's system, against which the system under test is being positioned, in the hope of demolishing it in the marketplace.

If your technical colleagues won't tell you what the product should do, perhaps your friends in sales and marketing will. In my experience, sales and marketing people live to create glitzy presentations showing where the product line is going. Although they can be general and imprecise, these documents might tell you which features and capabilities the product should support. If you're testing a product for which questions about supported features are harder to answer than questions regarding correct behavior, these documents might suffice for a somewhat vague but useful oracle.

Your colleagues in customer support might not have much information about what the product *should* do, but they probably know what they *don't* want the product to do. Since your testing stands between them and the hellish scenario outlined in the previous section, they are usually happy to tell you.

Unless the product is truly unique, you can use inductive reasoning to figure out what constitutes reasonable expectations and correct behavior in many cases. The generic categories into which products fit tell you a lot about what the products are supposed to do: a word processor, a Web browser, a PC, a laptop, a server, an operating system. Some esoteric questions might arise, but a core dump, a system crash, a burning CPU, garbage on the screen, an error message in the wrong language, and abysmal performance are indisputably bugs.

If in doubt, you should consider any suspect behavior buggy. Because you don't have a crisp way of determining pass and fail conditions, you will make mistakes in result interpretation. Remember that calling correct behavior a bug and working through the bug life cycle is less detrimental to product quality than failing to report questionable behavior that does turn out to be a bug. Be sure to file bug reports when questions arise.

One thing to keep in mind about this situation is that you are definitely not alone. Many people are struggling with the right amount of documentation to gather, and errors are made on both sides. I try to maintain an open mind, even though the "twenty questions" approach to defining expected results is somewhat frustrating. It is a good idea, if you're working in a poorly specified situation, to make sure that management understands that your test development will be less efficient due to the need to pull information from other groups. My usual rule of thumb is that the lack of clear requirements and design specifications imposes a 20- to 30-percent inefficiency on test development, and I estimate accordingly.[7]

Pink Slips:
Layoffs and Liquidation

According to Denis Meredith, 20 to 30 percent of testing and quality assurance organizations are disbanded within two years of their formation.[8] Informal discussions on Internet testing discussion groups like SWTEST-Discuss during the early 2000s recession has suggested that testers bear a disproportionate burden in layoffs, especially in

---

[7]Right around the time I was writing the first edition of this book, Johanna Rothman coincidentally wrote an article called, "Testing in the Dark." It can be found on her Web site, www.jrothman.com, and contains some additional excellent ideas for those of us struggling with vaguely specified products.

[8]See materials prepared for Denis Meredith's training course "Software Testing: An Integrated Approach," presented September 23–27, 1991, at the University of California at Los Angeles, p. I–19.

economic downturns. Anecdotally, I can attest to the credibility of these observations, having experienced multiple layoffs as a test manager. In some cases, I was asked to wield the ax; in others, I—along with most or all of my test team—got the ax.

For obvious reasons, companies don't tend to post big notices around the cube farm six months before a layoff, saying, "Get your résumés ready; here comes Chainsaw Al." In some instances, even the line managers might not know what's coming, although they usually do get a few clues. Based on my admittedly limited experience, and the shared experiences of some of my colleagues, I recount here some worrisome warning signs:

Being asked to participate in an employee ranking exercise, especially if this procedure involves every manager in the company. I have never seen these rankings used for anything other than whacking the bottom rungs off the ladder.

Noticing a decline in your company's revenues. In one firm, everyone knew that layoffs were coming when their biggest client stopped signing up new work and started to withdraw existing work. In another company, people were laid off from departments that still produced revenue, while the people who worked on a struggling, unprofitable product survived. Why? The company saw the success of that product as a "bet the farm" proposition; some bystanders lost that bet.

Noticing a sudden, unexplainable invasion of accountants or consultants, especially if they're working with the human resources department. Ask yourself whether the task at hand is figuring out severance packages.

Hearing any rumors of a layoff list. It might well include you or members of your test team. A test manager I know heard from other managers that they had seen a "list of developers" slated to go. He naïvely assumed that this couldn't mean testers, without asking himself how the other managers would choose to drop him a hint if it *did* mean testers.

Seeing signs that the independent test team will be reorganized into smaller units that will be integrated into the individual development teams. At least one or two positions are likely to be overhead should that happen, especially the test manager's position.

Test operations can bear a disproportionate burden when it comes to layoffs. Although you can't always escape layoffs in a company that is doing poorly, the keys to keeping your test operation viable are aligning your testing with customer usage, crisply reporting the problems you find to the right people, practicing some of the political skills described elsewhere in this chapter, and demonstrating a return on investment (as discussed in Chapter 11).

Presenting the Results: The Right Message, Delivered Properly

As you run tests, you will find bugs. Moreover, because your test lab is the place where the product hits something like the "real world" for the first time, you will find all sorts of logistical snafus and poorly thought-out processes. This is especially the case when multiple development teams are involved.

Neither situation should take you by surprise. The bugs are actually your quarry, and when you find one, you and your team should feel satisfied. The "Laurel and Hardy" routines that ensue when people fail to think through processes and logistics are less desirable, but they are hardly your fault, either. Nevertheless, you might find yourself received with dismay when the time comes to report your findings.

In ancient times, the messenger who brought bad news was sometimes executed, suggesting a human tendency that remains to this day. When you come to a meeting or approach a developer with news of bugs or unworkable test equipment, the first response might be defensiveness, anger, denial, or attack. I had a client who, in response to all the worrisome findings by a third-party test lab, seized on a few mistakes the lab had made. Every time bugs found by these folks were mentioned, the client would become infuriated at the mention of the lab's name, once sending me an email that said (paraphrased), "Get these [idiots] out of our life."

As dysfunctional as these behaviors are, you will have to deal with them. Even if others recognize the attacks as more appropriately directed at the problem rather than at the reporter (you), they probably won't leap to your defense. After all, they have their own problems, and getting involved in your quarrels will antagonize people. While you can't make the attacks go away, you can take certain courses of action to make the situation better—or worse.

Good Ways to Deliver Bad News

It's critical to avoid antagonizing your project teammates when discussing bugs, missed delivery schedules, support issues, and the like. Chapter 8 advocated professional pessimism, but too much pessimism approaches paranoia. The selfless, noble whistleblower who stops the evil, corrupt project team from shipping fatally flawed systems has become a mythical figure in the engineering world. When overplayed, however, such a role makes the test group the loose cannon of the development project. Loose cannons do not roll around on the corporate deck in the tempest of development for long before they fall overboard.

Likewise, you should guard against melodramatic reporting of results. It's important to maintain a sense of perspective about how a bug will actually affect a customer or user, which can differ significantly from how it affects you, your testers, and your test system. Holding up the shipment of a commercial product that is as good as or better than its competitors is a bad business decision and can cause real political damage for you. In an IT environment, delaying the deployment of an impaired but imminently useful business process automation application is likewise unwise. As a professional tester, you must keep an open mind during reasoned discussions about the business realities of delayed ship dates.

Expressing any opinion about the progress of bug-fixing efforts is also dangerous. I once made the mistake of commenting on a marathon, all-weekend bug isolation experiment undertaken by a set of developers, saying that it was "beyond my ability to understand why anyone would think that such an effort would actually locate the bug." The fact that I was right—the undertaking was indeed fruitless—did not win me any points from the developers involved, who were quite upset with me for making the comment.

Remember Don Quixote when you're presenting your findings. Although a bug can appear quite dangerous to testers, developers often see the same bug as benign. While the truth lies somewhere between the extremes, you can easily come off as an alarmist. Worse yet, you can be accused of not being a team player if you perpetually hold the product up to unrealistically high standards of quality and rail against moving the schedule forward because the product isn't ready yet. Sometimes you must make this argument, because it's true. However, you have to recognize that it will make you very unpopular, especially when people's bonuses are tied to hitting schedule dates. I engage in this argument only when it's likely to prevail on its own merits—the "emperor's new clothes"—or when failing to do so would approach professional malpractice. As the Jesuit historian Juan de Mariana wrote, "The greatest of follies is to exert oneself in vain, and to weary oneself without winning anything but hatred."[9]

Institutionalizing a Test Dashboard

One way to depersonalize the bad news is to tell the story using numbers and metrics such as the ones discussed in Chapters 3, 4, and 5. While the mechanics of gathering metrics and presenting clear, meaningful charts were discussed in those chapters, there're still strong political elements that you'll need to manage to institute a successful, useful, informative test dashboard.

First things first. The test team exists to generate useful information and effectively communicate that information to key testing stakeholders. The results reporting process is the method by which this happens, and the dashboard is the format in which the information is transmitted. Therefore, to succeed with a dashboard, we need to know who the key stakeholders are, what questions they need us to help them answer, and how best to communicate those answers to them. You already know who the key stakeholders are: the people involved in your quality risk analysis, the people who reviewed and commented on your test plan, the peer and upper managers discussed in this chapter, and the people who will attend the project status meetings. Talk to these people about the type of information you can provide to them, the charts, graphs, and reports you can present this information in, and the frequency with which they'd like to receive the information.

Based on these conversations, you can build a first-draft test dashboard. Maybe it will look like the dashboard in Chapter 5, "Managing Test Cases: The Test Tracking Spreadsheet," but most likely, it will be different. Be sure to make the charts follow the questions you need to answer, not the other way around.

Once you have a first draft of the dashboard, take it back to your stakeholders. Explain the charts and what they mean. Make sure that you also explain the limitations of the charts. I have seen a lot of misinterpretation of test status reports—often of the wishful-thinking variety—so it's important to make sure that people know how to read the charts. It might help to also show people some examples of good and bad indicators using the charts. The sample data in the case studies, the SpeedyWriter and DataRocket charts, and the exercises at the end of this chapter can help you do that. Make sure that everyone knows what bad news looks like. Fine tune the dashboard based on feedback from your stakeholders, but make sure people don't send you off on a wild goose chase

---

[9]Cited in Henry Kamen, *The Spanish Inquisition,* p. 127.

trying to produce charts that you can't from data you don't have. This happened to me once when one of my client's managers kept asking for a Rayleigh chart, which requires a defect removal model that didn't exist for the system we were building.

As you use the charts in status reporting, make sure that you continue to manage and fine-tune the dashboard. Ask your stakeholders about the dashboard. Is this providing useful information to you? Are you getting it often enough? Assess the credibility and accuracy of your status reports, too. Do you feel that people are taking your findings seriously? Are they acting on the reports? Do the reports paint a truthful picture of project status based on accurate data?

Don't fool yourself or others about the infallibility of the metrics, either. Since metrics can be "gamed" to advance a personal or political objective—anyone who's observed democracy in action is familiar with the distortion of statistics that fills each election campaign—quantitative results reporting by itself will not necessarily insulate you from your own biases or from a perception that you are biased. Therefore, even with the best dashboard, credibility is an issue.

While defining the dashboard is something you should do at the beginning of the project, the task is never completely finished. You should continue to adjust and improve your dashboards from project to project, and during each project. Think of your dashboard as a newspaper. Done right, it can be your most effective and efficient tool for delivering your assessment of quality to the project management team. As with a newspaper, credibility is key.

The Importance of Accuracy and Audience

A large part of credibility is consistent correctness. No mistake draws more attention and ridicule than telling someone else he has done something wrong when in fact *you* are the one who is wrong. You must ensure a high degree of accuracy in the test and defect data your team generates and in the information you collect and summarize from that data. The further up the corporate ladder you intend to escalate a particular bug report, defect analysis metric, or test status summary, the more critical this accuracy becomes.

Never send out a set of reports without reading every word first. Remember that typos and jargon can render your meaning unclear, causing your message to misfire. Time spent rereading these reports and fixing the errors is time well spent. Sending out accurate reports to your peers and managers is part of managing upward and outward, two key responsibilities.

Of course, accuracy is worthless if no one reads your reports or looks at your charts. This can happen if you send the wrong level of detail to your audience. For example, senior managers who need to look at trends will want to see just the dashboard. They'll also need your help understanding these reports, so you should provide high-level narrative with each chart, either as a cover sheet, as part of a presentation, or as part of the email to which the report package is attached. Individual developers, however, need to see detailed bug reports and might not care about the higher-level abstractions such as defect metrics. suggests target audiences for the reports and charts mentioned in this book. (I assume that you will provide these items freely to your own test organization

Table 9.1 Reports and Their Target Audience

ITEM	TARGET AUDIENCE
Failure mode and effects analysis (FMEA) or informal quality risks analysis	Developers, development managers, project managers, sales and marketing managers, customer and technical support managers, executive management
Test project Gantt chart	Development managers, project managers, executive management
Budget	Project managers, executive management
Test plans	Development managers, project managers, sales and marketing managers, customer and technical support managers, executive management
Hardware allocation plan or HW/SW logistics database reports	IT/MIS managers, facilities managers, project managers, executive management
Test coverage analyses	Development managers, project managers, sales and marketing managers, customer and technical support managers, executive management
Test- and defect-analysis dashboard	Development managers, project managers, sales and marketing managers, customer and technical support managers, executive management
Bug detail report	Developers, development managers, project managers
Bug summary report	Development managers, project managers, sales and marketing managers, customer and technical support managers, and executive management
Test case details	Developers, development managers, project managers
Test case summary	Development managers, project managers, sales and marketing managers, customer and technical support managers, executive management
Test suite summary	Development managers, project managers, sales and marketing managers, customer and technical support managers, executive management
Lab layout	Facilities managers, IT/MIS managers, project managers, executive management
Staffing plan	Project managers, executive management, human resource managers
Test organization chart	Development managers, IT/MIS managers, project managers, executive management

and expect your staff to understand at least the test status reports, bug reports, defect and test charts, and test logistics and how these reports affect their assignments.)

In addition to keeping in mind the appropriate audience, you should also consider the frequency of updates. Sending executive managers a daily update on test status, including all the items recommended in , is likely to exceed their ability to absorb and cope with the material. Developers, in contrast, might need access to these reports in real time; an intranet Web site, updated every few hours, might be appropriate for critical reports. Ideally, of course, you could simply give the entire company access to the tools used to generate the reports and then send out a formal update package once a week or so.

Note that "accuracy" has a different meaning to each audience listed in Table 9.1. A developer will probably tolerate jargon and less polished grammar, provided that your data is solid and your premises and conclusions sound. However, a senior manager is much more focused on a solid summary line for a bug report, consistency between charts, and up-to-the-minute timeliness.[10]

"You Can Tell the Pioneers"... The Effect of Early Adoption on Test

As the saying goes, you can tell the pioneers in computer technology by all the arrows sticking out of their backsides. Whether they represent the first of a family of CPUs, a new way of connecting peripherals, a new generation of software, or a faster telecommunications process, complex software and hardware systems just never work as advertised early in their life cycles—a fact that creates major headaches for test managers.

As you might have noticed, sales and marketing staff love to have the latest technology bundled in their products. Nothing makes their hearts beat faster than to be able to say to a prospect or print in an advertisement, "We're first to market with this supercalifragilisticexpialidocious technology, and you can only get it from us!" Don't get me wrong. I appreciate sales and marketing people, without whom I would have far fewer job opportunities. And, in fact, they are right: being first to market with exciting new technology can make a huge difference in a product's success and, by extension, the success of the company.

Nevertheless, there's a price to pay during test execution for trying to evaluate this stuff before it is in wide use. It should come as no surprise to any test manager that some companies release products before they are fully tested and debugged. This is just as true of your vendors as it is of your employers. New products contain bugs, some subtle, some glaring. If your company incorporates those products into its products, or relies on them to produce products, it will suffer the consequences.

In addition, a new product might be fine by itself but suffer when it is integrated into another product. I once worked on a laptop computer project that was the first to incor-

---

[10]For more on the hard and soft sides of instituting a metrics program, see Anna Allison's excellent article, "Meaningful Metrics," first published in Software Testing and Quality Engineering, Volume 3, Issue 3 (May/June 2001),, now found on www.stickyminds.com. (Tragically, Allison's life and contributions to the field of software quality were cut short on the morning of September 11, 2001.)

porate Intel 166 MHz MMX CPUs into its systems. These chips worked well, but the increased speed and functionality meant increased power consumption, which affected battery life and increased thermal radiation, which in turn affected the heat dissipation design. These were not bugs in Intel's chip per se, but rather in our usage of it.

If you concede that lots of bugs are encountered in new technology, the logical next step would be to spend a little more time testing it. This is where yet another headache for test managers kicks in. Figure 9.6 shows what the Gartner Group refers to as the "Hype Curve." When you are testing new technology during the "Bandwagon Effect" or "Peak of Expectations" period, all anyone reading the trade magazines hears about is how great this new technology is. Guess what that means? When you go to your management with a request for several thousand additional dollars to test the new technology in the product, you might be met with incredulity or distrust. Even some otherwise reasonable managers who have had painful past experience as early adopters can get caught up in the hype. As a result, you can end up woefully underbudgeted.

It's critical that you, as the test manager, remain the polite pessimist, dubious about the new technology, regardless of the enthusiasm raging around you on the project. Don't get sucked into the hype. People whose jobs involve being visionaries, product architects, and implementers must buy into it to some extent; after all, the desire to achieve the nearly impossible is a desirable attribute in these folks. However, test managers are professional skeptics. Even if you don't get the budget and the schedule to test new technologies properly, make the request on the record, and explain your concerns. You might manage to temper the hype a bit, and you might obtain enough resources to do a passable job of testing the new technology. At the very worst, you'll

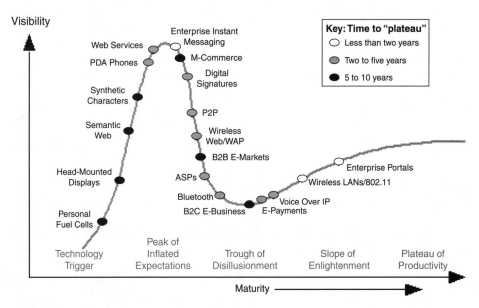

Figure 9.6 The Hype Curve.

© Gartner, Inc. "2001 Hype Cycle of Emerging Trends and Technologies," A. Linden, J. Fenn, K. Haley, July 2001.

have the solace of knowing that you did your best to test the new technology thoroughly should it blow up in the customers' hands.

Note that not all companies face the risks of new technology the same way. As seen in Figure 9.6, Gartner Group identifies three types of organizational behaviors. Type A companies pursue new technologies aggressively, in spite of risk, to achieve predominance in a specific niche. Type B companies wait until the earliest adopters have shaken out the most serious glitches, and then move in, mitigating some risk, but missing opportunities as well. Type C companies linger the longest, avoiding all the risk associated. In high technology, type C behavior is even more dangerous than type A behavior: the business history of computing is rife with the corpses of once-strong companies that jumped at just one key technology just a little too late, and many companies have had near-death experiences this way. Again, keep in mind the greater good of the company. An organization that optimizes its processes for type A behavior, while making your tasks more challenging, is less risky to your job security than a complaisant employer who waits until everyone else has worked out the glitches.

Ultimately, all the political advice and suggestions in this chapter come back to that theme. To feel good about your contributions as a test manager, you need to create an environment in which you and your team can do your best to find bugs. Most of the challenges are technical or managerial. Other challenges, however, are political. Any time people get together to solve problems and create products, even in the most tightly knit teams, politics are involved. Sometimes the solution is not necessarily consistent with the technical needs of the team.

Roland Huntford, author of *The Last Place on Earth*, tells the story of two teams, one English, one Norwegian, that competed to reach the South Pole in the early 1900s. The Norwegian team was the better organized and prepared, and it prevailed. However, during the expedition one of the members of the team, a man named Johansen, attacked the authority of the team leader, Amundsen. For this political offense, Johansen was excluded from the sprint to the pole and had to remain at the base camp on the Ross Ice Shelf, in spite of his skills and experience as a polar explorer, which might have been critical to the expedition's success. (It was by no means a foregone conclusion that the Norwegians would beat the English.) This story illustrates the inescapable fact that, even in the best of teams, under the most perilous of circumstances, political problems will arise. You can be prepared to handle them and succeed in your overarching aims, or you can try to ignore them, which will expose you, no matter how talented you are, to the possibility of failure.

Exercises

1. What is the difference between "Quality Control" and "Quality Assurance" for software systems? Give an example of each.[11]

---

[11]This exercise was contributed by Dr. Deepti Suri of Milwaukee School of Engineering.

2. For the following three exercises, find a partner or a small group of people who will role-play a project management team for you. In each case, you will be presenting a test status report that indicates a project in trouble. Present the status report using the dashboard charts and a verbal explanation. (The dashboard charts are available at www.rexblackconsulting.com for convenience, and show a variation on the quality risk coverage chart that uses absolute numbers instead of percentages.) While each of the three exercises is in a slightly different situation, some common elements apply. The project is our familiar SpeedyWriter example, the browser-based word processing application. Second, the development team ran the Component and Integration Test phases, Component Test from December 11 through December 29 and Integration Test from December 18 through January 12. The project is now in the System Test phase. Cycle one ran from January 8 through January 14, and today is January 15. The System Test Phase Exit Meeting is planned for January 29, which leaves two more one-week test cycles.

- **Too many bugs.** In the first scenario, the dashboard for which is shown in Figures 9.7 through 9.10, the Test team is working productively and finding a few more bugs than expected. A large backlog of known bugs (about 30) exists. Given the current bug find rate—which is not decreasing—and the backlog, the plan to finish testing in two weeks is in jeopardy. Furthermore, the high bug-find rate forced you to skip a large number of tests in cycle one.

- **Inadequate component and integration testing.** In this scenario, the dashboard for which is shown in Figures 9.11 through 9.14, the Test team is finding a lot of bugs, even in basic areas that adequate component and integration testing would have found. The test manager has found out through a hallway conversation or two that component and integration testing were done very poorly if at all due to a schedule crunch in the development phase. Even with extra testers to try to get through all the tests, the number and nature of the problems block many of the sophisticated test cases.

- **No stable test environment.** In this final scenario, the dashboard for which is shown in Figures 9.15 through 9.18, the test team is totally blocked from running tests. The operations and development teams were unable to install a working test release in the test environment all week. On Monday, the wrong software version was found to be on Web server. On Tuesday, the Operations team discovered that a complete operating system reinstall was required to get the Web server working. On Wednesday, five different uninstallable test releases were delivered, one after another. On Thursday, the server cluster appeared to be up, but the browser clients couldn't see the Web server on the network. On Friday, the application crashed the database server repeatedly whenever it was started. On Saturday and Sunday, when the testers came in to try to catch up from the unproductive week, the browser GPFed repeatedly during testing. Pages and cell phone calls to the Operations support staff were not returned, and the manager of the Operations team did not respond to escalation requests, either. Consequently, after dozens of false starts, no testing was completed during the week.

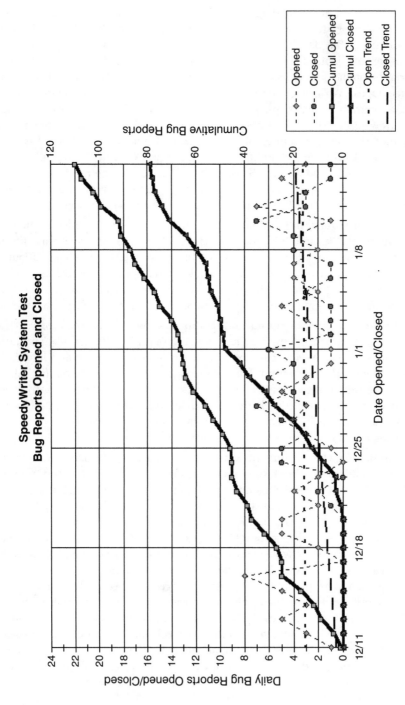

Figure 9.7 Bug reports opened and closed (too many bugs).

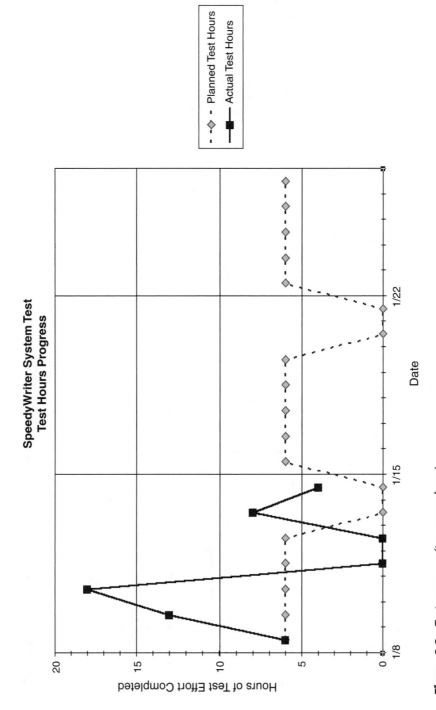

Figure 9.8 Test progress (too many bugs).

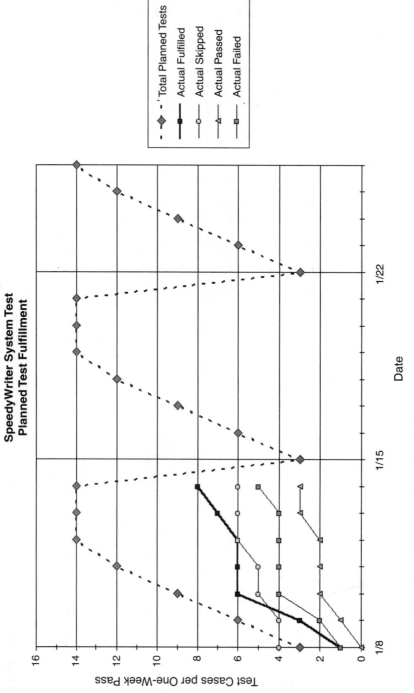

Figure 9.9 Planned test fulfillment (too many bugs).

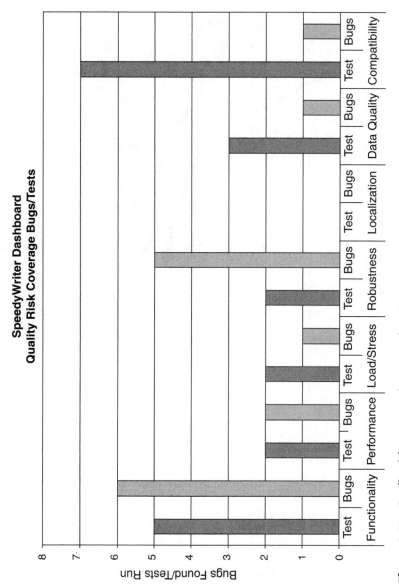

Figure 9.10 Quality risk coverage (too many bugs).

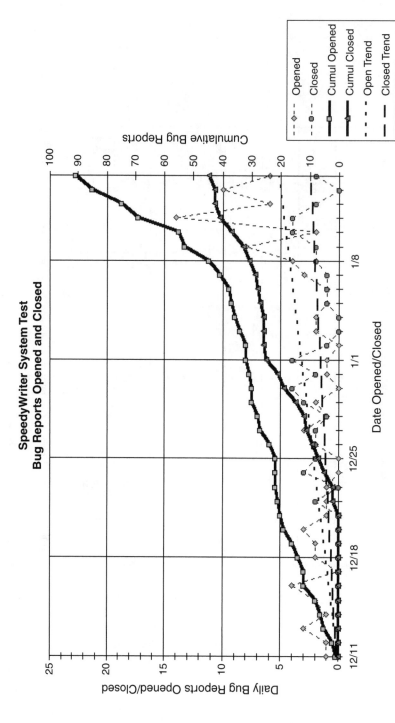

Figure 9.11 Bug reports opened and closed (inadequate integration and component testing).

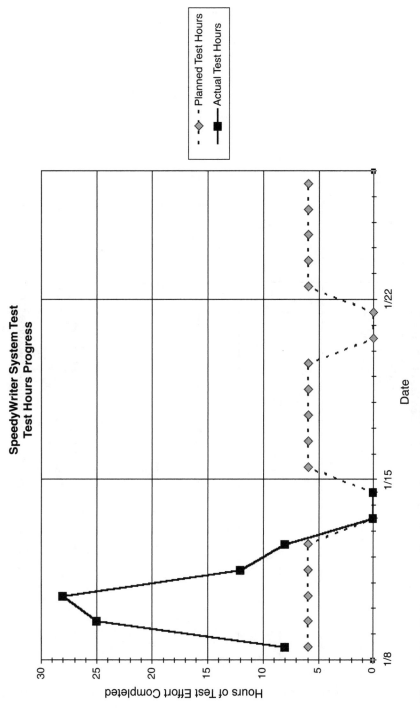

Figure 9.12 Test progress (inadequate integration and component testing).

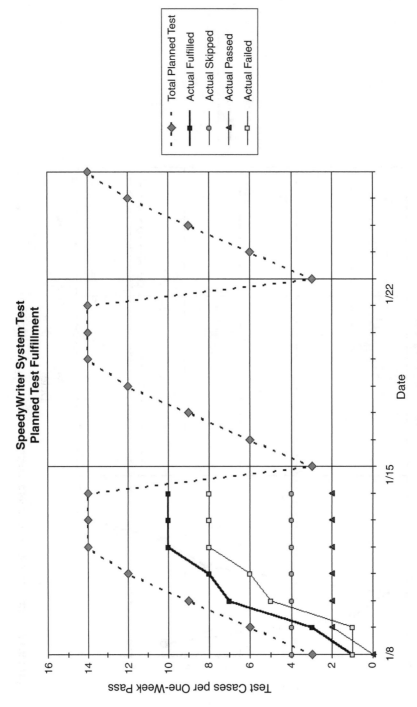

Figure 9.13 Planned test fulfillment (inadequate integration and component testing).

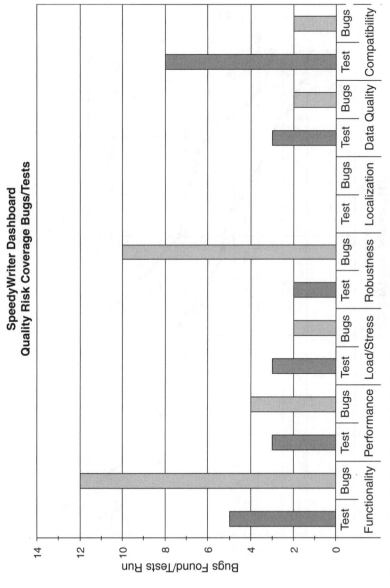

Figure 9.14   Quality risk coverage (inadequate integration and component testing).

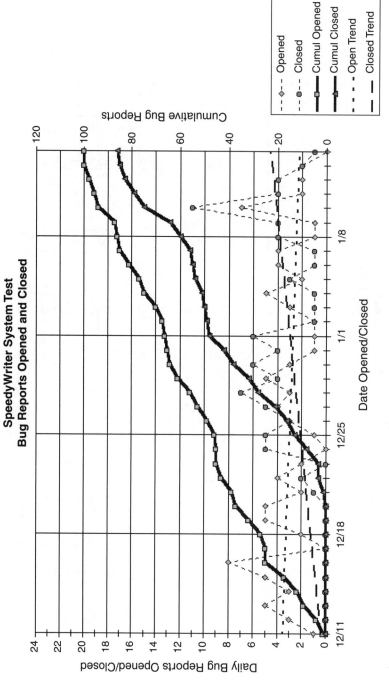

Figure 9.15 Bug reports opened and closed (no stable test environment).

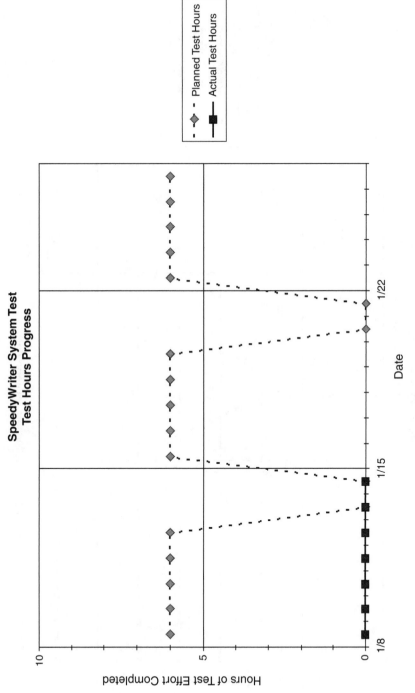

Figure 9.16   Test progress (no stable test environment).

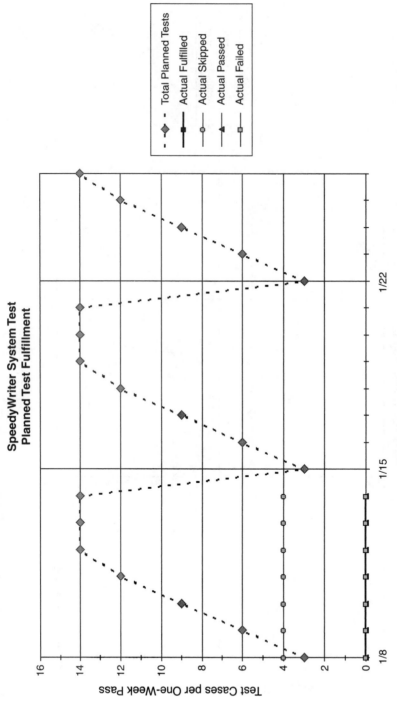

Figure 9.17 Planned test fulfillment (no stable test environment).

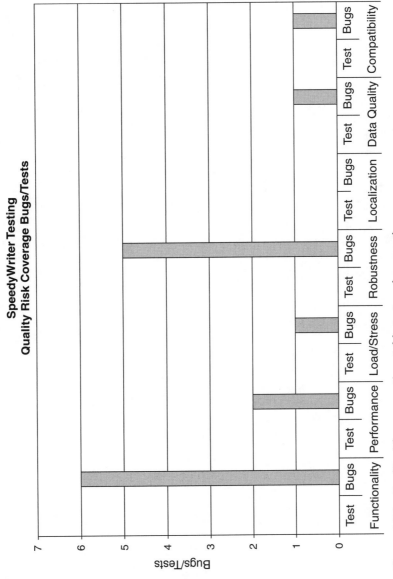

Figure 9.18 Quality risk coverage (no stable test environment).

Involving Other Players: Distributing a Test Project

Throughout this book, I've mentioned that various people and organizations in a company in addition to the test group have test-related responsibilities. Similarly, occasions arise when it makes sense to involve people and teams outside the company to help with particular test challenges. Assembling a distributed testing effort involves creating a hybrid project-matrix/skills-matrix test organization, consisting of the test team, other contributors within the company, and people who work in other companies.

Distributed testing comes in four basic flavors:

- Your vendors (those companies that provide components that will be integrated into your systems)

- Independent test organizations (especially for capital-intensive endeavors such as hardware and compatibility testing, or for test design, execution, tool, or management expertise)[1]

- Your sales or marketing offices (especially foreign offices for localization testing)

- Your business analysts, help desk or technical support, target customers or users (for alpha, beta, pilot, and acceptance testing)

[1]In the interests of full disclosure, note that my consultancy, Rex Black Consulting Services, Inc., is a third-party test organization. See www.rexblackconsulting.com for more details on our services.

Distributed test endeavors are also referred to as "virtual test teams."[2]

In some cases, distributed testing happens outside the scope of the test organization. Marketing teams often run the beta test program in mass-market software and system organizations. For in-house IT projects, the accepting user organization might insist on running the acceptance tests itself. Since this book is about managing *your* testing processes, not others, I'll focus on situations where vendors, independent test labs, sales offices, customers, or users perform some part of the test work that is within the scope of your organization. Distributing testing in such situations means that you have extended your test operation, with all the benefits and challenges that it implies.

To distribute testing successfully, you need to perform three sequential steps:

1. Choose your test partners, based on the specific testing you need to distribute and why you need to do so.

2. Plan the distributed test effort.

3. Manage the external testing as if it were your own.

The following sections examine each of these steps as well as suggest ways in which the tools introduced in this book can be extended to assist you.

Choosing Your Partners

If you choose a Texas BBQ joint to cater your wedding, you should not be surprised when brisket and beer, rather than caviar and champagne, appear on the menu. Likewise, it helps to consider your motivations and goals when choosing your test partners. Let's start with the question of why you want to use outside test resources rather than your own team exclusively.

You might want to get business analysts, help desk or technical support, target customers or users, or sales and marketing staff involved in testing to build their confidence in the quality of the system that's about to be released—or the testing that your team or some other team performed on that system. In some cases, the motivation is political, to make up for credibility deficits in the development team or your own team of testers. In other cases—especially customer involvement in acceptance testing—the motivation is contractual, since many outsource development efforts include a period of acceptance testing by the customers prior to final payment. I have worked on in-house IT projects that likewise included a user-executed acceptance test where a little bit of both applied.

More typically, though, my use of distributed testing, especially during system test, arose from one (or both) of two managerial motivations: either I was trying to leverage an external party's strength, especially one that I couldn't or didn't want to recreate in-house; or I was off-loading work that I couldn't handle quickly enough. For example, suppose that you are the test manager on the SpeedyWriter project and that you have

---

[2]For example, see Eric Patel's paper, "Getting the Most from Outsourcing," first published in Software Testing and Quality Engineering magazine, Volume 3, Issue 6, now available on www.stickyminds.com.

approached an external test lab, STC, about the possibility of performing some localization testing. Later you decide that some compatibility testing must be done with various hardware and applications, and you want to use STC for that. As for the localization efforts, Software Cafeteria's sales partner in Tokyo is willing to do the Far East localization, and your partner in Bonn can handle European localization. Your management decides that these folks will do a better job (and for free) and tells you to use them instead of STC for this aspect of testing. Finally, the marketing manager mentions to you that she has located a half-dozen customers with unusual use cases (workflows and documents) that she thinks would make good beta test candidates.

In addition, suppose that around September 9 you receive an unpleasant surprise: Maria, a key engineer for system testing, hands in her resignation. She agrees to stay through September 30 to finish developing the system test suite, but now you will need help running the suite. Because of the staffing and ramp-up turnaround time, you decide it's too late to bring a contractor on board, so you decide to have your STC test partners work with you during the system test phase, running the capacity/volume and network tests. See Figure 10.1 for a Gantt chart that shows test execution with these resources in place.

In the case of localization, compatibility, and unusual use case testing, you are leveraging the strengths of external resources. Your sales partners overseas have access to multilingual people who can help you with localization. Like most external test labs, STC has access to more hardware than you want—or possibly can even afford—to maintain in your in-house lab. The customers' unique use cases consist of special documents they have handy and workflows they are used to performing. In this instance, it makes sense to use foreign sales offices, external labs, and users for these tasks, even if you could handle the work in-house.

In the case of other system test tasks included in the three cycles of testing, you are primarily off-loading excess work to STC. It's also true that the capacity/volume and network tests are probably good fits for an external lab, given the abundance of hardware these labs generally contain. However, your principal motivation is getting the work off your plate to avoid overloading your staff. You might have chosen to use a contractor, but that would have meant trying to staff a position in three weeks and then hoping that the person could hit the ground running in a critical situation three weeks before the planned release date. Using a proven test resource such as STC is a less risky approach. And since the amount of work to be off-loaded is fairly small, the cost difference between using STC and using a contractor is probably minimal.

As this example shows, you can choose to distribute testing based on the factors of strength and necessity, with each decision involving different amounts of each factor. In some cases, though, necessity can tempt you to make outsourcing decisions that are deleterious to the success of your test effort. To avoid this, you should understand the strengths and weaknesses of various prospective test partners, as discussed in the following sections.

Your Vendors

There is a trend that has developed over the last few years in software and hardware systems engineering to outsource development of one or more key components in the system. Almost every major project I've worked on the last decade has involved one or

ID	Task Name	Duration	Start	Finish
39				
40	Execution	40 days	7/1	8/23
41	Component Test	18 days	7/1	7/24
42	Build C1 Rdy	0 days	7/1	7/1
43	Cycle One	1 wk	7/4	7/10
44	Cycle Two	1 wk	7/11	7/17
45	Cycle Three	1 wk	7/18	7/24
46				
47	Integration Test	15 days	7/15	8/2
48	Build I1 Rdy	0 days	7/15	7/15
49	Cycle One	1 wk	7/15	7/19
50	Cycle Two	1 wk	7/22	7/26
51	Cycle Three	1 wk	7/29	8/2
52				
53	System Test	20 days	7/29	8/23
54	Build S1 Rdy	0 days	7/29	7/29
55	Localization	2 wks	7/29	8/9
56	Compatibility	2 wks	7/29	8/9
57	Use cases	2 wks	7/29	8/9
58	Cycle One	1 wk	8/5	8/9
59	Cycle Two	1 wk	8/12	8/16
60	Cycle Three	1 wk	8/19	8/23

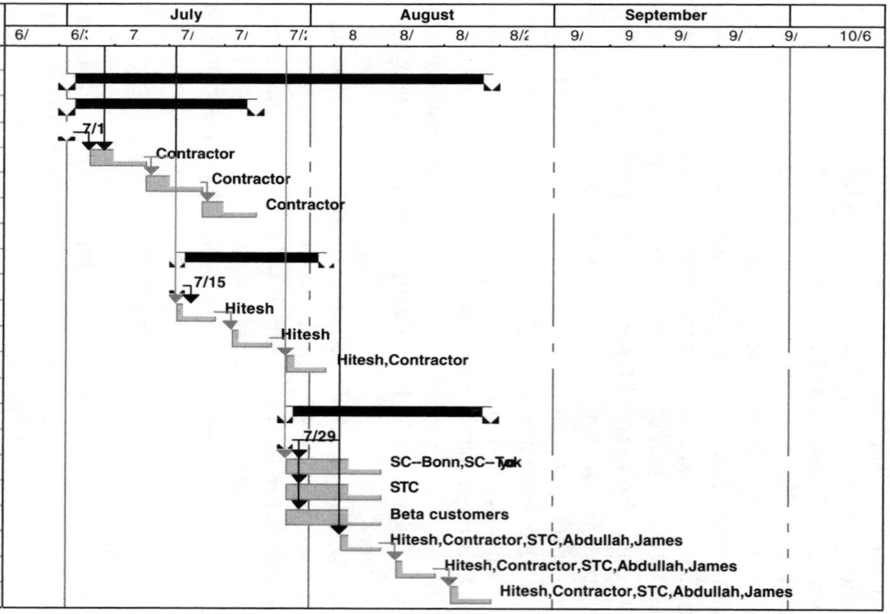

Figure 10.1 A Gantt chart for test execution, showing staff resources, a contractor, foreign sales offices, and an external test lab.

more outsourced components. I'm counting a couple of merger and acquisition situations as a form of outsourcing, since the assimilation of the two company's staff, culture, and technology was incomplete. With the ongoing trends toward bundling applications with other applications and with computers, focusing on core competencies, using cheaper offshore development options, and bringing on consulting firms to help with implementation of in-house IT systems, I don't expect to see an end to this any time soon.

I am a big fan of using outsourced teams to provide key components and services as part of a project. If I didn't believe in it, my consultancy wouldn't be in the business of providing outsource testing tool development, test execution, staff augmentation, and consulting services. However, I have had occasions where management assumed that outsourcing could be done without any risk, without any management or oversight, without any implications to the outsourcing company's practices and processes. I have seen more than one manager, beguiled by clever marketing and sales presentations, impressive client lists, or low hourly rates, who then lost control of key risks to the project. Risks to system quality are among them. When vendors are producing key components for your systems, clear-headed assessments of component quality and smart testing strategies are key to mitigating those risks.

If you are the test manager for DataRocket, some of the obvious participants in your distributed test effort are your vendors. The SCSI card, purchased from a Taiwanese vendor, and the LAN card, purchased from a U.S. vendor, must work properly with your motherboard, with each other, with the hard drives, with any other integrated hardware devices, and with the software—but first and foremost they must work by themselves. What assurance do you have that the vendors are selling you a product that works? And, if you believe the product works, do you need to repeat the vendors' testing?

These questions apply not only to hardware, but also to software. Increasingly, software companies are outsourcing development work to third parties, some of whom are separated from the main office by thousands of miles. Whether the outsourced effort includes hardware, software, or both, you have by definition distributed the testing. The question then becomes whether you can leverage the distributed testing to play to strengths and avoid wasted effort.

Component vendors tend to understand the testing process for their specific components. For example, I had a client who purchased custom modem subsystems from a large U.S. vendor. I audited the vendor's test process to ensure that the modem company was testing sufficiently and to determine what testing my client could omit. I found that the vendor was doing a great job of testing the modem itself. The testing was focused inward, and the modem as a modem worked well.

From the outward perspective of a modem as part of an overall system, however, the testing was less complete. For example, the vendor did thermal testing on the modem, recognizing that it would be installed in a laptop computer. However, the test used an artificial case that didn't approximate the setting in my client's system very well. When I pointed this out, the vendor politely but firmly declined to alter the test specifications. I received the same response concerning questions of software compatibility: the vendor wasn't interested in modifying its testing process to include the software operating environments we intended to bundle on the hard drive. The modem vendor felt that testing the integration of the modem into the system and its behavior as part of that system was clearly my client's concern.

In the case of a component such as a modem, this limited focus might be acceptable. Because a modem's interface to the system is usually serial, software integration is through a standard interface. However, if your vendor is selling SCSI cards, integration is a bigger issue for you. Compatibility issues arise between SCSI devices. You can't simply assume that connecting a hard drive, a tape drive, a removable mass-storage device, and maybe a scanner to a SCSI chain will work. Integration testing is important and should begin early.

Likewise, if you buy a significant portion of your system, such as a motherboard, from a vendor, your project's success depends on the proper functioning of the component; it's fundamental to the success of your platform. Even if some parts of the system are not quite mature, you might need to begin system testing early. A fully functional prototype—even if it's missing the "fit and finish" aspects—is required before you assume that it will work.

Most vendors take a narrow, targeted view of their testing: they might test very deeply in certain areas, but they aren't likely to test broadly. (By this I mean testing across the entire range of features, not just those provided by the vendor's component.) Unless your product performs only limited functions—as an ATM machine does, for example—you probably need to complement vendors' testing with broad testing. Even if a vendor does a certain amount of broad testing, the tests are not likely to be as detailed as you need.

What is the risk to your system's quality related to your vendors' components? In addition to the normal considerations of risks to system quality discussed in Chapter 1, "Defining What's on Your Plate: The Foundation of a Test Project," there are four additional factors, shown in Figure 10.2.

Component irreplaceability. If a component such as a PCI LAN card or an ISA modem is a problem, you can replace it easily; a motherboard, on the other hand, might prove harder to replace in your system. If you need a database in your software, you should have no trouble finding various database options you can use.

Component essentiality. Some systems include add-on components that are extraneous bells and whistles, nice to have if they work, but not key features for customers. For example, every laptop computer I've bought included a half-dozen bundled applications and other software doodads, few if any of which I've ever used. Many applications include add-on components that I know are there by the copyright notices and the packaging, but I've never used most. However, if you have outsourced the writing of the server-side software for a networked application, you are entirely dependent on that software working properly.

Component/system coupling. If a vendor's component is basically standalone—a modem, for example—and doesn't interact with the system in unique (and possibly far-flung) ways, the component is not tightly coupled. However, if it influences the overall behavior of the system, as a BIOS does, it is tightly coupled. Software that interacts with common tables and records in a shared system database is tightly coupled. The coupling might be more than technical, too: marketing sometimes imposes constraints that couple your product to certain components.

Vendor quality problems. How much confidence do you have in the quality of the vendor's components? Smart outsourcing includes a careful assessment of the vendor's capabilities, strengths, and weaknesses—called "due diligence" in the merger and acquisition world—and that should include looking at quality issues such as development and maintenance practices and processes, teams and technology, including testing. Does the test team consist of bright people, working in an orderly, planned fashion, with measurable results and repeatable processes, using appropriate tools? Are their findings taken seriously by management and used to guide the delivery of a quality product?

You have a number of options for dealing with increased risk to the quality of your system caused by one or more of these factors. You can use the techniques described in this chapter to integrate your vendor's testing into a distributed test project starting with component testing—yours and theirs—which you track and manage. To the extent that vendor quality problems are not an increased risk factor, you can trust their testing to deliver a working component, but make time for plenty of integration and system testing with the integrated component in your system. Most of the time, one of these two options has worked for me.

However, sometimes vendor quality problems are a significant risk factor. From a strictly problem-solving perspective, you have a couple of paths open to you. If you have the time and energy, you can fix their broken testing and quality processes by not only integrating them into a distributed test project, but also requiring the vendor to adopt process improvement measures. As a last resort, if you think the risks to system quality are huge and the vendor can't be trusted to help mitigate them, you can disregard their testing and repeat it. From a political perspective, either recommendation is likely to be greeted uncheerfully by management. They are probably under the impression that the vendor is selling them a solid, tested component. In addition, if the vendor has a solid relationship with management, the vendor might put you in a tough political situation by accusing you of being an obstructionist or protecting your turf. Of course, you know better than to let either of these charges *be* true or *appear to be* true, right? Seriously, if you find yourself in this situation, I advise a cautious, circumspect, and politically astute approach to dealing with it.

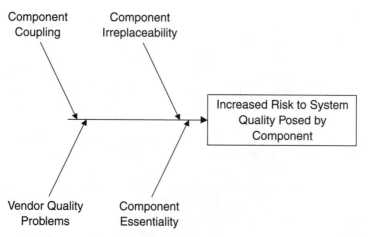

Figure 10.2 Key factors influencing component risk to system quality.

Whichever option you end up with, you should plan on handling the bulk of the integration and system testing yourself and with other testing partners rather than your vendors. In my experience, my clients' vendors have not been good choices for outsourcing these phases, with the exception of some of the functional testing of their component. Just because the component functions properly doesn't mean you have no potential problems in interfaces between the component and the rest of the system, end-to-end operations, capacity, volume, and performance effects, data quality, and most of the other integration and system test phase risks to system quality mentioned in Chapter 1.

Another essential is to make sure that a process exists to ensure that processes and technology support timely, conscientious, and unambiguous reporting, isolation, prioritization, and repair of bugs found either by the vendor or by the rest of the distributed test team. Organizational boundaries make great black holes for bug reports to fall into, never to be seen again. We'll look at some of the logistical problems associated with information flows later in the chapter. However, note that when we're talking about vendors, not only test results flow back to you, but fixes to problems must also. It can be frustrating as the test manager to get caught in the middle of an argument between your vendor and your development peers about where the bug lives. Make sure that the bug lifecycle discussed in Chapter 4, "An Exciting Career in Entomology Awaits You: A Bug Tracking Database," is expanded to accommodate the need for vendors to fix problems you find, and for your development peers to fix problems your vendors find.

Third-Party Testing Organization

Third-party test resources include any organization that offers test services to paying clients. These services can be provided off-site, on-site, or both. I am excluding generic staff-augmentation firms ("body shop" or temporary agency) from my definition of a third-party testing organization, since they do not generally put skilled test managers on the project, offer seasoned, specialized testing experts, build turnkey test teams, or provide expert test training and consulting as part of their services. If a company merely gives you a contractor with the word *test* on the résumé here and there, and you direct that person as you see fit, you're likely dealing with a temp agency, not a third-party test company.

A true third-party test organization brings several key strengths to the table. The most important is expertise in test project management and seasoned skills in technical testing. The company's skills might also be specialized, tightly focused, or unique. For example, some test consultancies do nothing but computer security work, while others have usability expertise. These skills are not common and are not mastered quickly; if you need such expertise, working with a good third-party organization might be your only choice.

Another advantage is that test companies can often begin running tests for you more quickly than you could do it yourself. Some organizations maintain a loose confederation of subcontractors who can jump in right away; others have a staff of test experts on salary. In addition, some of these companies maintain extensive hardware inventories or software libraries that you either can't afford or don't want to replicate. For example, some test labs specialize in environmental testing, which can involve large and expensive equipment such as thermal chambers and shock tables.

A third-party testing company, whether lab or consultancy or whatever, might also be able to offer expert consulting and training services. For example, they might be able to help you through the hiring process, including putting a temporary team in place to bootstrap your growing test organization. They might have training materials for testing and test project management. They might be able to put you on the telephone with skilled and seasoned test consultants—or put those consultants on-site as needed—to help solve particularly thorny testing challenges.

A common theme runs through all these strengths: for certain assets, it's better to rent than to own. If that sounds counterintuitive, consider the following example. If you are a stable citizen of at least moderate means, you can rent a truck, a trailer, and some landscaping equipment and redo your backyard over the weekend. Alternatively, you could hire a landscaping company to come in and do it for you. Either option is somewhat expensive—the latter much more so than the former—but less expensive than buying a truck, a backhoe/trenching machine, and all the other equipment than a professional landscaping firm owns. If you only want to landscape your yard from time to time, why pay to have all that equipment sit in your garage for the rest of the year?

That said, arrangements with third-party test labs can contain significant pitfalls. For the most part, these pitfalls are similar to the hazards encountered in hiring a consultant as discussed in Chapter 8, "Staffing and Managing a Test Team." When you contract with an external test organization, you are the one bearing the risk should that organization prove incapable of discharging your distributed test needs. You might sue, but most likely a nonperforming external lab would simply walk away with one project's worth of dough and an unhappy client. You, however, could lose your job for choosing the wrong partner.

The way to avoid such a situation is for you to exercise due diligence the first time you do business with an external test team. When you hire an employee or a contractor for your own staff, you interview the individual, check references, and scrutinize the person's résumé. Retaining the right third-party test organization is not terribly different.

You begin with an interview, which is likely to be multitiered. In some cases, you'll speak to a salesperson first. This might strike you as a waste of time, but it's not. At this meeting, you can qualify (or disqualify) the company in terms of business issues such as price, turnaround time, and facilities. Remember that the salesperson is checking you out, too, gathering information about similar issues from that company's perspective.

If the results of this interview are positive for both sides, you should proceed to discussions with the project manager and the technical staff. Don't skip this step, and do insist that you talk directly to the people who will work on your project. (If the company won't commit specific individuals at this point, it might not warrant killing the deal, but you should inform the primary contact, whomever that might be, that you insist on approving any and all changes in personnel.) You already know how to hire good test project leads, test engineers, and test technicians, so you can apply similar standards to the individuals involved here. In fact, in this situation your standards should be even higher: these people will cost your company more money than the salaries of your own comparable employees, so you have a right to expect a superior level of expertise.

Be aware that the hourly rate paid for services from a third-party test organization can be more than for that for the same resource through a standard body-shop. Premiums can vary from a few percent over the standard 33- to 50-percent margins of staffing agencies, to the whopping $300 to $400 per hour rates I have seen from some particularly well-known consulting companies. Such premiums can be justified when lab infrastructure, significant amounts of bundled consulting and training, or unique skills are involved. However, as a minimum the organizations should be reputable, provide seasoned people, and demonstrate a serious ability to reduce the risks to your testing project. While you will pay for quality, if you blindly pay, you might well not get quality.

Additional considerations come into play if the work is to be performed off-site. In this case, you are paying not only for people, but also for facilities and access to equipment. If you hire a test lab to perform environmental testing, for example, you are renting thermal chambers and shock and vibration tables, along with the skilled professionals who operate them.[3]

Finally, consider the facility itself. I recommend an on-site visit if you are working with a purely off-site resource. What are your security needs? Do you require a separate lab? Do your competitors use the same facility? Is the facility geographically convenient or inconvenient? Does its location give you access to a less expensive pool of talent than you could find locally? For example, the lower labor costs you'll often find in an overseas test lab might make up for its lack of geographic proximity and the occasional trips you might have to make to coordinate the work, provided that they meet your skill requirements.

This might sound like quite an undertaking, but with luck you will need to do it only once. After you establish a solid working relationship with an external test organization, you can use it repeatedly. This trusted relationship can benefit you not only at your current place of employment, but repeatedly throughout your career. If you find a partner with whom you work well, keep the relationship going.

Sales Offices

If you sell a product internationally, you might have a local sales office or a sales partner (such as a distributor) in various regions. Alternatively, you might have a "virtual" sales office, with a staff member in the main sales office handling foreign sales. Either way, the sales office is singly aware of and qualified to evaluate the unique quality risks of the foreign market.

Chapter 1's list of quality risks included localization as a major category of risk for any product sold or used internationally. In some cases, testing this quality risk at the home office is well beyond challenging. With DataRocket, for example, you might need testers fluent in Japanese, Korean, Mandarin, Thai, Cantonese, German, Dutch, French, Russian, Spanish, Italian, and Polish to vet your documentation and startup guides. How will you simulate foreign electrical power? If you include an optional modem, how about foreign dial tones? Which colloquialisms and symbols might be cultural taboos or just plain ridiculous? For example, in certain parts of Spanish-speaking South America, the verb *coger*, meaning "to get," takes on a crude connotation and

---

[3]Kaner, et al., in *Testing Computer Software* cite markups of four times the hourly rate to the tester at some independent test labs. So, if the lab is charging $60 per hour for testing, the bulk of the work is likely being done by $15 per hour technicians.

THE GARTNER GROUP ON OUTSOURCING

In the September 1998 edition of *Executive Edge* magazine, the Gartner Group describes three areas of effort that are good fits for the outsourcing of information technology functions: utility functions, which are nonstrategic but necessary roles; enhancement functions, which make a strategic position better; and frontier functions, which allow a company to move into new technologies.

Although the focus of the Gartner Group's article was on in-house IT efforts for banks and the like, the point is equally valid for outsource testing work to vendors and third-party testing companies. For example, routine but critical test operations such as shock and vibration tests for DataRocket might fit into the utility category. Add-on testing for SpeedyWriter in areas such as broad-ranging hardware compatibility or interface usability might be considered enhancement. If your product incorporates leading-edge (frontier) technology, it's often useful to bring in an external resource such as a consultant or an outside test lab with special expertise in this area.

The Gartner Group also points out certain risks associated with outsourcing:

- Poor communication with the external organization concerning the business objectives and the reasons for outsourcing.
- Jumping the gun on the process of selecting an external resource, perhaps in a hurried attempt to toss work over the fence.
- Failing to manage the work, assuming that it will take care of itself.
- Not integrating the data—in this case, test results and bug reports—back into your centralized tracking system.

Distributed testing, like development outsourcing, does offer many benefits, but you must also be sure to manage these risks.

---

must be avoided in polite discourse. In some countries, using an index finger as a pointer is considered rude. Every now and then you hear of a humorous translation of less-than-successful foreign advertising campaigns such as the soft drink that apparently claimed, in some Chinese dialect translations, to "bring your ancestors back to life." Few besides local people are likely to be aware of such distinctions.

As fellow employees, the staff members in a sales office have the same goals and objectives you do—they have a stake in ensuring that the test effort is successful. For example, the folks in your Tokyo sales office will want to do good job of testing the Far East localization of SpeedyWriter, so that their sales numbers look good.

Unfortunately, these sales and marketing people might not have technical sophistication or a particular skill with testing. If you are responsible for the results of the testing and want specific items tested, you will need to spell out these details. Any test cases you give to nontechnical colleagues must be precise and unambiguous. As Chapter 3, "Test System Architecture, Cases, and Coverage," explained, writing such test cases involves a great deal of hard work.

You must also remember that the salespeople, marketing staff, and sales partners do not work for you directly. They are typically peer or a peer-level manager's direct reports rather than your direct reports. Although you are responsible for ensuring the quality and completion of the testing they perform, you cannot structure their jobs, and you cannot specify standards of behavior, ways of interacting with your team, or circumstances under which you will end the relationship. As a practical matter, you might have to go to some amount of trouble to get results from them.

Users and User-Surrogates

In this category, I include business analysts, help desk, customer support, and technical support personnel along with actual target customers and users. Most commonly, these folks participate in alpha, beta, pilot, or acceptance testing efforts. (One of my clients, though, invites its customers' most-expert users of its system to participate in system test, using their own unique data and workflows.) As mentioned previously, testing by users and user-surrogates can result from considerations of credibility, contractual obligation, or from a need to broaden test coverage.

In the case of credibility problems or contractual obligation, your objective for such testing is reversed from the usual: you do not want the test partner to locate any bugs that you haven't already seen. If you've been having trouble convincing the project team of the seriousness of some of the bugs you've found, you might want the users and user-surrogates to find those bugs, but watch out for getting on the wrong side of the project management team if you deliberately create such incidents. Ideally, involving such partners in your test effort should confirm what you and the project team already know about the quality of the system.

The most common examples of this type of testing are acceptance and pilot testing. Acceptance testing should demonstrate conformance to requirements and fitness for use. Pilot testing demonstrates readiness for production, either in terms of literally firing up an assembly line or starting to use the system to do real work. Clarity and precision about the meaning of the words *requirements*, *fitness*, and *readiness* are key to such efforts. I've seen a project founder when the project team could not agree on the acceptance test exit criteria. To the extent that you, as the test manager for the overall development project, are involved in this, it's generally a supporting role. However, sometimes users or user-surrogates will witness acceptance testing performed by the test team, or use test cases, data, or tools developed by the test team.

If you need to broaden test coverage, then the focus is generally on finding bugs again. (Since users or user-surrogates are doing the testing, concerns might surface if "too many" bugs are found, especially bugs that indicate serious problems with readiness near the scheduled project end date.) Most alpha and beta programs are in this category. This type of testing can provide coverage of workflows, data sets, configurations, and deployed field conditions that might be tough to replicate in the test lab. For example, when I tested an Internet appliance, we used beta testing in part to understand how various telephone line conditions might influence connection speed and stability. These tests also give you a sense of usability issues that might not occur to testers, especially if your testers differ significantly from the users in application domain or technological expertise.

Like acceptance and pilot testing, alpha and beta testing might not be the test manager's effort to manage. For any user or user-surrogate testing, if you don't manage the effort, be cautious about taking on the responsibility of tracking their results. Since users and user-surrogates are generally not experienced testers, the quality of the testing and test result reporting can be inconsistent. I've had people tell me that they've had great luck with such programs, and I have on occasion as well, but I've also seen indecipherable bug and test reports come out of alpha and beta programs. I also had problems with test engineers having to spend a lot of time supporting one alpha test effort that was considerably more trouble than the limited information we obtained was worth. However, with careful planning and management, you might find involving users and user-surrogates to be a valuable and economical way to leverage the substantial stores of application domain knowledge and real-world usage that they can provide.

Planning a Distributed Test Effort

You need to plan distributed testing with the same level of detail you use to plan your internal effort. It should be a straightforward process, given that you have your own operation under control. The starting point is completion of the high-level test planning discussed in Chapters 1 and 2. You should also have your own test suites fairly well defined, although a few details might remain to be settled. Your test tracking and bug tracking processes should be worked out, including a plan for deploying the bug tracking system.

Assessing Capabilities

Once you've learned enough about a potential test partner to select the organization for the project, as outlined earlier, you next need to assess that partner's specific test capabilities as part of planning your overall test effort. You should approach this exercise as you approach any business meeting: with a certain expected outcome in mind. Compile a proposed list of contributions that you can check off as you go through the assessment, focusing especially on questions related to the areas of skills, staffing, and physical setup.

This is especially important when talking to your vendors or potential third-party test organizations. For each proposed task, can the test partner produce an expert—or at least an experienced, competent person with the requisite skills—who will do the work? In many cases, you will be pleased with the skill levels of the people the vendor and third-party test partner candidates will propose. However, in some cases the person you interview is not up to your expectations. This is not necessarily a reason to eliminate the prospective partner from further consideration, especially if the person they are proposing is better qualified than any other candidates you've spoken with. Holding out for the ideal set of experts at the ideal test partner might mean having no resource available in time. (As the Chinese proverb says, "The perfect is the enemy of the good.") If you must settle, make a note of this to use as a bargaining chip when price comes into the picture. In addition, as Chapter 8 warned concerning consultants, beware of bait-and-switch tactics, in which the vendor or third-party test organization substitutes people with less skill than you have been promised.

With sales and marketing people, users, user-surrogates, or other coworkers or colleagues with no direct responsibility for running tests, the assessment must look not only at capability, but also at commitment. Can you be sure that, when the time comes to run tests, these folks won't be busy doing other things?

Adequate staffing is critical. It's often tempting to see vendors and testing companies as bottomless wells of skilled test experts, especially if that's what you need. However, every company has its staffing limitations. Some test labs keep client costs down by using primarily subcontractors and temporary labor, so you might find that they specialize in ramping up for test projects. Others rely on full-time staff. Assure yourself that your partner will be able to provide the entire team. It's not uncommon for a software or hardware engineering company that performs outsourced work to try to win business by overcommitting to clients in terms of the staffing resources it can bring to a project. Then, having won the business, the company is unable to execute. This is a disheartening experience for those in the company in question, but it could prove politically fatal to you if major elements of your test effort go uncompleted because you didn't fully check out your test partner.

Your assessment of your partner's physical setup should include equipment, facilities, and location. Does the company own the equipment it needs to perform the work? If not, will it be able to buy or lease it in time? Does the company have room, physically, to perform the work? Is security adequate? Is the location suitable for the tasks you are contemplating?

If the testing work will happen off-site, your assessment should be performed at the test partner's facility. For foreign sales offices and the like, you should try to travel to the remote site. Contrary to accountants' wishes, on-site assessment becomes more important the further the partner is from your home office. A partner at a less remote site is less likely to try to snow you concerning test capabilities because it is easy for you to show up unannounced.

Understanding the Cost

Before you proceed further with detailed planning, a vendor or third-party test organization might require that you begin to pay for the project. An independent test company, of course, makes its money selling test services, not talking with prospects about test services. Your vendors might assume that further discussions are part of their deal with your company, but then again, they might not. Foreign sales partners, users, and user-surrogates might be willing to do certain testing for free, but you can't assume that their time is worth nothing.

From vendors or third-party test companies, you can request a bid, which can be either a fixed-cost bid or a time-and-materials bid. If you receive a time-and-materials bid, you will need to estimate a weekly or monthly cost for your own budgeting purposes. Make sure that the bid includes some flexibility or contingency fund, not only for the inevitable changes that will occur, but also to allow for alterations you will make in the next step when you create a unified test program (as described in the following section).

In addition to the fees the test partner might charge, certain expenses are necessarily associated with distributed testing itself. Later in the chapter, we'll discuss the mapping issues that can impose some of these costs. Besides these outlays, you will have other overhead such as communication and travel. Gather all these associated costs and incorporate them into your budget.

This budgetary work might be tedious and can slow the process, but it's important to take care of it at an early stage to avoid getting stuck with a program you can't afford. Money always matters, and it figures significantly in distributed test efforts.

Collating, Coordinating, and Partitioning the Test Program

Your next task in distributed testing is to merge two or more test projects into a single unified test program. In general, you can think of this process as analogous to cooking and cutting up a pie. Various ingredients are involved in preparing the pie, but when the pie is served, a little of each ingredient will be on each person's plate.

Let's use another DataRocket example. Ignoring localization for the moment, assume that the players in a distributed test effort include your test team at Winged Bytes; the SCSI card vendor, Lucky Bit; and an environmental test lab, System Cookers. The goal is to produce a single set of test cases, organized into a collection of test suites, with each suite run by one of the three teams. Figure 10.3 shows the steps involved.

The first step, collation, involves creating a single list of all the test cases that will be run. You'll need to collect each team's list of test cases and add it to your test tracking spreadsheet (discussed in Chapter 5, "Managing Test Cases: The Test Tracking Spreadsheet"). Use the spreadsheet's Owner column to keep track of which team is currently responsible for each test.

In the second step, coordination, you eliminate redundant test cases. For example, you notice that Lucky Bit was planning to run a thermal test on the SCSI card, but you would prefer to have System Cookers run a thermal test of the entire system with the SCSI card installed. Perhaps Lucky Bit can calculate the airflows required to keep each component operating within specifications and dispense with the test. System Cookers can attach thermal sensors to the active components and run the tests later. (Watch out, though, for partially overlapping test cases, as discussed in the section, *Dealing with Mapping Issues*.)

In the test tracking spreadsheet, you can assign a *Skipped* status to each redundant test case, noting in the Comments column that the test is skipped because another team is running a preferable test. Don't forget to include the test identifiers in the comment so that people can cross-reference the other case. For example, a comment might read: *Covered by Sys. Cook. Test 3.005.*

Your third step is to partition the work, reviewing the test tracking spreadsheet and reassigning test cases to new owners. Much of this work is done by default as you coordinate the testing, since skipped test cases are removed from a team's workload and eliminated from the list. In other cases, you simply might want a different participant to run the test case. Perhaps it is better to provide Lucky Bit with a system for thermal testing than to try to get one to System Cookers, because of engineering sample limitations.

This three-step process must take into account more than just technical matters. Budgetary concerns will surface if you change the scope of a partner's involvement drastically. Politics and turf issues can also come into play. A vendor might be happy to have you accept most of the test burden, but the vendor's test manager could feel threatened; the test manager might want to do more testing, but that could be counter to the vendor's business interests. Independent test labs always want more work, but only if you're willing to pay.

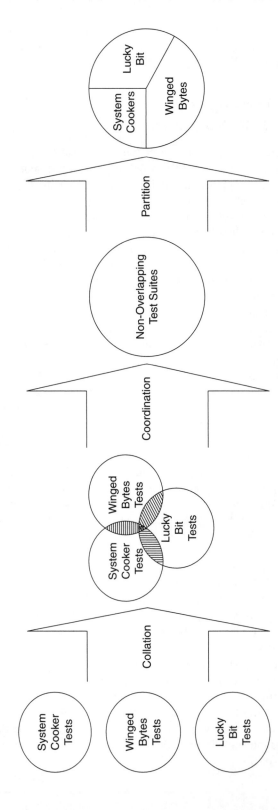

Figure 10.3 Integrating three distinct test programs into one.

Organizing Logistics

One of the advantages of distributed testing, when the test suites are partitioned properly, is that each partner plays to its strengths. This situation tends to minimize logistical problems. For example, if you use System Cookers to do your environmental testing for DataRocket, you have solved the logistical problems you would otherwise have in setting up your own thermal chambers, shock and vibration tables, and so forth. For SpeedyWriter, using STC to do compatibility testing frees you from having to stock and manage an extensive inventory of software and hardware.

In some cases, however, distributed testing creates unique logistical problems. The most difficult obstacles arise when a project includes one or more custom pieces of hardware, engineering samples, or other limited-availability equipment. On one project, custom-made parallel-port dongles were in short supply, limiting us to two testers. In a typical laptop project, only one or two dozen prototypes are hand-built for the first test cycle. Adding partners increases the number of engineering samples needed, thus putting an extra strain on the development organizations. Expect to have to negotiate your share of the samples, and plan on making compromises.

Since these components are engineering samples, they break more easily than production hardware does. Because field support won't have any idea how to handle a damaged piece of hardware they've never seen before, a failed component must be repaired by development. This imposes an additional burden because either the item must come back to its point of origin for repair, or an engineer must travel to the remote partner's location.

Speaking of traveling hardware, someone must coordinate the delivery and return of these items. Shipping is hardly an art form, but it does require planning and consideration. A test partner of mine once returned three laptop computers—irreplaceable first-stage engineering samples out of a total population of 25 or so—that were broken beyond repair. The person who sent them neglected to use packing foam or "peanuts," and instead placed the computers in a box, loose, and shipped them 5,000 miles. When confronted with the situation, this individual was surprised that anything had gone wrong—and expected the carrier's insurance to pay for the damage.

If computer equipment crosses an international border, you will have to deal with customs. Unlike shipping, this *is* an art form. Don't fly across the Pacific with four laptop computers in checked luggage, expecting to show up at a Taiwanese customs desk with a credit card, pay the duty, and go on your merry way, as your humble narrator once naïvely tried to do. Even with an experienced and competent customs broker, the process takes time and is not always transparent.

For these reasons, you'll want to keep the number of partners involved in your test project limited when you have custom hardware. In some cases, you might be able to give your test partners remote access to your custom hardware if their testing is primarily on the software side.

Even the software aspects are not without pitfalls, however. The problems in this area generally have to do with configuration and release management. For example, I participated in a project in which a remote test lab needed to have the custom software configuration of a laptop. We were forced to deliver physical disk drives because no one could come up with a workable method for delivering CD images or allowing a network download. (Such methods exist, of course, but in this case, no one had the time to figure out the potentially complicated process.) If your test partners need to receive multiple software releases, you will have to spend time thinking through the delivery process.

One aspect of this release management challenge involves security. If you come up with a method of sending your software releases over the Internet, you might be concerned about someone intercepting that software. To handle that problem, you might decide to encrypt the software. However, if that encrypted software is going to be crossing an international border, all sorts of laws govern the sending of encryption technology to different countries, or using encryption within a country. (U.S. export laws classify some encryption tools as military weapons; France, until quite recently, actually prohibited the private use of encryption; and the U.K. is considering laws requiring key escrow.) Government licenses might be required. The same applies if your system includes bundled encryption functionality, which might be hiding in unsuspected places. One client whose system included a browser—which has 128-bit encryption in the secure socket layer—had to get a license from the U.S. Department of Commerce to send the master system image to Taiwan to be put on systems there as they were produced.

You can use the logistics database discussed in Chapters 6 and 7 to help manage and keep track of the logistics of distributed testing. (You might recall that Chapter 6, "Tips and Tools for Crunch Time:Managing the Dynamic," included an example of distributed testing for SpeedyWriter, with testing being performed at Software Cafeteria's home office, at STC's lab location, and at John Goldstein's home office.) Of course, when you have remote partners, you don't need to use the lab logistics capabilities added in Chapter 7's ("Stocking and Managing a Test Lab") version of this database; organizing their own lab is part of what you're paying your test partners for.

Dealing with Mapping Issues

If every test operation worked exactly the same way—according to the model presented in this book, for example—your planning work would be finished once the test program was unified, the work was partitioned appropriately, and the logistical problems were handled. The truth is, however, that each test team uses a different approach. You can't (and needn't) make every test partner work the same way, but you do need to recognize and manage the differences. I call these "mapping issues" because you are trying to map your partners' test efforts onto your own.

The first mapping issues usually arise during coordination, as you are comparing and sorting test cases. Figure 10.4 illustrates some of the possibilities you might encounter. Some test cases are completely unrelated to one another, and you must keep them all to maintain the desired level of coverage. In other instances, truly redundant test cases exist: either two test cases serve exactly the same purpose, or one test case completely covers another's conditions (along with additional conditions). Still other test cases overlap one another partially: test case A covers some but not all of test case B's conditions, and vice versa, but you can't drop either one without compromising coverage.

When you discover partial overlap, you can sometimes drop one test case and then redesign another to cover the missing conditions. Often, however, you must resign yourself to some redundancy of coverage at the test case level. The amount of wasted time and effort is usually very low in comparison to the parameters of the overall project.

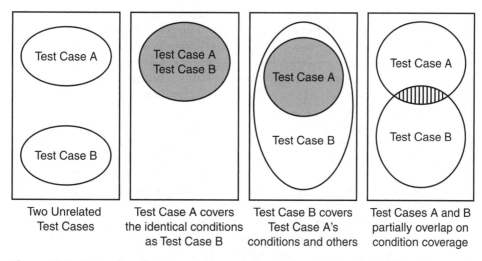

Figure 10.4   Examples of test case independence, redundancy, and partial overlap.

Test size, in terms of duration, effort, or both, can also complicate coordination and partitioning. Some test engineers write long test cases; others write shorter ones. Some test cases by nature require long duration or more effort. For example, reliability and environmental tests often run over a period of days. A three-day-long test case might happen to include some but not all of the conditions covered by a test case run elsewhere. You can't drop the test case, unless you're willing to recreate all the work at the remote site.

You'll encounter other mapping issues during test execution, and you should plan solutions ahead of time. The most important is creating a process for getting all the bug reports into a single bug tracking system. With the database presented in Chapter 4, you can use the replication feature in Microsoft Access to distribute the database to your partners, or they can dial up and access the data on your servers. (To facilitate this, you can split the database into a front end consisting of the forms, queries, and reports, and a back end consisting of the tables.) Alternatively, you or an administrative assistant can receive bug reports from partners and enter them in the database. Either approach will work, provided that you ensure minimal turnaround time.

Because multiple partners are testing, you will see more than the usual number of duplicate bug reports. Even if you do a good job of coordinating and partitioning the test cases to avoid overlap, certain bugs will manifest themselves on multiple tests. (If you do independent two-party testing, in which each party is unaware of what the other is doing, you can use the number of duplicate bug reports to estimate the effectiveness of the overall program. The more duplicates, the better.)

Language can also be a major issue when it comes to bug tracking and test tracking. You can expend a lot of effort setting up a process for sharing data electronically, only to find that the teams can't communicate in the same language anyway. Unfortunately, using a nontechnical translator or administrative assistant won't suffice, since many of the questions that arise might be technical. Language can become an insurmountable barrier in some distributed test efforts; you should be sure to look into the matter before you set up such a program. Not every tester at every partner's site must speak a common language, however; usually, one or two people from each team can do the lion's share of communication work. I have successfully managed distributed test programs with vendors and test labs in Taiwan in which only one or two people on each test team spoke English.

Other mapping issues can stem from intercompany differences in work hours, conference calls, telecommuting policies, and the like. Technical challenges such as email system incompatibilities can create difficulties. Even unexpected legal and trade barriers sometimes present challenges. For example, if you plan to encrypt sensitive documents to be shared with an overseas partner, you end up in the same bind mentioned earlier in regard to sending encrypted releases.

It's impossible to list every conceivable mapping issue. The fundamental point is that during the planning stages of a distributed test program, you must anticipate the differences, both formal and informal, between the processes you and your test partners follow and try to put plans in place to minimize the difficulties. Once test execution starts, you will have little time to resolve these issues on-the-fly.

Managing a Distributed Test Effort

Once you become accustomed to it, managing your virtual test team as the work proceeds is not that different from managing your own company's team. You will find, however, that these five areas require special attention: tracking the test project and its findings; communicating test status and changes in direction; handling the political realities; being sensitive to disparate cultures; and establishing and maintaining trust.

Monitoring Test Execution

Chapter 6 stresses the importance of keeping the bug tracking and test tracking mechanisms accurate and current during crunch periods. You will probably find this more challenging in a distributed test effort, even if you have done a good job of attending to the mapping issues discussed earlier. Distance, time zones, and language barriers can all get in the way. If you are updating the test tracking spreadsheet, for example, and find that you have questions about a set of test case failures found by your test partner, you could lose a few hours tracking down the person who can provide the information. If you need the data for an urgent presentation to management, this becomes a bigger problem.

Generally, you should plan for a certain lag in receiving results from external test partners, from a few extra minutes to as much as several days, depending on location. For example, when I worked with partners in Taiwan, our limited window for telephone conversations (early morning and early evening) meant that a miscommunication could go uncorrected for a full day. Email asynchronicity is convenient, but it also allows miscommunications to fester for days on end, especially when you're asking someone to carry out a task he doesn't really want to perform.

If you have a remote test partner whose work is on the critical path, there is no substitute for being on-site. A travel budget is important: a 10-day, $5,000 trip to Tokyo or Taipei starts to look pretty affordable when a loss of momentum by your test partner risks slipping the ship date by three or four weeks.

Although this might be seen as an argument against distributed testing, don't forget that there is also an upside to your test partners' isolation. Many dysfunctional events can occur at the home office during test execution, and having some of your testers insulated from the effects of those events can keep them focused on the tasks at hand. I once had a client who moved the test operation from one side of the building to another at the start of a critical 10-day test period; this was a major distraction that hurt productivity for the first two days of that period. I've also seen plenty of testers demotivated by the politics and frenzy attending crunch mode. An outside team, operating in a less crisis-driven environment, might make more headway than your own team, who is forced to react to the crisis of the moment.

Communicating Status and Changing Direction

None of your test partners can operate in a vacuum. You need a way to keep them apprised of what's going on, a way to allow them to bring problems to your attention, and a way to adjust course based on changing circumstances and test findings.

Email is not a bad communication channel for these purposes, but it can easily degenerate into "flame wars" and tangential discussions. If you use email to communicate status, it's useful to format messages as either a status report or a list of action items. A daily update of a short (one- or two-page) document from each test partner should suffice as a status report. (To keep it from being a running report, allow old items to drop off.) Alternatively, you can keep a specific list of numbered action items, each with an owner and a due date.

The action item list is most effective when combined with a regular conference call at least once a week. During crunch mode, you'll probably find that such calls are necessary daily. A conference call should always have a structured agenda, with each partner reporting status and problems to the group in turn, followed by a review of the action items. At the end of every conference call, all the participants should agree on the current status of the test project and what is to happen next (i.e., action items).

These conference calls are also the right place to communicate changes of direction that affect multiple partners. Changes that affect only one partner can be communicated either by telephone or by email, depending on urgency. Be sure to track any alterations in plan in your change management database (discussed in Chapter 6). Changes affecting your test partners are just as important as those affecting your own team.

I've assumed throughout this discussion that none of your test partners compete with each other directly. If they do, keep the two sides separated. In one project with some logistical pressures, I needed to use two competing independent labs for testing, one in Taiwan and one in Los Angeles. I explained the arrangement to each lab manager, and both understood, although neither was happy about it. I had to build a "firewall" between the two in terms of conference calls, email threads, and project findings to ensure that no industrial espionage or unproductive sniping could take place.

If you end up in this situation, avoid the temptation to play one side against the other. Agitating situations in which conflicting interests exist is liable to have unforeseen and negative outcomes. In addition, both of the organizations being manipulated will come to resent and dislike you. Building up reservoirs of ill will between you and people with whom you hope to do business in the future is hardly a wise move.

Handling Political Considerations

While your off-site test partners might be insulated from the turmoil and intrigue of your development project, you will inherit their political issues. Everyone in a development project must be seen as an active, positive participant. Because third-party test companies and vendors are off-site, however, an image of them as noncontributive can gain currency. In addition, questions of competency and diligence can arise when the inevitable mistakes are made. (Certainly, such concerns arose among my client's project managers after the laptop-shipping incident mentioned earlier in this chapter.)

Since you selected the test participants and planned the test effort, you have a stake in their success—not only their technical success (finding bugs and covering important test points), but also their political success (being perceived by the rest of the development team as effective, committed, and hard-working). It is up to you to champion the external test partners among your internal colleagues on the development team.

It sometimes happens, however, that negative perceptions of the external test partners are correct. In some cases, they are a net drag on the project. Test organizations can win contracts for which they are unqualified or understaffed. Vendors can prove unwilling to be frank about serious bugs they discover in their own products. Users, user-surrogates, and salespeople can turn out to be less interested in making a positive contribution to product quality than in carping about the lack of it—or even taking potshots at your testing effort. In these unfortunate circumstances—in which, I should point out, you might never find yourself—you need to act resolutely to mitigate the risk.

Such actions might include pulling the distributed testing back in-house—a painful solution, because you will likely discover the problem in the midst of the most pressure-filled part of the test schedule. This is not a conspiracy to make your life hell. People and organizations fail under pressure, not when the going is easy.

You might also want to shift some distributed testing to other external partners. Working with two test labs, as I described in the preceding section, did make my task of managing the project somewhat tricky. However, in addition to the logistical benefits, it also gave me a safety net. If one lab had proven unable to carry out its commitments, I could have moved its work to the other partner.

Either way, severing a relationship with a test partner is likely to prove unpleasant. Lots of money is at stake, and people get emotional under these circumstances. Since you had a hand in selecting the participants and planning the effort, you stand to lose face as well. You might also fear damaging an established relationship with the test staff of the vendor or test company. It's important, however, to keep your interests clear and consistent. Your ethical and fiduciary obligations are to your employer or client. If you handle it professionally, you can end the participation of a test partner without excessive rancor or unfairness.

Fairness in ending a relationship requires not only meeting financial considerations, but also maintaining an open mind in making the decision. Move slowly on such decisions, and consider the source of derogatory information you hear about external test partners. Distributed testing, while undoubtedly a good idea under many circumstances, encounters internal resistance in most organizations. Some people will resent the work being sent outside the company. These people sometimes act, both overtly and covertly, to damage the image of the distributed test program. Bashing the participants is one easy way to accomplish this. Do not disregard the concerns of such Cassandras, for they can be right, but do check out the story before making a final decision.

Being Sensitive to Culture Clashes

Any time your test organization relies on an external partner, cultural issues will become relevant, whether based in local culture or in the culture of a company. This is guaranteed by the fact that testers must, as discussed in Chapters 8 and 9, hold different perspectives than other technical contributors.

My own background provides some examples. I changed from being a programmer and a system administrator to being a tester and test project leader when I took a job with an independent test lab. All my colleagues at the lab were testers. We worked on projects for clients who were developing hardware and software, but usually we interacted with only one or two client contacts. This all served to shield me from the political and cultural cross-currents that roil test groups in broader organizational settings.

I was forced to adapt rapidly a few years later when I became a test manager in a small custom software development shop. Chapter 9 dealt with the political realities of testing within the context of a development organization, lessons I learned to a great extent in that first test manager position. I have since relearned those same lessons, with a few variations, with subsequent employers and clients.

When you implement a distributed test program, you will experience these cultural issues writ large. Perspectives, priorities, and values differ from one team to the next even within a company, depending on the personalities of the team members, the leadership skills of the manager, the integrity of the perceived technical and moral leaders of the team (not just the manager), and, not least, the mission that team serves. When you deal with external organizations, these cultural issues are intensified by the fact that the leaders of the partner companies can instill different values. Although I always emphasize the importance of individual contributors to the success of a team, I am often reminded, sometimes shockingly, of how much the vision, ethics, and leadership skills of a handful of top managers in a company can profoundly influence the way in which even the most mundane tasks are performed.

In terms of distributed testing, such differences can mean that some individuals who would fail as test technicians, test engineers, or test managers in your company are seen as consummate test professionals perfectly aligned with the company culture in your test partners' organizations. For example, I place great value on cooperative relationships between testers and developers. In contrast, however, some successful organizations use an adversarial approach, with test managers encouraging testers to "catch" developers in errors. I would find it too emotionally draining to work in an organization where employees sought to undermine each other's successes, but if I worked with a test partner that used such an approach, it would hardly be within my purview to try to change that culture. Nevertheless, I might find the internecine quarrels distracting, to the extent that they spilled over into my life.

More subtle but equally challenging cultural clashes can occur. For example, I had a client who (at my recommendation) used an external lab in Taipei to handle some compatibility testing. The client's vendor was also located in Taipei. The test lab's corporate culture encouraged flexible but long hours, as my client did. The vendor involved had an "8-to-5" culture. Ironically, when we needed to institute regular conference calls, the vendor's culture and my client's culture meshed, but the time difference worked against the test lab. We had to schedule the calls for 8:30 A.M. Taipei time, which was fine for the vendor but troublesome for the project leader in the test lab, who worked from noon to midnight by choice. Ultimately, I decided to excuse him from the call, making sure I understood their results and could represent their findings. This allowed the test manager to continue working his comfortable schedule. Had I insisted that he start working cumbersome hours, that could have damaged our relationship.

Building and Maintaining Trust

More fundamental than congruent cultures is the question of whether you can trust your test partners. Trust is an even more slippery concept than culture, but we all recognize people we trust or distrust. Even those who spend time building trust with us can lose it at a moment's notice. Suppose that you are the manager at Winged Bytes, working on DataRocket. A colleague of yours, the test manager for the SCSI card vendor, has been scrupulous about reporting any problems the vendor's test team finds, not just on this project but also on two previous projects. Suppose now that the test manager delays or conceals news of a fatal bug in the card's BIOS. That trust, built up over years, will suffer a serious, perhaps fatal, setback.[4]

All the tools and tips discussed in this chapter cannot resolve this problem. If you partition your test program to have test partners execute critical tests, you must establish a relationship of trust. You have to trust that the test lab won't skip a few tests because it's running behind schedule and fears that it will lose money on your project. You have to trust your vendor to be frank about even the most embarrassing bugs. You have to trust your colleagues in the foreign sales office to follow up with test results so that you aren't scrambling at the last minute to deal with critical bugs. You have to trust users and user-surrogates not to use testing results to slam your team—or the project.

Trust also involves more than ensuring that your partners won't take advantage of you. You must look out for them, too. For example, I have helped test partners on my projects work through problems with invoices and contracts. There is, of course, a narrow path to tread in such matters, as you have fiduciary responsibilities to your employer. However, assisting your chosen test partners in dealing with a nebulous or sluggish accounts payable problem shows good faith and a concern for your partner's success. When people know you are looking out for them, they'll usually look out for you.

In closing this chapter, it's worthwhile to point out that trust isn't an issue only for your external test partners. It is critical for the entire project team, whether those peo-

---

[4]See Rajiv Sabherwal, "The Role of Trust in Outsourced IS Development Projects," for an interesting discussion of the importance of building and maintaining a trusting relationship with outsource partners. While this article addresses development resources, it could just as easily have been written about working with external test partners.

ple work at one company or at several. You have to assume that people are all pulling for the success of the project, by playing their individual roles to the best of their abilities. You must also assume that people are pulling for the success of their collaborators.

The cliché about a few bad apples spoiling the barrel applies especially to trust in an organization, but it's also true that key leaders in a firm, by setting an example of trustworthiness, can set a company-wide standard. People who consistently apply their best efforts create passion and dedication. People who support all their colleagues and cooperate for the good of the team foster an environment filled with confidence and good will. No one, though, can contribute as much to a trusting and open company culture as a manager can. Managers who keep their commitments, who never let underlings take the fall for their own failings, who support and celebrate the successes of their star players, their team, and the company as a whole, who balance the company's needs with the personal needs of their subordinates and colleagues, and who consistently give and expect the truth from their staff, their peers, or their own managers, cultivate a corporate culture of trust and integrity. As a test manager, you must participate in creating and upholding an environment of trust, both within your team and across the company. The standard you set in your team is as important as anything else you do.

Case Study

On the information appliance project cited in Chapter 8, I put together an in-house test team that focused on four areas: server farm testing, information appliance testing, usability testing, and test tool development. To make sure the custom hardware worked correctly, I asked the vendor who built the system to thoroughly test the hardware. I also had a third-party test lab run some of the most critical hardware tests to make sure the quality was sufficient in these areas. Finally, the marketing manager administered various forms of user and user-surrogate testing, which, while not under our direct control, resulted in some interesting bug data that both confirmed some of our findings and added new information, especially in the area environmental issues such as telephone line conditions. Figure 10.5 shows the organizational chart for the distributed test team on this project. (The names have been changed to mask the project's identity.)

I thank my client, who wishes to remain anonymous, for permission to discuss this project here. I also thank my client contacts for their excellent support and steady leadership on this project. Finally, thanks to my test team, the vendor, and the independent test lab for their professionalism and excellence on this project.

Exercises

1. Suppose that an external test lab, located in Taiwan, and a vendor, located in India, are participating in your test effort. (Your offices are located in the central time zone of the United States.) They send you bug reports by email and you have a test technician enter them into the bug tracking system.

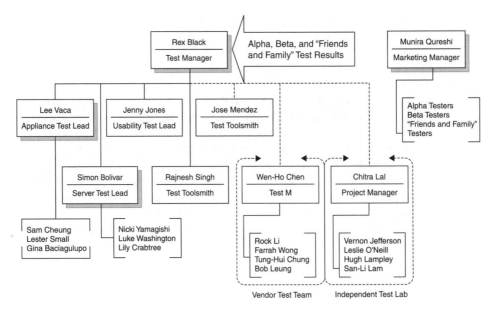

Figure 10.5   A distributed test project.

- Due to the time difference, bug reports get into the bug tracking system after almost a full day's lag. How will this affect your test dashboard? Is the effect significant?

- Assume a test release comes out once a week on Monday morning. It takes two days for the release to be transmitted securely to the vendor and the test lab. Assuming they both work from 9:00 A.M. to 5:00 P.M. local time, when is the earliest you would expect confirmation, regression, and planned testing to commence (in terms of central U.S. time) at each location?

- Assuming that confirmation testing concludes in a day and bugs identified in the test release notes are reported by email as fixed or not fixed by the end of the day, how does this lag affect your test dashboard? Is the effect significant?

2. One of the frequently cited concerns about outsourcing testing to third-party test company is that the consultancy's or lab's testers might not have sufficient knowledge of the application domain of the system. Based on the critical skills discussion in Chapter 8, do you feel that would necessarily be an issue for your company? Are there certain tests that your company could outsource even if application domain knowledge was in some cases an issue? Is your company sufficiently organized in terms of the areas discussed in this chapter to gain benefit from outsourcing testing?

Testing in Context: Economics, Life Cycles, and Process Maturity

In the last ten chapters, I explained the key tools, techniques, and approaches that I use to manage my testing projects. At the risk of sounding arrogant, I would say that, based on the response to the first edition of this book, people at my test management courses, and others to whom I've sent these templates, these ideas have worked for lots of test managers in some form of another. Therefore, I trust that you too will find a way to put them to work.

An important part of adapting these ideas to your particular situation is understanding the context in which you're working. Testing does not happen for its own sake, in a vacuum, because we're merely intellectually curious about the quality of some system—at least I've never been paid to do that. Rather, organizations pay for testing—they *invest* in testing—to realize benefits. If the project management team has realistic expectations, they'll invest in testing as part of a larger investment in quality. (In other words, the project management team should understand that the mere act of testing does not make bugs go away or reduce the number of bugs developers put in the system.) This investment in quality can yield benefits such as an improved reputation for quality; lower post-release maintenance costs; smoother release cycles; increased confidence that the system will work well for users and satisfy customers; protection from lawsuits initiated by unhappy customers, users, or those otherwise affected by system failure; or, to reduce the risk of loss of entire missions and even lives. Your management team might want you to help them realize some of these benefits, all of these benefits, or even some benefits not on this list. As I started to become aware of the motivating factors behind my test team's existence, I started to realize the difference between the tactical perspective on testing and the strategic one. Tactically, testing is the search for bugs in the system and for knowledge about what works and what doesn't work. Strategically, though, testing is a risk management activity that reduces the likelihood of the organization having to bear unanticipated future costs related to poor quality. Testing is something like insurance, but without actuarial certainty or the ability to make the company whole for a loss. A good testing group provides value in this regard by providing a timely, accurate assessment of system quality to the organization. This assessment is usually delivered in the context of a development or maintenance project.

Various risks threaten the success of a project:

Features. Can we deliver the right set of functions to the users and customers?

Schedule. Can we deliver those features soon enough?

Budget. Can we deliver those features in a profitable or at least financially acceptable way?

Quality. Can we deliver those features with the predominant presence of satisfying behaviors and attributes and a relative absence of dissatisfying behaviors and attributes?

Successful projects mitigate and balance these risks, and the four elements converge for a successful delivery as shown in Figure 11.1.

Because of the need to mitigate the risks and balance these competing elements, the test subproject must integrate smoothly into the sponsoring project. I discussed one aspect of this integration, aligning testing with the critical risks to the quality of each of the features in the system and the system as a whole, in Chapter 1, "Defining What's on Your Plate: The Foundation of a Test Project," and Chapter 2, "Plotting and Presenting Your Course: The Test Plan." I also discussed the need to fit the test subproject within the economic, schedule, and process parameters of the project from a micro or local sense; in other words, the way these project parameters affect the test subproject. In this chapter, though, I'll look at the macro or global view of testing within these economic, schedule, and process parameters.

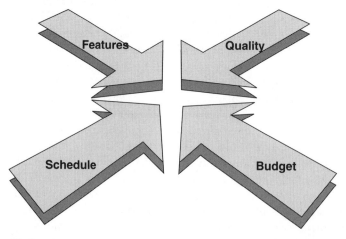

Figure 11.1   Project elements converging for a successful delivery.

Is Quality Free?
The Economic Justification
for the Testing Investment

Let's start with economics. There's a really fascinating apparent dichotomy lurking in this topic. On the one hand, improved quality is either usually—or always, depending on whom you ask—a good investment, and this can be demonstrated through a simple model called *cost of quality*. On the other hand, it is often very difficult to get adequate funding for testing, for reasons both economic and non-economic.

What Does Testing Really Cost?

Nothing. Zilch. Nada. Zero. Quality is free—at least that's what Phillip Crosby wrote in his book of the same name. Frank Gryna did his first cost/benefit analyses on quality at General Electric in 1949. Later, Gryna, together with J. M. Juran, wrote the *Quality Control Handbook*, which describes a model referred to as cost of quality or quality costs. Crosby, Gryna, and Juran refer primarily to service industries and manufacturing, but recently Sandra Slaughter, David Harter, and Mayuram Krishnan's paper, "Evaluating the Cost of Software Quality," published in the *Communications of the ACM*, made the same "quality is free" claim for software quality. Likewise, Campenella and his co-authors, in *Principles of Quality Costs*, include a case study of cost of quality at Raytheon's Electronic Systems group. Raytheon's Electronic Systems group reduced their costs associated with poor quality from a high of over 40 percent of the average project cost to 6 percent over the course of eight years. (This was done in conjunction with a process maturity initiative called the Capability Maturity Model; I'll return to the topic of process maturity in the last third of this chapter.)

Creative accounting strikes again, you say? Not really. To reach this rather startling conclusion, let's look at the costs of quality model. This model says that we can divide quality costs into two categories: the *costs of conformance* and the *costs of nonconformance*.

$$C_{quality} = C_{conformance} + C_{nonconformance}$$

The costs of conformance include any expenditure taken to ensure quality. This includes *prevention costs*—in other words, quality assurance—such as training, process improvement, and so forth. The cost of conformance also includes much of the testing budget, such as planning the test effort, designing and developing a test system, installing and configuring a test environment, and running each test (the first time). These test expenses are called *appraisal costs*.

$$C_{conformance} = C_{prevention} + C_{appraisal}$$

The costs of nonconformance arise from system problems (i.e., bugs) and process failures (such as the delays, bad test releases, and others discussed later in the section *Process Brake Pedals*). These bugs and process breakdowns result in rework, repairs, slowdowns, and other inefficiencies. In the testing effort, a common example arises any time a test case fails. You must repeat the test that found the bug or bugs to verify and isolate them, repeat tests to confirm fixes to the bug or bugs, and repeat some number of previously passed tests to check for regression due to the fixes. All this effort spent repeating tests is basically wasted time due to the presence of defects in the initial system. The time and money expended represent one cost of nonconformance arising from *internal failures*. Costs of nonconformance also include *external failures* (what happens when a bug affects a customer, end user, or society). These costs include much of the technical support group's budget, the expenses associated with creating, testing, and deploying field fixes, product recalls and refunds, liability costs, and lost sales.

$$C_{nonconformance} = C_{failure(Internal)} + C_{failure(External)}$$

Crosby, Gryna and Juran, and Slaughter, Harter, and Krishnan, and Campenella and his co-authors all demonstrate that, if you invest testing and quality assurance budgets wisely, the costs of conformance plus the costs of nonconformance related to internal failures will be less than the costs of nonconformance related to external failures.

$$C_{failure(External)} > C_{prevention} + C_{appraisal} + C_{failure(Internal)}$$

A SpeedyWriter Case Study

Cost of quality is a concept that's much easier to grasp when you see an example. Let's suppose that we're working with SpeedyWriter. To keep things simple, we'll look at testing as the only cost of conformance; in other words, there are no quality assurance or prevention costs of quality, only appraisal. For nonconformance costs, we'll consider only the cost of fixing bugs either before or after release, without trying to quantify intangibles. The plan is for a quarterly release, which, based on defect data from past projects and the estimated size of the SpeedyWriter releases, the project management team estimates will contain 1,000 must-fix (i.e., customer impacting) bugs. Finally, let's assume that we know that costs of failure, on average, are:

- $10 for bugs found and fixed by programmers during informal testing (unit and component) of their own or each other's code.
- $100 for bugs found by testers during formal testing (integration and system), fixed by programmers, and confirmed fixed by the test team.
- $1,000 for bugs found by customers after release, reported to technical support, fixed by supporting programmers, and run through confirmation and regression testing by the test team prior to release to customers.

Our initial situation, before an independent test team is formed, is shown in the "No Formal Testing" column in Figure 11.2. The programmers do a fine job of testing, finding 25 percent of the bugs, but customers still find 750 bugs per release. Our cost of nonconformance—mostly external failure—is $750,000, with a total cost of quality of $752,500. I said I'd ignore intangibles, but let me point out as an aside that it's not as if we're buying happy customers with this sizeable tab, but to the contrary, customers are quite upset with us. This is sometimes referred to as "adding insult to injury."

Suppose that in response to this situation the project management team decides to institute a test team to do manual testing, in addition to maintaining the same standard of unit and component testing by the programmers.[1] The analysis of this situation is shown in the "Manual Testing" column in Figure 11.2. Between the testing environment and the staff, this represents an investment of $70,000 per quarterly release. (The test environment can be amortized over multiple releases, let's say one year, so this represents a $40,000 initial test environment setup cost.) Assume this test team does a good job of testing and finds about half of the bugs that remain in the system during integration and system testing. Now customers find only 400 bugs—still a sizeable number, but quite an improvement—and our total cost of quality has fallen to a little over $500,000. So, what is our return on our $70,000 investment?

$$ROI = \frac{Net\ Benefit}{Investment} = \frac{752,500 - 507,500}{70,000} \cong 350\%$$

A	B	C	D
1 **Testing Investment Options: ROI Analysis**			
2			
3	No Formal	Manual	Automated
4 Testing	Testing	Testing	Testing
5 Staff	$0	$60,000	$60,000
6 Infrastructure	0	10,000	10,000
7 Tools	0	0	12,500
8 Total Investment	0	70,000	82,500
9			
10 Development			
11 Must-Fix Bugs Found	250	250	250
12 Fix Cost (Internal Failure)	2,500	2,500	2,500
13			
14 Testing			
15 Must-Fix Bugs Found	0	350	500
16 Fix Cost (Internal Failure)	0	35,000	50,000
17			
18 Customer Support			
19 Must-Fix Bugs Reported	750	400	250
20 Fix Cost (External Failure)	750,000	400,000	250,000
21			
22 Cost of Quality			
23 Conformance	$0	$70,000	$82,500
24 Nonconformance	$752,500	$437,500	$302,500
25 Total CoQ	$752,500	$507,500	$385,000
26			
27 Return on Investment	#N/A	350%	445%

Figure 11.2 SpeedyWriter testing investment ROI.

[1] I've mentioned in previous chapters the importance of good unit and component testing as part of a complete test effort. You may also want to refer to Elisabeth Hendrickson's paper, "More Testing, Worse Quality," available at www.qualitytree.com, for more thoughts on the dangers of programmer test abdication after the establishment of an independent test team.

Well, that's certainly a solid and respectable return on a fairly modest initial investment, right?

If you recall the Defect Detection Percentage (DDP) metric from Chapter 4, "An Exciting Career in Entomology Awaits You: A Bug Tracking Database," and Chapter 8, "Staffing and Managing a Test Team," we can put a metric on the effectiveness of our test team, too.

$$DDP = \frac{bugs_{testers}}{bugs_{testers} + bugs_{customers}} = \frac{350}{400 + 350} \cong 47\%$$

Is this good? Well, it's certainly a better situation than before, and establishes a baseline for future improvement.

Perhaps we can improve both the ROI and the DDP? One common technique for improving the effectiveness and efficiency of testing is to introduce automated testing tools for functional regression, load, performance, and reliability testing, among other areas. The "Automated Testing" column shows the analysis of that situation.

Assume we've invested $150,000 in test tool licenses, training, and expert consulting and contractor services to get our automated test effort off the ground. The licenses include three years of maintenance and upgrades, and the tests are expected to be usable on the average over 12 releases, so this represents a $12,500 investment per release. Thus, the overall test investment goes up to $82,500 per quarterly release. Assume this test team now finds about two-thirds of the bugs that remain in the system during integration and system testing. Now customers find only 250 bugs, which is perhaps a number we can live with at this point. Our total cost of quality has fallen to under $400,000.

Our new return on investment, including the test automation investment, is

$$ROI = \frac{Net\ Benefit}{Investment} = \frac{752,500 - 385,500}{82,500} \cong 445\%$$

Our new DDP has also improved significantly, becoming

$$DDP = \frac{bugs_{testers}}{bugs_{testers} + bugs_{customers}} = \frac{500}{500 + 250} \cong 67\%$$

It's important to recognize that returns like this on the testing investment might be above or below what you will get. (See also the *Comments on Exercise 1* sidebar in the Exercises for this chapter for further limitations on the cost of quality technique as a way to capture the business value of testing.) In addition, your returns will be negative if you test the wrong things. Finding bugs that do not relate to customer usage or critical quality risks distracts the project team from fixing real problems and can give a false sense of confidence that things work when in fact the system is teeming with bugs. However, if you follow the risk-based approach outlined in this book, apply good test system design, development, and implementation practices, and are responsible for test phases where finding bugs is the norm and the goal (i.e., not acceptance or pilot testing), then you are likely to consistently see a demonstrable, positive return on investment.

Management Obstacles to Test Funding

Given the business case we demonstrated in the preceding section, we should have no trouble getting adequate funding for our test efforts, right? Well, even armed with a convincing business case that includes a solid return on investment, you might find that you still have problems. There are a number of obstacles to getting adequate funding for testing. Some of these we create ourselves as test managers. Some are inherent in the testing reality. And some are the result of management blind spots to testing realities, usually compounded by our own mistakes. To do a decent job of testing, you must receive sufficient money, hiring requisitions, and lab equipment. However, the figure you consider adequate and the figure your managers will accept seldom coincide. In a typical situation, you will have to put together an organization that is both lean and effective.

Test Manager Budgeting Faux Pas: Obstacles the Test Manager Creates

Communication is a two-way street, as the saying goes, but as a test manager requesting funding for your test effort, the burden lies mostly on you to make the communication that occurs between you and your superiors effective. You have to explain to your manager, in terms she can understand, why you should receive a substantial sum of money to find bugs in the product. There are a number of ways to make this case, as I'll explain in a minute, but one way to *not* make this case is to argue from a moral perspective. Okay, if you're writing software where personal or public safety is involved, you have the right to play the "moral imperative" card. However, most of the time, banging the quality gong and pretending to be Don Quixote, Lone Defender of Quality, will just come off as self-righteous and disconnected from project realities. Usually, the test manager's job is not to be the lone defender of quality, but rather to put together an operation that can assess quality—as the customer will experience it—so that management can act on that information.[2]

Try to see testing through management's eyes. What motivates them to want testing? Can you make the information you can provide as a tester even more desirable to them? Do they see your testing budget as excessive? If so, why? The better you can understand the obstacles in your management's minds to giving you what you consider sufficient funds—and the forces that make them want to give you what they consider sufficient funds—the better you'll be able to communicate with them about this hotly debated topic. After all, selling is the art of making a product or service desirable to a customer, and then overcoming the customer's objections to the sale.[3]

---

[2]For more thoughts on the counter-productive nature of a moral argument for testing, see James Bullock's article, "Calculating the Value of Testing," originally published in Software Testing and Quality Engineering, Volume 2, Issue 3, now available on www.stickyminds.com.
[3]I learned this succinct description from Cem Kaner, who, as part of his Renaissance-man background, once worked in his family's retail store as a young man. The process of selling a developer on the effort involved to fix a bug is described in *Testing Computer Software*.

Regrettable Necessity: Obstacles the Testing Reality Creates

As you start to see testing from a management perspective, you'll also start to see that testing is, to paraphrase Winston Churchill's comment about democracy, the worst possible form of ensuring quality in computer products, except for all the others. Ideally, business analysts, marketing managers, software designers, engineers, and developers could, by applying preventive techniques, produce perfect systems that would require no testing.

Imagine a world where there was no crime. We wouldn't have to pay for police officers, would we? Imagine a world where houses couldn't catch fire. We wouldn't have to pay for firefighters then, right? Imagine a world where people settled their differences without fighting—okay, I'm getting into John Lennon territory here, so I promise to stop in just a second—but seriously, if people didn't fight wars to solve political problems, then we wouldn't need militaries.

The reason I bring this up is not to espouse some utopian society—I don't believe in the perfectibility of humanity, so I don't believe in utopias—but to introduce the economic concept of the *regrettable necessity*. A regrettable necessity is a cost that, from an economic point of view, would be nice to do without, because that money could be spent more productively elsewhere. It's very unfortunate that people commit crimes that victimize their fellow citizens, that houses catch fire, that people, say, attack innocent civilians of a tranquil country on otherwise-peaceful September mornings, but these things do happen. It's too bad that we need to spend money on governments at all, because government is another form of friction and economic loss. If we all could agree on the right thing to do and simply do so, without someone forcing us to be nonviolent and honest with laws, that would be cheaper, wouldn't it?

Okay, blue sky aside, the human condition is that we play the hand we're dealt. In software and hardware engineering, programmers and other engineers can't help but create bugs. They tend to do a reasonable job of finding some of those bugs during unit and component testing, but a fairly poor job of finding those bugs during integration and system testing. This means that test teams, which can consume as much as 50 percent of the human resources budget for a project, must exist to catch these bugs. Even if you are fortunate enough to work in an organization whose executive managers understand the necessity of testing, don't expect them to be thrilled about paying for it. Testing is expensive. If the ratio of testers to developers is one-to-three, somewhere between 15 and 35 percent of the development organization's human resources budget is going to people who, from the senior managers' bottom-line perspective, do nothing but find problems created by the people who receive the other 65 to 85 percent of the paycheck budget.

Some bugs are shy, as discussed in Chapter 6, "Tips and Tools for Crunch Time: Managing the Dynamic." This means that we have to construct production-like or customer-like test environments to find these bugs. The test environments can be extensive, costly, and hard to maintain. In terms of resources such as hardware and software, the ratio of costs for development environments versus test environments is tilted toward the test team. Developers can usually work on a subset or scaled-down version of the operating environment, but to be truly effective, testing must replicate end-user settings as much as possible. It's not unheard of for test labs to require resources valued at 10 times those needed by the development team. One attendee at my test management seminar told me that in his test lab he had single pieces of equipment valued at over $1,000,000, and that he had figured he would have to spend well over $1,000,000,000 to thoroughly represent the different field configuration options.

Time is money, too. Each additional test cycle is another day, week, month, or however long that cycle takes that the system will not be out in the real world. Delaying deployment or release means that some beneficial features or functions aren't being delivered. This could mean inefficiencies in some internal process for IT shops, which means lost money. This could mean lost sales—perhaps forever—in mass-market situations where someone chooses the product currently on the market and then is no longer looking to buy that product. This could mean contractual penalties in a custom-development shop where your managers agreed to deliver to the customer on a particular day.

So, when a manager is looking at a testing budget, he sees all these costs that he wishes weren't there. He also probably sees—if he's been around once or twice—that testing might well end up taking twice as long as planned. Hopefully, he recognizes that this isn't the test manager's fault, usually, at least when an abysmally bad product is snuck into the testing environment. However, slips in the schedule mean more staffing costs, more test environment costs, and more opportunity costs.

Hang on, you say, didn't you just get done telling me less than half a dozen pages ago that quality is free? If so, what are all these economic objections to the huge return on investment that I can offer?

Well, yes, I did say that quality is free, but only in the long run. Since we're talking economics, the dismal science, I'll quote John Maynard Keynes, who said that, "in the long run, we're all dead." A limited pile of cash is available for any given project. Once that money's gone, it's gone. (Ask any former employee of a dot-bomb firm about this fact of life.) Managers have to make prudent decisions—often trade-offs—about where to spend money. This puts limits on how much money can be spent on quality-related activities for any given project, positive return on investment notwithstanding.

Communication Breakdowns: Management Blind-Spots and the Difficulty of Education

Sometimes test budgets are not approved—or retroactively unapproved—because the management team doesn't understand the benefits of testing. Even seasoned high-tech managers occasionally fall into the rut of complacently thinking, "Oh, what could possibly go wrong?"

Some managers never get out of this rut. When you hear of organizations in which developers do all the testing, small test groups are assigned unachievable test loads and held responsible for quality, or management doesn't pay attention to the test dashboard, then you know that such organizations are run by a team of senior managers who fail to understand the complexity of software and hardware development. Frankly, there are many buggy products on the market today, and not understanding the need for an independent test organization, how it should function, or how to appropriately respond to test results has a lot to do with that.

However, I think that we test professionals need to accept our share of the responsibility for this situation. If we can't effectively articulate the test plan, doesn't that reinforce the idea that testing isn't really that hard? If we can't produce a clear set of system quality metrics, how will we convey our concerns about system quality to managers? If we can't measure defect removal trends, then how do we demonstrate how long it really takes to fix bugs—and thus to exit a test phase? If we fall into adversarial relationships, won't we come across as disruptive and negative rather than as people providing a valuable service to the project team?

Surmounting the Obstacles. . . Then Doing What We Can

I don't claim to know exactly how to communicate to your managers about the testing budget. Everyone is different. I'm an independent consultant, and I don't win every engagement I propose, so I guess I haven't figured out all these angles, either. However, there are some techniques I try to get people on board. Then there are some follow-through steps I think are important.

Testing is about risk management, and you must explain the risks as part of selling management on your budget. Because a risk is the possibility of a bad outcome, your pitch for each budget item might sound something like this: "If you don't test A, you might have failures X, Y, and Z in the field; and I can't test A without buying C." Some salespeople refer to this technique as "fear, uncertainty, and doubt," which makes it sound pretty low. However, it serves the greater good of shipping a better product, and, frankly, some managers just won't listen to you unless you use this technique to get their attention. Don't be an alarmist, though. Describe some realistic scenarios of bugs that could cost the company a lot of money but that could be caught by testing. The time you've spent understanding the important risks, using the techniques discussed in Chapter 1, should pay off here. Express those risks in terms of possible user experiences: "unable to complete a sale," "prevented from printing the file," "taking 10 seconds to respond to a keystroke." Avoid those dry and slightly mystical technical phrases such as "core dump," "blue screen of death," "surface overtemp condition," and other jargon.

If you consider it crass to raise alarms, at least understand that it is not dishonest. Testing can only add value when it helps the company mitigate risk. You are tying one hand behind your back if you decide to "take the high road"—whatever that might mean in this context—and eschew discussions of what could go wrong. If at some later point, you end up with so many people on your staff that everyone is playing video games or surfing the Internet half the time, then perhaps you should feel guilty.

Anecdotes are convincing, and you should use them. You should also use figures and data, too, in spite of the cliché that figures don't lie but liars do figure. Build credibility for your data, and then use defect removal models, past test results, and cost of quality to justify your budget. Just as with explaining your test results, using data to explain your resource needs can help make your presentation dispassionate.

It's important, too, to recognize that project funds are limited, so you're playing something of a *zero sum game*—in other words, a game whose outcome involves moving around existing money, like Poker or Blackjack, rather than creating new wealth, like free-market capitalism—with the other managers on the project. Money allocated to testing is money your fellow managers don't have in their budgets. But don't panic. Money I spend on food, airline tickets, trash pickup services, auto maintenance, and every other thing I write checks for every month is money I don't have in my savings account either, but I don't resent the people who sell me these goods and services. On the contrary, I feel that they are providing me with useful economic options and I'm glad to pay for those options.

This is something we need to master as test professionals. How can we convince our peer managers that we are providing them with a useful service? First, let's focus on being service oriented, on building strong alliances with our peer managers, as I discussed in Chapter 9, "The Triumph of Politics: Organizational Challenges for Test Managers." Developers need help finding bugs. Sales, marketing people, and business analysts want to sell or deliver quality to users and customers. Help desk, technical support, and customer support people don't want angry customers. Every one of these teams—and their managers—are obvious allies to help you help them.

Finally, I'm particularly careful these days to advocate, but never pontificate. Even when senior managers understand the need for testing, they might not realize why it costs so much. It's not always simple to explain. Because I've been testing for many years, all these facts of testing life have become paradigmatic to me. These facts are seldom obvious to my managers. Senior managers who understand and value the need for independent testing always give me an opportunity to justify each line item in my budget, but I am not excused from that exercise. It's up to me to respond to these legitimate questions by providing clear, to-the-point answers.

It's also up to me to do what I can with whatever I ultimately get. If I react to attempts to trim my budget by saying, "Fine, cut my budget and I'm outta here," then I'll probably spend a lot of my time adjusting to new cubicle space. Just as I said in Chapter 1, there's usually a difference between what I *should* test and what I *can* test. The difference: features, schedule, quality, and budget realities. When my wife and I had a house custom-built, we left out many features in the house that we wanted. We'll probably add these features over the coming years, and the features will cost us more than they would have if included during construction. However, we couldn't wait six or 12 more months to move in and we didn't want to spend another $100,000 or $200,000 on the house.

As a test manager, I make trade-offs. I always do. I'll be asked to focus on what's most critical, what no one else is testing. That's part of my job. Often, I'll make a pitch to management for some amount of testing and I'll be told to do a bit less testing with a bit less money and time. That's what usually happens. Doing a bit less testing than I'd really like to is always part of testing in the contexts in which I've worked. If I want to work as a test manager in such a context, I can't let what I can't do stop me from doing what I can.

Where Testing Fits into the Life Cycle

Another part of understanding project context is thinking about where the testing to be done fits into the overall system life cycle, the various phases, constituent activities, and dependencies among those activities. This is important because strategies, plans, and activities for test system development and test execution that would be ideal for one life cycle can be less helpful or even counterproductive for others. Since there are so many different life-cycle models defined, it's beyond the scope of this book to try to discuss each in detail. However, in the following subsections, I'll outline some of the major varieties I have encountered or that attendees at my test management seminars most often mention.

Common Life-Cycle Themes

Regardless of the specific life cycle chosen, the most successful projects I've worked on have some common themes in this area. One is that the testing is divided into phases (also referred to as "levels") as discussed in Chapter 1. Ideally, each phase should find all the bugs it can, leaving only those bugs specific to the subsequent phase to be found. For example, logic errors in specific functions or objects should be found during component testing, leaving data flow errors between functions or objects to be found during integration testing, which in turn leaves system performance problems to be found during system testing. The degree of formality and the number of phases tend to vary, but at a minimum should usually include a unit or component test phase and a system test phase. Using the right phases helps keep the testing process efficient. Think of test phases as steps in a cleaning process, each of which uses a type of cleanser and cleaning approach that removes a particular type of dirt, grime, or soil. For example, you can remove bacon grease from a plate with a clean dry towel, but you'd be better off washing the plate in hot water with dishwashing detergent and a sponge first, then rinsing the plate with warm water, and finally using the towel to dry the plate.

In most organizations in which I've worked, the developer of a unit or component was the owner of the unit or component testing for his or her unit or component. The component testing approach was primarily structural ("white-box"). The independent test team handled system testing. The system testing approach was primarily behavioral ("black-box"), with some live testing (especially live data, but also beta testing) and some structural testing (especially test tools) thrown in.

For complex systems, I highly recommend having an integration test phase as well. If you don't have the time and resources to do the type of formal, risk-driven integration testing I mentioned in Chapter 1, with integration or build plans along with integration test plans, at least do informal testing of as much of the system as exists as the components are completed, looking for bugs that could arise in interfaces and dataflows for various reasons. Without integration testing of some sort, the first phase of system test is a de facto "big bang strategy" integration test phase. I have seen this approach cause entire weeks of testing downtime when key components that seemed to work fine on their own failed to communicate—or sometimes even to compile and link—correctly when put together.

Integration testing is often an orphaned test phase. It requires some amount of structural testing and some amount of behavioral testing, so broader skills are required of a test team engaged in integration testing than one engaged in either component or system testing. It looks for bugs between pairs of components, but often programmers do not want to spend the time testing their component with other programmers' components. However, it can help to ask, "Who are the immediate beneficiaries of good integration testing?" The people charged with system testing are, because, as mentioned earlier, they are the people who will be blocked if poor or omitted integration testing results in a nonworking system being delivered for system test. (Even if you require the system to pass entry criteria and/or a smoke test before entering system test, as discussed in Chapter 2, you'll still end up scrambling to find productive work to do if the day before system test was to start the system fails to meet the entry criteria or to pass the smoke test.) Therefore, if integration testing is an orphan in your organization, I encourage you to work with management to get the resources you need to adopt it.

In systems to be delivered to in-house or contractual (as opposed to mass-market) customers, there is often an acceptance test phase of some sort. Pilot testing is another post-system-test phase that occurs in some organizations. Often, the test manager is not responsible for the acceptance test phase directly. However, the organization will reasonably expect that good component, integration, and system testing will result in a system ready for acceptance and pilot testing when the time comes. (In some cases, though, risks to system quality covered in acceptance and pilot testing go beyond the scope of the previous testing phases. For example, pilot testing of laptop computers tests the production line capability, but usually the previous test phases used hand-built engineering prototypes.) During the planning process, then, look at what the acceptance or pilot testing phases involve, and escalate to management if you see any gaps in the component, integration, and system test phases that could lead to last-minute discovery of critical bugs in acceptance or pilot testing. These types of findings can create a serious conundrum for the project—sometimes even outright project cancellation—along with real political problems for the test manager if these are seen as test escapes.

Entry and exit into test phases should represent major transitions in the readiness of the system, especially in terms of quality. If the system leaves one test phase and enters the next with all the appropriate bugs detected and repaired that could be detected and repaired in that phase, the subsequent phase will go smoothly. If a phase is done poorly or not at all and the system enters a subsequent phase buggy and untested, that subsequent phase will tend to proceed inefficiently. The subsequent phase might also be ineffective at finding the bugs it should find, due to the distraction posed by the leftover bugs that should have been found earlier. This can lead to a cascading or snowballing effect on to the next phase and ultimately on the quality of the delivered system. This is part of the reason for the importance of adopting good definitions for exit and entry criteria, as discussed in Chapter 2.

Another reason is that entry into a test phase owned by a different group than the previous test phase represents a significant hand-off point in the organization. If you use the right set of test phases with the proper entry and exit criteria, these hand-offs will be smooth and a feeling of teamwork fostered. If key test phases are omitted, if criteria are poorly defined, or if criteria are defined but not abided by in the event, then phase transitions will be more a matter of some poor-quality system being hurled over an organizational wall, resulting in a "gotcha" experience for the receiving party. In the long-run, repeated botched hand-offs will lead to personal ill will and distrust between members of the project team, especially between developers and testers or between users and user-surrogates and testers.

Selecting the right set of phases, defining proper criteria for them, and abiding by those criteria (or at least only waiving any of them through mutual consent of the stakeholders) is a key part of fitting the testing effort into the project life-cycle context. But how do we know what the right phases and criteria are? To some extent, that is a function of the life-cycle model being used, which can also have other effects on the test project.

The V Model

One common life-cycle model of software development is called the *V model*, shown in Figure 11.3. The development work proceeds in sequential phases down the left side of the V, while test execution phases occurs up the right side of the V. Tests are planned and developed, and the appropriate test environments acquired and configured, starting as soon as the corresponding development phase begins. The three arrows crossing the V show these activities. For example, requirements being the basis for behavioral and live acceptance tests, preparatory work for that phase of test execution can commence immediately. (Of course, requirements also figure in system testing, and to a lesser extent integration and component testing, too.) Some versions of the V model allow for overlap of phases, while other call for pure sequentialism; in other words, the entry criteria for one phase always include exiting from the previous phase.

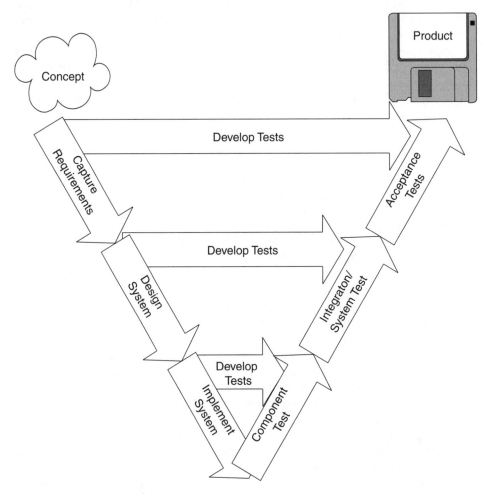

Figure 11.3   The V model.

This is a very intuitive model, and one that has in many ways become institutionalized in a lot of software engineers' minds and in many software development organizations. To many testers, it just looks right when they first see it. Most software engineers who received their degrees prior to 1990—which would therefore include many of the people in project management now—probably learned this model or its less test-explicit variant, the waterfall model, when they were in college.[4]

One chief danger with this model is that it's hard to plan accurately that far in advance. To announce that the project team will deliver a given set of features—which are often cast in stone in the minds of project managers, users, or user-surrogates by the end of the requirements phase—on a specific date that might be two or three years in the future and for a specific amount of money is to presume a level of prescience most human beings don't have. Capers Jones, in *Estimating Software Costs*, cites the incidence of significant delay or even cancellation in moderate-sized development efforts as around 20 percent, and for large efforts that figure can balloon to as large as 70 to 90 percent. As Jones puts it, "[T]here is almost an infinite number of ways to fail in building software applications, and only a few ways to succeed."[5]

This life-cycle model is basically driven by schedule and budget risks, with quality often taking a back seat. If the requirements, design, or implementation take longer than expected—and they often do—the "pivot point" at the bottom of the V starts to slide to the right, but the end date anchoring the top of the right arm of the V remains stuck in place. This leads to what I often refer to as the "ski slope and cliff" variant of the V model. The project glides down the implementation ski slope right into the quality cliff of the test execution phases at the end of the project, which were compressed in a haze of wishful thinking about how all those test cycles planned won't be needed after all.

Nevertheless, there are some ways to mitigate the risks inherent in the V model and use it successfully. Testing tasks should start as early as possible, be cooperative between all the participating groups, and should include feedback mechanisms. For example, on one project my team started working on test cases with early drafts of the requirements document. In this process, we discovered a whole raft of requirements problems that the project team then had a chance to resolve before they resulted in design and code defects.

Test execution cycles must also be planned realistically, especially in terms of how many cycles will be required to find all the bugs for each phase and give the developers ample time to repair those bugs. Defect removal models such as those discussed in Chapter 4 are a real help here, but if you don't have data, at least trust your gut instincts and the collective wisdom of the test team. Resist the urge to put in place patently silly plans such as two cycles of component, integration, or system testing on the assumption that the first will find all the bugs, which the developers will fix in short order, and then the second cycle will simply confirm the fixes and the lack of regression. (This might be a reasonable plan for acceptance testing, since you shouldn't really find any bugs during

---

[4]I have two copies of Roger Pressman's *Software Engineering*. The Second Edition, published in 1987, includes eight pages of discussion on life cycles, primarily focused on the waterfall or variations on it. The Fourth Edition, published in 1997, includes an entire chapter on the topic.
[5]See Caper Jones, *Estimating Software Costs*, Chapter Seven for his figures on project success and failure. The specific quote is found on page 114.

acceptance testing at all.) Such test phases might happen on some projects, but it's never happened on a project I've worked on.

While good entry and exit criteria are important regardless of the life-cycle model, on the V model they're even more critical, because test phase entry and exit points tend to be where the project team gets its best indicators that the project is off track in terms of schedule and budget. Be very clear about the risks to the quality of the system and perhaps to the project itself if people start talking about violating those criteria in the name of staying on track. (See the section *Process Brake Pedals*.) If you are allowing overlap between phases, fine, but then you should have smoke tests defined that demonstrate readiness to enter each phase. These smoke tests, if automated, also make a handy tool for keeping broken releases out of the test environment, because you can run them before starting a given test cycle.

Finally, rather than violating or waiving entry criteria, see if you can't set up a process where the project team revisits the feature set at test phase entry points. Change control boards (CCBs) are particularly useful for this process. If a feature is not completed or is completely bug-ridden, and that will delay the start of some test phase or activity, then that feature should be postponed to a later release. Realistic feature triage like this can mitigate some of the most nasty failures of the V model.

The Spiral Model

In some cases, it's hard to determine in advance what features exactly are needed—or can be feasibly built. The spiral model relies on quick prototyping to discover and manage key project risks early in the effort. In this model, shown graphically in Figure 11.4, the initial concept is quickly translated into a prototype of some or all of the system, focusing usually on those features and design elements considered most at risk in terms of technical feasibility or satisfying the users. The prototype is put through some limited testing, again focusing on the high-risk areas. What is learned from that prototype informs a subsequent round of design, prototyping, and testing. This continues until a final set of features, known to be feasible, is selected, at which point the model becomes much like the V, with design and implementation followed by the appropriate test phases, which might be just component and system test as shown in Figure 11.4 or might include unit, integration, and acceptance testing, too.

This model solves the V model problem of predicting the future on limited knowledge, because we don't commit to any particular feature set until we know what's feasible. If the prototypes include user interface prototypes and we can get the users involved in the early testing, then this model also mitigates the user interface and usability risks.

However, sometimes people get confused about which model they're following. I worked on one project that was clearly operating on a nice spiral-driven life cycle, but none of the senior project managers seemed to understand that. With each of the early testing phases, they became excited that we were about ready to deploy. They thought we were on a V model. This created lots of political problems when we went back to the redesign stages at the end of each test period.

Another risk of this model is that schedule and budget can be hard to control. This can result in the same type of problem described for the V model, namely the immovable end date. If someone decides by fiat that the system simply *shall* ship on a partic-

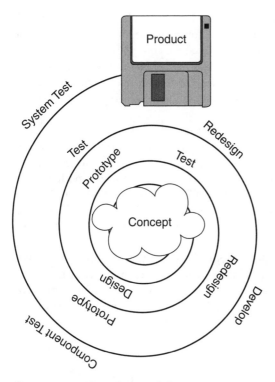

Figure 11.4 The spiral model.

ular date, then testing can once again get squeezed at the end. This brings us back to the same old conundrum: Ship a lousy product on time and budget, or slip the project to allow further testing, bug repair, and higher quality.

With expectations set clearly for all the stakeholders, though, this model can work really well. My associates and I built an automated test harness for a client once using this model. Every two or three weeks we polished up what we were working on into a stable prototype that included some new set of features, and then did a demo for the test team that showcased those features. As the prototypes matured, the testers started using the test tool a bit, too, to get some hands-on experience. Based on the feedback from the users, we would repair, redesign, and then add some new features. There is no way that a V model would have worked in that environment, because we could never have gotten the time and focus from the testers to write good requirements. However, they were happy to attend the demos and give us input as the test tool grew organically.

Evolutionary or Incremental Models

A broad and increasingly popular family of life-cycle models can be considered evolutionary or incremental in the sense that a given release grows up around a core of features that are delivered, often on a predetermined date. While that might sound like the V model, the difference is that features are added in chunks to a stable core. As the features drop in, this new system is stabilized through testing and debugging, and only then are more features added. At any point once the core features are stable, you can ship a system. The only question is what features it will include. Various methods can be used to select the order of feature inclusion, including user or market importance, technical risk, system architecture or consistency, or some mix of all of these and other considerations.

This model covers a broad spectrum of formality, from Rapid Application Development to the agile methods like Extreme Programming. (Some purists might object to my including Extreme Programming and other agile methods in this category, but it seems to me that the core characteristics of evolutionary or incremental models apply to these methods. The only question is the amount of "ceremony" involved, as the agile proponents would say.) The more formal variations will include what look like "mini-V-models" for each delivered increment (see Figure 11.5), while the less formal models will look more like a sequence of spirals.

The fixed release dates do resemble the V model in one way, in that there's always a temptation to ship a product where the last incremental set of features really isn't quite ready. Not to pick on the 800-pound gorilla of PC software, but Microsoft is said to follow an incremental method. I can often guess when using their products which fea-

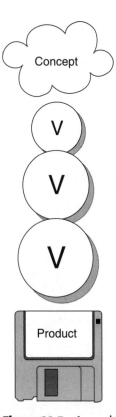

Figure 11.5 An evolutionary model, with formal increments.

tures were in the last increment![6] However, in general, the core features of their products are stable. Therefore, provided you pick the right set of core features and add additional increments in the right order, lingering quality issues in the final increment might be an acceptable business decision.

One aspect of incremental methods is that you'll need more testers, especially test technicians and other test execution resources, than you would for a V model, at least one of any size. Testing, including the expansive and expensive system test phase, tends to start earlier, because we need to thoroughly test the core before adding new increments. Therefore, where the entry criteria for system test for a V model project might specify that all features are complete and unit tested and the requirements frozen, in an incremental model you can only ask that the core features are complete and unit tested. The requirements won't be frozen until the decision is made about which is the last (i.e., shipping) increment. An automated regression testing tool can reduce the need for extra staff, but be aware that it takes very talented automated test engineers to develop automated tests for a system or parts of a system that are in the initial development (as opposed to on-going maintenance) stage of their life cycle.[7]

For smaller incremental life-cycle projects, especially those working with the emerging agile methods such as Extreme Programming, the software engineering community seems to be feeling its way toward an understanding of where and how testing in general—and independent testers and test teams in particular—fit in.[8] On the one hand, I find in the agile methods positive and encouraging ideas such as writing tests first and then writing code only until those tests pass. A couple associates and I built an automated testing harness and defined a lightweight but comprehensive process for component and integration testing for a client using freeware tools; I'm not sure they would have taken such care in this regard had they not been following an agile method.[9] On the other hand, I've heard remarks from agile method practitioners with no knowledge of or training in the field of testing that were along the lines of, "we test everything that could break." Upon closer scrutiny, this statement turned out to mean that they tested whatever came to mind as particularly risky in a technical sense. That approach to testing is about as far away from what I'm advocating in this book as almost anything could be. I think the onus is on us as professional testers to help develop a proper role for systematic but lightweight test processes and adapt the best practices of testing within the context of agile methods. Hopefully, this will happen before the end of this decade.

---

[6]See Richard Selby and Michael Cusumano's book, *Microsoft Secrets*.
[7]You may want to see Dorothy Graham and Mark Fewster's book, *Automated Software Testing*, for ideas on how to handle this and other challenges of test automation.
[8]To learn more about Extreme Programming from the tester's perspective, see Lisa Crispin's articles, "eXtreme Rules of the Road," published in Software Testing and Quality Engineering magazine, Volume 3, Issue 4 (July/August 2001), and "Is Quality Negotiable?" published in *The Proceedings of the STARWest 2001 Conference*. Both are now available on www.stickyminds.com.
[9]See our article, "Mission Made Possible," published in published in Software Testing and Quality Engineering magazine, Volume 4, Issue 4 (July/August 2002), and now available on www.stickyminds.com.

Code and Fix

Even though I said that a testing approach epitomized by statements like, "We test everything that could break" was almost as far from what I'm advocating as anything could be, there is one approach that is even further. It occurs within the context of a particular approach to software development known sometimes as *code and fix*.

Here's the process in a nutshell:

1. On the first day of the project, developers immediately sit down to write and debug code. There is no requirements gathering or design. Often, there is no unit testing, or each developer might pick a standard to follow, with little hope of sharing or reuse and no way to automate.

2. Within a few days, developers start to release code to an informal test team, often junior developers or other people with no training or experience in testing.

3. Even without the benefit of professional testing, the testers find many bugs. Often, these bugs are debugged and fixed in the test environment by developers, with the corresponding changes not always making it into the code repository. If there are test releases, these can come hourly or more frequently, often from the developers' own systems rather than out of the build and release engineering environment.

4. The project team repeats all of the preceding steps at the same time.

This process continues until time, money, or patience runs out. Whatever is in hand at the end of this maelstrom of chaos is shipped or deployed, unless it's really bad, in which case the project might be cancelled. Sometimes the end result of this frenzy is that the company goes out of business without deploying anything of value. The late 1990s dot-bomb phenomenon featured plenty of ill-conceived and poorly executed Internet applications that fit in this category.

What's interesting is that, in small projects, with a few minor tweaks, this process can work. Practice good source code control and release engineering and a major source of chaos goes away. Use professional testers instead of people with no talent or motivation to do the testing and the critical risks to system quality can be identified and tested. Establish a shared vision—on as little as a cocktail napkin—of the system's requirements and design, and keep people on the same page through frequent dialog. This degree of structure might be enough to avoid the "pushme-pullyou" that can break out between developers writing interfacing or interacting components.

The trouble is that this model does not scale—at least, I've not seen it scale well—in situations where there are large or distributed development teams working on complex projects. Once you get more than a half-dozen people working together on a project, it seems that you have to start writing things down and adopting orderly processes, or chaos and confusion will begin to eat dangerously into project team efficiency and effectiveness. I have seen people try to follow the code-and-fix approach as their companies grew, and often bad things happened. I had a colleague years ago who worked at Ashton-Tate, once the predominant player in PC database software. They apparently followed the code-and-fix approach. Basically, this became a game of quality roulette. They got away with it for a while, but finally in one release enough catastrophically bad bugs were missed that the marketplace abandoned their product in droves. I have had more than one of my test management seminar attendees tell me similar stories.

If you work in a code-and-fix environment, I would recommend that you at least adopt some of the ideas in this book to try to instill some order in the testing part of your projects. (It's hard to say without knowing your context where you'll get the most value in improving your process, but bug and test tracking—described in Chapters 4 and 5—are often good candidates.) You might serve as a shining beacon of order and efficiency to the rest of the project, or you might just eliminate some of the madness and frustration from your own domain, but at least you'll know that you're no longer part of the problem.

Testing Maintenance Releases

So far, I've been talking mostly about system development projects, but that's just the beginning of the software life cycle. Once software is released, it must be maintained. These maintenance releases must also be tested. From a task list and schedule perspective, a typical maintenance release might appear as shown in Figure 11.6.

A major risk for a maintenance release is regression. It is important that the new features or bug fixes in the maintenance release work, true, but you sure don't want to break an important system feature or capability that has become integrated into critical workflows by users or customers. Some organizations, through a variety of analytical methods such as module-to-feature tracing matrices try to anticipate where the regression risk is highest for any given change. They then rerun only those tests that cover those modules (which implies that they also have to have a tracing matrix from tests to features, and that they write test cases against each release that are reusable against subsequent maintenance releases). The trouble with these matrices and other analytical regression-predicting methods is that the paperwork and recording-keeping is time-consuming and complex. Programmers and testers alike often perceive it as low-priority drudgery. These facts can combine to results in near-instantaneous obsolescence. Furthermore, software can interact in unexpected ways, especially in the risky areas of reliability and performance or when shared databases exist. So, just because no one touched a given feature doesn't mean that a bug can't magically appear in it.

The more brute-force but less hazardous way to address regression risk is to repeat a lot of tests against each release. (Note that I'm still assuming you have reusable tests from the original release where the feature first appeared. One of the dangers of a purely exploratory approach that doesn't capture what was tested is that you have very limited alternatives in terms of regression testing.) There are two common approaches to doing this.

The first, more whiz-bang approach is to use automation for your regression testing. You either buy a commercial test tool or build one yourself, and then automate as many of your tests as you can. You can start small, and then gradually build up to having every test that can practically be automated in your automated suite. Some tests, such as usability tests, error handling and recovery tests, compatibility tests, and the like are not often automatable, so the same considerations of what you should and can test discussed in Chapter 1 should drive your testing, not what the tool can and can't do. You also have to avoid letting the tool and the automated test suite become, as James Bach memorably puts it, "the magic oak tree" that says pass and fail for reasons no one fully understands.[10]

---

[10]For this and other thoughts on automation, see James Bach's paper, "Test Automation Snake-Oil," found on www.satisfice.com.

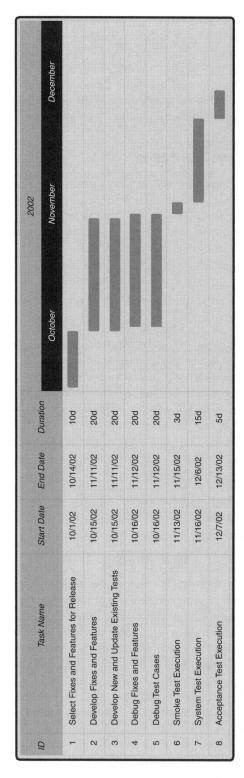

ID	Task Name	Start Date	End Date	Duration
1	Select Fixes and Features for Release	10/1/02	10/14/02	10d
2	Develop Fixes and Features	10/15/02	11/11/02	20d
3	Develop New and Update Existing Tests	10/15/02	11/11/02	20d
4	Debug Fixes and Features	10/16/02	11/12/02	20d
5	Debug Test Cases	10/16/02	11/12/02	20d
6	Smoke Test Execution	11/13/02	11/15/02	3d
7	System Test Execution	11/16/02	12/6/02	15d
8	Acceptance Test Execution	12/7/02	12/13/02	5d

Figure 11.6 A maintenance release task list and schedule.

Some people have had real trouble with automated testing, and others might not have the budget for it. In this case, you might prefer adopting a slower release schedule. If you try to have a maintenance release every two weeks, then the time available for manual retesting outside the new and changed areas might be minimal. What if the maintenance releases happened every two months, though? Yes, there'll be five times or so as much content in terms of new features and bug fixes to test, but there's an interesting thing that happens: tests often cover more than you expect.

One of my clients has a complete set of tests that takes about two person-decades of effort to run. With a test team of 20, they can get through all the tests in a year. They were concerned about regression risk, so they started measuring rolling four-week code coverage during testing. They were surprised—pleasantly so—to discover that in a given four week period they were consistently exercising over 50 percent of the code while running less than 10 percent of the test set. Over the course of their entire course of testing, they achieved 100-percent cumulative coverage for the entire project, but, the more coverage that had already been achieved, the less likely each subsequent test case was to add anything to the cumulative number.

This is nothing but the old "80/20" rule of management; in other words, 80 percent of your payoff comes from the first 20 percent of your effort, and the remaining 20 percent of your payoff requires the remaining 80 percent of your effort. Perhaps you can settle for something closer to 80 percent than 100 percent? The moral of this anecdote to me is that, by combining less-frequent releases with some intelligent assessment of what you might be missing and selection of appropriate test cases to fill those gaps, you can probably mitigate regression risk very effectively without test automation.

Whether you adopt a slow or rapid release schedule, one constant problem I've encountered in maintenance testing is the pressure to squeeze too much content into one given release. To each user, customer, salesperson, business analyst, help desk technician, or marketer, the bug fixes or new features important to them or their constituents are the most critical. Collectively, this results in a tremendous amount of pressure on the development team to increase the size of a maintenance release, but that just puts us right back in the painful trade-off of quality versus schedule and budget. This is particularly bad in maintenance testing, because delays often are acceptable only if the size of the maintenance release is increased, while shipping bad maintenance releases only further damages company credibility with customers and users and digs a deeper hole for the sustaining team to climb out of. Both of these are forms of vicious cycles that the organization's management team must break by establishing realistic estimation processes for maintenance releases.

Part of that process must include sufficient time for development of new tests or upgrading existing tests based on the maintenance release content. In the case of one company with an automated functional regression test harness, we received data and procedures to replicate a bug from technical support at the beginning of each maintenance release effort. We added new automated tests based on this material. We then waited to see which tests failed in the first test run, and then checked those failed tests to see which failures were actually correct results due to the changes made. That allowed us to reestablish the expected results and run the tests again. This took about a week once we got it all down.

Sometimes, though, a fairly small change can result in a big impact on the tests, especially automated tests. In the same company, a change to some file reading and database record-sorting logic resulted in literally hundreds of test results needing to be revalidated, along with an entire new test suite that had to be written. The test development effort was probably almost equivalent to the programmer effort.

System, Subsystem, Commercial Off-the-Shelf Software, and Component Integration

Not every major system project involves a whole lot of system development or maintenance. Especially with the rise of outsourcing (see Chapter 10, "Involving Other Players: Distributing a Test Project"), many projects primarily center on acquiring, integrating, and perhaps customizing existing software or hardware within a new or existing system. These projects—regardless of what any vendor's salesperson said during the sales process—require testing commensurate with the business and technical risks associated with the integrated system's potential failures.

These risks tend to increase in the presence of one or more of the following factors:

■ The criticality of the integrated component to the intended business purpose, operation, or mission of the overall system.

■ The coupling between the integrated component and any critical component, especially if the integrated component is "upstream" in terms of workflow or data processing.

■ A large degree of component customization or adaptation to a unique use.

■ Any unusual or unique workflows, use cases, or data sets that the component will encounter in your environment.

■ A large number of supported configurations in your environment.

■ A large number of configurations supported by the component. (For example, if the vendor tells you the component supports every version of Windows, ask yourself how much testing they could have practically done on your particular desktop configuration.)

■ A relatively small installed customer base for the component, especially if that customer base does not include anyone using the system in ways or configurations remotely like yours.

■ A brand-new major release (e.g., release 1.0 as opposed to release 1.4).

■ A large number of service patches, maintenance releases, and minor upgrades for the component.

■ Poor vendor testing practices. (How do you know? Well, you'll be prudent to tactfully assume these practices are poor, politely but firmly asking for documentation to disprove that assumption).

As discussed in Chapter 10, you can try to leverage your vendors' testing and tools to some extent, but you should remain in control of the testing and be vigilant about what's being done. The more your project involves integration of existing subsystems and components, the more you are—as a practical matter—limited to an acceptance testing role for those components. However, I'd encourage you to try to get as much visibility as possible into the vendor testing as early as possible, and adopt a "test to fail" outlook in this case, rather than the usual "test to pass" perspective of acceptance testing.

Hardware/Software Systems

Finally, projects often include hardware and software components, some custom, some integrated from other vendors, and some commercial off-the-shelf items. This can create some complications that affect the test effort. For one thing, the critical skills you identify for your test team will expand to include some amount of hardware knowledge, even if you're not directly responsible for hardware testing. As discussed in Chapter 2, you'll also need to ensure sufficient hardware—especially scarce engineering prototypes, if applicable—to provide for all your testing. Finally, it's often the case that custom hardware might not be as testable as a lot of off-the-shelf hardware; in other words, internal states, especially error states, might not be easy to detect without tools or special skills.

Especially with custom-developed hardware, you'll see some extra time and money required during estimation. Usually, projects that involve custom hardware reveal bugs not just in software, but in the hardware, too. There's some amount of extra time required to handle each bug, of course, but it also means that proportionately more test cases will fail, which adds to the overall test time as well. When tests fail, it's often important to isolate bugs across multiple platforms to make sure that you don't have a defective unit, rather than software, causing the bug. In some cases, hardware shortages will occur when engineering prototype units die, which can block tests or require that you institute second or third shifts to utilize the hardware that remains continuously.

After you file bug reports, you might see longer turnaround times (i.e., closure periods as discussed in Chapter 4) on bugs if confusion (or outright obfuscation) arises over whether the bug resides in the hardware, the firmware, some software component, and so forth. A properly authorized CCB, bug review committee, bug triage team, or whatever name these folks go by in your organization should have the ability to assign a bug to a particular team for repair, to keep the test team out of the middle of any debate on what's broken. For test teams with a primarily behavioral testing charter, once the testers have identified a quality problem in the system, prioritizing the bug, determining the root cause, ascertaining the most appropriate subsystem in which to fix the bug, and implementing that fix are all tasks that live most properly outside of the test team.

If you're a new test manager with a primarily software background approaching a test project that involves hardware, don't worry. You don't need to become a hardware engineer overnight—if at all. The techniques and tools outlined in this book are ones that I've used for plenty of hardware/software system projects ranging from stand-alone laptops to complex, distributed custom-interactive-voice-response/call center systems. A little time spent brushing up on statistical quality control and possibly reliability engineering if you can spare it will make you all the more effective, but most important are thoughtful advance planning, hiring an appropriate test team, managing execution carefully, and arranging for good hardware testing by a vendor or test lab as discussed in Chapter 10.[11] For a very basic introduction to what goes on in typical consumer-product or IT-system hardware test, see Appendix A, "Hardware Testing Fundamentals: An Introduction for Software Testing Professionals."

---

[11]You may want to consider Kauro Ishikawa's *Guide to Quality Control* and Steven Zimmerman and Marjorie Icenogle's *Statistic Quality Control Using Excel*, and O'Connor's *Practical Reliability Engineering* for hardware reliability.

Process Maturity

With all these different variations of life cycles, schedule and budgetary considerations, and other context issues affecting testing, surely every project is a unique beast, huh? Well, every project is a new thing in the sense that it's an endeavor to fill a heretofore unfilled need with a product or service. But, as King Solomon is said to have written, "What has been is what will be, and what has been done is what will be done; and there is nothing new under the sun." While Ecclesiastes is often seen as a disheartening poem, perhaps this is good news to us? Since the days of the great Egyptian Pyramids and even before, people have been working together to accomplish spectacular things, to implement useful tools, to make life better for each other. Perhaps there are lessons we can learn from the past, and from each other?

"But We're Different. . .": The Commonality of Solutions

In the opening sentence of his novel *Anna Karenina*, Leo Tolstoy observed that "all happy families are alike, but each unhappy family is unhappy in its own way." In commenting on this passage, the historian Paul Johnson disputes Tolstoy by claiming that, in reality, the sources of unhappiness in families—alcoholism, infidelity, violence, poverty—are tiresome and common and lead to tiresome, common, and sad results.[12] This might be a blessing in disguise, however, because the commonality of the afflictions allows common approaches to alleviating dysfunction, such as the 12-step programs developed for alcoholics.

The same is true of software and hardware development companies, development projects, and test organizations. When you talk about test concepts that might help to get your organization under control, management might respond, "Oh, but we're different. That will never work here. We have to be more creative than that." Balderdash! In fact, many corporate dynamics are common not only among companies in similar sectors, but even among organizations whose only similarities are that they are groups of people working together. As Peter Drucker writes, "The differences between managing a chain of retail stores and managing a Roman Catholic diocese are amazingly fewer than either retail executives or bishops realize...whether you are managing a software company, a hospital, a bank, or a Boy Scout organization, the differences apply to only about 10% of your work. This 10% is determined by the organization's specific mission, its specific culture, its specific history and its specific vocabulary. The rest is pretty much interchangeable."[13]

I have worked with companies and clients in various areas of the computer business, from big hardware companies and small integrators to shrink-wrap software houses and custom programming shops working for huge clients. Although the level of maturity of the processes and the skill levels of the staff influenced the types of problems I saw, the company's particular product or service mattered not a whit. There's probably very little if anything unique about your test management predicaments. You are not alone, and you

---

[12]Paul Johnson, *Intellectuals*, pp. 121, 122.
[13]Peter Drucker, "Management's New Paradigms," p. 156.

can apply solutions such as those you find in this book and others to solve your problems. Anyone who says, "Oh, but we're different…" is either uninformed or resisting change.

Nevertheless, you can't rush the process of change. The idealized test project models presented in this book represent organizations operating at a significant level of management maturity. The word *maturity* in this context doesn't mean that a company's senior managers are of a particular age; rather, it refers to companies that are in a continuous process of adopting and adapting the best—or at least the better—practices of software and hardware development professionals. In other words, they have learned from the cumulative mistakes of past software and hardware organization managers, and are continuing to learn from their own mistakes.

The Software Engineering Institute's Capability Maturity Model (CMM) measures five levels of process maturity. Level one is characterized by an approach that is completely ad hoc, devoid of any real processes whatsoever. People work according to management's whim of the moment. At the first sign of a crisis, managers drop any pretense of process and simply make up something on-the-fly. According to the Software Engineering Institute, "In an immature organization, there is no objective basis for judging product quality or for solving product or process problems. There is little understanding of how the steps of the software process affect quality, and product quality is difficult to predict. Moreover, activities intended to enhance quality, such as reviews and testing, are often curtailed or eliminated when projects fall behind schedule."[14]

The really pernicious aspect of an immature organization is that many managers who operate at that level have made a conscious choice to do so. They tend to react viscerally to suggestions that adopting a set of processes, rather than relying on intrepid improvisation, might make life better. If you work in an immature organization, you need first to recognize it and then to understand whether the situation results from an unawareness of the opportunity to do better or a denial of software engineering realities. The former situation is reparable through hard work and determination from the senior executive level on down, while the former is a matter of attitudes and belief systems that are sometimes resistant to empirical data and logical reasoning.

The tools and techniques in this book work best in an organization striving to become a mature one, applying industry best practices. To apply the approaches described here, you must be able to control the deployment of resources and the methods of work in your test group. If your organization remains stuck in deliberately chosen immaturity, proclaiming individual heroics the only way, and managers—both those above you and your peers—insist on micromanaging your resources, it will be very difficult to improve your situation. Depending on your place in the organization and your personal credibility with senior management, you might not be well-positioned to be an agent of significant change to your company's processes. However, the survival of the test organization depends on your ability to educate people about—and achieve—tangible benefits from testing. This can be a daunting task without some degree of formal process, both internal to the test group and at the test team's interfaces with other groups and managers.[15]

---

[14]*The Capability Maturity Model*, page 7.
[15]Boris Beizer has argued against doing the kinds of testing return on investment exercises I discussed earlier in this chapter, largely because chaotic organizations will not have enough data to do a meaningful job of such an analysis. See his paper, "Software Quality Reflections," found on Software Research's Software Testing Techniques archive, www.soft.com.

Test organizations are very sensitive to abrupt changes in plan. A sudden about-face by management can blow away significant investments of time and money in test suite development, undermining your return on investment. The change management database introduced in Chapter 6 can help you track the impact of such changes, but you might find that no one wants to hear explanations (a typical situation in immature organizations). If, after giving it the old college try, you decide that the organization will not change, and you feel as if the test team is treated like the poor relation of the company, you might want to find a job that will give you an opportunity to succeed.

The Test Team Is Not an Island: External Effects on Your Productivity

Various organizational behaviors and attributes, which I call *gas pedals* and *brake pedals*, can speed up or slow down test progress. In general, all of them exercise incremental influence on your test operation: a single tap on the brake won't bring the test project to a dead stop, just as a jab to the gas won't send the system under test rocketing through the test exit criteria in a single pass. Overall, however, to make testing proceed smoothly, your company needs to press on the gas pedal and lay off the brake pedal. Although each single incident or behavior is incremental, lots of brake lights should send a signal that a troubling trend is arising.

Your test project can easily suffer the death of 10,000 cuts from many little braking events. In a reactive sense, when the project takes a significant hit, document it in the change management database introduced in Chapter 6. However, the broader theme of this chapter, context, suggests that you understand how these contextual influences affect your testing effort. See if you can recognize any trends of inhibitors that develop, and try to reduce their occurrence in the future. Likewise, actively promote the behaviors that make your job easier. Help your peers and colleagues understand the importance to your productivity of following certain courses of action and eschewing others.

Process Gas Pedals

The following organizational behaviors and attributes tend to accelerate the test process. Encourage these activities and values among your peers, and jump at the opportunities to perform them yourself where appropriate.

Testing throughout the project. I use the phrase *testing throughout the project* in a three-dimensional sense. The first dimension involves time: in order to be properly prepared, and to help contain bugs as early as possible, the test team must become involved when the project starts, not simply at the end. The second dimension is organizational: the more a company promotes open communication between the test organization and the other teams throughout the company, the better the test group can align its efforts with the company's needs. The third dimension is cultural: in a mature company, testing as an entity, a way of mitigating risk, and a business management philosophy permeates the development projects. I also call this type of testing "pervasive testing."

Employing plenty of good technicians. As Chapter 8 explained, you can get qualified test technicians from the computer science and engineering schools of local universities and colleges as well as from technical institutes. Try to use these employees to perform any tasks that do not specifically require a test engineer's level of expertise. Since they are an inexpensive resource, you'll tend to have success at getting two or three on staff, when management would deny you an additional test engineer.

Automation. The more automated the test system, the less time it takes to run the tests. Automation also allows unattended test execution overnight and over weekends, which maximizes utilization of the system under test and other resources, leaving more time for engineers and technicians to analyze and report test failures. The basic tools provided with this book will allow you to automate some key test management activities, and you can expand these tools to be even more automated. You should apply a careful balance, however. Generating a good automated test suite can take many more hours than writing a good manual test suite. Developing a completely automated test management system is a large endeavor. If you don't have the running room to thoroughly automate everything you'd like to before test execution begins, you should focus on automating a few simple tools that will make manual testing go more quickly.

Good test system architecture. Spending time in advance understanding how the test system should work, selecting the right tools, ensuring the compatibility and logical structure of all the components, and designing for subsequent maintainability really pay off once test execution starts. The more elegant the test system, the more easily testers can use it.

Clearly defined test-to-development hand-off processes. As discussed in Chapter 4, two closely related activities, bug isolation and debugging, occur on opposite sides of the fence between test and development. On the one hand, test managers must ensure that test engineers and technicians thoroughly isolate every bug they find and write up those isolation steps in the bug report. Development managers, on the other hand, must ensure that their staff does not try to involve test engineers and technicians, who have other responsibilities, in debugging activities.

Clearly defined development-to-test hand-off processes. The project team must manage the release of new hardware and software revisions to the test group. As part of this process, the following conditions should be met:

- All software is under revision control.
- All test builds come from revision-controlled code.
- Consistent, clear release naming nomenclatures exist for each major system.
- A regular, planned release schedule exists and is followed.
- A well-understood, correct integration strategy is developed and followed during the test planning stages.

Automated smoke tests run against test releases, whether in the development, build (or release engineering), or testing environments (or all three), are also a good idea to ensure that broken test releases don't block test activities for hours or even days at the beginning of a test cycle.

Another hand-off occurs when exit and entry criteria for phases result in the test team commencing or ending their testing work on a given project. The more clearly defined and mutually accepted these criteria are, the more smoothly and efficiently the testing will proceed.

A clearly defined system under test. If the test team receives clear requirements and design specifications when developing tests and clear documentation while running tests, it can perform both tasks more effectively and efficiently. When the project management team commits to and documents how the product is expected to behave, you and your intrepid team of testers don't have to waste time trying to guess—or dealing with the consequences of guessing incorrectly. (See Chapter 9 for tips on operating without clear requirements, design specifications, and documentation when the project context calls for it.)

Continuous test execution. Related to, and enabled by, test automation, this type of execution involves setting up test runs so that the system under test runs as nearly continuously as possible. This arrangement can entail some odd hours for the test staff, especially test technicians, so everyone on the test team should have access to all appropriate areas of the test lab.

Continuous test execution also implies not getting blocked. If you're working on a one-week test cycle, being blocked for one just day means that 20 percent of the planned tests for this release will not happen, or will have to happen through extra staff, overtime, weekend work, and other undesirable methods.[16] Good release engineering and management practices, including smoke testing builds before installing them in the test environment, can be a big part of this. Another part is having an adequate test environment so that testers don't have to queue to run tests that require some particular configuration or to report test results.

Adding test engineers. Fred Brooks once observed that "adding more people to a late software project makes it later," a statement that has become known as Brooks' Law.[17] This law does not hold true as strongly in testing as it does in most areas of software and hardware engineering, however. Brooks reasoned that as you add people to a project, you increase the communication overhead, burden the current development engineers with training the new engineers, and don't usually get the new engineers up to speed soon enough to do much good. In contrast, a well-designed behavioral test system reflects the (ideally) simpler external interfaces of the system under test, not its internal complexities, which allows a new engineer to contribute within a couple of weeks of joining the team. (Structural test systems, however, do require an understanding of system internals.)

My usual rule of thumb is that, if a schedule crisis looms six weeks or more in my future, I can bring in a new test engineer in time to help. However, I have also added test engineers on the day system testing started, and I once joined a laptop

---

[16]As Tom DeMarco put it in *The Deadline*, "There are infinitely many ways to lose a day...but not even one way to get one back." Page 94.

[17]See Frederick Brooks' software engineering classic *The Mythical Man-Month* for this and other useful observations. Published initially in 1975, this book still has a lot to say about software engineering and software project management. A new edition was just published for 1995.

development project as the test manager about two weeks before the start of this phase. In both cases, the results were good. (Note, though, that I am not contradicting myself. Testing does proceed most smoothly when the appropriate levels of test staffing become involved early, but don't let having missed the opportunity to do that preclude adding more staff.) Talk to your test engineers to ascertain the amount of time that'll be required, if any, to ramp up new people, and then plan accordingly.

Process Brake Pedals

The following project behaviors and attributes tend to decelerate the test process. You should avoid these behaviors yourself, and help your organization avoid them as well.

Getting too clever. Because many previously independent pieces of the product come together in testing, test schedules have myriad dependencies, an elaborate critical chain (critical-path and near-critical-path task networks), and single points of failure. Even with the collective knowledge of the entire project team, test and project managers cannot easily identify all of these before they come whistling out of nowhere and whack you on the forehead. Avoid the temptation to "accelerate" the test schedule by piling one seemingly reasonable assumption on top of another, thereby building an insupportable house of cards. When the assumptions fail, the project is left de facto without a schedule, and chaos and improvisation ensue.

Unrealistic project schedules. The same types of problems associated with getting too clever also arise when project schedules are totally disconnected from reality. This situation occurs when management confuses business priorities with technical possibilities, and it is especially prevalent when marketing windows and bonuses are involved. When your managers start telling you that they intend to make up earlier schedule slips during test execution, something bad is about to happen, and you will be intimately involved.[18] (This is what I meant by the "ski slope and cliff" comment in regard to the V model.)

Failure to provide test deliverables. Such failures include shortages of hardware or software, the release to test of incomplete software systems, software releases that are impossible to install or that are improperly packaged, incompatibilities, releases outside strict revision control, and so forth. The frequent follow-up to such delays can take the form of project management dictating that the test team must meet its original schedule, hobbled though it is. Therefore, proactive efforts to anticipate and prevent such problems in the first place is key.

Lack of system administration, infrastructure, and developer support. The test lab infrastructure will often require expert system administration support. An

---

[18]Robert Glass, in his Practical Programmer column in the *Communications of the ACM*, writes of consulting with a client who had put such a schedule in place: "I said things like, 'The approach you are taking to accelerate the schedule is actually costing you long term, in that enhancements and system testing are taking such unpredictably long periods of time that it is not possible to achieve any anticipated schedule.' (Things had literally crawled to a halt in system testing, with each new bug fix generating enough new bugs that almost no forward progress was achieved)."

experienced system administrator can resolve in five minutes a problem that a test engineer might take five hours to figure out. For the same reason, support from facilities management is important—for example, having people on call to unlock doors that no one expected to be locked. Developer support is necessary, too. For example, during the early stages of testing, testers sometimes need to confirm with developers that anomalous behavior is really a bug rather than a configuration change test forgot to make or some other trivial glitch. A test team must have prompt support available from these various sources whenever tests are being run, which sometimes means 24 hours a day, seven days a week, once test execution begins in earnest. Testers should have contact lists, with home, cell phone, and pager numbers, including, as a last resort, the names and numbers of managers. Defining an escalation process, as discussed in Chapter 2, is important, and following that process when support breaks down is essential.

Scrimping on tools. Test tools, especially test automation tools, almost always pay for themselves when used wisely. Trying to economize by building your own tools, quashing the idea of purchasing a new tool because of budget constraints, and sending test engineers on snipe hunts for bargain tools waste the test team's time, thus delaying the project *and* costing more money.

It's true that sometimes you need to build your own test tools, because no commercial tool can accomplish what you need done. In this case, a separate toolsmith (or toolsmiths) should be hired to provide the tool-building support. It's a prime example of unrealistic scheduling to assume that someone will cobble up a test tool in her spare time while writing test cases, developing test data, getting the test environment configured, hiring test technicians, and all the other tasks that test engineers do while getting ready for test execution.

Unrealistic test execution schedules. Test schedules must allocate sufficient time for each test case, understanding that the discovery of bugs will increase the time needed to run the test cases. The schedules must also include sufficient cycles, in advance, for the resolution of problems found in the first cycle. I have participated in too many projects whose schedules were blown when management assumed that test would find no must-fix bugs. As soon as the first must-fix bug surfaced, these projects had no schedule. The estimation techniques discussed in Chapter 1 are part of putting realistic test execution schedules in place.

Slow development response. As mentioned in Chapter 4, a key metric for development response to test-reported bugs is the average turnaround time from the opening of a bug report to its resolution and closure, the closure period. Only development, by promptly debugging and fixing problems, can influence the closure period. (There are, though, process overheads such as test release schedules that introduce natural delays.) The longer development takes to resolve a bug, especially for the high-severity issues that can block test progress, the slower the test effort moves. This can include not getting through all the planned tests in a cycle and, ultimately, delaying finding bugs until late in the test phase, possibly with insufficient time to resolve the bugs.

Use of the test lab for debugging. Sometimes, development is forced to use the test lab equipment to reproduce bugs because the development environment is insufficiently complex. However, every minute that development uses a piece of test lab equipment for debugging is a minute that the test team can't run tests. There is also time required to bring the test lab back to a known configuration after debugging, which can include reinstalling software, changing network configurations, and other labor-intensive activities. Make sure project managers understand that testing is blocked while the test lab is in use for debugging and afterwards while the configuration is restored. Escalate these situations when they occur, and make notes in your change management database (see Chapter 6).

Buggy deliverables. The more bugs in the system under test, the slower testing goes. The time that test technicians and engineers spend in bug identification and isolation is several orders of magnitude greater than the time it takes to kick off automated tests and collect passing results.

Violations of test plan entry criteria. Project management often justifies entering a test phase before the system under test is ready by arguing that this will accelerate testing. It usually does not. Most commonly, the test team must abort the first cycle as a result of rampant stability bugs that prevent any forward progress. During hardware testing, equipment can actually be damaged because it can't "live" in the test lab environment.

Violations of test plan exit criteria. Leaving a test phase before the bug find rate has leveled off and all other exit criteria are met just passes along an immature system to the next phase of testing. This next phase will do a less efficient and less effective job of identifying the test escapes from the previous phase, because the test system operates at a coarser level of granularity as it progresses from one phase to the next.

Scope creep, crawl, and redefinition. Changes in system scope (e.g., features, capabilities, etc.) result in changes in test project scope. Test scope itself is sometimes subject to abrupt change, usually when the schedule begins to falter. Both increases and reductions in scope can create problems. Test engineers who design the test system must make certain assumptions about the pieces of functionality that will be contained in the product. If one of these pieces later drops out, a domino effect can result that compromises the test system, partially or completely breaking it.

For example, suppose that you design tools and cases to test stress, volume, and capacity loads of a system based on a particular driver or interface in the system, and then that driver or interface changes. What if you invest person-months of effort in building a test tool that can scale up to hundreds of simultaneous load-generating connections, only to find that the design capacity has been dropped, in response to bugs found by your team, to an order of magnitude less? Was the time spent building a tool that could scale to that capacity wasted? Maybe not, in the long run, but it will surely feel that way in the midst of a furious schedule crunch, when those two person-months could have been devoted to many other priorities.

Test suite or phase cancellation. Like system scope shrink, test scope shrink can waste time, although in this case it's usually retroactive: the time spent developing or preparing to run a test suite or phase proves to have been wasted. No bugs will be found by that testing, so the return on investment is shot, but most of the heavy lifting was already done. Fortunately, it's not impossible to see this coming. If a test phase or cycle drags on well beyond its originally scheduled exit date, start to plan proactively to shut it down and catch up the testing later, if possible.

Tester mistakes. Simply put, test managers, test engineers, and test technicians make mistakes. Clearly, as the test manager, you are responsible for minimizing these types of goofs. They include, among others, the following notable examples from my own experience:

- Failing to understand the dependencies while planning.
- Developing tightly coupled, unstable, unmaintainable, incompatible, or erroneous test systems.
- Picking the wrong test tools.
- Doing poor or inefficient bug isolation.
- Wasting time on trivial matters while the critical areas fall apart.
- Reporting bugs that aren't bugs.
- Failing to report bugs that are bugs.
- Running automated tests with the wrong parameters or in the wrong configurations.
- Skipping critical test cases.

Did I put this item last on the list of "brake pedals" on purpose? You bet. I've worked on a few troubled projects, and tester mistakes were always the least important of the problems. However, they can attract a lot of attention, especially when someone's looking to distract the project management team from his or her own problems, or when someone has a vested interest in undermining the credibility of the information coming out of the test team. (Sorry to sound so cynical, but I've seen it happen on some of the troubled projects I've worked on, and heard corroborating stories from many of the attendees of my test management seminar.) As I said in Chapter 9, if we are to point out the errors of others, it really does help to be right. Therefore, part of running a mature, credible test operation is working to minimize these tester errors, even if you have irrefutable evidence in your change management database that test errors are the least of the project's problems.

Process Maturity Models

If you wanted to gauge the maturity of your development or maintenance process—at least as it affects the testing process—and the maturity of your testing process, too, you could use the "gas pedals" and "brake pedals" to informally score your last few projects. The type of data captured in the change management database would be helpful, too. However, I didn't come up with the "pedals" or with the change management database as methods for measuring process maturity. Let me wind down this discussion of context by looking more closely at the concept of process maturity, and then introducing some techniques you can use to measure test process and company-wide process maturity.

When I say, "process," what I mean can be summed up as, "the way things are done around here." Your processes might be written, passed on through oral tradition, embedded in institutional knowledge, or made up by each participant from scratch as needs demand and fancy suits.

A number of factors influence the maturity of a process. One is the degree to which all the participants and stakeholders understand and support what is going on. Successful process maturity projects don't involve management dictates about how things will be done, but rather arise from ground-level consensus about how the team can effectively and efficiently execute projects. (Management can and should provide guidance, support, and direction in achieving process maturity.)

A mature process should also be reproducible and measurable. Reproducibility means that we do the same thing the same way on subsequent projects. Measurability means that we gather important project management and engineering metrics on the process. Measurability supports reproducibility because we can use those metrics to estimate and guide the upcoming projects.

We also should use these metrics not only to reproduce the processes from one project to the next, but also to improve them. W. Edwards Deming and Shewhart, two of the fathers of modern quality control, described a four-step process for continual improvement:

1. **Plan.** Develop a plan for improving the process, either to improve quality, save money, accelerate schedules, or some combination of all three. Set quantifiable goals to measure whether the plan succeeded.

2. **Do.** Execute the plan, gathering metrics that will allow you to judge process improvement success.

3. **Check.** Evaluate the metrics at key points to check the success of the change.

4. **Act.** Course-correct the plan to make it more effective in implementing improvements.

This cycle should repeat throughout the project and especially from one project to the next. In the most mature organizations I've seen, this Plan/Do/Check/Act process has become permanently engrained in "the way things are done around here."

For example, one of my clients analyzes the bugs reported by customers within the first six months of the release of their computers. (Such bugs are called *initial field incident reports*, or IFIRs.) They do a Pareto analysis of the bugs, the affected subsystems, and their root causes to see where to focus their attention. Then, for the most significant problems, the most likely-to-fail subsystems, the most frequently root causes, they introduce what they call "closed loop corrective actions" to ensure that these problems do not occur on future systems.

Over the last few years, a number of ways to measure test process maturity have become available to test managers. Tim Koomen and Martin Pol's technique, the Test Process Improvement model, seems to be growing the most popular, at least based on what I read and what I hear in my test management seminars. (See the case study at the end of this chapter for an example of applying it to a real project.) If TPI is not to your liking, you can also look at David Gelperin and Aldin Hiyashi's Testability Maturity Model; Susan Burgess and Rodger Drabick's Testing Capability Maturity Model; and Illene Burnstein, Robert Carlson, and Taratip Suwannasart's Testing Maturity Model (TMM).[19] You can have a formal assessment performed using any of these models by various consultants—myself included, if you will pardon the self-promotion—but you can also use self-assessment to check the maturity of your processes and set goals for improvement.

---

[19]For more information on the Test Process Improvement technique, see Koomen and Pol's book of the same name. A concise synopsis of all these maturity models can be found in Rodger Drabick's article, "Growth of Maturity in the Testing Process" on the Internet at www.softtest.org/articles /rdrabick3.htm.

Two cautions apply to any test process maturity model. The first is a generic rule that applies to any process improvement effort, which is that you shouldn't undertake process improvement or any change simply for its own sake or because someone not familiar with your particular context says you should. (To paraphrase a 2,000-year old quote from Petronius Arbiter, a Roman author, change can be a wonderful way to introduce inefficiency while appearing to be making progress [I thank Ed Kit and Rick Craig for teaching me this wonderful aphorism].) Process improvement should target the most critical processes that affect the way an organization or group adds value. Most or all of the processes I covered in these 11 chapters—quality risk analysis, test system development, test and bug tracking, results reporting, lab management, change management, staffing, and distributing testing—tended to be critical on most test projects I worked on. However, there certainly were projects where spending time perfecting our test distribution processes would have made no sense because we did all the testing with one small team inside a single test lab. As I said in the Introduction, this book is intended to be a toolbox; use what's useful to you where you can.

I'll give you another caveat on test process maturity models, this one specific to testing. When I first read about the Testing Maturity Model, I thought, hey, I'm a pretty organized, methodical test manager, I'll self-assess a few of my projects and see how great I am. I was disappointed to find that I scored mostly threes and fours, rather than fives, the maximum. As I thought about why I had scored low in certain areas, I realized that testing processes are in general very collaborative and contextual. For example, I can only finish all the planned tests if I'm in control of the test release process, especially timing. If I get test releases at the whim of the development manager—say every hour or so like we did on one project—then I'll have no time to do anything but confirmation testing. If someone asks later, "Why didn't you run all the tests you planned?" my answer will be, "Because I spent all my time reacting to bug fixes." A mature process should be proactive, not reactive, but sometimes the test manager is not in control of the upstream and downstream processes that influence the testing process.

Therefore, test process maturity models can be useful as a way to institute incremental improvements in your critical processes, but the only way to achieve world-class levels of test process maturity is in concert with a company-wide process maturity effort. Some formal models for company-wide process maturity improvement include the International Standards Organization's ISO 9000 and 14000 family of standards, the Software Engineering Institute's Capability Maturity Model (CMM), and the United States Department of Commerce's Malcolm Baldrige National Quality Award, along with others such as SPICE, TickIT, and Six Sigma.[20]

Like test process maturity models, these models can be used in a self-assessment fashion to implement process improvements. One of my clients had a small team who were focused on working with the entire organization to define and improve processes. This was not one of the test managers, but she reported to the same vice president as the test managers. The existence of a separate organization focused entirely on process improvement, reporting to an executive level in a company, is one

---

[20]If you're interested in these topics, you may want to check out Pankoj Jalote's *CMM in Practice*, Mark Paulk, et al.'s *The Capability Maturity Model*, and Charles Schmauch's *ISO 9000 for Software Developers*, as a few starting points.

sign of organizational commitment to improving quality by improving processes. Another sign of organizational commitment is when everyone recognizes—and managers and executives articulate—that process improvement is a serious, prolonged undertaking. Case studies in *The Capability Maturity Model* book indicate that up just one level takes on average between 12 and 18 months.

Once your organization has achieved a certain level of maturity through self-assessment and a diligent effort to institute on-going process improvement, then it might make sense to have that process maturity certified by an outside assessor. These consultants will come in and verify compliance with whatever maturity model you have followed. If you meet the criteria, they will certify you to be ISO 9000 compliant, CMM level 4, or whatever approach you've chosen. Bear in mind that these assessors don't work cheap. Moreover, in this case, the customer is *not* always right. Assessors can't afford to be push-overs, as their reputations are at stake as much as yours is when they do an assessment. A successful certification effort allows the organization to use that certification and the certifying organization's name in sales and marketing material.[21]

Over the years, a certain amount of cynicism has grown in regard to these company-wide process improvement programs. I recall hearing a company president in the early 1990s say to his management team that he was committed to winning the Malcolm Baldridge National Quality Award the next year. This comment revealed a significant level of unawareness, as the company would have scored at best a two out of five on the Capability Maturity Model. IBM, whose Rochester, Minnesota development team that created the AS/400 has actually won the Malcolm Baldridge National Quality Award, also had a division that was rated as CMM level five, which gives you an idea of the type of serious and mature organizations that actually win this award. Mercifully, this executive's plan for world-class quality in world-record time was silently dropped a few months later, but this further fed the skepticism many of us felt.

Eileen Shapiro, in her book *Fad-Surfing in the Boardroom*, described in ruthless—and humorous—detail how total quality management, right-sizing, reengineering, and other management trends have blown into organizations—often along with lots of high-priced consultants—and then blown out again after a few months. Then the next big thing comes along, escorted by its coterie of consultants and sycophants. Scott Adams, creator of the *Dilbert* characters, ran a sequence of cartoons lampooning the efforts of Dilbert's employer, a fictional high-tech company, to achieve ISO 9000 certification. People in organizations with will o' the wisp executive management develop a defensive posture of agreeing (often unenthusiastically) to whatever the new trend is, but then doing as little as possible in regard to the effort and waiting for it to go away. This type of behavior is what Deming describes as *lack of constancy of purpose*, which he includes in his list of Seven Deadly Sins in *The Deming Management Method*.

Such fickle management behavior and the justifiable cynicism it breeds are unfortunate and sad, I think. These process improvement models *can* work. I mentioned Raytheon's

---

[21]The American Society for Quality's monthly journal, Quality Professional, general includes a number of advertisements for assessor consultancies. As with any consultant, interview carefully and check references if you are involved in the assessor selection process. If you are pursuing certification in order to do business with a particular client—e.g., the United States Department of Defense—then you should probably check with your client to see if they have "preferred-assessor" or "recognized-assessor" lists.

Electronic Systems group earlier in the discussion on cost of quality. Raytheon, as part of the CMM process improvement and cost of quality programs, reduced their overall cost of quality from about 70 percent of project cost to down around 20 percent. Those types of improvements add up to saving around $500,000 on a medium-sized, million-dollar project. I consider myself a professional pessimist and a somewhat cynical guy, but I can get pretty optimistic and not a bit cynical about half a million dollars.

Managing the Testing Process: A Retrospective Conclusion

Whew! That's it. Just the case studies and exercises at the end of this chapter to go, and you have finished the book. (The Glossary and the appendices are more for your reference than to read word for word.) I hope you enjoyed reading this second edition of *Managing the Testing Process* as much as I enjoyed writing it. Before you put it down, though, let me spend a few final paragraphs looking back at the book and putting it all in context.

A couple of my test management course attendees remarked, at the end of the seminar, "Nice course, but where was the test process?" I responded that the entire course was about the test process, but then I realized that I've really told the story from the inside without ever looking at it from the outside.

To tie this all together, let me outline a test process as it might appear from the outside, and refer each piece of that process back to the chapter that addressed it.

1. Create a context for testing.
   A. Understand the broader context of the testing effort (Chapter 11).
   B. Assess and prioritize the risks to system quality (Chapter 1).
   C. Estimate testing tasks, cost, and time (Chapters 1 and 11).
   D. Develop a test plan (Chapter 2).
   E. Assemble the testers (Chapters 8 and 10).
   F. Build the test system (Chapter 3) and the test environment (Chapters 6 and 7).
2. Assess the quality of the system under test.
   A. Acquire a test release (Chapter 2).
   B. Execute tests (Chapters 3, 5, and 6).
   C. Document test results (Chapters 4, 5, and 6).
3. Communicate the test results.
   A. Identify stakeholders' needs (Chapter 9).
   B. Create the test dashboard (Chapters 4, 5, and 9).
4. Refine the testing process.
   A. Adjust testing for the current project (Chapters 3 and 6).
   B. Institute long-term improvements (Chapters 3 and 11).
This is shown graphically in Figure 11.7.[22]

The point of this book is to give you some basic tools, tips, and techniques that you can use to manage this process and each constituent activity. These approaches have worked well for me over my career as a test manager, and I hope you find them useful as well. As you continue to build your own career as a test manager, I'm sure you'll come up with your own methods and practices. To the extent that you build off my ideas, I'm honored to have been able to help you. Perhaps someday, you'll share some of your own ideas on testing and test management with me, too, whether by email, in a conference presentation, an article, or a book. I'd like that.

This book is by no means the last word on the topic. There's a lot of work to do still, figuring out all the ins and outs of managing testing of hardware and software systems. It's our unique privilege to be working in the early days of an emerging discipline, computer systems engineering. The ancient Egyptians that built the pyramids were pioneers in the field of civil engineering. The construction of a pyramid was an enormous project, involving a small city of workers and incredible logistics, made all the more complicated by the fact that the only real power available was human power. However, some of the management techniques—assembling specialized teams to handle particular tasks and adopting a hierarchical management structure to organize and control the work—would be familiar to civil engineers today. Likewise, some of our current test management techniques will be abandoned, just as today civil engineers use large trucks to move stone rather than having people roll the stones over logs. Nevertheless, like specialized teams and hierarchical management, some of what we do now will survive this first full millennium of systems engineering, becoming part of the best practices of the future.

I'm not sure how many of the ideas in this book will end up in that future body of knowledge, if any. Even if none do, I feel fortunate to be working in this unique field at this moment of its development. I also feel fortunate to be working among colleagues like the others who are writing on this topic, the people who've attended my test management seminars, and the people like you who've read this book.

Case Study

Table 11.1 shows the return on investment for three test projects. The first column is the type of project. Test development includes all costs associated with developing test cases, data, scripts, and other reusable intellectual property in the test system. Test environment includes systems, tools, and other reusable real property in the test lab. Both test development and test environment are amortized over three years. (The laptop computer project did not include any test development or environment because we used two outside test labs for our effort, which allowed us to capture this amortization as built-in overhead on test execution.)

Test execution includes the effort spent running the tests, gathering the results, reporting the results, responding to changes, and so forth; this is not amortized as it applies to the project itself. "Bugs" is the number of bugs found in testing. I calculate return on

[22]For those interested in a process-centric view of the testing process, please look for my next book, *Critical Testing Processes*.

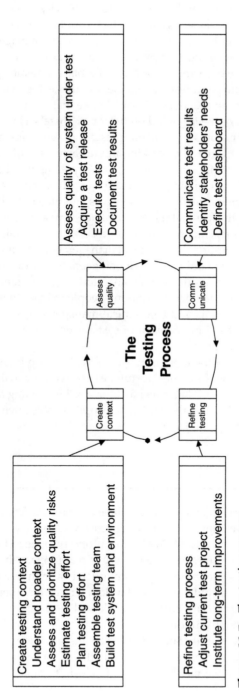

Figure 11.7 The testing process.

investment assuming an internal cost of failure associated with the must-fix bugs of $100 versus an external cost of failure of $1,000. This is also an estimate because precise cost of quality accounting data was not available. (See exercise 2 for a demonstration of why this is a conservative assumption.) Therefore, the return on investment is calculated as:

$$ROI = \frac{(900 \times Bugs_{testing}) - Cost_{testing} \cdot}{Cost_{testing}}$$

Retrospectively, I have self-assessed the maturity of the test process we used for the information appliance project using Tim Koomen and Martin Pol's Test Process Improvement. The Testing Maturity Matrix is shown in Figure 11.8. (The source spreadsheet, "Case Study TPI Test Maturity Assessment.xls," which includes the worksheets that assess compliance to each of the levels in each key area, is available at www.rexblackconsulting.com.)[23]

While we did not achieve a perfect score in some of the areas—we missed out in the area some long-term metrics and quality assurance for the test effort—the maturity of the test process we built and handed over to the client at the end of the project was quite good and certainly fit for their purposes. At the risk of pounding our own drum too strenuously, please allow me to point out that the level of maturity measure in was achieved by an outstanding team of test professionals who applied the tools, tips, and techniques described in the last 11 chapters.[24]

While I don't have enough insight into all the details of the project and organization to assess my client's Capability Maturity Model level, intuitively I would place it at a

Table 11.1 Cost of Quality Return on Investment Analysis for Three Projects

PROJECT TYPE	TEST DEVELOPMENT	TEST ENVIRONMENT	TEST EXECUTION	BUGS	ROI
IVR/Call Center	95,000	50,000	300,000	1,600	220%
Laptop Computer	0	0	150,000	240	44%
Information Appliance	$17,000	$11,000	$652,000	1,000	30%

[23]I thank Will Franklin and Allen Sell for sharing their Microsoft Word template for TPI assessment with me. It and Koomen and Pol's book formed the basis of the worksheet provided on the RBCS' Web site.

[24]Lest I seem boastful, let me point out that this achievement was, as always, more a reflection on the test team than on the manager. The fine group of test professionals who joined me on that project, in alphabetical order, were Dan Allred, Laurel Becker, Bret Grant, Amos Hare, Barton Layne, Joe Mata, Asif Moksud, Ivory Patterson, Frank Raymond, Lori Tolar, and Sunita Venketeswaran, along with hardware test professionals working with our vendor, Quanta Computer in Lin Kuo, Taiwan and our independent test lab, NTS/XXCAL in Boxborough, Massachusetts, USA. I thank each of you for all you taught me on that project. It was a privilege to serve as the manager of such a team.

ID	Key Area	0	1	2	3	4	5	6	7	8	9	10	11	12	13
	Koomen and Pol's Test Process Improvement Test Maturity Matrix														
	Internet Appliance Case Study														
								Scale							
		Ad Hoc		Controlled					Efficient				Optimizing		
1	Test Strategy		A					B				C		D	
2	Lifecycle Model		A			B									
3	Pervasiveness			A				B				C		D	
4	Estimation and Planning				A							B			
5	Test Specification Techniques		A		B										
6	Static Test Techniques					A		B							
7	Metrics						A			B			C		D
8	Test Tools					A			B			C			
9	Test Environment				A				B						C
10	Office Environment				A										
11	Commitment and Motivation		A				B						C		
12	Test Functions and Training					A			B		C				
13	Scope of Methodology					A						B			C
14	Communication			A	B								C		
15	Reporting		A			B		C					D		
16	Defect Management		A				B		C						
17	Testware Management			A			B				C				D
18	Test Process Management		A		B								C		
19	Evaluation							A			B				
20	Low-level Testing					A		B		C					

Figure 11.8   An assessment of test maturity based on the TPI model.

conservative two (repeatable) or a liberal three (defined). (You could classify the project as level three if you took a slightly relaxed view on how much documentation and formalism you require to meet the criteria for that level.) Illustrating one of the criticisms of the Capability Maturity Model, the one-dimensional nature of the scale, the project did include many of the process and quality metrics required for level four (managed). Koomen and Pol's Test Process Improvement metric avoids that problem for testing by using a multidimensional scale.

There's an interesting fact I should point out about this case study. For the three projects with returns on investment shown in Table 11.1, this project has the lowest return on investment but certainly the highest level of maturity both in testing and at the project level. The laptop computer project would probably rank a close second to the information appliance project in testing maturity, and, to a lesser extent, project maturity. It likewise has a relatively low return on investment. The lesson I take away from this case study is that, as the testing and the project processes mature, a particular way of quantifying test return on investment based on defects detected, as presented in this chapter, might become an inaccurate measure of the true return on the testing investment. Looking at the overall reduction in total cost of quality and the role a mature testing process can play in that, as shown in the Raytheon Electronic Systems group case study in Campenella, et al.'s, *Principle of Quality Costs*, might prove a more useful tool in such circumstances.

The IVR/Call Center shows the highest return on investment. In the case study change management database from Chapter 6, I measured about 20-percent inefficiency in that project due to various external changes. Excluding those inefficiencies would result in an even higher return on investment.

I thank my clients on these projects for the opportunity to work with them and for letting me to share these examples with readers of this book. My client contacts have asked that their organizations remain anonymous.

Exercises

Figures 11.9, 11.11, and 11.13 show three budgets for testing operations, one purely exploratory, one scripted manual, and one using both manual and automated scripts. Figures 11.10, 11.12, and 11.14 show the corresponding return on investment analyses for these budgets, using cost of quality. The source spreadsheet for these worksheets, "Exercise SpeedyWriter Budget.xls" is also available at www.rexblackconsulting.com.

1. Some common threads among the three projects are that each release will include 200 must-fix bugs that are either found and fixed during testing or delivered to the customers. In other words, we're not assuming any changes to the development process that would prevent defects. There will be quarterly maintenance releases and one major release every year. This allows you to amortize the test environment, test development, and any tools across three years, or 12 releases. For test engineer time, assume that half the time is spent developing tests or capturing testing done for later re-use, while the other half is spent in execution. Finally, assume that the test team is engaged from the start of the project in November. (Realistically, many major release projects would be longer than three months, but let's keep the exercise as simple as possible to focus on the key concepts.)

   - If you have two colleagues or fellow students available, take turns role-playing the test manager while the other two act as the skeptical project and executive managers. Present and defend the budget using the return on investment analysis.

   - If you don't have anyone to do exercise 1.a with, write down the justification you would use for each budget.

2. Suppose that we want to calculate the expected average cost of external failure for DataRocket. We know from past projects that the average server has 50 must-fix bugs lurking undiscovered when it ships. Customers report and receive fixes for 90 percent of these bugs within six months of first customer delivery. One full-time supporting engineer is assigned for each server during those six months, assuming the supporting engineer can fix on average 7.5 bugs per month. Each bug generates on average 10 calls to technical support, and each call requires one person-hour of technical support time, including any follow-up research, discussions with the supporting engineer, and providing information to the test team to create a confirmation test for the bug. Bug fixes are bundled in weekly support packs that require 20 person-hours of testing and five person-hours of release engineering time. Assume that the cost of a person-month, including the burden

rate, is $10,000. Based on 22 workdays a month and six productive work hours in a day, assume that a person-hour costs $76.

- What is the expected average cost of external failure during the first six months for DataRocket?

- Suppose you also knew that, on average for each technical support call, the customer spent one hour before calling trying to fix the problem and one hour during and after the call implementing a workaround, installing the fix, or otherwise mitigating the effect of the bug on the system. Further suppose that for every customer who did call, one other customer chose to fix the problem herself without calling, spending on average three hours. One other customer chose to return the server for a full refund of the $2,000 purchase price. Recalculate the expected average cost of external failure during the first six months based on this additional information.

- In exercise 1.b, did you include the customers' lost time? Why or why not?

- Are any categories of external failure costs missing in this exercise?

COMMENTS ON EXERCISE 1

You might have noticed in working through exercise 1 that the return on investment is significantly lower than the 350 percent and 445 percent shown in Figure 11.2, and that it went down as we added more resources rather than up. Why?

The reason the return on investment is lower is because the cost of conformance *per bug found* is different. In the example illustrated in Figure 11.2, the investment in testing (cost of conformance), normalized by the number of bugs found, came to about $175 per bug. In exercise 1, the cost of conformance per bug found is about $500 per bug, which is approximately three times higher. If we reduce staff costs—for example, through wise use of test technicians—we could increase the return on investment. However, it's also the case that, the worse the system under test is in terms of quality, the better the return on investment will look (at least, as long as we can run enough tests to find most of the bugs). This is another example of metrics being potentially misleading and dysfunctional. If, as the test manager or as the test team, you are given a bonus based on the return on investment calculated by cost of quality, then your incentive is to file an excessive number of bugs reports, ask the development team not do any unit or component testing, or both.

The reason for the declining return on investment is the shape of the cost of quality curve. Traditional cost of quality curves look something like Figure 11.15. If such is the shape of your cost of quality curve, at some point the cost of conformance and the cost of nonconformance curves intercept. Spending exactly that amount on costs of conformance minimizes the cost of quality. (Newer thinking on cost of quality now suggests that, if you invest your money in quality assurance and testing wisely, the cost of conformance never exceeds the cost of nonconformance.[25]) As you approach the cost of quality minimum, the return on investment might fall off, because each additional dollar investment in testing results in less of a reduction in the cost of nonconformance.

---

[25]See Campenella, et al.'s *Principles of Quality Costs.*

3. For as many current and past positions, engagements, or projects as practical, use a testing maturity model to assess the maturity of your test effort, and a project-wide or company-wide maturity model to assess the maturity of your project. I recommend using Koomen and Pol's TPI, because of its flexibility, and also because you can download the Do you see positive correlation between test maturity and company maturity? (NB: If you do not, I'd appreciate an email from you regarding your fascinating findings.)

4. Refer to the case study change management database from Chapter 6, and to the lists of "brake pedals" and "gas pedals" in this chapter. In a spreadsheet, classify the delaying problems against one of the brake pedals and the accelerating events against one of the gas pedals. (Add an "other" category for anything that doesn't fit.) Create a Pareto diagram of the influences of project process maturity issues on that project.

COMMENTS ON EXERCISE 1 *(Continued)*

You already have seen an example of this phenomenon at work. If you think back on the opened/closed charts shown in Chapter 4, imagine using that data along with the daily tester effort figures gathered in Chapter 5 to graph, on a daily basis, the number of person-hours required to find the next bug. You would get a curve that, instead of leveling off as you approached the end of system test, would instead go from a flat curve when bugs were easy to find to an upward-sloped and parabolic curve as bugs became more difficult to find.

As you think about these topics, you might start to ask yourself, as I did at one point, a nagging question. "Gee," I thought, "isn't something missing in this approach to calculating the return on investment of testing?" The answer to this question occurred to me in the form of another question: "Is the only value of testing in finding bugs?"

I believe the answer to that question is, "No." Testing is a form of quality risk management, something like insurance. Most people who own cars carry car insurance. At the end of a policy year, if a driver hasn't made any claims, would that driver go out and run a car into a lightpost to achieve a positive return on investment on the insurance policy? Of course not.

Using the insurance model, we might attempt to quantify the value of a passed test. In insurance, the expected payout is the probability of a loss times the cost of the loss. Therefore, if we know the average cost of particular types of field failures, we can justify spending some fraction of the total costs of those types of failures that could occur, based on the chance that those bugs *could* be present in the system. The return on investment would come not from finding the bugs, but from knowing whether the bugs were there. In other words, the return on investment would come from the reduced chance of unanticipated future costs.

I certainly haven't read every paper and book on software engineering economics, so I might have missed something. However, to my knowledge, no one has done a lot of digging into this topic yet. If you are an aspiring software engineering student looking for a senior year project or graduate thesis, this could well be fertile ground for research.

	A	B	C	D	E
1	**SpeedyWriter Test Budget**				
2	Exploratory Testing				
3					
4		Nov	Dec	Jan	Total
5	**Staff**				
6	Lin-Tsu Wong–Test Engineer	8,333	8,333	8,333	$25,000
7	**Total Staff**	**$8,333**	**$8,333**	**$8,333**	**$25,000**
8					
9	**Tools**				
10	Web loading/stress tool	$0	$0	$0	$0
11	**Total Tools**	**$0**	**$0**	**$0**	**$0**
12					
13	**Test Systems**				
14	Solaris Client	$1,500	$0	$0	$1,500
15	Windows 95 Client	1,000	0	0	1,000
16	Windows 98 Client	1,500	0	0	1,500
17	Mac Client	1,500	0	0	1,500
18	Solaris Server	2,500	0	0	2,500
19	Windows NT Server	2,500	0	0	2,500
20	Novell Server	2,500	0	0	2,500
21	**Total Test Systems**	**$13,000**	**$0**	**$0**	**$13,000**
22					
23	**Grand Total**	**$21,333**	**$8,333**	**$8,333**	**$38,000**

Figure 11.9 SpeedyWriter test budget (exploratory testing only).

	A	B	C
1	**SpeedyWriter Test Budget**		
2	Exploratory Testing ROI		
3			
4	**Testing**	Baseline	Testing
5	Staff (test development amortized)	0	$13,542
6	Systems (amortized)	0	1,083
7	Tools (amortized)	0	0
8	**Total Investment**	**$0**	**$14,625**
9			
10	**Development**		
11	Must-Fix Bugs Found	100	100
12	**Fix Cost**	**$1,000**	**$1,000**
13			
14	**Testing**		
15	Must-Fix Bugs Found	0	30
16	**Fix Cost**	**$0**	**$3,000**
17			
18	**Customer Support**		
19	Must-Fix Bugs Found	100	70
20	**Fix Cost**	**$100,000**	**$70,000**
21			
22	**Cost of Quality**		
23	Conformance	$0	$14,625
24	Nonconformance	$101,000	$74,000
25	**Total CoQ**	**$101,000**	**$88,625**
26			
27	**Return on Investment**	**#N/A**	**85%**
28			
29	**Defect Detection Percentage**	**0%**	**30%**

Figure 11.10 SpeedyWriter test ROI (exploratory testing only).

	A	B	C	D	E
1	**SpeedyWriter Test Budget**				
2	Scripted Manual Testing				
3					
4		Nov	Dec	Jan	Total
5	**Staff**				
6	Jamal Brown—Test Manager	$10,000	$10,000	$10,000	$30,000
7	Lin-Tsu Wong—Test Engineer	8,333	8,333	8,333	$25,000
8	**Total Staff**	$18,333	$18,333	$18,333	$55,000
9					
10	**Tools**				
11	Web loading/stress tool	$0	$0	$0	$0
12	**Total Tools**	$0	$0	$0	$0
13					
14	**Test Systems**				
15	Solaris Client	$1,500	$0	$0	$1,500
16	Windows 95 Client	1,000	0	0	1,000
17	Windows 98 Client	1,500	0	0	1,500
18	Mac Client	1,500	0	0	1,500
19	Solaris Server	2,500	0	0	2,500
20	Windows NT Server	2,500	0	0	2,500
21	Novell Server	2,500	0	0	2,500
22	**Total Test Systems**	$13,000	$0	$0	$13,000
23					
24	**Grand Total**	$31,333	$18,333	$18,333	$68,000

Figure 11.11   SpeedyWriter test budget (manual scripted testing primarily).

	A	B	C
1	**SpeedyWriter Test Budget**		
2	Scripted Manual Testing ROI		
3			
4	**Testing**	**Baseline**	**Testing**
5	Staff (test development amortized)	0	$29,792
6	Systems (amortized)	0	1,083
7	Tools (amortized)	0	0
8	**Total Investment**	$0	$30,875
9			
10	**Development**		
11	Must-Fix Bugs Found	100	100
12	Fix Cost	$1,000	$1,000
13			
14	**Testing**		
15	Must-Fix Bugs Found	0	60
16	Fix Cost	$0	$6,000
17			
18	**Customer Support**		
19	Must-Fix Bugs Found	100	40
20	Fix Cost	$100,000	$40,000
21			
22	**Cost of Quality**		
23	Conformance	$0	$30,875
24	Nonconformance	$101,000	$47,000
25	**Total CoQ**	$101,000	$77,875
26			
27	**Return on Investment**	#N/A	75%
28			
29	**Defect Detection Percentage**	0%	60%

Figure 11.12   SpeedyWriter test ROI (manual scripted testing primarily).

	A	B	C	D	E
1	**SpeedyWriter Test Budget**				
2	Manual and Automated Testing				
3					
4		Nov	Dec	Jan	Total
5	**Staff**				
6	Jamal Brown—Test Manager	$10,000	$10,000	$10,000	$30,000
7	Lin-Tsu Wong—Test Engineer	8,333	8,333	8,333	$25,000
8	Emma Moorhouse—Test Engineer	9,167	9,167	9,167	$27,500
9	**Total Staff**	**$27,500**	**$27,500**	**$27,500**	**$82,500**
10					
11	**Tools**				
12	Web loading/stress tool	$20,000	$0	$0	$20,000
13	**Total Tools**	**$20,000**	**$0**	**$0**	**$20,000**
14					
15	**Test Systems**				
16	Solaris Client	$1,500	$0	$0	$1,500
17	Windows 98 Client	1,000	0	0	1,000
18	Windows 2000 Client	1,500	0	0	1,500
19	Mac Client	1,500	0	0	1,500
20	Solaris Server	2,500	0	0	2,500
21	Windows NT Server	2,500	0	0	2,500
22	Novell Server	2,500	0	0	2,500
23	**Total Test Systems**	**$13,000**	**$0**	**$0**	**$13,000**
24					
25	**Grand Total**	**$60,500**	**$27,500**	**$27,500**	**$115,500**

Figure 11.13 SpeedyWriter test budget (automated and manual testing).

	A	B	C
1	**SpeedyWriter Test Budget**		
2	Manual and Automated Testing ROI		
3			
4	**Testing**	**Baseline**	**Testing**
5	Staff (test development amortized)	0	$44,688
6	Systems (amortized)	0	1,083
7	Tools (amortized)	0	1,667
8	**Total Investment**	**$0**	**$47,438**
9			
10	**Development**		
11	Must-Fix Bugs Found	100	100
12	**Fix Cost**	**$1,000**	**$1,000**
13			
14	**Testing**		
15	Must-Fix Bugs Found	0	90
16	**Fix Cost**	**$0**	**$9,000**
17			
18	**Customer Support**		
19	Must-Fix Bugs Found	100	10
20	**Fix Cost**	**$100,000**	**$10,000**
21			
22	**Cost of Quality**		
23	Conformance	$0	$47,438
24	Nonconformance	$101,000	$20,000
25	**Total CoQ**	**$101,000**	**$67,438**
26			
27	**Return on Investment**	**#N/A**	**71%**
28			
29	**Defect Detection Percentage**	**0%**	**90%**

Figure 11.14 SpeedyWriter test ROI (automated and manual testing).

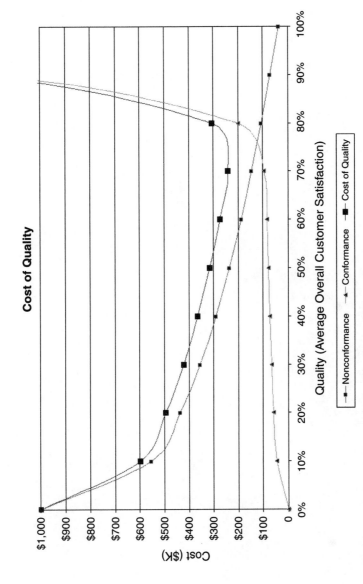

Figure 11.15   A hypothetical cost of quality graph.

Hardware Testing Fundamentals: An Introduction for Software Testing Professionals

Many people involved in computer hardware testing, myself included, fell into that role as part of testing systems that consist of both hardware and software, while having primarily a software background. While I did take some electrical, electronics, circuit, and engineering materials courses in college, I certainly don't consider myself a computer hardware or electronics engineer. However, I've found that, armed with a few basic concepts, those of us with extensive software test management experience can usually manage hardware testing as well, provided the right people are put in charge of the actual testing. The following brief introduction will give you some ideas of what to look for in a competently executed hardware testing effort. If you need to become a competent hardware tester yourself, I recommend that you read O'Connor's *Practical Reliability Engineering* and Ishikawa's *Guide to Quality Control* as a starting point.

Test Management

From a purely test management point of view, the same tools I introduced in the last eleven chapters will work for a test project that involves both hardware and software. You still have to track tests and bugs, assemble a test environment and team, get releases into the test environment, and possibly work with a distributed test team. That doesn't go away.

However, if you are a big test-automation buff, know that many of these tools won't help you in the hardware and systems testing world. You can use load generators of various sorts as part of a reliability test (more to come), but the failures you see will be different from the type of functional regression bugs most people use the automated tools to catch.

That's not to say you won't need tools. On the contrary, whomever ends up doing the actual hardware testing—the hardware vendor, a third-party test lab, someone else, all of the above—will need lots of tools: thermal chambers, oscilloscopes, voltage/amperage meters, shock and vibration tables, mechanical life harnesses, and more.

When testers find bugs with these tools, you'll soon learn that sometimes hardware systems behave differently, one to the next. Bad unit failures happen. They can be perplexing until you stop and think about the nature of a "bug" in hardware instead of software. In two hardware systems, bugs can arise because one system has a bad solder connection, a broken write, a faulty chip, or any other number of unique reasons. In software, the copy of the CD-ROM or floppy you use to install the software under test doesn't matter. That's hard for some software professionals to get used to, so internalize that fact as soon as possible.

It's also important to understand that test conditions can take longer to create in hardware testing. Some thermal tests can last days. A classic hardware reliability demonstration can take weeks. It's important to plan accordingly. Just because you'd like all the tests to last the same length of time—and indeed I encouraged such a standard in Chapter 3, "Test System Architecture, Cases, and Coverage"—doesn't mean that's practical for all hardware test cases.

Basic Functionality and Self Tests

The most fundamental hardware tests are those tests, often embedded in a system's read-only-memory (ROM) or basic input/output system (BIOS), that run whenever the system reboots or powers up. The tests generally are nothing more than a basic subsystem sanity test. A good test will cover not just one subsystem, but all of them. (I have seen embedded modems be especially problematic in this area.) It's also a good idea for the test team—possibly through a "magic keystroke combination" if you want to hide this capability from users—to be able to launch these tests. A basic subsystem sanity check should be the first line of defense in isolating bad unit failures.

Electrical Testing

This is one type of testing that, unlike almost all software tests, poses an actual risk of physical danger to the test and the system under test. Even a system that is not powered up can have potentially deadly electrical charges stored in capacitors or batteries. Only qualified professionals should perform any type of test, but in running electrical tests, this fact is especially critical.

Electrical tests come in many flavors. One type of electrical test is making sure the signal waveforms are correct on running systems. This type of testing, called "signal quality" testing, also includes checking for inappropriate voltages or potential current flows in various places, especially externally accessible ports. With systems supplying power to external devices such as USB ports and peripherals, the possibility exists for dangerous (to the hardware) situations.

Another type of electrical testing is checking to see how the system responds to various types of power conditions. In the United States, Canada, and Taiwan, 120 volts and 60 hertz are the nominal voltage and frequency coming out of the wall, but in Europe and much of Asia, 240 volts and 50 hertz are the norm. Temporary losses in voltage ("sags" or "brownouts") happen in various locations around the world, including even the high-tech state of California in 2001. How will voltage spikes affect your system? The best software in the world doesn't do any good if the host system crashes every 15 minutes because it can't eat the AC power coming out of the wall.

Some systems, such as laptops, mobile phones, and other portable devices, spend a lot of time away from the AC power coming out of the wall—or the DC power coming out of the car dashboard or the airplane armrest. For these devices, how they work—and how long they work—under battery power is a major concern. It also matters how long they take to charge. Do the batteries maintain consistent performance over multiple charge/discharge cycles? Does power run out without warning?

Environmental Tests

Environmental tests are those tests designed to see how the system responds to various types of insults and strenuous conditions the system will encounter in the real world. One type of such tests involves shocks and vibrations. Systems tend to get bumped, transported across rough roads, shaken, swung around in briefcases, and so forth. Rather than try to mimic these conditions exactly, the usual procedure is to mount the system under test to a shock table or vibration table, and then subject the system to certain accelerations and vibrations. The intensity of these shocks and vibrations are calibrated often in "G's" (for gravitational acceleration, like jet pilots measure tightness of turns at high speed).

Vibrations happen across various frequencies, with a gradual change usually (sweeping) across the frequencies in the course of the test. Shocks, occurring as incidents rather than over a period of time, have pulse shapes and durations. It is often somewhat difficult to imagine exactly how a particular shock or vibration test relates to an actual (potential) field incident, but most of the hardware test labs and reputable vendors have standard tests that they run. You'll need to consult an expert to understand how two different tests relate to each other, especially if they're measured in different units.

A related type of test is a drop test. Unlike the somewhat mystifying shock and vibration tests, this test involves simply dropping a system from a given height onto various types of surfaces in various configurations to see what happens. For example, a laptop computer might be dropped with the lid shut and the lid open onto a carpeted and a cement floor from a foot or two in the air onto its flat surfaces, edges, and corners.

Environmental tests can also include other nasty surprises the system is likely to encounter. For example, on several laptop and information appliance projects, the systems were subjected to juice, coffee, water, and cola poured into the device. The test involves not only correct operation during or after the spill, but also a reasonable cleanup process that does not damage the unit, strip legends off of keys on the keyboard, warp or crack mice, trackballs, pointers, and the like, or cause any other physical damage to the unit. According to some of my test management course attendees, battlefield computers are often subjected to smoke, sand, bullets, fire, and other severe insults.

Altitude is another potential factor, especially in systems that rely on convection cooling rather than cooling fans. For example, the information appliance we tested did not include a fan on its CPU, but rather had special vents and heat sinks designed to wick heat away from active components. Thin air at altitude can reduce the effectiveness of such schemes. PDAs, mobile phones, and other such devices might need such testing. Systems that operate at high altitudes or in space—for example, aeronautical systems on jets, especially supersonics jets that can operate in extremely thin air, and satellites must be tested in such environments.

The effect of pollutants might be another factor to consider. A home telephone system or information appliance designed to work in a kitchen will be subjected to smoke from hot or burned food, including smoking oil, which leaves heavy deposits behind.

One last environment test to mention is electrical conductivity and resistance. Can a simple static discharge onto a user interface or user-accessible component route through to a sensitive component such as a chip, causing damage? One way to find out is to test static discharges onto the exterior of the system. Can the device create dangerous shorts? If the system somehow comes in contact with a hot wire or electrified surface, that voltage should not travel through the case to a point where the user might receive a shock.

All of these environmental tests can—and perhaps in your case should—involve both operating (powered up) and non-operating units. The non-operating tests are generally of at least equal intensity as the operating tests, since it is assumed that non-operating units will be moved, while operating units tend to be more sedentary. This assumption does not hold for laptop computers, battlefield computers, integrated weapons electronics, cellular phones, PDAs, and other portable devices. In addition, for such portable devices, the shock, vibration, and drop tests should be considerably more severe than those used for a non-mobile system such as a server, a telephone switch, a rack-mounted router, or the like.

These tests generally destroy one or more units. Therefore, if such tests must be run against scarce engineering prototypes (see Chapter 2, "Plotting and Presenting Your Course: The Test Plan"), you might want to make sure those tests are run toward the end of a hardware test cycle, when new systems are soon to come. Of course, if environmental risks are considered a particularly high risk, then these tests should be run right away. Plan for extra units. Do not plan to use a system that has been through an environmental testing for any other testing, especially not any of the testing discussed in this appendix. Even if the unit is not destroyed, it might be damaged in subtle ways that influence the outcome of other tests, including software tests.

Mechanical Life

Any part of the system that can move, flex, rotate, bend, latch and unlatch, plug and unplug, toggle, switch, open and close, click, press and depress, or is in any way subject to opposing forces will be subject to strains and wear. Prime examples of this are hinges and latches, keyboards, touchpads, touchscreens, mice, trackballs, power switches, removable drives, CD-ROM/DVD-ROM/CD-RW players, floppy drives, and so forth. These items can have multiple moving parts. For example, a CD-ROM drive has the spindle, the laser and read head, the soft eject button (that works when the system is on), the hard eject button (that works when the system is off), and the platter. The floppy drive has many of these components and often a hinged cover. Any connector (e.g., telephone for a modem, network for a LAN) or a regularly touched surface such as a keyboard or trackpad or touchscreen is subject to the wear associated with regular use.

For any of these moving parts, the hardware test experts must make some reasonable assumption about how many motion events the part will experience over the course of its life. For keyboards, for example, test cases are often based on an assumption that each key will be pressed between 1 to 10 million times. Range of motion is another consideration, especially for latches, hinges, and the like. The test cases should also take force of motion into account. Often, frustrated computer users will bang on or sharply actuate computer keys or buttons during failure of the system. Finally, consider shearing or torque forces. For examples, suppose a user of a laptop always tends to open the lid by one corner or the other rather than the middle?

Thermal Tests

Thermals tests check to see whether the system can stand up to the temperature and humidity conditions it will experience in both operating and nonoperating modes. The testers place the system in a thermal chamber and run it through a series of temperature and humidity cycles as shown in Figure A.1. (Temperature is shown on the Y-axis in Centigrade scale, humidity is shown in percentages above the temperature graph, and durations of the dwells [flat lines] and transitions [sloped lines] in hours are show on the X-axis.) Often, active and heat-producing components such as CPUs and power supplies are instrumented with thermal sensors to check, over the course of the test, whether these components exceed their maximum operating temperatures. These tests are sometimes referred to as "four corners" tests, because graphs of maximum and minimum temperatures and humidity under operating and non-operating conditions produce a rectangle or parallelogram with four corners.

Another type of thermal test involves thermal shocks, where temperatures are changed rapidly. For example, consider the circuitry in a satellite, where ambient temperatures and humidity will go from the balmy launch pad to frigid and desiccated upper atmosphere and then outer space in a period of minutes.

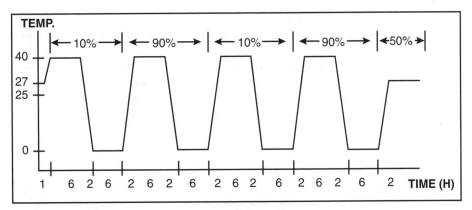

Figure A.1   A graph of temperature and humidity of time in a thermal test.

Reliability

Hardware systems, unlike software, wear out and fail over time. When software works under a particular condition it tends to work under that same condition indefinitely, but hardware can work under a particular condition one day and then fail the next. These failures can often be repaired and the unit put back into service, although the very act of repair tends to result in a lessening of future reliability. The rate of failure in a population of systems is often measured in terms of the *mean time between failures* (MTBF). If the more important consideration is availability rather than paucity of failures, then this can be measured in terms of uptime, which is a function of the mean time between failure and the mean time to repair (MTTR). A test for reliability is often referred to as a "reliability demonstration" or "MTBF demonstration."

One common technique for such a test is to gather a fairly large number of units, power them up, and then leave them in a running state, with some load test cycling indefinitely, under periods of maximum operating temperature and humidity. Given a desired level of statistical MTBF in the production units, some small number of units can fail during the demonstration period, which generally lasts weeks. The higher the level of reliability to be demonstrated, the larger the sample, the longer the demonstration, and the fewer the units that can fail. These tests are based on an assumption that failure rates are constant over time, which is generally valid during the expected life of the system.

Understanding reliability is very important if you intend to offer a free warranty on your systems, because you can predict, with great statistical accuracy, the exact cost associated with returns over the life of the warranty. Extended warranties sold with the system can be a significant profit center for your company, provided that you know the MTBF and can charge customers well above the expected payout per unit in repair costs. This is why consumer electronics stores tend to push these warranties so heavily, and why, statistically, you are rooking yourself out of good money if you let them talk you into buying one.

Another way to predict the reliability and the lifetime of a system is to use what are called highly accelerated life tests (HALT). These tests subject a small sample of systems to extreme operating temperatures, humidity, shock, and vibrations until they fail. Not only is the time to fail interesting in predicting the longevity of the system, but the failure mode is often interpreted as indicating which component or components are most likely to fail. Because of the elevated temperature, the lifetime of the system is accelerated (hence the name) according to the Arrhenius equation, which calculates the speeding-up of chemical reactions under conditions of higher temperature. Unlike a traditional MTBF demonstration, which involves a basic grasp of statistics, a highly accelerated life test involves a very sophisticated understanding of the system under test and the specifics of running a valid HALT test.[1]

---

[1] O'Connor's *Practical Reliability Engineering* explains the standard MTBF demonstration process, while McLean's *HALT, HASS & HASA Explained,* uh, like the title says, explains HALT tests.

Packaging Tests

An important variant of thermal, shock, drop, and vibration testing involves a nonoperating test of the system in its packaging, especially for computer electronics and computer systems such as telephones, laptop and desktop computers, PDAs, and the like. In these tests, the systems are placed in their packaging as they will be shipped to the customer and are run through a sequence of tests designed to check for problems that could occur during shipping and delivery to the customers. The circumstances of shipping and delivery affect this testing. A system shipped on an airplane will experience different modes of vibration than one shipped on a boat or a train. Propeller-driven planes have different vibrations in their frames than jet planes do. This might seem picayune, but the wrong vibration over a period of hours can shake a board, a chip, or a screw loose, resulting in reliability problems—and potentially warranty costs—after the system is delivered and installed. A system shipped in a heated truck and then transported by forklift to a warehouse in Alaska or Siberia in the winter will undergo dramatic thermal shocks, and might undergo significant mechanical shocks if the forklift operator is less than gentle when removing the palette of systems from the tines of the forklift. I once saw two movers drop a $250,000 IVR server in its packaging off the lip of a loading ramp. It fell two inches and hit with a loud boom. I made sure to get the number of the moving truck just in case; fortunately, the system powered up and worked fine in the test lab later.

The packaging tests are run much like the corresponding nonoperating thermal, shock, drop, and vibration tests, except that the system is inside its packaging. Thermal, humidity, and motion sensors are generally attached to the inside of the package, and then the test is run. These sensors record maximums and minimums and can be examined after the test is over. The system will also be powered up and given a basic functionality test, along with receiving a visual inspection.

Acoustics

Systems with built-in speakers and microphones are supposed to reproduce and capture sound with some level of quality. That is subject to testing, often in anechoic chambers with precise instruments for measuring sound across the audible spectrum of frequencies.

Systems also tend to produce sounds, especially the noise of spinning hard disks, CD-ROMs, floppies, and other drives. Cooling fans are generally not silent, either. Keyboards, mice, and other mechanical parts can make noise as they move. Sometimes, warning noises are irritating or disruptive. For example, my current laptop computer emits a very loud, repetitive tone when the battery gets low, which has frequently disturbed fellow passengers on airplanes. There is no way to customize the volume or type of warning tone emitted. I don't think anyone tested for this particular problem.

The best systems will have limits on how much noise they can produce, and these systems should be tested against these limits. Testing should take into account any factor that affects the noise a system makes. For example, to save power, some laptop computers, rather than switching on a fan to cool a CPU, will downshift the processor speed when operating on battery power. An acoustics test run on a laptop not connected to AC power will fail to detect a noisy fan.

Safety

Systems are often used by people or in an environment in which people are present. This means that systems can hurt people, especially when they fail or are used in an unusual way. Understanding customer usage, the environment, and potential failure modes is key to running a safety test. For consumer products, a classic example is small parts such as keys on a keyboard that can fall off or be plucked off and subsequently swallowed by a small child, resulting in choking.

Many portable computers contain batteries, which frequently include dangerous substances. Cadmium and nickel, for example, are potentially toxic metals found in some rechargeable batteries. Adequate care must be taken to ensure that these devices do not leak dangerous chemicals under foreseeable failure modes, and that warnings are included for safe disposal of the units after their life cycle is complete.

The NEBS test for telephony servers, telephone switches, and other devices to be located in central telephone offices specifies a fire test that actually involves taking a gas torch to various components on the system in a sealed chamber. (The tester should have a safety suit and an outside air supply for this test.) The resulting fumes are tested for toxicity, and the system is watched carefully for any signs of combustibility.

Radiation

In the course of operation, most system will emit—and be subject to—various forms of radiation, especially electromagnetic radiation in the radio spectrum due to the frequencies in clocks that control bus speeds, CPU speeds, screen refresh rates, and so forth. Emitted radiation must be limited to avoid interference with other devices, and incoming radiation that is within normal limits should not interfere with the operation of this device.

Some radiation can be more magnetic than electromagnetic. Computer-controlled magnetic resonance imaging (MRI) medical systems have been involved in fatalities when their powerful magnetic fields caused ferrous (iron-based) metal objects to abruptly fly through the air and strike occupants and bystanders with tremendous force. One patient was killed by a flying oxygen tank, and a police officer's gun was involved in another incident.

Some systems are designed to emit radiation, such as nuclear medicine devices like the Therac-25. You might recall the horrifying anecdote I related about this device's failures in Chapter 1, "Defining What's on Your Plate: The Foundation of a Test Project," where software bugs interacted to result in fatal dosages delivered to some patients. The United States Department of Defense in now considering the construction of extremely high-powered lasers mounted on aircraft for the purposes of shooting down ballistic missiles, and the United States Department of Energy is replacing the nuclear testing of bombs with simulated nuclear explosions through the action of very precisely computer-controlled lasers at the Lawrence-Livermore Labs in California. Understanding usage conditions, the environment, and potential errors and failure modes is important to thorough testing of any system, especially such complex computer-controlled systems that have the potential to affect human safety and health.

Standards and Regulations

Especially in the case of safety and radiation, testers have standards that specify the testing to be performed or at least what constitutes success or failure. In telecommunications, the NEBS standard applies to servers or other systems to be installed in telephone system central offices. Most governments have standards for safety and radiation, such as the United States Underwriters Laboratories and Federal Communication Commission, respectively. The bottom of a portable system to be sold in many countries often looks like a high-tech alphabet soup of the seals and logos of various regulatory agencies scattered around the globe.

One thing to remember about standards enforced by regulatory bodies is that government bureaucracies are not stakeholders in the success of your product. They will not care much if, say, your system's failure to pass a particular test is blocking its delivery to paying customers and costing your company thousands of dollars per day while the window of opportunity to capture the market closes. As a test manager, this means you must pay careful attention to these standards, allow for plenty of time to complete testing (including cycle time should the tests fail), and escalate blockages to management quickly. No matter how well-functioning your bug triage committee is, it cannot decide to waive or defer a bug related to the failure to meet government regulatory standards.

Not all regulations and standards are enforced by governments. For packaging, the International Shipping and Transportation Institute has voluntary standards that you can apply for testing. While no one will force your company to adhere to these standards, they represent good ideas that you won't need to reinvent for your testing. Why not give them a try?

Components and Subsystems

Complicating this whole matter of hardware testing is that systems are often comprised of various components and subsystems. These need to be tested separately before they're integrated into your system, but they also need to be tested in the system. Special tests might be required, depending on the subsystem.

Video cards, modems, networking cards, USB controllers, and other I/O components are a prime example of this. Signal quality testing of the incoming and outgoing signals is important, even on pins that are supposedly not used. I once worked on a project where the vendor had assumed that that words *not used* associated with a particular pin in the requirements specification for the connection to a monitor meant they could use that pin to adjust the monitor's image size on the assembly line. The vendor learned during testing that the words should have been *not to be used*, because an internal video chip controller signal was present on that pin, causing sporadic resizing of the image!

Thermal testing can also be a concern. On the IVR project I've referred to in this book, the telephony cards included high-speed processors. These cards were packed together in a VME bus in the system rack with four fans to move air over the cards. During thermal testing, I had the testers instrument these chips so that I could check for overtemp conditions during high heat portions of the test cycle.

Systems often include screens—ranging from simple LCDs to advanced TFT color displays—and these are subject to testing for defective pixels, contrast, color, power consumption, and readability under various lighting conditions. Screens also have implications for other tests, especially shock, vibration, drop, environmental, and battery life tests. Finally, a touchscreen, being both an input and an output device, needs special testing of the input facilities, including mechanical life testing.

External mice, keyboards, printers, monitors, and other bundled devices should also be considered for testing. In many cases, you can rely on the vendor's testing if this is a widely used commercial product, but you still must consider any unique usage conditions or environments. For example, if you're testing a battlefield system, just assuming that you can plug a standard monitor, keyboard, and mouse into that system and have those components work correctly with sand, smoke, bullets, and bombs flying around is probably a mistake.

Shocks and vibration can damage or loosen components and subsystems. Drops might cause bending or warping, even if the subsystem isn't at the point of impact, due to transmitted vibrations. Radiation might affect the component, and, if the component is inside your system, it might not be protected by radiation screening installed in the chassis or case of the system. Components might have moving parts, like my PC-Card modem in my laptop, that are subject to mechanical life tests. The failure of a component can affect the overall reliability of your system.

Integrated Software

While not directly related to hardware testing, it bears mentioning that many components of your system will have integrated software, especially firmware or BIOS code that starts the system or guides its operation during use. This includes networking cards, video cards, modems, hard drives, CD-ROMs, and other items. I mention this because insufficient testing or unmanaged change in these software elements can seriously affect the reliability and functionality of the subsystem, which can ripple through to affect your system. It can also affect the interfaces that a subsystem presents to your system or other subsystems within your system. On one project, poor testing and a total lack of configuration management and change control practices resulted in the firmware on a modem causing all sorts of connection reliability issues for the system under test. When talking to hardware vendors about their testing, don't forget to ask about how they control the quality of their firmware. Even the most diligent and careful hardware engineers might not understand good software engineering practices, especially if the company is too small to have a dedicated software engineering team.

Supplier Quality Engineering

The best way to deal with vendor quality issues—including testing of hardware and software—is to build long-term relationships with vendors, apply the distributed testing ideas I discussed in Chapter 10, "Involving Other Players: Distributing a Test Project," and also assign someone to work with the vendor to ensure the quality of their products during design, development, and production. This practice is often referred to as *supplier quality engineering*. A supplier quality engineer works with the vendor to ensure thorough testing and prompt resolution of any quality problems that arise throughout the life cycle of the subsystem. My most successful clients who buy subsystems to integrate in their systems have mature, well-run supplier quality engineering programs as part of their design, development, and production processes.

Pilot Testing

Once software is written and run through final system and perhaps acceptance testing, production is often as simple as copying bits onto a CD-ROM or floppy, or posting the software to a Web site. However, there is a distinct difference in hardware between skilled engineers hand-assembling an engineering prototype system and multiple people on a semi-automated assembly line doing the same thing for dozens or hundreds of systems per hour. Production of hardware systems is a complex endeavor. The quality of the outgoing products is influenced by the quality of the components and subsystems, the assembly process, the production environment, the training given to the assembly line team, and potentially myriad other factors.

To figure out what these factors are and whether the vendor is able to manufacture systems of an acceptable quality level and in an acceptable volume, a pilot test is often run during the initial production period. During the pilot test, heavy sampling and testing of the systems—sometimes as high as 100 percent—is performed. The appropriate period for burn-in testing (i.e., tests run to screen out those systems that will suffer infant mortality) is determined. I have sometimes been involved in this testing, even though my official role was as the development system test manager.

Case Study

On the information appliance project discussed in earlier case studies, we had to test not only the client and server software, but also the information appliance hardware. That testing involved primarily the vendor's test team and an external test lab. However, as shown in Figure A.2, testing also involved the vendor's engineering team, the vendor's production test team, and the two subsystem vendors making the keyboard and the power adapter (a.k.a. "brick"). The case study hardware test tracking spreadsheet, "Case Study Info Appliance Device Test Tracking.xls," is available at www.rexblackconsulting.com.

Owner	Test ID	Test Suite/Case	Status	System Config	Bug ID	Bug RPN	Bug Status	By	Plan Date	Act Date	Plan Hrs	Act Hrs	Test Hrs	Comment
				Device Test Case Tracking Worksheet										
Owner														
Vendor Test	1.000	Electrical												
Vendor Test	2.000	Reliability												
Vendor Engr.	3.000	Regulatory/Standards												
Vendor Engr.	4.000	Engineering Test												
NTS	5.000	Reliability/Correlation												
Vendor Test	6.000	Functionality												
Vendor Prod.	7.000	Manufacturability												
Kbd Vendor	8.000	Keyboard												
Brick Vendor	9.000	Power Adapter												

Figure A.2 Information appliance hardware test suites and assigned organizations.

I thank my client, who wishes to remain anonymous, for permission to discuss this project here. I also thank my client contacts for their excellent support and steady leadership on this project. Finally, thanks to my test team, the vendors, and the independent test lab for their professionalism and excellence on this project.

Bibliography, Related Readings, and Other Resources

Where Do I Go Next, Rex?

While this book should provide you with enough information to manage a test project, it is by no means a compendium. I encourage you to continue to augment your knowledge. The following subsections provide you with some places to go for more information, including the bibliography of references and recommended readings. Like the book, this appendix is not complete, nor does the presence or absence of a particular company, book, organization, or individual reflect my endorsement or opinion.

Bibliography and Related Readings

The following is my "suggested reading" list for test managers. Most of these books and articles are referenced somewhere in *Managing the Testing Process*. However, some I have included simply because I feel that you might benefit from a familiarity with the material presented, or with the author's point of view. Until fairly recently, there was a paucity of materials for the test professional, but that has begun to change. I encourage you to stay current and involved with the latest thinking and research in the field. Today's wacky idea is tomorrow's best practice, and the day after's expected minimum skill-set.

Batini, Carlo, Stefano Ceri, and Shamkant Navathe. *Conceptual Database Design.* Redwood City, CA: Benjamin/Cummings, 1992.

Beizer, Boris. *Black Box Testing.* New York, NY: Wiley, 1995.

Beizer, Boris. "The Black Box Vampire, or Testing Out of the Box." Closing speech at the 15th International Conference on Testing and Computer Software, Washington, DC, June 11, 1998. (Sponsor: United States Professional Development Institute, 1734 Elton Road, Silver Springs, MD 20903.)

Beizer, Boris. "Software Is Different." *Software Quality Professional* 1, no. 1 (1998): pp. 44–54.

Beizer, Boris. *Software System Testing and Quality Assurance.* New York, NY: International Thomson Computer Press, 1996.

Beizer, Boris. *Software Testing Techniques, Second Edition.* New York, NY: Van Nostrand Reinhold, 1990.

Berry, Thomas. *Managing the Total Quality Transformation.* Milwaukee, WI: ASQC, 1991.

Black, Rex and Greg Kubaczkowski. "Mission Made Possible," *Software Testing and Quality Engineering*, Volume 4, Issue 4, (now available on www.stickyminds.com.)

Brooks, Frederick P., Jr. *The Mythical Man-Month.* Reading, MA: Addison-Wesley, 1975.

Brooks, Frederick P., Jr. "No Silver Bullets—Essence and Accidents of Software Engineering." *Computer,* April 1987, pp. 10–19.

Bullock, James. "Calculating the Value of Testing." *Software Testing and Quality Engineering*, Volume 2, Issue 3, May/June 2000.

Campenella, Jack, editor, with the American Society for Quality's Quality Costs Committee. *Principles of Quality Costs: Principles, Implementation, and Use, Third Edition.* Milwaukee, WI: ASQ Quality Press, 1999.

Conway, Richard. *An Introduction to Programming: A Structured Approach Using PL/I and PL/C.* Boston, MA: Little, Brown, 1982.

Craig, Rick, and Stefan Jaskiel. *The Systematic Software Testing Handbook.* Orange Park, FL: STQE Publishing, 2002.

Crispin, Lisa. "eXtreme Rules of the Road." *Software Testing and Quality Engineering* magazine, Volume 3, Issue 4 (July/August 2001).

Crispin, Lisa. "Is Quality Negotiable?" *The Proceedings of the STARWest 2001 Conference.*

Crosby, Phillip. *Quality Is Free: The Art of Making Quality Certain.* New York, NY: McGraw-Hill, 1979.

DeMarco, Tom. *The Deadline.* New York, NY: Dorset House, 1997.

Dobbins, James. *Software Quality Assurance and Evaluation.* Milwaukee, WI: ASQC, 1990.

Drucker, Peter. *The Practice of Management.* New York, NY: Harper and Row, 1986.

Drucker, Peter. "Management's New Paradigms." *Forbes,* October 5, 1998, pp. 52–76.

Edwards, Owen. article "Rewriting the Geek Tragedy" in *Forbes ASAP,* August 24, 1998, p. 108.

English, Larry. *Improving Data Warehouse and Business Information Quality: Methods for Reducing Costs and Increasing Profits.* New York, NY: Wiley, 1999.

Ensworth, Patricia. *The Accidental Project Manager.* New York, NY: Wiley, 2001.

Fewster, Mark and Dorothy Graham. *Software Test Automation.* Harlow, England: Addison-Wesley, 1999.

Freedman, Daniel and Gerald Weinberg. *Handbook of Walkthroughs, Inspections, and Technical Reviews.* New York, NY: Dorset House, 1990.

Gartner Group. "When Should You Outsource IT Functions." *Executive Edge,* September 1998, p. 54.

Gartner Group. "The Hype Curve" illustration taken from "Surfing the Hype Curve." *Executive Edge*, September 1998, p. 16.

Gilbreath, Robert. *Winning at Project Management.* New York, NY: Wiley, 1986.

Gisselquist, Richard. "Engineering in Software." *Communications of the ACM,* 1998. Volume 41. Number 10, October 1998, pp. 107–108.

Hetzel, Bill. *The Complete Guide to Software Testing.* New York, NY: Wiley-QED, 1988.

Ishikawa, Kaoru. *Guide to Quality Control.* Tokyo, Japan: Asian Productivity Organization, 1982.

Jalote, Pankoj. *CMM in Practice.* Reading, MA: Addison-Wesley, 2000.

Johnson, Paul. *Intellectuals.* New York, NY: Harper and Row, 1988.

Jones, T. Capers. *Estimating Software Costs.* New York, NY: McGraw-Hill, 1995.

Juran, J. M. *Juran on Planning for Quality.* New York, NY: Free Press, 1988.

Juran, J. M., and Frank Gryna. *Quality Control Handbook.* New York, NY: McGraw-Hill, 1988.

Kan, Stephen. *Metrics and Models in Software Quality Engineering.* Reading, MA: Addison-Wesley, 1995.

Kaner, Cem, Jack Falk, and Hung Quoc Nguyen. *Testing Computer Software.* New York, NY: International Thomson Computer Press, 1993.

Kaner, Cem, James Bach and Bret Pettichord. *Lessons Learned in Software Testing.* New York, NY: Wiley, 2001.

Karat, Clare-Marie. "Guaranteeing Rights for the User" *Communications of the ACM* Volume 41, Number 12 (December 1998): pp. 29–31.

Lyu, Michael, ed. *Handbook of Software Reliability Engineering.* New York, NY: McGraw-Hill, 1996.

Mayer, John. "Test Engineers Finally Earn Respect," Contract Professional, July/August 1998, pp. 22–26.

McConnell, Steve. *Software Project Survival Guide.* Redmond, WA: Microsoft Press, 1998.

McConnell, Steve. *After the Gold Rush.* Redmond, WA: Microsoft Press, 1999.

McLean, Harry. *HALT, HASS & HASA Explained: Accelerated Reliability Techniques.* Milwaukee, WI: ASQ Press, 2000.

Moore, Geoffrey. *Crossing the Chasm.* New York, NY: Harper Collins, 1999.

Myers, Glenford. *The Art of Software Testing.* New York, NY: Wiley, 1979.

Neumann, Peter. *Computer-Related Risks.* New York, NY: Addison-Wesley, 1995.

Nielsen, Jakob. *Usability Engineering.* San Francisco, CA: Academic Press, 1993.

Norman, Donald. *The Invisible Computer.* Cambridge, MA: The MIT Press, 1999.

O'Connor, Patrick. *Practical Reliability Engineering.* New York, NY: Wiley, 1996.

Patel, Eric. 2001. "Getting the Most from Outsourcing: How to Choose the Right Provider and Evaluate Their Work." Software Testing and Quality Engineering, Volume 3, Issue 6 (November/December): pp. 34–40.

Patton, Ron. *Software Testing.* Indianapolis, IN: SAMS Publishing, 2001.

Paulk, Mark C., Charles V. Weber, Bill Curtis, and Mary Beth Chrissis. *The Capability Maturity Model: Guidelines for Improving the Software Process.* Reading, MA: Addison-Wesley, 1995.

Perry, William. *A Structured Approach to Systems Testing.* Wellesley, MA: QED Information Sciences, 1988.

Perry, William, and Randall Rice. *Surviving the Top Ten Challenges of Software Testing*. New York, NY: Dorset House, 1997.

Pressman, Roger. *Software Engineering: A Practitioner's Approach*, Second Edition. New York, NY: McGraw-Hill, 1987.

Pressman, Roger. *Software Engineering: A Practitioner's Approach*, Fourth Edition. New York, NY: McGraw-Hill, 1997.

Rubin, Jeffrey. *Handbook of Usability Testing*. New York, NY: Wiley, 1994.

Ruhl, Janet. *The Computer Consultant's Guide*. New York, NY: Wiley, 1997.

Sabherwal, Rajiv. "The Role of Trust in Outsourced IS Development Projects." *Communications of the ACM*, volume 42, Number 2 (February 1999): pp. 80–86.

Sabourin, Robert. *I am a Bug!* Roxboro, Quebec: Self-published, 1999.

Schmauch, Charles. *ISO 9000 for Software Developers*. Milwaukee, WI: ASQC, 1994.

Selby, Richard and Michael Cusumano. *Microsoft Secrets : How the World's Most Powerful Software Company Creates Technology, Shapes Markets, and Manages People*. New York, NY: Simon and Schuster, 1998.

Shapiro, Eileen. *Fad Surfing in the Boardroom: Reclaiming the Courage to Manage in the Age of Instant Answers*. New York, NY: Perseus Press, 1995.

Slaughter, Sandra, David Harter, and Mayuram Krishnan. "Evaluating the Cost of Software Quality." *Communications of the ACM* 41, no. 8 (August 1998): pp. 67–73.

Splaine, Steven, and Stefan Jaskiel. *The Web Testing Handbook*. Orange Park, FL: STQE Publishing, 2001.

Stamatis, D. H. *Failure Mode and Effect Analysis*. Milwaukee, WI.: ASQC Quality Press, 1995.

Voas, Jeffrey, and Gary McGraw. *Software Fault Injection*. New York, NY: Wiley, 1998.

Walton, Mary. *The Deming Management Method*. New York, NY: Putnam Publishing Group, 1986.

Weinberg, Gerald M. *Secrets of Consulting*. New York, NY: Dorset House, 1985.

Wilson, Larry Todd, and Diane Asay. "Putting Quality in Knowledge Management." *Quality Progress* None January (1999): pp. 25–31.

Wysocki, Robert, Robert Beck, Jr., and David Crane. *Effective Project Management*. New York, NY: Wiley, 1995.

Zimmerman, Steven and Marjorie Icenogle. *Statistic Quality Control Using Excel*. Milwaukee, WI: ASQ Press, 1999.

Zuckerman, Amy. *International Standards Desk Reference: Your Passport to World Markets*. New York, NY: Amacom, 1996.

Zuckerman, Amy. "Standards Battles Heat Up Between United States and European Union." *Quality Progress* None January (1999): pp. 39–42.

Help on the Internet

A recent Internet search under the words *software test* turned up almost 1,000 matches, and *hardware test* turned up 200. Clearly, the Internet can be a powerful resource for help. As a starting point, let me suggest some sites, newsgroups, and mailing lists of general interest that will help you home in on the best online resources for you:

- The newsgroup comp.software.testing and the FAQ sheet, www.faqs.org/faqs /software-eng/testing-faq/.

- The newsgroup comp.software-eng and the FAQ sheet, www.qucis.queensu.ca/Software-Engineering/.
- The U.S. Air Force's Software Technology Support Center, http://stsc.hill.af.mil/.
- The newsgroup comp.risks, also available as a mailing list risk-request@csl.sri.com.
- The mailing list SWTEST-Discuss, available at www.testfaqs.org/swtest-discuss.html.

Nonprofit Organizations

You might want to consider contacting the following nonprofit organizations for more information, in some cases, for information on certification programs related to testing and quality. (Certification might advance your career, but, in the interests of full disclosure, I am not a certified test or quality professional.)

- The Association for Computing Machinery is a professional organization that caters to academics, practitioners, and consultants, www.acm.org.
- The American Society for Quality is a professional organization with computer software- and hardware-related interest groups and quality-related certification programs, and is concerned with testing, quality control, and quality assurance. They also publish two journals of interest to hardware and software test professionals, *Quality Progress* and *Software Quality Professional*, www.asq.com.
- The Institute of Electrical and Electronic Engineers (IEEE) is a professional organization with interest groups in the areas of hardware and software, as well as other electronics, http://ieee.org.
- The Japanese Union of Scientists and Engineers provides resources in Japan and Asia, www.juse.or.jp.
- The British Computer Society provides resources in the UK and Europe, www.bcs.org.uk.

Publications

The following periodicals and magazines might be of interest to those working in the areas of software and hardware testing and quality assurance. Nonprofit publishers include:

- The Association for Computing Machinery, *Communications of the ACM*, www.acm.org.
- The American Society for Quality, *Quality Progress* and *Software Quality Professional*, www.asq.org.

■ The Institute of Electrical and Electronic Engineers (IEEE) also publishes various periodicals through their Special Interest Groups that pertain to testing and quality assurance. See ieee.org.

For-profit publishers include:

■ Software Quality Engineering, *Software Testing and Quality Engineering*, www .stqe.net.

■ Software Dimensions, *Journal for Software Testing Professionals*, www.softdim.com.

■ QBIT, *Professional Tester*, www.qbit.com.

Of course, not all publications are on paper anymore. The following online journals and periodicals might be of interest to those working in the areas of software and hardware testing and quality assurance. Publishers include:

■ Software Quality Engineering, *STQe-Letter*, www.StickyMinds.com.

■ VerticalNet, *Test and Measurement.com*, www.testandmeasurement.com.

■ QAI India, *Software Dioxide.com*, www.softwaredioxide.com.

Many, many, many others exist. New ones come about every day. Search the Internet to find these and others. However, check out their backgrounds. Who is sponsoring the site? How do they make money? Can they offer unbiased advice?

Contacting Me

I am, as I've mentioned before, a consultant, and I am the principal consultant in Rex Black Consulting Services, Inc. My associates and I practice test and quality assurance consulting for software and hardware development internationally. Specifically, we provide expert services in the following areas:

Test team bootstrapping. We can put a test team in place in a short timeframe, execute a complete test project against your current release, and then hand a running test process off to a full-time test staff.

Turnkey test project execution. We can also just perform a test project for your company, and then go away if there's no need for a full-time test team.

Test automation. We use commercial test tools, custom developed tools, and integrated combinations of the two.

Test execution and management tools. We have extensive experience building custom test tools for our clients.

Test training. We offer an ever-increasing variety of training programs for testers and test managers, including the popular three-day and two-day seminars based on this book.

Test project and process consulting. We can help you improve the effectiveness and efficiency of your testing through expert consulting.

Distributed test coordination. We can help you properly leverage outside groups to do some or all of your testing without increasing risk to your project.

Test staff augmentation. We can provide junior test technicians, senior test project managers, and all manner of skilled testing staff in between.

These services are available throughout the world. Should you have questions about these materials, or an interest in discussing ways in which RBCS can help your organizations, please contact me.

Rex Black Consulting Services, Inc.

Address:	31520 Beck Road
	Bulverde, TX 78163-3911USA
Phone:	+1 (830) 438-4830
Fax:	+1 (830) 438-4831
Email:	Rex_Black@RexBlackConsulting.com
Web:	www.RexBlackConsulting.com

I thank you for reading my book. I hope this material proves helpful to you when you manage your own testing processes.

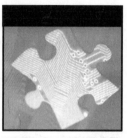

Glossary

acceptance testing A software or hardware development test phase designed to demonstrate that the system under test meets requirements. This phase is unique in all test activities in that its purpose is to demonstrate sufficiency and correctness, not to find problems. Acceptance testing is usually the last test phase before a product is released.

ad hoc testing Testing without written test cases, documented expected results, a checklist, a script, or instructions. Ad hoc tests often are not captured, which leads to questions about coverage and makes it impossible to do proper regression testing. Ad hoc testing can, however, be useful as a way to develop tests if records are kept. Also called *ad-lib testing*. Contrast with *exploratory testing*.

behavioral tests Tests based on what a computer system, hardware or software, is supposed to do. Such tests are usage-based and functional, at the levels of features, operational profiles, and customer scenarios. Also called *black-box tests* or *functional tests*.

black-box tests See **behavioral tests**.

bug A problem present in the system under test that causes it to fail to meet reasonable expectations. The reasonableness of an expectation can be determined by iterative consensus or management fiat if it is not obvious or defined (in the design specification or requirements documents). Notice that the test team usually sees only the failure, the improper behavior, but the bug itself is the flaw that causes the failure.

bug crawl A meeting or discussion focused on an item-by-item review of every active bug reported against the system under test. During this review, the participants can assign bug priority fix dates, defer insignificant bugs, and assess the progress of the development process. Also referred to as a *bug scrub,* change control board (CCB) meeting, bug triage meeting, bug review meeting, and many other different names.

closure period   For an individual bug that has been fixed and closed, the time between the initial bug report and the confirmation of the fix. The daily closure period is the average number of days between the opening of a bug report and its resolution for all bug reports closed on the same day, and the rolling closure period is the average for all closed bug reports. Closure period is a measure of development's responsiveness to test's bug reports.

component testing   A software development test phase (often referred to as *subsystem testing* in hardware development) that finds bugs in the individual pieces of the system under test before the pieces are fully integrated into the system. Component testing can require support structures such as stubs or scaffolds.

confirmation tests   A selected set of tests designed to find ways in which a bug fix fails to address the reported issue fully. A typical confirmation test involves rerunning the test procedure and isolation steps, per the bug report.

congruent   A description of test system architecture in which all elements of a test system align with one another and with the objectives of the test system. In a congruent test system, each component contributes to the functioning of the test system, without contradictory or destructive interfaces, outputs, or side effects.

continuation criteria   A set of decision-making guidelines that indicate whether a particular phase of testing is proceeding effective and efficiently. Conversely, when called *stopping criteria,* these guidelines are expressed in terms of determining whether testing should stop due to poor quality of the SUT or logistical problems related to performing tests. Continuation or stopping criteria tend to become more rigorous in later test phases such as *integration testing* and *system testing.* See also **entry criteria** and **exit criteria**.

debugging   The process in which developers determine the root cause of a bug and identify possible fixes. Developers perform debugging activities to resolve a known bug either after development of a subsystem or unit or because of a bug report. Contrast *isolation.*

deployment   For in-house IT systems, the point at which the first system under test, now a completely tested, finished product, ships to the first paying customer. Also called *release, cut-over,* or *migration,* among other names.

distributed testing   Testing that occurs at multiple locations, involves multiple teams, or both.

due diligence   Informally, the requirement that responsible employees and business associates, especially managers, not be negligent of the consequences of their decisions and the attendant risks to their employers or clients. This term has legal connotations; you should consult legal counsel for a precise definition.

entry criteria   A set of decision-making guidelines that indicate whether the project is ready to enter a particular phase of testing. Entry criteria tend to become more rigorous in the later phases such as *integration testing* and *system testing.* See also **continuation criteria** and **exit criteria**.

error seeding   A theoretical technique for measuring the bugs remaining in the system under test and thereby measuring the effectiveness of the test system itself, by deliberately inserting known defects (hidden from the testers) into the system under test, and then checking the proportion of these defects that are detected. Not commonly used and subject to widespread doubts about its accuracy.

escalate   To communicate a problem to a higher level of management for solution.

exit criteria   A set of decision-making guidelines that indicate whether the project is ready to exit a particular phase of testing, either to move on to the next phase or to complete the project. Exit criteria tend to become more rigorous in later phases such as *integration testing* and *system testing*. See also **continuation criteria** and **entry criteria**.

experience of quality   The customers' and users' opinions about whether a system is fulfilling their expectations and needs.

exploratory testing   Simultaneous design, development, and execution of tests, usually coupled with learning about the system under test, with generally lightweight testware documentation. Exploratory testing can be entirely self-guided, but can also proceed according to a high-level direction about the area to test (called a *test charter*). Contrast with *scripted testing* and *ad-hoc testing*.

fault injection   A theoretical technique for measuring the effectiveness of a test system, in which errors are created in the system under test by deliberately damaging, or perturbing, the source code, the executable code, or the data storage locations and then analyzing the test results. This technique is limited to finding bugs present in code that exists; in other words, bugs arising from missing, ambiguous, or incorrect items in requirements or design specification can generally not be detected. Not commonly used.

first customer ship   For mass-market systems, the point at which the first system under test, now a completely tested, finished product, ships to the first paying customer. Also called *release* or *general availability*.

fidelity   With respect to a test system, the degree to which it accurately models end-user hardware, software, and network environments and simulates end-user activities.

field-reported bug   A failure in a released, deployed, or shipping product, usually reported by a customer or a salesperson, that either affects the ability of the customer to use the product, or involves side effects that impair the customer's ability to use other products on the same system.

flexibility   The extent to which a test component can handle minor changes in the system under test's behavior without reporting bugs that don't exist or failing to report bugs that do exist.

FMEA   Acronym for *failure mode and effects analysis,* a technique for identifying and defining potential quality risks, ranking them by risk priority, and assigning action to prevent and/or detect related problems.

functional tests   Sometimes this phrase has the same meaning as *behavioral tests*, but it can also connote testing that focuses strictly on correctness of functionality. In these cases, it must be augmented with other test approaches to deal with potentially important quality risks such as performance, load, capacity, and volume, and so forth.

GA   Acronym for *general availability*. See **first customer ship**.

goat rodeo   Any confused, disorganized, and chaotic group event, generally held under pressure or duress, that results in little forward progress, thus frustrating many participants. Derived from the children's rodeo events where youngsters attempt to rope and tie goats, calves, and other small farm animals.

granularity Fineness or coarseness of focus. A highly granular test allows the tester to check low-level details; a structural test is very granular. Behavioral tests, which are less granular, provide the tester with information on general system behavior, not details.

integration testing A software development test phase (often referred to as *product testing* in hardware development) that finds bugs in the relationships and interfaces between pairs and groups of components in the system under test, often in a staged fashion. This test phase ideally occurs as all the constituent components of the system under test are being integrated, and is closely coordinated with and also helps coordinate the integration plan.

isolation Repeating the steps needed to reproduce a bug, possibly many times, with precise changes in system configuration, permission levels, background load, environment, and so forth, in an effort to understand the levers that control the bug and its behavior—in other words, to confirm that the bug is a real problem and to identify those factors that affect the bug's manifestations. Good isolation draws a bounding box around a bug. Isolation requires the tester to make intelligent guesses about the root cause of the problem. Contrast *debugging*.

kludge Any ill-advised, substandard, or temporary fix applied to an urgent problem in the (often misguided) belief that doing so will keep a project moving forward.

MEGO Acronym for *my eyes glazed over*; referring to a loss of focus and attention, often caused by an attempt to read a particularly impenetrable or dense technical document, or attending a meeting where off-agenda discussions and minutiae dominate the proceedings.

maintainable In terms of the test system, the extent to which a test engineer versed in the operation of the system can make changes in a test component without undue risk of damaging that component or other components.

MTBF Acronym for *mean time between failures*. Demonstrating a particular MTBF or discovering a statistically meaningful MTBF is often an important part of a hardware development project, as this figure predicts the financial impact of various warranty policies and has important implications for field defect rates and a company's reputation for quality.

MTTR Acronym for *mean time to repair*. Like MTBF, this figure has implications for a company's warranties and reputation. A problem that takes longer to repair will generally be a higher priority than one that takes less time to repair, all other factors being equal.

oracle Any way of determining the expected (correct) result for a test case, a test suite, or a test operation. This term is usually synonymous with *output oracle*, which, for a given input under a given set of test conditions, tells the tester what the expected output should be. However, oracles are also needed to describe non-output behaviors, especially when testing performance, load, capacity and volume, and error handling.

orthogonal A description of the relationship between two or more variables or set members in which the value of one does not influence the values of others.

peer review A quality improvement idea common in software development, in which one or more testers read and comment on a test deliverable such as a bug report, a test suite, or a test plan. The reading is followed by a review meeting in which the deliverable is discussed. Based on this discussion, the deliverable is updated, corrected, and re-released.

pilot testing   In hardware development, a test phase generally following or accompanying acceptance testing, which demonstrates the ability of the assembly line to mass-produce the completely tested, finished system under test. In software development, pilot testing is a test phase that demonstrates the ability of the system to handle typical operations from live customers on live hardware. First customer ship or deployment often immediately follows the successful completion of the pilot testing phase.

priority   The business importance of a bug, especially its effect on the viability and acceptability of the system from a user and customer perspective. Contrast *severity*.

product testing   See **integration testing**.

quality risk   The possibility of undesirable types of behaviors, or failure modes, in which the system under test does not meet stated product requirements or end users' reasonable expectations of behavior; in plain terms, the possibility of a bug.

quality risk management   The process of identifying, prioritizing, and managing risks to the quality of the system under test, with the aim of preventing them or detecting and removing them.

railroading   A technique that continues test execution in test suite order when a new test cycle starts. Rather than restarting the testing or moving on to a new set of suites, the testing simply continues from where it was when the test cycle began. The goal of this and similar techniques is to achieve an acceptable level of test coverage and minimize regression test gaps when coverage cannot be exhaustive.

ramp-up   A hardware production phase that immediately follows a product release, in which the assembly line learns the process and product foibles associated with mass-producing the completely tested, finished system under test. This phase usually is accompanied by a spike in *field-reported bugs*.

regression   A problem that occurs when, as a result of a change in the system under test, a new revision of the system, S_{n+1}, contains a defect not present in revisions S_1 through S_n. In other words, regression occurs when some previously correct operation misbehaves. (If a new revision contains a new piece of functionality that fails without affecting the rest of the system, this is not considered regression.) Usually, you'll detect regression when test cases that previously passed now yield anomalies.

regression test gap   For any given change or revision in the system under test, the difference between the areas of test coverage provided by the entire test system and the test coverage provided by the portion of the test system that is actually rerun. For a system release, a regression test gap is the extent to which the final release version of every component and change in the system did not experience the full brunt of the test system.

regression tests   A set of tests selected to find regression introduced by changes in component, interface, or product functionality, usually associated with bug fixes or new functionality. Regression is a particularly insidious risk in a software maintenance effort, because there is seldom time for a full retest of the product, even though seemingly innocuous changes can have knock-on effects in remote areas of functionality or behavior.

reporting logs   Raw test output produced by low-level test tools, which is human-readable in varying degrees. Examples include text files containing test condition pass/fail results, screen shots, and diagnostics.

reporting tools   Special test tools that can process reporting logs into reports and charts, given some information about the context in which the log was produced.

root cause   The underlying reason why a bug occurs, as opposed to the observed symptoms of the bug. Root cause data is most useful in the aggregate: analyzing a breakdown of the root causes of all bugs found in a system under test can help to focus the attention of both test and development on those areas that are causing the most serious and frequent problems.

scalable   The extent to which a test component's parameters of operation can expand without necessitating major changes or fundamental redesign in the test system.

scripted testing   Manual testing that follows a written test procedure, test case, or test script. These tests are written to some level of precision; the less precise the test script, the greater the number of details that are left to the discretion of the tester. I would be hard pressed to distinguish chartered exploratory testing from imprecise scripted testing. Confusingly enough, since automated tests are often implemented in interpreted programming languages (called *scripting languages* in programming parlance), the programming instructions to an automated test tool are often called *test scripts*.

SCUD release   A software or hardware release, hastily prepared by programmers and system engineers in a crisis atmosphere, that might or might not fix some number of critical bugs. Like their namesake *missiles*, such releases seldom hit their targets, arrive with little warning but lots of noise, cause a great deal of panic, and don't contribute much to ultimate victory.

severity   The impact of a bug on the system under test, regardless of the likelihood of its occurrence under end-user conditions or the extent to which the failure impedes use of the system. Contrast *priority*.

shotgunning   A technique that distributes test suites randomly across test cycles, or distributes test configurations randomly across test suites throughout a test phase. Shotgunning test suites across test cycles means that the test suites are preassigned to each cycle and are run as the new cycles begin. Shotgunning test configurations across test suites means that test system configurations (combinations of hardware, software, operating system, and infrastructure) are arbitrarily selected to run specific test suites. In both cases, the goal is to achieve an acceptable level of test coverage and minimize regression test gaps when coverage cannot be exhaustive.

spinning disk release   A software revision that is sent by development to test so hastily that supposedly the floppy disk is still spinning. See also **SCUD release**.

straw man plan   Any lightweight or incomplete plan, such as the first draft of a test plan or a hardware allocation plan, that serves as a starting point for discussion and a framework for coalescing a more concrete plan.

string testing   A software development test phase that finds bugs in typical usage scripts and operational or control-flow strings. This test phase is fairly unusual.

structural tests   Tests based on how a computer system, hardware or software, operates. Such tests are code-based or component-based, and they find bugs in operations such as those that occur at the levels of lines of code, chips, subassemblies, and interfaces. Also called *white-box tests, glass-box tests, code-based tests,* or *design-based tests*.

subsystem testing   See **component testing**.

SUT   See **system under test**.

SWAG   Acronym for *scientific wild-ass guess;* an educated guess or estimate. SWAGs abound in test estimation activities early in the development process.

system testing   A software or hardware development test phase that finds bugs in the overall and particular behaviors, functions, and responses of the system under test as a whole operating under realistic usage scenarios. These various system operations are performed once the system is fully integrated.

system under test The entirety of the product, or system, being tested, which often consists of more than the immediately obvious pieces; abbreviated *SUT*. Test escapes can arise through misunderstanding the scope of the system under test.

TBD Acronym for *to be determined*; a useful placeholder in test documents to indicate a work-in-progress.

test artifacts Behaviors arising from the artificiality of the test environment or from a test process that diverges from the way the system will behave in the field; misleading behaviors or incorrect results reported by the test system. Note: I use this phrase in the scientific experimentation meaning of the word *artifact*, but others in the test business use it in the archeological meaning of the word. These folks use the phrase *test artifact* to refer to the test documentation, test processes, test plans, test cases, test data, and other items that I generally call the *test system*.

test case A sequence of steps, substeps, and other actions, performed serially, in parallel, or some combination of consecution, that creates the desired test conditions that the test case is designed to evaluate. In some styles of documentation, particularly IEEE 829, these elements are referred to as *test specifications* and *test procedures*.

test case library A collection of independent, reusable test cases.

test case (suite) setup The steps required to configure the test environment for execution of a test case or test suite.

test case (suite) teardown The steps required to restore the test environment to a "clean" condition after execution of a test case or test suite.

test condition A system state or circumstance created by proceeding through some combination of steps, substeps, or actions in a test case. The term is sometimes also used to refer to the steps, substeps, or actions themselves.

test coverage 1. In a structural sense, the extent to which the test system covers, or exercises, the structure—the code or components—in the system under test. The metric is usually expressed as a percent of the total count of whatever structural element is being covered, such as lines of code or function points.
2. In a behavioral sense, the extent to which the test system covers, or exercises, the behavior—operations, activities, functions, and other uses—of the system under test. Coverage can be measured qualitatively against the uses to which the users and customers will subject the system, or quantitatively against requirements, quality risks, design specification elements, configurations, and so forth. Achieving thorough test coverage both behaviorally and structurally is necessary for good testing.

test cycle A partial or total execution of all the test suites planned for a given test phase as part of that phase. A test phase involves at least one cycle (usually more) through all the designated test suites. Test cycles are usually associated with a single release of the system under test, such as a build of software or a motherboard. Generally, new test releases occur during a test phase, triggering another test cycle.

tester failure Any failure caused by a tester using the test system, often the misinterpretation of a test result. Tester failures can result in reporting bugs that don't exist, or failing to report bugs that do exist, or they can simply be irritating yet immaterial.

test environment The setting in which testing happens, including the test platforms, the test infrastructure, the test lab, and other facilities.

test escape   Any field-reported bug that could reasonably have been caught during testing but was not. The term can also refer to a bug that makes its way into a subsequent phase of testing, although it should have been caught in a previous phase. A field-reported bug that was found during testing but that was not fixed because of a project management decision is not a test escape. A bug that could be found only through unusual and complicated hardware configurations or obscure operations is often not considered a test escape, either.

test pass   A period of testing consisting of the complete set of all the test suites planned for a given test phase. A test pass includes one or more test cycles, depending on the frequency of test releases and how long it takes to run all the tests.

test phase   A period of testing that addresses a particular set of quality risks and consists of one or more test passes.

test platform   Any piece of hardware on which a test can be run. The test platform is not necessarily the system under test, especially when testing software.

test release   Some subset of the overall system to be developed that is delivered for installation in some test environment and subsequent testing during a single test cycle. In later phases such as system and acceptance testing, a test release should be as close as possible to identical with the final customer release in terms of process, format, and completeness.

test system failure   Any failure of the test system. A test failure can result in reporting bugs that don't exist, or failure to report bugs that do exist, or it can simply cause unpleasant side effects that nevertheless do not compromise the validity of the test results.

test suite   A framework for the execution of a group of test cases; a way of organizing test cases. In a test suite, test cases can be combined to create unique test conditions.

test yield   The degree to which a test case or test suite finds bugs. A high-yield test suite, for example, results in many bug reports of a serious nature, while a low-yield test suite results in few or trivial bug reports.

test to fail   The mind-set involved in designing, developing, and executing tests with the aim of finding as many problems as possible. This attitude represents the right way to think while designing, developing, and executing tests.

test to pass   The mind-set involved in designing, developing, and executing tests with the aim of proving compliance with requirements and correctness of operation. Such an attitude not only misses opportunities to increase product quality, but also is demonstrably futile. It represents the wrong way to think while designing, developing, and executing tests (except in the case of acceptance testing).

test system   An integrated and maintainable collection of items used to find, reproduce, isolate, describe, and manage bugs in the software or hardware under test. The items consist of the *test environment*, the test processes, and the testware.

test tool   Any general-purpose hardware, software, or hardware/software system used during test case execution to set up or tear down the test environment, to create test conditions, or to measure test results. A test tool is separate from the test case itself.

unit testing   A software development concept that refers to the basic testing of a piece of code, the size of which is often undefined in practice, although it is usually a function or a subroutine. Unit testing is generally performed by developers.

white-box tests   See **structural tests**.

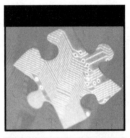

Index

A

acceptance testing, 7–8, 376, 386, 413, 461
acoustics, testing of, 457–458
action item list, 395
Action Results column, FMEA, 29
ad hoc testing, 94
ad lib testing, 94
administrative staff, 348
After the Gold Rush, McConnell's, 288
air conditioning, test lab and, 253
alpha tests, 8, 20, 375, 386–387
altitude, hardware and, 454
American Society for Quality, 288, 467
anechoic chambers, 457
applications, need for variety of in
    test lab, 255
appraisal costs, 403
The Art of Software Testing, Myers',
    5, 163, 283
assertiveness, testers and, 280
asset tags, 261, 263

asset tracking systems, 260, 261–263. *See
    also* logistics database
assignments, planning staff with logistics
    database, 228–233
Association for Computing Machinery
    (ACM), 21, 467
audition interviews, 299
audits, bug report, 216–217
author (Rex Black), 468, 469
automated testing
    of maintenance releases, 421, 423
    reducing regression test gaps via,
        103–104
    reducing test system errors via, 219
    speeding the test process via, 429
availability, testing for, 17

B

Bach, James, 93, 94, 206
background music, workplace, 267
Bad Unit bugs, 147